The Art of the Critic

The Art of the Critic
Literary Theory and Criticism from the Greeks to the Present

Volume 2
Early Renaissance

EDITED WITH AN INTRODUCTION BY
HAROLD BLOOM
Sterling Professor of the Humanities, Yale University

1986
CHELSEA HOUSE PUBLISHERS
NEW YORK   NEW HAVEN   PHILADELPHIA

Project Editor: James Uebbing
Editorial Coordinator: Karyn Gullen Browne
Editorial Staff: Perry King, Bert Yaeger
Research: Kevin Pask
Design: Susan Lusk

Copyright © 1986 by Chelsea House Publishers, a division of Chelsea House Educational Communications, Inc. Introduction copyright © 1986 by Harold Bloom

All rights reserved. No part of this pulication may be reproduced or transmitted, in any form or by any means, without the written permission of the publisher

Printed and bound in the United States of America

Library of Congress Cataloging in Publication Data
Main entry under title:

The Art of the Critic

    Includes bibliographies.
    Contents: v. 1. Classical and medieval—v. 2. Early renaissance.
    1. Criticism—Collected works. 2. Literature—Philosophy—Collected works.
I. Bloom, Harold.
PN86.A77   1986   809   84–15547
ISBN 0–87754–495–6

Chelsea House Publishers
Harold Steinberg, Chairman & Publisher
Susan Lusk, Vice President
A Division of Chelsea House Educational Communications, Inc.

133 Christopher Street, New York, NY 10014

345 Whitney Avenue, New Haven, CT 06510

5014 West Chester Pike, Edgemont, PA 19028

Contents

Introduction · vii ·
Boccaccio · 1 ·
    From *The Life of Dante* · 3 ·
    The Genealogy of the Gentile Gods · 6 ·
Petrarch · 65 ·
    Selected Letters · 67 ·
Erasmus · 85 ·
    From *The Antibarbarians* · 87 ·
Giangiorgio Trissino · 105 ·
    From *Poetica* · 107 ·
Giraldi Cinthio · 121 ·
    An Address to the Reader by the Tragedy of Orbecche · 123 ·
    From *The Apology for Dido* · 126 ·
    From *On the Composition of Romances* · 130 ·
Joachim du Bellay · 139 ·
    From *The Defence and Illustration of the French Language* · 141 ·
Julius Caesar Scaliger · 157 ·
    From *Poetics* · 159 ·
Antonio Minturno · 169 ·
    From *L'Arte Poetica* · 171 ·
Roger Ascham · 185 ·
    From *The Schoolmaster* · 187 ·
Lodovico Castelvetro · 211 ·
    From *On the Poetics* · 213 ·
George Gascoigne · 241 ·
    The Making of Verse · 243 ·
Michel Eyquem du Montaigne · 251 ·
    On Books · 253 ·
"E.K." · 263 ·
    In Praise of the New Poet · 265 ·
Sir Philip Sidney · 271 ·
    An Apology for Poetry · 273 ·
Jacopo Mazzoni · 313 ·
    From *On the Defense of the Comedy of Dante* · 315 ·

George Puttenham · 333 ·
    From *The Art of English Poetry*   · 335 ·
Nash and Harvey   · 357 ·
    A General Censure (Nash)   · 359 ·
    A Commendation of Sidney (Nash)   · 367 ·
    From *Four Letters* (Harvey)   · 370 ·
    From *Strange News* (Nash)   · 376 ·
Sir John Harington   · 379 ·
    A Brief Apology for Poetry   · 381 ·
Torquato Tasso   · 399 ·
    From *Discourses on the Heroic Poem*   · 401 ·
    Minturno, or On Beauty   · 435 ·
Giambattista Guarini   · 453 ·
    From *The Compendium of Tragicomic Poetry*   · 455 ·
George Chapman   · 477 ·
    On Homer   · 479 ·
Francis Meres   · 487 ·
    From *Palladis Tamia*   · 489 ·
Thomas Campion   · 499 ·
    Observations in the Art of English Poetry   · 501 ·
Samuel Daniel   · 521 ·
    A Defense of Rhyme   · 523 ·
Bibliography   · 541 ·

Index and Glossary are contained in Volume 11

Earlier Renaissance Literary Criticism: Humanism and the Vernacular

Harold Bloom

1

TO ASSERT THAT the triumph of Western humanism, and the ascendancy of the vernacular in high literature, were achievements of the earlier Renaissance was once to utter commonplaces, and now would be regarded as rather naive. The sequence of Dante, Boccaccio, and Chaucer hardly yields to their early Renaissance followers, whether as humanist sages or as great writers in the native tongues. Like all cultural ages, the Renaissance exalted itself as what we would now call a Modernism, and like all Modernisms, from the initial one at Hellenistic Alexandria through our own current so-called post-Modernism, the Renaissance suffered, and masked, an acute sense of belatedness in regard to the force of the cultural past. The anxiety of influence intensified as an aesthetic phenomenon during the post-Enlightenment era, but it is strongly present in the Renaissance from Petrarch on, and is at least as old as Euripides among the ancient Greeks, and Jesus ben Sirach (Ecclesiasticus) among the ancient Hebrews.

Thomas Greene, in his powerful study of "imitation and discovery in Renaissance poetry," *The Light in Troy*, seeks to distinguish between Renaissance and Romantic or Modern anxieties and polemics concerning the agon between cultural pasts and presents:

> The problem of the precursor is that he is not lost and not dead, thus not available for resurrection. His text has not suffered from any errancy, and thus no etiological itinerary away from it into the present is possible. The precursor constitutes the present; he determines the atmosphere the poet breathes. Between the precursor and the follower no discontinuity can intervene, since . . . discontinuity would be freedom. This is doubtless why Petrarch could make more controlled use of Virgil than he could of Dante. The discovery of the ancient world imposed enormous anxiety upon the humanist Renaissance, but its living poetry represents a series of victories over anxiety, based upon a

courage that confronts the model without neurotic paralysis and uses the anxiety to discover selfhood. The relationship to the subtext is deliberately and lucidly written into the poem as a visible and acknowledged construct.

This is a beautiful idealism, and is appropriately Humanist in its ideology. It assumes that an achieved poem is a victory over anxiety, and that the precursor can be confronted openly. Courage, a Humanist virtue, is thus extolled, and the darker motives for all poetic figuration are evaded. "Controlled use" is a key phrase, since it implies that everything which matters is in Petrarch's conscious and willed control. There is also a suggestion that the Romantic or modern poet, afflicted by an Oedipal "neurotic paralysis," lacks the classical virtues of the Humanist poet. A later passage in Greene's superb book makes the suggestion quite explicit:

> The passage of history will never be as simple as the *rite de passage* suggests. But by the reductive simplifications of its historical construct, the poem confronts the threat of history and asserts its own limited freedom from it. There is a term for the courage of the ancient or Renaissance artist who followed this strategy, who faced the threat of history and thereby found his artistic poise: the term is *classical*. The humanist poet is not a neurotic son crippled by a Freudian family romance, which is to say he is not . . . Romantic. He is rather like the son in a classical comedy who displaces his father at the moment of reconciliation.

The idealism of the Humanist self-estimate is continued here, and courage is again exalted as the classical virtue for the poet. Even a slight touch of Nietzschean skepticism is more than enough to expose this cultural celebration as another instance of the will to power. The pragmatic, Nietzschean question is: Who is the interpreter and what power does she or he seek to gain over the text? The answer here is that the interpreter is the Humanist, Renaissance or contemporary academic, and the power is a defense of the institutions of Western or Renaissance Humanism, including the modern university as it performs its clerical function for its society. The classical comedy of displacement, with father and son reconciled, is the serious working premise of the university, and is the principal service that the university is required to perform in our society.

2

Montaigne, until the advent of Shakespeare, was the great figure of the European Renaissance, comparable in cognitive power and in influence to Freud in our century. His mordant essay "Of Books" is marked by a genial irony that is profoundly skeptical of the Humanist program that ostensibly (and rather off-handedly) is endorsed:

INTRODUCTION

> Let people see in what I borrow whether I have known how to choose what would enhance my theme. For I make others say what I cannot say so well, now through the weakness of my language, now through the weakness of my understanding. I do not count my borrowings, I weigh them. And if I had wanted to have them valued by their number, I should have loaded myself with twice as many. They are all, or very nearly all, from such famous and ancient names that they seem to identify themselves enough without me. In the reasonings and inventions that I transplant into my soil and confound with my own, I have sometimes deliberately not indicated the author, in order to hold in check the temerity of those hasty condemnations that are tossed at all sorts of writings, notably recent writings of men still living, and in the vulgar tongue, which invites everyone to talk about them and seems to convict the conception and design of being likewise vulgar. I want them to give Plutarch a fillip on my nose and get burned insulting Seneca in me. I have to hide my weakness under these great authorities. I will love anyone that can unplume me, I mean by clearness of judgment and by the sole distinction of the force and beauty of the remarks. For I who, for lack of memory, fall short at every turn in picking them out by knowledge of their origin, can very well realize, by measuring my capacity, that my soil is not at all capable of producing certain too rich flowers that I find sown there, and that all the fruits of my own growing could not match them.

This hardly seems a matter of "classical courage" but rather of cunning, humor, skill, and a deliciously bland disarming of one's critics. It is also, rather clearly, a knowingly defensive irony, directed against a literary anxiety that Montaigne insists is universal, and not merely individual. Montaigne at this time (1578–80) is well underway to his final stance, where he forsakes the high Humanist doctrine in favor of the common life, so as to affirm the exuberance of natural existence, and the enormous virtue of being the *honnête homme*, thus establishing a new norm against which Pascal would rebel, or perhaps an influence that Pascal could neither escape nor accept. What "Of Books" subverts most audaciously is the Humanist scheme of benign displacement by imitation. When Montaigne writes of his unsavory critics, "I want them to give Plutarch a fillip on my nose and get burned insulting Seneca in me," he not only accurately names his prime precursors, but he asserts his own power of contamination. In contrast, consider Ben Jonson, more truly Greene's hero of "classical courage":

> The third requisite in our poet or maker is imitation, *imitatio*, to be able to convert the substance or riches of another poet to his own use. To make choice of one excellent man above the rest, and so to follow him till he grow very he, or so like him as the copy may be mistaken for the principal. Not as a creature that swallows what it takes in, crude, raw, or undigested; but that feeds with an appetite, and hath a stomach to concoct, divide, and turn all into nourishment. Not to imitate servilely,

as Horace saith, and catch at vices for virtue, but to draw forth out of the best and choicest flowers, with the bee, and turn all into honey, work it into one relish and savour; make our imitation sweet; observe how the best writers have imitated, and follow them: how Virgil and Statius have imitated Homer; how Horace, Archilochus; how Alcæus, and the other lyrics; and so of the rest.

Here one imitates precisely as the precursors imitated, which seems to me an apt reduction of the Humanist argument. It is no surprise that Jonson goes on to say of reading that it "maketh a full man," borrowing from his truest precursor Sir Francis Bacon in the essay "Of Studies." Admirable essayist in his narrow mode, Bacon is about as adequate to compete with Montaigne as Jonson was to challenge Shakespeare. It takes a singular perversity to prefer Bacon's essays to Montaigne's, and yet Jonson could insist persuasively that he was being loyal to the Humanist doctrine of imitation:

Some that turn over all books, and are equally searching in all papers; that write out of what they presently find or meet, without choice. By which means it happens that what they have discredited and impugned in one week, they have before or after extolled the same in another. Such are all the essayists, even their master Montaigne. These, in all they write, confess still what books they have read last, and therein their own folly so much, that they bring it to the stake raw and undigested; not that the place did need it neither, but that they thought themselves furnished and would vent it.

Bacon's essays certainly do not "confess still what books they have read last," and Montaigne is anything but formalist in his use of quite immediate reading. Greene is wiser, I think, when he recognizes that ambivalence and the antithetical haunt all imitation, however Humanist:

The process called imitation was not only a technique or a habit; it was also a field of ambivalence, drawing together manifold, tangled, sometimes antithetical attitudes, hopes, pieties, and reluctances within a concrete locus.

At the heart of Humanism was an ambivalence, even an antithetical will, that perhaps still makes the phrase "Christian Humanist" something of an oxymoron. Most simply, Humanism entailed a love of Greek and Latin wisdom and humane letters, a desire to know qualities uniquely available in antiquity. Christianity, in the early Renaissance, indeed became Greek and Latin in its culture, at a certain cost. The morality of the Christian Bible is scarcely Greek or Latin, and the God of Christianity remained the God of Abraham, Isaac, and Jacob, rather than the gods of Achilles, Odysseus, and Aeneas. Imitation or mimesis, whether of nature or of a precursor, is a Greek notion, rather than an Hebraic postulate. We cannot image an ancient Greek or Latin author confronting the stark text of the Second Commandment.

Erich Auerbach, in his *Mimesis: the Representation of Reality in Western*

INTRODUCTION

Literature, finds in Rabelais and Montaigne an early Renaissance freedom of vision, feeling, and thought produced by a perpetual playing with things, and hints that this freedom began to decline not so much in Cervantes as in Shakespeare, the two writers who by paradox may be the only Western authors since antiquity clearly surpassing the powers of even Rabelais and Montaigne. As Auerbach emphasizes:

> In Rabelais there is no aesthetic standard; everything goes with everything. Ordinary reality is set within the most improbable fantasy, the coarsest jokes are filled with erudition, moral and philosophical enlightenment flows out of obscene expressions and stories.

This extraordinary freedom of representation in Rabelais is matched by Montaigne in Auerbach's description of his emancipation not only from the Christian conceptual schema but from the cosmological view of his precursors Cicero, Seneca, and Plutarch:

> His newly acquired freedom was much more exciting, much more of the historical moment, directly connected with the feeling of insecurity. The disconcerting abundance of phenomena which now claimed the attention of men seemed overwhelming. The world—both outer world and inner world—seemed immense, boundless, incomprehensible.

Shakespeare, "more consciously aristocratic than Montaigne" in Auerbach's view, grants the aesthetic dignity of the tragic only to princes, commanders, and eminent figures in Roman history. To the Humanist heritage Auerbach attributes Shakespeare's sense that there is more than a temporal gap between contemporary life and the heroic past:

> With the first dawn of humanism, there began to be a sense that the events of classical history and legend and also those of the Bible were not separated from the present simply by an extent of time but also by completely different conditions of life. Humanism with its program of renewal of antique forms of life and expression creates a historical perspective in depth such as no previous epoch known to us possessed.

Of Cervantes Auerbach beautifully remarks: "So universal and multilayered, so noncritical and nonproblematic a gaiety in the portrayal of everyday reality has not been attempted again in European letters." It is as though Humanist perspectivism—not yet developed in the rambunctious Rabelais, a powerful shadow in Shakespeare, forsaken for the common life by Montaigne—had been set aside by a genial power of acceptance of the mundane in Cervantes. But these in any case are the Renaissance writers as strong as Homer, Dante, and Chaucer. With lesser writers (lesser only as compared with these), the opening to the past carried with it a perspectivism that generated anxieties both of influence and of representation. Paradoxically, Humanism both exalted and burdened writers by proclaiming that the vernacular could achieve what the ancients had achieved, by the aid of an antique greatness that carried its own implicit force of inhibition.

3

It would be difficult to argue that any major literary criticism was generated in the early Renaissance, with the single exception of Sidney's shrewd and subtle *Apology for Poetry*. And even Sidney enjoys only mixed esteem among modern scholars and critics. The great formalist critic W. K. Wimsatt judges Sidney's *Defence of Poesie* (its alternate title, in another early edition) a brilliant epitome of what is best in the poetics of the sixteenth century, but then charmingly dismisses it:

> It is a kind of formal beginning of literary theorizing by the English man of letters, and a brilliant enough one—written in the high, enthusiastic, occasionally a-syntactic style of the gifted amateur champion, headlong to outdazzle the lowness and myopia of professional moral grumblers.

A more effective, and less loving dismissal is performed by Richard Lanham in his brilliant study of Renaissance literary rhetoric, *The Motives of Eloquence*:

> A rhetorical perspective may help, also, to sort out some confusions in Renaissance poetics, it may show how someone like Sidney, for example, could in defending poetry confound its two contradicting kinds. A serious reality will suggest a didactic sugarcoating conception of poetry; rhetorical reality needs something more like Sidney's "golden" poetry, maker of a new reality. The rhetorical/serious dualism, that is, can clarify the relationship of moral to formal theories of poetry. Both finally address themselves to behavior, as Sidney wanted to believe. But the sugarcoating of conventional Renaissance didacticism addresses itself to the central self and to a reality poetry can but imitate. The golden poetic which he set over against such sugarcoating addresses itself to the rhetorical self, attempts to teach by addressing the histrionic pleasures we draw on in remaining ourselves. The Horatian *delectare* turns out to be a *prodesse* addressed to a different reality and thus speaking a different language. It is thus that formal and moral theories of poetry always find their relationship. They refer to the two aspects of the self and, like those two aspects, they can be held together in oscillation but never permanently unified. Sidney's confusion is an archetypal one, then; perhaps this accounts for *The Defense of Poetry's* continued high reputation.

The seeming contradiction between Sidney's two themes falls away when we see his attempt, more inclusive than he knew, as an attempt to encompass two realities he did not fully discriminate. Surely just in this failure, in fact, lies his inability to finish the *New Arcadia*. The *Old* was built upon rhetorical coordinates, but the *New* was to be serious.

INTRODUCTION

> The change in premises was too much for both plot and character. Sidney was stymied, aware, like Ariosto, Spenser, and Shakespeare, that the old epic seriousness would not do, but at a loss for something to put in its place. He seems to have made a similar mistake in his life as well, failing at critical junctures to discriminate between rhetorical and serious reality.

This is a severe judgment, informed by Lanham's clean distinction between the "fundamental strategies" of Plato and Ovid. Plato's "serious man" with his "central self" challenges Ovid's "rhetorical man" with his "social self." At once Platonic and Ovidian, Sidney has it both ways. Yet, as Lanham knows, this is altogether characteristic of Renaissance literature; Spenser doubtless is the great instance of this ambivalent, double stance. If *The Faerie Queene* survives Spenser's interplay of central and social selves, so surely does Sidney's *Apology*.

The strongest defense of Sidney's defense of poetry is in Margaret W. Ferguson's *Trials of Desire*, which analyzes the three crucial Renaissance defenses of poetry—those by the poet Joachim du Bellay, by the even more illustrious Torquato Tasso, author of the romantic epic *Jerusalem Delivered*, and by Sidney. Ferguson's case for Sidney is formidable:

> As a poet intent on protecting his "title," Sidney has obvious reasons for identifying his own cause with that of "poor poetry." But there is another facet of his identification which arises from what he calls the "affinity" between poetry and oratory as modes of discourse. "Persuasion," as Neil Rudenstine remarks, "lies at the heart of Sidney's entire theory of poetry." Sidney is perfectly aware that as an effort of persuasion his treatise is in crucial respects a double of the poetry it defines and defends. He is, moreover, aware that the affinity between his own rhetoric and the "moving" force of poetry raises questions about the use and abuse of power. When he echoes Aristotle's defense of rhetoric to formulate a definition of poetry as a morally ambiguous power, he invites us to see that, in this trial, the lawyer is as guilty or innocent as his client. Modern scholars of Renaissance literature who chide Sidney and his peers for their "erroneous" transgression of the Kantian boundary between aesthetic and practical discourse lead one to surmise that the modern anxiety about the abuse of verbal power has blinded critics to the subtlety with which Sidney handles his own anxiety about power. It is an irony of literary history that those who rely on Kantian, Aristotelian, or other theories of aesthetic formalism to fence off a sphere for innocent art (and innocent criticism) simply repeat a defensive strategy which Sidney himself employs in a dialectical and self-reflexive way. When, toward the end of the *Defence*, he presciently expresses his fear that he will be "pounded" for "straying from poetry to oratory," he is engaged, as he is throughout the treatise, in both establishing and transgressing the boundary between a language of play and a language of power.

Sidney's complex awareness of his dangerous balance pervades his *Apology*. Like his Italian critical precursors, he apprehends the curious Humanist puzzle in which one seeks to improve the vernacular by employing antique models, and like the best of the Italians, Sidney knows better. As the Italians already had their vernacular masterpiece in Dante, so the English had Chaucer:

> *Chaucer* undoubtedly did excellently in hys *Troylus and Cresseid*; of whom, truly I know not, whether to mervaile more, either that he, in that mistie time, could see so clearly, or that wee, in this cleare age, walke so stumblingly after him. Yet had he great wants, fitte to be forgiven in so reverent antiquity.

That last sentence is the Humanist party line, as it were, but what comes before is the truth. Imitation, the Humanist mode of evading the darker consequences of influence while accomodating it nevertheless, appears in Sidney's *Defence* as the art that takes place between philosophy and history, between the precept and the example. A fiction therefore does not follow the example of a prior fiction, which would make the history of poetry only a repetition, nor does it follow the precept of an aesthetician, be he Plato or Aristotle. By intervening between precept and example, the new poet mediates between what ought to be and what was, in order to establish a new text as what is, or rather as what will be. Defending poetry against both philosophy and history, Sidney shrewdly also defends the Humanist idealizing of the process of literary influence.

4

The literary criticism of the sixteenth century, since it is so entirely part of what can be called a Humanist manifesto, now demands to be read in a certain spirit of affectionate de-idealization. The greatest writers of the century accomplish this de-idealization by themselves, and if such an activity be considered criticism (and it is), then Montaigne, rather than du Bellay or Sidney or Tasso, becomes the great critic of the early Renaissance. To call the *Essays* a vast work of literary criticism is a revisionary act of judgment, but only in the sense of seeing now that Sigmund Freud, who died in 1939, appears in 1986 to have been the crucial critic of the twentieth century. Montaigne's defense of the self is also an analysis of the self, and Montaigne appears now to have been the ancestor not only of Emerson and Nietzsche, both of whom acknowledged him, but also of Freud, who did not.

Returning to Montaigne then, in a wider compass than just the essay "Of Books," is to encounter a poetics of the self that is also a relentless (for all its casual mode) critique of the Humanist, idealized poetics of the self. Petrarch, du Bellay, even the more pragmatic Sidney, and most of all the tormented Tasso—all of them idealize their stance in relation to vernacular precursors, and also in regard to ancient wisdom. Montaigne, once past his Humanist first phase, and his skeptical transition, does not deceive either himself or others when it comes to the problems of writing:

INTRODUCTION

> I have not had regular dealings with any solid book, except Plutarch and Seneca, from whom I draw like the Danaïds, incessantly filling up and pouring out. Some of this sticks to this paper; to myself, a little or nothing.

This, from near the start of the 1579–80 essay "Of the Education of Children," is one of the most astonishing sentences even in Montaigne. Terence Cave, in *The Cornucopian Text*, reads this sentence in the manner of Derrida and Barthes:

> The fullness of two model-texts is here designated, it would seem, as a source; the labour of the Danaides would thus represent the activity of transmission or exchange ('commerce'), by which the textual substance of Plutarch and Seneca is displaced into a discourse bearing the signature 'Montaigne'. But this sentence is marked from the beginning by a negation. Plutarch and Seneca appear in a concessive phrase made possible only by the absence of any 'livre solide': a characteristically Montaignian insistence on the emptiness of discourse (particularly the written discourses of pedagogy) allows provisional access to certain privileged texts whose unsystematic, open-ended form endorses that of the *Essais* themselves. The negation is not, however, limited to the unnamed texts Montaigne claims to have neglected. The Danaides are, after all, not a wholly reassuring figure of plenitude. Rabelais cites them as a counter-example of cornucopian productivity, a sign of despair, and the uselessness of their labours is made explicit in the following sentence: 'J'en attache quelque chose à ce papier; à moy, si peu que rien.' The *locus* is closed, as it began, in negation. The *moi*, in a place outside discourse, is scarcely touched by the language even of Plutarch and Seneca; its integrity is preserved, as at the beginning of the passage, by a repudiation of books. Alien discourse cannot be "attached" to the self, is external to it. Hence the gesture of transference, endlessly repeated, appears as an empty mime. The only thing to which fragments of another text may be attached is 'ce papier', a mediate domain which clearly concerns the *moi* (since the sentences inscribed on it have a habit of beginning with 'je'), but is no less clearly different from it. The paper on which the text of the *Essais* appears is, indeed, a place of difference: it allows the rewriting and naturalization of foreign texts; it thereby permits the search for the identity of a *moi* in contradistinction from what is 'other'; but at the same time it defers any final access to the goal of the search, since the self is expressly an entity dissociated from the activity of writing.

If read in that deconstructionist manner, then Montaigne is achieving an awareness that the experiential fullness he seeks outside language, and which he hopes to represent in his own language, is no more a true presence in Plutarch and Seneca than in his own pages, or in his own self. Like the Danaïds, all writers are condemned to carry the waters of experience in the sieve of language. But Montaigne (unlike Cave) *does* regard the *Moral Essays* of Plutarch and the *Epistles* of Seneca as "solid books." They are not merely privileged texts or sources, but pragmatically, experientially, they have, *for Montaigne*, a different status than his own writing possesses. They are the fathers, true authors and authorities; they do augment because they do not go back to the foundations, but for Montaigne they *are* the foundations. And some of their reality does stick to Montaigne's manuscript and printed page, even if some does not. Montaigne's self is as formidable as the selves of Plutarch and Seneca; his self repels influences. Yet he does grant priority to the text of the fathers, because his text, as opposed to his self, cannot have authority without some transference from the fathers.

Cave concludes his very useful study of Montaigne by turning to the text of the culminating essay, the magnificent "Of Experience" (1587–88). After observing that there is envy and jealousy between our pleasures, so that they clash and interfere with one another, Montaigne opposes himself to those who therefore would abandon natural pleasures:

> I, who operate only close to the ground, hate that inhuman wisdom that would make us disdainful enemies of the cultivation of the body. I consider it equal injustice to set our heart against natural pleasures and to set our heart too much on them. Xerxes was a fool, who, wrapped in all human pleasures, went and offered a prize to anyone who would find him others. But hardly less of a fool is the man who cuts off those that nature has found for him. We should neither pursue them nor flee them, we should accept them. I accept them with more gusto and with better grace than most, and more willingly let myself follow a natural inclination. We have no need to exaggerate their inanity; it makes itself felt enough and evident enough. Much thanks to our sickly, kill-joy mind, which disgusts us with them as well as with itself. It treats both itself and all that it takes in, whether future or past, according to its insatiable, erratic, and versatile nature.
>
> > Unless the vessel's pure, all you pour in turns sour.
> >   HORACE
>
> I, who boast of embracing the pleasures of life so assiduously and so particularly, find in them, when I look at them thus minutely, virtually nothing but wind. But what of it? We are all wind. And even the wind, more wisely than we, loves to make a noise and move about, and is content with its own functions, without wishing for stability and solidity, qualities that do not belong to it.

Cave deconstructs this:

> Full experience is always absent; presence is unattainable. All that the *Essais* can do, with their ineradicable self-consciousness, is to posit paradigms of wholeness as features of a discourse which, as it pours itself out, celebrates its own inanity. The Montaignian text represents the emptying of the cornucopia by the very gesture of extending itself

INTRODUCTION

indefinitely until the moment of ultimate *egressio* or elimination: the figures of abundance play a prominent part in the closing pages of *De l'experience*. Whatever plenitude seems to have been proper to the past, whatever festivity is assigned to these terminal moments, Montaigne's writing is both the only place in which they can be designated, and a place from which they remain inexhaustibly absent.

The plenitude of the textual past, of Plutarch, and of Seneca, and of Horace, is certainly present here, but so is the pragmatic presence of an achieved text, a newness caught in its annunciation. If we are all wind, and Montaigne's *Essays* nothing but wind, why then let us be as wise as the wind. The text, like ourselves, makes a noise and moves about. Like the wind, we and our texts ought not to seek for qualities not our own. But an unstable and fluid text, always metamorphic, can be viewed as positively as a mobile self. If Montaigne declares limitation, he also asserts a freedom, both for his text and for himself.

Montaigne, like the characters of Shakespeare's plays, changes because he listens to what he himself has said. Reading his own text, he becomes Hamlet's precursor, and represents reality in and by himself. His power of interpretation over his own text is also a power over the precursors' texts, and so makes of his own belatedness an earliness. What Petrarch and du Bellay and Tasso longed for vainly, what Sidney urbanely courted, is what Rabelais first possessed in the Renaissance, and is what culminates in Montaigne's "Of Experience," before it goes on to triumph again in Don Quixote, Falstaff, and Hamlet. Call it a Humanist reality rather than a Humanist idealization: an exaltation of the vernacular that authentically carried representation back to its Homeric and Biblical strength. In that exaltation, the writer makes us see regions of reality we could not have seen without him. As Wallace Stevens said of the poet, the enterprise of the Renaissance Humanist author:

> tries by a peculiar speech to speak
> The peculiar potency of the general,
> To compound the imagination's Latin with
> The lingua franca et jocundissima.

Boccaccio
1313–1374

Giovanni Boccaccio, a leading figure of the Italian Renaissance, was born in Florence in 1313, the illegitimate son of an Italian merchant and an unknown woman. Boccaccio would later represent his mother as a Frenchwoman of noble birth, a claim which is thought to be dubious. In any case, his father accepted him into his household and set him up in the banking world in Naples.

Boccaccio does not seem to have taken to banking; instead he persuaded his father to allow him to enroll at the University of Naples as a student of canon law. During his stay in Naples he made many connections at court and had the run of the Royal Library.

At this point in the early Renaissance Dante's tributes to Beatrice and Petrarch's to Laura had already established a tradition of infatuation among Italian poets, and Boccaccio was soon ready to inscribe his own name into that tradition. He first saw Fiametta on an Easter Sunday sometime in the early 1330's. This experience was his poetic point of departure. He claimed that it inspired his *Filocolo*, which is considered the first prose romance in Western literature. Throughout the 1330's he completed a number of works, including the *Filostrato*, the *Teseida*, the *Vision of Love*, and the *Comedy of the Florentine Nymphs*.

His father's business reverses forced Boccaccio to return to Florence before the end of 1341. In Florence he turned from the romance form and began to compose the kind of didactic allegory which Dante had contributed to Tuscan literature. The Black Death came to Florence in 1348, killing close to a third of the citizens, including Boccaccio's stepmother. His father died less than a year later. The plague serves as the gruesome backdrop to *The Decameron*, begun in the same year. It is considered one of the central literary works of the Renaissance.

Boccaccio first met his great precursor, Petrarch, in 1350, and the two poets became close friends. In an attempt to emulate Petrarch, Boccaccio abandoned his vernacular fictions for Latin works such as *The Fate of Illustrious Men* and *Concerning Famous Women*.

King Hugo of Cyprus, concerned about the lack of a comprehensive treatment of the mythology of antiquity, commissioned Boccaccio in the 1340's to write what became known as *The Genealogy of the Gentile Gods*. Boccaccio probably had the book in mind during much of his life, but the bulk of it was composed between 1350 and 1363.

Boccaccio set out in this work to revive and rationalize the enormous amount of classical material which was unknown or neglected during the Middle Ages. Even more difficult was the task of showing that the use of classical material was appropriate to the Christian poet. The latter Boccaccio accomplished through his insistence that secular poetry contained a truth. This truth, he said, could be obtained through allegorical interpretation. He demonstrates just such a method, albeit not very consistently, throughout the first thirteen books of the *Genealogy*, attempting to convince the reader that the pagan myths contain an obscured, sometimes even a Christian, truth. In his *Life of Dante*, Boccaccio justified the obscurity of poetic meaning by remarking that "anything gained with fatigue is sweeter than what is understood without effort. The plain truth, since it is understood easily, delights us and passes from the mind."

Book Fourteen of the *Genealogy* constitutes Boccaccio's defense of poetry against "cavillers." He claims that poets were the first theologians. Moses, says Boccaccio, "wrote the largest part of Pentateuch not in prose but in heroic verse." Boccaccio even suggests that Moses may in fact be the same person as Museaus, the mythical father of Greek poetry. All poetry, then, assumes a status which is, at the very least, complementary to scripture.

During the late 1350's, the dire warnings of a Carthusian monk almost convinced Boccaccio to give up literature entirely, but Petrarch intervened and persuaded him to continue his work. Petrarch died in the summer of 1374, and Boccaccio's greatest sonnet envisions Petrarch and Laura united at last in heaven. Boccaccio did not long outlive his great friend and died on December 21, 1374.

The selections from *The Life of Dante*, translated by Allan H. Gilbert, are reprinted with his permission from *Literary Criticism: Plato to Dryden*, edited by Allan H. Gilbert (Detroit: Wayne State University Press, 1962). ©1962 by Allan H. Gilbert. *The Genealogy of the Gentile Gods*, translated by Charles G. Osgood, is reprinted by permission of Bobbs-Merrill Educational Publishing from *Boccaccio On Poetry*, edited by Charles G. Osgood (Indianapolis: The Bobbs-Merrill Company, Inc., 1956). ©1956 by The Liberal Arts Press, Inc.

The Life of Dante

FROM
Chapter XXI

Since many who do not understand such matters think that poetry is nothing else than a mere fabulous narrative, I have decided to exceed my promise and show that it is theology. . . .

FROM
Chapter XXII

If we wish to lay aside the passions and look reasonably at the matter, I believe that we shall easily enough be able to see that the ancient poets, so far as it is possible to human capacity, followed in the footsteps of the Holy Spirit, which, as we read in the sacred Scriptures, revealed its lofty secrets to future times through the mouths of many writers, making them beneath a veil speak what it intended at the proper time to show in deeds, without any veil. Therefore, if we look well at their writings, we shall see that these men, wishing the imitator to be not unlike the thing imitated, under the cover of fictions described what had been, or what was in their time, or what they desired or presumed would come about in the future. Hence, without assuming that all kinds of writing have the same end, but considering only their method, with which I am now most concerned, the same praise can be given to both Scripture and profane writings, in the words of Gregory. He says of the sacred Scriptures what can also be said of poetry, namely, that in relating anything it explains the text and the mystery subordinated to it in the same words. Thus at the same time it occupies the wise and gives comfort to the simple; in the obvious sense there is something to sustain babes, and in the hidden sense it keeps that with which it holds in admiring awe the minds of the wisest hearers. Thus it appears to be a river, if I may use the figure, both shallow and deep, in which the tiny lamb can go on its feet and the great elephant has ample room to swim. But I must go on to prove what I have stated.

The sacred Scripture, which we call theology, in the guise of a story, now with the seeing of some vision, again by hearing some lament and in many other ways, sets out to show us the high mystery of the incarnation of the divine Word, his life, the events of his death, his victorious resurrection, his miraculous ascension, and all his other acts. If we are instructed by these, we can come to that glory which he, by dying and rising, opened to us after it had long been shut to us through the sin of the first man. Likewise the poets in their works, which we call poetry, with fictions about various gods, with transmutations of men into varied forms, and with pleasant persuasions show us the causes of things, the effects of virtues and vices, and what we should avoid and what we should follow, in order that by working righteousness we may attain that end which they who did not fully know the true God thought was complete blessedness. In the green bush in which Moses saw God like a burning flame, the Holy Spirit wished to show us the virginity of Her who was purer than any other creature, and that she was to be the dwelling and shelter of the Lord of nature and that she would not be defiled by the conception or the birth of the word of the Father. By Nebuchadnezzar's vision of the statue made of several metals struck down by a rock that was changed into a mountain, the Spirit wished to show all succeeding ages that they ought to submit to the doctrine of Christ, who was and is the living rock, and that the Christian religion born of this rock would become a thing immovable and eternal, as we see that the mountains are. In the lamentations of Jeremiah the Spirit intends to set forth the future destruction of Jerusalem.

Similarly our poets, when they feigned that Saturn had many children and devoured all but four of them, wished to have understood from this fiction nothing else than that Saturn is time, in which everything is produced, and as everything is produced in time, it likewise is the destroyer of all and reduces all to nothing. Of the four children that he did not devour, the first is Jove, that is the element of fire; the second is Juno, the wife and sister of Jove, that is the air, by the means of which fire works its effects below; the third is Neptune, god of the sea, that is the element of water; the fourth and last is Pluto, god of the inferno, that is the earth, lower than any other element. Likewise our poets feigned that Hercules was changed from a man into a god, and Lycaon into a wolf. By this they wished to show that by acting virtuously, as Hercules did, man becomes a god by participation in heaven, and that by acting wickedly, as Lycaon did, though he appears a man, he is truly to be called by the name of that beast which is known by everyone to have the quality most like his vice. So because of his rapacity and avarice, qualities like those of a wolf, it is feigned that Lycaon was changed into a wolf. Likewise our poets feign the beauty of the Elysian Fields, by which I understand the sweetness of paradise. From the darkness of Dis I learn the pain of the inferno. Hence I infer that attracted by the pleasures of one and frightened by the woe of the other we should follow the virtues that will lead us to the Elysian Fields and avoid the vices that will cause us to be hurled into Dis. I omit more particular expositions of these things, though they would be pleasing and would make my argument stronger, because I fear they would take me further than my chief subject demands and than I wish to go. And surely if no more were said than has been said, it ought to be well enough understood that theology and poetry are in agreement as to their form of working, but in subject I say that they are not merely wholly diverse, but in some parts contradictory. The subject of sacred theology is divine virtue; the ancient poets treat the gods of the Gentiles and men. They are contradictory in so far as theology brings forward from the beginning nothing unless it is true;

poetry brings forward things as true that are wholly false and erroneous and against the Christian religion. But because some foolish men rise up against the poets, saying that they have composed disgusting and wicked fables that have no harmony with truth, and that in some other way than by fables they should show their ability and give their teaching to men, I wish to go somewhat farther with the present discussion.

Let men of this sort, then, consider the visions of Daniel, those of Isaiah, those of Ezekiel, and the others in the Old Testament that were written by the divine pen and presented by Him to whom there has been no beginning and will be no end. Let them consider also the visions of the evangelists in the New Testament, full of marvelous truth to the understanding, and, if any poetic story is found so far from truth and from the verisimilar as these in many places appear on the surface, it may be conceded that the poets alone have written fables because they were unable to give delight or benefit. Without saying anything on the charges they bring against the poets, in so far as they have presented their teaching in fables or under a fabulous veil, I could properly pass on, since I know that when they foolishly blame the poets for this, they rashly stumble into blaming that Spirit that is none other than the way, the truth, and the life. Still I intend to give them some satisfaction.

It is obvious that anything that is gained with fatigue seems sweeter than what is acquired without any effort. The plain truth, since it is quickly understood with little difficulty, delights us and passes from the mind. But, in order that it may be more pleasing, because acquired with labor, and therefore be better retained, the poets hide the truth beneath things apparently quite contrary to it. For that reason they produce fables, rather than some other covering, because their beauty attracts those whom neither philosophical demonstrations nor persuasions would have been able to allure. What then shall we say about the poets? Shall we hold that they are madmen, as their senseless adversaries, saying they know not what, have thought them? Certainly not; on the contrary they employ in their productions the most profound thought, which is equivalent to everything hidden in the fruit, and admirable and splendid language, which corresponds to the rind and the leaves. But let us resume the thread of our discourse.

I say that theology and poetry can be called almost the same thing, when they have the same subject; I even say that theology is none other than the poetry of God. What else is it than a poetic fiction when the Scripture in one place calls Christ a lion, in another a lamb, and in another a worm [perhaps a reference to Job 25:6, "the son of man, which is a worm"], here a dragon and here a rock, and many others that I omit for the sake of brevity? What else do the words of Our Savior in the Gospels come to if not a sermon that does not signify what it appears to? It is what we call—to use a well-known term—allegory. Then it plainly appears that not merely is poetry theology but that theology is poetry. And surely if in so important a matter my words deserve little reliance, I am not disturbed by it; for I put my trust in Aristotle, an excellent authority in any important matter, who affirms he found that the poets were the first to write theology [*Metaphysics* 3. 4. 1000a9].

The Genealogy of The Gentile Gods

PREFACE

If I have understood aright, O famous King, the words of your distinguished soldier, Donino of Parma, you particularly wish to have compiled a Genealogy of the Gentile Gods and of the heroes who, according to ancient mythology, sprang from them. At the same time you desire an explanation of the meaning which various eminent men have perceived beneath the surface of these myths. Furthermore, from your exalted position, you have chosen me, as one supposed to enjoy deep and wide erudition in such matters, to be the author of this vast work. I will not dwell upon my wonder at your desire, for it becomes not a humble person to scrutinize the motives of a King; and I refrain from uttering my misgivings at your choice of me, for in showing my insufficiency to the task I might seem by subterfuge to try to escape that office which you impose. But before I express my opinion of this task, I should like, most Serene King, to relate at least a part of the conversation between your eminent soldier Donino and me, in which he imparted to me the commands of your Highness; so that, as you read it over, you may see your opinion of me set over against my temerity in obeying your Majesty.

He began with an eloquent description of your Majesty's studies in sacred subjects, of your wonderful acts as King, and a long and witty account of your eminent and distinguished titles. At last he endeavored with no little pains to bring me to your opinion by citing many reasons, some of which, I admit, seemed valid. When he paused, I answered at some length as follows:

"My eloquent soldier, perhaps you, or your King, who, by the grace of God, will soon be ours too, have supposed that this infatuate wish of the Ancients to be considered descendants of gods prevailed in only a small corner of the earth, that, being so absurd, it lasted but a short time, and that it can as easily be reduced to a description as any modern subject. But—always by indulgence—may I say that the fact is quite different. For the tinder of this foolishness blazed up not only on the Cyclades and other Aegean islands, but in Achaia, Illyria, and Thrace, especially during the days of the Greek Republic. It further infected the shores of the Black Sea, the Hellespont, the coast of Maeonia, Icaria, Pamphylia, Cilicia, Phoenicia, Syria, and Egypt. Even Cyprus, the fair adornment of our King, was not immune. It lapped all the shore of Lybia, the Syrtes, Numidia, the coast of the Atlantic, the western ocean and even the far-remote gardens of the Hesperides. Not content with Mediterranean shores, it penetrated to nations far inland. Together with the peoples of the coast all those along the sourceless Nile fell into this error, the pest-ridden sands of Lybia and the solitudes of most ancient Thebes. So too the upper Egyptians, the people of torrid Garamantia, the hot and hairy Ethiopians, the perfumed Arabs, the rich Persians, the people of the Ganges and handsome blacks of India, the Babylonians, they who dwell upon the lofty heights of Caucasus, and its rough slopes toward the torrid south as well as the icy north; the peoples by the Caspian Sea, at Tanais and Rhodope in its eternal snow; the grim Hyrcani, and the gross barbarians of Scythia. When finally it had tainted the waves of the eastern ocean and the islands of the Red Sea, it turned at last to us in Italy, so that Rome, Mistress of the World, was also wrapped in this cloud. Not to mention all the regions into which this ignorant belief managed to penetrate, there was, as you can see, only a small corner of the earth to the northwest which, unlike the others, was not dignified by any heaven-descended family, though, like the rest, it was infected with unspeakable cruelty.

"All this belongs not to our age. Abraham was yet a youth when such ideas began to creep among the Sicyoni, and insinuate themselves into the minds of ignorant men. In the heroic period they grew in fervor, attained at length their greatest splendor and vogue, and persisted as late as the fall of Troy; for I remember reading that in the Trojan war there fell certain sons of the gods, and that Hecuba was changed to a dog and Polydorus to a twig. That indeed is very remote—many centuries ago. In short this foolish faith without doubt flourished everywhere, and great tomes were written to commemorate for posterity the divine nobility of the Ancients. I always supposed the number of men ambitious for such fame was not small, but Paul of Perugia, a serious man, a very learned and eager investigator of such matters, has repeatedly said in my hearing what he had learned from Barlaam the Calabrian, a scholar of the first rank in Greek literature—that, during the florescence of that fatuity, there was never a man of distinction, political or otherwise, who did not try to prove his descent from one or another of the ancient gods. What then, am I to do, or you, in view of an error so widespread, so ancient, so persistent, recorded in so many documents, and propagated at large among so many men? Do you think I can possibly carry out the King's wishes? Doubtless—if mountains offer easy passage and trackless deserts an open and travelled road; if rivers are fordable and seas tranquil; if Aeolus from his cave sends me in my course strong and favorable winds; or, better still, if a man might have on his feet the golden sandals of Argeiphontes, to fly withersoever he pleased for the asking. Hardly then could he cover such extent of land and sea, though his life were never so long, and he did nothing else. Nay, further, let us suppose that a man could visit all these places in a moment, and by God's grace could understand the characters and idiom of various peoples and find entire libraries ready and waiting, who would there be in all the world—not to mention myself—strong enough, keen enough, and with good enough memory, first to observe what is relevant, then to understand it, retain it, note it down, and finally reduce it to order? You added a further request, that I explain the meaning which wise men had hidden under this cover of absurd tales, on the ground that his renowned Majesty thought it a stupid notion for men learned in nearly every doctrine to spend time and labor merely telling stories which are untrue and have only a literal meaning.

"Well, I will not deny it—the royal discernment which you report has won me, and given me a very definite subject, since, as you were saying, his genius is really divine; and it has impelled me to grant his wish, if only my powers are adequate. Such interpretations are harder than you think; they are properly the business of a theologian, for Varro, in treating of many matters both divine and human, holds that such subjects as this constitute a sort of theology which may be called 'mythical,' or as others would say—more accurately, perhaps—'physical.' In view of such an opinion, and of the large element of absurd untruth in mythology, there is the more need of skill in separating true from false.

"Wherefore, my learned warrior, a man's powers must be weighed and his abilities carefully considered, if fit and commensurate burdens are to be laid upon them. Atlas was able to uphold the heaven on his head, and Alcides was equal to relieving him of the weary load—divine men both and both invincibly strong. But me? What am I but a little fellow, weak, slow-witted, forgetful. And here you are trying to pile on my shoulders not heaven alone, which was enough for those old heroes, but earth too, and the seas, nay, the very gods with all their notable train! Why, it's nothing but a proposal to crush and destroy me. But great as was the King's conception of this work, if any human being was really equal to it, it is that distinguished man Francis Petrarch, at whose feet I have long been a listener. He is really a man of godlike genius, unfailing memory, and wonderful eloquence, thoroughly familiar with the history of the various nations, and learned in the meaning of myths; one, moreover, who understands every secret in the bosom of sacred Philosophy."

Here I paused. After a bit he went on, serene of feature and urbane of speech.

"I suppose that what you say is truer than I realize, and I can see the difficulties. But, my dear Giovanni, do you think, pray, that our King is without circumspection? Why, he is a ruler with his eyes open, well-disposed, and of laudable, royal good nature! Far be it from him wittingly to oppress you or anyone else; rather it has long been his habit to lighten the people's burdens; and in precisely that intention must his commands be understood and accepted.

"I can well believe that those nations you mention are inaccessible, and that such records as they possess are wholly unknown to the Latins. But whatever has passed by way of Greek literature among the Latins, or whatever can be found in Latin writers themselves, who in early times won no little distinction and glory in literature, let it all be brought to light, and, if all of it is not available, then King Hugo asks for at least so much as your endeavors can procure. Therefore please undertake this task without misgiving, and with lively hope in God. Do as well as you can, for no one asks of you the impossible. It has not been my good fortune to meet that noble man, Petrarch, nor has he visited Cyprus, though his fame is universal. I suppose God wills that a man so busy with affairs of utmost importance should be spared this work, and that I should suggest this honorable task to you, a young man, that from it your reputation may soon rise higher and shine even in Cyprus."

"I see, my valiant soldier," I replied. "You suppose this book can be compiled from Greek and Latin sources, without recourse to the recondite books of the barbarians. Dear me, Donino, do you not see for yourself that by such a concession you take back the greatest part of the work? But grant that, as the Roman rulers long since divided the empire into an eastern and western half, we distinguish two bodies of this monster—the one, barbarian, and the other Greek and Latin. Let us, then, suppose that books in Greek and Latin such as you yourself mention, have really existed. Next consider, please, how many enemies these books have had during the passing centuries. Not to cite particular instances, you will admit that a great many collections have perished by fire and flood. Even had the Alexandrian library, which Philadelphus long since collected with utmost care, been the only one lost, the loss would have been appalling, since it contained, according to the Ancients, any book you might want. Furthermore as Christ's most glorious name grew in power, and the pure and radiant light of Truth drove away the shades of the deadly Gentile error; as the glory of the Greeks declined, and the messengers of Christ cried out against the doomed religion and drove it to extermination, there is no question that these zealots destroyed ere they died many books replete with material on this subject, while they were showing by true and pious preaching that instead of many gods and their offspring there was but one God the Father and His only-begotten Son. You will admit that avarice, whose force is very great, has been another enemy of learning. They who are skilled in the study of poetry certainly get no money by it; and the avaricious man values nothing that does not get money; hence he not only neglects anything that gets no money but despises and rejects it. Now as nearly all men are in the race for wealth with both feet, books dealing with our subject have fallen into disuse, and straightway quickly perished. With other forces of destruction was joined the hatred of princes who conspired against books as against their enemies. The number which perished thus, not merely on mythology, but on various arts, could not easily be computed. But if all these enemies had relented, they would never have escaped the silent and adamantine tooth of fleeting time, which slowly eats away not books alone, but hardest rocks, and even steel. It has, alas, reduced much of Greek and Latin literature to dust. And yet, though these and many other losses have occurred, including that of books which would be particularly useful to a task like mine, I cannot deny that much is left. But there is no one book that I know of which contains all this matter about which you are so very curious. The names and tribes of gods and their progenitors are scattered hither and yon all over the world. Here a book and there another has something to say on the subject. But pray who is there that would wish, for no useful result, or at least very little, to hunt them all up, read, and finally gather a few notes? More than this I should not say."

Steadfastly and gravely he looked at me; then he said:

"I had not overlooked your probable objections to my moderate request. But they will not cut off my every escape. I will not deny the truth of what you say; and yet I repeat, do what you can! It is only the bit you *can* gather here and there that the King is asking for. You surely cannot refuse him that, can you? But alas, I am afraid that unworthy indolence invents such reasons. You are trying to get out of some hard work. There is nothing worse than an idle young man. If work must be done—and we are all born to it—to whom can you devote your labors more wisely than to this best of kings? Arise, then, shake off this inertia, and gird up your good wits for the task. Thus you will at once obey the King, and make for yourself a path to high renown. You will surely arrive, if you are careful, at the point whither I am urging you. You know how courage and hard work win in everything; you know how fortune favors the brave, and above all else how God never fails those who trust in Him. Come, then, with so much in your favor, turn the books over, nay, inside out; seize your pen, and in the same act serve the King and make your name reverberate to remotest time."

Then I:

"I am vanquished—more by the charm of your plea than by the force of your reason. You urge, drive, yes, force me to comply, willing or unwilling."

And thus, O most merciful King, to address you in person, after contending, your Donino and I, for some time, at last, whether equal to this task or not, I am perforce won to your view—how fitly you shall see. At your behest, then, I leave behind the mountain snails and barren soil of Certaldo, and, raw seaman that I am, embark in my frail little craft on a stormy sea all involved with reefs, little knowing whether my voyage will be worth the trouble. For I may trace every shore and traverse every mountain grove; I may, if need be, explore dyke and den afoot, descend even to hell, or, like another Daedalus, go winging to the ether. Everywhere, to your heart's desire, I will find and gather, like fragments of a mighty wreck strewn on some vast shore, the relics of the Gentile gods. These relics, scattered through almost infinite volumes, shrunk with age, half consumed, well-nigh a blank, I will bring into such single genealogical order as I can, to gratify your wish.

And yet I shudder to embark on so huge a task; why, if another Prometheus should appear, or the very one who, as poets tell, upon a time made men from clay, I hardly think they would be equal to the task, let alone me. Therefore, illustrious King, to prevent future surprise and disappointment on your part, I would warn you now not to expect, even after great outlay of time and midnight oil, that a work of this sort will have a body of perfect proportion. It will alas, be maimed—not, I hope, in too many members—and for reasons aforesaid distorted, shrunken, and warped. Furthermore, O excellent Prince, to arrange the members in any order, I must proceed to tear the hidden significations from their tough sheathing, and I promise to do so, though not to the last detail of the authors' original intentions. Who in our day can penetrate the hearts of the Ancients? Who can bring to light and life again minds long since removed in death? Who can elicit their meaning? A divine task that—not human! The Ancients departed in the way of all flesh, leaving behind them their literature and their famous names for posterity to interpret according to their own judgment. But as many minds, so many opinions. What wonder? There are the words of Holy Writ, clear, definite, charged with unalterable truth, though often thinly veiled in figurative language. yet they are frequently distorted into as many meanings as there are readers. This makes me approach my own task with less misgiving. Where I do not perform it well, at least I shall arouse a wiser man to do it better.

It is, therefore, my plan of interpretation first to write what I learn from the

Ancients, and when they fail me, or I find them inexplicit, to set down my own opinion. This I shall do with perfect freedom of mind, so that men who are ignorant and fastidiously despise the poets whom they do not understand, may see that the poets, though not Catholics, were so gifted with intelligence that no product of human genius was ever more skilfully enveloped in fiction, nor more beautifully adorned with exquisite language, than theirs. Whence it is clear that they were richly imbued with secular wisdom not often found in their jealous accusers. And these interpretations will enable you to see not only the art of the ancient poets, and the consanguinity and relations of the false gods, but certain natural truths, hidden with an art that will surprise you, together with deeds and moral civilization of the Ancients that are not a matter of every-day information. Furthermore, as the work will prove to be far more extensive than you suppose, I think it will be convenient both for purposes of reference and of memory to divide it into several parts or books. Before each book I plan to set a tree; at the root sits the father of the line, and on the branches, in genealogical order, all his progeny, so that you may have an index of what you are looking for in the book that follows. These Books you will find divided into chapters with proper and fuller rubrics corresponding to the mere name which you have already noted on the tree.

I shall conclude with two books, in the first of which I shall reply to certain objections that have been raised against poetry and poets. In the second—and last of all—I shall endeavor to remove such criticisms as may possibly be levelled at me. But for fear you may think it my fault, I must not fail to explain that it is the Ancients who are to blame, not I, if you often meet in reading my work with statements that are so wide of the truth, so discrepant, that you could never suppose them the utterances of philosophers, no, not even the inventions of rustics; other inconsistencies you will observe in their chronology. All these discrepancies and more I do not purpose to reconcile or correct, unless they naturally submit to some order. I shall be satisfied merely to write down what I find and leave learned disputation to the philosophers.

Finally, it has long been a wise and fitting custom, as Plato advises, in entering upon even the least of ventures, to invoke God's help, and set out in His name. Without it any initiation, Torquatus tells us, is fundamentally unsound. I can quite realize this labor to which I am committed—this vast system of gentile gods and their progeny, torn limb from limb and scattered among the rough and desert places of antiquity and the thorns of hate, wasted away, sunk almost to ashes; and here am I setting forth to collect these fragments, hither and yon, and fit them together, like another Aesculapius restoring Hippolytus. If I trust my own strength I should stagger under this overload. Wherefore to the most merciful Father, the one true God, Maker and Ruler of all things, in whom we mortals have our being, I humbly pray that He favor and aid this vast, ambitious work of mine. May He shine upon my way, a fixed and radiant star, and rule the helm of my little boat as she plows an untried sea. May He at right seasons spread her sails to the wind, that I may follow a course redounding to the splendor, laud, honor, and eternal glory of His name; but to all detractors confusion, ignominy, disgrace, and eternal damnation!

FROM
Book XIV

VI. *Poetry is a Useful Art*

I am about to enter the arena, a manikin against these giant hulks—who have armed themselves with authority to say that poetry is either no art at all or a useless one. In the circumstances, for me first to discuss the definition and function of poetry would be hunting a mare's nest. But since the fight must be fought I wish these past masters of all the arts would declare upon what particular point they desire the contest to bear. Yet I know full well that with a sneer and a brazen front they will unblushingly utter the same ineptitudes as before. Come, O merciful God, give ear to their foolish objections and guide their steps into a better way.

They say, then, in condemnation of poetry, that it is naught. If such is the case, I should like to know why, through generation after generation, so many great men have sought the name of poet. Whence come so many volumes of poems? If poetry is naught, whence came this word poetry? Whatever answer they make, they are going out of their way, I think, since they can give no rational answer that is not directly against their present vain contention. It is absolutely certain, as I shall show later, that poetry, like other studies, is derived from God, Author of all wisdom; like the rest it got its name from its effect. From this name "poetry" at length comes the glorious name of "poet"; and from "poet," "poem." In that case poetry apparently is not wholly naught, as they said.

If then it prove a science, what more will those noisy sophists have to say? They will either retract a little, or rather, I think, flit lightly over the gap thus opening in their argument to the second point of their objection, and say that if poetry *is* a mere art, it is a useless one. How rank! How silly! Better to have kept quiet than hurl themselves with their frivolous words into deeper error. Why, do not the fools see that the very meaning of this word "art" or "faculty" always implies a certain plenitude? But of this elsewhere. Just now I wish that the accomplished gentlemen would show how poetry can reasonably be called futile when it has, by God's grace, given birth to so many famous books, so many memorable poems, clearly conceived, and dealing with strange marvels. They will keep quiet at this, I think, if their vain itch for display will let them.

Keep quiet, did I say? Why they would rather die than confess the truth in silence, not to say with the tip of their tongues. They will dart off on another tack, and by their own arbitrary interpretation, will say, with slight addition, that poetry must be regarded a futile and empty thing, nay, damnable, detestable, because the poems which come of it sing the adulteries of the gods they celebrate, and beguile the reader into unspeakable practices. Though this interpretation is easy to refute—since nothing can be empty that is filled with adulteries—in any case it may be borne with a calm mind; nay their contention based upon it may be granted in all reason, since I readily acknowledge that there are poems of the kind they describe, and if the bad kind were to corrupt the good, then the victory would be theirs. But, I protest; if Praxiteles or Phidias, both experts in their art, should choose for a statue the immodest subject of Priapus on his way to Iole by night, instead of Diana glorified in her chastity; or if Apelles, or our own Giotto—whom Apelles in his time did not excel—should represent Venus in the embrace of Mars instead of the enthroned Jove dispensing laws unto the gods, shall we therefore condemn these arts? Downright stupidity, I should call it!

The fault for such corruption lies in the licentious mind of the artist. Thus for a long time there have been "poets," if such deserve the name, who, either to get money or popularity, study contemporary fashions, pander to a licentious taste, and at the cost of all self-respect, the loss of all honor, abandon themselves to these literary fooleries. Their works certainly should be condemned, hated, and spurned, as I shall show later. Yet if a few writers of fiction erred thus, poetry does not therefore deserve universal condemnation, since it offers us so many inducements to virtue, in the monitions and teaching of poets whose care it has been to set forth with lofty intelligence, and utmost candor, in exquisite style and diction, men's thoughts on things of heaven.

But enough! Not only is poetry more than naught, but it is a science worthy of veneration; and, as often appears in the foregoing as well as in succeeding pages, it is an art or skill, not empty, but full of the sap of natural vigor for those who would through fiction subdue the senses with the mind. So, not to be tedious, it would seem that at the first onset of this conflict these leaders have turned tail, and, with slight effort on my part, have abandoned the arena. But it is my present duty to define Poetry, that they may see for themselves how stupid they are in their opinion that poetry is an empty art.

VII. *The Definition of Poetry, Its Origin, and Function*

This poetry, which ignorant triflers cast aside, is a sort of fervid and exquisite invention, with fervid expression, in speech or writing, of that which the mind has invented. It proceeds from the bosom of God, and few, I find, are the souls in whom this gift is born; indeed so wonderful a gift it is that true poets have always been the rarest of men. This fervor of poesy is sublime in its effects: it impels the soul to a longing for utterance; it brings forth strange and unheard-of creations of the mind; it arranges these meditations in a fixed order, adorns the whole composition with unusual interweaving of words and thoughts; and thus it veils truth in a fair and fitting garment of fiction. Further, if in any case the invention so requires, it can arm kings, marshal them for war, launch whole fleets from their docks, nay, counterfeit sky, land, sea, adorn young maidens with flowery garlands, portray human character in its various phases, awake the idle, stimulate the dull, restrain the rash, subdue the criminal, and distinguish excellent men with their proper meed of praise: these, and many other such, are the effects of poetry. Yet if any man who has received the gift of poetic fervor shall imperfectly fulfil its function here described, he is not, in my opinion, a laudable poet. For, however deeply the poetic impulse stirs the mind to which it is granted, it very rarely accomplishes anything commendable if the instruments by which its concepts are to be wrought out are wanting—I mean, for example, the precepts of grammar and rhetoric, an abundant knowledge of which is opportune. I grant that many a man already writes his mother tongue admirably, and indeed has performed each of the various duties of poetry as such; yet over and above this, it is necessary to know at least the principles of the other Liberal Arts, both moral and natural, to possess a strong and abundant vocabulary, to behold the monuments and relics of the Ancients, to have in one's memory the histories of the nations, and to be familiar with the geography of various lands, of seas, rivers and mountains.

Furthermore, places of retirement, the lovely handiwork of Nature herself, are favorable to poetry, as well as peace of mind and desire for worldly glory; the ardent period of life also has very often been of great advantage. If these conditions fail, the power of creative genius frequently grows dull and sluggish.

Now since nothing proceeds from this poetic fervor, which sharpens and illumines the powers of the mind, except what is wrought out by art, poetry is generally called an art. Indeed the word poetry has not the origin that many carelessly suppose, namely *poio, pois*, which is but Latin *fingo, fingis*; rather it is derived from a very ancient Greek word *poetes*, which means in Latin exquisite discourse (*exquisita locutio*). For the first men who, thus inspired, began to employ an exquisite style of speech, such, for example, as song in an age hitherto unpolished, to render this unheard-of discourse sonorous to their hearers, let it fall in measured periods; and lest by its brevity it fail to please, or, on the other hand, become prolix and tedious, they applied to it the standard of fixed rules, and restrained it within a definite number of feet and syllables. Now the product of this studied method of speech they no longer called by the more general term poesy, but poem. Thus as I said above, the name of the art, as well as its artificial product, is derived from its effect.

Now though I allege that this science of poetry has ever streamed forth from the bosom of God upon souls while even yet in their tenderest years, these enlightened cavillers will perhaps say that they cannot trust my words. To any fair-minded man the fact is valid enough from its constant recurrence. But for these dullards I must cite witnesses to it. If, then, they will read what Cicero, a philosopher rather than a poet, says in his oration delivered before the senate in behalf of Aulus Licinius Archias, perhaps they will come more easily to believe me. He says: "And yet we have it on the highest and most learned authority, that while other arts are matters of science and formula and technique, poetry depends solely upon an inborn faculty, is evoked by a purely mental activity, and is infused with a strange supernal inspiration."

But not to protract this argument, it is now sufficiently clear to reverent men, that poetry is a practical art, springing from God's bosom and deriving its name from its effect, and that it has to do with many high and noble matters that constantly occupy even those who deny its existence. If my opponents ask when and in what circumstances, the answer is plain: the poets would declare with their own lips under whose help and guidance they compose their inventions when, for example, they raise flights of symbolic steps to heaven, or make thick-branching trees spring aloft to the very stars, or go winding about mountains to their summits. Haply, to disparage this art of poetry now unrecognized by them, these men will say that it is rhetoric which the poets employ. Indeed, I will not deny it in part, for rhetoric has also its own inventions. Yet, in truth, among the disguises of fiction rhetoric has no part, for whatever is composed as under a veil, and thus exquisitely wrought, is poetry and poetry alone.

VIII. *Where Poetry First Dawned Upon the World*

If you inquire, O King, under what sky, in what period, and by whose agency Poetry first came to light, I hardly trust my ability to answer. One group of writers thinks it arose with the holy rites of the Ancients, that is, among the Hebrews, since Holy Writ records that they were the first to offer sacrifice to God; for we read that the brothers, Cain and Abel, the first men born on earth, sacrificed to God; so also did Noah when the flood subsided and he went forth from the ark; and so Abraham for victory over his foes, when he offered Melchisedek the priest wine and bread. But since these accounts do not yield altogether the desired answer, writers of this opinion—rather by divination than proof, it must be said—insist that these rites were accomplished with some sort of formal discourse. They add that Moses, when, with the people of Israel, he had passed the Red Sea dry-shod, performed a complete sacrifice, since we read that he established rites, priests, and a tabernacle like the temple that was to be, and appointed prayers to placate the Divine Will. So it seems that poetry had its origin among the Hebrews not earlier than Moses, leader of the Israelites; and he led the people forth and performed his rites about the time that King Marathius of the Sicyoni died, which was the three thousand, six hundred and eightieth year of the world.

A second group would give the Babylonians the glory of inventing poetry. Among these the Venetian, bishop of Pozzuolo, a tremendous investigator, was wont to argue at length in bantering fashion, that poetry was far older than Moses, having had its origin about the time of Nembroth. Nimrod, he said, was the founder of idolatry, for when he saw that fire was useful to men, and that he could, to some extent, foretell the future from its various motions and sounds, he averred that it was a god; wherefore he not only worshipped it instead of God, and persuaded the Chaldeans to do likewise, but built temples to it, ordained priests, and even composed prayers. Now, according to the Venetian these prayers showed that he employed formal, polished discourse. Possibly; but the Venetian never clearly showed his authority for his statement. Yet I have read often enough that religious worship, the study of philosophy, and the glory of arms all had their origin among the Assyrians. But I cannot easily believe, without more trustworthy evidence, that an art so sublime as that of poetry arose first among peoples so barbarous and wild.

The Greeks also maintain that poetry originated with them, and Leontius supports this view with all his might. I am a little inclined his way, as I recollect hearing my famous teacher once say that among the primitive Greeks, poetry had some such origin as this: While they were still rude, some of them, above the rest in intellectual power, began to wonder at the works of their Mother

Nature; and as they meditated they came gradually to believe in some one Being, by whose operation and command all visible things are governed and ordered. Him they named God. Then, thinking that He sometimes visited earth, and considering Him holy, they raised buildings for Him at enormous expense, that He might on His visits find abiding places consecrated to His name. These we now call temples. Then, to propitiate Him, they devised peculiar honors to be rendered Him at appointed seasons, and called them rites. Finally, in their belief that, as He excelled all others in divinity, so ought He in honor also, they had silver tables made for His rites, and fashioned of gold the drinking-cups, candelabra, and whatever other vessels they used; they also selected men from among the wisest and gentlest of the people, whom they afterwards called priests, and these they would have appear in no common garb at the celebration of rites, but made them resplendent in costly robes with tiaras and crosiers. Then, since it seemed absurd for the priests to perform rites to the Deity in utter silence, they had certain discourses composed to show forth the praise, and great works of the Deity himself, to express the petitions of the people, and offer him the prayers of men in their various needs. And since it would appear inappropriate to address the Deity as you would a farmhand, an underling, or a familiar friend, the wiser among them wanted a polished and artistic manner of speech devised, and they committed this task to the priests. Some of these, though few—and among them, it is thought, were Musaeus, Linus, and Orpheus—under the prompting stimulus of the Divine Mind, invented strange songs in regular time and measure, designed for the praise of God. To strengthen the authority of these songs, they enclosed the high mysteries of things divine in a covering of words, with the intention that the adorable majesty of such things should not become an object of too common knowledge, and thus fall into contempt. Now since the art thus discovered seemed wonderful and wholly new, they named it, as I have said, from its *effect*, and called it poetry or *poetes*, that is, in Latin *exquisita locutio;* and they who had composed the songs were named poets. And, as the name favors the effect, the belief is that both the musical accompaniment of poetry and all its other accoutrements arose among the Greeks.

But the date of its origin is very doubtful. Leontius, for one, used to say that he had heard his teacher, Barlaam of Calabria, and other learned authorities on the subject, more than once assign the date to the time of Phoroneus, King of Argos, who came to the throne in the three thousand, three hundred and eighty-fifth year of the world. They also said that Musaeus, whom I mentioned above as one of the inventors of poetry, was eminent among the Greeks, and that Linus flourished about the same time; their fame, which is still great, bears witness even in our day that they presided over the rites of the Ancients. To these is added Orpheus of Thrace; they are therefore considered the earliest theologians.

But Paul of Perugia used to infer from the same ancient authorities, that poetry was much younger, and alleged that Orpheus, who is recorded as one of the earliest poets, flourished in the reign of Laomedon, King of Troy, when Eurystheus ruled Mycenae, about the three thousand, nine hundred and tenth

THE GENEALOGY OF THE GENTILE GODS

year of the world, that he was the Orpheus of the Argonauts, and not only a successor of Musaeus, but the teacher of the same Musaeus, son of Eumolpus. Such, at least, is the testimony of Eusebius in his *Liber Temporum.* Whence Paul's statement, cited above, that poetry was more recent among the Greeks than his opponents held. Leontius, however, in reply maintained that learned Greeks thought there were several by the name of Orpheus and Musaeus, but that the ancient Orpheus was a Greek contemporary with the ancient Musaeus and Linus, whereas it is a younger one who is called the Thracian. Indeed, since this younger Orpheus invented the rites of Bacchus, and the nocturnal gatherings of the Maenads, and made many innovations in the liturgy of the Ancients, and especially had great powers of eloquence—all of which won him high esteem in his generation—he was therefore regarded as the great Orpheus by posterity. Perhaps this is the right view especially since some of the Ancients bear witness that there were poets before the birth of the Cretan Jove, and it is known from Eusebius that Orpheus the Thracian flourished after Jove's rape of Europa.

But with scholars thus at variance, and me unable to find reliable evidence in ancient authors to support their theories, I cannot tell which to follow. It is at least evident from all accounts that, if one is to follow Leontius, poetry originated with the Greeks before it did with the Hebrews; if the Venetian, then with the Chaldeans before it did among the Greeks; but if we prefer to believe Paul, it follows that Moses was a master of poetry before either Babylonians or Greeks. Aristotle, to be sure, perhaps for reasons just urged, asserts that the first poets were theologians, by that meaning Greeks; and herein he favors somewhat the opinion of Leontius. Nevertheless I cannot believe that the sublime effects of this great art were first bestowed upon Musaeus, or Linus, or Orpheus, however ancient, unless, as some say, Moses and Musaeus were one and the same. Of the beast Nimrod I take no account. Rather was it instilled into most sacred prophets, dedicated to God. For we read that Moses, impelled by what I take to be this poetic longing, at dictation of the Holy Ghost, wrote the largest part of the Pentateuch not in prose but in heroic verse. In like manner others have set forth the great works of God in the metrical garment of letters, which we call poetic. And I think the poets of the Gentiles in their poetry—not perhaps without understanding—followed in the steps of these prophets; but whereas the holy men were filled with the Holy Ghost, and wrote under His impulse, the others were prompted by mere energy of mind, whence such a one is called "seer." Under fervor of this impulse they composed their poems. But since I have nothing further to say on the origin of poetry, do thou, O glorious King, choose whichever opinion accords with thy serene judgment.

IX. *It Is Rather Useful Than Damnable to Compose Stories*

These fine cattle bellow still further to the effect that poets are talemongers, or, to use the lower and more hateful term which they sometimes employ in their resentment—liars. No doubt the ignorant will regard such an imputation as particularly objectionable. But I scorn it. The foul language of some men cannot infect the glorious name of the illustrious. Yet I grieve to see these revilers in a purple rage let themselves loose upon the innocent. If I conceded that poets deal in stories, in that they are composers of fiction, I think I hereby incur no further disgrace than a philosopher would in drawing up a syllogism. For if I show the nature of a fable or story, its various kinds, and which kinds these "liars" employ, I do not think the composers of fiction will appear guilty of so monstrous a crime as these gentlemen maintain. First of all, the word "fable" (*fabula*) has an honorable origin in the verb *for, faris,* hence "conversation" (*confabulatio*), which means only "talking together" (*collocutio*). This is clearly shown by Luke in his Gospel, where he is speaking of the two disciples who went to the village of Emmaus after the Passion. He says:

"And they talked together of all these things which had happened.

"And it came to pass, that, while they communed together, and reasoned, Jesus himself drew near, and went with them."

Hence, if it is a sin to compose stories, it is a sin to converse, which only the veriest fool would admit. For nature has not granted us the power of speech unless for purposes of conversation, and the exchange of ideas.

But, they may object, nature meant this gift for a useful purpose, not for idle nonsense; and fiction is just that—idle nonsense. True enough, if the poet had intended to compose a mere tale. But I have time and time again proved that the meaning of fiction is far from superficial. Wherefore, some writers have framed this definition of fiction (*fabula*): Fiction is a form of discourse, which, under guise of invention, illustrates or proves an idea; and, as its superficial aspect is removed, the meaning of the author is clear. If, then, sense is revealed from under the veil of fiction, the composition of fiction is not idle nonsense. Of fiction I distinguish four kinds: The first superficially lacks all appearance of truth; for example, when brutes or inanimate things converse. Aesop, an ancient Greek, grave and venerable, was past master in this form; and though it is a common and popular form both in city and country, yet Aristotle, chief of the Peripatetics, and a man of divine intellect, did not scorn to use it in his books. The second kind at times superficially mingles fiction with truth, as when we tell of the daughters of Minyas at their spinning, who, when they spurned the orgies of Bacchus, were turned to bats; or the mates of the sailor Acestes, who for contriving the rape of the boy Bacchus, were turned to fish. This form has been employed from the beginning by the most ancient poets, whose object it has been to clothe in fiction divine and human matters alike; they who have followed the sublimer inventions of the poets have improved upon them; while some of the comic writers have perverted them, caring more for the approval of a licentious public than for honesty. The third kind is more like history than fiction, and famous poets have employed it in a variety of ways. For however much the heroic poets seem to be writing history—as Vergil in his description of Aeneas tossed by the storm, or Homer in his account of Ulysses bound to the mast to escape the lure of the Sirens' song—yet their hidden meaning is far other than appears on the surface. The better of the comic poets, Terence and Plautus, for example, have also employed this form, but they intend naught other than the literal meaning of their lines. Yet by their art they portray varieties of human nature and conversation, incidentally teaching the reader and putting him on his guard. If the events they describe have not actually taken place, yet since they are common, they could have occurred, or might at some time. My opponents need not be so squeamish—Christ, who is God, used this sort of fiction again and again in his parables!

The fourth kind contains no truth at all, either superficial or hidden, since it consists only of old wives' tales.

Now, if my eminent opponents condemn the first kind of fiction, then they must include the account in Holy Writ describing the conference of the trees of the forest on choosing a king. If the second, then nearly the whole sacred body of the Old Testament will be rejected. God forbid, since the writings of the Old Testament and the writings of the poets seem as it were to keep step with each other, and that too in respect to the method of their composition. For where history is lacking, neither one concerns itself with the superficial possibility, but what the poet calls fable or fiction our theologians have named figure. The truth of this may be seen by fairer judges than my opponents, if they will but weigh in a true scale the outward literary semblance of the visions of Isaiah, Ezekiel, Daniel, and other sacred writers on the one hand, with the outward literary semblance of the fiction of the poets on the other. If they find any real discrepancy in their methods, either of implication or exposition, I will accept their condemnation. If they comdemn the third form of fiction, it is the same as condemning the form which our Savior Jesus Christ, the Son of God, often used when He was in the flesh, though Holy Writ does not call it "poetry," but "parable"; some call it "exemplum," because it is used as such.

I count as naught their condemnation of the fourth form of fiction, since it proceeds from no consistent principle, nor is fortified by the reinforcement of any of the arts, nor carried logically to a conclusion. Fiction of this kind has nothing in common with the works of the poets, though I imagine these objectors think poetry differs from it in no respect.

I now ask whether they are going to call the Holy Spirit, or Christ, the very God, liars, who both in the same Godhead have uttered fictions. I hardly think so, if they are wise. I might show them, your Majesty, if there were time, that difference of names constitutes no objection where methods agree. But they may see for themselves. Fiction, which they scorn because of its mere name, has been the means, as we often read, of quelling minds aroused to a mad rage, and subduing them to their pristine gentleness. Thus, when the Roman plebs seceded from the senate, they were called back from the sacred mount to the city by Menenius Agrippa, a man of great influence, all by means of a story. By fiction, too, the strength and spirits of great men worn out in the strain of serious crises, have been restored. This appears, not by ancient instance alone, but constantly. One knows of princes who have been deeply engaged in important matters, but after the noble and happy disposal of their affairs of state, obey, as it were, the warning of nature, and revive their spent forces by calling about them such men as will renew their weary minds with diverting stories and conversation. Fiction has, in some cases, sufficed to lift the oppressive weight of adversity and furnish consolation, as appears in Lucius Apuleius; he tells how the highborn maiden Charis, while bewailing her unhappy condition as captive among thieves, was in some degree restored through hearing from an old woman the charming story of Psyche. Through fiction, it is well known, the mind that is slipping into inactivity is recalled to a state of better and more vigorous fruition. Not to mention minor instances, such as my own, I once heard Giacopo Sanseverino, Count of Tricarico and Chiarmonti, say that he had heard his father tell of Robert, son of King Charles,—himself in after time the famous King of Jerusalem and Sicily—how as a boy he was so dull that it took the utmost skill and patience of his master to teach him the mere elements of letters. When all his friends were nearly in despair of his doing anything, his master, by the most subtle skill, as it were, lured his mind with the fables of Aesop into so grand a passion for study and knowledge, that in a brief time he not only learned the Liberal Arts familiar to Italy, but entered with wonderful keenness of mind into the very inner mysteries of sacred philosophy. In short, he made of himself a king whose superior in learning men have not seen since Solomon.

Such then is the power of fiction that it pleases the unlearned by its external appearance, and exercises the minds of the learned with its hidden truth; and thus both are edified and delighted with one and the same perusal. Then let not these disparagers raise their heads to vent their spleen in scornful words, and spew their ignorance upon poets! If they have any sense at all, let them look to their own speciousness before they try to dim the splendor of others with the cloud of their maledictions. Let them see, I pray, how pernicious are their jeers, fit to rouse the laughter only of girls. When they have made themselves clean, let them purify the tales of others, mindful of Christ's commandment to the accusers of the woman taken in adultery, that he who was without sin should cast the first stone.

X. It Is a Fool's Notion That Poets Convey No Meaning Beneath the Surface of Their Fictions

Some of the railers are bold enough to say, on their own authority, that only an utter fool would imagine the best poets to have hidden any meaning in their stories; rather, they have invented them just to display the great power of their eloquence, and show how easily such tales may bring the injudicious mind to take fiction for truth. O the injustice of men! O what absurd dunces! What clumsiness! While they are trying to put down others, they imagine in their ignorance that they are exalting themselves. Who but an ignoramus would dare to say that poets purposely make their inventions void and empty, trusting in the superficial appearance of their tales to show their eloquence? As who should say that truth and eloquence cannot go together. Surely they have missed Quintilian's saying; it was this great orator's opinion that real power of eloquence is inconsistent with falsehood. But this matter I will postpone that I may come to the immediate subject of this chapter. Let any man, then, read the line in Vergil's *Bucolics:*

> He sung the secret seeds of Nature's frame,

THE GENEALOGY OF THE GENTILE GODS

and what follows on the same matter: or in the *Georgics*:

> That bees have portions of ethereal thought
> Endued with particles of heavenly fires.

with the relevant lines; or in the *Aeneid*:

> Know first that heaven and earth's compacted frame,
> And flowing waters, and the starry frame, etc.

    This is poetry from which the sap of philosophy runs pure. Then is any reader so muddled as not to see clearly that Vergil was a philosopher; or mad enough to think that he, with all his deep learning, would, merely for the sake of displaying his eloquence—in which his powers were indeed extraordinary—have led the shepherd Aristeus into his mother Climene's presence in the depths of the earth, or brought Aeneas to see his father in Hades? Or can anyone believe he wrote such lines without some meaning or intention hidden beneath the superficial veil of myth? Again, let any man consider our own poet Dante as he often unties with amazingly skilful demonstration the hard knots of holy theology; will such a one be so insensible as not to perceive that Dante was a great theologian as well as philosopher? And, if this is clear, what intention does he seem to have had in presenting the picture of the griffon with wings and legs, drawing the chariot on top of the austere mountain, together with the seven candlesticks, and the seven nymphs, and the rest of the triumphal procession? Was it merely to show his dexterity in composing metrical narrative? To mention another instance: that most distinguished Christian gentleman, Francis Petrarch, whose life and character we have, with our own eyes, beheld so laudable in all sanctity—and by God's grace shall continue to behold for a long time; no one has saved and employed to better advantage—I will not say, his time, but every crumb of it, than he. Is there anyone insane enough to suppose that he devoted all those watches of the night, all those holy seasons of meditation, all those hours and days and years—which we have a right to assume that he did, considering the force and dignity of his bucolic verse, the exquisite beauty of his style and diction—I say, would he have taken such pains merely to represent Gallus begging Tyrrhenus for his reeds, or Pamphilus and Mitio in a squabble, or other like pastoral nonsense? No man in his right mind will agree that these were his final object; much less, if he considers his prose treatise on the solitary life, or the one which he calls *On the Remedies for all Fortunes*, not to mention many others. Herein all that is clear and holy in the bosom of moral philosophy is presented in so majestic a style, that nothing could be uttered for the instruction of mankind more replete, more beautified, more mature, nay, more holy. I would cite also my own eclogues, of whose meaning I am, of course, fully aware; but I have decided not to, partly because I am not great enough to be associated with the most distinguished men, and partly because the discussion of one's attainments had better be left to others.

    Then let the babblers stop their nonsense, and silence their pride if they can; for one can never escape the conviction that great men, nursed with the milk of the Muses, brought up in the very home of philosophy, and disciplined in sacred studies, have laid away the very deepest meaning in their poems; and not only this, but there was never a maundering old woman, sitting with others late of a winter's night at the home fireside, making up tales of Hell, the fates, ghosts, and the like—much of it pure invention—that she did not feel beneath the surface of her tale, as far as her limited mind allowed, at least some meaning—sometimes ridiculous no doubt—with which she tries to scare the little ones, or divert the young ladies, or amuse the old, or at least show the power of fortune.

XI. Poets Prefer Lonely Haunts As Favorable to Contemplation

I have remarked above the objection of my clamorous opponents that poets, for lack of urbanity and manners, prefer the open country, the mountains and woods, as a habitation. Boors! Why they are too mad and blind to see that, in trying to prove truth by a false opinion, they have actually turned liars. I admit that poets seek the country, mountains and woods, and if my opponents hadn't spoken of it, I was resolved to myself, and may have done so already. The reason, however, is not, as these windbags allege, a lack of sophistication; indeed the poets' own works witness enough to the contrary. But, if these cavillers scorn to trust such evidence, let them turn the pages of the Ancients, the annals of philosophers; there they are sure to find many instances of poets who enjoyed at their pleasure the friendship and domestic intercourse of kings and nobles, such as never fall to the lot of crude and oafish men. In proof whereof not a few examples occur to me off hand. I could if I wished show that the poet Euripides was a tent-comrade of Archelaus, King of Macedon, Ennius of Brundisium lived with the Scipios, and Vergil was a very intimate friend of Octavius. And, if ancient instances do not appeal to them, there are enough modern ones. Our Dante was a friend to Frederick of Arragon, King of Sicily, and to Can Grande della Scala, the illustrious duke of Verona. I know, and in fact so does everybody, that Francis Petrarch has been on terms of great intimacy and affection with the Emperor Charles, with John, King of France, with Robert, King of Jerusalem and Sicily, and with many an exalted prelate besides, and will continue to be, as long as he pleases, and they are alive.

But these mutterers probably are not aware that poets have sought and still seek their habitation in solitudes because contemplation of things divine is utterly impossible in places like the greedy and mercenary market, in courts, theatres, offices, or public squares, amid crowds of jostling citizens and women of the town. Yet unless such contemplation is practically uninterrupted, the poet can neither conceive his works, nor complete them.

But all this aside, I should hardly expect their charges, had they ever in a moment of sanity read Horace's words to Florus. After he has reviewed in his own elegant manner certain disadvantages of life in the city, he asks,

> At Rome, amidst its toils and cares,
> Think you that I can write harmonious airs?

THE GENEALOGY OF THE GENTILE GODS

meaning thereby that it cannot be done. Not content with this, he adds other of the inconveniences that for ever disturb the lives of city people, and then says with some irony,

> Go then, and bustle through the noisy throng,
> Invoke the Muse, and meditate the song,

as much as to say—if you can! Then come the quizzical lines:

> How then in noise unceasing tune the lay,
> Or tread, where others hardly find their way?

Then, with some indignation,

> What then—at Rome? in this tumultuous town,
> Toss'd by the noisy tempest up and down,
> Can I, though even the willing Muse inspire,
> Adapt the numbers to the sounding lyre?

So, without going further, the reason why poets seek to dwell in sylvan spots is clear. We read also that Paul the Hermit did thus, and Antonius, Macharius, Arsenius, and many other reverend and holy men, not from want of sophistication, but to serve God with a freer mind. It seems then that it is no such abomination as these critics appear to think, to dwell in the woods where there is nothing artificial nor counterfeit, nor noxious to the mind, for all nature's works are simple.

There the beeches stretch themselves, with other trees, toward heaven; there they apread a thick shade with their fresh green foliage; there the earth is covered with grass and dotted with flowers of a thousand colors; there, too, are clear fountains and argent brooks that fall with a gentle murmur from the mountain's breast. There are gay song-birds, and the boughs stirred to a soft sound by the wind, and playful little animals; and there the flocks and herds, the shepherd's cottage or the little hut untroubled with domestic cares; and all is filled with peace and quiet. Then, as these pleasures possess both eye and ear, they soothe the soul; then they collect the scattered energies of the mind, and renew the power of the poet's genius, if it be weary, prompting it, as it were, to long for contemplation of high themes, and yearn for expression—impulses wonderfully reinforced by the gentle society of books, and the melodious bands of the Muses moving in stately dance. In the light of all this what studious man would not prefer remote places to the city?

But it is not the reproach of poets in preferring lonely spots—if reproach is the right word—that moves these insolent men to recrimination; it is rather a reprehensible ambitious infection of their minds; and because poets differ from them in this respect they call them abominable. It is a trait of abandoned characters to wish above all that others should be like them, either in self-defense, or to enjoy the privilege of being shocked at another's crime. Let them blush then and be still, if the poet's ways are not theirs. Decent men detest and abhor their trick of disfiguring their faces with artificial pallor. They detest and abhor this constant strolling about the cities. They detest and abhor this purchase of cheap popularity among idlers, of notoriety among the ignorant, by foul and hideous hypocrisy. They abhor not merely to ask, but even to desire the badges of office, or to haunt the halls of kings, to flatter any man with a head higher than the rest, to be on the track of pontifical robes, for pure idleness and their bellies' sake to flatter poor women into a deposit of money from which they graft, and get by foul means what they could never get on their merits. They detest and abhor with all their hearts this practice of sending souls of usurers to heaven for a price, and assigning them seats in glory according to their contributions.

But the poets whom these fellows blaspheme are content with plain living and little sleep, with constant speculation and the laudable exercise of composition; thus they aspire to a glorious fame that shall endure to the end of time. O strange sort of men, so easily defiled with the hubbub of towns; O hateful solitude!

Enough! I could say more, were not the shining purity, the eminent virtue, the commendable lives of the great poets a stronger defence against such enemies than I can urge.

XII. *The Obscurity of Poetry Is Not Just Cause for Condemning It*

These cavillers further object that poetry is often obscure, and that poets are to blame for it, since their end is to make an incomprehensible statement appear to be wrought with exquisite artistry; regardless of the old rule of the orators, that a speech must be simple and clear. Perverse notion! Who but a deceiver himself would have sunk low enough not merely to hate what he could not understand, but incriminate it, if he could? I admit that poets are at times obscure. At the same time will these accusers please answer me? Take those philosophers among whom they shamelessly intrude; do they always find their close reasoning as simple and clear as they say an oration should be? If they say yes, they lie; for the works of Plato and Aristotle, to go no further, abound in difficulties so tangled and involved that from their day to the present, though searched and pondered by many a man of keen insight, they have yielded no clear nor consistent meaning. But why do I talk of philosophers? There is the utterance of Holy Writ, of which they especially like to be thought expounders; though proceeding from the Holy Ghost, is it not full to overflowing with obscurities and ambiguities? It is indeed, and for all their denial, the truth will openly assert itself. Many are the witnesses, of whom let them be pleased to consult Augustine, a man of great sanctity and learning, and of such intellectual power that, without a teacher, as he says himself, he learned many arts, besides all that the philosophers teach of the ten categories. Yet he did not blush to admit that he could not understand the beginning of Isaiah. It seems that obscurities are not confined to poetry. Why then do they not criticise philosophers as well as poets? Why do they not say that the Holy Spirit wove obscure sayings into his works, just to give them an appearance of clever artistry? As if He were not the sublime Artificer of the Universe! I have no doubt they are bold enough to say such things, if they were not aware that philosophers already had their defenders, and did not remember the punishment prepared for them that blaspheme against the Holy Ghost. So they pounce upon the poets because they seem defenseless, with the added reason that, where no punishment is imminent, no guilt is involved. They should have realized that when things perfectly clear seem obscure, it is the beholder's fault. To a half-blind man, even when the sun is shining its brightest, the sky looks cloudy. Some things are naturally so profound that not without difficulty can the most exceptional keenness in intellect sound their depths; like the sun's globe, by which, before they can clearly discern it, strong eyes are sometimes repelled. On the other hand, some things, though naturally clear perhaps, are so veiled by the artist's skill that scarcely anyone could by mental effort derive sense from them; as the immense body of the sun when hidden in clouds cannot be exactly located by the eye of the most learned astronomer. That some of the prophetic poems are in this class, I do not deny.

Yet not by this token is it fair to condemn them; for surely it is not one of the poet's various functions to rip up and lay bare the meaning which lies hidden in his inventions. Rather where matters truly solemn and memorable are too much exposed, it is his office by every effort to protect as well as he can and remove them from the gaze of the irreverent, that they cheapen not by too common familiarity. So when he discharges this duty and does it ingeniously, the poet earns commendation, not anathema.

Wherefore I again grant that poets are at times obscure, but invariably explicable if approached by a sane mind; for these cavillers view them with owl eyes, not human. Surely no one can believe that poets invidiously veil the truth with fiction, either to deprive the reader of the hidden sense, or to appear the more clever; but rather to make truths which would otherwise cheapen by exposure the object of strong intellectual effort and various interpretation, that in ultimate discovery they shall be more precious. In a far higher degree is this the method of the Holy Spirit; nay, every right-minded man should be assured of it beyond any doubt. Besides it is established by Augustine in the *City of God*, Book Eleven, when he says:

"The obscurity of the divine word has certainly this advantage, that it causes many opinions about the truth to be started and discussed, each reader seeing some fresh meaning in it."

Elsewhere he says of Psalm 126:

"For perhaps the words are rather obscurely expressed for this reason, that they may call forth many understandings, and that men may go away the richer, because they have found that closed which might be opened in many ways, than if they could open and discover it by one interpretation."

To make further use of Augustine's testimony (which so far is adverse to these recalcitrants), to show them how I apply to the obscurities of poetry his advice on the right attitude toward the obscurities of Holy Writ, I will quote his comment on Psalm 146:

"There is nothing in it contradictory: somewhat there is which is obscure, not in order that it may be denied thee, but that it may exercise him that shall afterward receive it," etc.

But enough of the testimony of holy men on this point, I will not bore my opponents by again urging them to regard the obscurities of poetry as Augustine regards the obscurities of Holy Writ. Rather I wish that they would wrinkle their brows a bit, and consider fairly and squarely, how, if this is true of sacred literature addressed to all nations, in far greater measure is it true of poetry, which is addressed to the few.

If by chance in condemning the difficulty of the text, they really mean its figures of diction and oratorical colors and the beauty which they fail to recognize in alien words, if on this account they pronounce poetry obscure—my only advice is for them to go back to the grammar schools, bow to the ferule, study, and learn what license ancient authority granted the poets in such matters, and give particular attention to such alien terms as are permissible beyond common and homely use. But why dwell so long upon the subject? I could have urged them in a sentence to put off the old mind, and put on the new and noble; then will that which now seems to them obscure look familiar and open. Let them not trust to concealing their gross confusion of mind in the precepts of the old orators; for I am sure the poets were ever mindful of such. But let them observe that oratory is quite different, in arrangement of words, from fiction, and that fiction has been consigned to the discretion of the inventor as being the legitimate work of another art than oratory. "In poetic narrative above all, the poets maintain majesty of style and corresponding dignity." As saith Francis Petrarch in the Third Book of his *Invectives*, contrary to my opponents' supposition, "Such majesty and dignity are not intended to hinder those who wish to understand, but rather propose a delightful task, and are designed to enhance the reader's pleasure and support his memory. What we acquire with difficulty and keep with care is always the dearer to us;" so continues Petrarch. In fine, if their minds are dull, let them not blame the poets but their own sloth. Let them not keep up a silly howl against those whose lives and actions contrast most favorably with their own. Nay, at the very outset they have taken fright at mere appearances, and bid fair to spend themselves for nothing. Then let them retire in good time, sooner than exhaust their torpid minds with the onset and suffer a violent repulse.

But I repeat my advice to those who would appreciate poetry, and unwind its difficult involutions. You must read, you must persevere, you must sit up nights, you must inquire, and exert the utmost power of your mind. If one way does not lead to the desired meaning, take another; if obstacles arise, then still another; until, if your strength holds out, you will find that clear which at first looked dark. For we are forbidden by divine command to give that which is holy to dogs, or to cast pearls before swine.

XIII. Poets Are Not Liars

These enemies of poetry further utter the taunt that poets are liars. This position they try to maintain by the hackneyed objection that poets write lies in their narratives, to wit, that a human being was turned into a stone—a statement in every aspect contrary to the truth. They urge besides that poets lie in asserting that there are many gods, though it is established in all certainty that there is but

One—the True and Omnipotent. They add that the greatest Latin poet, Vergil, told the more or less untrue story of Dido, and allege other like instances. I fancy they think their point is already won, and so indeed it would be, were there no one to repel their boorish vociferations with the truth. Yet further discussion seems hardly necessary for I supposed that I had already answered this objection above, where at sufficient length I defined a story, its kinds, what sorts the poets employ, and wherefore.

But if the matter is to be resumed, I insist that, whatever those fellows think, poets are not liars. I had supposed that a lie was a certain very close counterfeit of the truth which served to destroy the true and substitute the false. Augustine mentions eight kinds of lies, of which some are, to be sure, graver than others, yet none, if we employ them consciously, free from sin and the mark of infamy that denotes a liar. If the enemies of poetry will consider fairly the meaning of this definition, they will become aware that their charge of falsehood is without force, since poetic fiction has nothing in common with any variety of falsehood, for it is not a poet's purpose to deceive anybody with his inventions; furthermore poetic fiction differs from a lie in that in most instances it bears not only no close resemblance to the literal truth, but no resemblance at all; on the contrary, it is quite out of harmony and agreement with the literal truth.

Yet there is one kind of fiction very like the truth, which as I said, is more like history than fiction, and which by most ancient agreement of all peoples has been free from taint of falsehood. This is so in virtue of their consent from of old that anyone who could might use it as an illustration in which the literal truth is not required, nor its opposite forbidden. And if one considers the function of the poet already described, clearly poets are not constrained by this bond to employ literal truth on the surface of their inventions; besides, if the privilege of ranging through every sort of fiction be denied them, their office will altogether resolve itself into naught.

Again: if all my preceding argument should deserve reprobation—and I hardly think it possible—yet this fact remains irrefutable, that no one can in the proper discharge of his duty incur by that act the taint of infamy. If the judge, for example, lawfully visits capital punishment upon malefactors, it is not called homicide. Neither is a soldier who wastes the enemy's fields called a robber. Though a lawyer gives his client advice not wholly just, yet if he breaks not the bounds of the law he does not deserve to be called a falsifier. So also a poet, however he may sacrifice the literal truth in invention, does not incur the ignominy of a liar, since he discharges his very proper function not to deceive, but only by way of invention.

Yet if they will insist that whatever is not literally true is, however uttered, a lie, I accept it for purposes of argument; if not, I will spend no more energy in demolishing this objection of theirs. Rather I will ask them to tell me what name should be applied to those parts of the Revelation of John the Evangelist—expressed with amazing majesty of inner sense, though often at first glance quite contrary to the truth—in which he has veiled the great mysteries of God. And what will they call John himself? What too will they call the other writers who have employed the same style to the same end? I certainly should not dare answer for them "lies" and "liars," even if I might. Yet I know well they will say what I myself in part am about to say—should anyone ask me—that John and the other prophets were men of absolute truthfulness, a point already conceded. My opponents will add that their writings are not fiction but rather figures, to use the correct term, and their authors are figurative writers. O silly subterfuge! As if I were likely to believe that two things to all appearances exactly alike should gain the power of different effects by mere change or difference of name.

But not to dispute the point, I grant they are figures. Then, let me ask, does the truth which they express lie on their surface? If they wish me to think it does, what else is it but a lie thus to veil the eyes of my understanding, as they also veil the truth beneath? Well then, if these sacred writers must be called liars, though not held such, since indeed they are none, no more are poets to be considered liars who lean with their whole weight upon mere invention.

Yet without question poets do say in their works that there are many gods, when there is but One. But they should not therefore be charged with falsehood, since they neither believe nor assert it as a fact, but only as a myth or fiction, according to their wont. Who is witless enough to suppose that a man deeply versed in philosophy hasn't any more sense than to accept polytheism? As sensible men we must easily admit that the learned have been most devoted investigators of the truth, and have gone as far as the human mind can explore; thus they know beyond any shadow of doubt that there is but one God. As for poets, their own works clearly show that they have attained to such knowledge. Read Vergil and you will find the prayer:

> If any vows, Almighty Jove, can bend Thy will—

an epithet which you will never see applied to another god. The multitude of other gods they looked upon not as gods, but as members or functions of the Divinity; such was Plato's opinion, and we call him a theologian. But to these functions they gave a name in conformity with Deity because of their veneration for the particular function in each instance.

But I do not expect these disturbers to hold their peace here. They will cry out the louder that poets have written many lies about this one true God—whom, as I have just said, they recognize—and on that count deserve to be called liars. Of course I do not doubt that pagan poets had an imperfect sense of the true God, and so sometimes wrote of him what was not altogether true—a lie, as their accusers call it. But for all that I think they should hardly be called liars. There are two kinds of liars: first, those who knowingly and wilfully lie, whether to injure another person or not, or even to help him. These should not be called merely liars, but, more appropriately, "wilful deceivers." The second class are those who have told a falsehood without knowing it. Among these last a further distinction is in order. For in some cases ignorance is neither to be excused nor endured. For example, the law forbids any man privately to hold a citizen prisoner. John Doe has detained Richard Roe, his debtor, and pleads exemption from fine through ignorance of the law; but since such ignorance of the law seems stupid and negligent, it can constitute no defense. Likewise a Christian who is of age should find no protection in ignorance of the articles of faith. On the other hand there are those whose ignorance is excusable, such as boys ignorant of philosophy or a mountaineer ignorant of navigation, or a man congenitally blind who does not know his letters. Such are the pagan poets who, with all their knowledge of the Liberal Arts, poetry, and philosophy, could not know the truth of Christianity; for that light of the eternal truth which lighteth every man that cometh into the world had not yet shone forth upon the nations. Not yet had these servants gone throughout all the earth bidding every man to the supper of the Lamb. To the Israelites alone had this gift been granted of knowing the true God aright, and truly worshipping Him. But they never invited anyone to share the great feast with them, nor admitted any of the Gentiles at their doors. And if pagan poets wrote not the whole truth concerning the true God, though they thought they did, such ignorance is an acceptable excuse and they ought not to be called liars.

But my opponents will say, that whatever ignorance occasioned the lie, he who told it, is none the less a liar. True; but I repeat, they who sinned in pardonable ignorance are not to be damned by the same token as the offenders whose ignorance was crass and negligent; for the law, both in its equity and its austerity, holds them excused, wherefore, they incur not the brand of a lie.

If these disparagers still insist in spite of everything that poets are liars, I accuse the philosophers, Aristotle, Plato, and Socrates of sharing their guilt. Now, I expect, these expert critics will again lift their voices to heaven and cry to the sound of harp and cithera that this objection of theirs has suffered no harm. Fools! Though one small shield be shattered, the whole front does not waver. Let them not exult, but remember how often they have now been belabored and beaten back.

Their objection to Vergil—that no wise man would ever consent to tell the story of Dido—is utterly false. With his profound knowledge of such lore, he was well aware that Dido had really been a woman of exceptionally high character, who would rather die by her own hand than subdue the vow of chastity fixed deep in her heart to a second marriage. But that he might attain the proper effect of his work under the artifice of a poetic disguise, he composed a story in many respects like that of his historic Dido, according to the privilege of poets established by ancient custom. Possibly someone more worthy of a reply than my opponents—perhaps even thou, O Prince—may ask to what purpose this was necessary for Vergil. By way of fitting answer let me then say that his motive was fourfold.

First, that in the same style which he had adopted for the *Aeneid* he might follow the practice of earlier poets, particularly Homer, whom he imitated in this work. For poets are not like historians, who begin their account at some convenient beginning and describe events in the unbroken order of their occurrence to the end. Such, we observe, was Lucan's method, wherefore many think of him rather as a metrical historian than a poet. But poets, by a far nobler device, begin their proposed narrative in the midst of the events, or sometimes even near the end; and thus they find excuse for telling preceding events which seem to have been omitted. Thus Homer, in the *Odyssey,* begins, as it were, near the end of Ulysses's wanderings and shows him wrecked upon the Phaeacian shore, then has him tell King Alcinous everything that had happened to him hitherto since he left Troy. Vergil chose the same method in describing Aeneas as a fugitive from the shore of Troy after the city was razed. He found no place so appropriate on which to land him before he reached Italy as the coast of Africa; for at any nearer point he had been sailing continuously among his enemies the Greeks. But since the shore of Africa was at that time still the home of rude and barbarous rustics, he desired to bring his hero to somebody worthy of regard who might receive him and urge him to tell of his own fate and that of the Trojans. Such a one above all he found in Dido, who, to be sure, is supposed to have dwelt there not then, but many generations later; yet Dido he presents as already living, and makes her the hostess of Aeneas; and we read how at her command he told the story of his own troubles and those of his friends.

Vergil's second purpose, concealed within the poetic veil, was to show with what passions human frailty is infested, and the strength with which a steady man subdues them. Having illustrated some of these, he wished particularly to demonstrate the reasons why we are carried away into wanton behavior by the passion of concupiscence; so he introduces Dido, a woman of distinguished family, young, fair, rich, exemplary, famous for her purity, ruler of her city and people, of conspicuous wisdom and eloquence, and, lastly, a widow, and thus from former experience in love, the more easily disposed to that passion. Now all these qualifications are likely to excite the mind of a high-born man, particularly an exile and castaway thrown destitute upon an unknown shore. So he represents in Dido the attracting power of the passion of love, prepared for every opportunity, and in Aeneas one who is readily disposed in that way and at length overcome. But after showing the enticements of lust, he points the way of return to virtue by bringing in Mercury, messenger of the gods, to rebuke Aeneas, and call him back from such indulgence to deeds of glory. By Mercury, Vergil means either remorse, or the reproof of some outspoken friend, either of which rouses us from slumber in the mire of turpitude, and calls us back into the fair and even path to glory. Then we burst the bonds of unholy delight, and, armed with new fortitude, we unfalteringly spurn all seductive flattery, and tears, prayers, and such, and abandon them as naught.

Vergil's third purpose, is to extol, through his praise of Aeneas, the *gens Julia* in honor of Octavius; this he does by showing him resolutely and scornfully setting his heel upon the wanton and impure promptings of the flesh and the delights of women.

It is Vergil's fourth purpose to exalt the glory of the name of Rome. This he accomplishes through Dido's execrations at her death; for they imply the wars between Carthage and Rome, and prefigure the triumphs which the Romans gained thereby—a sufficient glorification of the city's name.

Thus it appears that Vergil is not a liar, whatever the unthinking suppose; nor are the others liars who compose in the same manner.

XIV. The Foolishness of Condemning What One Does Not Readily Understand

Furthermore my opponents curse the poet and clamor for the extinction of poetry as replete with pranks and adulteries of pagan gods. Besides they can in no way bear the practice of the poets who assign many forms and names to one and the same god, such as Jove and the like. My adversaries come on like a foolish soldier, who is so fierce and eager to hunt the enemy that he does not look out for himself; with the usual result that he bares himself to the blows he intended for another. I supposed that these objections taken in the lump had already found their answer above where I remember saying time and again that in various licentious or grotesque incidents and names are implied many wise and pure thoughts; and these I am aware of having revealed to the best of my ability by removing the outer mythological covering.

But those seductive performances of the gods presented chiefly by comic poets, in whatever way, I neither praise nor commend, but detest, and I hold such writers to be as execrable as the scenes themselves. Wide indeed is the field of fiction, and Poetry's horn as she advances overflows with her many inventions; wherefore fair and decent disguises have never been lacking for any possible thought which an author may wish to express.

Indeed this complaint has long since been laid to rest and removed. At one time outrageous songs were sung on the stage of the theatre by mimes and actors and spongers and the like; but, according to Cicero, the ancient Romans abolished and repudiated them, condemned both the stage and its debased art, punished those who practised it with the censor's brand, and erased them from the roll of their tribes. Furthermore warning was published by Pretorian edict that whoever went upon the stage for the purpose of acting in such plays should in so doing lose his good name. Then after the time of the Emperor Constantine and Pope Sylvester, as the Catholic faith sprang up everywhere and waxed daily, the songs of such comic purveyors to the stage disappeared from the world, and left the writings of noble and worthy poets; wherein they exhibited the works of both men and nature in a nobler style, in artistic form, in more eloquent diction, under an appropriate guise of myth and image. But those whom the godly Plato would have expelled from the city, and whom my present adversaries in their ignorance really revile, are now cast out and abolished.

In reply to the second clause of my adversaries' objection, I may say that, if they had exercised some prudence in the onset, and been more alert to discover where they were exposed to attack, they would have been sure to see that the weapon they cast at the Gentile poet rebounds upon themselves. They would cease to wonder that the poets call Jove, now god of heaven, now lightning, now an eagle, or a man, or whatever, if they had only reminded themselves that Holy Writ itself from time to time represents the one true God as sun, fire, lion, serpent, lamb, worm, or even a stone. Likewise our most venerable mother the Church is prefigured in the sacred books, sometimes as a woman clothed with the sun, or arrayed in varied garb, sometimes as a chariot, or a ship, or an ark, a house, a temple, and the like. No less is this true of the

Virgin Mother, or of the Great Enemy of mankind, as I remember to have read, time and again. I can say the same also of the multiplicity of sacred epithets; those applied to God alone are indeed innumerable at present, as are those of the Virgin Mary and the Church. Such forms and epithets are not devoid of mystic meaning; no more are those employed by poets.

Why then keep up this bray? They suffer from a morbid envy that will not endure what it cannot explain.

XV. Detestable Judgment of the Incompetent

Yet another charge is urged by these zealots—that poets seduce their readers into criminal practices. If they urged this charge with some distinction, I might concede it in part. It is, of course, a well-known fact that long ago there were comic poets of doubtful honor who were such either at the prompting of their own unrighteous minds, or at the demand of an age as yet corrupt. For example, Ovid, the Pelignian, a poet of great eminence but licentious imagination, wrote a book on the Art of Love in which, to be sure, he suggested many a wrong practice; yet it was in no respect really dangerous, since no youth is so mad with passion, and no young woman so simple, that under the impulse of carnal appetite they are not much keener in inventing an expedients to achieve their desires than he who thought to make himself an eminent advisor in such matters. If, then, poets like these, who, I admit, should in some cases be rejected, have not kept fair the fame of the art of poetry, why, pray, should others of resplendent fame incur the same taint, and share the blame of the guilty? Why, it is not to be endured!

Yet to show why these objectors attack the really great poets, I beg them to tell whether they have ever read a book of Homer, or Hesiod, or Vergil, or a poem of say Horace or Juvenal? If they say yes, will they then tell what prompting to criminal practices they find therein; thus we who are blind may profit by their insight, and likewise condemn the blameworthy.

But such questions are vain. Who can hear their charge without seeing that they never have read these poets? We may rest assured that, if they had, they would never have arrived at their absurd conclusion. I am afraid, however, that such interrogation as this may only move them to add one sin to another; for they cannot keep still, so great is their fear that silence will impair their reputation for omniscience. They will talk away with bold effrontery, puffed cheeks, and unblushing brow, as if they were traveling the straight road to the summit of praise.

But why listen to such nonsense? Foh! I neither do, nor wish to—something better claims my interest. Great God, now mayest Thou rest from Thine eternal labor. If Thine eyes, O God, long for slumber, Thou mightest now be satisfied. For these creatures assume Thine office; nightly they watch in Thy place, and sweat in Thy stead. Among their greater duties, they very likely will drive the Primum Mobile. Tremendous undertaking! And they are equal to it, if Thou, O Lord, wilt suffer it.

Base perverted souls, that in petty disparagement of others miserably lay bare their own ignorance! We can, if we are not the greater fools, easily see how just, holy and acceptable is this charge of theirs. And that no one may think the answer I am about to make proceeds from mere idle speculation, let me say that it derives from most accurate deduction. Some time ago I heard several men engaged in making perhaps too scrupulous a reply to cross-questioning of this very sort; and—what was of especial interest to me—a certain venerable man, in other respects of eminent sanctity and learning, did not stop at a mere answer, but launched into a gratuitous diatribe in the worst of bad taste. God knows, I speak the truth. O King! This man, as it seemed, was so fierce an enemy of the poet's name that he apparently could not endure the word without retching. He once exhibited this prejudice on an occasion not altogether to his credit. For it happened one morning in our University that he was reading from the desk the Gospel according to St. John to a large audience when suddenly he came upon the name of poet. Forthwith he became flushed, his eyes took fire, and raising his voice, he broke into a perfect frenzy and poured out one false charge after another against poets. And finally, to show the justice of his case, he averred—nay, almost swore: "I never have seen, nor do I wish to see, a volume of poetry!" Good God! What may we expect from the ignorant, if an aged and revered man, and, in other respects, learned, spake thus? Could a madman speak worse nonsense? I should like to know of these censors extraordinary, if they can spare a moment from their greater concerns, how, if they haven't seen, much less become acquainted with the poets, they make out that poets are corruptors of morals. Why then, do they keep up this ignorant yelping? Why do such incompetents usurp the bench to judge that of which they know nothing? Why thunder out their verdict where one side of the case has never been examined, let alone heard? Perhaps they will say the Holy Spirit inspires them to this harsh judgment against poets. So I might suppose, if I thought the Holy Spirit ever enters, not to say dwells, in souls so foul. O base impiety, vile offence, hateful presumption—that a child born blind should openly attempt to distinguish colors. The practice of these venerable judges, forsooth, is that reported of Phoroneus among the Argives, Lycurgus among the Lacedaemonians, Minos among the Cretans, and Aeacus among the Myrmidons.

But to come now to my main point. The prattle of these reverend judges notwithstanding, poets are not corruptors of morals. Rather, if the reader is prompted by a healthy mind, not a diseased one, they will prove actual stimulators to virtue, either subtle or poignant, as occasion requires. Not to appear content with insufficient proof, I should like to call the attention of these noisy objectors to a few examples which may enable them, if they will, to acknowledge this fact. I will not pause with Homer, who being a Greek writer, is less familiar to the Latins. But let them, if they will, read, yes, and re-read those lines in the *Aeneid* where Aeneas exhorts his friends to endure patiently their labors to the last. How fine was the ardor of his wish to die a fair death from his wounds, to save his country! How noble his devotion to his father when he bore him to safety on his shoulders through the midst of the enemy and a shower of flying weapons, while buildings were ablaze and temples crashing down at every turn! What gentleness he showed to his enemy Achaemenides! What strength of character in spurning and breaking the chains of an obstreperous passion! What justice and generosity, too, in distributing well-earned rewards among friends and aliens alike, at the conclusion of the anniversary games to Anchises at the court of Acestes! What circumspect wisdom he showed in his descent into Hades! What noble exhortations to glorious attainment were those of his father! There too was his tact in cultivating friendly relations, and his high and loyal courtesy in keeping them afterwards; and there were his devoted tears for the death of his friend Pallas, and his frequent admonitions to his friend's son. But enough! I crave their attention—these who bray at the name of poetry: let them weigh carefully both the words and thought of this poet, and, if they are intelligent enough, derive from them all possible fruition. Please God, they will then see whether the poet allures the reader to eat the fruit of sin. Surely if Vergil could have known and worshipped God in due form, nothing but that which is holy could be found in his works. But if my opponents object that legally nothing is proved by one witness, they may add Horace of Venusia, Persius of Volterra, and Juvenal of Aquinum. For the satires of these poets inveigh against vice and the vicious with such righteous energy that they seem likely to do away with them. If then, these several examples suffice, let them who accuse poets of corrupting their readers be silent, subdue their rage with gentleness, nor scorn to learn, before they pass absurd judgment upon the labors of others; lest in hurling the darts of their dull injustice at others, they call down the thunderbolts of divine vengeance upon themselves.

XVI. *The Reading of Poets Conduces to Righteousness*

In the next place, they who so spitefully lie in wait for the poet, say that he is an allurer of the mind, since the charming music of his verse, his polished language, his ornate discourse, inspire folly in his readers, or what is worse, seduce the unsophisticated. Now any ignoramus as unfamiliar with the poets, particularly the great poets, as these know-nothings, or one who has glanced at them, but was too feeble of mind to appreciate them, will readily believe that these men are most righteous, just, and holy in their attack upon poetry. May God, and they to whom he has granted the light of intelligence, behold this! Thou, heavenly harper, thou, O David, who art wont to quiet Saul's rage with thy sweet song, if ever thou didst utter a soft, melodious note, silence now thy song. And thou, O Job, who hast recorded thy labors and longsuffering in heroic verse, if it should prove agreeable or fair, do thou likewise. And ye too, all holy men besides who have sung the divine mysteries in exalted notes, do ye accordingly. In like manner would I call upon Orpheus, Homer, Vergil, Horace, and the rest—when we reach the point where men are heard to say with impunity that the practice of framing metrical discourse sweetly, agreeably, and with care, is one and the same with perverting the minds of men. Ah, Bavius and Maevius, rejoice when these great names are fallen; for ample time and room have been conceded to you when least I expected it.

My antagonists will now say, I know, that it was the practice of writing and reading nonsense in sonorous verse that they called pernicious. I grant this qualification is of no small moment, unless I have already shown too often the nature of the absurdities in great poets which they now attack. Yet, for the sake of giving a direct answer to the charge that poets seduce the mind, I should first like to know—since there are many poets—which of them my opponents accuse. Of course they can mention only those they study themselves. But their own accusation shows which these are. Why, bless me, these zealots love, and are loved, make eyes at laughing girls, dictate love-notes, write verses, dash off ditties, which they charge with their thrills and sighs, and when their own ingenuity fails, resort for timely aid to professors in the art of love. Wherefore they search the pages of Catullus, Propertius, and Ovid, and from the foolish suasion of such, expressed in sweet-sounding verses, and in easy but ornate style, with whole-hearted inclination they surrender to its influence, are deluded, seduced, and enthralled. Thus it is they have discovered the allurements of the poets, thus they ungratefully turn and accuse their teachers, and thus they call them seducers of the mind, whom they have followed uninvited and of their own free will. Great, thrice great, employment for our opponents. And worthy indeed is their homage to Love, whose power overcame first Phoebus, then Hercules—each victorious over monsters. Ah, how much better it would have been for these ignorant men to hold their peace, rather than speak to their own undoing. With a little thought, they may see that in the act of accusing the poets they have only proved themselves to blame. Whence we readily infer the true worth of their studies, their desires, their so-called justice. What might one expect of them in case a girl by licentious glance and gesture, and soft utterance, held out an unholy promise to them, if they are allured by unuttered verses perused in silence? Well may the wretches blush and revise their mad counsel, considering how Ulysses, noble soul, spurned the sound, not of songs read in the closet, but the dulcet music of the Sirens, whom he passed by for fear of harm at their hands.

As for the force of this epithet "allurer" which these men hurl at the poets in hope of disparagement, they might have seen that, though Jews hurled it at Christ our Savior when they called him "allurer," yet not for ever was it destined to vilify Him. For these rascal perverters could not rob the word of its pristine force. It may, at times, have a good connotation. Skilful herdsmen may, for example, lure from an infected herd the cattle as yet untainted; much more do cultivated men by their instruction lure away nobler souls from those foundering under moral disease. Thus, I think, do the great poets most frequently lure the credulous to their improvement, while these unjust judges are lured and deluded into an evil course more by their own wickedness than by that of even the less honorable poets, and they try their utmost to show it. O blessed Jesus, turn aside this plague from the ignorant and credulous! Take these babblers and so instruct them that by Thy example they may be willing first to do, then to teach!

XVII. *That Poets Are Merely Apes of the Philosophers*

A few of the enemies of poetry who would outdo the rest in their attack say that poets are but apes of the philosophers. I cannot make sure whether such eructation comes from a wish to raise a general laugh, like their cheap jokes among silly girls, or whether it rises from real conviction, or from a mere low and idle desire to ridicule. If the first, then the wise should suffer it to pass, though with some feeling of indignation. For they often see eminent men bantered by the ignorant, who at many a street corner appear disguised as filleted asses, or hogs in their trappings, or in fringed and variegated skins of different beasts; and thus disguised freely utter, with less impropriety, any ribald lampoons they can make up. But if this charge against poets comes from conviction or from desire to ridicule, it is, in either case, both stupid and vicious. The apes' natural and invariable habit (as I remember saying elsewhere) is to imitate as far as they can everything they see, even to the actions of men. Whence these men speciously infer that poets, being imitators, are therefore apes of the philosophers: now this is not so absurd, even if it were true; for philosophers have been for the most part honorable men, and inventors of noble arts. But the ignorant deceive themselves. If they but understood the works of the poets, they would see that, far from being apes, they should be reckoned of the very number of the philosophers, since they never veil with their inventions anything which is not wholly consonant with philosophy as judged by the opinions of the Ancients. And then, too, the pure imitator never sets foot outside his model's track—a fact not observed in poets. For though their destination is the same as that of the philosophers, they do not arrive by the same road. The philosopher, everyone knows, by a process of syllogizing, disproves what he considers false, and in like manner proves his theory, and does all this as obviously as he can. The poet conceives his thought by contemplation, and, wholly without the help of syllogism, veils it as subtly and skilfully as he can under the outward semblance of his invention. The philosopher as a rule employs an unadorned prose style with something of scorn for literary embellishment. The poet writes in metre, with an artist's most scrupulous care, and in a style distinguished by exquisite charm. It is, furthermore, a philosopher's business to dispute in the lecture-room, but a poet's to sing in solitude. With such discrepancy between them, the poet cannot prove to be "the ape of the philosopher." If they called them apes of nature, the epithet might be less irritating, since the poet tries with all his powers to set forth in noble verse the effects, either of Nature herself, or of her eternal and unalterable operation. If my opponents care to consider it, they will perceive the forms, habits, discourse, and actions of all animate things, the courses of heaven and the stars, the shattering force of the winds, the roar and crackling of flames, the thunder of the waves, high mountains and shady groves, and rivers in their courses—all these will they find so vividly set forth that the very objects will seem actually present in the tiny letters of the written poem. In this sense, I admit, the poets are apes, and I hold it a task full of honor to attempt with art what nature performs in the fullness of her power. So much upon this point. It would be better for such critics if they would use their best efforts to make us all become apes of Christ, rather than jeer at the labors of poets, which they do not understand. Sometimes people who try to scratch another's itching back feel someone's bloody nails in their own skin—and not so pleasantly either!

XVIII. It Is Not A Deadly Sin to Read the Poets

These judges of equity—or rather of iniquity—in the heat of their mad desire to destroy the name of poet, as if they had not already said enough, keep shrieking and bellowing to this effect: "O ye distinguished men, ye redeemed of the blood of the Lord, ye chosen people of God, if in your hearts is piety, devotion, love of Christianity, fear of God, cast from you these unhallowed books of the poets; burn them with fire; scatter their ashes to the winds! For to have them at home, to read them, or even incline to read them is a mortal sin! They infect the soul with deadly poison, they drag you down into hell, and hurl you into endless exile from the heavenly kingdom!" Then with a louder voice they call Jerome to witness and allege his words in the *Epistle to Damasus* on the Prodigal Son: "The songs of poets are the food of devils." This and much else of the same sort they yell at the top of their voices at their poor ignorant hearers. O piety! O pristine faith! O great and patient God! How longsuffering art Thou! Thou Founder of all things, why dost Thou aim Thy thunderbolts at high towers and lofty mountain-tops? These, most Holy Father, these are Thy proper mark who with a treacherous tongue and false pursue empty celebrity through the destruction of others who are innocent. Doctors bury their mistakes in the ground. These charlatans try to hide their ignorance in prohibitions and flames. What ingenuous man could listen to these impostors without thinking that poets are most pernicious, nay, enemies of the name of God, familiars of demons, cruel, evil-doers, always ready for crime, heedless of every good, utterly devoid of piety, faith, or holiness? By such ignorant and unfair procedure, men of real distinction are brought to ignominy which they least deserve. I hope God will some day find them out.

Let us now consider, as we can, the real nature of this inexpiable sin which, they keep roaring, consists in posessing, looking at, or reading the songs of poets. I have already explained clearly enough what their books contain—the tendency of their influence, and what they teach and what they condemn. But, all that aside, I grant for the moment what is in reality untrue, that poets describe all manner of crimes, and make them attractive to their readers. What of it? They were Gentiles, who knew not Christ, and who upheld their own religion, because they regarded it as holy, and in publishing their works, they often held out to others the fruit that was most pleasing and acceptable to their own palates. And if further excuse were required, I wish these most exquisite babblers would tell me whether any teaching, ancient or modern, has forbidden their describing the wickedness of their gods in any style they choose. Surely not, if the Christian has not been forbidden to write such poetry as yields nothing, under intelligent scrutiny, contrary to Catholic Truth. If not, and if neither the Law, nor the Prophets, nor the holy rulings of the pontiffs, forbid the perusal of poetry, what harm is there in possessing and reading them? My opponents will say again that they seduce the mind with their sweetness. But this objection I have answered just above. And if these imbeciles are in any wise tractable, let them recall the saw about stones and glass houses and take care.

Yet I grant freely that it would be far better to study the sacred books than even the best of these works, and I suppose they who do so are more acceptable to God, to the high Pontiff, and to the Church. But we are not all at all times subject to one inclination, and occasionally some men incline to poetical writers. And if we so incline, or turn to them of our own accord, what sin or harm is there in that? We can in all innocence hear of the customs of barbarians, or, if we please, actually receive them among us, treat them hospitably, give them the benefit of our justice, if they ask it, and make of them friends and feast-mates. And yet—God's will! These learned men forbid us to read the poets! Why, there are Manichaeus, Arius, Pelagius, and such heresiarchs. No one forbids our knowing their vile errors, so that we may recognize them. Yet it is a frightful thing to read poetry, they keep clamoring "nay, a deadly sin." We may watch wandering clowns doing their low tricks at the corner; or hear entertainers sing their dirty songs at banquets, or buffoons at restaurants, or panderers in the brothels—yes, even let them blaspheme—and still escape hell. But poetry! Alas, it drives us forth into exile from the Kingdom of Heaven! It is thought proper for the painter to paint, within the holy precincts of the church itself, pictures of the triple dog Cerberus guarding the gate of Pluto, or sailor Charon plying the waters of Acheron, or the Furies with snaky fillets and flaming brands, or even Pluto himself, prince of the unhappy realm, in the act of visiting punishment upon the damned. Then is it wrong for poets to describe them in resounding verse, and is the reader guilty of unpardonable sin? The painter has even been permitted to decorate the palaces of princes and nobles with subjects chosen from the amours of ancient myth, the crimes of gods and men, and all sorts of fabrications, without an interfering word from the Fathers; and anyone who will may look at these pictures all he pleases. But a poet's creations, blazoned in ornate letters, they find more vicious to the wise than are pictures to the ignorant.

Well, I confess I could not, in spite of me, tell how violent and stubborn are the consuming spleen and ignorance which have driven these cattle so mad. Certainly they should know the testimony of the Vessel of Election, that sin consists not in the knowledge of evil, but in the act.

But not thus content, these raw and upstart pedagogues make bold to say—perhaps to gain more reputation for wisdom among their female admirers, and so get the fatter leavings—they make bold to say, that it is most pernicious even to read the poets, much more to know them. What bores! If poets are altogether to be scorned, then it will be wrong to pick up a pearl from the mud, since the dirt, though it may be wiped off, will make it less precious. Nor do these expounders blush, though their arrogant and sweeping prohibition would turn the truth to a lie, provided it comes from the mouth of a poet; they will deny at the top of their voices that poets ever speak the truth. It is absurd to say that the devil, the enemy of man, can utter a good word, but that the poets can never do so. For though I granted a moment ago, only for argument's sake, that they *are* evil, yet many of them can not justly be accused of any dishonor but that of being Gentiles. Yet the devil's testimony is frequently cited by holy men, while to cite the poets is, on the authority of these accusers, an unpardonable sin.

At this point I beseech these prohibitors and proscribers of poets to tell in what way Poetry has sinned worse than Philosophy. For while Philosophy is without question the keenest investigator of truth, Poetry is, obviously, its most faithful guardian, protecting it as she does beneath the veil of her art. If Philosophy errs, Poetry cannot keep in the right path. She is Philosophy's maidservant, and must follow in the steps of her mistress; so that necessarily the error of the one makes the other deviate. What right, then, have we, if we constantly cite the pagan philosophers, and cherish their thoughts, and consider nothing really well founded unless it rests upon their authority—what right have we fearfully to shun the poets and their words and condemn them in scorn? Socrates is lauded, Plato honored, Aristotle studied, not to mention the rest; and yet they were pagans, and often capable of erroneous and condemned opinion. But Homer is driven off with reproaches, Hesiod condemned, Vergil and Horace despised, though their creations carry no other meaning than do the dissertations of the philosophers. But since these cavillers have studied the philosophic writings a little, and, by dint of slight but painful effort, have caught certain very elementary fragments from them, they commend them as if they fully understood them. Yet the poets, whose works they neglect, and therefore do not appreciate, they despise and condemn. In spite of all this howling and barking, exhorting and pleading, if philosophical writings, and the life and customs of barbarians, and the perverted teaching of heretics, are allowable, certainly the works of the poets may be read, kept, and listened to with impunity, yet with a pure and steadfast mind, lest the poets, being, as it were, aliens from the orthodox faith, should now and then say something contrary to it, and the reader should slip unawares.

Finally, the last point of these noisy upstarts calls for really sharp and extended reproof; for they think that they have established their whole contention thus far by the authority of one devout and famous man. They keep shouting the dictum of Jerome to Pope Damasus, that the songs of poets are the food of devils. But a moment's consideration of my previous words would have shown them that I myself confirmed this point, particularly in condemning and repudiating more than once the obscenity of the comic poets. But since they are too obfuscated with envy to make any distinction between poets, and only rush hither and yon in their blindness; their cheap prejudice ought to be repelled and silenced for ever. If they had read carefully the epistles and other works of Jerome, or even this particular one they call to witness, they would find the real meaning of his dictum explained by Jerome himself, and their objection removed. I have in mind particularly the figure of the captive woman described as naked, shaven, and with closely pared nails; the Israelitish bride with hair close-cropped. If they would not appear more fastidious in their piety than these holy doctors they will find that this "food of devils" is not only snatched from the fire into which they have ordered it to be cast, but kept with care, and dressed and tasted by no less a person than Fulgentius, the Catholic doctor and pontiff; the fact is proved by his book which he himself has named the *Book of Myths,* and in which he recounts and explains the fables of the poets in highly finished style. In like manner they will discover that the great teacher Augustine was not afraid of poetry and its creations, but indeed studied it with patience and sagacity, and understood it. Certainly they could not deny it, in spite of themselves, for the holy man often cites Vergil and other poets; in fact he almost never mentions Vergil without a laudatory epithet. To repeat, then; the great and most holy Jerome, master of three languages, whom these men in their ignorance cite with so much ado, studied and remembered the poets with such care, as they may see, that their contention gains practically nothing by citing him. If they are not convinced, let them note for example the preface of his *Hebraicae Quaestiones* on Genesis, and see whether it is not throughout in the manner of Terence, and whether he does not frequently cite Horace and Vergil as his advocates, so to speak, or even Persius and others. Let them read beside Jerome's eloquent letter to Augustine, and see that the learned author there numbers among illustrious men the very poets that these men try in every possible way to overwhelm with their clamor. And if they are still unconvinced, they may read through the Book of Acts and see how studiously Paul, the Vessel of Election, sought acquaintance with the words of the poets. In his attempt to persuade the obstinate Athenians, on the Areopagus, he did not disdain, they will find, to cite the testimony of poets; and in another place he quotes a verse of Menander, the comic poet: "Evil communications corrupt good manners." I think it is the poet Epimenides whose line he cites elsewhere: "The Cretans are always liars, evil beasts, slow bellies"—a good description, by the way, of my opponents. Thus he who was caught up into the third heaven, unlike these more pious persons, thought it neither a sin nor a shame to read and teach the works of poets. Again, let them examine the words of Dionysius the Areopagite, a disciple of Paul, and glorious martyr of Christ, in his book on the *Celestial Hierarchy*. He takes the matter up from the first premise, and gives complete proof that divine theology employs, with its other instruments, poetic inventions. He says: "For in truth Theology with much skill hath employed sacred poetic forms and figures to convey non-figurative meaning, at the same time opening our minds, as I have already said, providing them with means of right conjectural interpretation, and presenting the Holy Scriptures to them in anagogical form"; and he continues with much more to the same effect. And lastly, to omit the other instances that I could cite against their bestial ravings, did not our Lord and Savior speak often in parable appropriate to the style of comic poet? Did he not, with his own voice, employ a verse of Terence against the stricken Paul—"It is hard for thee to kick against the pricks?" Far be it from me to suppose that our Lord took these words from Terence, though Terence lived long before they were uttered. It serves to prove my point that our Savior ever willed that a word and thought of His own should have been first uttered through the mouth of Terence, showing that the songs of poets are not wholly the food of devils.

What now have these cattle left to bellow about? Will they keep on howling and hurling their insults at poetry, though refuted by their own evidence, and vanquished by the testimony of many saints? They will, I suppose, make as much noise as ever, so incurable is their madness; but the justice of their claim thou, O excellent King, and others, may judge, who are friends of reason, and love not their shameless obstinacy. But God is a just judge and will in time visit proper punishment upon these envious and arbitrary destroyers; and the same measure shall be measured unto them that they mete unto others.

XIX. It Is Untrue That Plato Would Abolish All Poets from His Republic

A mere trifle it seems to these barkers—the exposure of their vain attempt to drive the poets out of the homes and hands of men. For see! they rally and rush to the attack, and flourishing like a weapon the authority of Plato they belch out with hideous roar, that Plato ordered the poets banished from the cities. Then, as if Plato were weak and needed help, they add as their own reason, that poets may vitiate the commonwealth with their immorality. Though I have already answered this objection at sufficient length, I shall not now shrink from a fuller reply. For I admit that the authority of this philosopher is of the highest order; and deserves all respect if rightly understood; but these men pervert or altogether misprise his meaning, as I shall prove.

I have said that the poets prefer to dwell in solitude, wherefore their disparagers called them backwoodsmen and boors. But if poets chose the hurly-burly of towns, what would these backbiters say of them? They would call them tyrants! It seems that they have changed their minds, and now call the poets dwellers in cities; if so, they are wrong. It is an established fact that Homer, after wandering the world over, settled at last in extreme poverty on the shore of Arcadia, amid crags and mountain-forests; and there, overtaken by blindness, but with "mind irradiate," conceived those great and marvellous works; works anointed not with the sweetness of Hybla, but of Castaly—the *Iliad* and the *Odyssey*. And Vergil, who was no less a genius than Homer, forsook Rome, then mistress of the world, and deserted Octavius, ruler of all the earth, whose friendship was the poet's peculiar and happy privilege, all to seek out an abode not far from the famous principality of Naples in central Campania, a spot even in that day abounding in beauty and comfort; and there, according to the account of John Barillus, a man of much intelligence, he chose a spot still and removed, near a lonely shore, between the cape of Posilipo and the old Greek colony Pozzuolo, whither none would come except to visit him. There he composed both his *Georgics* and the divine *Aeneid*. And when at Vergil's death, Octavius wished to commemorate his choice of this lonely spot, he caused his bones to be brought from Brundisium, and buried close by his favorite retreat near the road still called the Puteolan Way; thus his bones lie near the abode of his choice.

But I will not confine myself to ancient examples, for, however happy and authentic, my opponents will none of them. Francis Petrarch, a man of heaven-sent genius, and the greatest poet of our time, scorned the western Babylon, and ignored the favor of the Pope, for which nearly every Christian longs and contends his utmost—not to say the favor of bonneted cardinals and other princes—and departed to a secluded valley, in an exceptionally lonely part of France, where the Sorga, the greatest of springs, takes its rise. There, in meditation and composition, he spent nearly the whole flower of his youth, content with one servant. The proofs of his deed still remain and will so remain for a long time—a little house and garden, and, as long as God pleases, a number of living witnesses. These examples suffice to show what a waste of effort it is to try to drive poets out of the city whence they have departed of their own choice.

I wish my opponents would say whether they think that Plato, in his *Republic,* passed the stricture they mention upon Homer, so that Homer would have been an exile from his ideal city. Whatever they say, I cannot think so, having read so much in praise of Homer. The most sacred laws of the Caesars call him father of all virtues; and time and again their proposers, to win reverence for them, and support them with holy testimonial have mingled with them lines from Homer. Thus at the close of the proem of the Justinian Code occurs such a quotation, as likewise under the titles, On Justice and Law, On Contract of Sale, On Legacies and Trusts, and so forth: the curious may see it for themselves in the Pandects of Pisa. It was Homer whom many of the leading cities of Greece would have dignified as their citizen, though he had died in poverty; nay, they contended with one another for this honor. This is clearly shown in Cicero's speech for Archias where he says: "Homer is claimed as their fellow-citizen by the men of Colophon, while the Chians demand, and the Salaminians aspire to the same honor; Smyrna also insists that he is here, and has gone so far as to dedicate a shrine to him. Many others are there who likewise strive and contend for the same honor." Nor is Cicero the only witness; I remember reading it in an old Greek verse familiar to the learned which says: "Seven cities dispute for the honor of Homer's birth—Samos, Smyrna, Chios, Colophon, Pylos, Argos and Athens." Nay Plato himself calls Homer to witness in the very book of the *Republic* in which he condemns poets, and elsewhere. If then the laws call him the father of virtues, and glory of the law, and if he is claimed as citizen of so many states, and if Plato, our very monitor, cites him to prove a point, isn't it utter folly to think so wise a man as he would have ordered such a poet to be excluded from his commonwealth?

Are we to believe that by the same token Ennius must be banished? He was a man who lived content in honest poverty, and yet was greatly endeared to the Scipios by his goodness; and they, besides their distinction of noble birth and exploits in war, were at home in philosophy, and singularly pure in character. They so loved the poet that at his death they desired that he be buried in the tomb of their family, and his ashes mingled with those of their fathers and their own. Then I for one will never agree with these idiots; nay, rather am I convinced that Plato would have wished his state brim-full of such as these. What of Solon, who in his old age, after he had made the laws of Athens, devoted himself to poetry? Must he be also expelled who restored a broken and ruined city to civil and moral health? There again is Vergil, who withal was so pure that he blushed in mind as well as in countenance when he overheard an indecent remark among his coevals or others, and thus won the nickname "Parthenias," that is, "virgin," or more correctly "virginity." It is often said that his works contain as many admonitions to virtue as they do words. To save his divine poem from being burned according to his own dying command, Octavius interrupted the cares of his vast empire to compose some prohibitory verses, which are still extant. The poet's name enjoys such honor at his native Mantua that when Augustus moved his ashes, and the Mantuans were not suffered to have the keeping of them as they wished, they began to honor the little farm where he had lived, and named it after him as if it had been alive; and the old men of the place still point it out to the younger generation as something sacred and venerable. They even take care to call strangers' attention to it, as if to augment their own glory. Such things do not happen unprecedented by conspicuous virtue. Shall we suppose then, that Plato would have men of such virtue expelled from the state? Blockheads! I could say as much of Horace, and Persius of Volterra, and Juvenal of Aquinum, all to prove that it never entered Plato's mind to expel such men. But it is my purpose to cite contemporary instances, immediately visible, so that they can not repudiate them by any possible tergiversation. Can one imagine that Plato would have been mad enough to banish Francis Petrarch? From his youth Petrarch has lived celibate, and such has been his horror at impure and illicit love, that his friends know him for a perfect model of saintly and honorable living. A lie is his mortal enemy, and he abhors all the vices. Truth finds in him her sanctuary, and virtue her adornment and delight. He is a pattern of Catholic piety—dutiful, gentle, devout, and so modest that he is called a second Parthenias. He is, besides, the present glory of the art of poetry, an eloquent and sweet-tongued speaker, a man to whom the whole heart of Philosophy is open and familiar, of penetration more than human, endowed with tenacious memory, and enjoying knowledge commensurate with the mind of man. His prose, and his more extensive works in verse, are so splendid, so redolent with sweetness, so loaded down with the bright bloom of his eloquence, so honey-sweet with rounded cadence, so pungent with the sap of his wonderful wisdom, that they seem like the creations of a divine not a human genius. What more could one say? For surely he exceeds human limits and far outstrips the powers of man. Such praise I utter not of an ancient who died centuries ago, rather of one who, please God, is alive and well; of one whom you, my snarling monsters, if you trust not my words, may see with your own eyes, and seeing, believe. I have no fear that he will share the common fate of great men, whose presence, as Claudian says, impairs their fame. Nay, rather, I insist that his actual presence far surpasses his reputation. So dignified is his bearing, so flowing and delightful his discourse, so gentle his manners, so tranquil his old age, that one may say of him what Seneca writes of Socrates, that his hearers were even more edified by his character than by his words. I pause in my eulogy of this great man to ask these objectors whether such are the poets Plato would banish from his state. If men of this kind are shut out, what sort would even Plato admit in their stead? Will they be panderers, body-snatchers, parasites, roisterers, fishmongers, or jailbirds and the like? Long life and happiness to Plato's state, if she rids herself of poets to receive such as the safeguards of life and morals. But let us never suppose the learned man meant what these "interpreters" say he did; for I can only believe that great poets and their kind are to be rightly regarded not as merely citizens of his state and all others, but as the princes and rulers thereof.

But they will spleen and say: "If not these, then what poets would Plato expel?" There is only one answer to such nonsense. Find out for yourselves, you incompetents! To be sure, allowance must be made for ignorance of all sorts.

Every art, like every liquor, hath its lees; the lees may be but so much foul draff; yet an art, like a liquor, without lees is cheapened. What, for example, is truer than Philosophy, mistress of all sciences and arts? Yet she hath had as her dregs, so to speak, the Cynics and Epicureans—not to mention any more—who having got themselves tangled up in unspeakable errors, proceeded in various ways to defame her more like enemies than supporters. But shall we say that for the sake of these we must abandon also Socrates, Xenocrates, Anaxagoras, Panetius, and others adorned with the fair title of Philosopher? Such is the way of the knave and the fool! What is holier than the Christian religion? Yet she hath her Donatists, her Macedons, her Fotini, and far worse dregs of heresy than they; and we do not therefore regard Basil, and St. John Chrysostom, and Ambrose, and Pope Leo, and many another holy and reverend man as profane. Thus also poetry, like the other arts, contains likewise its dregs. There have been certain so-called comic poets, who, to be sure, included a few upright men such as Terence and Plautus, but who for the most part defiled the bright glory of poetry with their filthy creations. Even Ovid at times makes one of these. Whether from innate foulness of mind, or greed for money, or desire of popularity, they wrote dirty stories and presented them on the stage, and thus prompted lascivious men to crime, unsettled those who were established in virtue, and weakened the moral order of the whole state. What was worst of all, though the pagan religion was already in other respects reprehensible, yet they seduced various peoples into the practice of such licentious rites that its own disciples had to blush for it. It is such poets, I repeat, that paganism no less than Christianity abhors, and such it is that Plato would banish. Indeed I think they ought to be not expelled, but exterminated. But for the sake of these, must Hesiod also go, and Euripides, and Statius, and Claudian, and the like? I think not. I beseech these cavillers, then, to make a distinction, to avoid their hateful and unworthy prejudice, to single out for their attacks the really undeserving, and leave honorable men in peace.

XX. *The Muses Not Injured by the Defect of a Single Genius*

Lastly, O noble King, these blasphemers of poetry have dared with unspeakable effrontery to invade the very threshold of the Gorgonian cave, so still, remote, and holy, and thrust themselves into the fair sanctuary of the adorable art, where maidens dance together and raise the divine song. Amid clamor and discord they flourish the words of the most holy and learned Boethius, particularly those found near the beginning of his book on *Consolation*. It is the point where Philosophy speaks saying: "Who hath let these drabs of the stage approach unto this sick man; for they apply no manner of remedy to his sufferings, but only nurse them with sweet poisons," etc. Thus they shriek in triumph, and fill the place with hubbub, and try with cowardly insult to frighten them who take innocent sport therein. Little do they understand Boethius' words: they consider them only superficially; wherefore they bawl at the gentle and modest Muses, as if they were women in the flesh, simply because their names are feminine. They call them disreputable, obscene, witches, harlots, and, forcing the meaning of Boethius' diminutive, they would push them to the bottom of society, nay in the lowest brothel make them supine to the pleasure of the very dregs of the crowd. From this slander they deduce their contention that poets are dishonorable; for if, according to Boethius, the Muses are lewd, and disreputable, so also must be their familiars, the poets; since friendship and familiarity rest only upon affinity of character, and hence the Muses obviously are close familiars of the poets, as their songs aver, and therefore share their shame. Here mayest thou see, O sapient King, to what end the cleverness of these busy-bodies allures them. But whatever that end may be, it spells confusion in the face of pure truth. The number, quality, and names of the Muses, and their significance as perceived by great men, I have shown, if I remember rightly, in the Eleventh Book of this work; but the impiety of my opponents is still alive and calls for further effort on my part. I think it safe to infer from previous demonstration that there are two kinds of poets—one worthy of praise and reverence, always acceptable to good men, the other obscene and detestable, who, I said, should be both expelled and exterminated. Now the same distinction holds of the Muses, of which there is one genus but two species. For though they all enjoy the same power, and are governed by the same laws, yet the fruits of their labors are unlike, since one beareth sweet, the other bitter. Accordingly one may be held in honor, the other in dishonor. The one deserves every title and epithet of praise; she dwells in laurel groves, near the Castalian spring, or in whatsoever places we hold sacred; she is the companion of Phoebus; she goeth forth adorned with garlands of flowers, and graced with the sweet sound of voices in song. The other is she who is seduced by disreputable comic poets to mount the stage, preempt theatres and street-corners: and there for a fee she calmly exhibits herself to loungers in low compositions, destitute of a single commendable grace. It is not hers to relieve or heal the sufferings of those who languish, with the consolations of goodness, and with holy remedies of salvation; she only enhances their suffering even unto death amid groans and complaints, and strangles them in the toils of sensual delight. Hence these poet-haters may learn what they were too stupid to see, that when Boethius called the Muses drabs of the stage, he spoke only of theatrical Muses. This the cavillers might have seen clearly enough, if they had understood what Philosophy says a little later. Her words are: "But leave him to the ministering and healing care of *my* Muses." And, by way of clearer proof that he was talking of the second sort of Muses, Philosophy later cites many a fragment of verse and poetic fable to soothe and console Boethius. So if these good Muses have a share in the healing art of Philosophy, they must be reputable perforce. And if reputable, so are their familiars, it would seem by my opponents' arguments. Thus both poets and Muses are honorable, in spite of this attempt to befoul and disgrace them.

XXI. *To the King*

With such reasons as I could command, O most beneficient King, have I now repulsed the obloquy of these skulking enemies. Had I less self-respect, I should have sharpened and barbed my shafts with far more deadly effect against their character and manner of life, as well as their bold presumption. But I suppose this would only have led to more of their talk, and the desire to answer it would protract my discourse beyond reason. Prolixity is usually distasteful to a mind taken up with great affairs, like a king's, and may offend even those that are free and at leisure. So I would not tire your Highness, nor seem bent on the utter extermination of my opponents; compassion for their ignorance is better even than their destruction, however deserved. I will therefore pause at this point, and in conclusion do for them, with your indulgence, what of their own accord they would not do: setting aside all the resentment they have earned, and overlooking their weaknesses, I will address to them a friendly word, if by chance I may convert them to a better course.

XXII. *The Author Addresses the Enemies of Poetry in Hope of Their Reform*

And now, O men of sense, ye will do wisely to calm your indignation and quiet your swollen hearts. Our contest has grown perhaps too bitter. You began by taking up the cudgel against an innocent class of men, with the intention of exterminating them. I came to their defence, and, with God's help and the merits of the case, did what I could to save deserving men from their deadly enemies. Yet, if the poets in person had fairly taken the field against you, you would see how far their powers surpass both yours and mine, and repent at the eleventh hour. But the fight is over; with some glory of war, and a good deal more sweat, we have reached the point where the lust for victory may be a bit qualified, and we may part company with a fair settlement. Come then, let us freely unite to rest from our labors, for the prizes of the contest have been awarded. You forfeit to me your theory, and I to you a bit of consolation; this leaves ample room for peace. I have no doubt you are willing, since you are sorry to have begun the contest, and by this arrangement we shall both enjoy its benefits. To prove my sincerity, I, who am the first to tire of it, will be the first to resume friendly relations; that you may do likewise, I beg of you to consider with fair and unruffled mind the few words which I, in all charity and friendship, am about to say to you.

You recall, gentlemen, that, as well as I could, I have shown you the nature of poetry, which you had counted as naught, who the poets are, their function, and their manner of life, whom you cried out upon as depraved liars, moral perverters, corrupt with a thousand evils. I have shown also the nature of the Muses, whom you had called drabs and consigned to the stews. Yet being actually so worthy of regard as I have shown, you should not only cease to condemn them, but should cherish, magnify, love them, and search their books to your improvement. And that old age may not prevent you, or the popularity of other arts, try your best to do what an aged prince was not ashamed to attempt; I refer to that shining example of all virtues, famous King Robert of Sicily and Jerusalem, who besides being king, was a distinguished philosopher, an eminent teacher of medicine, and an exceptional theologian in his day. Yet in his sixty-sixth year he retained a contempt for Vergil, and, like you, called him and the rest mere story-tellers, and of no value at all apart from the ornament of his verse. But as soon as he heard Petrarch unfold the hidden meaning of his poetry, he was struck with amazement, and saw and rejected his own error; and I actually heard him say that he never had supposed such great and lofty meaning could lie hidden under so flimsy a cover of poetic fiction as he now saw revealed through the demonstration of this expert critic. With wonderfully keen regret he began upbraiding his own judgment and his misfortune in recognizing so late the true art of poetry. Neither fear of criticism, nor age, nor the sense of his fast expiring lease of life were enough to prevent him from abandoning his studies in the other great sciences and arts, and devoting himself to the mastery of Vergil's meaning. As it happened, an early end broke off his new pursuit, but if he might have continued in it, without doubt he would have won much glory for the poets, and no little advantage for the Italians engaged in such studies. Will you, then, hold that gift not worth the taking which was holy in the sight of this wise king? Impossible! You are not mere tigers or huge beasts, whose minds, like their ferocity, cannot be turned to better account.

But if my pious expectation is doomed to disappointment, and the heat of your hatred still burns against them who deserve it not, then whenever your tongues itch to be at it again, I beseech you, for the sake of your own decency, mind my words. I adjure you, by the sacred breast of Philosophy, which haply in other days has nourished you, not to rush in headlong fury upon the whole company of poets. Rather, if you have sense enough, you must observe right and timely distinction among them—such distinction as only can bring harmony out of discord, dispel the clouds of ignorance, clear the understanding, and set the mind in the right way. This you must do if you would not confuse the poets we revere—many of them pagans, as I have shown—with the disreputable sort. Let the lewd comic writers feel the stream of your wrath, the fiery blast of your eloquence; but be content to leave the rest in peace. Spare also the Hebrew authors. Them you cannot rend without insulting God's majesty itself. I have already cited Jerome's statement that some of them uttered their prophetic song in poetic style as dictated by the Holy Ghost. By the same token must Christian writers escape injury; for many even of our own tongue have been poets—nay, still survive—who, under cover of their compositions, have expressed the deep and holy meaning of Christianity. One of many instances is our Dante. True, he wrote in his mother tongue, which he adapted to his artistic purpose; yet in the book which he called the *Commedia* he nobly described the threefold condition of departed souls consistently with the sacred teaching of theology. The famous modern poet Petrarch has, in his *Bucolics*, employed the pastoral guise to show forth with marvellous effect both the praise and the blame visited by the true God and the glorious Trinity upon the idle ship of Peter. Many such volumes are there which yield their meaning to any zealous inquirer. Such are the poems of Prudentius, and Sedulius, which express sacred truth in disguise. Arator, who was not merely a Christian, but a priest and cardinal in the church of Rome, gave poetic form to the Acts of the Apostles by recounting them in heroics. Juvencus, the Spaniard, also a Christian, employed the symbolic device of the man, the ox, the lion, and the eagle, to describe all the acts of Christ our Redeemer, Son of the Living God. Without citing further examples, let me say that, if no consideration of gentleness can induce you to spare poets of our own nation, yet be not more severe than our mother the Church; for she, with laudable regard, does not scorn to favor many a writer; but especially hath she honored Origen. So great was his power in composition that his mind seemed inexhaustible and his hand tireless; so much so that the number of his treatises on various subjects is thought to have reached a thousand. But the Church is like the wise maiden who gathered flowers among thorns without tearing her fingers, simply by leaving the thorns untouched; so she has rejected the less trustworthy part of Origen, and retained the deserving part to be laid up among her treasures. Therefore distinguish with care, weigh the words of the poets in a true balance, and put away the unholy part. Neither condemn what is excellent, as if, by raising a sudden hue and cry against poets, you hoped to seem Augustines or Jeromes to an ignorant public. They were men whose wisdom equalled their righteousness; they directed their attack not against poetry, or the art of poetry, but against the pagan errors contained in the poets' works. At these they hurled fearless and outspoken condemnation because it was a time when Catholic truth was surrounded and beset with harassing enemies. At the same time they cherished them and ever recognized in these works so much art, and polish, such seasoning of wisdom and skilful application of ornament, that whoever would acquire any grace of Latin style apparently must derive it from them.

Finally in the words of Cicero pleading for Archias: "These studies may engage the strength of our manhood and divert us in old age; they are the adornment of prosperity, the refuge and solace of adversity; delightful at home, convenient in all places; they are ever with us through the night season; in our travels; in our rural retreats. And if we may not pursue them ourselves nor enjoy them in person, yet should we admire them as seen in others," etc. Poetry, then, and poets too, should be cultivated, not spurned and rejected; and if you are wise enough to realize this there is nothing more to say. On the other hand, if you persevere in your obstinate madness, though I feel sorry for you, contemptible as you are, yet no writing in the world could help you.

Thus ends the Fourteenth Book of the
Genealogy of the Gentile Gods.
Here happily begins the
Fifteenth and Last Book,
wherein the Author
clears himself
of Various
Charges.

THE GENEALOGY OF THE GENTILE GODS

FROM
Book XV

Proem

I have now steadied and trimmed my little craft, O most clement King, by such means as I could, for fear she be driven ashore by the wash of a stormy sea or the counterforce of the wind, with joints sprung and timbers crushed. And I have spread above her such protection as seemed opportune against lowering clouds that dissolve in rain or deadly flashes of lightning, lest she be either swamped or burned. Finally I have made her fast to the rocks, with stays and hawsers, that the ebb tide might not drag her into the depths. But mortal precaution avails naught against the wrath of God; and I have therefore resolved that the fate of my venture must be left in His hands without Whose favor naught shall endure. May He in His mercy keep her!

It now remains to offer some protection to the exhausted sailor from the weapons of his enemies, and in some way save him, if I can. No doubt he is pursued of many. But though aforetime I may have seemed impatient of the false charges against poetry and poets, yet shall I endure with the utmost patience the attacks upon the sailor, however violent. Such a course is perfectly reasonable; for in my opinion, the vituperative attack upon fair poetry and the skilful practicers of that art was unworthy, proceeding as it did from either pride or ignorance, I am not sure which. Not so with the sailor. For if he have put forth his utmost strength and nautical skill to bring his craft past roaring whirlpools and rocky shoals to safety, one can find no just fault with him. But I am fully aware of his great ignorance, and haply he deserves reproof for many an error of inadvertence. I will do my best, then, with God's help, to make his endeavor look less arrogant. And may He who snatched the young Israelites unscathed from the fiery furnace, save me from the jaws of my malignants, and bring me to the end of this my last work to the glory and honor of His holy name.

I. That Which at First Has Little Use May Some Day Be of Great Price

I am well aware that the aforementioned cavillers, or others of the sort, will glance sharply about this scene of our contest, and will then say—perhaps with pious intention, for mind-reading is difficult enough—"Such an immense work, of no utter use either now or in time to come!" Thus briefly they in effect demolish the whole book, especially as their objection seems colored by, or rather founded upon, a half-expressed fact. Of course anyone would at first glance say that the tales of the poets that make up this whole work are useless and even superfluous. But this, I think, is a mistake. I admit the work consists altogether of fables; and if I grant that such material is of little present use, yet will I show that many things of little present use, and among them this work, will eventually be of great worth. Then will I prove that, affording as it does, public and private benefits, it must be reckoned among useful things. Much then that we possess is of the very highest value, though not useful in the ordinary sense; and this applies as well to nature's products as to the inventions of man. When we wish to build a house we engage stone-workers, and masons, and carvers, and distinguished architects; yet for all practical purposes a common overseer could make as good a house out of mud and wattles. We build temples, and capitols, and royal palaces at tremendous cost both to people and prince, and adorn them with unnecessary painting. We use vases of gold and relief work, when cheap Samian ware would serve all needs. So with crowns and gay clothes, and gold armlets; we enjoy wearing them, when a plain woollen cloak is enough for any man. Thus artistic embellishment acquires value though it is of no practical use whatever. But since it derives this value from human ambition and pretence, let us see whether Nature, who is in every thing most prudent and discerning, has not also her desire for superfluous decoration. For example, of what use is the hair on the head? None, as all agree. Yet many claim such value for it that, if Venus were without it, she could not please Mars, for all her attendant graces. Caesar, as dictator, set such value upon hair, that he asked the senate for the perpetual privilege of wearing the laurel to cover his baldness. What use has a man for a beard? Yet if he come of age without one, he blushes for it before his fellows. Why does a stag have horns, or birds gay plumage? For embellishment and nothing else. This is enough to show that a thing precious for no other reason, may become so for ornament's sake. And if this is true of other things it certainly will be so of this book of mine. What is fairer in the oral intercourse of men than an occasional story mingled with the substance? What is more fitting than to unite with such discourse the pregnant meaning of a myth? Both of which—myth and meaning—this book offers in abundance. Great beauty accrues to weighty and elaborate speeches, as one may see who reads the works of Cicero or Jerome and other wise men, wherein myth and fable are mingled throughout. And this is enough to prove my work a valuable one merely on the score of ornament.

But there remains its usefulness, public and private, in which its greater value resides. Some men have thought that the learned poet merely invents shallow tales, and is therefore not only useless, but a positive harm. This is because they read discursively and, of course, derive no profit from the story. Now this work of mine removes the veil from these inventions, shows that poets were really men of wisdom, and renders their compositions full of profit and pleasure to the reader. And thus if poets who seemed to have perished through want of appreciation are now brought back to life, as it were, and to a high place in the state, while their usefulness to the individual, which was ignored because it was unrecognized, is now revealed by this work of mine, thus they rouse the reader's mind to higher feelings. Furthermore, I hope that, God willing, men will rise up as they have done in the past who will devote themselves to the study of poetry. As they peruse the memorials and remains of the Ancients they cannot fail to derive much help from this work of mine, which will prove valuable to them, if not to others. But enough. For, though these words of mine fail with everyone else, yet if your desire, O excellent Prince, by whose order I began the

THE GENEALOGY OF THE GENTILE GODS

work, is satisfied, that in itself I hold a measure of high value, however praiseworthy success at large may be. Yet if my book shall have failed to please your Highness, though it be favorably received by others, it will be worth little to me. It lies with you, then, to give the book its value, or, if it be your pleasure, to reject it.

II. Things Which Seem Perishable Often Endure Longest

With the same pious intention, some will say, as soon as they see how loose and inarticulate my work is, that a thing so full of holes and rifts is doomed not to last. My hearty thanks to these prognosticators; for they wake me up, and make me alert to the immediate necessity of precaution. If you remember, O renowned King, I anticipated this possibility even before I began my work, and at the outset showed as well as I could my reasons for thinking that the book must needs be fragmentary and mutilated. It appears from their comment, and in other ways, that I was not mistaken. Therefore I claim a just excuse for this defect. I have reinforced the work with such support as I could command, and, once fortified in this manner, it has developed no new or unexpected seams; as for the old and expected ones, I do not look for the sudden collapse that my critics forecast. If we may surmise the future in the usual way, this work will last a long time. One has often seen a fortress founded upon a rock fall to ruin sooner than a fisherman's hut on the marshes. But a man who knows his house is not very strong keeps constant watch, and as necessity demands, renews his foundation, stops the cracks in his walls, props his roof with timbers, and reinforces his galleries; so that the building that seemed on the point of collapse often lasts for ages. Who otherwise can be sure of his strength? For, while he rests secure, lo, one huge stone, loosened by its weight, slips, comes crashing down, and drags the whole house into a heap of ruins.

Decay is not the only fate of a great building: envy skulks in palaces, and hatred contrives their destruction; but a small house, with few inmates, familiar to its owner and his few friends, may last as long as God wills. Who could have thought that Ilium, the new-built city of Priam, fortified as it was, rich, gorgeous, the glory of all Asia's realm, the menace of all Greece, would fall before the hut of Aglaus of Psophis? In like manner we have seen a strong young man, full of life and health and beauty, by a slight fever or other accident, plunge to sudden death, while many an infirm old man drags out his life far beyond his wish.

But there is little need of discussion; human life teems with illustrations. Say what they please, I cling to my preference. Of one thing, at least, I am sure—"except the Lord keep the city, the watchman waketh but in vain." His is the power to save or destroy: His, and His alone is the knowledge of the term of all things mundane, whether long or short. The hope of the wise is in Him alone; the eye of the Lord be upon me! Knowing as I do the defects of my work, and that He "giveth grace to the humble," I have prayed Him to bestow all humility upon it.

But I have said enough. For defective, fragmentary, and full of gaps as my composition may be, the best is that it can at least reach your hands, my King, and prove to you my obedience, if not my scrupulous care. Such brief fame will be enough; but if my book survives, then shall I have God's goodness, and the King's favoring fortune to thank for it.

III. The Various Parts of the Book Could Not Be Arranged in Better Order

There will be other critics, I suspect, who, after examining what the rest have examined, will say that a sensible man would rather have the whole compilation perish than live on and on, since destruction will undo its defects, but survival only exhibit them. They will, above all point to a defect of construction—a broad chest protruding from the pate, legs from the chest, and feet from where the head ought to be. Think of Socrates' saying—"O happy physicians, whose blunders are hidden underground!" But with authors how different! For their choice utterances are exposed to the fangs of hounds, or at least harassed by their yelps. So this work of mine, wrought with the utmost pains of selection and composition, backed as far as possible by illustrious authority, is struck down by the words of passers-by. Yet patience is needful, if insolence is to be overcome of humility. I have no answer to such talk except that I was aware from the beginning of this *Genealogy* that many men would have many opinions, and that at the opening of the First Book I had not neglected to show that I chose the most ancient of the gods, which would lead naturally to some mention of the others. To this most ancient head, as my researches enabled me, I have joined in order the chest and other members. If other genealogies are truer or better arranged—and I admit that it is quite possible—I confess I have not seen them, though I have taken great care and gone through many volumes. And I know not in what order and relation the members of so vast a body could be combined. Let my critics also bring forth their knowledge, and, if in view of that my treatise deserves to be condemned, then the reader may give them his whole confidence. But if they merely assert without proof that I have joined the breast to the pate, it amounts only to unjust detraction, not fair rejoinder nor useful emendation.

IV. What Is Omitted Is Irrelevant

Besides thus urging the book's crudity, a charge already rebutted, these critics—or others—will say that I have left out much that ought to be included. I cannot deny this, even if I would, especially when I recall that, in dealing with the external matter of the myths, I said near the beginning of this work that for lack of proper books I should omit many human descendants of the gods. And though such books should prove to exist, who in the world will ever be hardy enough to come out and say that he has seen and read them all? Since I have not seen some which others have, I am not ashamed to admit that many authorities will be missed, perhaps in some cases even from lapse of memory. I cannot remember everything I have seen. Wherefore I beg that with this in mind they will temper their judgment, and not set down to deliberate error what really comes of ignorance or forgetfulness.

There is another consideration upon which perhaps men of higher attainments will be ready to criticize. I refer to the interpretations of the myths. Far be it from me to withstand their strictures. Indeed I think the criticism very likely is just, since I would never have dared on my own initiative to undertake such a task, aware as I was of my unfitness. But who will expect a perfect performance from imperfect man? God only can create the perfect thing, since He alone is perfect. If I have ventured too boldly, it has been at your command, O excellent King. And if in this respect my work is inferior, let the blame rest with your Highness. But I implore these more learned critics in the holy and venerable name of Philosophy, for which, I think they have regard, that, as they are impelled by some authority of the wise to make a savage attack upon an imperfect piece of work, so likewise they temper their wrath with humane considerations. Though the learned more often perceive that which escapes the unlearned, yet it sometimes happens that an unlearned man may see what the learned have overlooked. I am human, and it is no new and strange thing for a human being to err. As Horace says:

> Now and then
> Short fits of slumber creep on Homer's pen.

Argus had a hundred eyes, waking and sleeping fifty at a time, turn and turn about; and yet on one occasion he could not help going to sleep in all of them. What wonder then, if I with only two am sometimes overcome? Let them, I pray, interpret such myths as I could not, altering any inadequate explanation, and correcting such as have been based upon erroneous opinion. If I have not written fully, I have tried at least to write piously. If I have failed in this, I am not too perverse humbly to confess my error and be grateful for correction. For I am one who, though I hasten with all speed towards old age, am not afraid to learn—nay, I rather desire and long so to do. If, then, these critics do as I beg of them, my work will be improved and I shall gain by their generosity, both in learning and in praise.

V. *The Book Contains Only Such Myths and Stories As Have Been Derived from Commentaries of the Ancients*

Others will rise up and complain aloud that I have herein included myths and stories never heard of before, simply to make my work more impressive and elaborate. I deny having mingled any new myths or stories with the old, but I do admit having derived some from numerous Latin sources—stories unknown in this day and generation. None of these, however, is derived from any source other than the commentaries of the Ancients; nor were they cited to make the book more impressive and elaborate, but under necessity. Yet such is the querulous plaint of these jaundiced critics, all at odds with themselves! You cannot satisfy them. If you write in a style that is easy to read, loose, and obvious, they call it pedestrian, say it smells of the schoolroom, and throw it down in disgust. If you employ a somewhat harder style, they tire at the first step because the meaning does not strike the mind out of hand; then they find fault with the author for being harsh, and, however perfect his art, they reject him in scorn. But I do not think my style is involved or ambiguous; nor do I see that any difficulty or obscurity necessarily accrues to my work from inserted myths however unfamiliar to them—no, not even if I had made them up myself.

But I suspect my critics mean quietly and adroitly to condemn as false the myths and stories with which they are unfamiliar under the pretext that they are mere padding. I have already said that they are drawn from ancient commentaries, as I have shown by citing in each instance the names of the respective authors; if they have never seen them before, they should not therefore condemn them, as if nothing were true but what they had read. I am very sure they have read much that is unknown to me, just as I too may have read what has never come to their notice. No one but God has ever been able to enjoy omniscience. Then let them read my discoveries with the same mind in which they would have others read theirs. If perchance the text ever seems hard, let them exert their wits, and they will find that what they thought obscure is perfectly clear.

VI. *The Modern Authors Herein Cited Are Eminent*

I suppose they will also complain that I have cited as my authorities both such Ancients as are obscure or unheard of, and such moderns as have no reputation—in neither case such as they are ready to trust. Indeed this criticism carries some weight. However recent they once may have been who are now the Ancients, yet that which has been preserved through many ages has been approved by great lapse of time, and thence gains its authority. But as to all moderns, the right verdict concerning them, whatever their merit, seems to many to be still in suspense. I am of opinion that no writer will last long whose very novelty is not approved, since their very novelty is the necessary source of approval. Thus I have dared cite as my authorities moderns whom I have known or know personally, or whom by their merits I recognize as exceptional and reliable men. I know by every sign that they have spent nearly their whole lives in sacred studies, that they have ever mingled with men eminent for their attainments both of learning and character, they have lived laudable lives, are without stain or taint of any kind, and that both their writings and conversation are approved by the wisest. On such terms, I think, their modernity should offset the age of others. But for fear anyone may think my cited authorities are without sufficient weight, or that I am trying to approve them by my own testimony, may I say something of each of the most modern of them, that, if I should speak with effect, others may also be judges of their excellence?

I have frequently cited that noble and venerable old man, Andalò di Negro of Genoa, who was once my teacher of astronomy. Thou knowest well, O excellent King, how great his prudence, how serious his manner of life, and how deep is his knowledge of his subject. He was, as he used to say, very intimately associated with you, through similarity of studies which you pursued when a young man. You could see for yourself that he not only knew the motions of stars according to the laws discovered by the Ancients—which is our way of learning them—but he had travelled nearly all over the world, visiting every clime and horizon, and had used his experience and observation to inform himself at first hand of what we learn by mere hearsay. I am therefore disposed to trust him on all matters, but particularly on everything pertaining to astronomy, just as I should trust Cicero on oratory or Vergil on poetry. Many of his studies explaining the motions of the stars and heavens are extant to show how eminent he was in that subject.

In like manner I have also occasionally cited Dante Alighieri, the great Florentine poet and citizen, and have done it in all justice. He was a man of noblest birth and position among his compatriots, and however slender his means, or however great his suffering from cares at home, and at last from his long exile, yet he always found time to pursue his studies in at least physics and theology; witness the city of Paris, where he often entered the hall to dispute upon any subject of the curriculum with anyone who wished to submit theses or objections. He was moreover a poet of great learning and achievements and nothing but his exile kept him from receiving the laurel crown. He had resolved that he would never accept it anywhere but in his native city, and that he was not allowed to do. But praise is superfluous. His greatness is proved by his famous work in rime, which he wrote in the Florentine dialect with amazing skill, and called the *Commedia*. In that he stands forth rather as a Catholic and sacred theologian than a mere mythographer, and since he is known nearly the whole world over, perhaps his reputation will have reached the ears of your Highness.

I have also cited, though rarely, Francis of Barberino, a man of truly honorable character and illustrious life. Though more proficient in knowledge of sacred canons than in the art of poetry, he was the author of several essays in brilliant vernacular verse, which bear witness to the high order of his genius, and are much prized by the Italians. He was a man of purest faith, deserving all reverence, whom Florence did not scorn to include among her honored citizens. I have ever considered him an excellent and trustworthy authority on all points and worthy of being ranked with any men of distinction.

Not infrequently I quote Barlaam, the monk of Basil Caesariensis, a Calabrian. Though his body was slight, he overtopped others in learning. Indeed he was so good a Hellenist that he enjoyed privileges at the hands of emperors and Greek princes and scholars, which show that neither in our time, nor for many a century, have the Greeks produced a man endowed with such vast and peculiar erudition. Shall I not do well to trust him, particularly in all that pertains to Greek? I have never seen any formal work from his hand, though I have heard that he has written several. I possess, however, some material derived from him, and, though it was never reduced to the form of a book with a title, and shows certain of Barlaam's deficiencies in Latin, yet it proves both his wide reading and observation, and his power in interpretative criticism.

Paul of Perugia, a man of highest authority, is another of those to whom I refer. Advanced in years, of great and varied learning, he was long the librarian of the famous King Robert of Sicily and Jerusalem. If there was ever a man possessed of the curiosity of research he was the one. A word from his prince was sufficient to send him hunting through a dozen books of history, fable, or poetry. He thus enjoyed peculiar friendship with Barlaam, and though it could not be based upon common interests in Latin culture, it was a means by which Paul drank deeply of Greek lore. He wrote a huge book which he called *The Collections;* it included much matter on various subjects, but particularly his ingatherings of pagan mythology from Latin authors, together with whatever he could collect on the same subject from the Greeks, probably with Barlaam's help. I shall never hesitate to acknowledge that when still a youngster, long before you drew my mind to this undertaking, I drank deep of that work, with more appetite than discretion. Especially did I prefer all that part set down under the name of Theodontius. But to the very serious inconvenience of this book of mine, I found that his saucy wife Biella, after his death, wilfully destroyed this and many other books of Paul's. In short I am convinced that at the time when I knew him no one was his equal in studies of this sort.

Leontius Pilatus, of Thessalonica, is another whom I often mention. By his own statement he was a pupil of the aforesaid Barlaam. He is a man of uncouth appearance, ugly features, long beard, and black hair, for ever lost in thought, rough in manners and behavior. For all that he is a most learned Hellenist, as any inquirer discovers, and a fairly inexhaustible mine of Greek history and myth. In Latin he is not as yet so well versed. I have never seen any work from his hand; and all my quotations from him I have made at his oral dictation. For nearly three years I heard him read Homer, and conversed with him on terms of singular friendship; but so immense was the measure of all he had to tell that my memory, quickened though it was by pressure of other care, would not have been good enough to retain it, had I not set it down in a notebook.

Then there is also Paul the geometrician, my fellow-townsman. I am sure, O illustrious King, that you know him well by reputation; for I am convinced that to him more than to any other man in this part of the world the sciences of arithmetic, geometry, and astrology have opened and revealed their very depths; indeed, it seems as if no detail of them had escaped him. Wonderful as it sounds, more wonderful yet is it to see him give immediate ocular proof to anyone who asks, of every word he utters about the stars or heavens. This he does by means of instruments that he has made for the purpose with his own hands. His reputation is not confined to his native city, nor even to Italy; his scholarship is more celebrated at Paris than at home, as it is also in England, Spain, and particularly in Africa, where this subject enjoys special importance. Happy, indeed, the man whose zeal was more intense, or who lived in a more liberal age than Paul.

Last and greatest of my authorities is Francis Petrarch, of Florence, my revered teacher, father, and master. Not many years ago at Rome, by vote of the senate and approval of the famous King Robert of Sicily and Jerusalem, he received the decoration of the laurel crown from the very hands of the senators. He really deserves to be counted not among the moderns, but among the illustrious ancients. His great eminence as a poet has been recognized by—I will not say merely all Italians, for their glory is singular and perennial—but by all France, and Germany, and even that most remote little corner of the world, England, and, I must add, many of the Greeks. Surely his great fame has reached Cyprus, and hence the ears of your Highness. Many memorable works from his hand in prose and verse yield patent proof to all the world of his heaven-sent genius. First is his divine poem *Africa,* written in heroics to extol the deeds of the first Africanus. It still lies in his drawer awaiting publication. Second, is his *Bucolics,* famous the world over. Third, the book of metrical epistles to his friends. Fourth are two great volumes of letters in prose, so replete with thought and fact, so resplendent with artistic embellishment, that no fair-minded reader would judge them in any respect inferior to Cicero's. Fifth are his *Invectives against the Physician.* Sixth his book *On the Solitary Life.* Last is one which will see the light in a few days—his book *On the Remedies of Fortune.* Besides these there are still in the works several, which at their early completion we shall yet read in his lifetime. Who then will repudiate his testimony? Who will refuse to trust him? Oh, had I not a little above written of him in my feeble way, how much and how high the praise I could add to win more abundant faith in his utterance! But let what I have said suffice.

So much, then, about the moderns. But something remains to be said of those Ancients who are unfamiliar to my critics, lest I appear guilty of serious omission. They charge me with citing authors they never heard of, as if none were trustworthy whose names *they* have never heard. It is a common trait of the uneducated man to believe nothing that he does not see in a book, as though mere reading a fact made it credible. I confess I have cited myths and comment from many authors whose names are not generally current at present, because, as I said, their very antiquity accredited them. All these I have either seen and read myself, or else found them quoted by later writers. If these cavillers have not seen them or even heard their names, it is not the author's fault, but that of their own idleness. They should blame themselves, not find fault with me. The books cannot of their own accord take wing from the libraries into the hands of sluggards; and it is not the duty of those who are familiar with them to act as proxies for those who are not. Let them read and study for themselves. They will discover much that is new to them, and be at home where before they were strangers. They will find that these unfamiliar authors carry as much weight as they assign to those they have read before. So much, then, concerning both the modern and the ancient authors herein adduced. If their merits did not justify my citations, necessity would.

The great text of both civil and canon law has grown in bulk throughout generations of human failing, by editorial apparatus from many a doctor. The books of the philosophers also carry with them their commentaries compiled with great care and zeal. The books of medicine are filled with marginal notes from countless pens that resolve every doubt, and so with sacred writings, and their numerous expositors; so also with the liberal and the technical arts—each has its own commentary, from which anyone may select on occasion according to his preference. Poetry alone is without such honor. Few—very few—are they with whom it has dwelt continuously. Money-getters have found it unprofitable. It has therefore been neglected and scorned for many centuries, nay even torn by many persecutions and stripped of the aids given to the other arts. Wherefore, wanting such range of selection as they enjoy, one is forced to resort to this and that authority and bring away such slight fragments as one can. A discerning reader will readily see how often this has happened, for I have not only appealed on occasion to modern authors, but have had recourse to anonymous notes.

Wherefore let these cavillers bow to expediency and accept the authority of both the unfamiliar Ancients and the moderns.

VII. Greek Poetry Is Quoted in This Work Not without Good Reason

It is safe to say that these critics and others will charge me with purely gratuitous and ostentatious quoting from Greek poetry. I am well aware, of course, that the objection implies not a spark of charity, but proceeds from the malice of a blasted, withered, and impious heart. So be it; yet with God on my side, I shall not waver, but will, as usual, venture a humble response. Let me say then for the enlightenment of those unworthy slanderers, that it shows lack of judgment to derive from the stream what may be got at the fountainhead. I owned Homer's works, and do yet, and drew from them much that was of great use to my work. A great deal of this, as anyone may see, has been quoted by the Ancients, from whom of course I could have got it, as it were from the stream of tradition; in fact, I have frequently done so. But sometimes it has seemed better to draw from the source than from the stream, and more than once I have failed to find in the stream that which abounded in the fountain itself. Hence I have been guided sometimes by predilection, sometimes by necessity.

Authors occasionally delight to introduce digressive passages, which may indeed somewhat retard their readers, but contribute to their delectation and comfort, and keep them from leaving off their reading because they are tired with constant application or the monotony of the style. Such may be the effect of an occasional quotation of poetry. Furthermore my own bald statement of a fact thus gains corroboration from the witness of others in the face of any possible objector; if anyone distrust the verse as quoted, he may consult the *Iliad* or the *Odyssey* to find out whether I quoted correctly; and if I was right, so much the greater certitude. Then, too, I am not the only one to quote Greek in a Latin discourse; the practice is old. Let them open the books of Cicero, or Macrobius, or Apuleius, or, to go no further, the *Opuscula* of Maximus Ausonius; these authors they will often find quoting Greek verses in their Latin writings, and their precedent I have followed.

But my objectors will now say that it may have been laudable in those days, but at present such pains are silly. Since nobody now knows Greek, the old custom must perforce be obsolete. I am sorry, then, for Latin learning, if it has so completely rejected the study of Greek that we do not even recognize the characters. Though Latin literature be sufficient unto itself, and enjoys the exclusive attention of the whole western world, yet without question it would gain much light through an alliance with Greek. Besides the ancient Latin writers have not by any means appropriated all that is Greek. Much yet remains unrevealed to us, and much by knowledge of which we might profit greatly. But I shall take up this matter again.

My objectors do not consider to whom I dedicate my labor upon this book.

If they did they would realize that he is a most erudite monarch, said to be versed in Greek as well as Latin literature, who has learned Hellenists ever about him. *Such* will hardly agree with these dunces that Greek poetry is superfluous!

Well, enough! But I will now humor my accusers a bit. Suppose I *have* quoted Greek poetry for mere ostentation. What of it? Must they therefore set their teeth in me? Whom do I hurt in the pure enjoyment of my natural right? They may not know it, but it is my peculiar boast and glory to cultivate Greek poetry among the Tuscans. Was it not I who intercepted Leontius Pilatus on his way from Venice to the western Babylon, and with my advice turned him aside from his long peregrination, and kept him in our city? Did not I receive him into my own house, entertain him for a long time, and make the utmost effort personally that he should be appointed professor in Florence, and his salary paid out of the city's funds? Indeed I did; and I too was the first who, at my own expense, called back to Tuscany the writings of Homer and of other Greek authors, whence they had departed many centuries before, never meanwhile to return. And it was not to Tuscany only, but to my own city that I brought them. I, too, was the first to hear Leontius privately render the *Iliad* in Latin; and I it was who tried to arrange public readings from Homer. And though I did not understand Homer any too well, I got such knowledge of him as I could; and if that wanderer had dwelt longer among us, I should certainly have learned much more. But little as I did gain of the vast whole, some passages I came to understand very well by frequent interpretation of my preceptor; these have I, on occasion, embodied in this work. Now what possible harm can come from this? Greek myths abound in this book, yet no one accuses me of ostentation in recording them. But let me insert a few verses in Greek letters, and down they come upon me! Why, Marius of Arpinum, after his several triumphs over the Africans, the Cimbri, and the Teutons, made bold to do his drinking from the cantharus like Father Bacchus himself. And so Caius Duellius, the first to beat the Carthaginians in a sea-fight, made it his practice to go home from a public dinner by the light of a wax torch. All this, however it exceeded the precedent of the city of Rome, the Romans calmly accepted. Yet here are swine who fly into a rage at me for mingling Greek verses with Latin contrary to the modern custom, and little glory do I get for my pains. I thought I was thus adding a certain grace to my Latin, but lo, I have brought down a storm of malice upon myself. I am sorry enough. But it is no matter; from the judicious I do not look for such objections, and as for the rest, if they claim my attention, patience will suffice to get along with them. Finally, I beseech all my readers to endure such annoyance unperturbed, mindful of Valerius' words that there is no life so lowly that the sweetness of glory does not appeal to it.

VIII. *The Pagan Poets of Mythology Are Theologians*

There are certain pietists who, in reading my words, will be moved by holy zeal to charge me with injury to the most sacrosanct Christian religion; for I allege that the pagan poets are theologians—a distinction which Christians grant only to those instructed in sacred literature. These critics I hold in high respect; and I thank them in anticipation for such criticism, for I feel that it implies their concern for my welfare. But the carelessness of their remarks shows clearly the narrow limitations of their reading. If they had read widely, they could not have overlooked that very well-known work on the *City of God*; they might have seen how, in the Sixth Book, Augustine cites the opinion of the learned Varro, who held that theology is threefold in its divisions—mythical, physical, and civil. It is called mythical, from the Greek *mythicon,* a myth, and in this kind, as I have already said, is adapted to the use of the comic stage. But this form of literature is reprobate among better poets on account of its obscenity. Physical theology is, as etymology shows, natural and moral, and being commonly thought a very useful thing, it enjoys much esteem. Civil or political theology, sometimes called the theology of state worship, relates to the commonwealth, but through the foul abominations of its ancient ritual, it was repudiated by them of the true faith and the right worship of God. Now of these three, physical theology is found in the great poets since they clothe many a physical and moral truth in their inventions, including within their scope not only the deeds of great men, but matters relating to their gods. And particularly, as they first composed hymns of praise to the gods, and, as I have said, in a poetic guise, presented their great powers and acts, they won the name of theologians even among the primitive pagans. Indeed Aristotle himself avers that they were the first to ponder theology; and though they got their name from no knowledge or lore of the true God, yet at the advent of true theologians they could not lose it, so great was the natural force of the word derived from the theory of any divinity whatsoever. Aware, I suppose, that the title "theologian" once fairly won, cannot be lost, the present-day theologians call themselves professors of sacred theology to distinguish themselves from theologians of mythological cast or any other. Such distinction admits no possible exception as implying an injury to the name of Christianity. Do we not speak of all mortals who have bodies and rational souls as men? Some may be Gentiles, some Israelites, some Agarenes, some Christians, and some so depraved as to deserve the name of gross beasts not men. Yet we do not wrong our Savior by calling them men, though with His Godhead He is known to have been literally human. No more is there any harm in speaking of the old poets as theologians. Of course, if any one were to call them sacred, the veriest fool would detect the falsehood.

On the other hand there are times, as in this book, when the theology of the Ancients will be seen to exhibit what is right and honorable, though in most such cases it should be considered rather physiology or ethology than theology, according as the myths embody the truth concerning physical nature or human. But the old theology can sometimes be employed in the service of Catholic truth, if the fashioner of the myths should choose. I have observed this in the case of more than one orthodox poet in whose investiture of fiction the sacred teachings were clothed. Nor let my pious critics be offended to hear the poets sometimes called even sacred theologians. In like manner sacred theologians turn physical when occasion demands; if in no other way, at least they prove themselves physical theologians as well as sacred when they express truth by the fable of the trees choosing a king.

IX. It Is Not Improper for Certain Christians to Study Pagan Antiquity

Others will say with equal emphasis that it is improper for a Christian to investigate or publish wicked, superstitious beliefs and genealogies of the pagans, since they tend to pervert the minds of readers to erroneous opinions and involve them in imminent danger of false doctrine. I grant it: the criticism proceeds from a most sacred source. A considerable number should, I doubt not, be kept from studies of this sort. But just as safely others can be admitted to them without the least danger of suspicion. If it had seemed necessary for every one to avoid them, doubtless our holy Mother the Church would have uttered a perpetual decree of prohibition against them. Indeed, in the days when the Church was just taking root among the pagans, the Christians found it expedient to press hard against the pagan rites and observances, colored as men's notions of religion were by the origin and by the very perseverance of paganism. It was a precaution lest readers of pagan literature be caught by the claw of antiquity, and return as a dog to their vomit. But today, by the grace of Christ, our strength is very great; the universally hateful doctrine of paganism has been cast into utter and perpetual darkness, and the Church in triumph holds the fortress of the enemy. Thus there is the very slightest danger in the study and investigation of paganism. Of course it is better for a boy of tenacious memory but of mind as yet callow to avoid them, especially as he is not yet wholly familiar with the Christian religion. And a neophyte whose faith is not yet confirmed might, if the rein slackened, deviate into slippery places. Though there may be some men less sensitive who might let themselves slip into so dreadful a mistake, I cannot think it could happen to me even though I pursued nothing else. From my mother's womb I was brought to be washed at the fountain of our regeneration, and what my sponsors promised for me, a catechumen, I have kept from that hour to this as well as human frailty allowed. I have always held the Creed as it is sung in the congregation of just men:

That there is one God in triple distinction of persons, true, eternal, Maker of all things, in perpetual reason their Governor, Preserver, and Ruler; containing all things within Himself, but contained of none. That, by a marvellous and unique creative act of this Divinity, through the adumbration of the Holy Ghost, His eternal Word was made to destroy the guilt of men incurred by the disobedience of our first parents. He was conceived of a pure Virgin, who was forewarned by the Heavenly Harbinger; He became incarnate, was born in due time of the Virgin, still a virgin, and was made mortal man. While yet an infant at His mother's breast He was adored by the Sabean Kings with their offerings. As He grew, He went among doctors of the Law explaining to them its hard obscurities; yet they held Him not God, but a boy of wonderful powers; for the unfading splendor of truth had not as yet withdrawn the mist from their minds that they might recognize here clothed in the flesh the God that had been promised unto them. And I believe that He who had thus left the heavenly mansions, and changed His Godhead for a servant's guise, and grew a man among men, in His thirtieth year was baptized in the River Jordan by the prophet, unkempt and uncouth, one filled from his birth with the Holy Ghost, and appointed to open the door of eternal salvation; and the noise of thunder was heard, and a clear sound from the overhanging cloud which was the voice of God saying: "This is my beloved Son in whom I am well pleased; hear ye Him." And I believe, and hold it proven, that first at Cana in Galilee He turned water into wine to reveal the divinity within Him; then taking the holy company of His apostles, He went throughout Judea, and the cities of Phoenicia, and Samaria and Galilee, and in temple and synagogue taught the people the heavenly truth, healed lepers, made the dumb speak, restored those who were blind by nature or accident, brought back souls from death to their bodies, made fevers, winds, and waves obey Him, and showed many other signs of His divinity. At length when His hour was come through the envy of the priests of the Jews, He washed His friends' feet, and celebrated the great feast whereat was wrought by His hands and words the ineffable sacrament of our communion, in which He changed His body into bread and His blood into wine, and revealed them so changed unto those present and unto all generations to come. Then was He sold by one of His disciples, and, as He prayed in solitude, He was sought out by the rabble, and taken with torches and staves, brought to the rulers, basely accused, yet bearing with patient humility the false witness of certain accusers; then He was mocked in the judgment-hall, and cut with rods, crowned with a crown of thorns, buffeted and spit upon, and at last condemned after the manner of thieves, hung high on the cross, and had vinegar and myrrh to drink. When His human strength was overcome by His punishment, His end came; or rather, I believe with Thomas Aquinas, that He gathered up His strength, and of His own will gave up the ghost. And the whole earth shook, and the light of the midday sun turned to darkness for three hours, and the moon opposite was darkened. I wonder that Dionysius the Areopagite, in writing to Polycarp explains it otherwise. Then with his spear a soldier, blind of heart, pierced the side of Jesus, and blood mingled with water gushed out, whence I believe proceeded all the sacraments of our salvation. And I believe withal that when He had been taken from the cross and buried, He visited in spirit the abodes of hell, where He broke the iron bonds and shattered the walls of that ancient prison, then subdued Pluto, and brought forth to freedom all the ancient spoil of the place. Then by power of His deity, as sung by the prophets of old, the third day He rose from the bowels of the earth, like Jonah from the whale's belly, and triumphed over death. Thereafter He appeared often among His own. At last, oppressed by no corporeal weight, in His true body that was sometime mortal, of His own strength He arose from before their eyes and ascended to Him who had sent Him forth. Hence He imparted to His brave champions the Heavenly Flame proceeding equally from Himself and His all-righteous Father, quickening all things and teaching all truth. In Its light they waged war upon the Prince of this world; and when they had sown the seed of truth by their blood and wounds, and won the victory, they followed their Captain in triumph back into their own country. I believe also in the devout congregation of the just established by this only-begotten Son of God; in the holy baptism of regeneration, whereby the sins of men are done away; and in the other rites and sacraments of the Church by which we become submissive to God, and rise again when, in our foolishness, we have fallen, and by our own choice seek reconciliation not accomplished by shedding human blood, as among heathen savages, nor in the ancient manner, by sacrifice of sheep and cattle. I have never ceased to believe, by testimony of the Fathers, in the last great day when all things perishable shall be done away, and by the might of God we who were once mortal shall in our bodies rise immortal, and enter into our appointed place. There Christ Himself wearing all the marks of His passion, shall sit enthroned as judge in His proper majesty, and we shall hear Him speak final sentence upon our merits. I believe also in the life to come, wherein I hope in the body, through no merit of mine, but by divine compassion, to behold God my Redeemer, and rejoice with the saints in the land of the living.

This, then, briefly, is the sincere faith and eternal truth which is so deeply implanted in my heart, that by no influence of pagan antiquity nor any other power can it be torn out, or be cut off, or fall away. Sinner that I am, I am not by grace of Christ like young Cherea, in Terence, who by looking at a picture of Jove falling in a shower of gold from the roof to the lap of Danae, was inflamed to the desire of a similar misdeed. Any weak susceptibility of that sort, if it ever existed—and I am not at all sure that it did—left me with my youth. But I knew well that our old adversary spreads snares and nets for us on every side, and, as a roaring lion, walketh among the paths of men, seeking whom he may devour. Like Mithridates, the aged king of Pontus, who, with great and bold spirit and a splendid outlay, waged fierce and memorable war against Rome full forty years, and ever from his youth up carried in his bosom an antidote to deadly poison; so I have armed my breast with the truth of the Gospel, the holy doctrine of Paul, and with the commands, advice, and admonitions of Augustine and many other very reverend Fathers. Wherefore little have I to fear from the weapons of paganism. If at thy bidding, O renowned King, I, a Christian, have handled the foolishness of the Gentiles, and so roused the disapproval of these credulous objectors, I have only done—to compare small things with great—what many saintly men have done with highest approval, such as Augustine, or Jerome, or among others the neophyte Lactantius. I have been fully aware from childhood, by the Psalmist's testimony, that all pagan gods were devils, and have therefore disapproved of their absurd misdeeds; but I admit that, their manner of worship aside, the character and words of certain ancient poets have delighted me, and I have both praised them and defended them as well as I could against their accusers; whereof this book is proof enough. This I have done to save from ignorant clutches men who, if they had known Christ, would have worshipped Him as reverently as the noblest of our faith. But, to go higher, some one will say: "You have done well; it is a commendable thing to forearm oneself. But remember, he that toucheth pitch shall be defiled. Many a man at the very height of his trust in his strength has fallen at the hand of a weak enemy. Even if examples did not abound, Solomon is certainly a convincing proof of human weakness. He enjoyed at God's hand all wisdom, all wealth, great empire, held the Gentiles in just tribute, built a wonderful temple to God, wrought many good works; and yet in his old age forgot the Giver of so many honors, went up into the mountain of offence, and adored the Egyptian idol Moloch on bended knee.

And will you prove stronger or more circumspect than Solomon?" True, we deceive ourselves who trust too much in our own strength; the fact is true and undeniable. But my contention with paganism differs from that between Solomon and his Egyptian wife. Well aware in her woman's guile that she ensnared the soul of an unhappy man with her beauty, and eager to glorify her own gods, she proceeded to ply him incessantly with amorous embraces, honeyed kisses, a woman's flattery, wantonness, prayers, and tears—a very ready means with her sex—nay, with assumed indignation; and thus kept up the attack upon her lover day and night as well. Ah, how strong and irresistible are the love assaults of women, especially at night. For fear of losing her favor whom he loved above all the rest, Solomon turned and succumbed without defence to the armed force of a woman's wiles. But my strife with the absurdities of paganism is quite otherwise, for their power is disarmed by many a true reason familiar to me, and with their force thus spent and routed the fight is easy. I am fully aware that over-confidence is at all times a sin; but my trust is not in myself, but in the grace of Jesus Christ by whose precious blood I was redeemed. I am sure He will not suffer me, who have followed in His very steps so many years, even from my youth, to go astray in my old age. And if I slip, He will stretch out the hand of His righteousness to me in my weakness, and lead my weary feet to quiet peace.

Finally, what I have said goes to show that while it is not desirable for everybody to study paganism, it is not equally improper for everybody.

Petrarch
1304–1374

Francesco Petrarca, master of Italian letters and architect of European Humanism, was born in Tuscany on July 20, 1304. The son of a lawyer, Petrarch was sent to Montpellier (and later Bologna) to study jurisprudence; after his father's death in 1326, however, he forsook law in favor of literature. He moved to Avignon, took minor orders, and pursued a career at court, where his elegance and scholarship soon made him a renowned figure.

While at Avignon, Petrarch entered the service of Cardinal Colonna, whose patronage and influence enabled Petrarch to pursue his academic interests. During the next decade (1330–40) Petrarch travelled throughout the continent, visiting monastic libraries and universities, and soon established himself as one of the foremost classicists of his era. He wrote a series of "letters" in Latin verse (the *Epistolae Metricae*) and began a collection of biographical sketches of figures from antiquity (the *De Viris Illustribus*).

It was at this time also that Petrarch came into contact with Laura, whom he was to immortalize in his verse (especially in his vernacular *Rime*). In spite of his (very public) adulation of Laura, he gave few details about her identity or background, and we know almost nothing about her today apart from what is recorded in the *Rime*.

Petrarch became increasingly disenchanted with the corruption and venality of the Avignon court, and when the Black Plague broke out in 1348, he left, moving from place to place in Italy in flight of pestilence and in search of preferment. At this time he revised his *Rime*, dividing it into two parts: the *Rime in Vita di Laura* and the *Rime in Morte di Laura*. Undoubtedly, the death of Laura of the Plague in 1348 gave new impetus to his work, and the entire composition is one of the most moving meditations on love and grief ever written.

Petrarch's skillful command of Latin made him a useful diplomat and he served various princes in this capacity until 1370, when the new pope, Urban V, invited him to Rome to enter his service. En route, Petrarch suffered an incapacitating stroke, which rendered him an invalid for the next four years. He died on July 18, 1374.

Petrarch's influence upon contemporary attitudes toward literature must not be underestimated. The use of the vernacular as a poetic medium—a phenomenon which the popular imagination associates more often with Dante or Boccaccio than Petrarch—was given new credibility at this time in large part because of Petrarch's unrivalled command of the classics. In many ways Petrarch was very much a divided man: moving between court and cloister, he could never decide whether he desired the active or contemplative life, a tension that shows in his later works (particularly the *Secretum Meum*). Though affecting to disdain his *Rime* as trifles written in the vulgar tongue, Petrarch spent years reworking and perfecting them. His scholarship, his precision, commanded respect in academic circles, and this respect carried over to his vernacular "trifles."

The selections from Petrarch's letters, translated in part by David Thompson, are reprinted by permission of Harper & Row Publishers from *Petrarch: A Humanist Among Princes,* edited by David Thompson (New York: Harper & Row, 1971). © 1971 by David Thompson.

SELECTED LETTERS

FROM

ON THE NATURE OF POETRY[1]

I judge, from what I know of your religious fervor, that you will feel a sort of repugnance toward the poem[2] which I enclose in this letter, deeming it quite out of harmony with all your professions, and in direct opposition to your whole mode of thinking and living. But you must not be too hasty in your conclusions. What can be more foolish than to pronounce an opinion upon a subject that you have not investigated? The fact is, poetry is very far from being opposed to theology. Does that surprise you? One may almost say that theology actually is poetry, poetry concerning God. To call Christ now a lion, now a lamb, now a worm, what pray is that if not poetical? And you will find thousands of such things in the Scriptures, so very many that I cannot attempt to enumerate them. What indeed are the parables of our Savior, in the Gospels, but words whose sound is foreign to their sense, or allegories, to use the technical term? But allegory is the warp and woof of all poetry. Of course, though, the subject matter in the two cases is very different. That everyone will admit. In the one case it is God and things pertaining to him that are treated, in the other mere gods and mortal men.

Now we can see how Aristotle came to say that the first theologians and the first poets were one and the same.[3] The very name of poet is proof that he was right. Inquiries have been made into the origin of that word; and, although the theories have varied somewhat, the most reasonable view on the whole is this: that in early days, when men were rude and unformed, but full of a burning desire—which is part of our very nature—to know the truth, and especially to learn about God, they began to feel sure that there really is some higher power that controls our destinies, and to deem it fitting that homage should be paid to this power, with all manner of reverence beyond that which is ever shown to men, and also with an august ceremonial. Therefore just as they planned for grand abodes, which they called temples, and for consecrated servants, to whom they gave the name of priests, and for magnificent statues, and vessels of gold, and marble tables, and purple vestments, they also determined, in order that this feeling of homage might not remain unexpressed, to strive to win the favor of the deity by lofty words, subjecting the powers above to the softening influences of songs of praise, sacred hymns remote from all the forms of speech that pertain to common usage and to the affairs of state, and embellished moreover by numbers, which add a charm and drive tedium away. It behoved of course that this be done not in everyday fashion, but in a manner artful and carefully elaborated and a little strange. Now speech which was thus heightened was called in Greek *poetices*; so, very naturally, those who used it came to be called *poets*.

Who, you will ask, is my authority for this? But can you not dispense with bondsmen, my brother, and have a little faith in me? That you should trust my unsupported word, when I tell you things that are true and bear upon their face the stamp of truth, is nothing more, it seems to me, than I have a right to ask of you. Still, if you find yourself disposed to proceed more cautiously, I will give you bondsmen who are perfectly good, witnesses whom you may trust with perfect safety. The first of these is Marcus Varro,[4] the greatest scholar that Rome ever produced, and the next is Tranquillus,[5] an investigator whose work is characterized always by the utmost caution. Then I can add a third name, which will probably be better known to you, Isidore. He too mentions these matters, in the eighth book of his *Etymologies*, although briefly and merely on the authority of Tranquillus.[6]

But you will object, and say, "I certainly can believe the saint, if not the other learned men; and yet the fact remains that the sweetness of your poetry is inconsistent with the severity of my life." Ah! but you are mistaken, my brother. Why, even the Old Testament fathers made use of poetry, both heroic song and other kinds. Moses, for example, and Job, and David, and Solomon, and Jeremiah. Even the psalms, which you are always singing, day and night, are in meter, in the Hebrew; so that I should be guilty of no inaccuracy or impropriety if I ventured to style their author the Christian's poet. Indeed the plain facts of the case inevitably suggest some such designation. Let me remind you, moreover, since you are not inclined to take anything that I say today without authority, that even Jerome took this view of the matter. Of course these sacred poems, these psalms, which sing of the blessed man, Christ—of his birth, his death, his descent into hell, his resurrection, his ascent into heaven, his return to judge the earth,—never have been, and never could have been, translated into another language without some sacrifice of either the meter or the sense. So, as the choice had to be made, it has been the sense that has been considered. And yet some vestige of metrical law still survives, and the separate fragments we still call verses, very properly, for verses they are.

So much for the ancients. Now as regards Ambrose and Augustine and Jerome, our guides through the New Testament—to show that they too employed poetic forms and rhythms would be the easiest of tasks; while in the case of Prudentius and Prosper and Sedulius and the rest the mere names are enough, for we have not a single word from them in prose, while their metrical productions are numerous and well known. Do not look askance then, dear brother, upon a practice which you see has been approved by saintly men whom Christ has loved. Consider the underlying meaning alone, and if that is sound and true accept it gladly, no matter what the outward form may be. To praise a feast set forth on earthen vessels but despise it when it is served on gold is too much like madness or hypocrisy. . . .

PETRARCH DISCLAIMS ALL JEALOUSY OF DANTE[7]

There are many things in your letter which do not require any answer; those, for example, which we have lately settled face to face. Two points there were, however, which it seemed to me should not be passed over in silence, and I will briefly write down such reflections concerning them as may occur to me. In the first place, you excuse yourself for seeming to praise unduly a certain poet, a fellow-citizen of ours, who in point of style is very popular, and who has certainly chosen a noble theme. You beg my pardon for this, as if I regarded anything said in his, or anyone else's praise, as detracting from my own. You assert, for instance, that if I will only look closely at what you say of him, I shall find that it all reflects glory upon me. You take pains to explain, in extenuation of your favorable attitude towards him, that he was your first light and guide in your early studies. Your praise is certainly only a just and dutiful acknowledgment of his services, an expression of what I may call filial piety. If we owe all to those who begot and brought us forth, and much to those who are the authors of our fortunes, what shall we say of our debt to the parents and fashioners of our minds? How much more, indeed, is due to those who refine the mind than to those who tend the body, he will perceive who assigns to each its just value; for the one, it will be seen, is an immortal gift, the other, corruptible and destined to pass away.

Continue, then, not by my sufferance simply, but with my approbation, to extol and cherish this poet, the guiding star of your intellect, who has afforded you courage and light in the arduous way by which you are pressing stoutly on towards a most glorious goal. He has long been buffeted and wearied by the windy plaudits of the multitude. Honor him now and exalt him by sincere praise worthy alike of you and of him, and, you may be sure, not unpleasing to me. He is worthy of such a herald, while you, as you say, are the natural one to assume the office. I therefore accept your song of praise with all my heart, and join with you in extolling the poet you celebrate therein.

Hence there was nothing in your letter of explanation to disturb me except the discovery that I am still so ill understood by you who, as I firmly believed, knew me thoroughly. You think, then, that I do not take pleasure in the praises of illustrious men and glory in them? Believe me, nothing is more foreign to me than jealousy; there is no scourge of which I know less. On the contrary, in order that you may see how far I am from such feelings, I call upon Him before whom all hearts are open to witness that few things in life have caused me more pain than to see the meritorious passed by, utterly without recognition or reward. Not that I am deploring my own lot, or looking for personal gain; I am mourning the common fate of mankind, as I behold the reward of the nobler arts falling to the meaner. I am not unaware that although the reputation that attaches to right conduct may stimulate the mind to deserve it, true virtue is, as the philosophers say, a stimulus to itself; it is its own reward, its own guide, its own end and aim. Nevertheless, now that you have yourself suggested a theme which I should not voluntarily have chosen, I shall proceed to refute for you, and through you for others, the commonly accepted notion of my judgment of this poet. It is not only false, as Quintilian says of the construction put upon his criticism of Seneca,[8] but it is insidious and, with many, out-and-out malevolent. My enemies say that I hate and despise him, and in this way stir up the common herd against me, for with them he is extremely popular. This is indeed a novel kind of perversity, and shows a marvelous aptitude for harming others. But truth herself shall defend me.

In the first place, there can be no possible cause for ill-will towards a man whom I never saw but once, and that in my very earliest childhood. He lived with my grandfather and my father, being younger than the former, but older than my father, with whom, on the same day and by the same civil commotion, he was driven from his country into exile. At such a time strong friendships are often formed between companions in misery. This proved especially true of these two men, since in their case not only a similar fate but a community of taste and a love for the same studies, served to bring them together. My father, however, forced by other cares and by regard for his family, succumbed to the natural influences of exile, while his friend resisted, throwing himself, indeed, with even greater ardor into what he had undertaken, neglecting everything else and desirous alone of future fame. In this I can scarce admire and praise him enough,—that neither the injustice of his fellow-citizens, nor exile, nor poverty, nor the attacks of his enemies, neither the love of wife, nor solicitude for his children, could divert him from the path he had once decided upon, when so many who are highly endowed are yet so weak of purpose that they are swerved from their course by the least disturbance. And this most often happens to writers of verse, for silence and quiet are especially requisite for those who have to care not only for the thought and the words but the felicitous turn as well. Thus you will see that my supposed hate for this poet, which has been trumped up by I know not whom, is an odious and ridiculous invention, since there is absolutely no reason for such repugnance, but, on the contrary, every reason for partiality, on account of our common country, his friendship with my father, his genius, and his style, the best of its kind, which must always raise him far above contempt.

This brings us to the second reproach cast upon me, which is based upon the fact that, although in my early years I was very eager in my search for books of all kinds, I never possessed a copy of this poet's work, which would naturally have attracted me most at that age. While exceedingly anxious to obtain other books which I had little hope of finding, I showed a strange indifference, quite foreign to me, towards this one, although it was readily procurable. The fact I admit, but I deny the motives which are urged by my enemies. At that time I too was devoting my powers to compositions in the vernacular; I was convinced that nothing could be finer, and had not yet learned to look higher. I feared, however, in view of the impressionableness of youth and its readiness to admire everything, that, if I should imbue myself with his or any other writer's verses, I might perhaps unconsciously and against my will come to be an imitator. In the ardor of youth this thought filled me with aversion. Such was my self-confidence and enthusiasm that I deemed my own powers quite sufficient, without any mortal aid, to produce an original style all my own, in the species of production upon which I was engaged. It is for others to judge whether I was right in this. But I must add that if anything should be discovered in my Italian writings resembling, or even identical with, what has been said by him or others, it cannot be attributed to secret or conscious imitation. This rock I have always endeavored to avoid, especially in my writings in the vernacular, although it is possible that, either by accident or, as Cicero says, owing to similar ways of thinking, I may ignorantly have traversed the same path as others. If you ever believe me, believe me now; accept this as the real explanation of my conduct. Nothing can be more strictly true; and if my modesty and sense of propriety did not seem to you sufficient to vouch for this, my youthful pride at any rate certainly might have explained it.

Today, however, I have left these anxieties far behind, and, having done so, I am freed from my former apprehension, and can now unreservedly admire other writers, him above all. At that time I was submitting work of my own to the verdict of others, whereas now I am merely passing my own silent verdicts upon my fellows. I find that my opinion varies as regards all the rest, but in his case there can be no reason for doubt; without hesitation I yield him the palm for skill in the use of the vulgar tongue. They lie, then, who assert that I carp at his renown; I, who probably understand better than the majority of these foolish and immoderate admirers of his what it is that merely tickles their ears, without their knowing why, but cannot penetrate their thick heads, because the avenues of intelligence are obstructed. They belong to the same class that Cicero brands in his *Rhetoric*, who "read fine orations or beautiful poems, and praise the orators or poets, and yet do not know what it is that has aroused their admiration, for they lack the ability to see where the thing is that most pleases them, or what it is, or how it is produced."[9] If this happens with Demosthenes and Cicero, Homer and Virgil, among learned men and in the schools, how will it fare with our poet among the rude fellows who frequent the taverns and the public squares?

As for me, far from scorning his work, I admire and love him, and in justice to myself I may venture to add that if he had been permitted to live until this time he would have found few friends more devoted to him than myself, provided, of course, that I had found his character as attractive as his genius. On the other hand, there are none to whom he would have been more obnoxious than these same silly admirers, who, in general, know equally little about what they praise and what they condemn, and who so mispronounce and lacerate his verses that they do him the greatest injury that a poet can suffer. I might even strive to the best of my powers to rescue him from this abuse, did not my own productions give me enough to think about. As it is, I can only give voice to my irritation, when I hear the common herd befouling with their stupid mouths the noble beauty of his lines.

Just here it may not be out of place to say that this was not the least of the considerations which led me to give up a style of composition to which I devoted myself in my early years. I feared for my writings the same fate which I had seen overtake those of others, especially those of the poet of whom we are speaking. I could not in my own case look for more musical tongues or more flexible minds among the common people than I noted in the rendering of those authors whom long favor and habit have made popular in the theaters and public squares. That my apprehensions were not idle is clear from the fact that I am continually tortured by the tongues of the people, as they sing the few productions which I allowed to escape me in my youth. I indignantly reject and hate what I once loved; and day by day walk the streets with vexation and execrate my own talents. Everywhere a crowd of ignorant fellows, everywhere I find my Damoetas ready at the street corner "to murder with his screeching reed" my poor song.[10]

However, I have already said more than enough concerning a trifling matter which I ought not to have taken so seriously, for this hour, which will never return, should have been devoted to other things. And yet your excuse did seem to me to have just a little in common with the accusations of these critics, some of whom are constantly asserting that I hate, some that I despise, this person,—whose name I have intentionally refrained today from mentioning, lest the mob, who catch up everything without understanding it, should cry out that I was defaming it. Others again claim that I am actuated by envy—men who are jealous of me and my fame; for although I scarcely am an object for envy, I yet have noticed late in life that there are those who entertain this feeling towards me, a thing that at one time I could not have believed possible. In answer to this charge of envy brought against me, I might reply that, many years ago, in the ardor of youth, and with an approving conscience, I ventured to assert, not in any ordinary manner, but in a poem addressed to a certain illustrious personage, that I envied no man.[11] Suppose, though, that I am not worthy of belief. Still, even then, what probability is there that I should be jealous of a writer who devoted his whole life to those things which with me were but the flower and first-fruits of my youth. What to him was, if not his only occupation, certainly the supreme object of his life, to me was mere sport, a pastime, the first essay of my powers.

What occasion is there here for rancor? What ground is there for even a suspicion of jealousy? When you say, in praising him, that he might have devoted himself to another kind of composition, had he wished, I heartily agree with you. I have the highest opinion of his ability, for it is obvious from what he has done that he would have succeeded in anything he might have chosen to undertake. But suppose that he had turned his powers in another direction, and successfully—what then? What would there be in that to make me jealous? Why should it not rather be a source of satisfaction to me? Who indeed could excite envy in me, who do not envy even Virgil?—unless perhaps I should be jealous of the hoarse applause which our poet enjoys from the tavern-keepers, fullers, butchers, and others of that class, who dishonor those whom they would praise. But, far from desiring such popular recognition, I congratulate myself, on the contrary, that, along with Virgil and Homer, I am free from it, inasmuch as I fully realize how little the plaudits of the unschooled multitude weigh with scholars. Should it be suggested that the citizen of Mantua is, when all is said, dearer to me than my fellow-citizen of Florence, I must urge that, although I will not deny that jealousy does flourish most rankly between neighbors, the mere fact of common origin cannot by itself justify such an inference. Indeed the simple fact of our belonging to different generations would make this latter supposition absurd, for as one has elegantly said, who never speaks otherwise than elegantly, "The dead are neither hated nor envied."[12]

You will accept my solemn affirmation that I delight in both the thought and style of our poet, nor do I ever refer to him except with the greatest admiration. It is true that I have sometimes said to those who wished to know precisely what I thought, that his style was unequal, for he rises to a higher plane of excellence in the vernacular than in poetry and prose. But you will not deny this, nor will it, if rightly understood, carry with it any disparagement of his fame and glory. Who, indeed—I will not say at the present time, when eloquence has so long been mourned as dead, but at the time when it flourished most—who, I say, ever excelled in all its various branches? Witness Seneca's *Declamations*![13] No one dreams of attributing inexhaustible versatility even to Cicero, Virgil, Sallust, or Plato. Who would lay claim to a degree of praise which must be denied even to such genius? It is enough to have excelled in one kind of composition. This being true, let those be silent who attempt to twist my words into calumnies, and let those who have believed my calumniators read here, if they will, my opinion of them.

Having disposed thus of one matter which has been troubling me, I come now to a second. You thank me for my solicitude for your health. While you do this from courtesy, and in accordance with conventional usage, you well know that such acknowledgment is quite unnecessary. For who is ever thanked for his interest in himself, or his own affairs? and you, dear friend, are part and parcel of myself.

Although, next to virtue, friendship is the most sacred, the most God-like and divine thing in human intercourse, yet I think that it makes a difference whether one begins by loving or by being loved, and that those friendships should be more carefully fostered where we return love for love than where we simply receive it. I have been overwhelmed in a thousand instances by your kindness and friendly offices, but among them all there is one that I can never forget.

In days gone by, I was hurrying across central Italy in mid-winter; you hastened to greet me, not only with affectionate longings, which are the wings of the soul, but in person, impelled by a wondrous desire to behold one whom you had never yet seen, but whom you were nevertheless resolved to love. You had sent before you a piece of beautiful verse, thus showing me first the aspect of your genius, and then of your person. It was evening, and the light was fading, when, returning from my long exile, I found myself at last within my native walls. You welcomed me with a courtesy and respect greater than I merited, recalling the poetic meeting of Anchises and the King of Arcadia, who "in the ardor of youth, longed to speak with the hero and to press his hand."[14] Although I did not, like him, stand "above all others," but rather beneath, your zeal was none the less ardent. You introduced me, not within the walls of Pheneus, but into the sacred penetralia of your friendship. Nor did I present you with a "superb quiver and arrows of Lycia," but rather with my sincere and unchangeable affection. While acknowledging my inferiority in many respects, I will never willingly concede it in this, either to Nisus, or to Pythias, or to Laelius. Farewell.

ENCOURAGEMENT FOR BOCCACCIO AND A DIATRIBE AGAINST IGNORAMUSES OF SEVERAL SORTS[15]

"I have somewhat to say unto thee," if a poor sinner may use the words of his Savior, and this something for which you are listening, what should it be but what I am wont to tell you? So prepare your mind for patience and your ears for reproaches. For, although nothing could be more alike than our two minds, I have often noticed with surprise that nothing could be more unlike than our acts and resolutions. I frequently ask myself how this happens, not only in your case but in that of certain others of my friends, in whom I note the same contrast. I find no other explanation than that our common mother, nature, made us the same, but that habit, which is said to be a second nature, has rendered us unlike. Would that we might have lived together, for then we should have been but one mind in two bodies.

You may imagine now that I have something really important to tell you, but you are mistaken—and, as you well know, a thing must be trivial indeed which the author himself declares to be unimportant, for our own utterances are so dear to us that scarcely anyone is a good judge of his own performances, so prone are we to be misled by partiality for ourselves and our works. You, among many thousands, are the only one to be betrayed into a false estimate of your compositions by aversion and contempt, instead of inordinate love—unless, mayhap, I am myself deceived in this matter, and attribute to humility what is really due to pride. What I mean by all this you shall now hear.

You are familiar, no doubt, with that widely distributed and vulgar set of men who live by words, and those not their own, and who have increased to such an irritating extent among us. They are persons of no great ability, but of retentive memories; of great industry, too, but of greater audacity. They haunt the antechambers of kings and potentates, naked if it were not for the poetic vesture that they have filched from others. Any especially good bit which this one or that one has turned off, they seize upon, more particularly if it be in the mother tongue, and recite it with huge gusto. In this way they strive to gain the favor of the nobility, and procure money, clothes, or other gifts. Their stock-in-trade is partly picked up here and there, partly obtained directly from the writers themselves, either by begging, or, where cupidity or poverty exists, for money. This last case is described by the satirist: "He will die of hunger if he does not succeed in selling to Paris his yet unheard *Agave*."[16]

You can easily imagine how often these fellows have pestered me, and I doubt not others, with their disgusting fawning. It is true I suffer less than formerly, owing to my altered studies, or to respect for my age, or to repulses already received; for, lest they should get in the habit of annoying me, I have often sharply refused to aid them, and have not allowed myself to be affected by any amount of insistence. Sometimes indeed, especially when I knew the applicant to be humble and needy, a certain benevolent instinct has led me to assist the poor fellow to a living, with such skill as I possessed. My aid might be of permanent use to the recipient, while it cost me only a short hour of work. Some of those whom I had been induced to assist, and who had left me with their wish fulfilled, but otherwise poor and ill-clad, returned shortly after arrayed in silks, with well-filled bellies and purses, to thank me for the assistance which had enabled them to cast off the burden of poverty. On such occasions I have sometimes been led to vow that I would never refuse this peculiar kind of alms; but there always comes a moment, when, wearied by their importunities, I retract the resolve.

When I asked some of these beggars why they always came to me, and never applied to others, and in particular to you, for assistance, they replied that so far as you were concerned they had often done so, but never with success. While I was wondering that one who was so generous with his property should be so niggardly with his words, they added that you had burnt all the verses which you had ever written in the vulgar tongue. This, instead of satisfying me, only served to increase my astonishment. When I asked the reason of your doing this, they all confessed ignorance and held their tongues, except one. He said that he believed—whether he had actually heard it somewhere or other, I do not know—that you intended to revise all the things which you had written both in your earlier days, and, later, in your prime, in order to give your works, in this revision, the advantage of a mature—I am tempted to say hoary—mind. Such confidence in the prolongation of our most uncertain existence, especially at your age,[17] seemed to both of us exaggerated. Although I have the greatest confidence in your discretion and vigor of mind, my surprise was only increased by what I had heard. What a perverted idea, I said, to burn up what you wished to revise, so as to have nothing left for revision!

My astonishment continued until at last, on coming to this city, I became intimate with our Donato,[18] who is so faithful and devoted a friend of yours. It was from him that I learned recently, in the course of our daily conversation, not only the fact which I had already heard, but also the explanation of it, which had so long puzzled me. He said that in your earlier years you had been especially fond of writing in the vulgar tongue, and had devoted much time and pains to it, until in the course of your researches and reading you had happened upon my youthful compositions in the vernacular. Then your enthusiasm for writing similar things suddenly cooled. Not content simply to refrain from analogous work in the future, you conceived a great dislike to what you had already done and burned everything, not with the idea of correcting but of destroying. In this way you deprived both yourself and posterity of the fruits of your labors in this field of literature, and for no better reason than that you thought what you had written was inferior to my productions. But your dislike was ill-founded and the sacrifice inexpedient. As for your motive, that is doubtful. Was it humility, which despised itself, or pride, which would be second to none? You who can see your own heart must judge. I can only wander among the various possible conjectures, writing to you, as usual, as if I were talking to myself.

I congratulate you, then, on regarding yourself as inferior to those whose superior you really are. I would far rather share that error than his who, being really inferior, believes himself to be on a higher plane. This reminds me of Lucan of Cordova, a man of the ardent spirit and the genius which pave the way alike to great eminence and to an abyss of failure. Finding himself far advanced in his studies while still young, he became, upon turning over in his mind his age and the successful beginnings of his career, so puffed up that he ventured to compare himself with Virgil. In reciting a portion of a work on the Civil War, which was interrupted by his death, he said in his introductory remarks, "Do I in any way fall short of the *Culex*?"[19] Whether this arrogant speech was noticed by any friend of the poet, or what answer he received, I do not know; for myself, I have often, since I read the passage, inwardly replied indignantly to this braggart: "My fine fellow, thy performance may indeed equal the *Culex*, but what a gulf between it and the *Aeneid*!" But why, then, do I not praise your humility, who judge me to be your superior, and praise it the more highly in contrast with the boast of this upstart, who would believe himself superior, or at least equal, to Virgil?

But there is something else here which I would gladly discover, but which is of so obscure a nature that it is not easily cleared up with the pen. I will, however, do the best I can. I fear that your remarkable humility may after all be only pride. This will doubtless seem to many a novel and even surprising name for humility, and if it should prove offensive I will use some other term. I only fear that this signal exhibition of humility is not altogether free from some admixture of haughtiness. I have seen men at a banquet, or some other assembly, rise and voluntarily take the lowest place, because they had not been assigned the head of the table, and this under cover of humility, although pride was the real motive. I have seen another so weak as even to leave the room. Thus anger sometimes, and sometimes pride, leads men to act as though one who did not enjoy the highest seat, which in the nature of things cannot be assigned to more than a single individual, was necessarily unworthy of any place except perhaps the lowest. But there are degrees of glory as well as of merit.

As for you, you show your humility in not assuming the first place. Some, inferior to you both in talents and style, have laid claim to it, and have aroused our indignation, not unmixed with merriment, by their absurd aspirations. Would that the support of the vulgar, which they sometimes enjoy, weighed no more in the marketplace than with the dwellers on Parnassus. But not to be able to take the second or third rank, does not that smack of genuine pride? Suppose for the moment that I surpass you, I, who would so gladly be your equal; suppose that you are surpassed by the great master of our mother tongue; beware lest there be more pride in refusing to see yourself distanced by one or the other, especially by your fellow-citizen, or, at most, by a very few, than in soliciting the distinction of the first place for yourself. To long for supremacy may be regarded as the sign of a great mind, but to despise what only approaches supremacy is a certain indication of arrogance.

I have heard that our Old Man of Ravenna, who is by no means a bad judge in such matters, is accustomed, whenever the conversation turns on these matters, to assign you the third place. If this displeases you, and if you think that I prevent your attaining to the first rank—though I am really no obstacle—I willingly renounce all pretensions to precedence, and leave you the second place. If you refuse this I do not think that you ought to be pardoned. If the very first alone are illustrious, it is easy to see how innumerable are the obscure, and how few enjoy the radiance of glory. Consider, moreover, how much safer, and even higher, is the second place. There is someone to receive the first attacks of envy, and, at the risk of his own reputation, to indicate your path; for by watching his course, you will learn when to follow it, and when to avoid it. You have someone to aid you to throw off all slothful habits through your effort to overtake him. You are spurred on to equal him, and not be forever second. Such a one serves as a goad to noble minds and often accomplishes wonders. He who knows how to put up with the second place will ere long deserve the first, while he who scorns the second place has already begun to be unworthy even of that. If you will but consult your memory, you will scarcely find a first-rate commander, philosopher, or poet, who did not reach the top through the aid of just such stimulus.

Furthermore, if the first place is to most persons a source of complacent satisfaction with themselves, and of envy on the part of others, it is certainly also liable to produce inertia. The student as well as the lover is spurred on by jealousy: love without rivalry, and merit without emulation are equally prone to languish. Industrious poverty is much to be preferred to idle opulence. It is better to struggle up a steep declivity with watchful care than to lie sunk in shameful ease; better and safer to trust to the aid of active virtue than to rely upon the distinction of an idle reputation.

These are good reasons, it seems to me, for cheerfully accepting the second place. But what if you are assigned to the third or the fourth? Will this rouse your anger? or have you forgotten the passage where Seneca defends Fabianus Papirius against Lucilius?[20] After assigning Cicero a higher rank, he remarked: "It is no slight thing to be second only to the highest." Then, naming Asinius Pollio next to Cicero, he added: "Nor in such a case is the third place to be despised." Lastly, placing Livy in the fourth rank, he concluded, "What a vast number of writers does he excel who is vanquished by three only, and these three the most gifted!" Does not this apply very well to you, my dear friend? Only, whatever place you occupy, or whomsoever you may seem to see ahead of you, it cannot, in my judgment, be I who precede you. So, eschew the flames, and have mercy on your verses.

If, however, you and others are, in spite of what I say, thoroughly convinced that I must, willy-nilly, be your superior in literary rank, do you really feel aggrieved, and regard it as a shameful thing to be ranked next to me? If this be true, permit me to say that I have long been deceived in you, and that neither your natural modesty nor your love of me is what I had hoped. True friends place those whom they love above themselves. They not only wish to be excelled, but experience an extreme pleasure in being outstripped, just as no fond author would deny that his greatest pleasure consisted in being surpassed by his son. I hoped and hope still that I am inferior to you. I do not claim to be like a dear son to you, or to believe that my reputation is dearer to you than your own. I remember, though, that you, in a moment of friendly anger, once reproached me for this. If you were really sincere, you ought to grant me the right of way with joy. Instead of giving up the race, you should press after me with all your might, and so prevent any other competitor from thrusting himself between us and stealing your place. He who sits in the chariot or runs by his friend's side does not ask who is first, but is only anxious that they two shall be as near as possible. Nothing is sweeter than the longed-for closeness of companionship. Love is everything, precedence next to nothing, among friends. The first are last and the last first, for all are really one in friendship.

So much for the case against you. Let us now turn to the excuses for your conduct. In spite of your own explanation and that which comes to me through such a very good friend of yours, I have tried to discover some higher motive for your action than that which you mention; for the same act may be good or bad according to the motives which dictate it. I will tell you, then, what has occurred to me.

You did not destroy your productions, in a manner so unfair both to you and to them, through false pride, which is quite foreign to your gentle character; nor because you were jealous of someone else, or dissatisfied with your own lot. You were actuated by a noble indignation against the emptiness and vanity of our age, which in its crass ignorance corrupts or, far worse, despises everything good. You wished to withdraw your productions from the judgment of the men of today, and, as Virginius once slew his own daughter to save her from shame, so you have committed to the flames your beautiful inventions, the children of your intellect, to prevent their becoming the prey of such a rabble. And now, my dear friend, how near the truth have I guessed? I have indeed often thought of doing the same for my own compositions in the vulgar tongue, few as they are; and it was my own experience which suggested this explanation of your conduct. I should perhaps have done so, had they not been so widely circulated as to have long ago escaped my control. And yet, on the other hand, I have sometimes harbored quite the opposite design, and thought of devoting my whole attention to the vernacular.

To be sure, the Latin, in both prose and poetry, is undoubtedly the nobler language, but for that very reason it has been so thoroughly developed by earlier writers that neither we nor anyone else may expect to add very much to it. The vernacular, on the other hand, has but recently been discovered, and, though it has been ravaged by many, it still remains uncultivated, in spite of a few earnest laborers, and still shows itself capable of much improvement and enrichment. Stimulated by this thought, and by the enterprise of youth, I began an extensive work in that language. I laid the foundations of the structure, and got together my lime and stones and wood. And then I began to consider a little more carefully the times in which we live, the fact that our age is the mother of pride and indolence, and that the ability of the vainglorious fellows who would be my judges, and their peculiar grace of delivery is such that they can hardly be said to recite the writings of others, but rather to mangle them. Hearing their performances again and again, and turning the matter over in my mind, I concluded at length that I was building upon unstable earth and shifting sand, and should simply waste my labors and see the work of my hands levelled by the common herd. Like one who finds a great serpent across his track, I stopped and changed my route—for a higher and more direct one, I hope. Although the short things I once wrote in the vulgar tongue are, as I have said, so scattered that they now belong to the public rather than to me, I shall take precautions against having my more important works torn to pieces in the same way.

And yet why should I find fault with the unenlightenment of the common people, when those who call themselves learned afford so much more just and serious a ground for complaint? Besides many other ridiculous peculiarities, these people add to their gross ignorance an exaggerated and most disgusting pride. It is this that leads them to carp at the reputation of those whose most trivial sayings they were once proud to comprehend, in even the most fragmentary fashion. O inglorious age! that scorns antiquity, its mother, to whom it owes every noble art—that dares to declare itself not only equal but superior to the glorious past. I say nothing of the vulgar, the dregs of mankind, whose sayings and opinions may raise a laugh but hardly merit serious censure. I will say nothing of the military class and the leaders in war, who do not blush to assert that their time has beheld the culmination and perfection of military art, when there is no doubt that this art has degenerated and is utterly going to ruin in their hands. They have neither skill nor intelligence, but rely entirely upon indolence and chance. They go to war decked out as if for a wedding, bent on meat and drink and the gratification of their lust. They think much more of flight than they do of victory. Their skill lies not in striking the adversary, but in holding out the hand of submission; not in terrifying the enemy, but in pleasing the eyes of their mistresses.[21] But even these false notions may be excused in view of the utter ignorance and want of instruction on the part of those who hold them.

I will pass over the kings, who act as if they thought that their office consisted in purple and gold, in scepter and diadem, and that, excelling their predecessors in these things, they must excel them likewise in prowess and glory. Although they were put upon the throne for the single purpose of ruling (whence their title, *rex*, is derived), they do not in reality govern the people over whom they are placed, but, as their conduct shows, are themselves governed by their passions. They are rulers of men, but, at the same time, slaves of sloth and luxury. Still ignorance of the past, the ephemeral glory that fortune bestows and the vanity that always attends undue prosperity, may serve to excuse in some measure even these. But what can be said in defence of men of education who ought not to be ignorant of antiquity and yet are plunged in this same darkness and delusion?

You see that I cannot speak of these matters without the greatest irritation and indignation. There has arisen of late a set of dialecticians, who are not only ignorant but demented.[22] Like a black army of ants from some old rotten oak, they swarm forth from their hiding-places and devastate the fields of sound learning. They condemn Plato and Aristotle, and laugh at Socrates and Pythagoras. And, good God! under what silly and incompetent leaders these opinions are put forth! I should prefer not to give a name to this group of men. They have done nothing to merit one, though their folly has made them famous. I do not wish to place among the greatest of mankind those whom I see consorting with the most abject. These fellows have deserted all trustworthy leaders, and glory in the name of those who, whatever they may learn after death, exhibited in this world no trace of power, or knowledge, or reputation for knowledge. What shall we say of men who scorn Marcus Tullius Cicero, the bright sun of eloquence? Of those who scoff at Varro and Seneca, and are scandalized at what they choose to call the crude, unfinished style of Livy and Sallust? And all this in obedience to leaders of whom no one has ever heard, and for whom their followers ought to blush! Once I happened to be present when Virgil's style was the subject of their scornful criticism. Astonished at their crazy outbreak, I turned to a person of some cultivation and asked what he had detected in this famous man to rouse such a storm of reproach. Listen to the reply he gave me, with a contemptuous shrug of the shoulders: "He is too fond of conjunctions." Arise, O Virgil, and polish the verses that, with the aid of the Muses, thou didst snatch from heaven, in order that they may be fit to deliver into hands like these!

How shall I deal with that other monstrous kind of pedant, who wears a religious garb, but is most profane in heart and conduct; who would have us believe that Ambrose, Augustine, and Jerome were ignoramuses, for all their elaborate treatises? I do not know the origin of these new theologians, who do not spare the great teachers, and will not much longer spare the Apostles and the Gospel itself. They will soon turn their impudent tongues even against Christ, unless he, whose cause is at stake, interferes and curbs the raging beasts. It has already become a well-established habit with these fellows to express their scorn by a mute gesture or by some impious observation, whenever revered and sacred names are mentioned. "Augustine," they will say, "saw much, but understood little." Nor do they speak less insultingly of other great men.

Recently one of these philosophers of the modern stamp happened to be in my library. He did not, like the others, wear a religious habit, but, after all, Christianity is not a matter of clothes. He was one of those who think they live in vain unless they are constantly snarling at Christ or his divine teachings. When I cited some passage or other from the Holy Scriptures, he exploded with wrath, and with his face, naturally ugly, still further disfigured by anger and contempt, he exclaimed: "You are welcome to your two-penny church fathers; as for me, I know the man for me to follow, *for I know him whom I have believed.*"[23] "You," I replied, "use the words of the Apostle. I would that you would take them to heart." "Your Apostle," he answered, "was a sower of words and a lunatic." "You reply like a good philosopher," I said. "The first of your accusations was brought against him by other philosophers,[24] and the second to his face by Festus, Governor of Syria.[25] He did indeed sow the word, and with such success that, cultivated by the beneficent plough of his successors and watered by the holy blood of the martyrs, it has borne such an abundant harvest of faith as we all behold." At this he burst forth into a sickening roar of laughter. "Well, be a 'good Christian'! As for me, I put no faith in all that stuff. Your Paul and your Augustine and all the rest of the crowd you preach about were a set of babblers. If you could but stomach Averroes you would quickly see how much superior he was to these empty-headed fellows of yours." I was very angry, I must confess, and could scarcely keep from striking his filthy, blasphemous mouth. "It is the old feud between me and other heretics of your class. You can go," I cried, "you and your heresy, and never return." With this I plucked him by the gown, and, with a want of ceremony less consonant with my habits than his own, hustled him out of the house.[26]

There are thousands of instances of this kind, where nothing will prevail—not even the majesty of the Christian name nor reverence for Christ himself (whom the angels fall down and worship though weak and depraved mortals may insult him), nor yet the fear of punishment or the armed inquisitors of heresy. The prison and stake are alike impotent to restrain the impudence of ignorance or the audacity of heresy.

Such are the times, my friend, upon which we have fallen; such is the period in which we live and are growing old. Such are the critics of today, as I so often have occasion to lament and complain—men who are innocent of knowledge or virtue, and yet harbor the most exalted opinion of themselves. Not content with losing the words of the ancients, they must attack their genius and their ashes. They rejoice in their ignorance, as if what they did not know were not worth knowing. They give full rein to their licence and conceit, and freely introduce among us new authors and outlandish teachings.

If you, having no other means of defence, have resorted to the fire to save your works from the criticism of such despotic judges, I cannot disapprove the act and must commend your motives. I have done the same with many of my own productions, and almost repent me that I did not include all, while it was yet in my power; for we have no prospect of fairer judges, while the number and audacity of the existing ones grow from day to day. They are no longer confined to the schools, but fill the largest towns, choking up the streets and public squares. We are come to such a pass that I am sometimes angry at myself for having been so vexed by the recent and warlike and destructive years, and having bemoaned the depopulation of the earth. It is perhaps depopulated of true men, but was never more densely crowded with vices and the creatures of vice. In short, had I been among the Aediles, and felt as I do now, I should have acquitted the daughter of Appius Claudius.[27] But now farewell, as I have nothing more to write to you at present.

FROM

LITERARY IMITATION[28]

An imitator must see to it that what he writes is similar, but not the very same; and the similarity, moreover, should be not like that of a painting or statue to the person represented, but rather like that of a son to a father, where there is often great difference in the features and members, and yet after all there is a shadowy something—akin to what our painters call one's *air*—hovering about the face, and especially the eyes, out of which there grows a likeness that immediately calls the father up before us. If it were a matter of measurement every detail would be found to be different, and yet there certainly is some subtle presence there that has this effect. In much the same way we writers, too, must see to it that along with the similarity there is a large measure of dissimilarity; and furthermore such likeness as there is must be elusive, something that it is impossible to seize except by a sort of still-hunt, a quality to be felt rather than defined. In brief, we may appropriate another's thought, and may even copy the very colors of his style, but we must abstain from borrowing his actual words. The resemblance in the one case is hidden away below the surface; in the other it stares the reader in the face. The one kind of imitation makes poets; the other apes. It may all be summed up by saying with Seneca, and with Flaccus before him,[29] that we must write just as the bees make honey, not keeping the flowers but turning them into a sweetness of our own, blending many very different flavors into one, which shall be unlike them all, and better. . . .

FROM
ON BOCCACCIO'S DECAMERON[30]

Your book, written in our mother tongue and published, I presume, during your early years, has fallen into my hands, I know not whence or how. If I told you that I had read it, I should deceive you. It is a very big volume, written in prose and for the multitude. I have been, moreover, occupied with more serious business, and much pressed for time. You can easily imagine the unrest caused by the warlike stir about me, for, far as I have been from actual participation in the disturbances, I could not but be affected by the critical condition of the state. What I did was to run through your book, like a traveller who, while hastening forward, looks about him here and there, without pausing. I have heard somewhere that your volume was attacked by the teeth of certain hounds, but that you defended it valiantly with staff and voice. This did not surprise me, for not only do I well know your ability, but I have learned from experience of the existence of an insolent and cowardly class who attack in the work of others everything which they do not happen to fancy or be familiar with, or which they cannot themselves accomplish. Their insight and capabilities extend no farther; on all other themes they are silent.

My hasty perusal afforded me much pleasure. If the humor is a little too free at times, this may be excused in view of the age at which you wrote, the style and language which you employ, and the frivolity of the subjects, and of the persons who are likely to read such tales. It is important to know for whom we are writing, and a difference in the characters of one's listeners justifies a difference in style. Along with much that was light and amusing, I discovered some serious and edifying things as well, but I can pass no definite judgment upon them, since I have not examined the work thoroughly.

As usual, when one looks hastily through a book, I read somewhat more carefully at the beginning and at the end. At the beginning you have, it seems to me, accurately described and eloquently lamented the condition of our country during that siege of pestilence which forms so dark and melancholy a period in our century.[31] At the close you have placed a story which differs entirely from most that precede it, and which so delighted and fascinated me that, in spite of cares which made me almost oblivious of myself, I was seized with a desire to learn it by heart, so that I might have the pleasure of recalling it for my own benefit, and of relating it to my friends in conversation. When an opportunity for telling it offered itself shortly after, I found that my auditors were delighted. Later it suddenly occurred to me that others, perhaps, who were unacquainted with our tongue, might be pleased with so charming a story, as it had delighted me ever since I first heard it some years ago, and as you had not considered it unworthy of presentation in the mother tongue, and had placed it, moreover, at the end of your book, where, according to the principles of rhetoric, the most effective part of the composition belongs. So one fine day when, as usual, my mind was distracted by a variety of occupations, discontented with myself and my surroundings, I suddenly sent everything flying, and, snatching my pen, I attacked this story of yours. I sincerely trust that it will gratify you that I have of my own free will undertaken to translate your work, something I should certainly never think of doing for anyone else, but which I was induced to do in this instance by my partiality for you and for the story. Not neglecting the precept of Horace in his *Art of Poetry*,[32] that the careful translator should not attempt to render word for word, I have told your tale in my own language, in some places changing or even adding a few words, for I felt that you would not only permit, but would approve, such alterations. . . .[33]

NOTES

1. From *Epistolae Familiares* X, 4 (from Padua, December 2, 1348), to his brother Gherardo. For a contemporary's exposition of much the same ideas, see *Boccaccio on Poetry*, ed. Charles G. Osgood (reprinted in the Bobbs-Merrill Library of Liberal Arts).

2. An allegorical eclogue which Petrarch explicates at some length in the body of this letter.

3. *Metaphysics* 2, 4, 12. Both Petrarch and Boccaccio follow the line of Mussato: see the chapter on "Poetry and Theology" in E. R. Curtius, *European Literature and the Latin Middle Ages*, trans. Willard R. Trask (New York, 1953), pp. 214–27.

4. Cf. Augustine, *De Civitate Dei* VI, 5.

5. There is nothing to this effect in the surviving works of Suetonius.

6. VIII, 7, 2: "De poeta."

7. *Epistolae Familiares* XXI, 15 (from Milan, probably June, 1359), to Giovanni Boccaccio. See Aldo S. Bernardo, "Petrarch's Attitude Toward Dante," *PMLA* LXX (1955), 488–517.

8. Quintilian X, 1, 125.

9. *Rhetorica ad Herennium* IV, 2, 3.

10. Virgil, *Bucolics* III, 27.

11. *Epistolae Metricae* I, 6, to Giacomo Colonna.

12. *Invective Against Sallust* II, 5 (wrongly attributed to Cicero).

13. By Seneca the rhetor (of whose existence Petrarch was unaware), father of Seneca the philosopher.

14. A series of allusions to Virgil, *Aeneid* VIII, 163–66.

15. *Epistolae Seniles* V, 2 (from Venice, August 28, 1364), to Giovanni Boccaccio.

16. Juvenal, *Satires* VII, 87.

17. Boccaccio was born in 1313, and his age might not strike us as terribly advanced; but see the interesting article by Creighton Gilbert, "When Did a Man in the Renaissance Grow Old?" *Studies in the Renaissance* XIV, 7–32.

18. Donato Albanzani.

19. *The Gnat*, a poem ascribed to Virgil by several ancient writers. This incident is recorded in Suetonius' *Life of Lucan*.

20. Seneca, *Epistulae Morales*, 100, 9.

21. Cf. chapter XII of *The Prince*.

22. With the following pages compare Petrarch's invective, *On His Own Ignorance and That of Many Others*, translated by Hans Nachod in *The Renaissance Philosophy of Man*, ed. Ernst Cassirer *et al.* (Phoenix paperback), pp. 47–133.

23. II Timothy 1, 12.

24. Acts 17, 18.

25. Acts 26, 24: "And as he thus spake for himself, Festus said with a loud voice, Paul, thou art beside thyself; much learning doth make thee mad."

26. For an interpretation of Renaissance humanism which is based largely on such texts, see the recent essay by Rocco Montano, "The Renaissance? *What* Renaissance?" *Umanesimo* I (May, 1967), 1–10.

27. She was fined for speaking against the Roman people.

28. From *Epistolae Familiares* XXIII, 19 (from Pavia, October 28, 1366), in which Petrarch tells Boccaccio about Giovanni Malpaghini, who in two years' service had copied the *Familiares*. This is the gist of advice Petrarch had given Giovanni, who was not only a fine copyist but a would-be poet.

29. Cf. Horace, *Odes* IV, ii, 27–32; and Seneca, *Epistulae Morales* 84, 5, 6.

30. From *Epistolae Seniles* XVII, 3, written late in the winter or early in the spring of 1373 (before *Seniles* XVII, 2) from Padua, to Giovanni Boccaccio. (All four letters in Book XVII were addressed to Boccaccio; apparently none reached him.)

31. The Black Death of 1348.

32. Lines 131–35.

33. Petrarch's Latin adaptation of the tale of patient Griselda forms the major portion of the letter. On the *fortuna* of this translation in the fourteenth century, see J. B. Severs, *The Literary Relationships of Chaucer's "Clerkes Tale"* (New Haven: Yale University Press, 1942), pp. 21–37. (Though Chaucer was in Italy in 1373, it seems unlikely that he went to Padua.)

Erasmus
c. 1466–1536

Desiderius Erasmus—itinerant scholar, sometime monk, sometime diplomat, satirist, humanist, and controversialist—was born in Holland in the late 1460s, the bastard son of a priest and a physician's daughter. He received his early education at the hands of the Brothers of the Common Life, an order which did much to spread throughout Northern Europe the humanist ideas which had such a profound influence upon such figures as Erasmus, Thomas à Kempis, and Martin Luther. In 1492 Erasmus was ordained a priest in the Augustinian order at Steyne, and devoted the next few years to the study of classical literature and Holy Scripture.

The monastic life, however, soon proved too constricting for Erasmus, and in 1494 he left to become Latin secretary to the Bishop of Cambrai; diplomacy does not appear to have suited him much better, though, for he shortly thereafter left this post and went to Paris to study theology. A pattern of frequent uprootings and travel soon established itself, a life whose restlessness reflected Erasmus' mind. When Lord Mountjoy invited Erasmus to England in 1499, he accepted gladly. Though he never "settled" in England in any real sense, it was here that he made many of his closest friends, and gained much of his fame as a scholar and wit.

While living with Thomas More, Erasmus wrote—as a tribute to his friend's hospitality—the *Encomium Moriae (The Praise of Folly)*. The most popular (and enduring) of any of his works, it is an excellent example of the classical facility and savage wit for which Erasmus was famed. The highly opinionated tone of the *Encomium* is typical of Erasmus: the personal enthusiasms and animosities of the author show through clearly in it, just as they do—still more clearly—in his *Colloquia Familiara*. Around the same time as the *Encomium* (1509), Erasmus published his great *Adagia*, a collection of proverbs and witticisms taken from the classical authors, which greatly enhanced his reputation as one of the foremost classicists in Europe.

Despite his aversion to the monastic life (in 1517 Erasmus sought and was granted a dispensation allowing him to live outside the cloister), Erasmus' religious sense was not entirely dormant, and he produced many fine translations of early Patristic texts, as well as a monumental new edition of the New Testament, translated directly from the Greek. A very influential work—both as a text and on account of its many incisive marginal notes and glosses—it immediately established Erasmus as a major New Testament scholar, and served as an official translation during the reign of Edward VI.

In addition, Erasmus carried on a public disputation with Martin Luther (via "open letters") on theological and ecclesiastical questions. In many regards highly sympathetic to Luther (Thomas More's quip "Erasmus planted, Luther watered, Satan gave the increase" is an indication of this), Erasmus began the exchange in an amicable and moderate tone. Luther's replies, however, were marked by the extreme violence and distemper that characterized his attitude towards any controversy. As a result, he discredited himself and his cause in the eyes of much of the academic community in Europe, and drove Erasmus into the camp of the Papal loyalists.

Erasmus remained peripatetic through most of his life, settling for a time at Basel, only to flee when the Protestants triumphed there in 1529. He returned in 1535, however, and died a year later on July 12.

The selections from *The Antibarbarians*, translated and annotated by Margaret Mann Phillips, are reprinted by permission of University of Toronto Press from *The Collected Works of Erasmus (Literary and Educational Writings 1)*, edited by Craig R. Thompson (University of Toronto Press, 1978). © 1978 by the University of Toronto Press.

FROM
The Antibarbarians

Opening of Batt's Speech

"If I did not know that I was to speak before most cultivated judges, and was not largely assisted by the very soundness of my cause, I should be afraid that, in the face of such hatred on the part of the stupidest people, literature was not going to have a very good advocate today. But, as it is, I am so far from any apprehension of not being able to refute all the objections that the anti-rhetoricians can ever raise that I do not think it necessary in such an easily won cause even to use an introduction. It is not only in front of you, my good friends, with all your learning, you who have begged me for this speech and who cannot, I know, be anything but kind, willing, attentive hearers,[1] but even among the Sauromates or whatever may be more barbarous, provided they are human beings, I can promise myself certain victory; human beings, I say, who follow the lead of reason and not the dictates of passion. For as to these brawlers who go on obstinately defending their obvious idiocy, I look on them as Diogenes looked on his public assembly. When several thousand men had come together there, he still declared he had not yet seen a man. They say that learning is deadly to mortals, and the thing to wish for is ignorance,

> Olive no stone shall have nor nut no shell.[2]

Sure as I am already of making my point, this one thing I ask: do not expect magnificent oratory on such a thorny and intractable subject; even on the most favourable topics you should not require this of a Batt. You will not even demand to be amused, except when the crass stupidity of the barbarians' reasoning makes you laugh."

Beginning with an apology, I said, "Is it permissible to interrupt you sometimes as you speak?"

"Certainly," replied Batt, "interrupt me as often as you like; we are not speaking by the clock,[3] and the cause will not be lost if a little time is spent on the way."

"You seem to me," I said, "to have dispensed with an introduction in such a way that not to have one is in itself an introduction. But go on, I beg, do not let us hold you up in your first stage any longer."

"That's just like you," retorted Batt; "it isn't my way; you have got by heart all those subtleties and rhetorical tricks, but it is enough for me, I think, to set forth the thing as it is in the fewest possible words. And so I shall not go back further to inquire how it happened that the learning of antiquity fell from such a pinnacle of honour into this pit of darkness, or try to find out what fate caused this, when it came about, by what stages, as you were trying to do just now. That could be better done at another time perhaps. It is not really important to decide how someone fell into a well; the main thing is how to get him out. We shall therefore plead the cause of the old learning against its new opponents, and I see that the trouble comes mainly from three types of enemy.

"There are those who want the Republic of Letters to be destroyed root and branch. Others are doing their best to get its power not exactly extinguished, but restricted within narrower limits. Lastly there are those who want to see the republic preserved but utterly ruined, by themselves becoming tyrants, abrogating the laws of our fathers, and introducing foreign magistrates and behaviour.

"The first-named of these, as I see it, are those quite uncouth people who detest the whole of literature (which they call poetry) on some vague religious pretext, whether from jealousy or stupidity I cannot say. The second lot I understand to be the educated who are really uneducated, the people who somehow find other studies acceptable (that is, their own), but as for the humanities, without which all learning is blind, they hate them worse than a snake. Then there are the last, and who else are they but the people who admire and approve of every kind of literature, especially poetry and rhetoric, but on condition that they themselves are considered the finest poets and orators—which is far from the case.

"It would not be easy to say which of these enemies does the most grievous and dreadful harm to the Republic of Letters, or which of them is to be credited with the largest share of its disasters. For the first (do not let us underestimate them) may have nothing in the way of weapons and knowledge of warfare, but, as a savage horde massed together from the fields and hills, I wonder whether any kind of enemy could be more dangerous. They do not march into battle; they throw themselves into it like ravening wild beasts, mistaking fury for fortitude. They have four strong points: fury (like the Andabatae[4]), noise (like Stentor[5] in Homer), numbers (in which they exceed even the army of Xerxes[6]), and lastly a kind of shield which is the pretence of religion; and under that they are always sheltering—it is all they can put up against all kinds of missiles. These people are entirely outside the world of literature, and have a burning hatred of the glory attached to men of letters; they think it proper and pious to carp at the finest studies of others, and it is amazing how cunningly they mask their sluggishness, their envy, and their pride under the attractive names of simplicity and religion.

"The second lot are rather better educated than these, and they attack us from far and near: from a distance with missiles, but quite laughable ones (they hurl at us tow, smoke, and dung); in hand-to-hand fighting they go for us with daggers, but leaden ones. They offer peace, but on obviously arrogant terms, on condition that we should get our learning without the humanities—though without these no literature can exist. They ban all culture, and whatever they themselves have not learnt. They are difficult to get hold of, and most troublesome on this account. They never make a stand; they are more elusive than the Parthians,[7] now saying yes and then no; they are always shuffling, getting away with a quibble, and like Proteus,

> Into all kinds of wondrous shapes they change.[8]

"The last group might perhaps be judged not very bitter enemies, because their offence comes from zeal, not hatred; but I find them far and away the most harmful. The others attack under hostile banners and can be driven from the ramparts, but these are living inside the walls, in our very strongholds, and by their weapons and badges look like our friends, but all the time they are planning for the eternal ruin of the republic under a deceptive appearance of devotion, and the more they strive to deliver their country, the more they entangle it in shameful slavery. One might almost warm to the first group of opponents, because their hatred of letters means that they never touched them. The second group are the less harmful for having kept away from the best writers, that is, the poets and orators, being content with their own state. The last want to know everything and meanwhile they have mixed up, corrupted, and ruined everything. It is said, and how truly, that there is nothing less kind[9] than a mistimed kindness. Just so, these people have tried to come to the rescue of literature in distress, and they have entirely wiped it out by their disastrous zeal. The thing to do was to measure their powers, to determine the range of their intellect, before taking up so strenuous a task. What they did was to prefer to imitate Phaethon,[10] the inexperienced driver who tried to manage his father's chariot, and upset it to his own downfall. And as they are like Phaethon in their folly, they deserve a similar calamity or even worse. It is by their rashness that philosophy, the great, old, and true, has been reduced to sheer nonsense, mere fantasy. Through them we have lost innumerable works of the early writers; the fact that corrupt textual readings abound, and abound the more the more learned the author, is something we owe to them; if the fine theology of the old days has so much degenerated, this is their doing and no one else's; if the grammarians write and teach nothing but sheer barbarism, we have them to thank. And to bring this to a close: it is their doing that in both verse and prose mute and inarticulate authors are prized above the most learned; one among them writes on grammar, another on rhetoric, another on dialectic, another on natural philosophy, another on theology; while this one writes commentaries on the best authors, shedding darkness on them, not light, not adorning but corrupting, and another one tries to emend what he does not understand, and a third turns into bad Latin what was in good Greek, though he knows practically nothing of either language; and so, I say, while they are vying with each other to make an uproar, they have managed to confuse, corrupt, and overturn everything with their futile efforts; and the more industriously each of them tries to do his part, the more ruin he causes. It is like someone trying to wipe a speck of dust off a purple robe with hands smeared with ordure—the harder he tries to help the more harm he does.

"But, leaving them aside (for to discuss the subject one would have to go on for ever), I shall fall on the other two lines in two separate offensives; and here I shall acquit myself so that you will swear I am more expert than Pyrrhus.[11]

"As to the army of yokels, I shall be content to have dispersed them with a hastily raised force, and put them to flight stripped of their shields of religious pretence; this will not need much doing. For they are an unwarlike crowd made up of old men, who, realizing that their time has been passed in self-indulgence and run out, are futilely jealous of the young who are advancing to better things. I shall first force them to turn tail, using the most cogent arguments as javelins, and then, when they turn again to fight, I shall stab them with swords—the testimony of Holy Writ.[12] When they are stunned by this barrage of instances, I shall drive them from their strongholds, and once these have been reduced I shall drive on in the same flush of battle to attack the stragglers, and, stripping them of all their arms, carry off the victory in every kind of warfare.

"But now the first lot are to be challenged, and we will suppose that the chief of the Fetial priests[13] has completed the ceremonies; for them, I think, the following declamation would be suitable, if the matter were carried out seriously.

Speech of the Fetial Priests

"'Hear, ye Goths! By what right have you crossed your frontiers and not only occupied the domains of the Latins—I mean liberal studies—but dared to invade the city which rules all, Latinity itself? What injury has been done to you, what are your demands? If you want war, decide the matter in open fight; give us the opportunity to do battle with you. If you shrink from the fray, cease to be troublesome, withdraw from the land, clear the country of your presence, remain within your own boundaries. If you would rather be called foes than brigands, come out of your lairs, join battle with us, and these feuds shall find a conclusion in open fight; either you will be defeated and quiet, or we shall admit that the victory is yours.'

If Literature Appears Objectionable to Many People, the Cause Lies Merely in Their Ignorance

"Now the Fetial priests, their plea unheard, have declared war by casting a spear; now the enemy must be challenged to battle."

Here I interrupted: "Take care you don't go too fast! You have not completed all the formalities—you have to kill a pig with a stone before you rush to arms."

"Quite right," said he; "I wish I were allowed to choose a fine specimen out of those sties where so many fat healthy porkers idle away and are stuffed with the food of the people. I would rather sacrifice a biped than any four-footed pig. But come on, let us take it as done, the thing we so ardently wish done, and go on with good auguries to attack the enemy. For at present I am going to behave exactly as if I had them face to face. You sit and watch, as the spectators of our skirmish. And as it would not do for my friend Erasmus to complain that we had no trumpet—I see he is a fastidious observer of ceremonies—let this blast of abuse take the trumpet's place.[14]

"Tell me, I say, you loutish fellows, race of Midas,[15] senseless blocks of marble,[16] what have letters done ('profane' letters as you call anything you have not learnt) to deserve that you should attack them with such obstinate virulence, as if men were born for one thing only, to hate learning? It annoys you that you learnt nothing, and cannot learn now, but must you choose to hate? If you have sunk into hopeless sloth, do you think it a fine thing to look on others with envy? Why not rather set vigorously to work, and wrest from us this glory which you envy? But you are afraid we shall poke the ancient jests at you, 'a donkey learning the fiddle, a bull in the wrestling ring; what has a jackdaw to do with a harp, or a pig with amaranth?'[17] But there is nothing remarkable in your hating—the wonder would be if you were to love. What the greatest of Peripatetic philosophers[18] wrote is true, as usual—'only the ignorant is an enemy to knowledge.' 'A cock[19] does not appreciate a bit of jasper, nor do pigs delight in roses; no picture pleases an ape, no light the purblind; for Midas there is no pleasure in the song of Apollo.' Why do you foolishly show off your asses' ears; you are even sillier than your father Midas who did try to keep them hidden. Why not rather bury the shame of your ignorance in the ground? Why not imitate the artfulness of some people who praise letters, to give themselves the air of knowing? Why not at least keep your mouths shut and look like philosophers? Now you are caught in your own accusation like squeaking mice.[20] But maybe you are so far advanced in your madness as to think it a clever thing to do to hate and envy and carp at the best things of all, which the wisest men think worth obtaining with many labours. That bit of glory, in case you don't know, you share with porters, cobblers, sailors, and grave-diggers; they hate cultivated studies too, and despise and curse them, but they are better than you for two reasons; their hate is less violent, and they despise our studies for love of their own skills. You detest the refined arts and have none of your own. They prefer one skill to another, one kind of study to another; you put ignorance before knowledge, madness before a sane mind, animals before men. You slavish herd of sneerers,[21] even the asses laugh at you!

"Now just look and see how unfair it is to hate without knowing what you hate or why you hate it. You condemn rhetoric, but what that might be you have not the foggiest idea. You hate poetry, without understanding what it is or what kind of thing. You hate antiquity, but the ancients mean nothing to you. In short, you pour scorn on the whole of what learned scholars toil for far into the night, and the whole of its greatness is unknown to you. For if you ever did learn these things yourselves why rebuke those who want to learn, and if you never learnt them (and this you not only admit but glory in) why pronounce judgment so ponderously on matters you know nothing about? You have heard, I think, that there is something bad in these studies. Of course you have, but from people like yourselves, envious, ignorant and hostile; it is like pig teaching pig, or the blind leading the blind.[22] But show me, if you can, one person who has found fault with this literature when he has thoroughly understood it, one person who has said that he regretted the time spent on it. Why should a dolt be believed, jabbering about things he does not understand, and a learned man disbelieved when he talks about what he knows? Do you think your jealousy is concealed from anybody? Do you think you are deceiving us with your pretences? or that we cannot see what disease is eating you up? Suppose we now give things their proper names: stop posing as devout and religious men instead of the jealous, sluggish creatures you are!"

It Is Malice and Not Piety to Hate Literary Studies of Which You Are Ignorant

The doctor said then: "As you have given leave, I will make use of it and interrupt you. You have shown yourself a valiant skirmisher, and I think you are rightly called Batt!"

When the other asked him why he thought so, he went on: "These are no riddles to you who know the fables so well. You have shown up the tricks of the barbarians so well that I could almost believe that a second metamorphosis had transformed you back from that legendary stone[23] into Batt again; and then your challenge to these fellows provoking them to fight was clever too. There is nothing which can so rouse their rage as to charge them as you do with stupidity, ignorance, envy—in fact, hearing some truths about themselves."

"You are right," said Batt, "and it really is no wonder if scabby fellows jump when you touch their sore places. You may see the arrogant men giving proof of their soul's rage by their flashing eyes and the savagery written all over their faces; even though in the midst of this they do not yield a step in their fake religious fervour—like characters in a play they act out their tragic parts. For religion, while it is the best of all things, is also, the famous historian[24] tells us, the most convenient cloak for any vice you like to name, because if anyone tries to draw attention to the vices themselves he appears to many people to be attacking religion, by which they are masked; and so it often happens that 'evil oft lurks, masked by its neighbour, good.'[25]

"These people are soaked in vice—in much worse vices than any other mortals, whom they, demigods as they are, regard as the common herd; yet they make attacks on others' lives with their impudent tongues and spare nobody, neither age nor sex nor nationality nor order, neither a man's person nor his good fame. But whenever anyone finds them drunk, or whoring, or committing some deed even worse than these, they put up excuses, they cover up, they will have it hushed up for the honour of their order, as they say—as if other mortals were outside all orders. When they bawl about the vices of the secular clergy, and preach revolt, and incite the ignorant mob to stone them, they never think of the risk of rousing the anger of Christ, the Founder of *that* order—for he was a priest,[26] but not a Dominican. If anyone dares to divulge any of their secrets and disturb the Augean stable, they announce that he is in danger of destruction from an irate Francis, or Dominic, or Elijah,[27] so help me! One of this flock recently gave high praise to a colleague of his order, because he shouted all manner of things in a public sermon against priests with concubines, and tried to persuade the people and the magistrates that priests' concubines should be compelled to wear a red cross on the left shoulder. As he was enjoying himself mightily over this story, someone asked him— with compliments about the other man's speech—what colour would he wish the cross to be for the Dominicans, the Carmelites, and the rest. Would he like the concubines of the Friars Minor to wear grey crosses, those of the Carmelites white, of the Dominicans black? At this the pious man crossed himself vigorously against the evil omen. The second man continued, 'You will never succeed, however big a sign of the cross you make, in hiding from many people what shameful things are sometimes perpetrated by your colleagues. It could not possibly be otherwise, given such a heap of offscourings of men and races. But perhaps it is not right to make all this public, for the sake of the order.' The first speaker agreed heartily with this. Then the other asked, 'And the priesthood, is not that an order?' As he could not deny it, the second man asked why he should think the wrongdoings of priests ought to be howled out in front of the people with such inflammatory uproar. Not to digress further from our subject, we may say that they use the same cloak for their crass ignorance as for the other shameful things in their lives.

"They hold out false piety everywhere as their shield, and they do it with such art and cunning that they manage to deceive not only other people, but themselves as well, clever fellows that they are! Not that they are moved by any real religious fervour—they have no wish to appear religious in anything but this one particular—but, as Quintilian puts it, they want to 'skulk in the shadow of a great name.' This is the religion of evildoers, of robbers and murderers, who have a habit of flying to the altar and the temple as soon as they have perpetrated any crime, like the wicked slave in Plautus.[28] Why do they do this? Because they are charmed with the religious feeling of the place? Not in the least—they do it to escape the cross, to go unpunished for their evil deeds. In the same way our severe critics—who may be Dionysius or Clodius[29] in other things—want to appear like Numa whenever it comes to discussing good studies; it is then that they remember they are Christians; it is then that they begin to chant the bits out of the Gospel, and wrap up ugly things in attractive words, and say they are inspired by zeal, not envy, and do not hate our studies but despise them—that being the special duty and honour of a Christian. They hold up before us the rustic simplicity of the apostles. They say that there is a high reward among the blessed which awaits those who for religion's sake can despise these heathen teachings, invented for ostentation and pride; ignorant piety, they say, is most pleasing to heaven; as if heaven were in any way gratified by our being boorish—in that case why do we not cherish stupidity more than anything?—or as if ignorance were useful to any aspect of the management of life; when the truth is that to despise in others the splendid thing which you have not got and never hope to have is utterly absurd and a mark of insanity. They are wildly wrong if they think a contempt for any kind of thing will redound to their own credit. Take Thersites,[30] the least of the Greeks: supposing that he in his utter cowardice were to declare that he despised the glory of Achilles, and the arms by which it was won (those arms which Ajax and Ulysses quarrelled about), would he not provoke a universal shout of laughter? Who would not smile if a snail despised the speed of the horse? or an owl mocked at the eagle's eyes, or a mole at a roebuck's? if a raven scorned the colours of a parrot? or a donkey belittled the intelligence of an elephant? or if a doltish fool despised the prudence of a wise man? That will never win him praise. And so I shall be doing the barbarians a good turn if I explain the rational basis of scorn, and thus prevent their using scorn as a means of self-glorification.

Things Which May Be Rightly Despised, and Others Which May Not

"In human affairs there are certain things which attract the minds of mortal men with a special ingrafted longing, whether because they look honourable and beautiful, or sweet, or useful, and in this category are wealth, fame, rank, pleasure; if you possess these, or if they are easily within your reach, to hold them lightly is an act worthy of a strong and upright man—at least in so far as they turn him away from virtue. It is equally praiseworthy to disdain the sad things and the sweet; that is, to be able to renounce the latter and go to meet the former. Plato does not altogether approve of the Spartan way of life, because while they made nothing of the hardest toil, they seemed less practised in the contempt of pleasure.[31] But these Catos[32] of ours are weaker than any woman on both counts; they only show themselves men when it comes to the contempt of literature. To make it even funnier, they pour scorn not only on the most admirable things, but on things entirely outside their knowledge. They scorn Ciceronian eloquence, being themselves as dumb as fish; they scorn the acuteness of Chrysippus,[33] and they themselves are as dull as a pounded pestle.[34] They scorn poetry, being uninitiated and, as Plato says,[35] foreign to the Muses. They scorn the refined literary style of the old theologians, which they cannot hope to follow, and if they were to hope for this they would be all the crazier. What a doltish herd of scorners! Just tell me, what new greatness of soul is this? What is this extraordinary type of contemptuousness? You cannot despise money, but you bask in the glory of despising erudition? For kissing and cuddling a whore you beat Hercules, silly childish lust is your master, any kind of adulation ravishes you, the least opposition dismays you, and you think you will cut the figure of a strong man if you manage to pour scorn on things more important than you could possibly understand? To take pride in a well-turned speech is not permitted, but you sell yourself to the womenkind with your well-cut gown; you prefer your speech to be empty and squalid but your skin is well filled and shining. You turn away in disgust from the mention of girls in the stories of the poets, but meanwhile you have no disgust at all about forcing other men's wives, even Vestal virgins.[36] The pen must not be sleek and shining, but the purse can. Listen, proud scorner, you must get learning first and then despise it; if you want to play the strong man, first acquire the object of your scorn; unless perhaps your boast is that you are imitating the apostles in this also, that your reputation of virtue rests on the relinquishment of desire, and not on the kind of thing relinquished. Come now, suppose there were no difference between wealth and learning: the apostles were indifferent to poverty or to the hope of greater wealth, and that without envy; stripped bare themselves, they did not envy the riches of others. You have not even a little learning, which you could claim to despise, but a great hopelessness, because learning is a matter of great difficulty and needs infinite toil, and your brains are heavier than lead.[37]

"Finally, supposing you were right to despise learning, why should you envy others? If you envy, that means you wish for something; and if you wish, why do you not come down with us into the arena, and try to be happy with us instead of being wretched because of us? Strive, win, triumph. But lazy men see how our learning is hedged in on all sides by hard labour and nightly vigils; if they were equal to making light of it, they would not talk so boastfully and stupidly about despising erudition. When I have mastered the whole of literature, that will be the time when I shall be right in despising it, not that I shall lose interest in it, but so as to avoid arrogance; and I will see to it that, though I excel all others in learning, I shall not put myself before anyone, not even the stupidest. I shall frankly encourage modest efforts; I shall congratulate the victor and not envy him. The greater I am, the greater will be my humility—the more I know, the more gently I shall tolerate the ignorance of others, and bearing with all I shall take care that no one has anything to bear from me. I shall vie with the studious in learning, and with all men in gentleness, courtesy, modesty; I shall conduct myself so that it is clear that I am better for being wiser. The more others look up to me, the more I shall look down on myself. Finally, when I have tried my best to learn everything, I shall not seem to myself to know anything.

"This is the way in which our scorn may be praiseworthy, if we are scorning not others' learning but our own. Looking at it this way, not erudition only but virtue itself is to be despised, and the thing above all to be scorned is scorn. Augustine 'despised' heathen culture in this way, but only after becoming a prince of learning in this field. Jerome's 'contempt' for the writings of Cicero and Plato did not debar him from an excellent mastery of them, and he used them continuously.[38] Basil and Chrysostom were so neglectful of the orators' and philosophers' talents that you have only to look at the documents to see that they knew all about them!

"To sum up, why on earth should these fellows glory in their scorn? Is it because, like the fox in the fable, they have vain longings? The fox began to be disgusted by the ass's testicles only when it had stopped hoping; 'what vile food,' it said, 'I could never have eaten that!'[39] But if we are to call things by their right names, this is sheer envy, not scorn. Or perhaps the reason is that they are weaklings, frightened by the difficulty of work, without which there is no approach either to virtue or to learning. Anyone can see that this is the attitude of a lazy man, and a spiteful one too. Or perhaps they have an innate uncouthness which makes them hate the elegance of literary studies? This seems to me not the attitude of a pious Christian (as they say), but of a clodhopping and actually brutish mind. Now let us have a little modesty, please; let them give way to those who are trying for better things. Let it be enough for them to acknowledge their own ignorance to themselves, and not go on making unnecessary trouble for us, and looking down on people they should respect and admire; and if they find nothing better or sweeter than sleep and idleness, let them show more justice as regards others; they can just leave the gloomy night-watchings and crazy toil to us, seeing that we have not the slightest envy of their delights. It is a worse kind of envy to be galled by other people's hard work.

It Is Absurd to Disapprove of Anything Simply Because It Was Discovered by the Ancients

"With this vinegar running through them, it is amazing how noisily they attack us, saying we are not Christians but heathens, idolaters, and more noxious than the heathens themselves. They ask if a person can really be considered Christian when he takes so much trouble and finds so much delight in irreligious exercises invented by wicked men to satisfy their pride, when he finds all his repose in these things and makes them into his leisure occupation, his business, his one solace? And is it not obvious to everyone that this is sacrilege, if a man who has once enrolled himself in the ranks of Christ's soldiers, once been admitted and pledged himself to the service of Christ as his leader, should desert to the enemy, the spirits of evil, and have dealing with the worshippers of idols? Surely those people deal with idols, they say, who delight to be called Ciceronian as speakers, Virgilian or Horatian as poets, or as philosophers Aristotelian, Academic, Stoic, Epicurean? This is the Chrysippean argument that you have heard, the two-horned syllogism. You see how they go about to tie you up all unawares in this sophistical trap. I see there is some need of that famous hellebore of Carneades.[40] What are you saying, you anti-Chrysippeans? Is everything which came out of the heathen world always to be bad, and forbidden to Christians? So we are not to be allowed to take over anything discovered by the pagans unless we cease forthwith to be Christian?

"In that case you had better preach to the carpenters and warn them not to dare to use any of their saws, axes, adzes, gimlets, nor their wedges, rules, plumblines, centring, nor straight edges.[41] Should you ask why, I'll tell you: this carpenter's art and its tools were invented by Daedalus, a heathen. The blacksmiths had better stop—it was the Cyclops, men-monsters, who discovered how to work iron. Let no one work in bronze—they say this was first taught by the Chalybes; and pottery by Choroebus, so the potters can have a holiday. A certain Boethus was the first cobbler, so let no Christian sew together a shoe; Niceas was the first fuller, so no one must wash the dirt out of his clothes. The Egyptians invented weaving: back we go to dressing in skins. The Lydians invented dyeing, so let no one tint the wool shorn from the sheep. Cadmus the Phoenician found out how to cast metal, so the furnaces had better cool off. As for sailors, we must get them to vow, if possible, that they will not use their customary tackle, and coachmen must be warned not to imitate Erichthonius.[42] Painters, carvers, glaziers, every kind of craftsman, in short, must find some other way of earning their living if they can, to avoid defilement of themselves and their families by these heathen arts; and if they cannot they must starve, rather than give up being Christians. Suppose we inspire the soldiers too—very pious fellows—with a religious scruple against using shields, breastplates, helmets, swords, greaves, crests, bows, arrows, lances, and spears? They ascribe the invention of all these things to the wicked. But who could bear to take away from the girls their devotion to Minerva and their tools at the same time—their bundles of wool, their distaffs, spindles, shuttles, and looms—none of these having been invented by Christians? And then the tillers of the soil—I see that you must put them out of work even if you starve for it: the plough was invented by Osiris; from now on let no one dare to turn the soil, or sow it when turned, or reap it when sown, for they say all this was due to Saturn. No one may cultivate the vine, for that was devised by Bacchus. No one may drink wine neat, or even watered down—it was Staphylus[43] who demonstrated this. Sick people must not send for the doctor: medicine is an invention of Apollo. And these were not merely wicked men but, according to popular belief, demons.

"So for you it is permissible to use things invented by evil spirits, but for us it will be forbidden to use the works of studious men? The fact is that those people are not ashamed (even those who want to figure as dialecticians and theologians) to throw up against the studious a kind of reproach which, if tried with diggers and reapers in the field, would bring the yokels out to finish them off with mattocks and scythes. If we are to be forbidden to use the inventions of the pagan world, what shall we have left I ask you, in the fields, in the towns, in churches and houses and workshops, at home, at war, in private and in public? To such an extent is it true that we Christians have nothing we have not inherited from the pagans. The fact that we write in Latin, speak it in one way or another, comes to us from the pagans; they discovered writing, they invented the use of speech.

"These people say, 'Am I to carry books by damned men in my hand and in my bosom, and read them over again and reverence them? Virgil is burning in hell, and is a Christian to sing his poems?' As if many a Christian were not burning there too, whose writings—if any good ones survive—would not be shunned for that reason by anybody. Really, who can bear this capricious way of sitting in judgment, waving a Mercurial wand[44] and sending off whoever they wish to hell, and calling up whom they wish to heaven? I will not enter here on that quarrelsome discussion about the pagans, which is unworthy even of women; it is not for us to discuss the damnation of the heathen, those, I mean, who lived before our faith. If we wished to indulge in guesswork, I could easily prove that the great men among the pagans are saved, or else no one is; let us concern ourselves with the fineness of their teaching, rather than ask ourselves how well they lived. The judge orders stage-actors to be heard as witnesses, even though anyone who knows their manner of life condemns it. The books of Origen, censured as heretical in many passages, are read by the Christian church with profit to scholarship; and yet we shun the divine writings of men on whose moral character we cannot pass judgment without the greatest impertinence. Or, to put it better, one may judge them favourably with credit, but one could not criticize them without great fault.

"'Be off!' they say. 'Am I to let myself be called a Ciceronian or a Platonist, when I have once and for all chosen to be called a Christian?' Why not call yourself a monster of a man? If you can truly be called a Sardanapalus[45] when you copy his abandoned luxury, or a Gnatho[46] because you are a flatterer, or a Thraso[46] when you are a stupid boaster, why should not someone who imitates Cicero's language be called a Ciceronian, or why, if I try to emulate something of Virgil's should I not be called Virgilian? You arrogate to yourself those barbarous titles and love to be called Albertist, Thomist, Scotist, Occamist,

Durandist as long as you take these names from Christians.[47] For my part, I will allow myself to be called after any pagan so long as he was deeply learned or supremely eloquent; nor shall I go back on this declaration, if only the pagan teaches me more excellent things than a Christian.

"To bring this discussion to an end at last: if our opponents were not made blinder than moles by their own envy, they would see what is clear even to the blind—they would see that among the inventions of the pagans there are distinctions to be made; some of them are useless, doubtful, unwholesome, while others are extremely useful, health-giving, and even necessary. Let us leave the bad things to them; why should we not take over the good for ourselves? This is what a Christian man should do, a prudent and studious man. But what we do, heaven help us, is just the opposite: we imitate the vices of the heathen all the time, in fact we beat them at lust, avarice, ambition, superstition: but the one thing it would be right to imitate, their learning, is the one thing we reject, whether from stupidity or pride I cannot yet tell. For if we have inherited from them, without doing wrong, things which were to be of general usefulness to us, what is there to hinder us from doing the same in the case of their arts? Nothing more useful or more excellent than these exists in the affairs of men, if we are to believe Jerome.[48]

The Pagans Perfected Systems of Knowledge According to the Divine Plan, Not for Us to Scorn Them, but for Our Use

"When I look a little more closely at the wonderful arrangement, the harmony as they call it, of things, it always seems to me—and not to me only: many of the weightiest authors have thought the same—that it was not without divine guidance that the business of discovering systems of knowledge was given to the pagans. For the great and eternal Disposer, who is wisdom itself, establishes all things with consummate skill, differentiates them with beautiful play of interchange, and orders them with perfect rightness, so that each balances another in a marvellous way; nor does he allow anything to move at random in all the immense variety of the world. It was he who willed that the Golden Age[49] in which he had chosen to be born was to be sovereign over all epochs which came before or followed after; it pleased him that whatever existed in nature should be put to use for increasing the happiness and glory of that time. He himself promised that this should be done: 'I, if I be lifted up from the earth,' he says, 'will draw all unto me.'[50] Here it seems to me that he most aptly uses the word *traho*, 'I draw,' so that one may understand that all things, whether hostile or heathen or in any other way far removed from him, must be drawn, even if they do not follow, even against their will, to the service of Christ. What of that great universal harmony, which in the eyes of St Augustine meant that not even bad things were created without intention? All those allegories, signs, and mysteries existing from the beginning of the world—in which direction did they point? Why, to the century of Christ. What about the whole Mosaic law, all those rites and ceremonies, those forms of worship, those promises and prophecies? Is not Paul the witness that all these things happened

THE ANTIBARBARIANS

to them for examples?[51] Not to speak of the transfer of empires, what was the purpose of 'founding the Roman nation with such vast effort,'[52] and through such great disasters and bloodstained victories subjugating the entire world to the City which held sway? Was it not according to the divine plan, so that when the Christian religion was born, it might spread abroad the more easily into different parts of the world, diffused as it were from one head into the separate members? And again, what was his intention in allowing almost the whole earth to be entangled with such lunatic, scandalous religions? Why, so that when the One arose, it would overturn all the others with the utmost glory. Nothing fine is ever done without struggle.

"It was Greece, devoted to study, which discovered the arts; then Latium[53] entered into rivalry with her, and was the victor as far as concerns war, but barely equalled her achievements in literature and oratory. Some concerned themselves with searching out the hidden causes of things; others, bound by the fetters of Prometheus, observed the regular revolutions of the heavenly lights. There were those who tried to explore divine mysteries; one discovered methods of argument and another laws of oratory; some portrayed the customs of men with great sagacity, and for some their great concern was to hand on to posterity the memory of past deeds. In law, in philosophy, how the ancients laboured! Why did all this happen? So that we on our arrival could hold them in contempt? Was it not rather that the best religion should be adorned and supported by the finest studies?

"Everything in the pagan world that was valiantly done, brilliantly said, ingeniously thought, diligently transmitted, had been prepared by Christ for his society. He it was who supplied the intellect, who added the zest for inquiry, and it was through him alone that they found what they sought. Their age produced this harvest of creative work, not so much for them as for us; just as every region cannot supply every commodity, nor (as Virgil says)[54] does every land grow everything, so it seems to me that every century is allotted its own gifts. Many of the philosophers wore out their lives and their brains in seeking the highest good; but the real highest good, the perfect gift, was reserved by Christ for his own time. However he did not intend all the rest to be useless and done to no purpose. We see with our own eyes how in material things nature takes care that no portion of time shall slip away uselessly. Look at the trees (the sight of them suggests this example to me): in early spring they supply sap to nourish the leaves, and now you see the leaves are joined by flowers, and how much pleasure it gives us to look at them. As summer comes, these little flowers swell out gradually into the pulp of the fruit; in autumn, the trees will stand weighed down with ripe apples, and, as soon as they let them fall, once again that season which passes from autumn into winter is spent in making new shoots for the coming summer. Even winter itself is not idle, but reestablishes things in an interval of quiet; the same effect is produced by the revolving of the heavenly bodies, disposed in such varying ways. There is a great discord in nature which is the completest concord. All things, both particular and universal, are carried in the same direction; they all face the same way, tend towards one thing. So while Christ, the greatest and best of disposers, allocated to his own century in a special way the recognition of the highest good, he gave the centuries immediately preceding a privilege of their own: they were to reach the thing nearest to the highest good, that is, the summit of learning. What could man acquire, by virtuous striving, that is more valuable than knowledge? Indeed, on this point God was willing to consult the laziness or the leisure of the Christians, by taking away a great deal of the hard work from us, who were likely to have much to do elsewhere. It is much easier to master a thing which is already worked out to the last detail[55] than to invent it. If they had not sown the seed of letters, perhaps we should have had nothing to reap; what should we have discovered by ourselves, we who have never added anything to their inventions, but have damaged many of them and thrown them all into confusion? This makes it all the more ungracious, in fact spiteful, that we should not be willing to accept things freely offered, which were to be of so much use to us, and which cost them so dearly; and we not only refuse a splendid gift, but treat the giver of the gift with contempt, instead of the gratitude we owe him."

It Is Ignorance Rather Than Erudition Which Makes Men Insolent

Here I said: "You speak most learnedly and truly, my dear Batt; and yet I could hardly believe that there was anybody so bereft of human reason as to think that the whole of literature should be separated from religion, provided it be Christian."

"As if there were any Christian erudition," said Batt, "which is not the very reverse of erudition! I am not speaking of the mysteries of our religion, but of invented systems of learning. If we are willing to admit the truth, can we say that since the time of those great pagans we have invented anything new, which was not at the same time crude? How could we be good at discovering anything when we are so bad at preserving the discoveries of others? In my opinion there is no erudition in existence except what is secular (this is their name for the learning of the ancients) or at least founded on and informed by secular literature; I would allow this to be called Christian (if we rule out perverse and wicked prejudice), although I meet a number of people who are religious in such a doltish fashion that they think little even of that so-called Christian, that is, ecclesiastical, learning. 'What does it matter,' they say, 'if we are not theologians? If you know Christ well it is enough; you need not know anything else. Eternal life is promised to the innocent, not to the learned. Am I to be condemned for it if I have no very lofty understanding of the writings of Paul? if I don't grasp Jerome's style of composition? if I have never even read Augustine and Ambrose, and don't even understand the Gospel?' You dunderhead, does it matter if you don't understand yourself, and whether you are a camel or a man? 'Don't worry, even the beasts will go to heaven.' What a race of men, to be sure—not only stupid, but irreligious. If only they did know Christ, those who congratulate themselves on knowing nothing of letters! But it often happens that people who wish to be credited with simplicity in this line are the knowingest of rogues in worldly affairs; however my business is not with them at present. I introduced this aside so that it will not surprise you if those people detest our kind of learning, which I have just described, when they also despise the Gospel. As I have just said, I am not dealing with these, but with people who want to appear learned in matters relating to the church, and yet abstain from all secular learning, like a Jew shunning unclean food. They have forgotten what Paul said, 'To the pure all things are pure.'[56] For my part, I consider the learning of these people so narrow that it is not learning at all, and worse than any sort of ignorance. These are the ones who detest our whole body of knowledge, and call it bad, pagan, and irreligious; what *they* know, they claim to have received not from the studies of men but from heaven. I am even told it is commonly remarked that if anyone is particularly well versed in literature he must be particularly immoral. And this is an insult which touches not only poets and orators but theologians, lawyers, dialecticians, and other studious men, and should be confuted by them all.

"If learning is bad, is it bad in itself or because of something else? If because of something else, why do we confine our reproaches solely to erudition? If it is bad in itself, why do the most serious authors judge it to be among the most honourable and valuable things? Why is it ranked above wealth, which is not in itself bad? Furthermore, truth can never be bad in itself, and since the liberal disciplines are truths, they must be good. If knowledge is good in itself, ignorance is bad; if knowledge is bad, it should be avoided, although if we listen to the voice of Nature, who would not rather be entirely knowledgeable than entirely ignorant? This is where our dialecticians begin to be barbarians. We do not rebuke learning, they say, as learning, but because it makes people wily, conceited, unmanageable, arrogant, and supercilious. They ask, 'What are you aiming at, if not to get away from the common herd, to stand out from the rest, to be lauded and celebrated and to treat us and our like as mere animals?' This tells you what is really biting these sanctimonious people: they are unwilling to be despised. They want to rule and lead, not to be led, not to obey, and so they come to think it is essential for keeping the peace that no one shall exist who can correct the ignorance of others. I think you can see that slander against learning proceeds from nothing else than pride. But it would be most unfair if a purblind man were to accuse the sun because its light irritated him. 'Knowledge puffs up,' they say, 'charity builds.'[57] Arrogance is a defect, but is it a defect of knowledge or of ourselves? They will not dare, I think, to say it is a defect of knowledge, because in that case no one would ever have been erudite who was not arrogant, and the more learned anyone became, the haughtier it would make him. Such a statement is not only absurd, it is manifestly slanderous. Against whom? Against Augustine, against Jerome, against many others—it would be wicked to accuse them of pride because they were great authors. 'But I am talking of profane learning,' you say. That is what we accept, what we admire and reverence as we find it in these princes of the Christian religion whom I have just named—a kind of learning very different from yours, you who profess to have the teaching of the church. Another point: if it is through our own fault that we grow haughty and not because of the fault of things round us, which is right: to correct our own character or to blame our environment, with no justification? Would you not be behaving more modestly, you who teach modesty to others, if you were to admit your ignorance frankly and not work up a slander against the most valuable things, merely in order to protect your own vice? In everything else you are clumsy, but this slander finds you eloquent. 'Secular learning,' you say, 'supplies the material for arrogance.' Who denies that? But that material can be procured from anywhere—even from the best and holiest things. So is it the things themselves which are to be blamed, or you yourself and your wretched misuse of the best? A mind which is inherently arrogant seizes every opportunity to swagger. How many vices are encouraged by money? Yet no one accuses it of being bad; it is the spirit of those who use it badly which is reproved. What can there be which is so good that it does not sometimes provide an occasion for evil? Not fasting, nor alms, nor chastity, nor virtue itself. The philosophers have their pride, the poets are pleased with themselves. Tell me, you, are there no proud theologians? Is there any haughtiness anywhere more arrogant than theirs? But who would dare to bring an accusation against sacred theology! Plenty of them are proud on this account, yet the fault is not theology's but theirs. Are there no cases of illiterate insolence? What makes such people overweening? Why, their own ignorance. What would they do then, if they had learnt letters?

Ignorance Is the Mother of Pride; It Is from Learning, on the Contrary, That Modesty Is Born

"What could be more untrue than to say that literature makes men wily, conceited, and supercilious? If by wiliness you mean prudence, I do not disagree, since we are commanded by the advice of the Gospel to imitate the wisdom of serpents.[58] As to superciliousness, anyone can see the absurdity there. What is it that leads those hard and boorish men towards a more humane type of life, towards a kinder outlook and gentler ways? Is it not letters? It is they which mould our character, quiet our passions, check our uncontrolled impulses, give mildness to our minds in place of savagery. When they talk of superciliousness, do they mean that we refuse to admire their barbarism? Or that we are unable to enjoy the silly nonsense of utter blockheads, and that we do not treasure dung as if it were diamonds? Is this the behaviour of a supercilious man, or is it not rather that of a sane one, able to distinguish the worst from the best? As to modesty, I think just as St Jerome does when he quotes the opinion of some Greek writer or other (and to me he seems to have thought rightly and written elegantly)—that inexperience produces self-confidence, but knowledge is accompanied by fear.[59] I perceive that Quintilian saw this clearly: 'the less a person's mind is worth,' he says, 'the more he tries to aggrandize himself and increase his importance.' We see many people who seem to themselves consummate scholars before they have any idea of what they know or do not know. By the time they have persuaded themselves, and through their folly made a bid for a certain reputation for erudition among the common herd, it is inevitable that they should have no little esteem for themselves and should despise others. They boldly teach what they do not know; they write, they speak, they explain; there is nothing they leave unattempted, nothing they do not dare; relying on the applause of their supporters, they pour scorn on the judgment of the learned and on their fewness in number; they are a pestilential race of men, and their mental outlook is in keeping with their stupidity. . . ."

NOTES

1. See the description of the mood of an audience in Cicero *De oratore* 2.19.80, and the *Rhetorica ad Herennium* 1.4.6.
2. Horace *Epistles* 2.1.31.
3. "By the waterclocks," an allusion to the method of timing cases in the Roman courts. See Erasmus, *Adagia* I iv 73.
4. The Andabatae bashed about with closed eyes; see *Adagia* II iv 33.
5. *Iliad* 5.785; *Adagia* II iii 37.
6. The size of Xerxes' army became proverbial: see Herodotus 7.60.
7. The Parthians were noted for deceptive manoeuvres in war; see Virgil *Georgics* 3.31, etc.
8. Virgil *Georgics* 4.441.
9. *Adagia* III x 35.
10. Ovid *Metamorphoses* 2.1–340. Phaethon borrowed the chariot of the sun, and by his loss of control brought drought and destruction upon the earth before he was finally burnt to death.
11. King of Epirus, famous for his talents as a general.
12. Eph 6:17: "The sword of the Spirit, which is the word of God."
13. The *Fetiales* were a body of priests in Rome whose duty it was to declare war and make peace.
14. This quip is an addition of 1520.
15. *Adagia* I iii 67.
16. *Adagia* IV iii 99.
17. Ancient jokes; see *Adagia* I iv 35, 37, 38, 62.
18. Aristotle.
19. The fable of the cock comes from Phaedrus; for pigs and roses see *Adagia* III vii 23. The story of Midas is told by Ovid (*Metamorphoses* 11.146–93).
20. *Adagia* I iii 65. The allusion is to the shrew, supposed to be shriller than the ordinary mouse and therefore prone to give itself away.
21. Horace *Epistles* 1.19.19.
22. *Adagia* I viii 40; Matt 15:14.
23. The Battus of legend was a shepherd of Pylos, turned to stone by Mercury (Ovid *Metamorphoses* 2.687–707).
24. Probably Livy.
25. This was an opportune moment for Erasmus to insert the attack on the monastic orders which expresses his feeling about the situation at Louvain. The following paragraph is an insertion of 1520.
26. Heb 6:20; 7:1–8:7.
27. Because the Carmelites took their name from Mount Carmel, where Elijah vanquished the prophets of Baal (1 Kings 18).

28. *Mostellaria* 1094.

29. Dionysius II, tyrant of Syracuse, and P. Clodius Pulcher, the enemy of Cicero, exemplify the dissolute life. Numa Pompilius, the early ruler of Rome (seventh century B.C.), typifies beneficent and wise government.

30. Thersites (*Iliad* 2.211–77) is used as a symbol of baseness. In post-Homeric tradition (as reflected in Sophocles *Ajax*) Achilles' arms were made a prize after his death.

31. *Laws* 1.633B ff.

32. Cato the Censor (second century B.C.), famous for his temperate way of life.

33. Stoic philosopher; cf 27:14n.

34. Dumb fish and beaten pestles are proverbial: *Adagia* prolegomena xiii (LB II 12E) and III vi 21.

35. For example, *Republic* 8.546D; *Adagia* II vi 18.

36. Nuns.

37. *Adagia* prolegomena xiii (LB II 12D).

38. The irony of this passage is increased in the 1520 version.

39. A variant of the fox and the grapes? Cf Stith Thompson *Motif-Index of Folk-Literature* (Helsinki 1932–6) J 2066.1.

40. *Adagia* I viii 51.

41. The catalogue of ancient inventors in this paragraph comes from Pliny *Naturalis historia* 7.56.196–202.

42. The fourth king of Athens, said to have invented chariots and harnessed horses to draw them.

43. A son of Silenus.

44. A reference to Hermes Psychopompus, escort of the dead in Greek mythology.

45. King of Assyria, notorious for effeminate luxury.

46. Thraso is a braggart soldier in Terence's *Ennuchus*, and Gnatho his flattering parasite.

47. Followers of the medieval Schoolmen Albertus Magnus, Thomas Aquinas, Duns Scotus, William of Occam, Durandus.

48. Cf Jerome Ep 53.5–6.

49. The fourth *Eclogue* of Virgil, prophesying the return of the primeval Age of Gold, was applied by Christian writers to the birth of Christ.

50. John 12:32.

51. 1 Cor 10:11.

52. Virgil *Aeneid* 1.33.

53. Italy.

54. *Eclogues* 4.39 prophesies that in the Golden Age every land will bear all fruits.

55. *Adagia* I v 91.

56. Titus 1:15.

57. 1 Cor 8:1.

58. Matt 10:16.

59. Jerome Ep 73.10.

Giangiorgio Trissino

1478–1550

With Giangiorgio Trissino Italian literary theory enters a period which is strongly classical in its orientation. In comparison with Dante or Boccaccio, Trissino is a mediocre figure, and his poetry is little read today. His introduction of Aristotelian principles to Italian poetry, however, was a decidedly influential moment in the development of Renaissance literary theory. Trissino is an essentially conservative figure who looked to the formalism of classical literary theory for inspiration.

Trissino was born into a wealthy family of noble status on July 8, 1478. He did not begin his serious education until he was twenty-eight, by which time he was already married with two children. He went to Milan and immersed himself in literary studies and Greek philosophy. His later critical work demonstrates a familiarity with both Greek and Latin criticism. He was briefly exiled from his native Vicenza in 1509 and spent some time in Germany. He returned, however, to become a favorite of Pope Leo X. He served Clement VII after Leo's death and was made a count by Charles V. Throughout his life Trissino used his poetry to win favor with his patrons, and he himself served as a patron to the great Renaissance architect Palladio. Trissino lived as a great noble at his villa at Cricole, and he died at Rome in 1550.

Trissino presented his tragedy, *Sofonisba,* in 1515. The work appears to have been something of a Neo-Classical manifesto since it rigidly maintained Aristotelian rules concerning the unity of action and time. It is also the first major Italian work of literature which is written in blank verse, another attempt to hew hard to the formal properties of Greek and Latin drama. It has been called a "lifeless demonstration of rules rather than a work of art." His other major poetic work, *Italia liberata dai Goti (Italy Liberated from the Goths),* was an attempt to create a Homeric epic based upon history. It has met with no more critical approval in this century than *Sofonisba*. Trissino used the epic to attack his son, Giulio, whom he also disinherited and accused of heresy.

Arte Poetica was probably written during the same period that Trissino was writing *Sofonisba*. He published the first four divisions in 1529. The fifth and sixth parts, which deal with more general ideas, were completed about twenty years after he originally composed the work, and they were not actually published until 1563, after Trissino's death. Had they been issued at the same time as *Sofonisba*, Trissino would have been the first to introduce the *Poetics* of Aristotle to Europe in the vernacular.

The selections from *Poetica* which are reprinted here primarily come from the last two parts of the work. They can be read as a kind of loose re-interpretation of Aristotle in which Trissino applied classical rules to Italian poetry liberally using his own poetry as *exempla*. What is perhaps most interesting to the modern reader is the section in which Trissino discusses the Aristotelian requirement that tragedy invoke both pity and fear in the audience. In Trissino's elaboration, the principle becomes an intricate discussion of the manipulation of power which is, as Allan Gilbert has noted, heavily indebted to Machiavelli's discussion of fear. Also interesting is the suggestion that ambiguity both puts identity into question and, as a form of comedy, weakens the distinction between the joker and the object of the joke.

The selections from the *Poetica*, translated by Allan H. Gilbert, are reprinted with his permission from *Literary Criticism: Plato to Dryden*, edited by Allan H. Gilbert (Detroit: Wayne State University Press, 1962). © 1962 by Allan H. Gilbert.

POETICA

FROM
Division I

It is a splendid thing to benefit humanity, and is thought the more noble not merely as the benefit extends to a larger number of persons, but also as the pleasure of those benefited is greater, as in the instance of the physician who is thought more skillful when he not merely restores many to health but also does it without pain and with pleasant medicines. Now the greatest benefit that can be rendered to human beings is to teach them to live well, because this gives them while they are alive a tranquil and pleasant existence without any perturbation, and after death secures them eternal felicity in that other very long existence. Since the greater part of men are of such nature that they unwillingly lend their ears to instruction and listen with delight to stories and pleasant things, I judge those ancient poets should be greatly praised who considering delight and general usefulness have mingled with fables and stories of battle the most excellent instructions on human life, and in that way have made them pleasing to the people, whereas if these teachings had been unadorned they would perhaps have pleased little. Since then the poets are those who mingle with delight precepts designed to make the lives of men perfect, poetry should of right be thought by everyone a most excellent thing. Now without this most just cause can it be believed that it would have been in such high repute as it has been in all ages and perhaps among all the nations of the world? Since it has been so fully treated by Greek and Latin authors in their tongues, I have formed the wish to deal with it also in our Italian language. . . .

FROM
Division V

Since we have spoken of all the modes of making rhymed verses and of all the species of poems that are made with them, it will be well to lay them aside, because verses without rhyme, that is without agreement of the termination of the last words, are more fitted to all sorts of poetry than those with rhyme.[1] It is true that in the choruses of tragedies and comedies and in poems whose matter is love or praise, where sweetness and attractiveness are especially desirable, rhymes with their rules are not to be given up, but ought to be received and adopted as principal causes of this attractiveness and sweetness; and perhaps for this reason alone that period of antiquity, in which as though through some heavenly influence not merely literature but all the fine arts were brought down to the lowest point, adopted rhyme with great eagerness, so that in the time of the decay of the Latin language men of unpolished abilities pursued it with great zeal, as the hymns of the church clearly show.[2] And although rhyme was invented by the Greeks, though not much used by them because of its defects, that age of which I have spoken, finding it in the Latin which was growing corrupt and disappearing, embraced it with so much ardor that it not only was established in the vulgar tongue of Sicily and Italy, but also passed into France and Spain, and even returned into Greece itself; one can say, perhaps without falsity, that it was received by most of the nations of the world, but by the languages of *si*, of *oc*, and of *oi*, as Dante calls them, rhyme was arranged and classified with abundant rules. Hence, since I wish to write the Art of Poetry in the language of *si*, that is in Italian, it appears necessary to treat of rhyme, in which almost all the poems of that language are composed, and it appears the more necessary to treat of it because after the age of Dante and Petrarch, poets of the highest order, rhyme has always been much used, but its rules, as it were, abandoned. Though our age has well begun to throw light on rhyme, the explanation of the craft has not gone so far that it needs no aid. Hence some men of noble and quick parts such as Sannazaro, Bembo, and others, composing in rhyme, have not dared to step aside from mere imitation of Petrarch, and if they did abandon this imitation and wander off by themselves, they made great mistakes, for some of them could not distinguish the madrigal from the ballata, nor the latter from the canzone, nor could they discern the *serventesi*[3] from other kinds of poetry, as can be easily seen in their writings. Hence for the sake of the Italian language I have set myself to explain rhyme at length, and in doing it I have not spared labor, for besides Dante's work *On the Vulgar Tongue* and the rules of Antonio da Tempo, I have read also almost all the ancient Sicilian and Italian poets, as well as the Provençals and Spaniards I have been able to find, among whom I have observed all who use the rules I have set forth in my third and fourth books. My labors will be less irksome in proportion as I shall learn that I have satisfied many excellent minds who have an eager desire to know of such things. So after a long voyage I have come to poetry, which if it abounds in beautiful and learned ideas, yet forces me to treat with all possible brevity every part of it, in order that I may keep the promise I made at the beginning. I will not part from the rule and the precepts of the ancients, and especially of Aristotle, who wrote divinely of this art. . . .

In the following division, where we shall discuss heroic poetry and comedy, in which moral qualities are equally useful and necessary, we shall treat them more particularly and fully than Aristotle has done in the *Poetics*. Hence in this part we shall follow the division of moral traits made by Dionysius of Halicarnassus,[4] which in my opinion is copious and excellent. Since tragedy is an imitation of the most important and greatest people, the composer of tragedy ought to act like the best painters, who in their pictures, although they give the true likeness of those whom they draw, nevertheless represent them as more beautiful;[5] so the poet, when imitating the wrathful, the timid, the lazy, and the like ought to make their moral traits better, that is, more gentle and more benign—not prouder and more malignant—as did Homer, who represented Achilles as wrathful, but loving and good; and Terence in the *Hecuba* made the mother-in-law pleasant to the nurse, and the harlot to the wife. Therefore the poet should observe what we have said, and afterwards take care of those things which of necessity come to the senses from poetry, that is, to the sight and the hearing. I say he should consider that the tragedy he is writing is to be recited, and the gestures seen, and the speeches and the melody heard. Hence he should treat the fable with words pleasing and fit, and in putting it together he should put everything before his eyes, and act as though he himself had a share in those actions, because if he does so he will see plainly all the moral traits, and will easily find what is suitable to each one, and things contrary and repugnant will not be concealed, and if he places as far as possible before his eyes the gestures and movements of those under the influence of the passions, he will as it were put himself under the influence of those passions, because those who are under the influence of the passions show through nature itself exactly how the tormented man is tormented and the troubled man is troubled. Therefore Aristotle says that those of the highest ability are suited to poetry, and those who are moved by violent feeling,[6] because the first know well how to investigate and the others how to form the passions.

It is necessary then that the poet, in order to do this, first lay out the speeches generally and then insert the episodes; to lay out the speeches generally is nothing other than to note the whole action that he wishes to imitate; this is exemplified in the *Sofonisba*, the action of which is that in a war between two republics one of them made a league with a king; the other republic, in order to detach the king from that league, gave him as wife the daughter of its general and thus did detach him. Then when the two republics fought together the one that had gained the king was routed in battle by the other, and the king was taken prisoner. Another king, an ally of the victorious republic, entering the city of the captive king, was besought by the wife of the prisoner not to give her into the hands of the conquering republic; he promised to do what she wished and, in order to do it better, took her for his own wife. After the wedding there arrived a messenger from the captain general of the victorious republic, who demanded the queen; the king who had espoused her did not wish to give her up and went to the captain general, who wished to send the queen as a prisoner to his republic. Therefore the king who had wedded her, not being able to keep his promise, sent her poison, saying that by taking it she could prevent herself from falling into the hands of her enemies; she accepted it, drank, and died. This then is the action, and the rest of the play is made up of the episodes; therefore the poet ought first to outline the simple action, and then insert the names and weave in the episodes; these episodes should be few and short, and suited to the action, as are in the *Sofonisba* the coming of Cato, the speech of Scipio with Syphax, and the sacrifice of Sofonisba, for these are few and brief and most suitable, and are in no respect like the episodes of heroic poetry, which are many and long, like those of the *Odyssey* of Homer and the *Aeneid* of Vergil.

The discourse or expression of thought in the play, the conceptions that Aristotle classes under *dianoia*,[7] ought to be taken from rhetoric, for it is proper to that art; to discourse pertain all those things which are necessary in preparing a speech the parts of which are to prove, to make clear, and to move the passions, such as pity and wrath, though such passions, and likewise greatness and littleness, are equally employed in preparing a play, which takes them from the same models as does an oration; but in this they are different: for a tragedy they are prepared from the nature of things without artifice, but in an oration they are made by the ability and the artifice of the speaker. Dionysius of Halicarnassus holds that the said discourses or speeches should be neither superfluous nor defective nor paradoxical; of the superfluous an example is furnished by Homer, who has Thersites utter much superfluous nonsense at which the Greeks laugh; so superfluous talk runs into chattering, defective into weakness, and paradoxical into peril. From this is manifest that eloquence does not consist in abundance but in proper and skillful arrangement; speeches should not be too brief, that they may not be weak, but should be enough to suffice, and this demands measure; which ought always to be preserved with security; security is gained by not saying contrary things and by proceeding always with propositions that are known and which all believe and admit, as that God is good and just, and that virtue is an honorable thing, and that one should revere his father and his mother; Plato and Xenophon say that Socrates always did this.

But because pity and fear are things with which tragedy is especially concerned, I wish to say something of their nature and origin, following the *Rhetoric* of Aristotle.

Fear then is a sorrow or perturbation through the imagination of some deadly or painful evil which is likely to come, for not all evils are feared, because no one is in fear of becoming unjust or slothful, though these are evils, but merely those evils are feared which can bring about death or the greatest pains and sorrows; and these are not always feared but merely when they appear near us and are likely to come on us, for when evils are uncertain or very distant they are not feared, such as death, which everyone knows he must undergo, but because it is not near we do not think about it. If this is what fear is, it is necessary that all things are fearful that seem to have great power to kill us or to do us the most painful injuries; therefore the apparent approach of them causes us fear, because the formidable appears to be near at hand; so the near approach of the formidable is properly called peril. Therefore, the enmity and wrath of those who are able to injure us is formidable, because, since they are enemies or angry at us, it is obvious that they are able and wish to injure us and therefore are on the point of doing it. Injustice also excites fear when it is strong because the unjust man is unjust through choice, which indicates he will do what he wishes so far as he can. Likewise a capable man injured is worthy of fear when he has power, because manifestly he always can do what he wishes when he is injured and has power; therefore, because of both will and power, evil is at hand. Fear on the part of those who are able to do evil is also an indication of danger because such as these are of necessity always prepared and because, moreover, most men are ill-disposed and allow themselves to be overcome by gain and are timid in perils; for this reason it is almost always a fear-inspiring thing to stand at the discretion of others; hence, those who are conscious of some serious misdeed committed by someone seem formidable to him because he fears they will reveal it or will abandon him; and those who can do injury are formidable to those who are likely to receive it because men are for the most part inclined to do injury when they can. And those who have been injured or think they are going to be injured are dangerous because they are ever watching their opportunity. And equally those who have done injury are to be feared if they have power because they fear vengeance from someone else and such vengeance is put among objects of apprehension. And those also are formidable who contend about things which they cannot possess together because such as these ever war one with another. Those also who are afraid of those more powerful than themselves are equally dangerous to the more powerful because they can easily injure those stronger than themselves. For the same reason they are to be dreaded who are feared by those stronger than themselves; and also those are to be dreaded who have killed men stronger than themselves, and those who have attacked men less powerful than themselves are dangerous at that time or when they are made great. Of those who have been injured, and enemies, and adversaries, the choleric and free are less to be feared than are the mild, and two-faced, and malignant, because it cannot be known when such as these are about to act and when they are far from it. Of all formidable things those are most to be dreaded which, though they cannot be carried out, yet cannot be changed either because change is impossible or because it is not in the power of the doers but in that of their adversaries. Formidable also are those things that cannot be helped, or against which aid, though possible, is not easy to obtain.

To put it very briefly, I say those things are worthy to cause fear that excite pity, when they are put into action or are about to be put into action. These then are all the things disposed toward terror, and to be feared, or at least the chief ones.

Let us see then who those are who fear them. It is manifest that, since fear is the expectation of undergoing some deadly or painful sufferings, those who think they are not going to suffer any evil do not fear, because they cannot fear either things they suppose they cannot undergo or men who cannot cause them suffering or at a time when no suffering can come to them. It is necessary, then, that those should fear who think that they can suffer evil, and that they should fear those who can make them suffer it, and such evil as can actually happen to them, and at the time when it can happen. The persons, then, who do not fear they will undergo any evil are those who are or who think themselves to be in great prosperity, and these are the rich, the strong, the powerful, those abounding in friends, and the like, and for that reason they are almost always proud, disdainful, and audacious. But those who have suffered the greatest ills do not fear they are going to suffer them, nor do those who are cold and as it were dead to the future, such as those under torture and near death, for he who fears must have some hope that he can deliver himself from what afflicts him; the indication of this is that fear makes a man take counsel because no one ever takes counsel about a thing that is beyond hope. Hence in giving counsel to another and in comforting his fear one usually says that men commonly suffer similar ills and that they have suffered others greater than these, and one usually points out that many like to them suffer and have suffered ills they have not foreseen, and at the hands of unexpected persons and at unexpected times. So what we have said will be sufficient in order to understand what fear is and what things are feared and who those are that fear.

Let us come then to pity, which is sorrow because of some evil, or what appears an evil, which may be deadly or painful, and comes to someone who does not deserve to suffer it, and the observer thinks this evil can come to himself or to some of his relatives; this is especially true when the evil seems near at hand. Whence it is manifest that he who would have pity must be such a person that either he or some of his can suffer such evils or similar or equal ones. For those who are totally ruined do not have pity because they think they can suffer no more, having already suffered so much; nor are the compassionate those who think themselves very prosperous, for such persons are rather contemptuous of the afflicted, because, believing they have everything that is good, they think they cannot suffer evil, for not to be able to suffer evil is surely to be placed among the good things of life. They feel pity, then, who think they themselves can suffer, having at other times suffered and been freed; also the old feel pity because of their prudence and experience. And so the weak and the timid and the practiced are liable to pity because they are governed by reason. They are also quick to show compassion who have fathers, wives, brothers, and children, because these appear to them able to suffer the things mentioned above. On the contrary they are not likely to feel pity who are subject to the passions of the strong, as wrath and audacity, because they do not think of what can come; nor do those feel commiseration who are by nature malicious and unjust, because such men do not consider that they are able to suffer. But they are subject to pity who stand in a middle place, that is, who are neither irascible nor audacious, nor malicious, nor unjust. The very timid also do not feel compassion, for when in terror they do not pity others because they are occupied with their own feelings, which arise from their belief that some of those who suffer are good and kind, since he who did not think anyone good would judge all men worthy of affliction. But generally those will be compassionate who remember that to themselves or to some of their relatives similar accidents can come, or who fear that they will come to themselves or some of theirs.

The things for which there can be commiseration are matters of suffering and sorrows that are death-bringing and excessive, and all those great ills of which Fortune is the cause. The things grievous and excessive are deaths, wounds, and afflictions of the body, such as old age, diseases, and need of necessary food. An evil of which Fortune is the cause is to have no friend or to have very few; therefore violent separation from friends and companions is full of misery. Pity is also caused by ugliness, weakness, the lack of some member of the body, and the receiving of evil from a person from whom good should be received—something that often happens. It also moves pity when to a man who has suffered greatly some good comes after he is dead. It is also pitiable never to have anything good, or to have had it without ever being able to use or enjoy it. These are the things that excite pity.

Pity is excited by those whom we know but are not closely connected with, for when our intimates suffer or are about to suffer we feel sorrow as for ourselves. Hence Aristotle says that Amasis did not weep for his son who had been condemned to death and did weep when he saw one of his friends begging, because to see his friend beg was pitiable and the fate of his son was atrocious; for atrocity is a thing diverse from pity and expulsive of it, and often is useful to bring about the contrary; yet there is pity when the horror of the evil is near at hand. We have pity for those who are like us in age or characteristics or disposition or dignity or race, because in such as these it clearly appears what things can happen to us. So it can be generally said that all those things which we fear as able to happen to ourselves move compassion in us when we see them happen to someone else. And when such sufferings appear near at hand, then are they most piteous, because things done ten thousand years ago or which will be done ten thousand years later, since we neither expect them nor remember them, do not move pity at all or very little. Hence it is needful for those who wish to excite commiseration with ancient stories that they should be made pitiable with masks, language, and clothing, and in a word with the stage presentation, for the evil which is done or about to be done, being placed before our eyes by the means just mentioned, comes to appear near us, and what is near at hand, being done at the moment or going to be done, is the more piteous. For that reason such things as the outer garments and shirts of those who have suffered, and the words of those who are under the influence of the passions, especially when it appears that at the same time they are deserving of love and are virtuous, move us greatly. All the things that show that sufferings are near us, and that those who suffer are suffering unjustly, produce the greatest pity. This will suffice us on pity. . . .

FROM

Division VI

It remains, then, to treat the imitation of actions and traits less dignified and of a worse sort, which may be done by deriding and censuring them, and in that way teach men virtue, something usually done by comedies, in which the poet does not speak for himself but, in the same way as in tragedy, always brings in persons to speak and act. So it is also in pastoral eclogues, though in these there is sometimes utterance by the poet, as is apparent in Theocritus and Vergil. Comedy, then, imitates worse actions with speech, rhythm, and harmony, as does tragedy; and it imitates an action single, complete, and large, which has a beginning, a middle, and an end. But in this it differs from tragedy, that as tragedy carries on its teaching by means of pity and fear, comedy teaches by deriding and censuring things ugly and vile. . . . It suffices to know that comedy is an imitation of the wicked and the vicious, yet not in every extremity of the vices, but merely of that which is ugly, whence springs the ridiculous, which is an ugly defect without pain and without deaths; of the ridiculous we shall treat at length in its place.

Comedy, then, has the same substantial parts as tragedy, that is, the fable, the human traits, the thought, the words, the stage presentation, and the melody, because to make a comedy that would be perfect it is necessary to represent it on the stage, where it needs the chorus and melody. The comic fable, then, is made up of actions diverse from those of tragedy, and as it were contrary to them, because tragedy produces the effect of its teaching with pity, with tears, and with fear, which are sad things, while comedy does it with jokes and with laughter, which are pleasant things; hence as for tragedy are sought out piteous acts of great and illustrious men, so in comedy it is necessary to use jocose acts of persons of low rank and unknown, and as in tragedy there come about sorrows and deaths and it almost always ends in unhappiness, so in comedy, though there are some disturbances, they do not involve wounds and deaths, and all terminate in good, as weddings, peaceful agreements, and tranquillity, through which characters issue in peace from the scene. . . .

The moral type is that in which morals are most prominent, as the *Hecyra* of Terence, and the ridiculous is that in which jokes and ridiculous things prevail, as the *Menechmi* of Plautus, from which we have adapted the *Simillimi*. And nothing forbids that the same comedy should be simple and moral, as is the *Adelphi*, and double and moral, as is the *Hecyra*, simple and ridiculous, as is the *Aulularia*, and double and ridiculous, as the *Simillimi*. But it cannot at the same time be simple and double, for they are contraries. So he who wishes to compose a comedy well should first arrange the fable, that is, find the action and write a summary of it, and put it before his eyes, and consider well the moral traits, and see what is fitting and what is contrary or repugnant, and then put in the names, and insert the episodes, and treat it with excellent sententious sayings, and with words familiar, ornate, and suitable, as we have said about tragedy.

But comedy will differ from tragedy in that while in tragedy the actions and names are true, either all or the greater part, in comedy the actions and names are all invented by the poet, though Plautus in his *Amphitryo* did not do it, whence it is called a tragicomedy. Yet such a thing was not afterward imitated either by himself or by any other, but rather they have all abandoned true names, especially since in Athens, to restrain the license of comedy, which unjustly blamed and derided worthy men, it was established by law that in comedies no one should be permitted to call anyone by name; thence was derived the custom of the new comedies, in which no real names are introduced, but all are invented by the poet. Such names are formed either from countries, as in *Mysis* from *Mysia*, *Syrus* from *Syria*, or from cities, as *Messenius* from *Messina*, or from mountains or rivers, as *Pachinus* and *Alesa*, or from qualities, as is *Phaedria* meaning *joyous*, *Sophrona* meaning *prudent*, *Chremes* meaning *avaricious*, and the like. The formation of such names from traits or qualities of men is the best way and the most suitable to comedies of all, and the plan of forming them from the Greek language is good, because they are formed more appropriately, although they are also appropriately derived from the Latin, *Mizio* from *mitis*,[8] and from the vulgar tongue, as *Scovoletto* from *scovolo*,[9] and the like.

In this place we shall especially treat of the ridiculous, which, as Aristotle says, pertains to comedy. Of the ridiculous Aristotle says in his *Rhetoric* that he has dealt with it in his *Poetics*; perhaps it was in the part dealing with comedy, which has been lost through the ravages of time, and with it the treatment of the ridiculous which was included in it. So it is necessary to investigate it, which we shall do according to a method other than that used by Marcus Tullius and Fabius Quintilianus, because their method was rather oratorical than philosophical. The ridiculous then, as Aristotle says, is a mild form of the ugly, and is a defect and an ugliness that is neither deadly nor painful. Tully then and Quintilian, who perhaps took their idea from Aristotle, say, not badly, that the place and seat of the ridiculous is in ugliness and deformity, but from what cause this ugliness moves laughter they do not say, and the part of Aristotle which perhaps gave it is lost. Hence we shall investigate it in the following manner.

It is evident that laughter comes from the delight and pleasure of him who laughs, and this pleasure cannot come to him except through the senses, that is from seeing, hearing, touching, tasting, and smelling, or from the memory of the pleasures they have had from something, or from the hope that they are going to have them. Such pleasure does not come from every object that delights and pleases the senses but merely from those objects that have some share of ugliness, for if a man sees a beautiful lady or a beautiful jewel or something similar that pleases him,[10] he does not laugh, nor does he laugh on hearing music in praise of him, nor on touching, tasting, and smelling things that to the touch, the taste, and the smell are pleasant and grateful; rather these together with pleasure bring admiration and not laughter. But if the object that is presented to the senses has some mixture of ugliness, it moves laughter, as an ugly and distorted face, an inept movement, a silly word, a mispronunciation, a rough hand, a wine of unpleasant taste, or a rose of unpleasant odor moves laughter at once, and those things especially cause laughter from which better qualities were hoped, because then not merely our senses but also our hopes are slightly offended, and such pleasure as this comes to us because man is by nature envious and malicious,[11] as is clearly seen in little children, for almost all of them are envious, and always delight to do evil, if they are able. It can be observed also that man never naturally delights in the good of others, except through accident, that is, through some good which he hopes from it for himself, as Plautus says:

> There is no one who would not envy the obtaining of something pleasant.

Hence if anyone sees that someone finds some money, he does not laugh or take pleasure, but rather is envious, but if he sees that someone falls into the mud and soils himself, he laughs, because that evil which does not come on ourselves, as Lucretius says, is always pleasant to observe in others. But if we have like sufferings, the sight of them in others does not move us to laughter, for no hunchback laughs at another hunchback nor a lame man at another lame man, unless he thinks that these ills are in him less ugly than in the other. If the evils, then, that we see in others are deadly and painful, as are wounds, fevers, and injuries, they do not move laughter, but rather pity through fear that similar ills may come to ourselves or to some of our circle, for we think those who belong to us parts of ourselves. The small ill, then, not painful or deadly, that we see or hear in others, as ugliness of body, and folly of mind, when it is not or we believe it is not in ourselves, is what pleases us or makes us laugh.

As man is composed of mind and body, so ugliness in him is double, of the mind and the body, and the special deformities of the mind are ignorance, imprudence, credulity, and the like, which often depend one on the other, and the therefore in jokes we laugh at the ignorance, imprudence, and credulity of someone else, and especially when we see them in persons who are thought substantial and of good intelligence, for in such as these many times opinion and hope are deceived. To such instances of ugliness may be reduced all the jokes and jibes written by Boccaccio and the Courtier, and likewise all the ridiculous stories and jokes and clever sayings gathered up by Tully, Quintilian, Boccaccio, Poggio, and the Courtier.[12] It is well to know that if the ugliness and deformity of mind we have spoken of are great, such as betrayals and perjuries, they do not move laughter, but disdain, and are condemned and rebuked, as are lies, exhibitions of ignorance, and similar awkward things of mind or body. But if they are slight, they move laughter and are mocked at and delight is taken in them. All these ridiculous deformities are either pointed out, or narrated, or observed with some urbanity. Those which are pointed out are of the sort that Tully assigns to Crassus, who, when speaking against Helvius Mancia, said: "Now I shall show you who you are." Mancia urgently answered: "Who will you show that I am?" Then Crassus, turning, pointed with his finger to a Cimbrian shield of Marius on a shop, on which was carved the face of a Frank, brutal and distorted, which certainly resembled the face of Mancia, at which everyone began to laugh.[13]

Deformities can also be shown in narrative only, as was that of Strepsiades in Aristophanes,[14] who was narrating the disagreements between himself and his wife; since he was a countryman and avaricious, and she a citizen and proud, they disagreed in many things, and especially in the name they were going to give the son who was born to them; Strepsiades wished to give him the name of Pennysaver, and the proud mother the name of Horsemaster; in the end they agreed to give each half a name, to wit Savehorse or Phidippides. Such a story as this excites laughter everywhere, because it throughout makes plain the ignorance and avarice of the countryman, and the pride and imprudence of the lady, which are all of them deformities of mind. Such deformities either of body or mind can be pointed out with some word, an action called urbanity;[15] an example appeared when someone indicated the deformity of body of Testio Pinario, who twisted his chin in speaking as if he had a nut in his mouth, and his adversary said to him: "Say what you wish, when you have cracked the nut you have in your mouth." Similarly a buffoon pointed out a deformity in the face of the Emperor Vespasian of such a sort that it appeared to strain to get away from the body; the emperor asking him if he were going to say something, the buffoon replied: "I will speak when you have got away from your body." Also M. Bartolomeo Pagello noted the deformity of mind in M. Lionardo da Porto, who said it was easy to provide so that the hail would not injure Vicentio by placing some cannon in certain mountains above which the hail-bringing clouds were accustomed to come, and when those clouds were seen coming to discharge the cannon into them so that they would burst and let out their water and the hail would not fall on the lower ground. Pagello then put his hand into his purse and took out two *marcelli* and gave them to M. Lionardo, saying: "Please take these, and say that it was I who have spoken of so fine a remedy." At this everyone laughed, and so with urbanity he made plain the folly of such a remedy, without answering at all. This urbanity is a thing brief, sharp, swift, and excellently fitted to keen and ridiculous sayings, and it appears in speaking and answering, and it is a good source for anything involving ridicule, such as ambiguity, deceiving the expectation, scoffing at the nature of another, comparison with something still more deformed, dissimulation, inept sayings, and rebuking the silly; and all of the aforesaid things have many parts that excite ridicule, either in denying or refuting or defending or diminishing; and these all move laughter because they point out some deformity either in oneself or in some other.

An example of ambiguity is that sonnet of Antonio Alemani on Alemano Salviati. This Alemano was with other citizens on a committee which did not wish to please the said Antonio in something he wished; so Alemano to excuse himself said to Antonio: "It is not I, that is, I am not the one who did not wish to please you." Antonio, feigning to think that he said that he was not Alemano Salviati, wrote as follows:

> Alemano says to me, I am not I,
> And this is not true, because he is he.
> But when he denies that he is himself
> He wonders whether he will speak the truth of my action.

Here the ridiculous rises from the ambiguity of *I am not I*, with which he feigns ignorance in himself and a lie in Alemano, both of which are deformities of the mind. Much like this was that circumstance of Scipio Nasica and Ennius the poet that Tully tells. Nasica, going to the house of Ennius and asking if he were at home, heard Ennius answer the servant that he was not. A few days later, Ennius, going to the house of Nasica, asked if he were there, and Nasica answered in a loud voice that he was not, and Ennius said: "What, do I not know your voice?" Then Nasica said: "You are not very courteous, for the other day when your servant told me you were not at home I believed him, and now you are not willing to believe me when I tell you myself." Here are two defects of mind that produce the ridiculous, one the ignorance that Nasica feigns in himself in wishing that Ennius should believe he was not at home when he heard he was there; the other is the lie which is revealed in Ennius who when he was at home had his servant say he was not there. Similar humor was that in a reply of Pievano Arlotto, who, finding himself on a street in Florence and passing a beautiful and bold girl, said to his companion: "This is a beautiful lady." The bold girl turned toward him and said: "I cannot say as much for you." Pievano instantly answered: "Yes indeed, since you wish to tell a lie of me, as I have of you." Thus Pievano, by feigning in himself deformity of mind that led him to lie, discovered the deformity of an ungrateful spirit in the lady who censured a man who praised her, and at the same time he made game of deformity of body in her. These two comic conditions are not very different from that above of Alemani, except that these do not come from ambiguity as does that.

Of this ambiguity there are many kinds, such as the changing of letters which by some is called a pun, as Garifilo to Garofolo, Luca Michiele to Licamelculo,[16] and the like; it is also done by means of some addition, as *moral* and *mortal*, as in that sonnet of Aretino as follows:

> Though you are, I confess it,
> Both poet and mortal philosopher
> Without a *sesino* and without natural.[17]

Here the ridiculous is produced not merely with the ambiguity, by saying *mortal* in place of *moral*, but also with irony, when he says, *Though you are, I confess it*, and with synecdoche, by saying *sesino*, which is a kind of money, in place of money, which is the genus, and then he turns again to ambiguity, saying *without natural*, in place of *without natural philosophy*, for ambiguity, as though always feigning ignorance in itself, reveals deformity in others, as equally irony does, with which Aretino and Bernia produced many ridiculous passages, and not merely with these but also with sarcasm, allegory, hyperbole, and the other things we have mentioned. . . .

That which deceives expectation is the mode most appropriate to the ridiculous, because it reveals the imprudence of the one who waits, as in the jest of Giovanni Cannaccio with Prior Pandolfini, who believed for a certainty that Frate Girolamo Savonarola was a saint and that though then dead he should rise up; therefore he said one day to Cannaccio, who was one of those who sentenced the Frate to death: "What will you say, Giovanni, when you see Frate Girolamo raised from the dead?" Cannaccio responded, contrary to the expectation of Pandolfini: "I shall say that next time we ought to have him hanged." But here since the expectation is deceived in so grave a matter, it does not move so much laughter as if the thing were less serious, because every slight thing in which a man deceives himself moves laughter not only in others but also in the man himself, when he understands it, that is, when he sees he has uttered one word instead of another or has taken up one thing for another. Therefore the *Amphitryo* of Plautus and *I Simillimi* are very gay comedies because the persons in them many times deceive themselves, and because of resemblance take one person for another, and speak to one when they think they speak to another; thus they reveal that they themselves and the others are in some slight way ignorant, and frequent ridiculous situations arise. . . .

A laugh is also roused by an acute response to some proverb that is uttered, such as was made by Maestro Gerardo Bolderico, a Veronese physician, to that lady of the Malaspini who asked from him a remedy for her only son. The physician answered nothing was wrong with the boy and she should not wish to have medicine given to him, but the lady still insisted that he should use some remedy, and wishing to excuse herself for such insistence, did it with a proverb, saying to him: "O sir, he who has but one eye often wipes it." The physician added: "And wipes it so much that he digs it out." The comedy sprang from the revelation of the imprudence of that lady, who believed that medicine would help one who was not sick.

And finally all the comic passages in Aristophanes, Plautus, Terence, Apuleius, and others, and in some Italian authors, as Boccaccio, Burchiello, Poggio, Pulci, Ariosto, Aretino, Bernia, and Mauro, all show and point out little or ordinary deformities of body or of mind of some person, and with pointing out or otherwise revealing in different ways those deformities, produce ridicule, and pointed sayings, and jests. And what we have said will suffice for the ridiculous, so far as it pertains to comedy. It is manifest, then, that words in comedy should not attempt to be lofty and sounding and lordly, as do those of tragedy, but should aim to be low, clear, and urbane, and that the metaphors and other figures should be easy and such as are common in ordinary speech, which comedy especially imitates. Comedy therefore should not have diversity of foreign expressions or things that may make it appear foreign, nor should it show too much pains or too much ornament, because, as we have said, words very splendid and labored hide ideas and human traits; moreover expressions not in common use produce elevation, a thing not fitting to comedy.

NOTES

1. Trissino's epic of *Italy Liberated from the Goths* is unrhymed, as is his tragedy of *Sofonisba*, except for irregular use of rhyme in the choruses and related passages, somewhat as in Milton's *Samson Agonistes*, though more generally.
2. For example the hymn by Thomas a Celano beginning

> Dies irae, dies illa
> Solvet saeclum in favilla,
> Teste David cum Sybilla.

3. These forms are explained by Trissino in Division IV.
4. Author of *On the Arrangement of Words* and other works. He taught oratory at Rome in the first century B.C.
5. Cf. Aristotle, *Poetics*, XV, 54b8.
6. The word is *furore*. He has in mind the *furor poeticus*, though the actual allusion is to more general passions. See Aristotle, *Poetics*, XVII, first par., above.
7. *Poetics*, XIX, first par.
8. Gentle.

9. Sponge.
10. Cf. Sidney, *Defense*, sect. 50.
11. Cf. Dryden, *Of Dramatic Poesy*, sect. 59.
12. Castiglione in the *Courtier*, Bk. II, secs. 42–89, discusses comedy, with illustrative examples. His discussion, like that of Trissino, owes much to Cicero's remarks in *De oratore* II, 54–71.
13. The story is told by Cicero, *De oratore*, II, 66, but assigned to Crassus by Pliny, *Natural History*, XXXV, 8.
14. In the *Clouds*.
15. In the Latin sense of cleverness.
16. *Garofolo* means *clove*; the English equivalent would be to call Mr. Clive, Mr. Clove. The modification of Luca Michiele seems to involve a diminutive of camel.
17. The pun on *natural* is obscene in both English and Italian.

Giovambattista Giraldi Cinthio
1504–1573

Giraldi Cinthio was born in Ferrara, where he taught rhetoric at the University of Ferrara from 1541 to 1562. He composed a number of tragedies, of which *Orbecche* (1541) is perhaps the most famous. Giraldi is the first Renaissance tragedian to stage atrocities in full view of the audience, thus violating Aristotle's dictum that they should be reported and not seen. He also wrote a collection of *novelle* entitled *Ecatommitti (The Hundred Stories)*, from which Shakespeare took the plots for *Othello* and *Measure for Measure*.

As a literary theorist, Giraldi made his reputation as a "modern." That is, he asserted the independence of contemporary literature from the principles of construction formulated by Aristotle and Horace. In his work on the romance form, Giraldi declares, "The laws given by Aristotle apply only to the forms of poetry which are of a single action; and . . . all poetic compositions which contain deeds of heroes are not included within the limits that Aristotle has set for poets who write poems having a single action." The consequence of this declaration is the liberation of the romance—Ariosto's *Orlando Furioso* was the preeminent, and highly controversial, example of this genre—from the rules governing Aristotelian tragedy. On an even broader level, Giraldi insists upon the principle that a work of art must be judged according to the standards of its own time rather than according to "eternal" principles of classicism. Giraldi writes in his work on the romance, for instance, that ". . . it would be a great error now to follow Homer in those things which, though suitable to his time, were unsuitable to the majority of Rome and similarly are unsuitable in our times. . . ." In such a manner, Giraldi went directly against the prevailing current of his own time, in which, as Allan Gilbert remarks, " . . . the theorist tended to look with veneration to the past and to consider the present as less authoritative."

In both the *Address* from *Orbecche* and *The Apology for Dido* Giraldi defends his tragedies against Aristotelian dictates. *On the Composition of Romances* occasioned a great controversy with Giovanni Battista Pigna, a former student. Pigna had his *I romanzi (The Romance)* published before Giraldi's, but Giraldi accused him of having stolen his ideas. Giraldi's work is modeled upon Aristotle's *Poetics* even though Giraldi opposes

Aristotle in most of his theory of the romance form. The centerpiece of his opposition to Aristotelian theory (with regard to the romance) lies in his privileging of variety in the plot over Aristotelian unity. It is Giraldi's contention that Aristotle's rules apply only to the unified action of the tragedy; in the romance, according to Giraldi, variety is the "spice of delight." Giraldi also declares the poets "should not so restrain their liberty within the bounds set by their predecessors that they dare not set foot outside the old paths," and comes down squarely on the side of artistic innovation. On the other hand, Giraldi believes that the principles of verisimilitude and decorum as well as the moral function of the literary work combine to restrain the excesses of artistic license.

An Address to the Reader by the Tragedy of Orbecche, and the selections from *The Apology for Dido* and *On the Composition of Romances,* all translated by Allan H. Gilbert, are reprinted with his permission from *Literary Criticism: Plato to Dryden,* edited by Allan H. Gilbert (Detroit: Wayne State University Press, 1962). © 1962 by Allan H. Gilbert.

An Address to the Reader

By the Tragedy of Orbecche

Now, dear reader, my sad conclusion has come about, and if I could have disposed of myself according to my wish, I would have remained in concealment and not have annoyed anyone with my plaints and lamentations. For though I know that the wisest set the royal gravity of tragedy ahead of every sort of poetry because they well understand that nothing exists in the world better fitted to enable the human race to live a more excellent life, yet I see wantonness so increased (thanks to the decline of the world) that not only is tragedy not in esteem but its regal name is odious to many. Yet since the wishes of others have conquered my will and I am constrained to issue out into the light in my own despite, if there is any pity in you I pray that you may be willing to be rather a kind and benignant censor than harsh and rude, in order that you may not add to my sorrow, which is of itself hard because of the affliction that lacerates me. And if perhaps it seems that I do not appear in the proud habit that befits me, let the force of my sufferings excuse me, for they have so deprived me of the desire to ornament myself that I have sometimes envied the rudest pastorals; in their humble garments there is repose, while the grave and royal are full of care.

And though I have sprung from a recent event and not from ancient history, I do not deserve the less praise, for he who with a just eye looks on the truth will see that without censure a new tragedy may be permitted to rise from new matter and new names. Nor should I be blamed because my prologue is separated from the acts themselves, for the times in which I am born and my novelty and some other special reason makes me carry the prologue with me. Indeed he would be insane who in his effort to use nothing except what was customary among the ancients should abandon what without dishonor the place and the time require. And if I am not in everything like the ancients, it is because I was born just now of a young father and can appear only as young; perhaps my green youth will remove the displeasure you feel at my deep sadness. Nor should it be held a fault that I am divided into acts and scenes, but it should make me appear much more pleasing, for as a man would make a strange figure in the world who did not have limbs distinct from each other, so I think it would be disagreeable to see me confused in one large whole. And indeed Seneca and the ancient Romans realized how wrong the Greeks appear in this. And that I should be large and have my parts great beyond what is proper is not natural. Yet, on the other hand, greater beauty reigns in bodies that are larger than others of their species.

And if there is anyone for whom it is hard to hear reasons able to move to pity a soul disposed to revenge, perhaps Malecche may seem tedious;[1] such a one may shorten that part as he wishes, for I shall not contend with him about it. Nor should it appear strange to you that the ladies I have in my company are wiser than some think is suitable for them, for in addition to the light that a woman like a man has from reason, the great wisdom possessed by that lady whose high and royal name in its splendor I hold hidden within me, with the greatest reverence and the greatest honor, has the power to make evident to every fair judgment not merely how much worth a gentle lady can have in herself, but that in prudence and in discretion (when the envy of others is banished) she can be the equal of the wisest man in the world. In addition let it not appear strange to you that I do not have Cyruses, Dariuses, and Statiras,[2] although I confess that I am from Persia. From such blame my birth can excuse me, if one looks closely, nor to a man who knows what desperation and deep sorrow can accomplish in the heart of a woman should it appear hard that a daughter plunged into sorrow without hope should have inflicted violent death on her cruel father. And though the savage tyrant comes to his death, no one will ever accuse me of wickedness who with a sane eye sees how much pity is roused in human hearts by the fate of those from whom I have my origin.

And if the Stagirite,[3] who saw and knew and wrote so much, and initiated the art of composing tragedies, has taught me to cause the queen from whom I take my name to die by her own hands on the stage to end her evil condition, there is nothing very strange in my departing from the laws of the Venusine at this point and wishing that in the sight of the people she should violently sla herself with a dagger on the stage.[4]

There are those who, intent on the matter of elocution, ever anxiously seek for swelling words and strong epithets and if they write a lament fill their pages with blind horrors and bloody dead men from Acheron, and with black and horrid nights, and if they write of gladness nothing other is heard than flowers, herbs, shadows, caves, waves, soft breezes, rubies, pearls, sapphires, topazes, and gold. I should say that to such selection the force of sorrow that oppresses me makes me unfitted, and I have wished rather to have for a guide nature with fit ornament than feigned art with pompous words. There are many today who write in the vulgar tongue and abandon the custom of approved authors, trusting in themselves, since they were born in a place where, as it seems to them, the vulgar speech is perfect, though in fact it is without value if ancient authors do not give it honor. To them you can easily respond, if perchance they wish to speak against me because in part I have followed the great Tuscan who for the sake of Laura exchanged the Arno for the Sorgue, and the good Certaldese, those two eternal and shining lights of the sweet vulgar speech,[5] that such was the Roman and such the Greek tongue as the vulgar is now, and both gained their renown not frrom common speech but from writers who showed themselves excellent in them. And they were esteemed in proportion as one or the other was like those three or four or six who have made the choice of the best from the speech of the illiterate vulgar, and whoever sought fame for his use of words followed those good authors and did not rely on having been born in Greece or in Rome. It is certainly true that since this pleasing common speech is alive, it is permitted to anyone who writes in this language to use some words (selected, however, with excellent judgment) that are not found in the aforesaid Tuscans. Therefore to those who have limited our language to the words used by the two famous Tuscans (and there are many today who hold such an opinion), I prefer that the divine Bembo should make response, if there is a word in me that is not found in them, the divine Bembo, who has freed the vulgar tongue from its dark prison and from the obscure kingdom of Dis with a plectrum of happier sound than Orpheus used for his beloved wife. And may there also be an answer from the gentle Trissino, who with his song was the first to bring tragedy from the Tiber and the Ilissus to the waves of the Arno. And from the great Molza, whose honored name flies everywhere with sounds of fame. And the good Tolomei, who with a new method has already adapted verses in the vulgar tongue to Latin numbers and the Roman form. And that one who from Thebes beyond the frozen Alps has put into Tuscan dress the piteous sister of Polynices; I mean Alamanni, who because of my rare good fortune saw me come on the stage. The happy and exquisite abilities of these men, with the others who have followed in their steps, as well as those two celebrated authors, should be esteemed as they deserve. Seeking to enrich this language with firm choice and sound judgment they have preferred to obtain by effort, in praiseworthy liberty, words that would set forth their thoughts rather than with fetters on their feet to remain silent in prison. Leaving then to you and to them such a burden, I shall wait under the secure protection of that nobleman through whose favor I have come out, hoping that some other, aroused by my words, may show tragedies in a more noble dress, more worthy of honor, and of rarer beauty; (if only it be not out of harmony with my sorrow) I shall seek with all my power to imitate their virtue, gifts, and rare and wondrous beauty.

NOTES

1. His part is that of a prudent adviser, a frequent, almost conventional, character in Renaissance tragedies presenting kings; his function is to utter "wise saws and modern instances."
2. First ed. *Satipne*.
3. Aristotle, *Poetics*, XI, end.
4. Horace (the Venusine), *Art of Poetry*, 185–7.
5. Petrarch and Boccaccio.

FROM

THE APOLOGY FOR DIDO

I shall now deal with the objections that have been made to my work. The first is that it would be better if I had composed this tragedy in prose rather than in verse. The second is that Aristotle objects to the introduction of gods into tragedy. The third is that it is blameworthy to divide plays suited to the tragic stage into acts and scenes, because it was never done by the Greeks, from whom should be taken the laws and the true rules for composing plays creditably as Aristotle worked them out. The fourth is that the objector does not praise the use of a great number of interlocutors. The fifth is that the speeches people make about themselves are not according to decorum. The sixth is that I do not give in my *Dido* that image of the *Oedipus Tyrannus* from which Aristotle has taken his precepts, as from the true idea of the perfection of tragedy. The seventh is that it is too long in the presentation. All of these I see are the result of the slight understanding of the objector.

Coming then to the objections, I say to the first that I do not know why this great censor should wish tragedies to be composed in prose, since not merely Aristotle in his *Poetics* says they should be composed in verse, and shows of what sort the verses should be, but we read the same thing in Horace, and besides this it can be seen that the tragic writers have all composed their works in verse. . . . But Ariosto revealed his ideas about material for the stage in his comedies, for though they were first issued in prose, on seeing their unfitness in that guise, he turned them into verse, for it appeared to him that prose was not at all suitable for such plays. It likewise appeared to Signor Trissino that prose was not at all adapted to tragedy. Therefore, he composed his *Sofonisba* in that sort of verses which he before anyone else most suitably gave to the stage in place of the iambic which the Greeks and Latins used. For it appeared to him that these verses loosed from the obligation of rhyme carried with them the same reason for being as the senarii, composed of iambics, in the Greek and the Latin tongues, namely, that they are similar to the familiar speech of our times, and fall, like the iambics, from the mouths of speakers (though they do not know it) in common speech. To the opinion of this excellent tragic writer Ruscelli conformed in his *Rosmonda*, which appeared with great acclaim soon after the *Sofonisba*, and I believe that in the future all those who give themselves to such compositions and seek honor from them will conform. And this is enough to answer anyone who ill says that our language does not have verses suitable to the stage.

Aristotle blames the introduction on the stage of gods who through their sole power and authority bring about the solution of the plot. This solution should come from the nature of the subject and the resourcefulness of the poet, and when both of these are lacking and the machine that carries the god is introduced to end the plot, as in the *Iphigenia among the Taurians* and in the

Andromache and the other similar plays, and in the *Philoctetes* of Sophocles, it merits no praise at all. And that this was the opinion of Aristotle is perfectly clear from the passage in which he accuses Euripides, for though he says that dramatist can be called supremely tragic and praises him for most ingeniously tying the knot of a plot, he says that nonetheless some of his solutions are inept, and Aristotle says this because Euripides in a solution resorts to the machine. Thence it appears that he does not condemn the introduction of the gods in the beginning and in the other parts of a tragedy, but only in the solution, if it is brought about merely by the intervention of the god. . . . But, returning to Aristotle, if he had so blamed the introduction of the gods in the beginning (as is seen in Sophocles and Euripides), he would not have said that Euripides tied the knot ingeniously and would not (as I have said) have blamed merely the solution but the beginning also and the other parts, since in the tying of the knot gods appear in many dramas. Besides that, it seems to me it can reasonably be said that when the solution necessarily requires a god, it is not merely not unfitting to introduce him but it would be an error to leave him out. In the *Io*, for example, Minerva was suitably brought in to make known that Io was a child of Apollo; in this way the knot is easily untied, as Mercury had suggested at the beginning.

Now passing from this objection to that on the division of tragedies into acts and scenes, I confess that the Greeks did not use this device; among them the stage never remained empty, because the chorus was always there, as is made clear not merely by the authority of Aristotle, but by the Greek plots that have survived the injuries of time. But I hold it certain that in this matter the Romans were much wiser than the Greeks, because it is not probable that great and lordly persons would wish to consider matters of great importance, such as appear in tragedy, in the midst of a multitude of people, even though these were their servants, but in matters which deal with honor or shame or the life or death of great persons, they have with them merely their secretaries, counselors, and other prudent and wise persons in whom they confide and who have been chosen by them for such matters, and surely they often speak with them alone of important affairs; nor is it probable that in the course of their activities and in their considertions pertaining to an important act they would speak of them to others about the court in the midst of a multitude. If the Greeks did not understand this matter of decorum, the Romans did, and knew how to give to the majesty of royal actions the persons who would manage them in such a way as would be fitting to so great majesty. . . . Homer sometimes did not consider what fitted the majesty of the actions he had in hand.

In regard to the fourth objection, that on the number of the speakers, it is manifest than in ancient tragedies their numbers is not certain and defined, for some of them have six, some seven, and sometimes eight and nine are seen, and sometimes ten and eleven, nor are those lacking which have twelve and thirteen; this has led me to think that the interlocutors can be as many as suffice to develop the parts of the plot to an end magnificently and without confusion. And I am the more confirmed in this opinion when I see that the ancients who have given their judgment on the Greek tragedies praise highly those that carry with them the largest number of persons; the reason for this number, as it seems to me, is that regal actions are on a grand scale and individuals of various conditions appear in them on the side of him who suffers as much as of him who is the cause of the action; such actions cannot be carried to an end without a great deal of speaking by the characters. Therefore it seems to me that the number of persons introduced represents in large measure the majesty of the action, if only that number of persons is judiciously brought in. This is especially true when the kings of diverse, nations with their courts appear on the stage, for I know that Your Excellency ⟨Ercole II, duke of Ferrara⟩ saw in the time of your illustrious father how unhappily that comedy turned out that was represented with but five actors, and with what great difficulty (though the argument was pleasing) it was carried to its conclusion, for the spectators were bored by having the same persons in their eyes and ears all the time. And if this monotony appears strange in comedy, where actions of the common people only and of not much importance are seen, how clearly should it be rejected in the presentation of regal affairs, and especially in our times, when the courts of great princes are crowded with a multitude of the most noble persons. Therefore, so long as unnecessary actors are not introduced and they do not make confusion but take the parts and produce the effects suitable to them, plenty rather than poverty of persons will make the conduct of the stage appear always more magnificent and more pleasing. The argument from the *Oedipus Tyrannus* is of no avail, for Aristotle does not adduce that story because of the number of the persons solely because of the quality of the knot and the solution of the argument and because if that tragedy could properly prescribe the number to all the others there would not be seen in some ancient tragedies a greater number and in others a smaller number. And this greater number is so much the more fitting to the *Dido* because it contains the suites of two royal persons of diverse nations who have courts befitting the rank they hold. . . .

And the objection of my critic that it is not according to verisimilitude that kings should discourse in public on their affairs and that they should walk alone reasoning within themselves is so foolish that I blush to respond to him truly; if his objection should hold, it would not be proper to introduce on the stage the discussions of kings and queens with their secretaries and councilors and their servants, for none of the said discussions are carried on in public and yet they are introduced on the stage. But poor fellow that he is, does he not understand that though the stage represents a city, such speeches are not thought of otherwise than if they were carried on in the most secret and concealed rooms of the rulers? Hence they are shown on the stage in the same way as if they spoke in their chambers, for so stage presentation requires. And this speech in soliloquy appears to me to bring so much of regal gravity to the action that the omission would be rather a fault than the reverse. And this was so thoroughly approved by Roman practice that in it soliloquies were very frequent, both in comedies and in tragedies. And they were able to do it properly, gradually bringing the actors on the stage according to the requirements of the play. Wherefore only those were found there (as it would be in our times) who were speaking either alone or accompanied, with the chorus completely off the stage except when it was introduced as a speaker or when it divided one act from another. And I do not know why, in confirmation of his opinion, he brings up the argument that the spectators hear them speak. For he should know that the spectators are not to be regarded by the actors, who speak as though they were in their own houses and in their private rooms where they would naturally speak of their affairs.

And because this is so manifest of itself that to set it forth completely is superfluous, I will turn to respond to the sixth objection that he has made against me, that is that the *Dido* is not like the *Oedipus Tyrannus*. And this I concede to him without question, with respect to the material, since the subject of the *Oedipus Tyrannus* is such that one like it has never existed before, does not now, and probably never will again. And if Aristotle selected this play as a sort of Idea for the composition of tragedy, he did it with the judgment he has used in all his other compositions, for this material is truly unique among the others. And he who was the author of the drama shows without any doubt a marvelous acuteness of ability, because the plot is excellently knit and loosed. And Sophocles found the material so disposed and had little trouble in making it into a tragedy, and needed only to ornament it with words fitting the subject. But if we wish to respect the judgment of this slanderer we shall be obliged to say that all the tragedies that have been composed before and after the *Oedipus Tyrannus* are of no value, for there is none that is like it in subject. And if all the other Greek and Latin plays must for this reason be of no value, I do not intend to feel shame if also this of mine and the others which I have composed on the commission of Your Excellency or because of the desire I have to be of avail to the men of this age and of our language, to the best of my knowledge and ability, suffer the same fate. But if the desire my critic has to oppose me does not blind the eyes of his intellect, he will be able plainly to see what is evident to all the judicious, namely that however much Aristotle esteemed the *Oedipus*, nonetheless he did not have so little esteem for the others that he did not avail himself also of them in giving ordinances and laws for the praiseworthy composition of tragic matter. I confess then without any concealment that the *Dido* in its matter is diverse for the *Oedipus Tyrannus*. But I do not wish to concede that in the parts which are proper to tragedy and in workmanship it is not of the same sort as the *Oedipus* so far as was permitted by the subject taken from Vergil that I had before me. And if perhaps I have sometimes departed from the rules given by Aristotle in order to conform to the customs of our times, I have done so after the example of the ancients, for it may be seen that Euripides did not begin his stories as did Sophocles and that, as I just said, the Romans arranged their plots in yet another way than did the Greeks, and besides this Aristotle himself has conceded it to me. For he does not forbid at all, when it is demanded either by place or time or the quality of the matters dealt with, to depart somewhat from those arts which he reduced to the precepts that he gave us.

FROM

ON THE COMPOSITION OF ROMANCES

If a good poet should set himself to treat the deeds of Hercules or of Theseus . . . and should wish in a single poem to describe the whole life and all the illustrious actions of either one in order to put before the eyes of the reader the honored and praiseworthy life of a brave man, as Xenophon did for Cyrus in his *Cyropaedia* and as perhaps Statius wished to do in his *Achilleid* and as Silius did for Hannibal, I do not believe it would be unfitting to commence from the beginning of their lives and go through them to the end, for such a poem would not be written without splendor in the composition and without the pleasure and profit of the reader. For if we are glad to read in prose the lives of Themistocles, Coriolanus, Romulus, and other excellent men, why should it be less pleasing and less profitable to read them when arranged in verses by a noble and wise poet who knows how the lives of heroes should be written in verse in the guise of history as an example to mankind? I believe also that Suidas had such a poem in mind when he said the epic, which is not other than heroic composition in verse, was history, for he does not hold it improper to set forth in verse, in the manner of history, the life of a man who fully deserves the name of hero. And as the composition of history begins with the beginning of things,[1] so works dealing with the whole life of a man open with the first of his illustrious deeds. And if in the cradle he gave sign of his greatness, with the cradle should begin the actions of his life. And if you say to me that Vergil did not do so for Aeneas nor Homer for Achilles in the *Iliad* and for Ulysses in the *Odyssey*, it seems to me proper to answer that both were attempting poems of a single action and not the poem that follows the style and manner of history. And though it appeared to Aristotle that if a man set out to produce such a composition it would be infinite, and therefore he did not praise it,[2] yet I am of the opinion (and I wish to speak with all the reverence I feel for so great a writer as Aristotle) this is not a sufficient cause to deter a judicious poet from undertaking such a work. There are a thousand means of shortening a work without giving up the description of the whole life of the man on whom the poet has set out to write, such as to have some things predicted by a diviner, to have others painted, and still others narrated. In this way can be treated all events not so splendid as to deserve such description as the others. By these means the poet will keep the work from surpassing its proper limits; for he should not wish to write of every thing so fully as to leave no place where the reader would not need to linger somewhat and exert a little effort to understand the passage. And that this can easily be done by an ingenious poet Ovid has shown in his *Metamorphoses*, for delivering himself with admirable skill from Aristotle's laws of art, he began the work with the beginning of the world and with astonishingly good sequence treated a great variety of things, and nonetheless covered them in a smaller number of books than Homer used in the *Iliad* and in the *Odyssey*, though each of these contained but a single action. Nor was Pisander among the Greeks unlike Ovid in treating a diversity of things, for he too began his work with the wedding of Juno and Jove and wrote in sequence all that happened up to his own times.[3] This is enough to show that the laws given by Aristotle have reference only to poems of a single action, and that all the poetical compositions that contain the deeds of heroes are included within the limits Aristotle gave the poets who wrote poems of single actions. . . .

If the subject of the work includes many and various actions of many and various men according to the make-up of the romances in our tongue, as we have indicated above, the work will take its origin from the matter that is of greatest importance and on which all the rest appears to depend; this appears in the practice of Ariosto and Boiardo. In this matter it should be considered that Ariosto, though he began his composition with Orlando and finished with Ruggiero, does not deserve on that account the censure that some give him, for he follows the order of the events that he has set before him. And just as Ruggiero was the last in the presentation, so his victory (if the intention of the writer is to be respected) concludes the whole work laudably. . . . It appears to me that if a poet is to deal with ancient material in the form of a romance it is better to apply himself to many actions of a man than to one only. For I think this method better suited to composition in the form of romances than is the use of a single action. Diversity of actions carries with it variety, which is the spice of delight, and gives the author wide scope for introducing episodes, or pleasant digressions, and for bringing in events which in poems dealing with a single action cannot come about save with some hint of blame. . . . And these digressions the poet should be very careful to treat in such a manner that one may depend on another and be well joined with a continuous thread and a continuous chain to the parts of the subject he has undertaken to treat, and that they may carry with them the probability that pertains to poetic fictions, as we shall show below in its place. For if these digressions were otherwise handled, the poem would become faulty and wearisome, just as it delights and pleases when they appear to arise in such a way as though born at the same birth with the main topic. . . . The writer should use great diligence that the parts of his work fit together like the parts of the body, as we said above. And in putting together the bony frame he will seek to fill in the spaces and make the members equal in size, and this can be done by inserting at suitable and requisite places loves, hates, lamentations, laughter, sports, serious things, beauties, descriptions of places, temples, and persons, fables both invented by the author himself and taken from the ancients, voyages, wanderings, monsters, unforeseen events, deaths, funerals, mournings, recognitions, things terrible and pitiable, weddings, births, victories, triumphs, single combats, jousts, tournaments, catalogues, laws, and other like matters, which perhaps are so many that no little effort must be made by him who would wish to recount them one by one. For there is nothing above the heavens or below,[4] nor in the very gulf of the abyss, which is not ready to the hand and choice of the judicious poet, and which cannot with varied ornaments adorn the whole body of his composition and bring it not merely to a beautiful but to a lovely figure, for such things give to all the parts their due measure and fit ornament in such proportion that there emerges a body well regulated and composed. . . .

And because I have said that the light of judgment should be one's guide in literary composition, I will make known that this judgment is acquired in two ways. One is conversation and discussion with men who are learned and accustomed to compose. . . . The other way in which judgment is acquired is to read and observe diligently what has been written by authors who have attained excellence in the narrative kind of poetry, and to select their virtues and seek with all diligence to follow them, because so doing will not only develop the judgment but also will stimulate the young poet to practice composition. For often there will work in him the spirit that caused the activity of the poet whose work he reads, and it will awaken in him a flame that little by little will set his mind on fire and fill him with the fury that the Greeks call enthusiam; roused by this, as though stung by a gadfly, he will be as it were forced to put on paper those things that are born in his mind because of his reading of that author. It has many times happened to me . . . that when I had no thought of composing anything, by the reading of some poet I have been forced in spite of myself to seize my pen and write out the things that have come into my mind. I believe this results from the sympathy of our souls with that of the poet, for since they are full of the seeds of things fit for harmony and the spirit of poetry, as soon as they are excited and aided they produce their fruit. Or it may be that this comes about because, as Aristotle says, poetry is natural to man, and our minds easily turn to that to which nature calls them. Therefore, the judicious reader should take the utmost care to flee from the vices of those he reads and to attend to their virtues only, for even in good authors are found things that should rather be avoided than followed. These, being mingled with other things that are full of good, enter unobserved, unless they are foreseen, into the minds of others, and at times because of the imperfection of our nature, which easily turns to the imperfect, have more power over readers than virtues have. Faults of this sort arise for the most part from the place where the good poets we read were born, or from the age in which they wrote, or from the nature of the poet. Vergil, by being too modest, has in matters of love often missed that graceful lasciviousness which went to excess in Ovid because he was of another nature than Vergil. . . . We see in the *Odyssey* of Homer many similar things, and specially where he has Nausicaä, the daughter of Alcinoüs, go to the river with other young women to wash clothes, which in our time would be impossible, I will not say to the daughter of a noble or a gentleman, but even of a simple artisan. This came about then because the poets of those early times followed a certain rough simplicity far remote from that majesty, with face royal and full of reverence, that appeared together with the excellence of the Roman empire; majesty which (though the greatness of the empire is past) has endured in a high degree even to our day. It would be a great error now to follow Homer in those things which, though suitable to his time, were unsuitable to the majesty of Rome and similarly are unsuitable in our times. . . . Though the age of Homer and the customs of his times and the singular virtue of that divine poet made such things tolerable in him, to do the same thing now would not be other than deliberately to select from the gold of his composition the dung (which came there not through the fault of the poet but through that of his age and time), and yet to suppose that one had selected the purest gold, as can be seen in the *Italia* of Trissino. . . . He who wishes to take literary material from Homer should therefore be careful to apply himself merely to those things which fit the age in which he writes and not to those which, though indeed they can be allowed in Homer for the reasons I have mentioned, appear very faulty today in those writers who need to have authority given to them that they may bestow it on things that are themselves lacking in it. . . . Though the compositions of Homer might offer material for composition to all the poets (as in fact they do give it to them), not all that Homer wrote was suitable in every time, in every age, in every condition of person. And what is taken from him needs to be better digested and brought to such perfection that it may fit in all its parts the time in which it is written, in such a way that what is taken from him may become better. This Marcus Tullius Cicero teaches us when he says that the Romans have taken many things from the Greeks, but that they then have made them better.[5]

Taking up again our discussion of arrangement . . . I say that when it is judiciously used it carries with it the chain with which one part is joined and combined with another just as the parts of the human body are bound together by the muscles and other ligatures. Hence it should be considered that the poetic romances have another sort of connection than the heroic poetry of the Greeks and the Latins, who composed poems of a single action, as did Homer and Vergil. . . . For these have joined one book with another merely in a continued narration with a certain relation which they have had with each other with respect to the matter. But the writers of romances of highest reputation have not been content merely with relation but have striven to do something further, namely to put in one canto after another, before they come to the continuation of the matter, something to prepare the way for what they intend to say. In this Ariosto has succeeded admirably. And because there are those who blame in him what to me appears worthy of the greatest praise, that is, the beginnings of his cantos,[6] it seems to me not out of place to give a reason for this and to show how much more praiseworthy it is to do this than to follow in this matter the order of Vergil and of Homer. And to make this plan better known, it will not be too much for me to run back to what I first said, namely that the romances are divided into cantos. For our poets either sing or pretend that they sing before great princes, according to the custom of the ancient Greeks and Latins. And so, because they promise at the ends of their cantos that they must at some other time sing what they have left unfinished and similarly at the beginnings of their cantos feign that they have come back to sing what they left unfinished, before they come to the matter that they wish to continue they need to dispose the minds of their hearers to attention. Therefore, they act like a good player on the lyre or the lute or any other similar instrument who, before he begins to play the tune for which he has taken up his instrument, seeks to catch the ears of those before whom he plays. So our poets, seeking to catch the attention anew from canto to canto, with some striking introduction rouse the minds of their hearers, and then come to the continuation of their matter, thus binding one canto to another with admirable workmanship. . . . There is also another difference to be found between the connections made by these poets of ours and by the ancient heroic poets. For as the writers of the romances set out to deal with the actions of many, they have not been able to continue one matter, fully connected, from one canto to another. But they have been obliged, in order to bring their work to any end, to speak first of one of their characters, then of another, and breaking off their first subject to enter upon the deeds of another character, and in this way to continue their materials to the end of the work, a thing they have done with remarkable skill. For, when they break off their narrative, they lead the reader to such a point before they make the break that they leave in the mind an ardent desire to return to take up the narrative again; this secures reading for the whole of their poem, since the principal matters always remain imperfect until the completion of the work. . . .

Perhaps the method of composition with a single hero deserves more praise than the other, for that beauty which the writers of romances seek to secure by means of variety in the actions of many men can in various ways properly be introduced into a poem which contains many actions by a single man, and so relieve the reader from the satiety of reading continually on the same subject. . . . Yet actions with a continuous thread can be arranged by an ingenious poet with admirable variety . . . but if this can be done by Homer and Vergil in the course of describing a single action in many books, how much better can it be done by him who describes many actions. . . . In the compositions of Homer and Vergil can be found loves, unexpected events, examples of courtesy and justice, injuries, liberality, vices, virtues, attacks, defenses, stratagems, faith, loyalty, fortitude, instances of worthlessness, hopes, fears, useful things, harmful things, and other episodes or digressions in great numbers, which in combination with the knitting together and disposition of the work can bring about so much variety and delight that the poem will become very attractive and pleasing, without those breaks in the action that have been used by our writers. Yet I do not blame the romancers, but rather praise them, since under the compulsion of the causes I have mentioned they cannot do otherwise if they wish to bring their works to an end. . . .

And now to speak generally, I say that authors who are judicious and skillful in composition should not so restrain their liberty within the bounds set by their predecessors that they dare not set foot outside the old paths. In addition to being a bad use of the gifts that mother nature has given them, such restraint would also prevent poetry from ever going beyond the bounds that one writer has given it, nor would it ever move its foot from the path in which the early fathers made it walk. Hence, knowing that it is permitted to architecture, to the military art, to rhetoric, to geometry, to music, and to the other arts that deserve the attention of a liberal spirit, to add, increase, diminish, and change, the great Vergil judged that such a procedure was still more appropriate to the poet in so far as to him is given the same power that the world has agreed to give to the excellent painter, of varying likenesses according to his own judgment as appears to him most to his purpose. Hence he shows in a great number of places how good writers, treading the same path in which the ancients have walked, can turn aside somewhat from the course already laid down, and leaving the beaten track, make their own ways to Helicon. Nor is this seen merely in the Latins but even in the Greeks, and among them in Homer, and much more in our Tuscan poets, whose compositions are of no less value in this language than were those of Greek and Latin poets in theirs, although the Tuscans did not follow in the ways of their predecessors, for, to speak truly, our tongue also has its forms of poetry, which are proper to it and do not belong to any other tongue or nation. Therefore no one should wish to confine the Tuscan poet within the limits to which the Greeks and the Latins are restricted . . . but he ought to walk in those paths which the best poets in our language have indicated with authority equal to that of the Greeks and Latins in their tongues.

And this is the reason why I have often laughed at those who have wished to bring the writers of romances under the laws of the art given by Aristotle and Horace, without considering that neither of them knew our language nor our manner of composing. Hence romances should not be subjected to classical laws and rules, but left within the limits set by those among us who have given authority and reputation to this species of poetry. As the Greeks and the Latins have derived the art of which they have written from their poets, so we should also take our art from our poets and hold to that form which the best writers or romances have given them. . . .

There is nothing marvelous in that which happens often or naturally, but there is in what appears impossible and yet is assumed to have happened if not in truth at least in fiction, such as the changes of men into trees, of ships into nymphs, of branches into ships, the union of the gods with men, and other such things which, though they are false and impossible, are still so accepted by custom that a composition cannot be pleasing in which these fables do not appear. And perhaps the poet is called poet for this more than for any other reason, for this name of poet signifies nothing other than maker.[7] And not because of his verses but chiefly through his subjects he is called a poet, in so far as these subjects are made and feigned by him in such a way that they are fit and suitable for poetry.[8] If he should merely take the things already made and not feign new ones, he would lose the name of poet, for he would not make but merely would recite what is made. . . .

While the historian is obliged to write only of deeds and actions that are true and as they really happened, the poet presents things not as they are but as they should be, that they may serve to instruct his readers about life.[9] And this is why, though the poets write of ancient affairs, they nonetheless seek to harmonize them with their own customs and their own age, introducing things unlike those of ancient times and suitable to their own.[10] This is seen in Vergil's account of Aeneas, for though he came from Troy, and the methods of sacrificing, conducting funeral ceremonies, and arming in Asia were not like those in Italy, yet Vergil has the Trojans sacrifice, bury, and fight according to Italian habits and not even according to the habits of the time before Rome was founded but those of the age of Octavian. And good poets have not merely taken this license, but have named things that did not exist in the time of the men of whom they write, not otherwise than as if in early times customs had been in use that appeared much later, as can be seen in Homer and Vergil. The writers of romances have also made some use of this method, for the reason that the poet (as I have said) does not write of things as they were or are, but as they should be, in order to give at once profit and delight by satisfying the men of that age in which they write,[11] a thing that is not permitted to those who write histories. . . .

I hold the belief of Aristotle, who says that the poet is far ahead of the historian in his power to benefit. And perhaps this is true because the historian, unable to part from the truth, is obliged to write of the vices no less than the virtues of men; hence he injures them as much as he benefits them. But the poet in his fictions imitates illustrious actions, presenting them not as they are but as they ought to be, and suitably accompanying things that have vice in them with the horrible and miserable (for the heroic poet does this as much as the tragic one when the material demands it), purges our minds from like passions and arouses them to virtue, as is seen in the definition that Aristotle gives of tragedy. . . .[12]

The function then of our poet, with respect to affecting morals, is to praise virtuous actions and to blame vices and by means of the terrible and the piteous to make them odious to the reader. In these two things the writers of the romances in our language are much more copious than were the Greek and Latin heroic poets, for, as they merely indicate blame and praise in such matters, our poets do it at length, especially in praising and blaming things of our times. This habit (so far as I can understand) was first introduced by Dante and passed on to the times that came after him.[13] It was then most happily taken up by our judicious Petrarch, not merely in his canzoni and his sonnets, as in the canzone on Italy and the sonnets on Rome, but in his *Triumphs*, in which he frequently passes into digressions of the type mentioned and then easily returns to the theme he has left.[14] And in the same thing Ariosto is great and wonderful, as he has also been very successful in treating in his poem subjects and events not included in his first intention but which add extraordinary beauty to his accomplished work. And the same things add beauty to the compositions of others who make use of them with judgment and grace. And here it is to be observed that in digressions that contain jousts, tournaments, loves, beauties, passions of the soul, fields of battle, buildings, and similar other things, the author of romances is much more copious than Vergil and Homer have been. . . .[15]

The poet should ever have his eye on decorum, which is nothing else than what fits places, times, and persons. And therefore it comes about that the ancient observers of the nature of things say that decorum was that beauty, that grace, which springs from the forms of speech that are joined together with judgment and with measure and carry with them some exposition of characters, which should shine out in words just as the beauty of color shines out in a beautiful body. In short, decorum is nothing other than the grace and fitness of things and should be considered not merely in actions but also in the speeches and answers of men among themselves. For we speak with a king in a way unlike that in which we speak with a gentleman. And a king replies to another king not as he does to his vassal or to another lesser prince. And he speaks in one way to his soldiers, to arouse them to battle, and in another to his people to quiet them when they have risen in armed rebellion. . . .[16] And this principle of decorum should be applied not merely to actions, persons, places, and circumstances, as we have said, but also to words. For words are without force when they do not serve as the covering for things, nor can things be made manifest without words. Nor should this decorum be considered merely in the work as a whole but in each part of it, as in expository passages, invocations, narrations, and other parts as they come, so that each part may have what is individually suitable to it. Therefore he who would acquire fame as an author must give much attention to decorum in things and in words, in the whole and in the parts, for the composition and arrangement of the parts will avail little if the parts are ineptly placed and show some lack of decorum, and they cannot help lacking decorum whenever the writer does not take prudence as his guide in things and in words. [He then deals with decorum in persons, developing Horace, *Art of Poetry*, 153 ff.[17]]

NOTES

1. Apparently a common theory. Sir Walter Raleigh began his *History of the World* with the creation.
2. This section is directed against the view expressed in *Poetics* VIII, and accepted by many Renaissance critics.
3. Pisander's work is now lost.
4. Cf. Sidney's phrase, *Defense of Poetry*, sect. 24.
5. Milton thought there was no plagiary if what was taken was "bettered by the borrower" (*Eikonoclastes*, chap. XXIII).
6. Cf. *Paradise Lost*, beginnings of III, VII, IX and beginnings of books in *Tom Jones*.
7. Cf. Sidney, *Defense*, secs. 8 and 9.
8. Cf. Sidney: "not rhyming and versing that maketh a poet. . . . But it is that feigning" (*Defense*, sect. 16).
9. "As they should be" is from Aristotle, *Poetics*, XXV, 60b32. The last clause, giving the moral purpose, is the conclusion of the Renaissance.
10. It has often been supposed that the anachronisms of Shakespeare and his contemporaries are the result of ignorance. This passage suggests that they may often be deliberate. To Renaissance dramatists history was subordinate to the higher purposes of poetry; the present age gives history relatively a higher position.
11. A good example of the Renaissance combination of Aristotle (see the beginning of this paragraph and the note) and Horace (*Art of Poetry*, 333) and a conclusion from it.
12. *Poetics*, VI. Giraldi assumes that Aristotle's catharsis implies the moral effect of tragedy.
13. Cf. Mazzoni, *Of the Defense of the "Comedy,"* Bk. IV, chap. XXXVI ff. He apparently

has in mind such passages as Dante's invectives against Florence, e.g., *Purgatorio*, XXIII, 94–108.

14. Canzone 16, *Italia mia*; Sonnets 105 (*Fiamma dal ciel*), 106 (*L'avara Babilonia*), 107 (*Fontana di dolore*); *The Triumph of Fame*, part II, ll. 142–4, furnishes an instance of a digression. Dante himself recognized his method as digressive (Letter to Can Grande, sect. 9).

15. Was it classical feeling that led Milton to say that he would not tell of
> tilting furniture, emblazoned shields,
> Impresses quaint, caparisons and steeds
> *Paradise Lost*, IX, 34–5.

as the romancers had done?

16. The king in *Hamlet* (IV, V, 119 ff.) addresses Laertes on his rebellion.

17. Decorum is also discussed in Giraldi's work on the drama, where it is made "what befits the disposition of the doer and the speaker." Cf. Milton's description of decorum as "the choice of such persons as he ought to introduce, and what is moral and decent for each one" (*Reason of Church Government*, sect. 3).

Joachim du Bellay
1522–1560

Along with Pierre de Ronsard, Joachim du Bellay was a founder of the French school of Renaissance poetry, the Pléiade, named after a group of seven tragic poets of ancient Alexandria. Born into an aristocratic family, du Bellay was orphaned at an early age and was subsequently left by his brother to run wild at the family estate of La Turmelière. At the age of 23, he went to study law at Poitiers, where he came into contact with a group of humanists and poets, including Jacques Peletier, who had published a translation of Horace's *Ars Poetica*. Du Bellay met Ronsard outside Poitiers in 1548 and returned with him to Paris in order to join a circle of students attached to Jean Dorat. He later spent four years in Italy in the service of his cousin, the Cardinal Jean du Bellay.

In 1548, Thomas Sibilet published *Art poétique,* a broad attack upon the sonnet and "modernism" in literature. Du Bellay wrote *The Defence and Illustration of the French Language* in 1549 as a rejoinder to Sibilet's work, although du Bellay is much more ambitious in his scope. *The Defence* is an exploration of the possibilities of the French language, particularly in its relationship to the Latin and Greek classics. He claims to write the treatise so "that our language, which still creeps along the ground, may lift its head and rise up on its feet."

Like many theoretical works of the sixteenth century, *The Defence* revolves around the question of to what extent literary innovation is desirable or even possible, considering the tremendous prestige maintained by the classics. Du Bellay's work is interesting precisely because of his equivocal stance on this question. He advocates the proper "cultivation" of the language through borrowing from the greatness of the Latin and Greek. (Michel Deguy has glossed du Bellay's assessment of the relationship between modernity and antiquity: "Do not imitate them in order to be like them; imitate them in order to arrive at the difference of equality.") At the same time, du Bellay is ambivalent about the proper relationship between the classics and modern French. At points he indicates a tremendous concern for what he calls "the sacred relics of antiquity," and at such points, writes Margaret Ferguson, "imitation is seen more and more not simply as the means to achieve inventive richness, but as an end in itself." At another point, however, he claims that it is precisely the study of the ancient authors which "sterilizes" his contemporaries, making them inferior to the classical authors. Du Bellay's opponent, Barthélemy Aneau, perhaps best summarized the complex nature of du Bellay's *Defence:* "Is this a defense and illustration, or rather an offense and denigration?" Throughout the work, du Bellay is keenly aware of the authority of the classical texts. He cites the classics even to insist that the French language must stand on its own, and he ignores the distinctive contributions already made to French literature by Rabelais, Scève and Villon.

The selections from *The Defence and Illustration of the French Language,* translated by Gladys M. Turquet, are reprinted by permission of J.M. Dent & Sons, Ltd. from *The Defence and Illustration of the French Language,* (London: J.M. Dent, 1939). © 1939 by J.M. Dent & Sons, Ltd.

FROM

THE DEFENCE AND ILLUSTRATION OF THE FRENCH LANGUAGE

Book I

Chapter I
The Origin of Languages

If nature (of whom a personage of high renown has not without reason doubted whether we should call her mother or stepmother) had given to men a common will and consent, besides the innumerable commodities which would have thereby resulted, human inconstancy would not have needed to forge for itself so many manners of speaking. Which diversity and confusion can rightly be called the Tower of Babel. For languages are not born of themselves after the fashion of herbs, roots, or trees: some infirm and weak in their nature; the others healthy, robust, and more fitted to carry the burden of human conceptions; but all their virtue is born in the world of the desire and will of mortals. That (it seems to me) is a great reason why one should not thus praise one language and blame the other; since they all come from a single source and origin, that is from the caprice of men, and have been formed from a single judgment for a single end, that is to signify amongst us the conceptions and understandings of the mind. It is true that in the succession of time, some from having been more carefully regulated have become richer than others; but this should not be attributed to the felicity of the said languages, but to the sole artifice and industry of men. So then all the things which nature has created, all the arts and sciences in the four quarters of the globe, are each in their own way the same thing; but since men are of diverse wills, therefore do they speak and write diversely. In this connection I cannot sufficiently blame the foolish arrogance and temerity of some in our nation who, being in no wise Greek nor Latin, misprize and reject with a more than stoical haughtiness all things written in French; and I cannot sufficiently wonder at the strange opinion of some learned men who think that our vulgar tongue is incapable of good letters and erudition: as if an invention for language alone should be judged good or bad. The former I undertake to satisfy. The latter I desire (if it be possible for me) to bring to change their opinion by means of a few reasons which I hope to deduce: not that I feel myself more far-seeing in that, or in other things, than they, but because the affection they bear towards foreign languages does not allow them to make healthy and complete judgment of their vulgar tongue.

Chapter II
That the French Language Should Not Be Called Barbarous

To begin, then, to enter the subject, concerning the meaning of this word barbarous: in ancient times they were called barbarous who spoke Greek incorrectly. For as strangers coming to Athens strove to speak Greek, they often fell into this absurd expression *barbaros*.

Afterwards the Greeks transported the name to brutal and cruel manners, calling all nations outside Greece, Barbarians. That should in no way diminish the excellence of our tongue; because this Greek arrogance, admiring only its own inventions, had neither law nor privilege to legitimize its own nation and bastardize all the others; as Anacharsis said: the Scythians were barbarians among the Greeks, but the Athenians were also barbarians among the Scythians, and even had the barbarity of the customs of our ancestors moved them to call us Barbarians, I do not see that things are so that we should now be considered as such; seeing that in civility of manners, equity of laws, magnanimity of heart, in short, in all forms and ways of living no less praiseworthy than profitable, we are not anything less than they; and still further, seeing that they themselves are now such that we may justly call them by that name which they gave to others. Still less should this happen because the Romans called us Barbarians, seeing that in their ambition and insatiable hunger for glory, they sought not only to subjugate but to render other nations vile and abject beside them: principally the Gauls, from whom they suffered more shame and hurt than from others.

In this connection, thinking many times, whence comes it that the deeds of the Roman people are so celebrated throughout the world, nay, so far more highly preferred to those of all other nations taken together, I find no greater reason than this: that the Romans did have so great a multitude of writers that most of their deeds (to say no worse) through the space of so many years, ardour in battle, laying waste of Italy, invasions of foreigners, have been preserved entire until our times. On the contrary, the actions of other nations, especially of the Gauls, before they fell into the power of the French, and the actions of the French themselves since they gave their name to the Gauls, have been so ill collected, that we have almost lost not only the glory of them, but even the memory of them. Thereto the envy of the Romans has aided, who, as if in a certain conspiracy conspiring against us, weakened, as they were able, our warlike glory, whose brilliance they could not endure, and not only have they done us wrong thereby, but, to render us still more contemptible, they have called us brutal, cruel, and barbarous. Someone will say: Why have they exempted the Greeks from this name? Because they would have done more harm to themselves than to the Greeks, from whom they borrowed all the good which they had, at least with regard to the sciences and the illustration of their language. These reasons seem to me sufficient to make any equitable adjudicator of things understand, that our language (though we have been called barbarians by our enemies and by those who had no right to give to us this name) should yet not be misprized, especially by those to whom it is proper and natural: and who are in nothing less than the Greeks or Romans.

Chapter III
Why the French Language Is Not So Rich as the Greek and Latin

And if our language be not so copious and rich as the Greek or Latin, that must not be imputed to it as a fault, as if of itself it could never be other than poor or sterile: but rather must one attribute it to the ignorance of our ancestors, who having (as someone says, speaking of the ancient Romans) in higher esteem well-doing than fair speaking, and liking to leave to posterity examples of virtue, rather than precepts, deprived themselves of the glory of their fine deeds, and us of the fruit of the imitation thereof: and by the same means have left us our language so poor and bare that it has need of the ornaments and (so to speak) the plumes[1] of other persons. But who would say that Greek and Latin were always in the state of excellence wherein they were seen in the time of Homer and of Demosthenes, of Virgil and of Cicero? And if these authors had judged, that never, whatever diligence and culture were brought thereto, would these tongues have been able to produce greater fruit, would they have laboured so much to bring them to that point where we now see them? So can I say of our tongue, which now begins to flower without fructifying; or rather, like a plant and small shoot, has not yet flowered, still less borne all the fruit that it might well produce. That certainly, not by any defect in the nature thereof, as apt to engender as others, but by the fault of those who have had the care of it, and have not sufficiently cultivated it; but like a wild plant in that same desert where it had begun to live, without ever watering it, or pruning, or guarding from brambles and thorns which shaded it, have let it grow old and almost die. And if the ancient Romans had been as negligent of the culture of their language when first it began to bud, certainly it would never in so short a time have become so great. But they, in the manner of good agriculturals, did first transplant it from a wild to a domestic place; then that it might the earlier and the better fructify, cutting off all round the useless twigs, in exchange for these did restore free and domestic branches, drawn in masterly fashion from the Greek tongue, which quickly were so well grafted and made like unto their trunk that henceforward they appeared no longer adopted but natural. Thence were born in the Latin tongue those flowers and those fruits coloured with the great eloquence, the numbers, and the artificial binding together of phrases, all which things, not so much by its own nature as by artifice, every language is accustomed to produce. Therefore if the Greeks and the Romans, more diligent in the cultivation of their languages than we in that of ours, were unable to find therein, except with great toil and industry, either grace or number or finally any eloquence, should we marvel if our vulgar tongue is not so rich as it well might be, and thereby take the opportunity to misprize it as a vile thing and of little price? The time will come (maybe), and I hope for it with the help of good French fortune, when this noble and puissant kingdom will in its turn obtain the reins of sovereignty, and when our language (if with Francis the whole French language be not buried), which now begins to throw out its roots, will emerge from the ground, and rise to such height and greatness, that it can equal the Greeks themselves and the Romans, producing, even as they, Homers and Demosthenes, Virgils and Ciceros, just as France has sometimes produced her Pericles, Nicias, Alcibiades, Themistocles, Caesars, and Scipios.

Chapter IV
That the French Language Is Not So Poor as Many Esteem It

I do not, however, consider our vulgar tongue, as it now is, to be so vile, so abject as do these ambitious admirers of the Greek and Latin tongues, who would not think, were they even Pitho, goddess of persuasion, that they could say anything good, unless it were in a foreign tongue, not comprehended of the vulgar. And he who will look closely, will discover that our French tongue is not so poor that it cannot render faithfully what it borrows from others, not so unfertile that it cannot produce of itself some fruit of good invention by means of the industry and diligence of its cultivators, if some are found who are such good friends of their country and of themselves, that they will apply themselves thereto. But to whom, after God, shall we render thanks for such a benefit if not to our late good king and father, Francis, the first of that name and first in all virtues? I say first, since he has in his noble kingdom first restored all the good arts and sciences in their ancient dignity: and our language, which before was harsh and ill-polished, he has thus rendered elegant, and if not so copious as it well might be, at least a faithful interpreter of all others. And it is in such wise that philosophers, historians, doctors, poets, orators, both Greek and Roman, have learned to speak in French. What shall I say of the Hebrews? The sacred writings give ample testimony of what I say. I leave aside here the superstitious reasonings of those who maintain that the mysteries of theology ought not to be laid bare and, as it were, profaned in the vulgar tongue, and that which those in the opposite camp allege. For this discussion is proper only for that which I have undertaken, which is solely to show that our language had not at its birth the gods and the stars in such enmity, that it cannot one day attain to the height of excellence and perfection as well as the others, since all sciences can faithfully and copiously be treated in it, as may be seen in the very great number of books, Greek and Latin, nay, even Italian and Spanish and others, translated into French by many excellent pens of our day.

Chapter V
That Translations Are Not Sufficient to Give Perfection to the French Language

In any case this most praiseworthy labour of translation seems not to me the only means, nor sufficient, to raise our vulgar tongue to be the equal and paragon of the other tongues. Which I claim to prove so clearly that none (as I believe) will wish to contradict, unless he be a manifest calumniator of truth;

and firstly: It is a thing agreed among all the best authors of rhetoric, that there are five parts of fair speaking: invention, elocution, arrangement, memory, and pronunciation. Now since the two last are to be learned, not so much by the benefit of tongues as they are given to each of us according to the fertility of his nature, increased and maintained by studious exercise and continual diligence, since also arrangement lies rather in the discernment and good judgment of the orator than in definite rules and precepts—seeing that the events of time, the circumstances of place, the conditions of persons, and the diversity of occasions, are innumerable—I will content myself with speaking of the two first: that is of invention and of elocution. The office then of the orator is to speak elegantly and copiously of each thing proposed. Now this faculty of speaking thus of all things, can be acquired only by the perfect understanding of the sciences, which were first treated by the Greeks, and next by the Romans, imitators of them. It is therefore necessary that these two tongues be understood by him who would acquire this copiousness and richness of invention, the first and principal piece in the harness of the orator. And touching this point, faithful translators can greatly serve and aid those who have not the sole means of devoting themselves to foreign tongues. But as for elocution, certainly the most difficult part, and without which all other things are, as it were, useless, and like a sword still covered with its sheath—elocution (say I) by which principally an orator is judged more excellent, and a manner of speaking better, than another—as for that elocution from which is derived the name of eloquence itself, and whose virtue lies in words which are proper to the common usage of speech used therein and not alienated therefrom; in the metaphors, allegories, comparisons, similitudes, energies,[2] and so many other figures and ornaments without which any oration or poem is bare, maimed, and weak, I shall never believe that this can be learned from translators, because it is impossible to render it with the same grace which the author used; since each language has a something proper to itself alone, of which if you strive to express the nativeness in another language, observing the law of translation, which is not to expatiate yourself beyond the limits of the author, your diction will be constrained, cold, and ungraceful. And to prove it be thus, read me a Demosthenes and a Homer in Latin, a Cicero and a Virgil in French, to see if they will engender such emotions, nay, if even as a Proteus, they will transform you in diverse sorts, as you feel, reading these authors in their own languages. You will seem to pass from the burning mountain of Etna to the cold summit of Caucasus. And that which I say of the Greek and Latin languages, should equally be said of all the vulgar tongues, of which I will cite as an example only a Petrarch, of whom I dare to say that if Homer and Virgil, born again, had undertaken to translate him, they could not render him with the same grace and naturalness as lies in his own native Tuscan. In any case, some in our time have undertaken to make him speak in French. These briefly are the reasons which have made me think that the diligent service of translators, in other ways most useful for instructing those ignorant of foreign tongues in the knowledge of things, is not sufficient to give to our own language that perfection, that final touch which painters give to their pictures, which we desire. And if the reasons which I have alleged seem not strong enough, I will produce for my guarantors and defenders the ancient Roman authors, poets principally and orators, who (as Cicero translated some books of Xenophon and Aratus, and as Horace gives the precepts of good translating) have devoted themselves to this part more for their study and particular profit than for the publication and amplification of their language, their glory, and the convenience of others. If any have seen some works of that time under the title of translations, I mean works of Cicero, of Virgil, and that most happy age of Augustus, they can deny what I say.

Chapter VI
Of Bad Translators, and of Not Translating the Poets

But what shall I say of some truly more worthy to be called traducers[3] than translators? For they traduce those whom they undertook to explain, robbing them of their glory, and by the same means seduce ignorant readers, showing them white for black; and, to acquire the name of savants, they translate on credit those languages of which they never understood the first elements, like Hebrew and Greek; and again, to make themselves the better known, tackle the poets—a race of authors certainly to which if I were able or wished to translate I would so little address myself, because of that excellence of invention which they have more than others, that grandeur of style, magnificence of words, gravity of sentences, audacity and variety of figures, and countless other lights of poetry: in short, that energy, and I know not what of spirit which is in their writings, which the Latins would call genius. All which things can as much be expressed in translating, as a painter can represent the soul with the body of him whom he undertakes to draw from nature. What I say is not addressed to those who by the command of princes and great lords translate the most famous Greek and Latin poets, because the obedience one owes to such personages admits of no excuse in this place, but indeed I mean to speak to those who from blitheness of heart (as we say) undertake such things lightly and in the same way acquit themselves thereof. O Apollo! O muses! thus to profane the sacred relics of antiquity! But I will say no more thereof. He then who would make a work worthy of price in his own tongue, let him leave this labour of translating, principally the poets, to those who from a laborious and little profitable thing, I would even say useless, nay, harmful, to the enrichment of their language, rightly get more of vexation than of glory.

Chapter VII
How the Romans Enriched Their Language

If the Romans (someone will say) did not devote themselves to this labour of translation, by what means then were they able to enrich their language, even to make it almost equal to the Greek? Imitating the best Greek authors, transforming themselves into them, devouring them; and, after having well digested them, converting them into blood and nourishment, taking for themselves, each according to his nature, and the argument he wished to choose, the best author of whom they observed diligently all the most rare and exquisite virtues, and these like shoots, as I have already said, they grafted and applied to their own tongue. By doing this (I say) the Romans did build those fine writings which we praise and admire so much, now equalling one of these writings with the Greeks and now excelling them.

And of what I say, give good proof Cicero and Virgil, whom willingly and for their honour I name always in the Latin tongue, of whom the one gave himself entirely to the imitation of the Greeks, counterfeited, and did express in so lively a fashion the fertility of Plato, the vehemence of Demosthenes, and the joyful sweetness of Isocrates, that Molo, the Rhodian, once hearing him declaim, cried that he brought Greek eloquence to Rome. The other did so well imitate Homer, Hesiod, and Theocritus, that it has since been said of him that of these three he surpassed the first, equalled the second, and approached so closely to the other, that if the felicity of the arguments he treated had been equal, it were doubtful to whom to give the palm. I therefore ask you who are busied only with translations, if these so famous authors had amused themselves with translating, would they have raised their language to the excellence and height wherein we now see it? Think not then by any diligence and industry that you may employ in this direction, to so do that our language, which still creeps along the ground, may lift its head and rise up on its feet.

Chapter VIII
Of Amplifying the French Language by the Imitation of the Ancient Greek and Roman Authors

Let him who would enrich his language then compose himself to the imitation of the best Greek and Latin authors, and let him direct the point of his style to their greatest virtues as to a certain end. For there is no doubt that the greater part of artifice is contained in imitation; and just as it was most praiseworthy in the ancients to invent well, so is it the most useful to imitate well, above all for those whose language is not yet very copious nor rich. But let him who would imitate understand that it is no easy thing well to follow the virtues of a good author, and, as it were, to transform himself into him, seeing that nature, even to things which seem most similar, has not been able so to do, that by some note or difference they may not be distinguished. I say this because in every language many there are who, without penetrating to the more hidden and innermost parts of the author whom they have chosen, attach themselves to what strikes the first glance, and, charmed with the beauty of the words, miss the force of the things. And certainly, as it is no vicious thing, but a praiseworthy, to borrow from a foreign tongue thoughts and words and appropriate them to our own, so is it reprehensible, nay, odious, for any reader of liberal nature to see in the same language such an imitation as that of some learned men who believe themselves to be the better when they most resemble a Héroet[4] or a Clément Marot. Therefore do I admonish thee (O thou who desirest the increasing of thy language, and wouldst excel therein) not to imitate lightly (*à pié leué* as someone lately said) the most famous authors therein, as ordinarily do for the most part our French poets, a thing indeed as vicious as it is profitless to our common speech, seeing that it is nothing other (O great liberality!) than to give unto it that which belonged to it. I would that our language were so rich in domestic examples that we had no need to have recourse to foreigners. But if Virgil and Cicero had remained content to imitate writers in their own language, whom shall the Latins have besides Ennius or Lucretius, besides Crassus or Antony?

Chapter IX
Reply to Some Objections

After having, as succinctly as I could, opened the way for those who desire the amplification of our language, it seems good to me, and necessary, to reply to those who esteem it barbarous and irregular, incapable of that elegance and fecundity which are in the Greek and Roman, since (they say) it has not its declensions, its feet, and its numbers like these two other languages. I will not allege in this place (though I could do so without shame) the simplicity of our ancestors who were content to express their ideas with bare words without art or ornament, not imitating the curious diligence of the Greeks to whom the muse had given a rounded mouth[5] (as someone said), that is to say, perfect in all elegance and beauty of words, as afterwards she gave to the Romans imitating the Greeks. But I will say that our language is not so irregular as some would declare, since it is declined, if not in nouns, pronouns, and participles, at least in verbs in all their tenses, moods, and persons. And if it be not so curiously regulated, or rather fettered and tortured in its other parts, also it has not so many heteroclites and anomalies, strange monsters of Greek and Latin. As for feet and numbers, I shall say in the second book[6] how we compensate for them. And certainly (as says a great author of rhetoric,[7] speaking of the felicity the Greeks have in the composition of their words) I do not think that such things are done by the nature of the said languages, but we always favour strangers. What would have prevented our ancestors from varying all the declinable parts of speech, from lengthening one syllable and shortening the other, or making feet or hands as they liked?[8] And who will keep our successors from observing such things, if a few men of learning and no less ingenuity in this age undertake to reduce them to an art as Cicero promised to do with civil law: a thing which to some seemed impossible and to others not so. We must not here allege the excellence of antiquity, and, as Homer complained that in his time bodies were too small, say that modern minds cannot be compared with ancient. Architecture, the art of navigation, and other ancient inventions are certainly admirable; not, however, if one looks to necessity the mother of arts, so great that one should believe that the heavens and nature spent therein all their virtue, vigour, and industry. I will produce as testimony of what I say only printing, sister of the muses and tenth of them, and this no less admirable than deadly thunderbolt of artillery, with many other inventions which are not ancient and which show veritably that through the long course of centuries the minds of men are not so bastardized as some would say. I say only that it is not impossible that our tongue may some time receive this ornament and artifice as curious in effect as it is with

DEFENCE OF THE FRENCH LANGUAGE

the Greeks and Romans. As for the sound and that natural sweetness (as they say) which is in their tongues, I do not see that we have it less, in the judgment of most delicate ears. It is very true that we use the prescription of nature, who for speaking has given us only the tongue. We do not vomit our words from the stomach like drunkards, we do not strangle them in our throats like frogs, we do not cut them up in the palate like birds, we do not hiss them through our lips like serpents. If in such manners of speech lies the sweetness of languages, I confess that ours is harsh and ill-sounding. But we have this advantage, not to twist the mouth in a hundred thousand ways as do the apes, nay, like many, ill remembering Minerva, who, playing on a time upon a flute, and seeing in a mirror the deformity of her lips, threw it far away, unhappy presage of presumptuous Marsyas, who afterwards was flayed for so doing.

What then (someone will say), wouldst thou, following the example of this Marsyas, who dared compare his rustic flute to the sweet lyre of Apollo, equal thy tongue with the Greek and Latin? I confess that the authors in these have surpassed us in learning and fecundity, in which things it was easy for them to vanquish those who did not defend themselves. But that we, by long and diligent imitation of those who have first seized that which nature nevertheless has not denied to others, cannot succeed so well in that as we have already done in the greater part of their mechanical arts, and at times in their monarchy, that I will not say; for such an insult would extend not only against the minds of men but against God, who gave as inviolable law to all created things, not to last perpetually, but to pass without an ending from one state to the other, the end and corruption of the one being the beginning and generation of the other. Some obstinate person will reply again: Thy tongue tarries too long in receiving this perfection. And I say that this retarding proves not that it cannot receive it, but I say that it may be certain to keep it long, having acquired it with so great toil, following the law of nature, which has willed that every tree which is born, flowers and fructifies very quickly, very quickly also grows old and dies, and that on the contrary that one lasts for long years, which toiled long to throw out its roots.

Chapter X
That the French Language is not Incapable of Philosophy, and Why the Ancients Were More Learned than the Men of Our Age

All that I have said for the defence and renowning of our language concerns principally those whose profession it is to speak well, as poets or orators. As to the other parts of literature and that circle of sciences which the Greeks called the encyclopaedia, at the beginning I touched on a part of this, as it seems to me; that is that the industry of faithful translators is in this place most useful and necessary; and, if they meet sometimes with words which cannot be received into the French family, this should not retard them, since the Latins did not oblige themselves to translate all the Greek expressions, such as rhetoric, music, arithmetic, geometry, philosophy, and almost all the names of the figures, herbs, maladies, of the sphere and its parts, and in general the greater number of the terms used in the natural sciences and mathematics. These words will then be in our language as strangers in a city; to whom, however, periphrases serve as interpreters. Yet would I be of the opinion that the learned translator should perform rather the office of paraphraser than of translator, striving to give to all the sciences which he will wish to treat the ornament and light of his tongue, as Cicero claims to have done in philosophy, and following the example of the Italians, who have translated almost the whole of it into their vulgar tongue, especially the philosophy of Plato.

And if any one will say that philosophy is a burden for other shoulders than those of our language, I have said at the beginning of this work, and I say it again, that all languages are of a like value, and formed by mortals to a like end with a like judgment. Wherefore thus, since without changing customs or nation, the Frenchman and the German, not only the Greek or Roman, can devote himself to philosophizing, so do I believe that to each man his language can competently communicate every doctrine. Therefore if the philosophy sown by Aristotle and Plato in the fertile Attic field were replanted in our French plain, it would not be casting it among the brambles and thorns, where it becomes sterile, but would be making it near rather than distant, and instead of a stranger a citizeness of our republic. And, peradventure, even as the spices and other oriental riches which India sends to us, are better known and better treated by us, and held of higher price than in the place of those who sow or gather them, similarly, philosophical speculations would become more familiar than they now are, and more easily understood by us, if some learned men had transported them from Greek and Latin into our vulgar tongue, than by those who go (if we must speak so) to gather them in the places where they grow.

And if someone should say that diverse tongues are fitted to signify diverse conceptions, some the conceptions of the learned, other those of the unlearned, and that the Greek principally is so well suited to the doctrines that it seems that it was formed for expressing them by nature herself and not by human foreseeing, I say that this nature, which in every age, in every country, in every habit, is always one same thing, as thus voluntarily it exercises its art throughout the world, not less on earth than in heaven, and though it is attentive to the production of reasonable creatures, yet does not forget the unreasoning, but with equal artifice engendering these and those, so is it worthy to be known and praised of all persons in all tongues. The birds and fishes and beasts on earth, in some manner, now with one sound, now with another, without the distinguishing of words, signify their emotions. Far more quickly should we then do the same, each with his own language, without having recourse to others. Writings and languages have been found, not for the conservation of nature, who (divine as she is) has no need of our aid, but only for our good and usefulness, so that present, absent, living, and dead, manifesting one to the other the secret of our hearts, we may the more easily arrive at our felicity, which lies in the understanding of sciences, not in the sound of words, and consequently those tongues and writings should be most in use which would be most easily learned. Alas, and how much better would it be that there were in the world a single natural language than to use so many years to learn words; and that until the age, very often, when we have no longer the means nor the leisure to devote ourselves to greater things, and certainly thinking many times whence comes it that the men of this century generally are less learned in all sciences, and of less price than the ancients, among many reasons I find this one which I would dare to call the principal: 'tis the study of the Greek and Latin languages. For if the time which we consume in learning the said languages were employed in study of the sciences, nature is certainly not become so sterile that she could not bring forth in our time Platos and Aristotles. But we, who ordinarily do affect more to appear learned than to be so, consume our youth not only in this vain exercise, but as we repent of having left the cradle and become men, we return again to childhood; and in the space of twenty or thirty years we do only the one thing, learn to speak, this man in Greek, that one in Latin, and the other in Hebrew. Which years being ended, and ended too with them that vigour and promptitude which naturally reigns in the mind of young men, then we procure that we are made philosophers, when by maladies or troubles of domestic affairs, and other hindrances which time brings, we are no longer fitted for the speculation of things, and often astonished by the difficulty and long time required for learning words only, we have it all through despair, and hate letters before we have tasted them or begun to love them.

Should we then leave the study of languages? No; since the arts and sciences are for the present in the hands of the Greeks and Latins. But it should be in future that one could speak of all things throughout the world, in every language. I well understand that the professors of languages will not be of my opinion: still less those venerable Druids, who through the ambitious desire they have to be amongst us what the philosopher Anacharsis was among the Scythians, fear nothing so much as that the secret of their mysteries, which must be learned from them, not otherwise than formerly the days from the Chaldaeans, be laid bare to the vulgar, and that the eyes of the crows (as Cicero says) be put out.[9] In this connection, I remember having many times heard some of their academy say that the King Francis, I mean that Francis to whom France owes no less than did Rome to Augustus, had dishonoured the sciences and left the learned in contempt. O times! O manners! O crass ignorance! not to understand that even as an evil, when it spreads further, is the more pernicious, so is a benefit the more profitable when it is common.

And if they will say (as they do also say) that by so much is such a benefit the less excellent and admirable among men, I will answer that so great an appetite for glory and such an envy ought not to reign in the columns of the Christian Republic, but rather in that ambitious king who complained to his master for that he had divulged the acroamatic sciences, which is to say those that can be learned only by hearing the teacher. What then? Would these giant enemies of heaven limit the powers of the gods and restrain that which by a singular beneficence they gave to men, and enclose it in the hand of those who know not how well to guard it? I am reminded of those relics which are seen only through a little window, and which it is not permitted to touch with the hand.

So do they wish to do with all disciplines,[10] which they keep shut up in Greek and Latin books, not allowing that they may be seen otherwise, or that they be transported from these dead words into those which are living and wing their way daily[11] through the mouths of men. I must have (it seems to me) sufficiently contented those who say that our vulgar tongue is too vile and barbarous to treat such high matters as philosophy. And if they are not yet well satisfied I will ask them: Why then did the ancient Greeks travel through so many lands and dangers, some to the Indies to see the gymnosophists, others to Egypt to borrow from those old priests and prophets those riches of which Greece is now so proud? And in any case these nations, wherein philosophy has so willingly dwelt, produced (as I believe) persons as barbarous and inhuman as we are, and words as strange as ours. Very little would I care for the elegance of speech which is in Plato and in Aristotle if their books were written without reason. Philosophy truly did adopt them for her sons, not because they were born in Greece, but because they did speak in a high sense and well wrote of her. Truth so well sought by them, the arrangement and order of things, the sententious brevity of the one, and the divine copiousness of the other, is proper to them and not to others; but nature, of whom they spoke so well, is the mother of all the others, and disdains not to make herself known to those who manage with all industry to understand these secrets, not in order to become Greek, but to be made philosophers. True it is that, since the arts and sciences were ever in the power of the Greeks and Romans, who were more studious of those things which might render them immortal than others, we believe that by them alone can they and should they be treated. But the time will come, peradventure (and I pray the great and good God that it may be in our age), when some good person, not less bold than ingenious and learned, not ambitious nor fearing envy nor hatred from any one, will remove from us this false persuasion, giving to our tongue the flower and the fruit of good letters; otherwise, in the affection which we bear to foreign tongues (whatever excellence there be in them) should prevent this great felicity, these tongues would be worthy, verily not of envy but of hatred, not of fatigue but of vexation, they would be worthy finally to be not learnt, but taken away from those who have more need of the lively understanding of the spirit than of the sound of dead words. So much then for disciplines. I come back to the poets and orators, the principal subject of the matter which I treat, which is the adorning and dignifying of our language.

Chapter XI
That It Is Impossible to Equal the Ancients in Their Languages

All persons of good wit will understand enough that what I have said for the defence of our language is not in order to discourage any one from the Greek or Latin; for so far am I from being of that opinion, that I confess and maintain that he cannot make an excellent work in his own tongue who is ignorant of these two languages, or, at least, does not understand Latin. But I should be strongly of the opinion, that after having learned them, he should not misprize his own;

and that he, who by a natural inclination (which one can judge by the Latin and Tuscan works of Petrarch and Boccaccio and of other learned men of our time), should feel himself more fitted to write in his own language than in Greek or in Latin, should study rather to render himself immortal among his fellows, writing well in his own vulgar tongue than writing ill in these two other languages, to be vile, equally to both learned and unlearned. But if there be still to be found some of those who of mere words make all their art and science, so that to name the Greek or Latin language seems to them to speak of a divine language, and to speak of their vulgar tongue to name an inhuman language, incapable of all erudition, if such were to be found (say I) who wished to flaunt themselves and misprize all things written French, I would fain question them in this wise. What think they then to do, these replasterers of walls, who day and night break their heads with striving to imitate? Do I say to imitate? nay, to transcribe a Virgil and a Cicero, building their poems with hemistichs of the one, and swearing fealty in their proses to the words and thoughts of the other, dreaming (as someone did say) of the conscript fathers, of the consuls, of the tribunes, of the comitia, and all ancient Rome, none otherwise than Homer, who in his *Batrachomyomachia* adapts to rats and frogs the magnificent titles of the gods and goddesses. These, indeed, deserve the punishment of him who, ravished to the tribunal of the great judge, replied that he was a Ciceronian.[12]

Think they, then, I say not to equal, but to approach only these authors in their languages, culling from this orator or from that poet, now a verb, now a line, and now a sentence, as if in the way in which one rebuilds an old edifice they expected to restore by the stones picked up in the mined fabrication of these languages its first greatness and excellence? But you will surely not be such good masons (you who are so great partisans of the Greek and Latin languages) that you can restore to them that form which these good and excellent architects first gave them, and if you hope (as did Aesculapius with the limbs of Hippolytus) that by these collected fragments they may be resuscitated, you cheat yourselves, not thinking that on the fall of so superb edifices, together with the fatal ruin of these two puissant monarchies, one part becomes dust and the other must be in many pieces, which to wish to reduce to one would be an impossible thing; not thinking besides that many other parts did remain in the foundations of the old walls, or being lost through the long course of centuries can be found by no one. Therefore, coming to rebuild this construction, you will be far from restoring to it its first greatness, when, where was once the hall, you would make peradventure the chambers, the stables, or the kitchen, confounding the doors and the windows, in brief, changing all the form of the edifice. Finally, I should be considering that art can express the lively energy of nature, if you could restore this renewed construction to the likeness of the ancient, since the idea whence it were necessary to draw the example in order to rebuild it would be imperfect. And this I add (to explain more clearly that which I have said), since the ancients used languages which they had sucked in with the milk of their nurse, and the unlearned spoke as well as the learned, except that these last studied the disciplines and the art of fair speaking, rendering themselves by this means more eloquent than the others. That is why their blessed ages were so fertile in good poets and orators. That is why even the women aspired to this glory of eloquence and erudition, like Sappho, Corinna, Cornelia, and a thousand others whose names are joined with the memory of the Greeks and Romans. Think not, then, imitators, servile flock,[13] to attain to the top point of their excellence, since with great difficulty did you learn their words, and the better part of your age is past. You misprize our vulgar tongue, peradventure not for any other reason that that from childhood and without study we did learn it, and the others with great trouble and effort. And if, like the Greek and Latin, it had perished and been put into the reliquary of books, I doubt not that it had been as difficult (or almost) to learn as they are. I did desire to say these words, because human curiosity admires far more things rare and difficult to find, even though they are less convenient for the usage of life, like perfumes and gems, than the common and necessary things like bread and wine. I do not see, however, that one should esteem one language more excellent than the other, simply because it is more difficult, unless one would say that Lycophron was more excellent than Homer because he was more obscure, and Lucretius than Virgil for this same reason.

Chapter XII
Defence of the Author

Let those who will think that I am too great an admirer of my language consult the first book *Of the Ends of Benefits and Evils*,[14] made by that father of Latin eloquence, Cicero, who at the beginning of the said book, among other things, replies to those who despise things written in Latin and like better to read them in Greek. The conclusion of the argument is that he esteems the Latin language not only not to be poor, as the Romans then esteemed it, but even to be richer than the Greek. What ornament (he says) of copious or elegant speech has been lacking, I will say to us, or to good orators, or to poets, since they have had someone whom they could imitate? I would not give such high praise to our tongue, because it has not yet its Ciceros and Virgils, but I dare well affirm that if the learned men of our nation deigned to esteem it as much as the Romans did theirs, it could at times, and right quickly, put itself in the ranks of the most famous. It is time to close this discussion in order to touch particularly on the principal points of amplification and ornament of our language. In which (reader) be not astonished if I speak not of the orator as of the poet. For besides the fact that the virtues of the one are for the most part common to the other, I am in no wise ignorant of the fact that Étienne Dolet,[15] a man of good judgment in our vulgar tongue, did formulate *The French Orator*, which, someone (maybe), a friend of the memory of the author and of France, will shortly and faithfully bring to light.

NOTES

1. The French *plumes* allows a pun here.
2. Aristotle, *energeia*.
3. The English cannot reproduce the neat Italian *traduttori, traditori*, nor Du Bellay's *traditeurs . . . traducteurs*.
4. Antoine Héroet, Bishop of Digue, author of Platonic love poems.
5. *Ore rotundo loqui*, Horace, A.P. vv. 323–4.
6. Bk II, chap. vii.
7. Quintilian.
8. *Faire des pieds ou des mains*. It is open to discussion whether Du Bellay here wished to make a pun, or whether he wished to say "using every means at their disposal."
9. *Pro Murena*, xi. 25. "From the crow's habit of attacking its prey in the eyes arises the proverb, *cornicum oculos configere*—to catch a weasel asleep." (Lewis and Short.)
10. *Eadem in litteris ratio est reliquisque rebus, quarum est disciplina.*—Cic. *Divin.* II. iii. 10.
11. Pater's translation: Ennius *ap.* Cic. *Tusc.* i, *Volito vivu' per ora virum*.
12. On St Jerome saying, when questioned, that he was a Christian, the judge replied: *Ciceronianus es, non Christianus*.
13. *O imitatores, servum pecus.*—Horace, *Ep.* I. xix. 19.
14. *De Finibus Bonorum et Malorum*.
15. Étienne Dolet, celebrated humanist and printer, condemned by the Sorbonne in 1546. *L'Orateur français* was never published.

Julius Caesar Scaliger

1484–1558

Julius Caesar Scaliger was an Italian classics scholar who moved to France in 1525 in order to become the physician to the Bishop of Agen. He settled there, taking a French wife who bore him 15 children. He made his name as a literary critic with two attacks upon Erasmus' *Ciceronianus;* when Erasmus made no reply to his initial attack, Scaliger issued an even sharper tract. Scaliger is also known for his work entitled *De Causis Linguae Latinae,* one of the first attempts to establish the principles for a Latin grammar. His most influential work, however, is the *Poetics* (1561), published three years after his death. During his lifetime, Scaliger was known for his works on botany and zoology as well as his literary works.

The *Poetics* is a systematic appraisal of Aristotelian theory. Bernard Weinberg has written of Scaliger's effect upon the course of sixteenth-century criticism:

> whereas in Minturno knowledge of other critical systems leads to eclecticism and disorganization, in Scaliger a different result is achieved. For he is basically an orderly thinker, capable of seeing the necessary consequences of his distinctions and of creating a subordination of his ideas to guiding principles. One remarkable effect of this quality is that he recognizes, after developing his own system, that it is contradictory to that of Aristotle.... This is highly significant for the history of the *Poetics* in the sixteenth century; for almost at the same time that Aristotle becomes the great "authority" on poetics, he becomes somebody with whom one may disagree if one has a solid critical approach of one's own. Especially if one is Scaliger.

Scaliger advances a poetics which is, if anything, harsher than Aristotle's. Like other critics of the same period, Scaliger does not acknowledge any difference between nature and art. The result, as Weinberg points out, is that "whatever is said about poetry must be equally appropriate to the natural sciences, on the one hand, or to the political (or "human") sciences, on the other." For this reason, Scaliger establishes Vergil as the absolute authority on the "nature" of poetry:

> These things, which are thus constituted by nature, must be discovered in the bosom of nature and, plucked out therefrom, must be exposed before the eyes of men. . . . If we would do this as conveniently as possible, we must ask examples from him who alone is worthy of the name of poet. I mean Vergil, from whose divine poem we shall establish the various kinds of persons.

This "deification" of Vergil had a lasting effect throughout the next three centuries.

Scaliger is primarily remembered for his strict interpretation of Aristotle's unities, an interpretation based upon his refusal to acknowledge any difference between nature and art. It is an interpretation which has been completely overturned in the last century and a half. George Saintsbury writes in his *A History of Criticism and Literary Taste* (1902) that "neither Scaliger nor any of his successors in purism has proved that we are, or ought to be, any more shocked by Aeschylus when he shifts from Delphi to Athens than by Thackeray when he transports us from Flanders to Chelsea."

The selections from the *Poetics*, translated by F. M. Padelford, are reprinted by permission of Harcourt Brace Jovanovich, Inc. from *Critical Theory Since Plato*, edited by Hazard Adams (New York: Harcourt Brace Jovanovich, 1971). © 1971 by Harcourt Brace Jovanovich, Inc.

FROM

Poetics

Everything that pertains to mankind may be classed as necessary, useful, or pleasure-giving, and by an inherent characteristic of all these classes the power of speech was implanted in man from the very beginning, or, as time went on, was acquired. Since man's development depended upon learning, he could not do without that agency which was destined to make him the partaker of wisdom. Our speech is, as it were, the postman of the mind, through the services of whom civil gatherings are announced, the arts are cultivated, and the claims of wisdom intercede with men for man. It is of course necessary to secure from others those things which we need, to give orders to have things done, to prohibit, to propose, to dispose, to establish, and to abolish. Such were the functions of early speech.

Then the usefulness and effectiveness of language were increased by rules governing construction, dimensions, as it were, being given to a rude and formless body. Thus arose the established laws of speech. Later, language was adorned and embellished as with raiments, and then it appeared illustrious both in form and in spirit. As to an undefined body the metric science appoints breadth, angles, and length—the masters of harmony also add proportion, the *rhythmoi* of the Greeks—so to an unordered language law first gave the so-called rules. Next, more careful cultivation added knowledge of windings, of valleys and hills, of retreats, of light and shade. To speak figuratively, such cultivation afforded the soldier his necessary armor, the senator his useful toga, or the more elegant citizen his richer pleasure robe. Not unlike these were the ends which language served, since necessity demanded language in the search of the philosophers after truth, utility dictated its cultivation in statesmanship, and pleasure drew it to the theater. The language of the philosophers, confined to exact, logical reasoning, was necessarily concise and adapted to the subject matter. On the other hand, in the forum and the camp less precise expression was permissible, governed by the subject, the place, the time, and the audience, and such speaking was called oratory. The third class contains two species, not very unlike, which in common employ narration, and use much embellishment. They differ, however, in that one professes to record the fixed truth, and employs a simple style of composition, while the other either adds a fictitious element to the truth, or imitates the truth by fiction, of course with more elaboration. While, as we have said, they are both equally narrative in character, the name *history* came to be applied to the former alone, since, I suppose, it was satisfied merely with that field of writing adapted to setting forth actual events. On the other hand, the latter was called *poetry*, or *making*, because it narrated not only actual events, but also fictitious events as if they were actual, and represented them as they might be or ought to be. Wherefore the basis of all poetry is imitation.

Imitation, however, is not the end of poetry, but is intermediate to the end. The end is the giving of instruction in pleasurable form, for poetry teaches, and does not simply amuse, as some used to think.[1] Whenever language is used, the purpose, of course, is to acquaint the hearer with a fact or with the thought of the speaker, but because the primitive poetry was sung, its design seemed merely to please; yet underlying the music was that for the sake of which music was provided only as a sauce. In time this rude and pristine invention was enriched by philosophy, which made poetry the medium of its teaching. Let it be further said that when poetry describes military counsels, at one time open and frank, at another crafty—the *stratēgēma* of the Greeks—when it tells of tempests, of wars, of routs, of various artifices, all is for one purpose: it imitates that it may teach. So in *The Frogs* of Aristophanes, to the one who asked him, "What merit in a poet can arouse the greatest admiration for him?" Euripides made a good answer when he replied, "The ability to impress adroitly upon citizens the need of being better men." Plato was less happy in the *Ion* in saying that a rhapsodist cannot satisfactorily represent military or nautical doings, because such arts are foreign to him.[2] For the rhapsodist will say nothing worse about such things than the poet has written of them, since, as is very well remarked in the same passage, while the poet is the imitator of things, the rhapsodist is he who acts out the imitation, and according as the poet represents, the rhapsodist can reproduce.

Now is there not one end, and one only, in philosophical exposition, in oratory, and in the drama? Assuredly such is the case. All have one and the same end—persuasion; for, you see, just as we were saying above, whenever language is used it either expresses a fact or the opinion of the speaker. The end of learning is knowledge, that is, knowledge, of course, interpreted in no narrow sense. An accurate and simple definition of knowledge is as follows: Belief based either upon conclusive evidence, or upon a loose notion. Thus we say, "I know that Dido committed suicide because Aeneas departed." Now we do not know any such thing, but this is popularly accepted as the truth. Persuasion, again, means that the hearer accepts the words of the speaker. The soul of persuasion is truth, truth either fixed and absolute, or susceptible of question. Its end is to convince, or to secure the doing of something. Truth, in turn, is agreement between that which is said about a thing and the thing itself.

By no means are we to accept the popular idea that eloquent speaking, rather than persuasion, is the end of oratory, for the arguments of the grammarians on this point are not valid. Clearly, if a man does not persuade, this is due to no fault of the art, but either to the issue, which it is beyond the power of the orator to control, wherefore he does not cease to be an orator, or to some defect of his own, which may either reside in his speaking or in the bad cause which he espouses. In this last case he is either no orator, or else he is a knave.

Eloquent speaking certainly cannot be the end, for obviously it is the means to an end, or a mode of the means. An end is not that which serves another end, but that which all serves, and so one uses eloquence that he may persuade. Moreover, you are not the arbiter of your eloquence, but the judge is, and if he does not think you eloquent, not only is your eloquence fruitless, but it is not eloquence at all. Therefore you may go away frustrated in your purpose, even though you have spoken eloquently. Further, it is not possible that both the defendant and the plaintiff should be equally eloquent; in fact it is necessary that one or the other should lose his cause, or should merit losing it. Therefore he will not be your orator whom you have picked out as eloquent.

Finally, in that treatise entitled *Eisagōgikos*, attributed to Galen, and in that other work on the science of medicine, the *Systasis*, which is more confidently attributed to him, two kinds of arts are recognized.[3] If Quintilian, by the way, had run across this idea in Plato, from whom Galen borrowed it, he would have changed his theory about the end of oratory. Two kinds there are, then. Arts of the one kind can attain their ends in and of themselves, such as shoemaking, carpentry, and the like; the others are not thus able, as oratory, medicine, and navigation. The latter arts the Greek denominate *stochastikai* ("conjectural"), because, as is stated in the *Philebus*,[4] they proceed, so to speak, by conjecture, not by fixed principle. Now, for my part, I take a different view. Medicine always cures curable diseases, but the physician does not always do so, because he is embarrassed by many obstacles; wherefore in that case he fails to be a doctor. In fact the physician does not accept an incurable case unless he be careless, or stupid, greedy for fees, or rash. Further, accidents are wont to befall the sick, either through their own instrumentality, or that of their servants, or through some chance happening, as of the atmosphere, the sun, dampness, anger, grief, fear, and the like. Here belong what Hippocrates and other physicians call external agencies—*ta exōthen*. Indeed, not even nature herself is a perfectly reliable workman, for occasionally she is embarrassed and fails of her end, as when she produces a monstrosity, or brings forth defective bodies.

The orator, then, speaks in the forum that good may be meted to good men, and punishment to evil men; in assemblies and councils that public affairs may be well administered; and in eulogies that we may be won from evil by good example, and may pursue and practice that which is set forth as honest. In this class, the epideictic, certain invectives are to be included. Other kinds of invectives, however, belong to judicial bodies, such as those uttered in the presence of witnesses; still others to deliberative bodies, as the speeches against Antony and Catiline,[5] and the addresses on consular provinces.

All of these different kinds of speaking have a common end. To be sure, there are those who contend that in judicial proceedings the end is justice; in deliberative proceedings, utility; and in eulogies, honesty; but such are properly rebuked by Quintilian. The ground of the rebuke should be noted rather carefully, for not only do these men reason superficially, but they even contradict themselves. In fact, in another passage they confound utility with honesty. But all that aside, be it observed that utility is the end of all the virtues, wherefore also of justice. And since justice is the righteous payment to a man of that which is his own or its equivalent, justice is the end of deliberative counsels. Justice is even the end of war, for the councils of war—they are very many—are held for the sake of justice. Finally, if the end of man is virtue, honesty is either a state of mind induced by virtue, or it is the soul of virtue. Of every human office, of every act and thought, honesty will be the end.

We must consider even more carefully than did Quintilian the basis for the classification of the different kinds of speaking. That he might simplify the threefold division, he classified as follows: cases either are subject for judicial investigation, or are outside of it. The latter relate either to the past or to the future. Those relating to the past are epideictic; those of the future, deliberative. But now who does not appreciate that in judicial proceedings the past is involved? Wherefore it is not possible for the latter to form a subspecies of the judicial. So I would have altered the statement as follows: a case is either in the past or in the future; the latter alone prescribes deliberation; the former divides into the forensic, or judicial, and the epideictic. Although that discerning man, the disciple of the first philosopher, classed them as forensic, deliberative, and epideictic, and accused man is never tried or defended without praise or censure either of a person, an event, an act, a word, or a policy, and in like manner never without deliberation. Indeed, it is deliberated whether to convict or to acquit the defendant. So you see that there cannot be species or genera of cases, because no species of one is able to be part of another species.

Finally, it is improper, as some do, to call speeches of a deliberative nature hortatory, for persuasion is the end of all speaking. What else does an orator do than create confidence, and this, to persuade? Quintilian makes an equally bad mistake when he interprets the word *epideiktikos* to mean ostentatious speaking, on the ground that the word usually had this meaning among the Greeks. So far is this from the truth, that the philosophers used it to define the most simple and exact exposition.

Let it be observed, while we are on the subject, that in deliberative and judicial speaking the orator depends upon his audience. Indeed, the accomplishment of that purpose in behalf of which he essays to speak hinges upon the favor of his hearers. Let it be further noted, that in epideictic speaking the case is the opposite of this, inasmuch as the mind of the hearer is surrendered to the speaker. It is, indeed, as if he who adjudges praise were himself relieved from judgment. These points in which we differ from the recognized opinions of the rhetoricians must, from the very nature of my undertaking, be dwelt upon, just as we have dealt more accurately with various other matters. Thus we might say that the translative state could be subsumed under the conjectural,[6] since in both, the fact being conceded, it is a question who is responsible for it. All kinds of speeches have this in common. The orator in the forum debates concerning life, vices, virtues, examining them in the state of quality, and in that in which inquiry is made concerning what is, just as in councils the question is what is to be preferred. But the philosopher and the poet deal with all such matters in the very same spirit, each in his own person or in that of another. As an illustration of the latter mode, Socrates introduces Diotima or Aspasia, and Plato brings forward Socrates; and the orator in like manner interjects personifications. If he would eulogize a man, he must needs touch upon the story of his life, his family, his nation; and this allies him with the historian. The historian, on his part, frequently adds a characterization, such as we read of Camillus, Scipio, Hannibal, Jugurtha, and Cicero; and, as it were, intersperses his decrees. But it is only poetry which includes everything of this kind, excelling those other arts in this, that while they, as we have said above, represent things just as they are, in some sense like a speaking picture,[7] the poet depicts quite another sort of nature, and a variety of fortunes; in fact, by so doing, he transforms himself almost into a second deity.[8] Of those things which the Maker of all framed, the other sciences are, as it were, overseers; but since poetry fashions images of those things which are not, as well as images more beautiful than life of those things which are, it seems unlike other literary forms, such as history, which confine themselves to actual events, and rather to be another god, and to create. In view of this fact, its common title was furnished it, not by the agreement of men, but by the provident wisdom of nature. I must express my surprise that when the learned Greeks had most happily defined the poet as the *maker*, our ancestors should be so unfair to themselves as to limit the term to candle-makers, for though usage has sanctioned this practice, etymologically it is absurd. . . .

We may make a threefold classification of poets, according to poetical inspiration, age, and subjects.[9] Plato first, and then Aristotle, said that there are diversities of inspiration, for some men are born inspired, while others, born ignorant and rude, and even averse to the art, are seized on by the divine madness, and wrested from their lowliness. It is the work of the gods, who, though divine, use even these as their servants. Thus Plato himself, in the *Ion*, calls such men the interpreters and expounders of the gods. Wherefore the dictum expressed in the *Republic*, which some crude and insensible men would construe to the exclusion of poets from the republic, would be taken less seriously, for though he condemns certain scurrilous passages in the poets, we are not on that account to ignore those other passages which Plato cites times out of mind in support of his own theories. Plato should remark how many impertinent and low stories he himself employs, what filthy thoughts this Greek rogue often forces upon us. Surely the *Symposium*, the *Phaedrus*, and other such monstrous productions, are not worth reading.

The poets invoke the Muses, that the divine madness may imbue them to do their work. Of these divinely possessed ones, two classes are to be recognized. The one class are those to whom the divine power comes from above, with no mental effort on their part except the simple invocation. Hesiod classed himself in this category, and Homer is placed there by universal consent. The other class is aroused by the fumes of unmixed wine, which draws out the instruments of the mind, the spirits themselves, from the material parts of the body. Horace said that Ennius was such a poet, and such we consider Horace himself. Tradition says the same of Alcaeus and Aristophanes. Alcman did not escape such censure, and Sophocles applied it to Aeschylus: "Wine," he said, "not Aeschylus, was the author of his tragedies."

Again, poets may be divided into three classes, according to the age in which they wrote. First, there was that pristine, crude, and uncultivated age, of which only a vague impression remains. No name survives, unless it be that of Apollo, as the originator of poetry. Then there is the second and venerable period, when religion and the mysteries are first sung. Among the poets of this period are numbered Orpheus, Musaeus, and Linus; Plato includes Olympus also. Of the third period Homer is the founder and parent, and it includes Hesiod and other such writers. If it were not for historical records, one could fancy that

Musaeus was later than Homer, for he is more polished and refined. Aelian states that Oroebantius of Troezen, and Dares the Phrygian, flourished before Homer, and that in Homer's time the *Iliad* of Dares was held in esteem. The same author has it that Syager the poet even antedated Musaeus and Orpheus, and that he was the first to write of the Trojan war.

The third classification is according to subject matter. This the Greeks call *hypokeimenon*; our uncultivated philosophers, most correctly, subject; and the Latin philosophers, somewhat inappositely, argument. Of this class of poets there are as many kinds as there are styles of subjects treated. Yet for the sake of treatment, the poets may be classed under three principal heads. The first is that of the religious poets. Such are Orpheus and Amphion, whose art was so divine that they are believed to have given a soul to inanimate things. The second is that of the philosophical poets, and these again are of two sorts—natural, as Empedocles, Nicander, Aratus, and Lucretius; and moral, including the political, as Solon and Tyrtaeus; the economical, as Hesiod; and the general, as Phocylides, Theognis, and Pythagoras.

Now all that we have been saying may be equally well applied to women authors. They too merit praise. Such authors are Sappho; Corinna, the mistress of Pindar; Hedyle, the mother of the Samian or Athenian poet Hedylus, who excelled in iambic poetry; Megalostrata, whom Alcman loved, and others.

I leave it to the judgment of each one to determine whether or no the poetry of Martius and of the Sibyls should be referred to such categories as the above. My preference is not to do so, for they do not narrate past events, but predict future ones. This part of theology is not simply learning about the gods, but actual utterance of the things disclosed by the gods.

As for our poetry,[10] Gellius is authority for the statement that it was born during the Second Punic War. Let me give his own choice words: "In the Second Punic War, with winged step the Muse bore herself to the warlike, rugged race of Romulus."[11] On the other hand, it is commonly received that Livius Andronicus wrote his dramas before Naevius, who gave his to the public in the year 519 (A.U.C.).[12]

Now that the poets are enumerated and classified, certain questions may receive attention. Why does Horace question whether or not comedy is poetry? Forsooth, because it is humble, must it be denied the title of poetry? Surely an unfortunate ruling! So far from comedy not being poetry, I would almost consider it the first and truest of all poetry, for comedy employs every kind of invention, and seeks for all kinds of material.

Another question: Was Lucan a poet? Surely he was. As usual, the grammarians deny this, and object that he wrote history. Well now! Produce a pure history. Lucan must differ from Livy, and the difference is verse. Verse is the property of the poet. Then who will deny that all epic poets go to history for their subjects? History, sometimes delineated only in semblance, sometimes idealized, and always with changed aspect, is made the basis of poetry. Is not this the practice of Homer? Do we not do this in the tragedies themselves? Such is the practice of Lucan. Instance the image of the country offering itself to Caesar, the spirit called forth from Hades, and other such episodes. Wherefore, indeed, it

POETICS

seems to me that it would be better to give the title of poet to Livy than to deny it to Lucan. For as the tragic poets base their plays upon true events, but adapt the actions and speeches to the characters, so Livy and Thucydides insert orations which were never recognized by those to whom they were attributed. Moreover, although Aristotle exercised this censure so severely that he would refuse the name of poet to versifiers, yet in practice he speaks differently, and says: "As Empedocles poetically wrote (*epoiēsen*)"; so he even calls Empedocles, who feigned not at all, a poet. . . .[13]

Tragedy and comedy are of the same genus, and share in common the name drama. Clearly this is not far from the thought that Plato touched upon, but did not elaborate, in the *Symposium*.

The grammarians did some more false teaching about comedy when they said that it was poetry based upon imitation, and consisted in gesticulation and delivery, for surely a comedy is no less a comedy if it be read in silence. Then gesture is confined to recitation, and not all who read, recite. Moreover, we hear too much about imitation being the end of poetry in general. So our definition would be: Comedy is a dramatic poem, which is filled with intrigue, full of action, happy in its outcome, and written in a popular style.

An inaccurate definition of the Latin comedy described it as "a plot free from the suggestion of danger, dealing with the life and affairs of the private citizen." In the first place, this definition covers other, nondramatic stories, which can be presented in simple narration. In the second place, there is always the suggestion of danger in comedy, although the outcome is invariably tame. What else is danger than the approach or the visitation of imminent danger? Further, there is not only danger in comedy, but violence at the hands of panderers, rivals, lovers, servants, or masters. Thus in the *Asinaria* and *The Ghost* even the masters themselves are ill treated. Once more, this definition would not admit the official class, wearers of the toga, for they are not private citizens. Finally, the definition would embrace mimes and dramatic satires.

Crates of Athens was the first to write comedy free from the shackles of meter.

Now since comedy and tragedy are of the same genus, it is important to know the extent of the similarity. We will first treat of tragedy in general, and then later we will discuss the characters and actions in comedy and tragedy respectively. . . .

The definition of tragedy given by Aristotle is as follows: "Tragedy is an imitation of an action that is illustrious, complete, and of a certain magnitude, in embellished language, the different kinds of embellishments being variously employed in the different parts, and not in the form of narration, but through pity and fear effecting the purgation of such like passions."[14] I do not wish to attack this definition other than by adding my own: A tragedy is the imitation of the adversity of a distinguished man; it employs the form of action, presents a disastrous dénouement, and is expressed in impressive metrical language. Though Aristotle adds harmony and song, they are not, as the philosophers say, of the essence of tragedy; its one and only essential is acting. Then the phrase *of a certain magnitude* is put in to differentiate the tragedy from the epic, which is sometimes prolix. It is not always so, however, as the work of Musaeus illustrates. Further, the mention of "purgation" is too restrictive, for not every subject produces this effect. *A certain magnitude*, to return to the phrase, means not too long and not too short, for a few verses would not satisfy the expectant public, who are prepared to atone for the disgusting prosiness of many a day by the enjoyment of a few hours. Prolixity, however, is just as bad, when you must say with Plautus: "My legs ache with sitting, and my eyes with looking. . . ."

The early orators had only one end in view, to persuade and move their hearers, and their language was correspondingly rude; the poets sought only to please, and they whiled away their leisure simply with alluring songs. In due time, however, orator and poet secured from each other that which they lacked respectively. Isocrates is credited with having first given graceful movement to a hitherto rude diction, though deeper students of the literary monuments award this distinction to Thrasymachus, and add that his diligent efforts were furthered by Gorgias, while the work of Isocrates was to add the finishing touch. As to poetry, on the other hand, it was rendered more thoughtful by being transferred from the country to the town, where plots were added to furnish warning examples, and sentiments to furnish precepts.

Horace most aptly said, "He carries every vote who mingles the useful with the pleasing,"[15] for poetry bends all its energies to these two ends, to teach and to please. Now to realize these ends one's work must conform to certain principles. In the first place his poem must be deeply conceived, and be unvaryingly self-consistent. Then he must take pains to temper all with variety (*varietas*), for there is no worse mistake than to glut your hearer before you are done with him. What then are the dishes which would create distaste rather than pleasure? The third poetic quality is found in but few writers, and is what I would term vividness (*efficacia*): there is also a Greek name for it which will be given in the proper place. By *vividness* I mean a certain potency and force in thought and language which compels one to be a willing listener. The fourth is winsomeness (*suavitas*), which tempers the ardency of this last quality, of itself inclined to be harsh. Insight and foresight (*prudentia*), variety, vividness, and winsomeness, these, then, are the supreme poetic qualities. . . .

Of well-governed conduct there is, as it were, a definite form, which the philosophers call right reason. Is there any form of evil conduct? No, there is not. But in the absence of such form we are either bad or else indifferent. What then does the poet teach? Does he teach actions, which arise from mental states or dispositions, the *diathēseis* of the Greeks? Or does he teach us how to become such men that the faculty of doing good is potent, and the principle of avoiding evil conduct is implanted?

Aristotle ruled that since poetry is comparable to that civic institution which leads us to happiness, happiness being nothing other than perfect action, the poet does not lead us to imitate character, but action. Surely he is right; we agree perfectly. But what he adds offers a little more difficulty. He says that there cannot be a tragedy without action, though there may be one without disposition. Under the circumstances, I would here translate *ēthos* by "character," for he says that the tragic poets of his day usually constructed plots that lacked delineation of character. Thus Zeuxis the painter gave no expression of character in his work, and Polygnotus excelled in character-drawing. But if now *ēthos* means "an inclination to a certain course of action," and this is excluded from tragedy, the action will be altogether fortuitous, and wholly dependent on chance. To illustrate: Orestes once committed murder by slaying his mother. Yet here there is no question of character, for it was not a characteristic action. On the other hand, Aegisthus was a murderer in character, and so were Polymnestor, Pylades, Euclio, Pseudolus, Ballio, and Davus. So our inquiry is not as to whether the poet teaches character or action, but as to whether he teaches a mental disposition, or the outward expression of it. Though many things are done contrary to character, they are not done without our being disposed to do them. The result of the inquiry is, then, that the poet teaches mental disposition through action, so that we embrace the good and imitate it in our conduct, and reject the evil and abstain from that. Action, therefore, is a mode of teaching; disposition, that which we are taught. Wherefore action is, as it were, the pattern or medium in a plot, disposition is its end. But in civil life action is the end, and disposition its *form*.

If anyone thinks that our distinctions are more subtle than the subject warrants, he need not take it to heart; he will find it very easy to leave the whole matter alone.

Aristotle was also illogical in attributing to tragedy alone that which was the common property of poetry, just as when he formulated metrical laws from words and the parts of words, and afterwards ignored those very laws themselves.

NOTES

1. Scaliger adopts the Horatian position here, particularly against those early churchmen who would disparage poetry as trivial entertainment. See Horace, *Art of Poetry*.
2. See *Ion*.
3. The two works mentioned by this Greek physician of the second century A.D. are probably *Introductio sive Medicus* and *On the Nature of Medicine*, respectively.
4. A dialogue of Plato's later years, primarily concerned with ethical questions.
5. Delivered by Cicero.
6. [Padelford] For these technical terms see Quintilian [*On the Training of an Orator*], III. vi. especially 45 *ff.*
7. See Horace, *Art of Poetry*.
8. See Sidney, *An Apology for Poetry*.
9. Scaliger includes in his threefold classification a number of legendary Greek poets: in the classification according to age, those who antedate Homer, and in the classification according to subject matter, Orpheus, Amphion, and the Sibyls. The

identity of Martius is unknown. The other Greek poets Scaliger mentions are known to have written between the seventh and first centuries B.C.

10. Roman poetry.
11. *Attican Nights*, XVII. xxi. 45.
12. The Roman year 519 is 235 B.C.
13. Aristotle does not refuse the name of poet to versifiers but asserts that to versify does not mean one has written a poem. See *Poetics*, I. 8–9.
14. *Poetics*, VI. 2.
15. *Art of Poetry*.

Antonio Minturno
1500–1574

Antonio Minturno followed an ecclesiastical as well as literary career. He studied philosophy and went to Rome, where he developed an interest in humanistic and vernacular poetry. While his critical career began to take shape, Minturno was also involved in the movement for reform of the Church, and he participated in the opening of the first Jesuit college at Naples. He became Bishop of Uggento in 1559, and he was a participant in the third session of the Council of Trent, which enacted widespread reforms in the Church in response to the threat of Protestantism.

Minturno wrote verse and prose in both Latin and the vernacular. He is, however, best known for his works of literary criticism, *De Poeta* (1559) and *L'Arte Poetica* (1564); the former is written in Latin while the latter is essentially a revision of the earlier material for the literature of the Tuscan vernacular. He refers to it, in fact, in the dedication as *Della toscana poesia* (*Of Tuscan Poetry*).

In our selections from *L'Arte Poetica*, Minturno is primarily concerned with the question of ancient versus "modern" literature as well as the role of imitation. He is extremely harsh when it comes to the comparison of the modern "romance"—as exemplified for him by Ariosto—with the ancient epic. Minturno practices a kind of genre criticism, but one in which the classic forms become linked to the "nobility" while the romance is tied to the "barbarism" of popular taste. Fundamentally, Minturno believes that art must correspond to an unchanging truth. He writes elsewhere in *L'Arte Poetica*:

> For truth is one; and that which is true once must be true forever and in every age, nor does any difference of times change it, as such difference is capable of changing customs and life; even through such change, truth remains in its unchanged state.

He is able to condemn the romance, then, precisely for its mutability of form and its lack of adherence to a single truth, using a clever pun on the "knight errant" of the romance:

> Since that sort of composition gives the deeds of errant knights, they obstinately affirm not merely that it is not fitting to write poetry in the manner of Vergil and Homer, but even that it is desirable that poetry also should be errant, passing from one manner to another, and binding together various things in one bundle.

This forms the basis of Minturno's negative appraisal of Ariosto (part of an ongoing controversy concerning the poet's merits in comparison with the ancients). Ariosto, says Minturno, has constructed a multiple plot, in contradistinction to Homer, who "makes all spring from one beginning, and directs all to one end."

In Book IV, on the other hand, Minturno replaces his strict precepts for the maintenance of classical genre with the question of the imitation of other authors, and here he is much more genial. He instructs the poet to feel free both to borrow from other poets and to change what he has borrowed—". . . for since the very model has taken many things from others, and yet has changed many words, our author permits himself to do only what the one imitated thought was permitted."

Minturno remains, however, a clearly conservative figure in Italian literary debate of the period, demanding that Italian vernacular literature conform to the standards of the ancients.

The selections from *L'Arte Poetica*, translated by Allan H. Gilbert, are reprinted with his permission from *Literary Criticism: Plato to Dryden*, edited by Allan H. Gilbert (Detroit: Wayne State University Press, 1962). © 1962 by Allan H. Gilbert.

L'Arte Poetica

FROM
Book I

Minturno. He will compose correctly the plot of an epic poem who imitates and describes excellently a subject that is entire and perfect, made up of actions that are illustrious and serious, and having suitable size, because, as has been said, the plot is the imitation of an action which is one and complete and of proper length; but by means of episodes a poem is increased in length, and an epic poem especially, because it has taken as its characteristics great size and length,[1] for it is a narration. But because every narrative is able to include many things at one time, the epic feigns that many of them happened at the same time in different places.... Hence by reason of this prerogative the heroic poem has in itself great magnificence, and because of the variety of matter taken from outside often refreshes the mind of the hearer with wondrous delight, and renews his attention, not to mention driving away the boredom that the length of the work might generate.... But though the epic has this prerogative of being carried to a great length, the plot should not be made up of more than one unit of material nor composed of actions that came about in a longer time than a single year,[2] for the epic narrative is not a history; the latter narrates not merely all the things that happen in the same time and all the things that happen to one or more persons, and which have come together by chance and without reason, but also things that have happened during many years and which come in order one after another.... But in a space of many years, as in the wars of the Romans with the Carthaginians, many things follow one after another of which it cannot be said that they terminate in a single manner. But the poet, as we have shown (since in one poem he comprehends those things which tend to one end), does not treat everything that happened to one man at the same time and in the same group of events, if they are varied and not of one sort.... Vergil did not set out to describe all that happened in ancient Latium as a result of the coming of the Trojans.... If he had described so many and so various things, the work would have become immense in size and not easy to understand, and even if it had not increased more than was fitting, it would have been in the utmost confusion because of its great variety. And if, according to the habit of the historians, the facts had been briefly narrated and the poem ornamented with no episode, the poetry would have been despoiled of its beauty.[3] As the most skillful of poets, they undertook to write about what among so many things was clearest and most suitable to be written about, and what would make up a unified and perfect action. And in order to enrich their works they interposed many and dissimilar things, but such as, even though they were introduced from without or were merely attached to the plot, were not so remote from it that they did not direct themselves to the same end. Hence those plots are thought the worst in which we see many things mingled neither according to verisimilitude nor necessity. Authors who fill up their pages with dreams commonly make this mistake.

Vespasiano. You are referring to the loves and the famous deeds of the Paladins, which indeed deserved to have their memory kept alive for eternal ages by the most noble writers.

Min. But do you not find in such books many episodes much removed from the principal action and the matter in hand and introduced there for no suitable reason, and are not their poems truly the idle tales of the romances?

Vesp. But for all that, people repeat or read some song of the loves and deeds of Rinaldo or Orlando more gladly than any of the more graceful *canzoni* or the better sonnets of Petrarch.

Min. True. But by whom is it done or with what judgment? Certainly by the common herd who do not know what poetry is nor understand in what the excellence of the poet consists. For my part I value a sonnet by Petrarch higher than all the romances; this indicates that the rabble is mistaken in its wishes.

Vesp. Is it not possible of that same material to compose a poetic plot and produce an excellent poem?

Min. Why not? But with another order and another method and another style. Anyone who carefully considers our argument will easily understand this.

Vesp. Since we have gone on so far in our reasoning, just what is the romance?

Min. I shall not deny that it is an imitation of great and illustrious actions that are worthy of epic poetry. But certainly the word is strange, and in the Spanish as well as in the Provençal I believe it refers to the vulgar tongue. In Spain and in Provence because of the Roman colonies Latin was generally diffused to such an extent that men spoke there in a Romanized fashion (for the Romans occupied both regions, and barbarous nations dwelt there). Since the Roman language persisting in those lands, though for the most part contaminated and destroyed, was nevertheless more regular and more graceful than the Gothic and the Alanic, their native tongues, they applied themselves to learning and retaining it, and called it Romance and wrote in it. Therefore, because they dealt in that language with the actions and the loves of the knights more than with any other subject, the compositions made on that theme were called romances. The same word passed into Italy, because our writers began to imitate the romantic and classical compositions of the barbarians. And since our authors, as Cicero teaches us, always improve what they find in others, they make also the poetry of the romances more graceful and beautiful, if in truth it is to be called poetry.

Vesp. Why is it not worthy of this name? Is not M. Ludovico Ariosto a most excellent poet, as he is a most noble writer of romances?

Min. Yes, indeed, nor do I judge that a lower estimate should be made of him. But I cannot affirm that his romances and those of the others contain the kind of poetry that Aristotle and Horace taught us.

Vesp. Of what consequence is it that the romance is not such poetry but another kind taken over from the Ultramontanes and made more splendid and more beautiful by the Italians, if the world is pleased with it and accepts and receives it with delight?

Min. I do not wonder about the common crowd, which oftentimes accepts things it does not understand; and when once it has adopted a thing with great pleasure, it always retains it and favors it; nor if anything better than that should present itself does it receive it willingly; such is the power of opinion firmly impressed on the human mind. But I cannot but be greatly astonished that there are some learned men, well versed in good literature and of excellent abilities, who (as I understand) acknowledge that there is not in the romances the form and the rule that Homer and Vergil follow, and that Aristotle and Horace command as appropriate, and who nevertheless labor to defend this error.[4] Nay more, since that sort of composition gives the deeds of errant knights, they obstinately affirm not merely that it is not fitting to write poetry in the manner of Vergil and Homer, but even that it is desirable that poetry also should be errant, passing from one manner to another, and binding together various things in one bundle.

Vesp. Will you teach us in what the romance differs from the heroic poem?

Min. The heroic poem, as I have said, sets out to imitate a memorable action carried to its conclusion by one illustrious person. The romance, they say, has as its object a crowd of knights and ladies and of affairs of war and peace, though in this group one knight is especially taken whom the author is to make glorious above all the others; he is to treat as many deeds by him and by the others as he thinks sufficient for the glory of those he is disposed to praise (though he may select the more memorable ones), and he takes for description diverse and contrasted lands and the various things that happened in them during all the time occupied by the fabulous story of the matter he sets out to sing.

Vesp: Does not the father of poetry do the same, since he deals with many very striking deeds of Ulysses, Diomed, the two Ajaxes, Menelaus, King Agamemnon, Nestor, and the other demigods, though he intends to praise Achilles above all the others?

Min: Yes, that is true; but he makes all spring from one beginning, and directs all to one end. This is not done in the romance. Homer takes as his subject the wrath of Achilles, and how injurious it was to the Greeks and how much damage it caused them, because while that demigod was fighting, none of the Trojans had the courage to issue out of the city. But when he turned against King Agamemnon because of the injury received from him and for that reason decided to fight no more against the enemy in aid of his own people, the Trojans took courage, summoned their energies, and many times came to combat to the disadvantage of the Greeks. Thus, treating with superhuman genius all that followed the wrath of Achilles, within that one action Homer included many things fitly joined to each other, such as the combat of Menelaus with Paris, of Hector with Ajax, and of Patroclus with Hector, and the plan

Ulysses made with Diomed to kill Rhesus and take away his horses, the burning of the ships, and other actions not a few, until the wrath of Achilles was changed by the death of Patroclus and turned against the Trojans, with the result that Hector was miserably killed.

In the *Orlando Furioso* the author could have followed the same order and method, if he had wished, and could have directed his poem to a similar end, for he could have undertaken to sing the amorous fury of Orlando and all that followed that madness, showing that the Moors did not have courage to undertake war against King Charles of France while Orlando was sane, but when he grew mad for love they passed into France and did very great damage to the Christians. In this he would have been able to treat the things done at that time because of love or any other cause, by the knights on one side or the other, who took part in that war. And after Orlando regained his first sanity, he was able to give the victory to the Christians through his valor.

Vesp. This was not the design of that poet, but he wished to show clearly that Ruggiero was worthy of praise above all the others, since from him the illustrious house of his patron, whom he intended to praise, had taken its origin.

Min. If he was not content to treat the deeds of Ruggiero, as of the most excellent of all the knights present in the war caused by the madness of Orlando, he could have composed another narrative about him, as Homer composed the *Iliad* in praise of Achilles and the *Odyssey* in praise of Ulysses, though Ulysses in the *Iliad* did many things greatly deserving praise. And so he would not have indicated by the title of the work that he was writing about Orlando and then written about another, as a principal character, nor would he have put forward a great number of persons and things, some of which are such that one of them alone would furnish a subject for an entire poem.

Vesp. Has not the *Iliad* its name from the place where the war was fought, and yet the subject of the work is the wrath of Achilles? And the tragedy entitled *Medea* and the other which is called *Tereus*, do they not have for their objects compassion directed to neither the one nor the other person named?

Min. The wrath of Achilles is not the subject of the divine *Iliad* in the sense of causing the action of the poem to show how great was the valor of the hero. While he appeared in the field the Greeks were victors, but after his wrath had so much power over him that he gave up bearing arms in their behalf, the victory went to the Trojans. And in the tragedies you speak of, what else is dealt with except the infelicity of the person from whom they have their names? I do not intend by what I have said to blame so great and noble a poem by so rare and excellent a poet, whose powers I marvel at; rather I exhort all to read the work, since it has power to give great delight and no little profit to those who understand it well. And I excuse the author, who, not because he did not know what was better but rather to give pleasure to the many, chose to follow the bad method he found in the romances. And if he put in the title of his poem the name of Orlando and not of Ruggiero, whom he set out to praise, he did it, as his defenders say, in order that the work should be more acceptable and more gladly read, because he thought the name of Orlando, as a more famous knight, would make it more pleasing than would that of Ruggiero or some other hero less known and less important in the romances. Ruggiero was so famous and well known from the romances of Boiardo that if Ariosto had written a book named after Ruggiero he would have been able to make it acceptable because of the beauty of his language, though the making of two separate poems, one on Orlando, the other on Ruggiero, would have been a heavy task and would have required a long time; nor, though he was not very old, did he have any certainty of so long a life that he would be able to finish both of them. Yet nonetheless he chose to base on the romances a single work in which these two heroes should be indicated as the chief and most glorious of all, the one to give his name to the poem, the other as providing the goal to which all might be directed.

Nor can it be believed that Ariosto was of the opinion that in the romances the form of Homeric poetry could not be kept, for the reason that in the *Odyssey*, to which the romance is more similar than to the *Iliad*, the only travelers introduced are Ulysses and Telemachus, the latter of whom pretends he is traveling in order to get news of his father, but in the romances many of the characters go on travels. Nor can it be believed for the reason that in the romances there are so many wandering knights they cannot be represented in any banquet or in any picture or in any guise whatever, as they are in the *Odyssey* in the case of Alcinous, Nestor, and Menelaus, and in the *Aeneid* in the case of Dido, Anchises, and Evander, and in the description of the shield, for the things the knights do can be narrated, as are in the *Iliad* the deeds of Ulysses and of Diomed and many other demigods. Nor can it be credited that Ariosto believed he could not follow the epic form on the ground that the epic founds its imitation on things that have truth in them or at least are accepted as true, because there can be no doubt that Aeneas came to Italy and acquired the kingdom of the Latins and the Rutulians, nor that the things described in the *Iliad* were the most memorable that happened in that war, nor that Patroclus was killed by Hector and Hector by Achilles, nor that after long wanderings Ulysses returned to his native land and his house and at last revenged himself on the suitors. On the contrary the writers of romances without any regard to the truth feign what never was, since neither written history nor fame gives any testimony to the love or the madness of Orlando, yet Boiardo feigned that he was in love and Ariosto that he was mad. Yet tragedy, which follows the truth or at least that which is held true, sometimes makes use of a novel event that has never really happened.[5] Nor, even though it always has been and always will be permitted to the poet to leave the path followed by the others, is it to be believed that the right to pass the bounds prescribed to poetry should be given him. Vergil rejected subjects to the narration of which idle spirits would have listened intently, as already written on by others and generally known, and set himself to follow that road by which he would be able

> To raise himself from earth, and, famous and victorious
> Through the praise of others, wheel in flight.

Yet he did not go so far as to abandon the bounds set down for the poet and preserved by the most worthy authors.

I do not believe that it ever came into the mind of Ariosto to think of the Italian language as so rustic and barbarous that it could not receive Homeric and Vergilian poetry, merely because the rabble had its ears prepared for the follies of the romances and because the verses of Italian are of other measure and other harmony than those of Greek and Latin, and the Christians have another religion, other laws, and other customs than the Gentiles did. God grant that a poet so judicious and of such excellence should not fall into such a thought! since it cannot be denied that Italian is so serious and graceful and fit to set forth in language every subject that can be expressed in words, that it can treat gracefully and seriously any sort of poetry.[6]

If modern melic poetry follows the footsteps of ancient poetry, though with a different harmony of words, and dramatic poetry in our time begins to appear beautiful for no other reason than it endeavors to assimilate itself to that of the ancients, cannot the epic, represented by the romances, take its example from the idea expressed in the books of Vergil and Homer? It cannot be denied that the *Teseid* of Boccaccio, which narrates deeds and loves not of knights but of heroes (although in it very little or no semblance of Homeric poetry can be seen), is no more pleasing to judicious and learned men than the *Ancroja*, or the *Spagna*, or the *Altobello*, or even the *Morgante*[7] or any other romance which in years past has gladly been read by the unlearned. This result would not have come about if the romances in themselves possessed such excellence as today some attribute to them in order to praise Ariosto. But they would assuredly praise him more if they would show that all their praise comes not from themselves but from the great powers of the noble genius of that author, who by his style made appear so beautiful and pleasing to all a thing in its nature barbarous and naked of all grace. Petrarch surely would not have called them dreams of sick men and follies of romance if in his times the opinion had been held that in them some vestige of poetry appeared. And it is not credible Dante would have said he could not find that any Italian up to his time had sung of arms, for the reason that no such composition was to be found in the hands of the common people, but rather because no person worthy of praise and esteemed for his pursuit of the muses had written of them, for it is held that the first writer of romances in whom some light of poetry shone was Boccaccio. Moreover Bembo would not have attempted,[8] as it is understood he did, to divert Ariosto from giving his efforts to romances and direct him to epic poetry if he had not thought the romances were ignoble. What shall we say of the verse? If it is worthy to have heroic matter sung in it, can we not infer that it also is such that he who writes in it can observe that law according to which, as poets of the first rank show us, an epic subject should be treated?

What shall we say of the diverse religion and of the different customs if not that, though the poet should properly harmonize himself with his times, he should not depart from the law of poetry? Antiquity had the celestial gods as well as those infernal and earthly; modern times have the angels and the saints in heaven and one God only, and on earth the monks and the hermits. Antiquity had oracles and sibyls; modern times have necromancers and magicians. Antiquity had enchanters, such as Circe and Calypso; recent times have the fates.

In ancient days the messengers of Jove were Mercury and Iris; but now some of the angels are sent by God.[9] But all this does not make it impossible that the subject matter of recent poetry should not and cannot be made up of one single entire and perfect action, as it was in ancient poetry. Though in Athens the judges conducted themselves in another manner than in Rome, the speech of those who accused or defended did not change its form and method. Marcus Tullius, wishing to teach the Romans the perfect manner of speaking, would not have translated what Aeschines and Demosthenes said to the judges, the one accusing and the other defending Ctesiphon, if, even though the form of managing a case in Greece was different from that which prevailed in Rome and some diversity is to be found in the words, he had thought he could not use their speeches as good examples.

Just because no other names in Italian poetry are so well known as those of Orlando and Rinaldo, it is not, I think, impossibe that a poem in the language now commonly written in Italy can be acceptable, even though it does not deal with one of those heroes, because I think that not the fame of the person celebrated in the verses but rather the ability of the poet gives a work authority and reputation. The name of Aeneas was known to but few (since no poem especially on him was read when Vergil commenced to write of him), but nonetheless the excellence of that divine poet made him famous and known to everyone, and gave the work composed on him so much favor that no other in the Latin tongue is so gladly read. Moreover the fame of Achilles and of Ulysses was not widespread until Homer, the prince of poets, wrote of them; and yet the *Iliad* and the *Odyssey* from the first day they were heard until the present have been most acceptable to all the world and ever will be. Even though it was not known in Italy what a paladin was and no one had heard such a name before men began to write of them, common readers did not at all hesitate to accept first a romance composed about some knight of the court of King Arthur of England, and then one on King Charles of France.[10]

Even if the giant is more beautiful than the pigmy, and he is better who is defective in being too big rather than too small in stature, still the animal which is great beyond measure and whose members are not proportionate with each other will not appear in the least beautiful. And though Ariosto and Boiardo, to whom either their own virtue or fortune (if it is indeed true that every poem like every other work has its fate) or both together have given a very great reputation, have chosen to follow the way discovered by crude and barbarous writers, their authority ought not to render it improper to walk on the road trodden by the best of the ancients, for I do not believe it is possible to deny that things invented take from their inventors authority, force, and vigor. . . . Now we see what sort of men are the inventors of epic poetry, of which we are speaking, and what sort invent romances. Certain it is that the most noble poets of the Greeks and Latins gave us the idea of epic poetry expressed in their works and the most excellent writers of either tongue composed the poetic art from it. The inventors of the romances were barbarians, men who never had any reputation for learning, but were as if guided by the light of nature. But all affirm that natural endowment without art is not able to make a perfect work. And it appears to me that those who endeavor to find in these dreams a new type of art are seeking for leafy trees and green herbs in the sands of Ethiopia. Certainly this is nothing other than to seek for law in people who are naturally at enmity with reason, for the truth in vanity, and for certainty in error. And though to show that they are strong in ability and learning they make an effort to introduce a new poetic art into the world, they are not therefore of so great authority that we should believe them rather than Aristotle and Horace.

But if these two, using Homer's poetry as their example, have taught a true art of poetry, I do not see how another diverse from that can be set up, for the truth is one, and that which is once true must of necessity be true always and in every age; nor can the differences between various ages change what is true, though they may be able to change customs and life, yet in all their mutations the truth still remains stable.[11] Hence the variety that comes from different times cannot bring about the possibility of treating in poetry more than one action that is entire and of suitable size, with which all the rest may truly and reasonably harmonize and join. Besides, this Art gives all her effort to the imitation of Nature, and does well in proportion as she approaches her. But in everything of every sort Art holds to a law with which she is regulated in her work and by which she directs everything. One also is the idea in which Nature is mirrored when she works, and one is the form on which Art looks in carrying out her function. Architecture always has one law to which she ought to hold fast even though the building is often varied. Equally in its imitation painting makes an effort to keep one law, and so does sculpture and every other imitative art. And though now this art and now that one has been subject to variety, there has been no change in its inner being but only in some accidental quality, or in the mode of imitating the ornaments. Though painting commenced by drawing outlines and then added color, and after that the art, distinguishing itself, found light and shade and that splendid quality which, because it is between the other two, is called tone by the Greeks, and found the law for adapting one color to another, yet in this art the imitation does not change so much that it is not, as it always has been, of one complete action. Nor because kinds of poetry are diverse (for we see that epic is one thing, dramatic poetry another and lyric another, and each holds to its own method, its own instrument, its own style, its own form, and its own way) do they therefore fail to guard in the same way the unity of the matter taken for imitation. And the epic, though it is much more extensive and takes in more things, never thought that it was permitted to depart from the same law. Colossi surely do not differ from pygmies in this. And what art, what science, what discipline can be found (not architecture, not music, not painting, not sculpture, not military affairs, not medicine) in which anyone works without endeavoring to follow the steps of the ancients, and in which he will not be most praised who follows them most closely? Only poetry presumes in our times to do what has always been blamed by wise men, and those are not lacking who hold it more beautiful and better than ever.[12] But it is according to reason that in every poem there should be treated one sole and single action which should be perfect and of suitable length since on searching through all the arts and all the sciences you will not find a written work which has more than one subject under which may be put all that is treated in it, and to which everything may be directed as to the unique object of that work.

Vesp. Not to contradict your opinion, the reasons for which seem to me conclusive, but to make the truth clearer, I shall ask you about this thing. How is it that the rule Aristotle gave us and Horace confirmed can be true if he who wrote the *Heracleid*,[13] and he who composed the *Theseid*, and Papinius, who wrote the *Achilleid*, and Ovid, who narrated the metamorphoses of the gods, of men, and of things, are by all looked on as poets? . . .

Min. . . . I surely will concede to you that those authors, who, you say, are put in the number of the poets, wrote stories in verse, and Ovid in the *Metamorphoses* made a fabulous story, since he brought together all the fables, knitting one after the other into the narration with wonderful power for arrangement, and much more appropriately than it had been done by those Greeks who wrote it in prose and left it for us to read. Yet as those Greeks are not for that reason reputed to be poets, so Ovid does not merit the name of poet because of it, just as he does not deserve it because he wrote the *Fasti*.

I shall never affirm that there is epic poetry in these works; why then are their authors to be called poets? I will explain to you. It is both because the common people attribute the name to all those who write in verse, whether they treat of agriculture, as Vergil and Hesiod, or of astrology, as Aratus, Manilius, and Pontanus, or of medicine, as Nicander, or of things done in war, as Quintus Calaber, . . . Silius Italicus, and Lucan, and because they adorn them with poetic splendors and add to them things feigned, as Vergil did in the *Georgics*[14] when he narrated the fable of Aristaeus. And all of this sort they call epic, as I said in my Latin treatise on the poet.

Vest. Cannot the romancers stand among these, since they write fabulous stories?

Min. You say what those content themselves with who presumptuously set Ariosto in many things before Homer and Vergil. And in truth it seems to me that romancers can reasonably be called neither by one nor the other name, since they set out to follow now these, now those, and now go by the way followed by neither one nor the other, for, like the pure epic poets, they narrate things of many persons and many years; like the true epic writers, who are called heroic,[15] they use recognitions and peripeties and depict customs and passions, and make choice of someone whom they present for praise before all the others, and increase the size of the poem with many episodes, and following their own peculiar custom often break the course of the narrative, and interrupt what they are dealing with, leaping from one part to another, and then take it up again, returning to the place whence they departed. This they do both when time allows and when it forbids. Time allows that when one action has been narrated, what has happened elsewhere at the same time should next be told, and that then returning to the narrative that was broken off the author should proceed with it; as was said above, the epic does this not without the pleasure of the auditor in the variety of things narrated, which naturally pleases. But time does not allow that when a battle has been joined or a tempest or some other thing commenced, it should be interrupted in the middle, and when the end of it is awaited, it should be left off for the sake of treating some other matter which happened to other persons in other places at the same time, as is the peculiar custom of the romancers without regard to what time demands or the desire of the reader, for they leave in the minds of their readers rather pain than delight, for it should reasonably please no one that a thing should be interrupted when it is most delightful. And I do not find it true that the attention is stimulated but rather that it is lessened, because it is fired with desire of knowing the end not when the narrative that has been begun is abandoned for another, but when the outcome is delayed by many accidents that pertain to the same subject. If that is a virtue the epic poet is not without it, because he is intent on a single principal action of a single man. For though he is not episodic, as are the romancers, yet he inserts so many episodes in his poem that if episodic structure were not a vice he would sometimes be able to use it. Vergil, for example, could have left Turnus shut up in the Trojan fort and passed to the council and to the assembly of the gods, and then returned to liberate Turnus, not without injury to his enemies, if he had thought that this leaving off of his narrative could reasonably delight; he could also have found occassion in other places for use of the same method.

FROM

Book II

Min. You will understand the end of tragic poetry when you have learned the function of the tragic poet, which is nothing other than to speak in verse in such a way that he may so teach, delight, and move[16] that he purges the passions from the minds of the spectators. Like every other dramatic poet, he is said to teach when he presents his poem in the theater, and in addition he brings especially before our eyes the example of the life and the manners of those who surpass others in greatness and in dignity and the favors of Fortune, and yet are through human error thrown into extreme unhappiness, so we may understand that in prosperity we are not to put our trust in worldly things, and that there is no one down here so long lived or so stable that he is not frail and mortal, no one so happy that he cannot become miserable, no one so great that he cannot become humble and low. And seeing in another so great a change of fortune, we should know how to guard ourselves that no unexpected evil may come upon us.[17] And if any evil does come upon us (since our nature is so subject to evil that it often molests us) we may know how with a patient spirit to sustain it. The same poet also, in addition to the pleasing quality of his verse, and the ornaments of speech, also delights us greatly with song, with the dance, and with spectacle, nor does he represent to us anything that does not please us, nor does he move us without delight;[18] but with the power of his words and with the weight of his thought he arouses passion in the mind and induces astonishment in it, both filling it with horror and moving it to pity. What is so tragic as to move another? And what moves so much as a terrible and miserable and unexpected happening, such as the cruel death of Hippolytus, the fierce and compassion-moving madness of Hercules, the unhappy exile of Oedipus? Yet this horror and this pity by delighting us surge us from like passions, because more than anything else they restrain the untamed fury of the human soul, for no one is so overcome by unrestrained appetites that if he is moved by fear and pity for the unhappiness of another, his soul is not purged of the passions which have been the cause of that unhappy state.[19] And the recollection of the grave misfortunes of others not merely makes us quicker and better prepared to support our own, but wiser and more skillful in escaping similar evils. A physician will not have greater capacity to expel with poisonous medicine the very poison of an illness which afflicts the body, than the tragic poet will to purge the mind of mighty perturbations with the force of the passions charmingly expressed in verses. And if music with the singing of words in the sacrifices purged the human soul, will not the harmony of the poet as well be able to do it?

Let us consider then how much assistance experience in adversity gives in bearing lightly the chances of human life, and how easily is sustained that fatigue to which one is accustomed. Now will not being accustomed to the passions make more easy the bearing of them? Neither is it true that in proportion as we listen to tragedies our passions are increased because the tragic stories move our spirits and perturb us.[20] On the contrary if it happens that we must be perturbed very seriously, we may bear our sufferings very lightly, for when we receive a wound we have foreseen, it must needs give us less pain, since no unexpected evil comes to him who is accustomed to be moved by the many and strange things that happen to others. Besides, if exercising ourselves with labors makes our bodies more apt to endure them without distress, and to this end the ancient laws and customs of Crete and Sparta are directed, will it be beyond reason that if we often hear and see in the theaters that which greatly disturbs us and horrifies us, our spirits may learn to bear easily the blows of fortune? Therefore, it may be held that no teaching is to be found which so much abates the passions of the mind as does tragic poetry, since she does not present before our eyes a single thing that cannot come about, and clearly presents to us the condition of man as though she were a brightly shining mirror;[21] and he who in this mirror sees the nature of things and the variety of life and the weakness of man does not grieve over it, when he thinks carefully on it, but wishing to act like a wise man, he will be able when fortune is adverse to console himself in three ways. First, because for a long time he will have considered that adversity might come upon him, and such a thought is excellent above every other remedy in its power to free the soul from every affliction. Next, because he understands that men must bear the accidents that happen to them. Lastly, because he knows nothing is evil except sin, and there should not be attributed to sin what does not proceed from a man's own will.

Angelo. From this discourse of yours I understand you have wished to show not merely that it is true that tragedy by means of pleasure purges the passions from the soul, as Aristotle thinks, but that one ought to hold the opinion of Plato false, for he blamed poetry because it fills the mind with perturbations.

Min. You have completely understood everything.

Ang. Since you have made the end of the tragic poet open and plain to us, tell us what his matter is.

Min. It cannot be doubted that it should be magnificent and serious, dealing with great and famous persons and marvelous and notable actions, since it represents to us what in ancient times chanced to the demigods and describes to us the things they did and suffered, yet not all of them, but only those that had a terrifying and miserable end. But because you will find that some men of this excellent type are good and some are evil and some partake of both qualities, being neither superior to the others in virtue nor so vicious that the responsibility for the unhappiness with which they are wounded by Fortune should be wholly attributed to them, it is not reasonable that the good, or even the evil, should be represented in the theater in whatever adversity they have fallen into; it is not merely unsuitable but is esteemed an unworthy and abominable thing to bring into the view of others those who, being of the best morals and ornamented with the greatest virtue, find themselves crushed by the blows of some wicked and horrible chance.... We may feel indignant, then, and have great displeasure at the adverse fortune of men famous for their virtue and perfect, but the ills of wicked and vile men do not appear to us worthy of pity.... Whence among those who are on a high level of glory and fortune, that man will be represented in the theater by the tragic poet who is not best and most excellent in virtue, nor altogether void of it; in fact, he will be rather more good than bad, and unhappy rather more through human error than through his own deliberate wickedness, as were Oedipus, Thyestes, and Creon. For this same reason the fortune of tragedy does not make a miserable and sorrowful man glad and happy, since there is nothing in such a change that is shocking or excites pity. This is confirmed by the fact that the business of the tragic poet is to put his reader into a condition of astonishment. And we consider those accidents astonishing that move us to compassion or horror, and yet the more when they come about with probability against our hopes and opinions, since events brought about by fortune, though of themselves they do not appear very worthy to cause astonishment, yet greatly excite us to wonder when we think they come about through the divine will or as the result of a plan.[22]

Min. That especially belongs to the tragic poet which fills the hearer with astonishment by horrifying him or moving him to compassion, and what we receive from an enemy is not so horrifying nor so pitiable that we ought to marvel at it, for it is not a very strange thing that one enemy should fiercely kill another, and evil that happens to the good excites in us anger and vexation rather than horror or compassion, as we have shown. You cannot deny, then, that if we are intent on what pure tragedy demands as suitable to it, we are forced to include its truly appropriate material within such narrow limits. Yet since tragedies are found of which the plots are double, as we shall explain, and many things happen which cause great astonishment not because of the person to whom they happen or by whom they are done, but in themselves, either through their

L'ARTE POETICA

novelty, as in the death of Macaria,[23] or because the action is full of inhumanity, as was the case of the miserable Trojan women,[24] we may widen the range of subjects suitable to tragedy and define it in such a way that whoever suffers a marvelous thing, if it is horrifying or causes compassion, will not be outside the scope of tragedy, whether he be good or whether he be evil.[25] As to Aristotle's saying that the finest tragedies are few for no other reason except that it comes to few to suffer or do things serious and terrible, you see clearly that in such cases one must consider him who suffers the ill and him who causes it. And with regard to him who causes it there is no doubt that the precept is true that he should be a friend or relative to him who receives death or wounds or similar afflictions. But considering him who suffers, even though he be an enemy and deserves pain, his case is not therefore wholly unworthy of compassion.

NOTES

1. Joachim du Bellay called the epic "the long poem" (*Defence and Illustration of the French Language*, Bk. II, chap. V).

2. This corresponds to the single day allowed to the drama.

3. The primary purpose of the episode is adornment. It falls among things that the poet uses for delight rather than for profit.

4. Perhaps Giraldi, *On the Romances*.

5. Aristotle, *Poetics*, IX, first par., above. Cf. Jonson's "truth of argument" (*Sejanus*).

6. Cf. Sidney's praise of English, sect. 55.

7. The *Morgante maggiore* of Pulci is the best known of the romances in this list; a translation of the first canto may be found in the works of Byron.

8. An Italian cardinal and literary dictator, as it were, in the early sixteenth century.

9. This passage may be said to foretell what was to be done by Tasso in *Jerusalem Delivered* and by Milton in *Paradise Lost*.

10. Charlemagne, who is important in the *Orlando Innamorato* of Boiardo and the *Orlando Furioso* of Ariosto.

11. On the permanence of artistic principles see Tasso, *The Heroic Poem*, secs. 28 ff.

12. As did Giraldi in the works given immediately above. In his epigram beginning "Three poets," Dryden asserted the superiority of Milton to Homer and Vergil. The claims of the ancients and the moderns were much discussed in the eighteenth century. See Swift's *Battle of the Books*.

13. For this and the *Theseid* see Aristotle's *Poetics*, chap. VIII, first par.

14. *Ibid.*, IV, 315 ff.

15. Cf. the distinction made by Edward Phillips, *Theatrum Poetarum*, sect. 8.

16. For the addition of *moving* to the Horatian *teach and delight* (*Art of Poetry*, 333, above) cf. Sidney, *Defense*, sect. 26.

17. The concept of Fortune is highly important in Renaissance tragedy, as is apparent on reading Jonson's *Sejanus*. Cf. Sidney's presentation of the tragic uncertainty of life and the overthrow of the great (*Defense*, sect. 32). Perhaps there was some influence of the line from Horace: "Then the fortune of kings, with their hands bound behind them, is dragged on the stage" (*Epistles*, II, I, 191).

18. See Aristotle, *Poetics*, VI, 49b20.

19. Horace, *Art of Poetry*, 344.

20. A marginal note indicates that this passage is a refutation of the opinion of Plato that tragic perturbations augment the passions (*Republic*, III).

21. Cf. the prologue to Marlowe's *Tamburlaine*:

> View but his picture in this tragic glass,
> And then applaud his fortune as you please.

22. This whole section may be compared with Aristotle, *Poetics* XIII, as an example of Renaissance modification of Greek theory.

23. In *De poeta*, Minturno writes: "In the *Children of Hercules* by Euripides, the Pythia answered that the brothers of Macaria would not be safe and victorious unless some virgin should be slain as a victim to Ceres. Therefore, that they might gain the victory, Macaria of her free will presented herself to be sacrificed."

24. Euripides, *The Trojan Women*.

25. In *De poeta*, Minturno argues for the death of Christ as a tragic subject: "Events are not lacking that can strike terror to our spirits."

Roger Ascham
1516–1568

Roger Ascham's *The Schoolmaster* (1570) profoundly shaped Elizabethan views on education, and Ascham's opinions concerning the role played by the imitation of the classical authors in a child's education are generally important to the criticism of the time.

Ascham was educated by Sir Humphrey Wingfield, who sent him to St. John's College, Cambridge in 1530. Cambridge at that time was at the height of its newly acquired enthusiasm for the classics, especially the Greek classics. After receiving his M.A., he was awarded a Greek readership at the university. He found higher patronage, however, in 1545 when he dedicated his treatise *Toxophilus* ("lover of the bow") to King Henry VIII. He later tutored Princess Elizabeth in Greek and Latin for two years before becoming the secretary to Sir Richard Moryson, English ambassador to the Emperor Charles V. In 1553 he became the Latin secretary to Edward VI, a position which he retained until his death, even during the reign of Queen Mary, who could have been expected to dismiss a Protestant such as Ascham.

Despite his classical education, Ascham favored the widespread use of English. Writing to Sir William Cecil in 1548, he urged him to cultivate the English language "so that men might understand that even our language allows a man to write in it with beauty and eloquence." At the same time, however, Ascham was convinced, as was du Bellay before him in his *Defence of the French Language*, that the true models of eloquence lay in the Greek and Latin authors. Thus, Ascham placed heavy emphasis upon his doctrine of imitation, which is essentially "following the best authors," among whom Cicero is most worth imitating. Ascham then places himself in the interesting position, characteristic of his time, of recommending classical models to form the basis of the vernacular as a literary language.

The Schoolmaster is also notable for the ferocity of its attack upon what he calls "rude beggarly rhyming" in poetry and its hostility to medieval forms such as the romance. It was, in fact, characteristic of the Renaissance literary critic to disparage the rich medieval literary tradition in favor of an idealized classical past. The extent of Ascham's feeling on the subject can be gauged from his statement that to continue rhyming would be "to eat acorns with swine when we might freely eat wheat bread amongst men." He favors the idea of reviving classical meters without providing any specific recommendations.

Ascham can be an excellent literary critic. He praises Chaucer for presenting "the inward disposition of the mind" of his characters. As might be expected, however, he is entirely blind to the merits of Malory's *Morte d'Arthur*, which he termed a work of "open manslaughter and bold bawdry." As a critic of contemporary literature, he is perhaps even more limited, proposing Watson's *Absalon* and Buchanan's *Jepthe* as the finest tragedies of the era.

The selections from *The Schoolmaster* are taken from *Elizabethan Critical Essays*, edited by G. Gregory Smith (Oxford University Press, 1904).

FROM

The Schoolmaster

OF IMITATION

Imitation is a facultie to expresse liuelie and perfitelie that example which ye go about to folow. And of it selfe it is large and wide: for all the workes of nature in a manner be examples for arte to folow.

But to our purpose: all languages, both learned and mother tonges, be gotten, and gotten onelie by Imitation. For as ye vse to heare, so ye learne to speake: if ye heare no other, ye speake not your selfe: and whome ye onelie heare, of them ye onelie learne.

And therefore, if ye would speake as the best and wisest do, ye must be conuersant where the best and wisest are: but if yow be borne or brought vp in a rude contrie, ye shall not chose but speake rudelie: the rudest man of all knoweth this to be trewe.

Yet neuerthelesse, the rudenes of common and mother tonges is no bar for wise speaking. For in the rudest contrie, and most barbarous mother language, many be found [that] can speake verie wiselie: but in the Greeke and Latin tong, the two onelie learned tonges, which be kept not in common taulke but in priuate bookes, we finde always wisdome and eloquence, good matter and good vtterance, neuer or seldom asonder. For all soch Authors as be fullest of good matter and right iudgement in doctrine be likewise always most proper in wordes, most apte in sentence, most plaine and pure in vttering the same.

And, contrariwise, in those two tonges, all writers, either in Religion or any sect of Philosophie, who so euer be founde fonde in iudgement of matter, be commonlie found as rude in vttering their mynde. For Stoickes, Anabaptistes, and Friers, with Epicures, Libertines, and Monkes, being most like in learning and life, are no fonder and pernicious in their opinions than they be rude and barbarous in their writinges. They be not wise therefore that say, "What care I for a mans wordes and vtterance, if his matter and reasons be good." Soch men say so, not so moch of ignorance, as eyther of some singular pride in themselues or some speciall malice or other, or for some priuate and parciall matter, either in Religion or other kinde of learning. For good and choice meates be no more requisite for helthie bodies than proper and apte wordes be for good matters, and also plaine and sensible vtterance for the best and depest reasons: in which two pointes standeth perfite eloquence, one of the fairest and rarest giftes that God doth geue to man.

Ye know not what hurt ye do to learning, that care not for wordes but for matter, and so make a deuorse betwixt the tong and the hart. For marke all aiges: looke vpon the whole course of both the Greeke and Latin tonge, and ye shall surelie finde that, whan apte and good wordes began to be neglected, and properties of those two tonges to be confounded, than also began ill deedes to spring, strange maners to oppresse good orders, newe and fond opinions to striue with olde and trewe doctrine, first in Philosophie and after in Religion, right iudgement of all thinges to be peruerted, and so vertue with learning is contemned, and studie left of: of ill thoughtes cummeth peruerse iudgement, of ill deedes springeth lewde taulke. Which fower misorders, as they mar mans life, so destroy they good learning withall.

But behold the goodnesse of Gods prouidence for learning: all olde authors and sectes of Philosophy, which were fondest in opinion and rudest in vtterance, as Stoickes and Epicures, first contemned of wise men and after forgotten of all men, be so consumed by tymes, as they be now not onelie out of vse but also out of memorie of man: which thing, I surelie thinke, will shortlie chance to the whole doctrine and all the bookes of phantasticall Anabaptistes and Friers, and of the beastlie Libertines and Monkes.

Againe, behold on the other side how Gods wisdome hath wrought, that of *Academici* and *Peripatetici*, those that were wisest in iudgement of matters and purest in vttering their myndes, the first and chiefest that wrote most and best in either tong, as Plato and Aristotle in Greeke, Tullie in Latin, be so either wholie or sufficientlie left vnto vs, as I neuer knew yet scholer that gaue himselfe to like, and loue, and folowe chieflie those three Authors, but he proued both learned, wise, and also an honest man, if he ioyned with all the trewe doctrine of Gods holie Bible, without the which the other three be but fine edge tooles in a fole or mad mans hand.

But to returne to Imitation agayne: There be three kindes of it in matters of learning.

The whole doctrine of Comedies and Tragedies is a perfite imitation, or faire liuelie painted picture of the life of euerie degree of man. Of this Imitation writeth Plato at large in 3. *de Rep.*, but it doth not moch belong at this time to our purpose.

The second kind of Imitation is to folow for learning of tonges and sciences the best authors. Here riseth, emonges proude and enuious wittes, a great controuersie, whether one or many are to be folowed: and, if one, who is that one; Seneca or Cicero; Salust or Cæsar; and so forth in Greeke and Latin.

The third kinde of Imitation belongeth to the second: as, when you be determined whether ye will folow one or mo, to know perfitlie, and which way to folow, that one; in what place; by what meane and order; by what tooles and instrumentes ye shall do it; by what skill and iudgement ye shall trewelie discerne whether ye folow rightlie or no.

This *Imitatio* is *dissimilis materiei similis tractatio*; and, also, *similis materiei dissimilis tractatio*, as Virgill folowed Homer: but the Argument to the one was Vlysses, to the other Æneas. Tullie persecuted Antonie with the same wepons of eloquence that Demosthenes vsed before against Philippe.

Horace foloweth Pindar, but either of them his owne Argument and Person; as the one, Hiero king of Sicilie, the other, Augustus the Emperor: and yet both for like respectes, that is, for their coragious stoutnes in warre and iust gouernment in peace.

One of the best examples for right Imitation we lacke, and that is Menander, whom our Terence (as the matter required), in like argument, in the same Persons, with equall eloquence, foote by foote did folow.

Som peeces remaine, like broken Iewelles, whereby men may rightlie esteme and iustlie lament the losse of the whole.

Erasmus, the ornament of learning in our tyme, doth wish that some man of learning and diligence would take the like paines in Demosthenes and Tullie that Macrobius hath done in Homer and Virgill, that is, to write out and ioyne together where the one doth imitate the other. Erasmus wishe is good, but surelie it is not good enough: for Macrobius gatherings for the Æneados out of Homer, and Eobanus Hessus more diligent gatherings for the Bucolikes out of Theocritus, as they be not fullie taken out of the whole heape, as they should be, but euen as though they had not sought for them of purpose but fownd them scatered here and there by chance in their way, euen so, onelie to point out and nakedlie to ioyne togither their sentences, with no farder declaring the maner and way how the one doth folow the other, were but a colde helpe to the encrease of learning.

But if a man would take his paine also, whan he hath layd two places of Homer and Virgill or of Demosthenes and Tullie togither, to teach plainlie withall, after this sort:

1. Tullie reteyneth thus moch of the matter, thies sentences, thies wordes:
2. This and that he leaueth out, which he doth wittelie to this end and purpose.
3. This he addeth here.
4. This he diminisheth there.
5. This he ordereth thus, with placing that here, not there.
6. This he altereth and changeth, either in propertie of wordes, in forme of sentence, in substance of the matter, or in one or other conuenient circumstance of the authors present purpose.

In thies fewe rude English wordes are wrapt vp all the necessarie tooles and instrumentes, where with trewe Imitation is rightlie wrought withall in any tonge. Which tooles, I openlie confesse, be not of myne owne forging, but partlie left vnto me by the cunningest Master, and one of the worthiest Ientlemen that euer England bred, Syr Iohn Cheke, partelie borowed by me out of the shoppe of the dearest frende I haue out of England, Io. St. And therefore I am the bolder to borow of him, and here to leaue them to other, and namelie to my Children: which tooles, if it please God that an other day they may be able to vse rightlie, as I do wish and daylie pray they may do, I shal be more glad than if I were able to leaue them a great quantitie of land.

This foresaide order and doctrine of Imitation would bring forth more learning, and breed vp trewer iudgement, than any other exercise that can be vsed, but not for yong beginners, bicause they shall not be able to consider dulie therof. And, trewelie, it may be a shame to good studentes, who, hauing so faire examples to follow, as Plato and Tullie, do not vse so wise wayes in folowing them for the obteyning of wisdome and learning as rude ignorant Artificers do for gayning a small commoditie. For surelie the meanest painter vseth more witte, better arte, greater diligence, in hys shoppe, in folowing the Picture of any meane mans face, than commonlie the best studentes do, euen in the vniuersitie, for the atteining of learning it selfe.

Some ignorant, vnlearned, and idle student, or some busie looker vpon this litle poore booke, that hath neither will to do good him selfe, nor skill to iudge right of others, but can lustelie contemne, by pride and ignorance, all painfull diligence and right order in study, will perchance say that I am to precise, to curious, in marking and piteling thus about the imitation of others; and that the olde worthie Authors did neuer busie their heades and wittes in folowyng so preciselie, either the matter what other men wrote, or els the maner how other men wrote. They will say it were a plaine slauerie, and iniurie to, to shakkle and tye a good witte, and hinder the course of a mans good nature, with such bondes of seruitude, in folowyng other.

Except soch men thinke them selues wiser than Cicero for teaching of eloquence, they must be content to turne a new leafe.

The best booke that euer Tullie wrote, by all mens iudgement, and by his owne testimonie to, in wrytyng wherof he employed most care, studie, learnyng, and iudgement, is his booke *de Orat. ad Q. F.* Now let vs see what he did for the matter, and also for the maner of writing therof. For the whole booke consisteth in these two pointes onelie: In good matter, and good handling of the matter. And first, for the matter, it is whole Aristotles, what so euer Antonie in the second and Crassus in the third doth teach. Trust not me, but beleue Tullie him selfe, who writeth so, first, in that goodlie long Epistle *ad P. Lentulem*, and after in diuerse places *ad Atticum*. And in the verie booke it selfe Tullie will not haue it hidden, but both Catulus and Crassus do oft and pleasantly lay that stelth to Antonius charge. Now, for the handling of the matter, was Tullie so precise and curious rather to follow an other mans Paterne than to inuent some newe shape him selfe, namelie in that booke, wherein he purposed to leaue to posteritie the glorie of his witte? yea forsooth, that he did. And this is not my gessing and gathering, nor onelie performed by Tullie in verie deed, but vttered also by Tullie in plaine wordes: to teach other men thereby what they should do in taking like matter in hand.

And that which is especially to be marked, Tullie doth vtter plainlie his conceit and purpose therein, by the mouth of the wisest man in all that companie: for sayth Scaeuola him selfe, *Cur non imitamur, Crasse, Socratem illum, qui est in Phaedro Platonis? etc.*

And furder to vnderstand that Tullie did not *obiter* and bichance, but purposelie and mindfullie, bend him selfe to a precise and curious Imitation of Plato, concernyng the shape and forme of those bookes, marke, I pray you, how curious Tullie is to vtter his purpose and doyng therein, writing thus to Atticus.

Quod in his Oratoriis libris, quos tantopere laudas, personam desideras Scaeuolae, non eam temere dimoui: sed feci idem, quod in politeia *deus ille noster Plato, cum in Piraeeum Socrates venisset ad Cephalum locupletem et festiuum senem, quoad primus ille sermo haberetur, adest in disputando senex: deinde, cum ipse quoque commodissime locutus esset, ad rem diuinam dicit se velle discedere, neque postea reuertitur. Credo Platonem vix putasse satis consonum fore, si hominem id aetatis in tam longo sermone diutius retinuisset.*

THE SCHOOLMASTER

Multo ego satius hoc mihi cauendum putaui in Scaeuola, qui et aetate et valetudine erat ea qua [esse] meministi, et his honoribus, vt vix satis decorum videretur, eum plures dies esse in Crassi Tusculano. Et erat primi libri sermo non alienus a Scaeuolae studiis: reliqui libri technologian *habent, vt scis. Huic ioculatoriae disputationi senem illum, vt noras, interesse sane nolui.*

If Cicero had not opened him selfe and declared hys owne thought and doynges herein, men that be idle, and ignorant, and enuious of other mens diligence and well doinges, would haue sworne that Tullie had neuer mynded any soch thing, but that of a precise curiositie we fayne and forge and father soch thinges of Tullie as he neuer ment in deed. I write this not for nought; for I haue heard some both well learned and otherwayes verie wise, that by their lustie misliking of soch diligence haue drawen back the forwardnes of verie good wittes. But euen as such men them selues do sometymes stumble vpon doyng well by chance and benefite of good witte, so would I haue our scholer always able to do well by order of learnyng and right skill of iudgement.

Concernyng Imitation many learned men haue written, with moch diuersitie for the matter, and therfore with great contrarietie and some stomacke amongest them selues. I haue read as many as I could get diligentlie, and what I thinke of euerie one of them I will freelie say my mynde. With which freedome I trust good men will beare, bicause it shall tend to neither spitefull nor harmefull controuersie.

In Tullie, it is well touched, shortlie taught, not fullie declared by *Ant.* in 2. *de Orat.*: and afterward in *Orat. ad Brutum*, for the liking and misliking of Isocrates: and the contrarie iudgement of Tullie agaynst Caluus, Brutus, and Calidius, *de genere dicendi Attico et Asiatico.*

Dionis. Halic. *peri mimēseōs* I feare is lost: which Author, next Aristotle, Plato, and Tullie, of all other that write of eloquence, by the iudgement of them that be best learned deserueth the next prayse and place.

Quintilian writeth of it, shortly and coldlie for the matter, yet hotelie and spitefullie enough agaynst the Imitation of Tullie.

Erasmus, beyng more occupied in spying other mens faultes than declaryng his owne aduise, is mistaken of many, to the great hurt of studie, for his authoritie sake. For he writeth rightlie, rightlie vnderstanded: he and Longolius onelie differing in this, that the one seemeth to giue ouermoch, the other ouer litle, to him whom they both best loued and chiefly allowed of all other.

Budæus in his Commentaries roughlie and obscurelie, after his kinde of writyng: and for the matter, caryed somewhat out of the way in ouermuch misliking the Imitation of Tullie.

Phil. Melancthon learnedlie and trewlie.

Camerarius largely with a learned iudgement, but somewhat confusedly, and with ouer rough a stile.

Sambucus largely, with a right iudgement but somewhat a crooked stile.

Other haue written also, as Cortesius to Politian, and that verie well: *Bembus ad Picum* a great deale better: but Ioan. Sturmius, *de Nobilitate literata et de Amissa dicendi ratione*, farre best of all, in myne opinion, that euer tooke this matter in hand. For all the rest declare chiefly this point, whether one, or many, or all are to be followed: but Sturmius onelie hath most learnedlie declared who is to be followed, what is to be followed, and, the best point of all, by what way and order trew Imitation is rightlie to be exercised. And although Sturmius herein doth farre passe all other, yet hath he not so fullie and perfitelie done it as I do wishe he had, and as I know he could. For though he hath done it perfitelie for precept, yet hath he not done it perfitelie enough for example: which he did, neither for lacke of skill, nor by negligence, but of purpose, contented with one or two examples, bicause he was mynded in those two bookes to write of it both shortlie, and also had to touch other matters.

Barthol. Riccius Ferrariensis also hath written learnedlie, diligentlie, and verie largelie of this matter, euen as hee did before verie well *de Apparatu linguae Lat.* He writeth the better in myne opinion, bicause his whole doctrine, iudgement, and order semeth to be borowed out of Io. Stur. bookes. He addeth also examples, the best kinde of teaching: wherein he doth well, but not well enough: in deede, he committeth no faulte, but yet descrueth small praise. He is content with the meane, and followeth not the best: as a man that would feede vpon Acornes, whan he may eate as good cheape the finest wheat bread. He teacheth, for example, where and how two or three late Italian Poetes do follow Virgil; and how Virgil him selfe in the storie of Dido doth wholie imitate Catullus in the like matter of Ariadna: Wherein I like better his diligence and order of teaching than his iudgement in choice of examples for Imitation. But, if he had done thus, if he had declared where and how, how oft and how many wayes, Virgil doth folow Homer, as for example the comming of Vlysses to Alcynous and Calypso, with the comming of Æneas to Cartage and Dido; Likewise the games, running, wrestling, and shoting, that Achilles maketh in Homer, with the selfe same games that Æneas maketh in Virgil; The harnesse of Achilles, with the harnesse of Æneas, and the maner of making of them both by Vulcane; The notable combate betwixt Achilles and Hector, with as notable a combate betwixt Æneas and Turnus; The going downe to hell of Vlysses in Homer, with the going downe to hell of Æneas in Virgil; and other places infinite mo, as similitudes, narrations, messages, discriptions of persons, places, battels, tempestes, shipwrackes, and common places for diuerse purposes, which be as precisely taken out of Homer as euer did Painter in London follow the picture of any faire personage; And when thies places had bene gathered together by this way of diligence, than to haue conferred them together by this order of teaching, as diligently to marke what is kept and vsed in either author, in wordes, in sentences, in matter, what is added, what is left out, what ordered otherwise, either *praeponendo, interponendo,* or *postponendo,* and what is altered for any respect, in word, phrase, sentence, figure, reason, argument, or by any way of circumstance: If Riccius had done this, he had not onely bene well liked for his diligence in teaching, but also iustlie commended for his right iudgement in right choice of examples for the best Imitation.

Riccius also for Imitation of prose declareth where and how Longolius doth folow Tullie; but, as for Longolius, I would not haue him the patern of our Imitation. In deede, in Longolius shoppe be proper and faire shewing colers, but as for shape, figure, and naturall cumlines, by the iudgement of best iudging artificers he is rather allowed as one to be borne withall than especially commended as one chieflie to be folowed.

If Riccius had taken for his examples where Tullie him selfe foloweth either Plato or Demosthenes, he had shot than at the right marke. But to excuse Riccius somwhat, though I can not fullie defend him, it may be sayd his purpose was to teach onelie the Latin tong; when thys way that I do wish, to ioyne Virgil with Homer, to read Tullie with Demosthenes and Plato, requireth a cunning and perfite Master in both the tonges. It is my wish in deede, and that by good reason: For who so euer will write well of any matter must labor to expresse that that is perfite, and not to stay and content himselfe with the meane: yea, I say farder, though it be not vnposible, yet it is verie rare, and meruelous hard, to proue excellent in the Latin tong for him that is not also well seene in the Greeke tong. Tullie him selfe, most excellent of nature, most diligent in labor, brought vp from his cradle in that place and in that tyme where and whan the Latin tong most florished naturallie in euery mans mouth, yet was not his owne tong able it selfe to make him so cunning in his own tong, as he was in deede, but the knowledge and Imitation of the Greeke tong withall.

This he confesseth himselfe; this he vttereth in many places, as those can tell best that vse to read him most.

Therefore thou that shotest at perfection in the Latin tong think not thy selfe wiser than Tullie was, in choice of the way that leadeth rightlie to the same: thinke not thy witte better than Tullies was, as though that may serue thee that was not sufficient for him. For euen as a hauke flieth not hie with one wing, euen so a man reacheth not to excellency with one tong.

I haue bene a looker on in the Cokpit of learning thies many yeares: And one Cock onelie haue I knowne, which with one wing, euen at this day, doth passe all other, in myne opinion, that euer I saw in any pitte in England, though they had two winges. Yet neuerthelesse, to flie well with one wing, to runne fast with one leg, be rather rare Maistreis moch to be merueled at than sure examples safelie to be folowed. A Bushop that now liueth, a good man, whose iudgement in Religion I better like than his opinion in perfitnes in other learning, said once vnto me: "We haue no nede now of the Greeke tong, when all thinges be translated into Latin." But the good man vnderstood not that euen the best translation is, for mere necessitie, but an euill imped wing to flie withall, or a heuie stompe leg of wood to go withall: soch, the hier they flie, the sooner they falter and faill: the faster they runne, the ofter they stumble, and sorer they fall. Soch as will nedes so flie, may flie at a Pye and catch a Dawe: And soch runners, as commonlie they shoue and sholder to stand formost, yet in the end they cum behind others and deserue but the hopshakles, if the Masters of the game be right iudgers.

Therefore, in perusing thus so many diuerse bookes for Imitation, it came into my head that a verie profitable booke might be made *de Imitatione*, after an other sort than euer yet was attempted of that matter, conteyning a certaine fewe fitte preceptes, vnto the which should be gathered and applied plentie of examples, out of the choisest authors of both the tonges. This worke would stand rather in good diligence for the gathering, and right iudgement for the apte applying of those examples, than any great learning or vtterance at all.

The doing thereof would be more pleasant than painfull, and would bring also moch proffet to all that should read it, and great praise to him [that] would take it in hand, with iust desert of thankes.

Erasmus, giuyng him selfe to read ouer all Authors, Greke and Latin, seemeth to haue prescribed to him selfe this order of readyng, that is, to note out by the way three speciall pointes, All Adagies, all similitudes, and all wittie sayinges of most notable personages: And so, by one labour, he left to posteritie three notable bookes, and namelie two, his *Chiliades, Apophthegmata*, and *Similia*. Likewise, if a good student would bend him selfe to read diligently ouer Tullie, and with him also at the same tyme as diligently Plato and Xenophon with his bookes of Philosphie, Isocrates and Demosthenes with his orations, and Aristotle with his Rhetorickes, which fiue of all other be those whom Tullie best loued and specially followed, and would marke diligently in Tullie where he doth *exprimere* or *effingere* (which be the verie proper wordes of Imitation) either *copiam Platonis* or *venustatem Xenophontis, suauitatem Isocratis* or *vim Demosthenis, propriam et puram subtilitatem Aristotelis*, and not onelie write out the places diligentlie, and lay them together orderlie, but also to conferre them with skilfull iudgement by those few rules which I haue expressed now twise before: if that diligence were taken, if that order were vsed, what perfite knowledge of both the tonges, what readie and pithie vtterance in all matters, what right and deepe iudgement in all kinde of learnyng would follow, is scarse credible to be beleued.

These bookes be not many, nor long, nor rude in speach, nor meane in matter, but, next the Maiestie of Gods holie word, most worthie for a man, the louer of learning and honestie, to spend his life in. Yea, I haue heard worthie M. Cheke many tymes say: I would haue a good student passe and iorney through all Authors both Greke and Latin; but he that will dwell in these few bookes onelie, first in Gods holie Bible, and than ioyne with it Tullie in Latin, Plato, Aristotle, Xenophon, Isocrates, and Demosthenes in Greke, must nedes proue an excellent man.

Some men alreadie in our dayes haue put to their helping handes to this worke of Imitation: As *Perionius, Henr. Stephanus in dictionario Ciceroniano*, and P. Victorius most praiseworthelie of all, in that his learned worke conteyning xxv. bookes *de varia lectione*: in which bookes be ioyned diligentlie together the best Authors of both the tonges where one doth seeme to imitate an other.

But all these, with Macrobius, Hessus, and other, be no more but common porters, caryers, and bringers of matter and stuffe togither. They order nothing. They lay before you what is done: they do not teach you how it is done. They busie not them selues with forme of buildyng. They do not declare, this stuffe is thus framed by Demosthenes, and thus and thus by Tullie, and so likewise in Xenophon, Plato, and Isocrates, and Aristotle. For ioyning Virgil with Homer I haue sufficientlie declared before.

The like diligence I would wish to be taken in Pindar and Horace, an equall match for all respectes.

In Tragedies (the goodliest Argument of all, and, for the vse either of a learned preacher or a Ciuill Ientleman, more profitable than Homer, Pindar, Virgill, and Horace, yea comparable in myne opinion with the doctrine of Aristotle, Plato, and Xenophon), the Grecians Sophocles and Euripides far ouer match our Seneca in Latin, namely in *Oikonomia et Decoro,* although Senacaes elocution and verse be verie commendable for his tyme. And for the matters of Hercules, Thebes, Hippolytus, and Troie, his Imitation is to be gathered into the same booke, and to be tryed by the same touchstone, as is spoken before.

In histories, and namelie in Liuie, the like diligence of Imitation could bring excellent learning, and breede stayde iudgement, in taking any like matter in hand. Onely Liuie were a sufficient taske for one mans studie, to compare him, first with his fellow for all respectes, Dion. Halicarnassaeus; who both liued in one tyme, tooke both one historie in hande to write, deserued both like prayse of learnynge and eloquence: Than with Polybius that wise writer, whom Liuie professeth to follow; and, if he would denie it, yet it is plaine that the best part of the thyrd Decade in Liuie is in a maner translated out of the thyrd and rest of Polibius: Lastlie with Thucydides, to whose Imitation Liuie is curiouslie bent, as may well appeare by that one Oration of those of Campania, asking aide of the Romanes agaynst the Samnites, which is wholie taken, Sentence, Reason, Argument, and order, out of the Oration of Corcyra, asking like aide of the Athenienses against them of Corinth. If some diligent student would take paynes to compare them togither, he should easelie perceiue that I do say trew. A booke thus wholie filled with examples of Imitation, first out of Tullie, compared with Plato, Xenophon, Isocrates, Demosthenes, and Aristotle, than out of Virgil and Horace, with Homer and Pindar, next out of Seneca, with Sophocles and Euripides, lastlie out of Liuie, with Thucydides, Polibius, and Halicarnassaeus, gathered with good diligence, and compared with right order, as I haue expressed before, were an other maner of worke for all kinde of learning, and namely for eloquence, than be those cold gatherings of Macrobius, Hessus, Perionius, Stephanus, and Victorius, which may be vsed, as I sayd before, in this case, as porters and caryers, deseruing like prayse, as soch men do wages; but onely Sturmius is he, out of whom the trew suruey and whole workemanship is speciallie to be learned.

I trust this my writyng shall giue some good student occasion to take some peece in hand of this worke of Imitation. And as I had rather haue any do it than my selfe, yet surelie my selfe rather than none at all. And by Gods grace, if God to lend me life, with health, free laysure, and libertie, with good likyng and a merie heart I will turne the best part of my studie and tyme to toyle in one or other peece of this worke of Imitation.

This diligence to gather examples, to giue light and vnderstandyng to good preceptes, is no new inuention, but speciallie vsed of the best Authors and oldest writers. For Aristotle him selfe (as Diog. Laertius declareth), when he had written that goodlie booke of the Topickes, did gather out of stories and Orators so many examples as filled xv. bookes, onlie to expresse the rules of his Topickes. These were the Commentaries that Aristotle thought fit for hys Topickes: And therfore to speake as I thinke, I neuer saw yet any Commentarie vpon Aristotles Logicke, either in Greke or Latin, that euer I lyked, bicause they be rather spent in declaryng scholepoynt rules than in gathering fit examples for vse and vtterance, either by pen or talke. For preceptes in all Authors, and namelie in Aristotle, without applying vnto them the Imitation of examples, be hard, drie, and cold, and therfore barrayn, vnfruitfull, and vnpleasant. But Aristotle, namelie in his Topickes and Elenches, should be not onelie fruitfull but also pleasant to, if examples out of *Plato* and other good Authors were diligentlie gathered and aptlie applied vnto his most perfit preceptes there. And it is notable that my frende Sturmius writeth herein, that there is no precept in Aristotles Topickes wherof plentie of examples be not manifest in Platos workes. And I heare say, that an excellent learned man, Tomitanus in Italie, hath expressed euerie fallacion in Aristotle with diuerse examples out of Plato. Would to God I might once see some worthie student of Aristotle and Plato in Cambrige, that would ioyne in one booke the preceptes of the one with the examples of the other. For such a labor were one speciall peece of that worke of Imitation, which I do wishe were gathered together in one Volume.

Cambrige, at my first comming thither, but not at my going away, committed this fault in reading the preceptes of Aristotle without the examples of other Authors: But herein, in my time, thies men of worthie memorie, M. Redman, M. Cheke, M. Smith, M. Haddon, M. Watson, put so to their helping handes, as that vniuersitie, and all studentes there, as long as learning shall last, shall be bounde vnto them, if that trade in studie be trewlie folowed which those men left behinde them there. . . .

Now to returne to that Question, whether one, a few, many, or all are to be followed, my aunswere shalbe short: All, for him that is desirous to know all: yea, the worst of all, as Questionistes, and all the barbarous nation of scholemen, helpe for one or other consideration: But in euerie separate kinde of learnyng, and studie by it selfe, ye must follow choselie a few, and chieflie some one, and that namelie in our schole of eloquence, either for penne or talke. And as in port[r]aicture and paintyng wise men chose not that workman that can onelie make a faire hand, or a well facioned legge, but soch one as can furnish vp fullie all the fetures of the whole body of a man, woman, and child, and with all is able to, by good skill, to giue to euerie one of these three, in their proper kinde, the right forme, the trew figure, the naturall color, that is fit and dew to the dignitie of a man, to the bewtie of a woman, to the sweetnes of a yong babe; euen likewise do we seeke soch one in our schole to folow, who is able alwayes, in all matters, to teach plainlie, to delite pleasantlie, and to cary away by force of wise talke, all that shall heare or read him, and is so excellent in deed as witte is able or wishe can hope to attaine vnto: And this not onelie to serue in the Latin or Greke tong, but also in our own English language. But yet, bicause the providence of God hath left vnto vs in no other tong, saue onelie in the Greke and Latin tong, the trew preceptes and perfite examples of eloquence, therefore must we seeke in the Authors onelie of those two tonges the trewe Paterne of Eloquence, if in any other mother tongue we looke to attaine either to perfit vtterance of it our selues or skilfull iudgement of it in others.

And now to know what Author doth medle onelie with some one peece and member of eloquence, and who doth perfitelie make vp the whole bodie, I will declare, as I can call to remembrance the goodlie talke that I haue had oftentymes of the trew difference of Authors with that Ientleman of worthie memorie, my dearest frend, and teacher of all the litle poore learning I haue, Syr Iohn Cheke.

The trew difference of Authors is best knowne *per diuersa genera dicendi* that euerie one vsed. And therfore here I will deuide *genus dicendi*, not into these three, *Tenue, mediocre, et grande*, but as the matter of euerie Author requireth, as

in Genus $\begin{cases} Poeticum \\ Historicum, \\ Philosophicum, \\ Oratorium. \end{cases}$

These differre one from an other in choice of wordes, in framyng of Sentences, in handling of Argumentes, and vse of right forme, figure, and number, proper and fitte for euerie matter; and euerie one of these is diuerse also in it selfe, as the first,

Poeticum, in $\begin{cases} Comicum, \\ Tragicum, \\ Epicum, \\ Melicum. \end{cases}$

And here, who soeuer hath bene diligent to read aduisedlie ouer Terence, Seneca, Virgil, Horace, or els Aristophanes, Sophocles, Homer, and Pindar, and shall diligently marke the difference they vse, in proprietie of wordes, in forme of sentence, in handlyng of their matter, he shall easelie perceiue what is fitte and *decorum* in euerie one, to the trew vse of perfite Imitation. Whan M. Watson in S. Iohns College at Cambrige wrote his excellent Tragedie of Absalon, M. Cheke, he, and I, for that part of trew Imitation, had many pleasant talkes togither, in comparing the preceptes of Aristotle and Horace *de Arte Poetica* with the examples of Euripides, Sophocles, and Seneca. Few men, in writyng of Tragedies in our dayes, haue shot at this marke. Some in England, moe in France, Germanie, and Italie also, haue written Tragedies in our tyme: of the which not one I am sure is able to abyde the trew touch of Aristotles preceptes and Euripides examples, saue onely two that euer I saw, M. Watsons *Absalon* and Georgius Buckananus *Iephthe*. One man in Cambrige, well liked of many, but best liked of him selfe, was many tymes bold and busie to bryng matters vpon stages, which he called Tragedies. In one, wherby he looked to wynne his spurres, and whereat many ignorant felowes fast clapped their handes, he began the *Protasis* with *Trochoeiis Octonariis*: which kinde of verse, as it is but seldome and rare in Tragedies, so it is neuer vsed, saue onelie *in Epitasi*: whan the Tragedie is hiest and hotest, and full of greatest troubles. I remember ful well what M. Watson merelie sayd vnto me of his blindnesse and boldnes in that behalfe, although otherwise there passed much frendship betwene them. M. Watson had an other maner care of perfection, with a feare and reuerence of the iudgement of the best learned: Who to this day would neuer suffer yet his *Absalon* to go abroad, and that onelie bicause, *in locis paribus, Anapestus* is twise or thrise vsed in stede of *Iambus*: A smal faulte, and such one as perchance would neuer be marked, no neither in Italie nor France. This I write, not so much to note the first, or praise the last, as to leaue in memorie of writing, for good example to posteritie, what perfection, in any tyme, was most diligentlie sought for in like maner, in all kinde of learnyng, in that most worthie College of S. Iohns in Cambrige.

Historicum, in $\begin{cases} Diaria, \\ Annales, \\ Commentarios, \\ Iustam\ Historiam. \end{cases}$

For what proprietie in wordes, simplicitie in sentences, plainnesse and light, is cumelie for these kindes, Cæsar and Liuie, for the two last, are perfite examples of Imitation: And for the two first the old paternes be lost, and as for some that be present and of late tyme, they be fitter to be read once for some pleasure than oft to be perused for any good Imitation of them.

Philosophicum, in $\begin{cases} Sermonem,\ \text{as}\ Officia \\ \quad Cic.\ et\ Eth.\ Arist. \\ Contentionem,\ \text{as the Dialoges of} \\ \quad Plato,\ Xenophon,\ \text{and}\ Cicero: \end{cases}$

Of which kinde of learnyng, and right Imitation therof, Carolus Sigonius hath written of late, both learnedlie and eloquentlie: but best of all my frende Ioan, Sturmius in hys Commentaries vpon Gorgias Platonis, which booke I haue in writyng, and is not yet set out in Print.

Oratorium, in $\begin{cases} Humile, \\ Mediocre, \\ Sublime. \end{cases}$

Examples of these three, in the Greke tong, be plentifull and perfite, as Lycias, Isocrates, and Demosthenes: and all three in onelie Demosthenes, in diuerse orations, as *contra Olimpiodorum, in Leptinem, et pro Ctesiphonte*. And trew it is that Hermogenes writeth of Demosthenes that all formes of Eloquence be perfite in him. In Ciceroes Orations *Medium et sublime* be most excellentlie handled, but *Humile* in his Orations is seldome sene. Yet neuerthelesse in other bookes, as in some part of his Offices, and specially *in Partitionibus*, he is comparable *in hoc humili et disciplinabili genere*, euen with the best that euer wrote in Greke. But of Cicero more fullie in fitter place. And thus the trew difference of stiles, in euerie Author and euerie kinde of learnyng, may easelie be knowne by this diuision:

in Genus $\begin{cases} \textit{Poeticum,} \\ \textit{Historicum,} \\ \textit{Philosophicum,} \\ \textit{Oratorium.} \end{cases}$

Which I thought in this place to touch onelie, not to prosecute at large, bicause, God willyng, in the Latin tong, I will fullie handle it in my booke *de Imitatione*.

Now, to touch more particularlie which of those Authors, that be now most commonlie in mens handes, will some affourd you some peece of Eloquence, and what maner a peece of eloquence, and what is to be liked and folowed, and what to be misliked and eschewed in them, and how some agayne will furnish you fully withall, rightly, and wisely considered, somwhat I will write as I haue heard Syr Iohn Cheke many tymes say.

The Latin tong, concerning any part of purenesse of it, from the spring to the decay of the same, did not endure moch longer than is the life of a well aged man, scarse one hundred yeares from the tyme of the last Scipio Africanus and Laelius to the Empire of Augustus. And it is notable that Vellius Paterculus writeth of Tullie, how that the perfection of eloquence did so remayne onelie in him and in his time, as before him were few which might moch delight a man, or after him any worthy admiration, but soch as Tullie might haue seene, and such as might haue seene Tullie. And good cause why: for no perfection is durable. Encrease hath a time, and decay likewise, but all perfit ripenesse remaineth but a moment: as is plainly seen in fruits, plummes, and cherries, but more sensibly in flowers, as Roses and such like: and yet as trewlie in all greater matters. For what naturallie can go no hier must naturallie yeld and stoupe againe.

Of this short tyme of any purenesse of the Latin tong, for the first fortie yeare of it, and all the tyme before, we haue no peece of learning left, saue Plautus and Terence, with a litle rude vnperfit pamflet of the elder Cato. And as for Plautus, except the scholemaster be able to make wise and ware choice, first in proprietie of wordes, than in framing of phrases and sentences, and chieflie in choice of honestie of matter, your scholer were better to play then learne all that is in him. But surelie, if iudgement for the tong, and direction for the maners, be wisely ioyned with the diligent reading of Plautus, than trewlie Plautus for that purenesse of the Latin tong in Rome, whan Rome did most florish in well doing, and so thereby in well speaking also, is soch a plentifull storeho[u]se for common eloquence, in meane matters, and all priuate mens affaires, as the Latin tong, for that respect, hath not the like agayne. Whan I remember the worthy tyme of Rome wherein Plautus did liue, I must nedes honor the talke of that tyme which we see Plautus doth vse.

Terence is also a storehouse of the same tong, for an other tyme, following soone after; and although he be not so full and plentiful as Plautus is, for multitude of matters and diuersitie of wordes, yet his wordes be chosen so purelie, placed so orderly, and all his stuffe so neetlie packed vp and wittely compassed in euerie place, as, by all wise mens iudgement, he is counted the cunninger workeman, and to haue his shop, for the rowme that is in it, more finely appointed and trimlier ordered than Plautus is.

Three thinges chiefly, both in Plautus and Terence, are to be specially considered: The matter, the vtterance, the words, the meter. The matter in both is altogether within the compasse of the meanest mens maners, and doth not stretch to any thing of any great weight at all, but standeth chiefly in vtteryng the thoughtes and conditions of hard fathers, foolish mothers, vnthrifty yong men, craftie seruantes, sotle bawdes, and wilie harlots, and so is moch spent in finding out fine fetches and packing vp pelting matters, soch as in London commonlie cum to the hearing of the Masters of Bridewell. Here is base stuffe for that scholer that should becum hereafter either a good minister in Religion or a Ciuill Ientleman in seruice of his Prince and contrie (except the preacher do know soch matters to confute them), whan ignorance surelie in all soch thinges were better for a Ciuill Ientleman than knowledge. And thus, for matter, both Plautus and Terence be like meane painters, that worke by halfes, and be cunning onelie in making the worst part of the picture, as if one were skilfull in painting the bodie of a naked person from the nauell downward, but nothing else.

For word and speach Plautus is more plentifull, and Terence more pure and proper: And for one respect Terence is to be embraced aboue all that euer wrote in hys kinde of argument: Bicause it is well known by good recorde of learning, and that by Ciceroes owne witnes, that some Comedies bearyng Terence name were written by worthy Scipio and wise Laelius, and namely *Heauton* and *Adelphi*. And therefore, as oft as I reade those Comedies, so oft doth sound in myne eare the pure fine talke of Rome, which was vsed by the floure of the worthiest nobilitie that euer Rome bred. Let the wisest man, and best learned that liueth, read aduisedlie ouer the first scene of *Heauton* and the first scene of *Adelphi*, and let him consideratlie iudge whether it is the talke of the seruile stranger borne, or rather euen that milde eloquent wise speach which Cicero in *Brutus* doth so liuely expresse in *Laelius*. And yet, neuerthelesse, in all this good proprietie of wordes and purenesse of phrases which be in Terence, ye must not follow him alwayes in placing of them, bicause for the meter sake some wordes in him somtyme be driuen awrie, which require a straighter placing in plaine prose, if ye will forme, as I would ye should do, your speach and writing to that excellent perfitnesse which was onely in Tullie, or onelie in Tullies tyme.

The meter and verse of Plautus and Terence be verie meane, and not to be followed: which is not their reproch, but the fault of the tyme wherein they wrote, whan no kinde of Poetrie in the Latin tong was brought to perfection, as doth well appeare in the fragmentes of Ennius, Cecilius, and others, and euidentlie in Plautus and Terence, if thies in Latin be compared with right skil with Homer, Euripides, Aristophanes, and other in Greeke of like sort. Cicero him selfe doth complaine of this vnperfitnes, but more plainly Quintilian, saying, *in Comoedia maxime claudicamus, et vix leuem consequimur vmbram*: and most earnestly of all Horace *in Arte Poetica*, which he doth namely *propter carmen*

Iambicum, and referreth all good studentes herein to the Imitation of the Greeke tong, saying,

Exemplaria Graeca
nocturna versate manu, versate diurna.

This matter maketh me gladly remember my sweete tyme spent at Cambrige, and the pleasant talke which I had oft with M. Cheke and M. Watson of this fault, not onely in the olde Latin Poets, but also in our new English Rymers at this day. They wished as Virgil and Horace were not wedded to follow the faultes of former fathers (a shrewd mariage in greater matters) but by right Imitation of the perfit Grecians had brought Poetrie to perfitnesse also in the Latin tong, that we Englishmen likewise would acknowledge and vnderstand rightfully our rude beggerly ryming, brought first into Italie by Gothes and Hunnes, whan all good verses and all good learning to were destroyd by them, and after caryed into France and Germanie, and at last receyued into England by men of excellent wit in deede, but of small learning and lesse iudgement in that behalfe.

But now, when men know the difference, and haue the examples, both of the best and of the worst, surelie to follow rather the Gothes in Ryming than the Greekes in trew versifiyng were euen to eate ackornes with swyne, when we may freely eate wheate bread emonges men. In deede, Chauser, Th. Norton of Bristow, my L. of Surrey, M. Wiat, Th. Phaer, and other Ientlemen, in translating Ouide, Palingenius, and Seneca, haue gonne as farre to their great praise as the copie they followed could cary them; but, if soch good wittes and forward diligence had bene directed to follow the best examples, and not haue bene caryed by tyme and custome to content themselues with that barbarous and rude Ryming, emonges their other worthy praises, which they haue iustly deserued, this had not bene the least, to be counted emonges men of learning and skill more like vnto the Grecians than vnto the Gothians in handling of their verse.

In deed, our English tong, hauing in vse chiefly wordes of one syllable which commonly be long, doth not well receiue the nature of *Carmen Heroicum*, bicause *dactylus*, the aptest foote for that verse, conteining one long and two short, is seldom therefore found in English; and doth also rather stumble than stand vpon *Monasyllabis*. Quintilian, in hys learned Chapiter *de Compositione*, geueth this lesson *de Monasyllabis* before me; and in the same place doth iustlie inuey against all Ryming; that if there be any who be angrie with me for misliking of Ryming may be angry for company to with Quintilian also for the same thing. And yet Quintilian had not so iust cause to mislike of it than as men haue at this day.

And although *Carmen Exametrum* doth rather trotte and hoble than runne smothly in our English tong, yet I am sure our English tong will receiue *carmen Iambicum* as naturallie as either Greke or Latin. But for ignorance men can not like, and for idleness men will not labor, to cum to any perfitenes at all. For, as the worthie Poetes in Athens and Rome were more carefull to satisfie the iudgement of one learned than rashe in pleasing the humor of a rude multitude, euen so if men in England now had the like reuerend regard to learning, skill, and iudgement, and durst not presume to write except they came with the like learnyng, and also did vse like diligence in searchyng out not onelie iust measure in euerie meter, as euerie ignorant person may easely do, but also trew quantitie in euery foote and sillable, as onelie the learned shalbe able to do, and as the Grekes and Romanes were wont to do, surelie than rash ignorant heads, which now can easely recken vp fourten sillabes, and easelie stumble on euery Ryme, either durst not, for lacke of such learnyng, or els would not, in auoyding such labor, be so busie as euerie where they be; and shoppes in London should not be so full of lewd and rude rymes, as commonlie they are. But now the ripest of tong be readiest to write: And many dayly in setting out bookes and balettes make great shew of blossomes and buddes, in whom is neither roote of learning nor frute of wisedome at all. Some that make Chaucer in English and Petrarch in Italian their Gods in verses, and yet be not able to make trew difference, what is a fault and what is a iust prayse in those two worthie wittes, will moch mislike this my writyng. But such men be euen like followers of Chaucer and Petrarke, as one here in England did folow Syr Tho. More, who, being most vnlike vnto him in wit and learnyng, neuertheles in wearing his gowne awrye vpon the one shoulder, as Syr Tho. More was wont to do, would nedes be counted lyke vnto him.

This mislikyng of Ryming beginneth not now of any newfangle singularitie, but hath bene long misliked of many, and that of men of greatest learnyng and deepest iudgement. And soch that defend it do so, either for lacke of knowledge what is best, or els of verie enuie that any should performe that in learnyng, whereunto they, as I sayd before, either for ignorance can not, or for idlenes will not, labor to attaine vnto.

And you that prayse this Ryming, bicause ye neither haue reason why to like it nor can shew learning to defend it, yet I will helpe you with the authoritie of the oldest and learnedst tyme. In Grece, whan Poetrie was euen as the hiest pitch of perfitnes, one Simmias Rhodius of a certaine singularitie wrote a booke in ryming Greke verses, naming it *hōon*, conteyning the fable how Iupiter in likenes of a swan gat that egge vpon Leda, whereof came Castor, Pollux, and faire [H]elena. This booke was so liked that it had few to read it, but none to folow it: But was presentlie contemned: and, sone after, both Author and booke so forgotten by men, and consumed by tyme, as scarse the name of either is kept in memorie of learnyng. And the like folie was neuer folowed of any many hondred yeares after, vntill the Hunnes and Gothians and other barbarous nations of ignorance and rude singularitie did reuiue the same folie agayne.

The noble Lord Th. Earle of Surrey, first of all English men in translating the fourth booke of Virgill, and Gonsaluo Periz, that excellent learned man, and Secretarie to kyng Philip of Spaine, in translating the Vlisses of Homer out of Greke into Spanish, haue both, by good iudgement, auoyded the fault of Ryming, yet neither of them hath fullie hit[t]e perfite and trew versifying. In deede, they obserue iust number, and euen feete: but here is the fault, that their feete be feete without ioyntes, that is to say, not distinct by trew quantitie of sillabes: And so soch feete be but numme feete, and be euen as vnfitte for a verse to turne and runne roundly withall as feete of brasse or wood be vnweeldie to go well withall. And as a foote of wood is a plaine shew of a manifest maime, euen so feete in our English versifing without quantitie and ioyntes be sure signes that the verse is either borne deformed, vnnaturall, and lame, and so verie vnseemlie to looke vpon, except to men that be gogle eyed them selues.

The spying of this fault now is not the curiositie of English eyes, but euen the good iudgement also of the best that write in these dayes in Italie: and namelie of that worthie Senese Felice Figliucci, who, writyng vpon Aristotles Ethickes so excellentlie in Italian, as neuer did yet any one in myne opinion either in Greke or Latin, amongest other thynges doth most earnestlie inuey agaynst the rude ryming of verses in that tong: And whan soeuer he expresseth Aristotles precepts with any example out of Homer or Euripides, he translateth them, not after the Rymes of Petrarke, but into soch kinde of perfite verse, with like feete and quantitie of sillabes, as he found them before in the Greke tonge; exhortyng earnestlie all the Italian nation to leaue of their rude barbariousnesse in ryming, and folow diligently the excellent Greke and Latin examples in trew versifiyng.

And you that be able to vnderstand no more then ye finde in the Italian tong, and neuer went farder than the schole of Petrarke and Ariostus abroad, or els of Chaucer at home, though you haue pleasure to wander blindlie still in your foule wrong way, enuie not others that seeke, as wise men haue done before them, the fairest and rightest way; or els, beside the iust reproch of malice, wisemen shall trewlie iudge that you do so, as I haue sayd and say yet agayne vnto you, bicause either for idlenes ye will not, or for ignorance ye can not, cum by no better your selfe.

And therfore, euen as Virgill and Horace deserue most worthie prayse, that they, spying the vnperfitnes in Ennius and Plautus, by trew Imitation of Homer and Euripides brought Poetrie to the same perfitnes in Latin as it was in Greke, euen so those that by the same way would benefite their tong and contrey deserue rather thankes than disprayse in that behalfe.

And I reioyce that euen poore England preuented Italie, first in spying out, than in seekyng to amend this fault in learnyng.

And here for my pleasure I purpose a litle by the way to play and sporte with my Master Tully; from whom commonlie I am neuer wont to dissent. He him selfe, for this point of learnyng, in his verses doth halt a litle, by his leaue. He could not denie it, if he were aliue, nor those defend hym now that loue him best. This fault I lay to his charge: bicause once it please him, though somwhat merelie, yet oueruncurteslie, to rayle vpon poore England, obiecting both extreme beggerie and mere barbariousnes vnto it, writyng thus vnto his frend Atticus: There is not one scruple of siluer in that whole Isle, or any one that knoweth either learnyng or letter.

But now, master Cicero, blessed be God and his sonne Iesus Christ, whom you neuer knew, except it were as it pleased him to lighten you by some shadow, as couertlie in one place ye confesse saying, *Veritatis tantum vmbram consectamur*, as your Master Plato did before you: blessed be God, I say, that sixen hundred yeare after you were dead and gone it may trewly be sayd, that for siluer there is more cumlie plate in one Citie of England than is in foure of the proudest Cities in all Italie, and take Rome for one of them. And for learnyng, beside the knowledge of all learned tongs and liberall sciences, euen you owne bookes, Cicero, be as well read, and your excellent eloquence is as well liked and loued, and as trewlie folowed, in England at this day, as it is now, or euer was, sence your owne tyme in any place of Italie, either at Arpinum, where ye were borne, or els at Rome, where ye were brought vp. And a litle to brag with you, Cicero, where you your selfe, by your leaue, halted in some point of learnyng in your owne tong, many in England at this day go streight vp, both in trewe skill and right doing therein.

This I write, not to reprehend Tullie, whom aboue all other I like and loue best, but to excuse Terence, because in his tyme, and a good while after, Poetrie was neuer perfited in Latin, vntill by trew Imitation of the Grecians it was at length brought to perfection: And also thereby to exhorte the goodlie wittes of England, which, apte by nature and willing by desire, geue them selues to Poetrie, that they, rightly vnderstanding the barbarous bringing in of Rymes, would labor, as Virgil and Horace did in Latin, to make perfit also this point of learning in our English tong.

And thus much for Plautus and Terence, for matter, tong, and meter, what is to be followed, and what to be exchewed in them.

After Plautus and Terence no writing remayneth vntill Tullies tyme, except a fewe short fragmentes of L. Crassus excellent wit, here and there recited of Cicero for example sake, whereby the louers of learnyng may the more lament the losse of soch a worthie witte.

And although the Latin tong did faire blome and blossome in L. Crassus and M. Antonius, yet in Tullies tyme onely, and in Tullie himselfe chieflie, was the Latin tong fullie ripe and growne to the hiest pitch of all perfection.

And yet in the same tyme it began to fade and stoupe, as Tullie him selfe, in *Brutus de Claris Oratoribus*, with weeping wordes doth witnesse.

And bicause emongs them of that tyme there was some difference, good reason is that of them of that tyme should be made right choice also. And yet let the best Ciceronian in Italie read Tullies familiar epistles aduisedly ouer, and I beleue he shall finde small difference for the Latin tong, either in propriety of wordes or framing of the stile, betwixt Tullie and those that write vnto him: As Ser. Sulpitius, A. Cecinna, M. Cael[i]us, M. et D. Bruti, A. Pollio, L. Plancus, and diuerse other. Read the epistles of L. Plancus in *x. Lib.*, and for an assay that Epistle namely to the *Coss.* and whole Senate, the eight Epistle in number; and what could be eyther more eloquentlie or more wiselie written, yea by Tullie himselfe, a man may iustly doubt. Thies men and Tullie liued all in one tyme, were like in authoritie, not vnlike in learning and studie, which might be iust causes of this their equalitie in writing: And yet surely they neyther were in deed, not yet were counted in mens opinions, equall with Tullie in that facultie. And how is the difference hid in his Epistles? verelie, as the cunning of an expert Seaman in a faire calme fresh Ryuer doth litle differ from the doing of a meaner workman therein, euen so, in the short cut of a priuate letter, where matter is common, wordes easie, and order not moch diuerse, small shew of difference can appeare. But where Tullie doth set vp his saile of eloquence, in some broad deep Argument, caried with full tyde and winde of his witte and learnyng, all other may rather stand and looke after him than hope to ouertake him, what course so euer he hold, either in faire or foule. Foure men onely, whan the Latin tong was full ripe, be left vnto vs, who in that tyme did florish, and did leaue to posteritie the fruite of their witte and learning: Varro, Salust, Caesar, and Cicero. Whan I say these foure onely, I am not ignorant that euen in the same tyme most excellent Poetes, deseruing well of the Latin tong, as Lucretius, Catullus, Virgill, and Horace, did write, but bicause in this litle booke I purpose to teach a yong scholer to go, not to daunce, to speake, not to sing (whan Poetes in deed, namelie *Epici* and *Lyrici*, as these be, are fine dauncers and trime singers): but *Oratores* and *Historici* be those cumlie goers, and faire and wise speakers, of whom I wishe my scholer to wayte vpon first, and after in good order and dew tyme to be brought forth to the singing and dauncing schole: And for this consideration do I name these foure to be the onelie writers of that tyme.

Varro

Varro, in his bookes *de lingua Latina et Analogia*, as these be left mangled and patched vnto vs, doth not enter there in to any great depth of eloquence, but as one caried in a small low vessell him selfe verie nie the common shore, not much vnlike the fisher men of Rye and Hering men of Yarmouth, who deserue, by common mens opinion, small commendacion for any cunning sailing at all, yet neuertheles in those bookes of Varro good and necessarie stuffe, for that meane kinde of Argument, he verie well and learnedlie gathered togither.

His bookes of Husbandrie are moch to be regarded and diligentlie to be read, not onelie for the proprietie, but also for the plentie of good wordes, in all contrey and husbandmens affaires: which can not be had by so good authoritie out of any other Author, either of so good a tyme, or of so great learnyng, as out of Varro. And yet, bicause he was fourscore yeare old whan he wrote those bookes, the forme of his style there compared with Tullies writyng is but euen the talke of a spent old man: whose wordes commonlie fall out of his mouth, though verie wiselie, yet hardly and cold[l]ie, and more heauelie also than some eares can well beare, except onelie for age and authorities sake. And, perchance, in a rude contrey argument, of purpose and iudgement he rather vsed the speach of the contrey than talke of the Citie.

And so, for matter sake, his wordes sometyme be somewhat rude, and, by the imitation of the elder Cato, old and out of vse: And beyng depe stept in age, by negligence some wordes do so scape and fall from him in those bookes, as be not worth the taking vp by him that is carefull to speak or write trew Latin, as that sentence in him, *Romani in pace a rusticis alebantur, et in bello ab his tuebantur.* A good student must be therfore carefull and diligent to read with iudgement ouer euen those Authors which did write in the most perfite tyme: and let him not be affrayd to trie them, both in proprietie of wordes and forme of style, by the touch stone of Caesar and Cicero, whose puritie was neuer soiled, no not by the sentence of those that loued them worst.

All louers of learnyng may sore lament the losse of those bookes of Varro which he wrote in his yong and lustie yeares with good leysure and great learnyng of all partes of Philosophie: of the goodliest argumentes perteyning both to the common wealth and priuate life of man, as *de Ratione studii et educandis liberis*, which booke is oft recited and moch praysed in the fragmentes of Nonius, euen for authoritie sake. He wrote most diligentlie and largelie also the whole historie of the state of Rome; the mysteries of their whole Religion; their lawes, customes, and gouernement in peace; their maners, and whole discipline in warre. And this is not my gessing, as one in deed that neuer saw those bookes, but euen the verie iudgement and playne testimonie of Tullie him selfe, who knew and read those bookes, in these wordes: *Tu aetatem patriae: tu descriptiones temporum: tu sacrorum, tu sacerdotum iura: tu domesticam, tu bellicam disciplinam: tu sedem regionum, locorum; tu omnium diuinarum humanarumque rerum nomina, genera, officia, causas aperuisti*, etc.

But this great losse of Varro is a litle recompensed by the happy comming of Dionysius Halicarnassaeus to Rome in Augustus dayes: who, getting the possession of Varros librarie, out of that treasure house of learning did leaue vnto vs some frute of Varros witte and diligence; I meane his goodlie bookes *de Antiquitatibus Romanorum*. Varro was so estemed for his excellent learnyng, as Tullie him selfe had a reuerence to his iudgement in all doutes of learnyng. And Antonius Triumuir, his enemie, and of a contrarie faction, who had power to kill and bannish whom he listed, whan Varros name amongest others was brought in a schedule vnto him to be noted to death, he tooke his penne and wrote his warrant of sauegard with these most goodlie wordes, *Viuat Varro, vir doctissimus*. In later tyme, no man knew better, nor liked and loued more Varros learnyng than did S. Augustine, as they do well vnderstand that haue diligentlie read ouer his learned bookes *de Ciuitate Dei*: Where he hath this most notable sentence: "Whan I see how much Varro wrote, I meruell much that euer he had any leasure to read; and, whan I perceiue how many thinges he read, I meruell more that euer he had any leasure to write," etc.

And, surelie, if Varros bookes had remained to posteritie, as by Gods prouidence the most part of Tullies did, than trewlie the Latin tong might haue made good comparison with the Greke.

Saluste

Salust is a wise and worthy writer; but he requireth a learned Reader, and a right considerer of him. My dearest frend, and best master that euer I had or heard in learning, Syr I. Cheke, soch a man as, if I should liue to see England breed the like againe, I feare I should liue ouer long, did once giue me a lesson for Salust, which, as I shall neuer forget my selfe, so is it worthy to be remembred of all those that would cum to perfite iudgement of the Latin tong. He said that Salust was not verie fitte for yong men to learne out of him the puritie of the Latin tong, because he was not the purest in proprietie of wordes, nor choisest in aptnes of phrases, nor the best in framing of sentences; and therefore is his writing, sayd he, neyther plaine for the matter, nor sensible for mens vnderstanding. "And what is the cause thereof, Syr?" quoth I. "Verilie," said he, "bicause in Salust writing is more Arte than nature, and more labor than Arte: and in his labor also to moch toyle, as it were, with an vncontented care to write better than he could, a fault common to very many men. And therefore he doth not expresse the matter liuely and naturally with common speach, as ye see Xenophon doth in Greeke; but it is caried and driuen forth artificiallie, after to learned a sorte, as Thucydides doth in his orations." "And how cummeth it to passe," sayd I, "that Caesar and Ciceroes talke is so naturall and plaine, and Salust writing so artificiall and darke, whan all they three liued in one tyme?" "I will freelie tell you my fansie herein," said he: "surely Caesar and Cicero, beside a singular prerogatiue of naturall eloquence geuen vnto them by God, both two, by vse of life, were daylie orators emonges the common people and greatest councellers in the Senate house, and therefore gaue themselues to vse soch speach as the meanest should well vnderstand and the wisest best allow, folowing carefullie that good councell of *Aristotle, loquendum vt multi, sapiendum vt pauci*. Salust was no soch man, neyther for will to goodnes nor skill by learning; but, ill geuen by nature, and made worse by bringing vp, spent the most part of his yougth very misorderly in ryot and lechery, in the company of soch, who, neuer geuing theyr mynde to honest doyng, could neuer inure their tong to wise speaking; but at last cummyng to better yeares, and bying witte at the dearest hand, that is by long experience of the hurt and shame that commeth of mischeif, moued by the councell of them that were wise, and caried by the example of soch as were good, first fell to honestie of life, and after to the loue of studie and learning; and so became so new a man that Caesar, being dictator, made him Pretor in Numidia, where he, absent from his contrie and not inured with the common talke of Rome, but shut vp in his studie and bent wholy to reading, did write the storie of the Romanes. And for the better accomplishing of the same, he red Cato and Piso in Latin for gathering of matter and troth, and Thucydides in Greeke for the order of his storie and furnishing of his style. Cato (as his tyme required) had more troth for the matter than eloquence for the style. And so Salust, by gathering troth out of Cato, smelleth moch of the roughnes of his style: euen as a man that eateth garlike for helth shall cary away with him the sauor of it also, whether he will or not. And yet the vse of old wordes is not the greatest cause of Salustes roughnes and darknesse: There be in Salust some old wordes in deed as *patrare bellum, ductare exercitum*, well noted by Quintilian, and verie much misliked of him; and *supplicium* for *supplicatio*, a word smellyng of an older store than the other two so misliked by Quint. And yet is that word also in Varro, speaking of Oxen thus, *boues ad victimas faciunt, atque ad Deorum supplicia*: and a few old wordes mo. Read Saluste and Tullie aduisedly together, and in wordes ye shall finde small difference; yea Salust is more geuen to new wordes than to olde, though som olde writers say the contrarie: as *Claritudo* for *Gloria*, *exacte* for *perfecte*, *Facundia* for *eloquentia*. Thies two last wordes *exacte* and *facundia*, now in euery mans mouth, be neuer (as I do remember) vsed of Tullie, and therefore I thinke they be not good: For surely Tullie speaking euery where so moch of the matter of eloquence would not so precisely haue absteyned from the word *Facundia* if it had bene good, that is proper for the tong, and common for mens vse. I could be long in reciting many soch like, both olde and new wordes in Salust, but in very dede neyther oldnes nor newnesse of wordes maketh the greatest difference betwixt Salust and Tullie, but first strange phrases made of good Latin wordes but framed after the Greeke tonge, which be neyther choisly borowed of them, nor properly vsed by him; than a hard composition and crooked framing of his wordes and sentences, as a man would say, English talke placed and framed outlandish like. As for example first in phrases, *nimius et animus* be two vsed wordes, yet *homo nimius animi* is an vnused phrase. *Vulgus, et amat, et fieri,* be as common and well known wordes as may be in the Latin tong, yet *id quod vulgo amat fieri,* for *solet fieri,* is but a strange and Grekysh kind of writing. *Ingens et vires* be proper wordes, yet *vir ingens virium* is an vnproper kinde of speaking; and so be likewise *aeger consilii, promptissimus belli, territus animi,* and many soch like phrases in Salust, borowed, as I sayd, not choisly out of Greeke, and vsed therefore vnproperlie in Latin. Againe, in whole sentences, where the matter is good, the wordes proper and plaine, yet the sense is hard and darke, and namely in his prefaces and oration[s], wherein he vsed most labor, which fault is likewise in Thucydides in Greeke, of whom Salust hath taken the greatest part of his darkenesse. For Thucydides likewise wrote his storie, not at home in Grece, but abrode in Italie, and therefore smelleth of a certaine outlandish kinde of talke, strange to them of Athens, and diuerse from their writing that liued in Athens and Grece, and wrote the same tyme that Thucydides did, as Lysias, Xenophon, Plato, and Isocrates, the purest and playnest writers that euer wrote in any tong, and best examples for any man to follow whether he write Latin, Italian, French, or English. Thucydides also semeth in his writing not so much benefited by nature as holpen by Arte, and caried forth by desire, studie, labor, toyle, and ouer great curiositie; who spent xxvii. yeares in writing his eight bookes of his history. Salust likewise wrote out of his contrie, and followed the faultes of Thuc. to moch; and boroweth of him som kinde of writing which the Latin tong can not well beare, as *Casus nominatiuus* in diuerse places *absolute positus,* as in that place of Iugurth, speaking *de Leptitanis, Itaque ab imperatore facile quae petebant adepti, missae sunt eo cohortes Ligurum quatuor.* This thing in participles, vsed so oft in Thucyd. and other Greeke authors to, may better be borne with all, but Salust vseth the same more strangelie and boldlie, as in thies wordes, *Multis sibi quisque imperium petentibus.* I beleue the best Grammarien in England can scarse giue a good reule why *quisque,* the nominatiue case, without any verbe, is so thrust vp amongst so many oblique cases." Some man perchance will smile, and laugh to scorne this my writyng, and call it idle curiositie thus to busie my selfe in pickling about these small pointes of Grammer, not fitte for my age, place, and calling to trifle in: I trust that man, be he neuer so great in authoritie, neuer so wise and learned, either by other mens iudgement or his owne opinion, will yet thinke that he is not greater in England than Tullie was at Rome, not yet wiser nor better learned than Tullie was him selfe, who, at the pitch of three score yeares, in the middes of the broyle betwixt Caesar and Pompeie, whan he knew not whither to send wife and children, which way to go, where to hide him selfe, yet, in an earnest letter, amongest his earnest councelles for those heuie tymes concerning both the common state of his contrey and his owne priuate great affaires, he was neither vnmyndfull nor ashamed to reason at large, and learne gladlie of Atticus, a lesse point of Grammer than these be, noted of me in Salust, as whether he should write *ad Piraeea, in Piraeea,* or *in Piraeeum,* or *Piraeeum, sine praepositione*: And in those heuie tymes he was so carefull to know this small point of Grammer that he addeth these wordes, *Si hoc mihi zētēma persolueris, magna me molestia liberaris.* If Tullie, at that age, in that authoritie, in that care for his contrey, in that ieoperdie for him selfe and extreme necessitie of hys dearest frendes, beyng also the Prince of Eloquence hym selfe, was not ashamed to descend to these low pointes of Grammer, in owne naturall tong, what should scholers do, yea what should any man do, if he do thinke well doyng better than ill doyng: And had rather be perfite than meane, sure than doutefull, to be what he should be in deed, not seeme what he is not in opinion. He that maketh perfitnes in the Latin tong his marke must cume to it by choice and certaine knowledge, not stumble vpon it by chance and doubtfull ignorance. And the right steppes to reach vnto it be these, linked thus orderlie together, aptnes of nature, loue of learnyng, diligence in right order, constancie with pleasant moderation, and always to learne of them that be best; and so shall you iudge as they that be wisest. And these be those reules which worthie Master Cheke dyd impart vnto me concernyng Salust and the right iudgement of the Latin tong.

Caesar

Caesar, for that litle of him that is left vnto vs, is like the halfe face of a Venus, the other part of the head beyng hidden, the bodie and the rest of the members vnbegon, yet so excellentlie done by Apelles, as all men may stand still to mase and muse vpon it, and no man step forth with any hope to performe the like.

His seuen bookes *de bello Gallico* and three *de bello ciuili* be written so wiselie for the matter, so eloquentlie for the tong, that neither his greatest enemies could euer finde the least note of parcialitie in him (a meruelous wisdome of a man, namely writyng of his owne doynges), nor yet the best iudegers of the Latin tong, nor the most enuious lookers vpon other mens writynges, can say any other but all things be most perfitelie done by him.

Brutus, Caluus, and Calidius, who found fault with Tullies fulnes in woordes and matter, and that rightlie, for Tullie did both confesse it and mend it, yet in Caesar they neither did, nor could, finde the like or any other fault.

And therfore thus iustlie I may conclude of Caesar, that where, in all other, the best that euer wrote, in any tyme, or in any tong, in Greke or Latin (I except neither Plato, Demosthenes, nor Tullie), some fault is iustlie noted, in Caesar onelie could neuer yet fault be found.

Yet neuertheles, for all this perfite excellencie in him, yet it is but in one member of eloquence, and that but of one side neither, whan we must looke for that example to folow, which hath a perfite head, a whole bodie, forward and backward, armes and legges and all.

Lodovico Castelvetro
1505–1571

A man of tremendous arrogance, Lodovico Castelvetro was also one of the most prominent critical and linguistic figures of the Italian Renaissance. His commentary on Aristotle's *Poetics* was a decisive influence in transforming Aristotle into the clear precursor of Italian literary criticism in the sixteenth century, and his work remained the most widely read commentary on the *Poetics* until the late eighteenth century.

It was Castelvetro's arrogance which fueled his famous quarrel with Annibale Caro, which led to Castelvetro's exile from Italy. Castelvetro's scathing criticism of Caro's canzone in praise of France, written in a private letter, was published, and Caro responded furiously, calling Castelvetro an enemy of God and man. Caro managed to have Castelvetro called before the Inquisition, but Castelvetro fled to Switzerland. He was condemned *in absentia* for doctrinal error in 1560, and died in exile at Chiavenna.

Most of Castelvetro's significant critical work was written in exile, including commentaries on Petrarch's *Rime* and the first 29 canti of the *Inferno*. He also composed a guide to Bembo's *Prose* in which he explored the derivation of Italian from Latin. His commentary on Aristotle's *Poetics*, first published in 1570, remains his best-known work, and his insistence upon a strict interpretation of the Aristotelian "unities" of time and place strongly affected the development of the European drama.

It was a particularly daring piece of work when it was first published. Castelvetro managed to offend Aristotelian critics by taking issue with the master as well as earning the expected enmity of those opposed to Aristotle. He quarrels with Aristotle, for instance, over the issue of catharsis, claiming that Aristotle proposes a moral utility for catharsis and therefore contradicts his own earlier explanation of the genesis of drama in pleasure.

This quarrel with Aristotle is related to another aspect of Castelvetro's daring, which is his rejection of the Horatian formula that poetry must both delight and please. Castelvetro states flatly, "Poetry has been discovered solely to delight and to recreate," and this definition leads him to propose what appears at first to be a radically "democratic" understanding of poetry's limitations: "It should have as its subject those things that can be understood by the common people and when understood can make them happy." In practice, Castelvetro uses this principle to sharply circumscribe the imaginative limits of literature. Bernard Weinberg has pointed out in his *A History of Literary Criticism in the Italian Renaissance* that Castelvetro tends to treat art as a natural object which must obey the rule of the senses—thus his insistence upon the tragic "unities." Weinberg writes:

> The challenge is not to produce a beautiful work of art through the ordering of all the parts to an artistically perfect structure. Questions of beauty rarely concern Castelvetro. Rather, it is the task of the poet to find some way of entertaining the audience while he keeps it convinced that what it sees (or reads) is true, that is, some way of striking a proper balance between the probable and the marvelous.

Castelvetro is also quite interesting on the relationship between art and imitation, claiming that any kind of borrowing from another poet is plagiarism while in another instance he approvingly cites the example of Michelangelo completing the beard of an excavated statue. In the example of Michelangelo, interestingly enough, Castelvetro appears to consider the statue an example of history rather than artifice, thus allowing the artist to "borrow" from it.

The selections from *On the Poetics*, translated by Allan H. Gilbert, are reprinted with his permission from *Literary Criticism: Plato to Dryden*, edited by Allan H. Gilbert (Detroit: Wayne State University Press, 1962). © 1962 by Allan H. Gilbert.

ON THE POETICS

FROM
Chapter I

Aristotle writes that the sciences and the arts and history are not subjects for poetry. And I, who in this matter hold an opinion not at all different from that of Aristotle and think it wholly true, believe that I can bring forward the reasons that have induced me to hold such beliefs, which, if they are not the very same as Aristotle presented, are perhaps not very different; I have already incidentally mentioned some of them and taken them for granted; they are these. Poetry is the similitude or likeness of history. Just as history is divided into matter and words, so poetry is divided into two principal parts, which are likewise matter and words, but in these two parts history and poetry differ from each other, because history does not have matter that is given to it by the abilities of the historian, but its matter is furnished by the course of worldly events, or by the will, either manifest or hidden, of God. It has, in truth, words given to it by the historian, but they are such as are used in reasoning. The matter of poetry is found and imagined by the ability of the poet, and its words are not such as are used in reasoning, since men do not generally reason in verse, but the words of poetry are composed in measured verse by the exercise of the poet's powers.

Now the matter of poetry should be like the matter of history and resemble it, but it ought not to be the same, for, if it were the same, it would not be like it or resemble it, and if it were not like it or did not resemble it, the poet in dealing with such material would not have labored at all, and would not have showed keenness of intellect in finding it; therefore he would not merit praise and especially he would not merit that through which he is reputed to be more divine than human, for he knows how to deal with a story, imagined by himself about things that have not happened, and yet to make it not less delightful nor less like the truth than is the history produced by the course of mundane events or by the infinite providence of God, whether manifest or hidden. In taking his matter from history, that is, from things that have already happened, the poet does not endure any fatigue, nor does it thence appear whether he is a good poet or a bad one, that is, whether he knows or does not know how skillfully to find things like the truth, and he cannot be praised for producing a resemblance of them; rather he is to be blamed and is thought of as endowed with but a weak judgment because he has not recognized this. Moreover he is thought to have a wicked and deceptive nature, because with the force and color of poetic language he has wished to dupe his readers or hearers, making them believe that beneath his words there was some poetic matter, and acquiring false commendation for it.

Therefore Lucan, Silius Italicus, and Girolamo Fracastoro in his *Joseph*[1] are to be removed from the ranks of the poets and deprived of the glorious title of poetry,[2] because they have in their writings dealt with matter already treated by historians; and even though it had not first been treated by the historians, it is enough that it had happened before and was not imagined by the authors mentioned.

From this it can also be comprehended that science and art cannot be matter for poetry and cannot well be included in a poem, since, so far as the poet is concerned, the science and the art which have already been considered and understood through reasons necessary and having the appearance of truth, and through long experience by philosophers and artists, take the same position as history and things that have already happened. The poet merely covers with poetical words a subject from science or from art that has been found and written about by others, and on which it can be said that history has already been composed; the poet has no part in it by reason of which he can boast himself a poet. Therefore one should not marvel of those versifiers, Empedocles,[3] Lucretius, Nicander, Serenus, Girolamo Fracastoro in his *Siphylis*, Aratus, Manilius, Giovanni Pontano in his *Urania*, Hesiod, and Vergil in the *Georgics* are not received into the number of the poets, for even though they have been the first to think out some science or art and have not taken it from any philosopher, they should not therefore be called poets, because if they have thought out the truth of some science or art, and have discovered something that was and will be perpetually in the nature of things, and with which that science is concerned and by which that art is constituted, they have still performed the function of a good philosopher and of a good scientist but not that of a good poet.

The poet's function is after consideration to give a semblance of truth to the happenings that come upon men through fortune,[4] and by means of this semblance to give delight to his readers; he should leave the discovery of the truth hidden in natural or accidental things to the philosopher and the scientist, who have their own way of pleasing or giving profit which is very remote from that of the poet. Besides, there is another reason more manifest to sense why the matter of the sciences and the arts cannot be the subject of poetry; poetry has been discovered solely to delight and to recreate,[5] I say to delight and to recreate the minds of the crude multitude and of the common people,[6] who do not understand the reasons and the divisions and the arguments, subtle and far from the practice of ordinary men, which the philosophers use in investigating the truth of things,[7] and professional men in their labors. It is not proper that a listener, when anyone addresses him, should feel irritation and displeasure, for it naturally annoys us excessively when anyone speaks to us in such a way that we are unable to understand him. Therefore if we concede that the matter of the sciences and of the arts can be the subject of poetry, we should concede also either that poetry was not discovered for delight or that it was not intended for the plain people, but in order that it might teach and for the benefit of persons well skilled in letters and in disputations. This will be recognized as false through what we shall prove as we go further.

Now because poetry has been discovered, as I say, to delight and recreate the common people, it should have as its subject those things that can be understood by the common people and when understood can make them happy.[8] These are the things that happen every day and that are spoken of among the people, and that resemble historical accounts and the latest reports about the world. For this reason we affirm, with respect to matter, that poetry is the similitude or resemblance of history; this matter, because it only resembles the truth, not merely renders its inventor glorious, and makes and constitutes him a poet, but delights more than does the history of things that have happened. . . . Because, then, the matter of the sciences and the arts is not understood by the people, not merely should it be avoided and shunned as the subject of a poem, but care must also be taken that no part of these arts and sciences is used in any part of the poem. In this matter Lucan and Dante in his *Comedy* have especially sinned without any necessity, for these poets by means of astrology show the seasons of the year and the hours of the day and the night.[9] Homer and Vergil in his *Aeneid* never fell into this error. I cannot do other than wonder somewhat at Quintilian, who thinks that no one can understand the poets well who is not versed in the art of astronomy and instructed in philosophy.[10]

Chapter III

The dramatic manner, which, as we said, employs things where the original had things, and words in direct discourse where the original had words, is different from the narrative, first, in that it uses words and things instead of the original words and things, while narrative used words alone in the place of things and indirect discourse in the place of direct discourse. It is further different in that the dramatic is less ample, in respect to places, than the narrative, for the dramatic method cannot represent places very far apart, while the narrative method joins together places that are widely separated. It is also different in that the dramatic method is less ample with respect to time, for the narrative method joins together diverse times, something the dramatic method cannot do. In addition there is between them the difference that the narrative method tells things that are visible and invisible, audible and not audible, and the dramatic represents only things that are visible and audible. Still further they seem different in that the narrative does not so much move the hearers in those things that are connected with the feelings as does the dramatic. They are also much different in that the narrative relates many things, even though they are connected with the feelings, much better and more fully than the dramatic method presents them.

Because of the difficulty of representing actions and making them verisimilar, dramas do not present on the stage murders and other things that it is difficult to represent with dignity, and it is proper that they should be done off stage and then narrated by a messenger.[11] Still they are different because the narrative is able to relate in a few hours many things that happened in many hours, and to relate in many hours a few things that happened in a few hours. But the dramatic method, which spends as many hours in representing things as was taken by the actions themselves, is able to do none of these things; thence it comes about that tragedy and comedy, which are members of the dramatic class, cannot last longer than the time allowed by the convenience of the audience, nor represent more things than those which come about in the space of time that the comedies and the tragedies themselves require. And as I say, there must always be regard to the ease of the people, for after some hours the people have to leave the theater because of the human necessities for eating, drinking, sleeping, and other things.

FROM
Chapter IV

Aristotle was not of the opinion that poetry was a special gift of God bestowed on one man rather than on another, as is the gift of prophecy and other similar privileges that are not natural and common to all. Without doubt he intends, though he does not say it openly, to refute the opinion that some attribute to Plato, that poetry is infused into men through divine madness. This opinion had its origin and source in the ignorance of the common people and has been increased and favored by the vainglory of the poets for the following reasons and in the following manner. Anything done by someone else is highly regarded and seems marvelous to those who have not the power to do it themselves, and because men commonly measure the forces of the body and of the ability of other men by comparison with their own, they reckon as a miracle and a special gift of God that which they do not know how to attain by their own natural powers, and see that others have attained. Hence the first poets were thought by the ignorant people to be full of the spirit of God and to be aided by God. For the people admired beyond measure the invention of the story in poetic compositions and likewise the long series of verses with which the story was set forth, and especially so when they saw that the divine responses of Apollo were given in such verses, for they thought that through these the gods spoke. . . . This belief of the people, though false, was pleasing to the poets, since through it great reputation came to them and they were looked on as dear to the gods. Hence they nourished it with their approval, and making it appear that the condition was as the people thought, they began at the beginnings of their works to call on the aid of the Muses and Apollo, the god set over poetry, and to make it seem that they uttered their poems as though with the mouths of the aforesaid gods. . . . It is wrong then to attribute to Plato this opinion of the *furor* infused into the poets[12] because, as I said, it originated with the people and the poets agreed to it for the sake of their own interests. Plato, when he mentions it in his books, surely is jesting, as in similar instances he often does; for example, in the *Phaedrus* he says that the lover is possessed by a *furor*. But since Plato wishes to prove that this does not mean that the poet is therefore in the power of something evil, he adds that it is a good madness which overcomes the priestesses in Delphi and the priests in Dodona, and the Sibyl and other diviners, and the poets. Yet by this he does not prove that the poets are possessed by a divine *furor*, but merely brings forward as examples some similar things, in harmony with the popular belief.... He writes in jest in the *Apology* of Socrates, when he says the poets do not understand what they write in their poems when moved by the divine *furor*.[13] This is clear enough, for if he were telling the truth and believed that their poems proceeded from divine inspiration, why did he forbid them in his republic? ...[14]

The imitation that is natural to men is one thing and that which is demanded of the poet is another.[15] For the imitation of others that is natural to men, that is in them from childhood and by means of which they first learn, and to which all men are more disposed than are the other animals, and which consequently they are much pleased to engage in, is nothing else than a following of the examples of others and a doing of the things the others do without knowing any cause why they should do so. But the imitation the poet is expected to use not merely does not follow the example laid down by another, or do the same thing that has already been done without knowing the cause for doing it, but does something completely separate from what has been done and sets before itself, so to speak, another example to follow. In following it, the poet must needs have an excellent knowledge of the causes why he does what he does and must spend time in reflection and careful reasoning, to such an extent that it can securely be affirmed that the imitation demanded from the poet is not and ought not to be called directly or properly imitation, but should be or can be called the strife of the poet and the disposition of fortune, or of the course of mundane things, in finding an incident of human conduct delightful to listen to and marvelous.

FROM

Chapter V

The second[16] class of pleasing things able to raise laughter in us consists of deceptions; I mean those deceptions by reason of which someone says or does or suffers things which he would neither do nor say nor suffer if he were not deceived. The deception of someone pleases us excessively, then, and delights us and constrains us to laugh for pleasure. The cause of this is our nature, corrupted through the sin of our first parents, which rejoices at the coming of evil upon someone else as at some benefit to ourselves, and especially rejoices at evil which proceeds from that part which is peculiar to man, that is from the natural intellect, for it appears to those who are not deceived, when they see others deceived, that they are themselves better and that they surpass them in that quality,[17] namely reason, in which men are nearest to God and greatly superior to all the other animals. This is known to be true because men do not laugh or take pleasure, or at least not so much, if a neighbor is constrained by force or chance to say or do or suffer things against his will, provided that in him is seen no diminution of reason or of intellect, though he may receive a great deal of injury or dishonor. Now the deceptions that are material for laughter can be divided in four ways. The first is of the deceptions that come about through ignorance of those things which are in ordinary use and in the common understanding of men, as through drunkenness or sleep or delirium. The next class contains the deceptions that come about through ignorance of the arts and the sciences and of the powers of the body or the mind, when someone, before he has correctly estimated his capacity, boasts of something he cannot do. The third class contains those deceptions that result from an unexpected movement of things in another direction or through a turning of the point of a jest against the person who is the author of it. The last class contains those deceptions that proceed from tricks or from chance. [Castelvetro then gives a number of illustrations from the *Decameron* of Boccaccio.]

The third type of amusing things that can move us to laughter comes from wickedness of the spirit and from defects of the body, with their results. Sometimes they are presented to us covertly, in such a way that we are able to appear to laugh at something else than such wickedness and defects and actions, for, as we have said, our nature, corrupted by the original sin handed down to us from our first parents, enjoys recognizing a defect in others, either because it appears less defective if it has many companions, or because the appearance of being much superior fills it with pleasure and pride, since it seems to itself to be without these defects. But it is true that such defects would not make us laugh if they were not revealed under some covering in such a way that anyone is able, by excusing himself and feigning, to give the appearance of laughing at something else. For no one would wish to have it appear that wickedness or the defect of someone pleased him, however much it might really please him, for so much of the light of God is given us that we would judge such pleasure to be evil. So when Master Ermino Grimaldi asked Guielmo Borsiere to tell him of something that had never been seen before to paint in his house, Guielmo said to him, indicating something that Ermino had never seen: "Have courtesy painted there."[18] It was possible to understand this saying literally, that Master Ermino had never seen courtesy, since it is not a thing that can be seen or subjected to the bodily eyes, and yet it can be otherwise understood, namely, that he had always been avaricious and never had exercised courtesy. . . .

The fourth and last kind of pleasing things that move us to laughter are all the things that pertain to carnal delight, as the secret parts of the body, lascivious connections, memories of them, and things that are like them. But it is to be noted that the aforesaid things do not make us laugh when they are set openly before the eyes of the body or of the mind in the presence of others; rather they overcome us with shame and make us blush, and especially if we are or can be such persons of whom under the circumstances there can be a suspicion that

ON THE POETICS

we enjoy such things and desire to do them or to experience them. For if we do not laugh or make some sign or say some word by which we give obvious testimony that this does not please us, it will be presumed that we would consent to similar indecencies and desire them because nature inclines us without restraint in their direction. . . . Then the aforesaid pleasing things make us laugh when they are presented in the presence of someone else under a veil by means of which we are able to give the appearance of laughing not at the indecency but at something else. This without any example is much more than obvious to everyone. They also make us laugh when they are presented without a veil, in fact or in word, in such a place that we are seen by no one.

FROM
Chapter VI

Since it appeared to Plato that tragedy through the example of the tragic persons might injure the citizens and lower their moral tone, making them vile, cowardly, and full of pity, he did not wish tragedy to be presented in his republic, for he thought, if the people heard and saw men of high reputation do and say the things they do on the stage, that the too compassionate, the timorous, and the vile would console themselves, and pardon in themselves their softness of mind and fear and pusillanimity, for they would see that they have companions among the great, such as kings, and would learn to allow themselves to be carried farther than is fitting by such passions.[19] But Aristotle, in order that men should not believe on the authority of Plato that he himself, when writing on tragedy, had set out to present an art injurious to the citizens and likely to contaminate their morals, in a few words rejects what Plato says, affirming that tragedy has just the opposite effect, that is, that with its example and its frequent representation it changes the spectators from vile to magnanimous, from fearful to firm, and from over-pitying to strict,[20] for it is the opinion of Aristotle that continual experience with things worthy of pity, fear, and baseness does not make men too pitying, nor fearful, nor vile, because tragedy by means of the aforesaid passions, terror and pity, purges and drives out of the heart of men the passions that have been mentioned. Now I wish to make clearly understood what Aristotle perhaps has wished to say, and says rather obscurely and scarcely indicates, either because, as has been often said, the things put in this book are brief notes to be used for a larger work,[21] or because he did not wish openly to blame the opinion of his master Plato, being restrained by a certain reverence. It must be understood, then, that as pure wine of a certain quantity, with which not a drop of water has been mixed, has more vigor and spirit than has the same amount of wine of the same quality with which a large proportion of water has been mingled, for though it exceeds the other in quantity, yet through the addition of so much water it becomes watery and loses all its original vigor and spirit, so the love of fathers for their children is much greater and more fervent and they take better care of them when they have a few of them, that is, three or two or one, than if they have a large number, as a hundred or a thousand or more. In the same way the compassion and the fear of men, when exercised on a few pitiable and terrible cases, are more vigorous and more moving than when they are scattered over a large number of events deserving of pity and fear. Then tragedy, which represents to us similar actions, and makes us see them and hear them much more frequently than we would see them or hear them without tragedy, causes fear and compassion to diminish in us, since we have to divide the effect of this passion among so many diverse actions. The clearest proof of this comes before our eyes in a time of pestilence, for at the beginning, when three or four persons die, we are moved with pity and terror, but when we see hundreds and thousands die, the emotion of pity and horror ceases in us. We know this also by experience in perilous skirmishes, for in these, new soldiers are at first terrified by the thunder of the guns and the arquebuses and have the greatest pity for those who are wounded and killed, but after they have been in several fights they stand firm and without being much affected by pity see before their eyes their companions wounded and die. These reasons, perhaps, though they are very strong, are not of so much importance that because of them the law forbidding tragedy should be annulled, for they are directed elsewhere, namely, toward what Plato had in mind in making his prohibition. And in order to see clearly how the matter stands, one must realize that there are persons who undergo experiences that are terrible and able to excite pity, such as those mentioned. These persons are of two sorts, that is the strong and the timid, and the actions in question are also of two sorts, namely the frequent and the infrequent, and the one and the other according to diversity of manners bring about diversity of effect. Hence if the persons who suffer are strong and enduring, with the example of their fortitude and endurance they affect the spirits of others and drive pity and fear away from them. But if the persons are timid and weak, with their example they increase the terror and the compassion of the beholders and confirm them in their fear and weakness of spirit. . . . Likewise, if terrible and pitiable actions are uncommon they move men the more to terror and to compassion, but if they are frequent they move them the less, and because of their frequency are able to purge the terror and the compassion of mortal hearts. This comes about through two causes, of which one is that when we see many misadventures come about, and none of them touch ourselves, little by little we grow secure and make ourselves believe that God, as he has guarded us many times in the past, will also guard us in the future. The other is that those mishaps which come about often and to many do not appear so terrible and consequently do not appear to us so deserving of compassion, though we may be certain that they will touch us when we see that they do not spare so many others.

If the plot is the end of tragedy,[22] and consequently of every sort of poem, for the plot holds the same place in every sort of poem as in tragedy,—if the plot is final and not a thing accessory to the morals of the agents, but on the contrary the morals do not hold the final place and are accessory to the plot, it follows that many authors of high reputation for letters among the ancients and the moderns, among whom is even Julius Caesar Scaliger,[23] have greatly erred, for they think the intention of good poets, like Homer and Vergil in their most famous works, the *Iliad*, the *Odyssey*, and the *Aeneid*, has been to depict and show to the world, let us say, a general portrayed in the most excellent manner that is possible, or a valorous leader, or a wise man, and their nature, and like absurdities.[24] For if this is true the moral habits of characters would not have been chosen by poets to second the action, as Aristotle says, but the action would have been chosen to second the characteristics. In addition, it would happen that if such material were principal and not accessory, it could not be poetic material, since it is naturally philosophical and taken from many philosophers, especially Aristotle and Theophrastus.[25]

FROM

Chapter VIII

Aristotle . . . firmly requires that the action making up the plot should be one and relate to one person only, and if there are more actions than one, that one should depend on the other. He brings forward no reason or proof for this except the example of the tragic poets and Homer, who in composing their plots have used a single action by one person. But it can easily be understood that in tragedy and in comedy the plot contains one action or two which because of their interdependence can be reputed one, and more often of one person than of one family, not because the plot is not fitted to contain more actions but because the space of time of twelve hours at most in which the action is presented and the limitation of the space in which it is acted do not permit a multitude of actions or even the actions of one family, nor indeed the complete presentation of one action, if it is somewhat long. This is the principal and necessary reason why the plot of tragedy and comedy ought to be one, that is, ought to contain one action of a single person or of two that through their dependence may be thought of as one. This reason of limited time and place could not cause Homer to take a single action of a single person in the epic, which can recount not merely one action but several very long ones that happened in diverse countries.

It is to be said that in the singleness of the action there is something else in view, namely, that he judges the plot will be more beautiful and the author more admired if he takes only a single action of a single person.[26] For it is not to be wondered at if a number of actions by one person, or one action of one people, or a number of actions by several persons delight us and render us eager to hear them, for because of the number of actions, variety, novel happenings, and multitude of persons and peoples, the plot carries with it pleasure and greatness and magnificence. Yet in that narration, though in itself it brings about the end of poetry, the ability of the poet does not show to much advantage. But in the narration of a single action of a single person, which at first sight does not appear to have power to cause an audience to listen with pleasure, there is revealed the judgment and the industry of the poet, since he does with one action of one person what others scarcely are able to bring about with many actions by many persons.[27] Therefore Homer is much to be commended, for with but one action by Achilles, and that of lesser importance, namely an instance of anger, he knew how to plan the fabric of so excellent a plot. Similarly from one action by Ulysses, that is, his return from Calypso to his native land, he planned a second web not less wonderful. From this it is to be concluded that the plot of a tragedy or of a comedy should of necessity contain one action of one person, or two that are mutually dependent, and the plot of an epic should contain one action by one person, not of necessity but to show the excellence of the poet.

FROM

Chapter IX

Tragedy and Epic Deal with Kings

In the plot of tragedy and of the epic there are necessarily to be found occurrences that happen to have taken place in the life of a particular man, and are known in outline, as for example, Orestes accompanied by Pylades his friend, and aided by him and by Electra his sister, kills Clytemnestra his mother, but no one knows in detail and exactly the ways he took and the methods he used in accomplishing this murder. Now the reason is manifest, and so clearly manifest that it can be spoken of as proved, because it is fitting that the plot of a tragedy and of an epic should accept such actual events as are common to it and to the truth of history. For the plot of the two kinds of poem mentioned should contain action not human alone but also magnificent and royal. And if it ought to contain action by a prince, the conclusion follows that it contains action that has happened and is certain, and that concerns a ruler who has been and who is known to have been, since we cannot imagine a king who has not been nor attribute to him any act, and so far as he has been and is known to have been, we cannot attribute to him an act that has not really happened. . . . For kings are known through fame or through history and equally their notable acts are known, and to introduce new names of kings and to attribute to them new actions is to contradict history and fame, and to sin against the manifest truth, a much greater sin in the composition of the plot than to sin in verisimilitude. Therefore the plots of all tragedies and all epics are and should be composed of happenings that can be called historical, though Aristotle had a different opinion. . . . [28] But these incidents should not be set forth by history or fame except briefly and generally, in order that the poet may be able to perform his function and show his ability in finding the ways and particular methods through which the aforesaid incidents were accomplished. For if the ways and special methods through which these incidents were brought to completion were also known, there would be no matter fitted for the plot and it would not pertain to the poet but to the historian. Nor withal should we allow anyone to form the opinion that it is easier to compose the plot of a tragedy or of an epic than of a comedy, because in the plots of the first two the poet does not find out everything for himself as he does in comedy. . . .

Comedy Is the Poet's Invention

Now to compose the plot of a comedy the poet searches out with his own powers a happening in its universal and particular aspects, and because everything is invented by him and no part is given to actual events or to history, he gives names to the persons as it pleases him and is able to do it with no inconvenience and in a reasonable way. He is able to shape a happening he has invented in all its parts, and therefore it should concern a private person of whom and of the things that have happened to him no one has any recollection, nor will they be given to the memory of the future through history or fame. Hence he who forms a complete and new experience of private persons and gives them names as he pleases cannot be rebuked by history or fame as a falsifier. And, if he wishes to be thought a poet in the true meaning of the word, that is an inventor, he ought to invent everything, because, since the private material makes it easy for him, he is able to do it. But no one should think that he who composes the plot of the comedy has license to make up for himself new cities that he has imagined, or rivers or mountains or kingdoms or customs or laws, or to change the course of the things of nature, making it snow in summer and putting harvest in the winter, and the like, for it befits him to follow history and truth, if in forming his plot it happens that he needs such things, just as it equally befits him who forms the fable of a tragedy or of an epic.

The Historical Plot Truly Poetic

It appears that if things that have happend cannot constitute a poem[29] and do not tend toward the constitution of a poem, they should tend toward the destruction and diminution of a poem, when they are mingled with things that can possibly happen and things devised by the poet, if with the mixture made up of the things that have come about and those that can come about we compare those that can come about by themselves alone. That is, it appears that the plot of a tragedy or of an epic, when it is formed from an action that has really happened and retains the real names, as we have shown that it ought to be formed, ought to render its maker less deserving of the name of poet than is he who, in forming the plot of a comedy or of a tragedy, devises for himself the entire action and all the names, as did Agathon for his tragedy named the *Flower*. For if the plot made up wholly of things that have happened does not permit the author to be a poet at all, the plot made up partly of things that have happened would in its proportion take from him his poetic being; consequently he would be less a poet than the man who is considered a complete poet because he uses plots entirely of his own devising and events that might happen. Nevertheless I judge that the man who forms the plot of a tragedy or an epic taken from history with real and true names is not the less to be esteemed a poet than the maker of a plot containing only imaginary things; on the contrary he should perhaps be thought greater. For things that have happened, which the aforesaid composer considers in forming the plot of the epic and of the tragedy, are not so many nor set out in such a way that they deliver him from the effort of invention, since everyone can imagine for himself such things without much cleverness of intellect. We may suggest something that any man can easily imagine, such as the outline that a son has killed his mother who has murdered her husband and driven her son from the realm that she may enjoy herself with her paramour. But the difficulty is to find the ways in which the son may come to this killing in a marvelous fashion such as has not happened before. This difficulty is greater than that of devising the action in general and the particular ways and means through which it came to a conclusion, since the outline devised by the poet is not so fixed and determined that it cannot be altered and changed, if it seems good to him, and that he is unable to make his characters clever or stupid or possessed of other qualities, as he judges these changes in harmony with the methods for constructing a good plot that earlier presented themselves to him. But he who takes his plot from things that have already happened cannot do that, because he is kept within certain bounds from which he cannot issue.

An Example from Sculpture

To show by an example what this difference is, I say that not many years ago, when excavations were going on in Rome, there was found a marble statue of a large and beautiful river god, with the beard broken and lacking, and yet, judged by the part that still remained on the chin, the beard if entire would, if properly proportioned, reach to the navel, though the point of the beard still remained high up on the breast without reaching any further; at this everyone marveled and could not imagine how that beard was arranged when it was complete. Michelangelo Buonarroti alone, a sculptor of great ability who was present, having stood solitary for a while, understood the state of things, and said: "Give me some clay." When he had it, he formed the part of the beard that was lacking of such a size as to be properly proportioned to the remainder, and joining it on drew it down as far as the navel. Then knotting it with one turn he showed clearly that the point of the beard formed by him touched high up on the breast in the very same place as the point of the broken beard. So to the wonder of all who were present he showed how the beard that was lacking was made and how it was knotted. And there was no one there who did not think that Michelangelo, for his quickness of wit in restoring so marvelously the lacking beard, was to be preferred to any other artificer who might have made a complete beard acceptable to his mind without regard to the pieces of the beard remaining.

Another Difficulty in the Historical Plot

There is another difficulty much greater than that mentioned in actions taken from history, which is not found in imaginary actions, namely, that it is true of the ways and means of bringing to completion the actions taken from history that they are of necessity few, and have often been employed by earlier poets, and the most fitting and marvelous and workable devices have been discovered by others to such an extent that one must needs be a very skillful inventor and almost transcend the state of man if he wishes to deserve the name of a worthy poet in an action taken from history. Truly then there is need of superhuman ingenuity on the part of one who wishes, for example, to use in his plot the killing of his mother by Orestes, since it has been handled so many times and so well by so many poets in the past, and to bring about this murder there have been found so many ways and methods and such verisimilar and extraordinary ones, none of which the new poet can employ without incurring the infamy attaching to theft. From this restriction the inventor of the action that has not happened is free. Hence he who forms the plot of a comedy or a tragedy from an action wholly imaginary is not more a poet or more to be esteemed than he who forms the plot of an epic or a tragedy from an action that has actually happened.

Plagiarism

"And if he should happen to write of what has happened, he is not for that less a poet" [*Poetics*, IX]. These words are to be understood sensibly, that is, if it happens that the poet, not knowing that things have happened, and having imagined them for himself, puts them in his poem, he will be a poet just as much as though those things had never happened, since he has undergone the labor by which others gain the title of poet. But if he had before known that it had come about, he would have undergone no labor in finding it out and would not be a poet, as for the same reason no one is a poet for turning into verse what has been written by Herodotus. Now this reason which forbids the poet to take things that have happened also forbids him from taking things that have been written and invented by another poet, even though they have not happened. In that instance he would undergo as little labor in taking over the things written by others, as he does in taking things that have happened, and it appears that it is a more blameworthy theft to steal what another man has found and which is his own product, than it is to steal what has been produced by the course of the world under the control of Fortune and therefore seems in some sense common and not the special property of anyone. Now not merely in poetry is it reputed a theft to steal something that has been found by another poet, but also in any other subject, when one publishes the discovery of his neighbor as his own. The lawyers say that a doctor of laws who, in lecturing or counseling, gives as his own an opinion on the laws acutely found out by another doctor is liable to the penalty pronounced against those who do injury and commit theft. And such thefts as these of the inventions of another are pointed out with the finger and jeered at by the world, in the same way as is the crow who adorns himself with the feathers of the other birds in order to appear worth looking at and beautiful beyond all the others, and then, when each one takes away from him its feathers, he remains without feathers and fit to be mocked at and base. But if any thief of the inventions of others ought to be mocked at and punished, the poet who is a thief should be, for the essence of a poet consists in his invention, since without invention he is not a poet.

Examples of Plagiarism

Nonetheless there are many poets greatly acclaimed who have borrowed from histories or other poets part or all of the inventions of their poems, and they find some men so stupid and so ignorant as to admire and commend them when they ought to blame and despise them. For example, Giovanni Boccaccio puts in the tale of the Count of Anguersa the love of Giacchetto for Gianetta,[30] taken from the story of the love of Antiochus for his mother-in-law. And Ludovico Ariosto, taking now one part from Ovid and now another from Statius and then another from Marullo and other from others, fills out his *Orlando Furioso*, especially stealing without changing anything the story of Zerbino from Heinrich the storyteller of the Emperor Henry the Fourth.[31] Nor does Petrarch guard himself from taking the invention of many of his sonnets from Latin and Italian poets, and that of the sonnet *O little chamber, that you were a port* from Pliny the Younger.[32] What more will you have? Vergil himself, if we believe Macrobius, stole various and not a few parts from Homer, which the critic gathers and tells about, and believing to exalt the poet by it, makes him out clearly a thief to no great credit of his. Entire comedies have been stolen from the Greek poets by Plautus and Terence, and entire tragedies by Seneca too from the Greek poets. And likewise entire tales of Boccaccio, such as the one on the Gascon lady, from ancient stories,[33] and that one about Guido Cavalcanti from Petrarch,[34] and those of Peronella and of Hercolano from Apuleius.[35] And Apuleius did not find it for himself but took from someone else the invention of his *Golden Ass*. But no more, for this is not the place to reveal all the blameworthy thefts of these and the other authors.

Plagiarism Justified

I shall merely add that some of these thieves, who wish to be thought poets, are found to be so shameless that they dare to affirm it is permissible to steal things found by other poets, because the theft is committed without any damage to those from whom something is taken, and mockingly they say: If you do not believe it, go to see if in their books anything is lacking because of our theft. Or at least they say: The theft is not made against the will of the master. And still mocking they say that those who do not guard their property cannot reasonably complain when they are robbed, and that of this sort are the authors who leave their poems unwatched and publish them too without sending with them any guardian who will defend them from theft. They have even greater presumption and affirm that they do not commit theft nor take anything from anyone whenever they write what others have already written in earlier poems, since the others do not find or are unable to find anything that has not been said before.

The Inventor Is Entitled to His Fame

To this it is possible to say in a brief response that when the invention which was the property of the inventor becomes, through the theft of someone, common to him also, and it is believed that the thief is as much its inventor as the one who found it, the glory that ought to be entirely that of the first finder and limited to him is diminished when it is shared with another. But when because of a theft the invention is attributed to him who stole it, the first finder wrongfully and completely is deprived of his deserved glory. Of this glory everyone who takes delight in the graceful labor of the inventor ought to be the eager and faithful guardian and conservator, holding in abomination the thieves of invention as ingrates and men without understanding who deserve heavy punishment. Now it is true that nothing is said which has not been said before, if we consider the fundamental parts of which each thing is composed and consists. But if we consider it as a whole, it is not true that everything has already been said. If so, we should have to say that all poems which from time to time have been made in succession are one, and that the *Odyssey* of Homer, which was made after the *Iliad*, is the *Iliad* or some poem composed before it, because the *Odyssey* has been first given either in the *Iliad* or in another poem composed before it.

FROM

Chapter XI

Artistic Use of Ignorance

Now Aristotle speaks of the recognition by means of which the plot is made beautiful and says nothing of the ignorance which nonetheless can have a place and a principal place in the plot and makes it become beautiful; at present we may treat this ignorance in two ways, one called ignorance of fact, the other ignorance of persons. Ignorance of fact is divided in two ways, according as there are two ignorant persons; to one of them the deed pertains, to the other it does not. If those chiefly concerned in the deed are ignorant, the plot has an attractive end and gives great delight because of the deception that comes about. There are many examples of this in the *novelle* of Boccaccio, as in the stories of Gianni Lotteringhi,[36] the husband of Peronella,[37] the husband of Madonna Agnese,[38] the husband of Madonna Isabella,[39] Egano de Gallucci,[40] the jealous husband,[41] and Nicostrato.[42] Though all these are husbands and those to whom more than to any others pertain the adulteries of their wives, they are ignorant of them and by their ignorance provide amusing material for the plot.

Ignorance of the fact in those persons to whom the deed does not pertain or pertains less than to all the others is also a cause of pleasure in the plot, as in Boccaccio it may be seen how much pleasure is given by the ignorance of the neighbors and relatives about the action of the wife of Tofano, for being deceived by the words of the lady they believe what they should not, speak insultingly to Tofano, and give him blows.[43] And how pleasant the story is made by ignorance of the deed of Monna Sigismonda on the part of her mother and brothers, for being ignorant of what has happened they think her husband is drunk.[44]

Ignorance of the persons has part in the story and sometimes brings consolation to the ignorant and sometimes sorrow. It brings consolation when the ignorant person suffers, after having obtained what he desired through a person unknown and believed by him to be of adequate station or higher, as, in Plautus, ignorance of the vile woman with whom was found Pyrgopolynices, the bragging soldier, did not permit him to grieve because he had paid so much money, since he believed her noble and was consoled because he made payment for a woman that he really enjoyed and who, as he was given to understand, deserved the payment.[45] It brings sorrow when the ignorant person is so impeded that he is not able to enjoy the person who being vile is reputed noble, being made to believe that a great felicity is denied to him, as in Boccaccio when Calandrino, believing himself to be with the wife of Philippo, and being with the woman without taking any pleasure with her, is let go with this false belief so that he may not temper his sorrow at not being able to enjoy her by knowing that she was a harlot.[46] This ignorance on the part of Calandrino is perhaps the result of skillful planning by Boccaccio and makes the plot very good, but it was not brought in so skillfully by Plautus in the case of Pyrgopolynices, nor does it cause the plot to come out so well, since he completes his enjoyment and is able to console himself for the injury and the scorn he suffers by means of the pleasure he has with the woman, for because of his ignorant love for her he would have no reason for regret if he had suffered something still greater. For after the injury of the payment of the money Plautus should take away the soldier's ignorance of the person in order to take away also his consolation, as Boccaccio does, for the latter takes away from the provost of Fiesole his ignorance of the person of Ciutazza, with whom he has lain, in order to remove the consolation he might have if he continued to suppose that he had been with the widow he was in love with.[47]

Defects in the Poetics

Now it is to be known, as we have said, that Aristotle does not say a word on ignorance of persons or ignorance of the deed, nor does he speak at all of the recognitions of which we have spoken, but he speaks merely of three kinds of recognition, that is, of the chief recognition of an unknown person, of the recognition that appears to be made by things without intelligence and the power of perception, and of the recognition of the act; of these three he speaks in such a way that his speech cannot easily be understood by everyone. By the words *either to love or hate*[48] he means that the principal recognition of unknown persons generates amity or enmity, as we have said above, that is, hate or love. Brotherly love is caused by the recognition of Iphigenia and Orestes. The recognition of Myrrha excites hate in Cinyras against her. The recognition of Oedipus and of Jocasta excites in each of them hate against himself. And because here Aristotle speaks only of the recognition of unknown persons, he does not need to give an example of the recognition of an unknown act. . . .

Why Recognition of Persons Is Superior

In saying that the best recognition is accompanied by a peripety, Aristotle indicates by the word *accompanied* that he has in mind the recognition of the chief persons who are unknown, . . . and that he does not have in mind the recognition of incidental persons, such as Orestes and Electra.[49] Now it is evident why Aristotle calls this recognition of unknown persons who play a chief part the best sort of recognition, when compared with the recognition of accessory unknown persons. But it is not evident why a little later he prefers it to the other recognitions and especially to the recognition of a fact, unless it is explained by means of other reasons than those he brings forward. For since he wishes to prove that such recognitions and reversals are more suitable to the plot than all the other recognitions and reversals, he says that they generate compassion and fear, and in them is found happiness or misery, and still the recognition of the unknown fact and the reversal in those actions that can be matter for tragedy generate compassion and fear, and in them is found happiness or misery neither to a more nor a less extent. Eolus through his recognition of the abominable union of Canace and Macareus, his children, passed from happiness to unhappiness; this can arouse in other fathers, to whom such misadventures might happen, compassion toward him and fear for themselves. The recognition of unknown persons is not therefore better nor more suitable for the story, for the reasons given, than the recognition of the unknown fact, but it should be considered better and set ahead of the other recognitions because the ignorance of persons comes about more seldom than the ignorance of a deed, because it is not usual to lose knowledge of persons closely joined in blood, and if it is lost or ignorance comes about through some accident, it is close to a miracle that among so many thousands of persons in the world a horrible deed should involve just these unknown persons, and besides it is not less a marvelous thing that they should be recognized by chance and through the indications given by words or things intended for some other purpose. And these are the causes that set this recognition ahead of the others. . . .

Discovery of an Action

Aristotle says: "It can also be discovered whether a person has or has not done something." The sentence refers to the discovery of an unknown action.

This . . . is divided into two classes; in one, what another has done is learned, as when Eolus learns what his children, Macareus and Canace, have done, namely their incest; in the other, it is learned that someone has not done something, as when Theseus learns what his son Hippolytus has not done, namely, that he has not done violence to his stepmother, nor done violence to his stepmother, nor done any deed or said any word to her that was not fitting for a modest stepson. Since it is to be observed that Aristotle said in his definition that, as the name signifies, the recognition is a change from ignorance to knowledge producing friendship or enmity in those who are ordained for happiness or unhappiness, it clearly appears that he did not mean that the recognition of which he speaks should be limited merely to those who have first had knowledge of the person or of the deed, and then through some accident have lost this knowledge, which they then regain; for example, Hercules, first having the clearest knowledge of Megara, his wife, and his children, when he became insane lost it, and because he did not know them killed them, but when he became sane once more he recovered the knowledge he had lost.[50] But Aristotle also extends this knowledge to those who had not first had any knowledge, but there is complete ignorance both of the person and the deed until the recognition. Hence it does not appear to be wrong to make a distinction between the recognition of unknown persons and that of unknown actions, and it may be said that there is a knowledge that is acquired and a knowledge that is recovered.

Acquired and Recovered Knowledge

The knowledge that is acquired must be of those persons and actions of which there is complete ignorance up to the point when they become known. For example, Alexander in Boccaccio was completely ignorant that the abbot was a woman until by touching her breasts he knew her to be one.[51] And in the same Boccaccio the unchastity of Ghismonda was wholly unknown to Tancred until the time when with his own eyes he saw Guiscard sporting with her.[52] Knowledge that is recovered has to do with those persons and deeds of which a person has in the past had knowledge, which through some accident he has lost and which later he recovers. An example of recovered knowledge may be seen in Hercules, who, as we said, having at one time clear knowledge of Megara, his wife, and his children, when he became insane forgot them and not knowing them killed them; then having become sane he recovered the knowledge he had lost. Another instance is found in Boccaccio, in the widow who, foolishly forgetting the injury done by her to the scholar, trusted him, but when she received the punishment due her she recovered what had passed from her memory.[53] It seems, then, that it is well to make the aforesaid distinction between knowledge that is acquired and knowledge that is recovered, because they are very different from each other; and perhaps superior ability is demanded from the poet if he will handle one of them well than if he will handle the other well, in accordance with necessity or probability.

Three Kinds of Ignorance

It also appears that each recognition of a person or of an unknown fact can and should receive a classification into three parts, according as there are three kinds of ignorance of persons or of facts, wholly separate and distinct one from the other in the mode in which the knowledge arising from ignorance has been concealed; without this preceding concealment there can be no recognition. The persons or the facts may be unknown because they do not appear in their own forms or those of anything else, or they may be unknown because they appear in the form of something else, or they may be unknown because they appear in their own forms as modified in some secondary way. The person of Guiscard, in Boccaccio's story, was unknown to Tancred while he was in the cave, not because he appeared in his own form changed in some secondary way or in the form of something else, but because he did not appear in any form at all, being in a place where he could not be perceived by the sight or by any other sense of Tancred.[54] Buffalmacco was represented to Master Simone under the form of a horned beast and was not recognized.[55] Lodovico, who kept his appearance and changed his secondary quality of being a gentleman into that of a servant, was not known by Egano de Gallucci.[56] An adultery, in order that we may give example of ignorance of a fact, is not recognized by the husband in question, since it is not apparent to the husband because it is in the form of some other action, and not in the form of adultery, because of some secondary change, as that of the lady of Master Francesco Vergellesi with Zima, in Boccaccio's story.[57] And some other adultery, or rather some other adulteries, are unknown to the husband, as are those of Madonna Isabella with Leonetto and with Master Lambertuccio, since it is presented to the husband under the form of another action, that is, of a fight between the adulterers.[58] Further, an adultery may not be recognized by the husband as adultery, even though it is presented under the appearance of adultery, since it has some secondary modification, like that of Lucretia with Tarquin, for neither her husband nor her parents looked on it as adultery because of the menaces of Tarquin which modified its character.

Comparison of Ignorance of Person and of Action

And it is to be considered that in the first case, when the person or the fact is unknown, because they do not appear in their form nor in the form of something else, ignorance of the person is not at all different from ignorance of the fact in the ease with which it is introduced. This is not true in the second case in which the person or the fact is unknown, because, when their aspect is concealed, they show themselves under the aspect of something else, and the person who conceals his aspect can make it appear in few forms of other things and with much difficulty, but the fact, when its true appearance is concealed, can be shown in the form of many things with little difficulty. And in order not to abandon the example I have taken of adultery, it can be seen how the adultery or the adulteries of Madonna Isabella with Leonetto and with Master Lambertuccio appear in the form of a fight between the adulterers,[59] and the adultery of the godmother with Brother Rinaldo in the form of an enchantment,[60] and the adultery of Peronella with her lover in the form of the sale of a cask,[61] and the adultery of Goody Belcolore with the priest of Varlungo in the form of the loan of a stone mortar,[62] and the adultery of the avaricious Milanese lady with Gulfardo in the form of the loan of money.[63] But why should I go to the length of giving more examples of this action of adultery alone, since there are innumerable forms of other things in the form of which it can appear in such a way that it has been and can be unknown?

Easy Concealment of Identity

But in the third instance the contrary comes about because the person who retains his own form is well supplied with means of concealing himself and bringing about ignorance through unessential changes, but an action is very poor in such means. Thus the fact of adultery, which in the form of other things finds many ways of concealing itself, when it appears in its own shape finds scarcely two methods of bringing about that it should not be recognized as adultery; one of these is force and the other the fear of death which is obviously impending. But a person, appearing in his own form, produces ignorance in others by means of so slight a thing as a change of costume; for example, the abbot, though really a woman, is supposed to be a man by Alexander,[64] and Achilles, though a man, is by Lycomedes supposed to be a woman.[65] And by the external change of a large number of attendants into a small number, great lords escape recognition, as in the instance of Saladin, who without being recognized came to see all the country of the Christians,[66] and Giglietta, who went from Roussillon to Florence without being known.[67] And merely by means of changing his garb from the secular to the religious, Tedaldo talks with his lady and is unknown.[68] And through so slight and external a thing as a change from Italian clothing to that of the Saracens, Master Torello remains unknown. Because of the external change from good light to bad through the coming of night, Tito is not known by Sophronia,[69] and since the windows of the chamber are closed, Catella does not recognize Ricciardo even at noon.[70] The changes brought about by time alone prevent Madam Beritola from recognizing her son,[71] nor does Fineo recognize Teodoro.[72] By reason of a change in belief that does not affect the reality, Lady Catalina, the wife of Nicoluccio Caccianemico, is not recognized by him because he thinks her dead,[73] just as Tedaldo is not recognized by his brothers. . . .[74]

The Best Recognition

In order that we may know which recognition is most worthy of praise, we must understand that when one person knows and the other does not, the recognition can come about in two ways, either with the desire of the one who knows or against his desire. If a recognition comes about through the desire of the person who knows, the recognition has nothing marvelous in it, for it is an easy thing for one who knows to cause himself to be recognized, if he wishes to, by the one who does not know, but if the recognition is against the will of the one who knows, it cannot be other than wonderful, since the one who knows makes an effort not to be recognized. But when both persons do not know, it is likely that the first recognition will be very excellent and new, because it can come about only by chance, but the second, because it can come about either with the desire or against the desire of the one who knows, is of slight excellence if it is according to his wish, and of great excellence if it is against his will; it can be seen in the *Iphigenia among the Taurians* how much more marvelous is the first recognition, that of Iphigenia by Orestes, which came about through chance, than the second, that of Orestes by Iphigenia, which came about by his desire after he recognized his sister.

FROM

Chapter XIII

Now whether it is true or false that tragedy can have no other material than the terrifying or the piteous, I will not now speak further on it. But it surely appears to me that this has not been proved by Aristotle by means of the things he has said up to now, even though he presupposes that they are proved. Since he has set out to contradict Plato, who had said that tragedy was injurious to the morals of the people, he does not wish to approve any other sort of tragedy than that which according to him is of value in giving the people good morals and purging with fear and compassion those passions and driving them from the minds of the people in the manner we have mentioned above. Aristotle was so intent on this that he did not take care not to contradict himself and the things he had said before. If it is true that poetry was invented chiefly for the sake of pleasure and not for the sake of utility, as he has shown when he speaks of the origin of poetry in general, why does he hold that in tragedy, which is one part of poetry, utility should chiefly be sought? Why is not pleasure chiefly sought for without any regard for utility? Either Aristotle should pay no attention to utility or he should at least pay so little that he would not reject all the other kinds of tragedy which do not have it, and he should limit utility to one kind alone, namely the bringing about of the purgation of terror and compassion.[75] And nonetheless, if utility is to be considered, it would be possible to present other kinds of tragedy, as, for example, those that contain the changes of good men from misery into happiness, or the change of the wicked from felicity into misery, in order that the people may be assured by the examples that are presented, and confirm themselves in the holy belief that God takes care of the world and exercises special providence over his own, defending them and confounding their enemies and his. . . . [76]

It is necessary to know that there are some things that reason shows to be of great efficacy in producing the effect of the art but which experience shows are of little efficacy, and indeed destroy the effect. For the sake of example and in order that we may not depart from the art of poetry, reason shows us that we are more moved by the sense of sight than by the sense of hearing, that is, that we are more moved when we see things with the eyes than when we hear them narrated and take them in with the ears, and that therefore poets should cause homicides and horrible things to be represented on the stage to be seen by the people, striving with all their power to cause the people to feel terror and compassion. Yet poets do not do so, and if they do so they are blamed, but they introduce either a messenger or another person who by way of narrative makes them hear merely, for experience has shown that such cruelty and horror cannot with verisimilitude be made to appear in action, and that when they do, they make people rather laugh than weep and that they produce the effect not of tragedy but of comedy. [Here a * indicates that something is omitted by the editor of 1576.] And there are some other things that reason shows should be of great efficacy in producing the effect of art, which experience likewise shows to be of the efficacy that has been mentioned, for through their power the effect that is desired is secured in an extraordinary fashion. Of this sort is the sad end of tragedy, which by reason is proved to be of great value in generating terror and compassion, and through experience the same thing is found to be true. Still further, in tragedy without a sad end reason does not suggest that there is generated nor is there generated, according to what experience shows, terror or compassion. Then, says Aristotle, since this is shown by experience, which is the strongest proof that can be brought forward in the arts and the one to which in dealing with the arts we should alone give heed, we ought not to doubt at all, even though reason induces us to believe otherwise. In this instance, however, as has been said, reason is in conformity with experience.

Chapter XIV

The pleasure especially belonging to tragedy is, then, that which is derived from the terror and the compassion coming from the change from happiness to misery, because of an error, of a person neither good nor bad. But anyone can ask what the pleasure is that is derived from seeing a good man undeservedly hurled from prosperity into misery, for according to reason we would derive from it not pleasure but displeasure. Now there is no doubt that Aristotle understood by the word *pleasure* the purgation and the removal of fear from human minds by the means of those same passions in the way which we have above set forth at length. This purgation and this driving away, if they proceed, as he affirms, from those same passions, are seen to be capable of being with the utmost propriety called *hedone*, that is, pleasure or delight, and it ought properly to be called utility, since it is health of mind acquired through very bitter medicine.

Then pleasure arising from compassion and fear, which is truly pleasure, is that which we have already called indirect pleasure. This appears when, feeling displeasure from the misery of another that has come on him unjustly, we realize that we ourselves are good, since unjust things displease us; this realization is a very great pleasure to us because of the natural love that we have for ourselves. To this pleasure is joined another that is not at all small, namely, that on seeing the tribulations beyond what is reasonable that have come on someone else and which can possibly come on us and others like us, we learn silently and without realizing it that we are subject to many misfortunes and that we cannot believe that the current of human events runs smoothly. This delights us much more than if some other man, acting as a teacher and openly presenting the subject, taught us the same thing. For experience of things that have happened impresses instruction more on our minds than does the mere voice of a teacher, and we take more pleasure in a little that we learn for ourselves than in much that we learn from others, for we cannot learn from others if we do not admit ourselves ignorant of that which we learn and under obligation to our teachers for what we learn from them. And perhaps the wise man had these things in mind when he said that it is better to go to the house of mourning than to go to the house of feasting.[77]

FROM

Chapter XVII

[Comment on "Poetic art is the affair of the gifted man more than of the madman."] It has been concluded that he who well understands how to transform himself into an impassioned person will know how to represent such a person properly; that is, he will know how to say and do well, without the aid of art, what is fitting to such a one. And yet not everyone is fitted to do that, but merely he who is of great ability; moreover it is possible to represent a person affected by strong feeling not in this way alone but also in another way, namely to consider diligently that which men under the influence of feeling do and say in expressing their passion, but this is not a method to be used by everyone but merely by a man of high ability. Therefore it follows that poetry is devised and produced by the man of ability and not by the madman, as some say, for the madman is not in a position to put himself into various states of feeling nor is he a careful investigator of the sayings and acts of those under excitement. But it is to be observed that in my opinion there is an error in the text, since the words *or of the madman* ought to be written *not of the madman*.[78] It is not strange that *not* should be made *or* by those who have already absorbed that opinion of the *furor poeticus*[79] which . . . is here by this argument refuted by Aristotle. It is true that it is possible to retain the reading *or of the madman* without departing far from the opinion just expressed if we interpret *or of the madman* as *rather than of the madman*, as is suggested by that verse of Homer:

I wish your people to live rather than to perish.

That is, Aristotle says poetry is the product of a man of natural ability rather than of a madman, but because *than* instead of *rather than* seems suitable to verse rather than to prose, we rest on what we first said.

Chapter XXV

There have been many in the past and also at present there are many well versed in letters and known to fame, who hold the belief that the poet should be excellently instructed in all the sciences and all the arts, and that without full knowledge of these he cannot be truly a poet. From this opinion Aristotle is far distant, so far as we can judge from the words he writes here. If he says there is one kind of correctness for poetry and another for every other art, and afterwards expresses the opinion that error and transgression in another art is another thing, and that therefore the poet should be unpunished for faults committed in other arts, it follows he believes poetry can be perfect and worthy of praise without depending on extraordinary or even moderate knowledge of the sciences and the arts.

NOTES

1. This passage raises the question of the suitability of the life of a Biblical hero for poetry. In England poems by Sylvester, Quarles, and Cowley (*Davideis*) are of this type. Milton must have been interested in the problem as well, for *Paradise Lost* is to some extent a poem on the life of Adam, though it also has affinities with the cosmological Biblical poem, such as that of Du Bartas.
2. Dante considered Lucan one of the five great poets of antiquity into whose company he represented himself as admitted in *Inferno* IV, 90. Dante's theory of poetry obviously did not deny the poet a well-known subject. His belief in allegory probably influenced him. See the selection from Dante, above. Ben Jonson said of Du Bartas "that he thought not Bartas a Poet but a Verser, because he wrote not Fiction" (*Conversations with Drummond*).
3. See Aristotle, *Poetics*, I, above. The authors mentioned all wrote on scientific subjects, such as astronomy, medicine, and agriculture.
4. Fortune would have no power over nature.
5. For Tasso's opposite opinion see *Of the Heroic Poem*, sect. 7, below. Castelvetro repeats this idea (122, 13; 275, 30; 279, 24; 295, 6; 505, 40; 552, 42; 592, 14; 696, 26; and elsewhere).
6. This belief is reiterated near the end of the work.
7. Cf. Sidney's remark on the "quiddity of *ens* and *prima materia*" (*Defense of Poetry*, sect. 42).

8. Milton invoked his muse thus: "Fit audience find, though few" (*Paradise Lost*, VII, 31). But he probably had in mind moral rather than intellectual fitness. When he addressed the learned, as in his *Christian Doctrine*, he wrote in Latin. For suggestions that he held a popular theory of poetry, see the *Reason of Church Government*, sect. 2.

9. Against the charge of too abstruse reference to astrology Dante is defended by Mazzoni (*Dalla difesa di Dante*, V, 12). A passage he especially vindicates is *Paradise*, I, 37–42: "The lantern of the world rises to mortals through divers openings, but from that which joins four circles with three crosses it issues with a more propitious course and joined with a more favorable star."

10. *Institutes*, I, 4.

11. Castelvetro says also (in chap. XIII): "Reason shows that we are more moved by the sense of sight than by the sense of hearing; that is, we are more moved when we see something with our eyes than when we hear it narrated and take it in with our ears [from Horace, *Art of Poetry*, 180 ff.]. Therefore the poets should have murders and horrible things represented on the stage and make the people see them, exerting their powers to the utmost to produce terror and compassion in the audience. Yet they do not represent these horrible things, and if they do they are blamed for it, but they introduce a messenger or some other person who by the method of narrative makes the audience hear only, for experience has shown that such cruelty and horror cannot with verisimilitude be shown in action and that when shown they make the audience rather laugh than weep and that they produce the effect not of tragedy but of comedy." Is this illustrated by O'Neill's *Mourning Becomes Electra*?

12. See especially Plato's *Ion*.

13. *Apology*, 22.

14. See Castelvetro's comment on *Poetics* in chap. XVII.

15. The Italian word here translated *imitation* is *rassomiglianza*, the equivalent of the English *resemblance*. I regret that the English word has lost the flexibility and breadth of meaning it once possessed, for it perhaps is less likely to mislead than the word *imitation*. *Imitation*, however, is now generally used to render the Greek *mimesis* in the passage Castelvetro is here considering (*Poetics*, IV, first par.).

16. He has been discussing laughter that is not comic, such as that of a mother on seeing her children.

17. This suggests the feeling of superiority in the theory of comedy associated with the name of Hobbes.

18. *Decameron*, I, 8.

19. See *Republic*, III.

20. This astonishing overstatement represents a common interpretation of the catharsis.

21. "We may, then, be certain of what we have many times said, namely, that this little book is a collection of confused matters and of memories of material from which a well-ordered art of poetry could be compiled" (Castelvetro, chap. XIII).

22. *End*, a logical word, indicates here determining component. Castelvetro is repeating Aristotle's statement (*Poetics*, VI, 50a15).

23. Scaliger entitles chap. III of his seventh book "Whether the poet should teach morals or actions." He agrees with Aristotle that "beatitude is nothing else than perfect action," and that a poem leads men toward that beatitude. He cannot, however, admit that there can be a poem without character, as Aristotle suggests (50a15), and decides that the poet teaches moral habits through actions. "Action is therefore a mode of teaching; and the moral habit is what we are taught to apply. Hence the action will be a sort of example of instrument in the narrative; the moral habit will be its end."

24. With his opinion that "the end of poetry is to teach pleasantly," Scaliger was forced into such a belief as Castelvetro assigns to him. He devotes several pages to showing that Aeneas is the perfect character in all functions (*Poetice*, III, 12, pp. 91 ff.) of both public and private life. Vergil showed extraordinary skill "when he set out to unite in Aeneas alone the fortitude of Achilles and the prudence of Ulysses, and added to them piety. He eliminated the rashness of the one and removed the craft of the second, and transferred rashness to Turnus and craft to Sinon" (*ibid*, III, 20, p. 107 BC$_1$). Cf. Spenser's letter to Raleigh.

25. The *Ethics* of Aristotle and the *Characters* of his pupil Theophrastus deal with typical characters and their traits. Their works and those of imitators apparently furnished suggestions to Renaissance dramatists. There are many points of contact between English works of the sort, such as Earle's *Microcosmography*, and the playwrights of the early seventeenth century.

26. Cf. Tasso, *Heroic Poetry*, sect. 32.

27. Cf. Giraldi, *Romances*, sect. 42.

28. *Poetics*, IX, first par.

29. Here and in two succeeding instances I have substituted the reading *poema* for the *poeta* of the text.

30. *Decameron*, II, 8.

31. *Orlando Furioso*, XX-XXIV.

32. The sonnet runs as follows: "O little chamber, once a port of refuge against the severe tempests of every day, now you are a nightly fountain of tears, which in the day I conceal for shame." In his comment Castelvetro writes: "This sonnet is taken from an epistle of Pliny, Bk. VII [no. 5], to Calpurnia: 'I lie awake a great part of the night with your image in my mind, and by day, as it is commonly but truly put, my feet of their own accord take me to your room, but knowing it is vacant I turn back from it in sorrow and disappointment like an excluded lover. I escape these torments only when I am in the forum engaged in the lawsuits of my friends.' And consider how much better advised than the words of Petrarch are those of Pliny, for the latter had been in the habit of visiting his lady in that room" (*Le rime del Petrarca*, esposte per Lodovico Castelvetro [Venice, 1756], Sonnet 198).

33. *Decameron*, I, 9.

34. *Decameron*, VI, 9.

35. *Decameron*, VII, 2, from Apuleius, *The Golden Ass*, IX, 5-7, and *Decameron*, V, 10, from Apuleius, IX, 22-29. The second story is much more modified by Boccaccio than the first.

36. *Decameron*, VII, 1.

37. *Ibid*, VII, 2.

38. *Ibid*, VII, 3.

39. *Ibid*, VII, 6.

40. *Ibid*, VII, 7.

41. *Ibid*, VII, 5.

42. *Ibid*, VII, 9.

43. *Ibid*, VII, 4.

44. *Ibid*, VII, 8.

45. Plautus, *Miles Gloriosus*.

46. *Decameron*, X, 5.

47. *Ibid*, VIII, 4.

48. *Poetics*, XI, 52a29.

49. The recognition of these two, in the *Electra* of Sophocles, does not in itself cause

tragic feeling, but merely leads toward the main tragic action, the murder of Clytemnestra.

50. See *Hercules Furens* by either Euripides or Seneca. The latter's Hercules arrives at the truth by process of reasoning; he sees his own bloody arrow and realizes that he alone was able to bend the bow that drove it (ll. 1196–1200). Cf. also Aristotle, *Poetics*.
51. *Decameron*, II, 3.
52. *Ibid*, IV, 1.
53. *Ibid*, VIII, 7.
54. *Ibid*, IV, 1.
55. *Ibid*, VIII, 9.
56. *Ibid*, VII, 7.
57. *Ibid*, III, 5.
58. *Ibid*, VII, 6.
59. See the preceeding note.
60. *Decameron*, VII, 3; not strictly correct, for the characters are mother and godfather.
61. *Ibid*, VII, 2.
62. *Ibid*, VIII, 2.
63. *Ibid*, VIII, 1.
64. *Ibid*, II, 3.
65. Achilles, disguised as a maiden to keep him from participation in the Trojan war, lived at the court of Lycomedes.
66. *Decameron*, X, 9.
67. *Ibid*, III, 9.
68. *Ibid*, III, 7.
69. *Ibid*, X, 8.
70. *Ibid*, III, 6.
71. *Ibid*, II, 6.
72. *Ibid*, V, 7.
73. *Ibid*, X, 4.
74. *Ibid*, III, 7.
75. It is strange that Castelvetro, with his certainty that Aristotle did not on the whole stand for utility rather than pleasure in poetry and with his own belief that it exists for delight rather than profit, should have felt so sure that the catharsis was a moral matter. Possibly he is an early instance of the critic misled by assuming a violent opposition between Plato and Aristotle.
76. Cf. Sidney, *Defense*, sect. 25.
77. Ecclesiastes 7, 4.
78. Castelvetro renders it *non da furioso* in his Italian translation. For opinion at present see Aristotle's *Poetics*, XVII, 55a22. Faustino Summo, in his *Discorsi poetici* (Padova, 1600) disagrees with Castelvetro (*Disc.* VIII, p. 57 r).

Dryden, said to be following Rapin, accepts Castelvetro's reading (Preface to *Troilus and Cressida*, in Ker, *Essays of Dryden*, I, 221–2, 319).

79. In chap. IV, commenting on *Poetics*, IV, Castelvetro writes: "From this can be understood that Aristotle did not think poetry a special gift of God conceded to one man sooner than to another, as is the gift of prophecy and other like privileges not natural and not common to all. And without doubt he intends, though he does not do it openly, to censure the opinion that some attribute to Plato, that poetry is infused into men by divine inspiration (*furore divino*)." Continuing, he declares that the notion of poetic fury should not be attributed to Plato, but is an invention of the ignorant, impressed by the powers of

the poet. In commenting on Aristotle's praise of Homer's skill in constructing the plot (chap. VIII), Castelvetro writes: "Aristotle does not recognize in Homer any poetic fury to which he attributes such skill in planning his poem, and if he does not recognize it in Homer, much less does he recognize it in any other poet."

On the *furor poeticus* see also Patrizi, *La deca disputata*, Bk. I.

George Gascoigne
1525–1577

George Gascoigne is one of the precursors of the Elizabethan literary renaissance in England, and his critical work, *Certain Notes of Instruction* (1575) is the first English treatise on prosody.

Gascoigne himself lived a rather dissolute life. He entered Gray's Inn in 1555, belonging to a group which insisted that he compose five poems as part of his initiation, the effective beginning of his poetic career. He ruined his finances attempting the life of a courtier, and his father eventually disinherited him. A petition, probably circulated by his creditors, prevented him from assuming his seat in Parliament in 1572. It stated: "He is a defamed person and noted as well for manslaughter as other great crimes" and also termed him a "common Rhymer." Perhaps because of this incident, he left the country and became a soldier in Holland. Returning in 1575, he published a book of poems called *The Posies*, to which he appended *Certain Notes*. In addition to his poetry, Gascoigne also authored "The Adventures of Master F. J." which is considered the first original prose narrative of the English Renaissance.

In contrast to much of the Italian criticism of the period, Gascoigne's suggestions appear eminently practical and he makes no attempt to construct a theoretical system. He insists that "pleasant words" should play a subordinate role to the theme in poetry. He recommends the use of words in ordinary use and suggests that the poet disregard any artificial distinction between figures of prose and poetry.

The work is perhaps most notable to the modern reader for its outline of verse forms in the English language. Conspicuous by their absence in this catalogue are the heroic couplet used by Chaucer in his *Canterbury Tales* and the blank verse already introduced to the language by Surrey.

The Making of Verse is taken from *Elizabethan Critical Essays,* edited by G. Gregory Smith (Oxford University Press, 1904).

THE MAKING OF VERSE

CERTAYNE NOTES OF INSTRUCTION CONCERNING THE MAKING OF VERSE OR RYME IN ENGLISH, WRITTEN AT THE REQUEST OF MASTER EDOUARDO DONATI.

Signor Edouardo, since promise is debt, and you (by the lawe of friendship) do burden me with a promise that I shoulde lende you instructions towards the making of English verse or ryme, I will assaye to discharge the same, though not so perfectly as I would, yet as readily as I may: and therwithall I pray you consider that *Quot homines, tot Sententiae*, especially in Poetrie, wherein (neuerthelesse) I dare not challenge any degree, and yet will I at your request aduenture to set downe my simple skill in such simple manner as I haue vsed, referring the same hereafter to the correction of the Laureate. And you shall haue it in these few poynts followyng.

The first and most necessarie poynt that euer I founde meete to be considered in making of a delectable poeme is this, to grounde it upon some fine inuention. For it is not inough to roll in pleasant woordes, nor yet to thunder in *Rym, Ram, Ruff* by letter (quoth my master Chaucer), nor yet to abounde in apt vocables or epythetes, vnlesse the Inuention haue in it also *aliquid salis*. By this *aliquid salis* I meane some good and fine deuise, shewing the quicke capacitie of a writer: and where I say some *good and fine inuention* I meane that I would haue it both fine and good. For many inuentions are so superfine that they are Vix good. And, againe, many Inuentions are good, and yet not finely handled. And for a general forwarning: what Theame soeuer you do take in hande, if you do handle it but *tanquam in oratione perpetua*, and neuer studie for some depth of deuise in the Inuention, and some figures also in the handlyng thereof, it will appeare to the skilfull Reader but a tale of a tubbe. To deliuer vnto you generall examples it were almoste vnpossible, sithence the occasions of Inuentions are (as it were) infinite; neuerthelesse, take in worth mine opinion, and perceyue my furder meanyng in these few poynts. If I should vndertake to wryte in prayse of a gentlewoman, I would neither praise hir christal eye, nor hir cherrie lippe, etc. For these things are *trita et obuia*. But I would either finde some supernaturall cause wherby my penne might walke in the superlatiue degree, or els I would vndertake to aunswere for any imperfection that shee hath, and therevpon rayse the prayse of hir commendacion. Likewise, if I should disclose my pretence in loue, I would eyther make a strange discourse of some intollerable passion, or finde occasion to pleade by the example of some historie, or discouer my disquiet inshadowes *per Allegoriam*, or vse the couertest meane that I could to auoyde the vncomely customes of common writers. Thus much I aduenture to deliuer vnto you (my freend) vpon the rule of Inuention, which of all other rules is most to be marked, and hardest to be prescribed in certayne and infallible rules; neuerthelesse, to conclude therein, I would haue you stand most vpon the excellencie of your Inuention, and sticke not to studie deepely for some fine deuise. For, that beyng founde, pleasant woordes will follow well inough and fast inough.

2. Your Inuention being once deuised, take heede that neither pleasure of rime nor varietie of deuise do carie you from it: for as to vse obscure and darke phrases in a pleasant Sonet is nothing delectable, so to entermingle merie iests in a serious matter is an Indecorum.

3. I will next aduise you that you hold the iust measure wherwith you begin your verse. I will not denie but this may seeme a preposterous ordre; but, bycause I couet rather to satisfie you particularly than to vndertake a generall tradition, I wil not somuch stand vpon the manner as the matter of my precepts. I say then, remember to holde the same measure wherwith you begin, whether it be in a verse of sixe syllables, eight, ten, twelue, etc.: and though this precept might seeme ridiculous vnto you, since euery yong scholler can conceiue that he ought to continue in the same measure wherwith he beginneth, yet do I see and read many mens Poems now adayes, whiche beginning with the measure of xij. in the first line, and xiiij. in the second (which is the common kinde of verse), they wil yet (by that time they haue passed ouer a few verses) fal into xiiij. and fourtene, *et sic de similibus*, the which is either forgetfulness or carelesnes.

4. And in your verses remembre to place euery worde in his natural Emphasis or sound, that is to say, in such wise, and with such length or shortnesse, eleuation or depression of sillables, as it is commonly pronounced or vsed. To expresse the same we have three maner of accents, *grauis, leuis, et circumflexa*, the whiche I would english thus, the long accent, the short accent, and that whiche is indifferent: the graue accent is marked by this caracte `, the light accent is noted thus ´, and the circumflexe or indifferent is thus signified ~: the graue accent is drawen out or eleuate, and maketh that sillable long wherevpon it is placed; the light accent is depressed or snatched vp, and maketh that sillable short vpon the which it lighteth; the circumflexe accent is indifferent, sometimes short, sometimes long, sometimes depressed and sometimes eleuate. For example of th' emphasis or natural sound of words, this word *Treasure* hath the graue accent vpon the first sillable; whereas if it shoulde be written in this sorte *Treasúre*, nowe were the second sillable long, and that were cleane contrarie to the common vse wherwith it is pronounced. For furder explanation hereof, note you that commonly now a dayes in English rimes (for I dare not cal them English verses) we vse none other order but a foote of two sillables, wherof the first is depressed or made short, and the second is eleuate or made long; and that sound or scanning continueth throughout the verse. We haue vsed in times past other kindes of Meeters, as for example this following:

No wight in this world, that wealth can attayne,

Vǹleśse hè bèléue, thàt áll ìs bùt váyne.

Also our father Chaucer hath vsed the same libertie in feete and measures that the Latinists do vse: and who so euer do peruse and well consider his workes, he shall finde that although his lines are not always of one selfe same number of Syllables, yet, beyng redde by one that hath vnderstanding, the longest verse, and that which hath most Syllables in it, will fall (to the eare) correspondent vnto that whiche hath fewest sillables in it: and like wise that whiche hath in it fewest syllables shalbe founde yet to consist of woordes that haue suche naturall sounde, as may seeme equall in length to a verse which hath many moe sillables of lighter accentes. And surely I can lament that wee are fallen into suche a playne and simple manner of wryting, that there is none other foote vsed but one; wherby our Poemes may iustly be called Rithmes, and cannot by any right challenge the name of a Verse. But, since it is so, let vs take the forde as we finde it, and lette me set downe vnto you suche rules or precepts that euen in this playne foote of two syllables you wreste no woorde from his natural and vsuall sounde. I do not meane hereby that you may vse none other wordes but of twoo sillables, for therein you may vse discretion according to occasion of matter, but my meaning is, that all the wordes in your verse be so placed as the first sillable may sound short or be depressed, the second long or eleuate, the third shorte, the fourth long, the fifth shorte, etc. For example of my meaning in this point marke these two verses:

I vnderstand your meanying by your eye.

Yoùr ḿeaniǹg Í vǹdérstànd ƀy yoùr éye.

In these two verses there seemeth no difference at all, since the one hath the very selfe same woordes that the other hath, and yet the latter verse is neyther true nor pleasant, and the first verse may passe the musters. The fault of the latter verse is that this worde *vnderstand* is therein so placed as the graue accent falleth upon *der*, and therby maketh *der* in this worde *vnderstand* to be eleuated; which is contrarie to the naturall or vsual pronunciation, for we say *ìndèrstánd*, and not *ìnderstaǹd*.

5. Here by the way I thinke it not amisse to forewarne you that you thrust as few wordes of many sillables into your verse as may be: and herevnto I might alledge many reasons. First, the most aunciente English wordes are of one sillable, so that the more monasyllables that you vse the truer Englishman you shall seeme, and the lesse you shall smell of the Inkehorne: Also wordes of many syllables do cloye a verse and make it vnpleasant, whereas woordes of one syllable will more easily fall to be shorte or long as occasion requireth, or wilbe adapted to become circumflexe or of an indifferent sounde.

6. I would exhorte you also to beware of rime without reason: my meaning is hereby that your rime leade you not from your firste Inuention, for many wryters, when they haue layed the platforme of their inuention, are yet drawen sometimes (by ryme) to forget it or at least to alter it, as when they cannot readily finde out a worde whiche maye rime to the first (and yet continue their determinate Inuention) they do then eyther botche it vp with a worde that will ryme (howe small reason soeuer it carie with it), or els they alter their first worde and so percase decline or trouble their former Inuention: But do you alwayes hold your first determined Inuention, and do rather searche the bottome of your braynes for apte wordes than chaunge good reason for rumbling rime.

7. To help you a little with ryme (which is also a plaine yong schollers lesson), worke thus: when you haue set downe your first verse, take the last worde thereof and coumpt ouer all the wordes of the selfe same sounde by order of the Alphabete: As, for example, the laste woorde of your firste line is *care*, to ryme therwith you haue *bare, clare, dare, fare, gare, hare*, and *share, mare, snare, rare, stare*, and *ware, &c.* Of all these take that which best may serue your purpose, carying reason with rime: and if none of them will serue so, then alter the laste worde of your former verse, but yet do not willingly alter the meanyng of your Inuention.

8. You may vse the same Figures or Tropes in verse which are vsed in prose, and in my iudgement they serue more aptly and haue greater grace in verse than they haue in prose: but yet therein remembre this old adage, *Ne quid nimis*, as many wryters which do not know the vse of any other figure than that whiche is expressed in repeticion of sundrie wordes beginning all with one letter, the whiche (beyng modestly vsed) lendeth good grace to a verse, but they do so hunte a letter to death that they make it *Crambe*, and *Crambe bis positum mors est*: therfore *Ne quid nimis*.

9. Also, asmuche as may be, eschew straunge words, or *obsoleta et inusitata*, vnlesse the Theame do giue iust occasion: marie, in some places a straunge worde doth drawe attentiue reading, but yet I woulde haue you therein to vse discretion.

10. And asmuch as you may, frame your stile to perspicuity and to be sensible, for the haughty obscure verse doth not much delight, and the verse that is to easie is like a tale of a rosted horse; but let your Poeme be such as may both delight and draw attentiue readyng, and therewithal may deliuer such matter as be worth the marking.

11. You shall do very well to vse your verse after thenglishe phrase, and not after the maner of other languages. The Latinists do commonly set the adiectiue after the Substantiue: As, for example, *Femina pulchra, aedes altae, &c.*; but if we should say in English a woman fayre, a house high, etc. it would haue but small grace, for we say a good man, and not a man good, etc. And yet I will not altogether forbidde it you, for in some places it may be borne, but not so hardly as some vse it which wryte thus:

> Now let vs go to Temple ours.
> I will go visit mother myne &c.

THE MAKING OF VERSE

Surely I smile at the simplicitie of such deuisers which might aswell haue sayde it in playne Englishe phrase, and yet haue better pleased all eares, than they satisfie their owne fancies by suche *superfinesse*. Therefore euen as I haue aduised you to place all wordes in their naturall or most common and vsuall pronunciation, so would I wishe you to frame all sentences in their mother phrase and proper *Idióma*; and yet sometimes (as I haue sayd before) the contrarie may be borne, but that is rather where rime enforceth, or *per licentiam Poëticam*, than it is otherwise lawfull or commendable.

12. This poeticall licence is a shrewde fellow, and couereth many faults in a verse; it maketh wordes longer, shorter, of mo sillables, of fewer, newer, older, truer, falser; and, to conclude, it turkeneth all things at pleasure, for example, *ydone* for *done*, *adowne* for *downe*, *orecome* for *ouercome*, *tane* for *taken*, *power* for *powre*, *heauen* for *heaun*, *thewes* for good partes or good qualities, and a numbre of other, whiche were but tedious and needelesse to rehearse, since your owne iudgement and readyng will soone make you espie such aduauntages.

13. There are also certayne pauses or restes in a verse, whiche may be called *Ceasures*, whereof I woulde be lothe to stande long, since it is at discretion of the wryter, and they haue bene first deuised (as should seeme) by the Musicians: but yet thus much I will aduenture to wryte, that in mine opinion in a verse of eight sillables the pause will stand best in the middest; in a verse of tenne it will best be placed at the ende of the first foure sillables; in a verse of twelue, in the midst; in verses of twelue in the firste and fouretene in the seconde wee place the pause commonly in the midst of the first, and at the ende of the first eight sillables in the second. In Rithme royall it is at the wryters discretion, and forceth not where the pause be vntill the ende of the line.

14. And here, bycause I haue named Rithme royall, I will tell you also mine opinion aswell of that as of the names which other rymes haue commonly borne heretofore. Rythme royall is a verse of tenne sillables; and seuen such verses make a staffe, whereof the first and thirde lines do aunswer (acrosse) in like terminations and rime, the second, fourth, and fifth do likewise answere eche other in terminations, and the two last do combine and shut vp the Sentence: this hath bene called Rithme royall, and surely it is a royall kinde of verse, seruing best for graue discourses. There is also another kinde, called Ballade, and thereof are sundrie sortes: for a man may write ballade in a staffe of sixe lines, euery line conteyning eighte or sixe sillables, whereof the firste and third, second and fourth do rime acrosse, and the fifth and sixth do rime togither in conclusion. You may write also your ballad of tenne sillables, rimyng as before is declared; but these two were wont to be most commonly vsed in ballade, which propre name was (I thinke) deriued of this worde in Italian *Ballare*, whiche signifieth to daunce. And in deed those kinds of rimes serue beste for daunces or light matters. Then haue you also a rondlette, the which doth always end with one self same foote or repeticion, and was thereof (in my iudgement) called a rondelet. This may consist of such

measure as best liketh the wryter. Then haue you Sonnets: some thinke that all Poemes (being short) may be called Sonets, as in deede it is a diminutiue worde deriued of *Sonare*, but yet I can beste allowe to call those Sonnets whiche are of fouretene lynes, euery line conteyning tenne syllables. The firste twelue do ryme in staues of foure lines by crosse meetre, and the last two ryming togither do conclude the whole. There are Dyzaynes, and Syxaines, which are of ten lines, and of sixe lines, commonly vsed by the French, which some English writers do also terme by the name of Sonettes. Then is there an old kinde of Rithme called Ver layes, deriued (as I haue redde) of this worde *Verd*, whiche betokeneth Greene, and *Laye*, which betokeneth a Song, as if you would say greene Songes: but I muste tell you by the way that I neuer redde any verse which I saw by aucthoritie called *Verlay* but one, and that was a long discourse in verses of tenne sillables, whereof the foure first did ryme acrosse, and the fifth did aunswere to the firste and thirde, breaking off there, and so going on to another termination. Of this I could shewe example of imitation in mine own verses written to the right honorable the Lord Grey of Wilton upon my journey into Holland, etc. There are also certaine Poemes deuised of tenne syllables, whereof the first aunswereth in termination with the fourth, and the second and thirde answere eche other: these are more vsed by other nations than by vs, neyther can I tell readily what name to giue them. And the commonest sort of verse which we vse now adayes (*viz.* the long verse of twelue and fourtene sillables) I know not certainly howe to name it, vnlesse I should say that it doth consist of Poulters measure, which giueth xii. for one dozen and xiiij. for another. But let this suffise (if it be not to much) for the sundrie sortes of verses which we vse now adayes.

15. In all these sortes of verses, when soeuer you vndertake to write, auoyde prolixitie and tediousnesse, and euer, as neare as you can, do finish the sentence and meaning at the end of euery staffe where you wright staues, and at the end of euery two lines where you write by cooples or poulters measure: for I see many writers which draw their sentences in length, and make an ende at latter Lammas: for, commonly, before they end, the Reader hath forgotten where he begon. But do you (if you wil follow my aduise) eschue prolixitie and knit vp your sentences as compendiously as you may, since breuitie (so that it be not drowned in obscuritie) is most commendable.

16. I had forgotten a notable kinde of ryme, called ryding rime, and that is suche as our Mayster and Father Chaucer vsed in his Canterburie tales, and in diuers other delectable and light enterprises; but, though it come to my remembrance somewhat out of order, it shall not yet come altogether out of time, for I will nowe tell you a conceipt whiche I had before forgotten to wryte: you may see (by the way) that I holde a preposterous order in my traditions but, as I sayde before, I wryte moued by good wil, and not to shewe my skill. Then to returne too my matter, as this riding rime serueth most aptly to wryte a merie tale, so Rythme royall is fittest for a graue discourse. Ballades are beste of matters of loue, and rondlettes moste apt for the beating or handlyng of an adage or common prouerbe: Sonets serue aswell in matters of loue as of discourse:

THE MAKING OF VERSE

Dizaynes and Sixaines for shorte Fantazies: Verlayes for an effectual proposition, although by the name you might otherwise iudge of Verlayes; and the long verse of twelue and fouretene sillables, although it be now adayes vsed in all Theames, yet in my iudgement it would serue best for Psalmes and Himpnes.

I woulde stande longer in these traditions, were it not that I doubt mine owne ignoraunce; but, as I sayde before, I know that I write to my freende, and, affying my selfe therevpon, I make an ende.

Michel de Montaigne
1533–1592

Michel Eyquem de Montaigne was born on February 28, 1533 at the Chateau de Montaigne near Bordeaux. The son of a minor nobleman, Montaigne was educated liberally in a household where Latin was spoken with greater frequency than French (indeed, French was Montaigne's second language, which he did not learn until the age of six). As the son of a public servant, Montaigne drifted naturally and without great excitement into politics, spending 13 fairly uneventful years in the newly formed royal court of justice, the Parlement de France.

Montaigne's duties allowed him ample time for private study and reflection, and he soon turned his attention to writing. In 1569, he translated *The Book of Creatures, or Natural Theology*, a philosophical work which attempted to prove God's existence using the evidence of the physical world. This was the first sign of Montaigne's interest in Sebond, a 15th-century Spanish philosopher. Montaigne improved the work in significant ways, editing it with great skill and employing a fine prose style.

When Montaigne assumed the family title upon the death of his father in 1568, he retired from public life to the family estate. Here he began to write in earnest, composing the first chapters of his mighty collection of *Essays*. Eventually encompassing three volumes, the *Essays* are broad-ranging in their subjects and idiosyncratic in their outlook, reflecting the attitudes of their author. The most famous chapter, "The Apology for Raymond Sebond," is an extended meditation on the reliability of human knowledge and perception—in actuality, it discusses Sebond only tangentially and in a minor way—and has often been seen as an example of that skepticism which is associated more often with the Enlightenment, but has its roots in the Renaissance.

Various chapters of the *Essays* (e.g., "On Education," "On Pedantry," "On Books," et al.) touch upon literary questions, and here as in most areas, Montaigne's views are *sui generis*. He criticizes the Pléiade movement in broad terms, but finds room nonetheless to praise du Bellay for his erudition and excellence. His admiration of the ancients is conventional and to be expected from a man of his period, but his disdain of the medievals is extreme. Having little ability in Greek, he passes no judgment upon Homer or Aristotle, but he makes it clear that Virgil is the Roman poet most worthy of fame. Interestingly, he makes no comment whatever on French verse.

The picture that emerges of Montaigne on the basis of his writings on literature is that of a pragmatist. He recommends the classical authors because he feels that Greek and Latin scholarship will make for an enrichment of the French language. In "On Books" he takes a deliberately nonchalant attitude towards literature in general, claiming an inability to remember what he reads, and maintaining that he reads primarily for personal amusement. The same skepticism which marks other aspects of his personality is brought into play here: always there is a sense of moderation, an unwillingness to be placed in any specific "camp"—the somewhat distant, somewhat superior attitude of one who has refused to enter the fray. It should come as no surprise that during the course of the frequently violent religious wars of the 16th century, Montaigne—though he remained always loyal to the old Faith himself—counselled toleration in dealing with the Protestants.

The *Essays* constituted Montaigne's life work. Although he occupied himself with political and military pursuits into his old age, he continued to expand and revise the *Essays* up to 1588. Little is known of his last years. He died on September 13, 1592.

The essay "On Books," translated by Donald M. Frame, is reprinted by permission of Stanford University Press from *The Complete Essays of Montaigne* (Stanford: Stanford University Press, 1958). © 1958 by the Board of Trustees of Leland Stanford Junior University.

OF BOOKS

I have no doubt that I often happen to speak of things that are better treated by the masters of the craft, and more truthfully. This is purely the essay of my natural faculties, and not at all of the acquired ones; and whoever shall catch me in ignorance will do nothing against me, for I should hardly be answerable for my ideas to others, I who am not answerable for them to myself, or satisfied with them. Whoever is in search of knowledge, let him fish for it where it dwells; there is nothing I profess less. These are my fancies, by which I try to give knowledge not of things, but of myself. The things will perhaps be known to me some day, or have been once, according as fortune may have brought me to the places where they were made clear. But I no longer remember them. And if I am a man of some reading, I am a man of no retentiveness.

Thus I guarantee no certainty, unless it be to make known to what point, at this moment, extends the knowledge that I have of myself. Let attention be paid not to the matter, but to the shape I give it.

Let people see in what I borrow whether I have known how to choose what would enhance my theme. For I make others say what I cannot say so well, now through the weakness of my language, now through the weakness of my understanding. I do not count my borrowings, I weigh them. And if I had wanted to have them valued by their number, I should have loaded myself with twice as many. They are all, or very nearly all, from such famous and ancient names that they seem to identify themselves enough without me. In the reasonings and inventions that I transplant into my soil and confound with my own, I have sometimes deliberately not indicated the author, in order to hold in check the temerity of those hasty condemnations that are tossed at all sorts of writings, notably recent writings of men still living, and in the vulgar tongue, which invites everyone to talk about them and seems to convict the conception and design of being likewise vulgar. I want them to give Plutarch a fillip on my nose and get burned insulting Seneca in me. I have to hide my weakness under these great authorities. I will love anyone that can unplume me, I mean by clearness of judgment and by the sole distinction of the force and beauty of the remarks. For I who, for lack of memory, fall short at every turn in picking them out by knowledge of their origin, can very well realize, by measuring my capacity, that my soil is not at all capable of producing certain too rich flowers that I find sown there, and that all the fruits of my own growing could not match them.

For this I am obliged to be responsible: if I get myself tangled up, if there is vanity and faultiness in my reasonings that I do not perceive or that I am not capable of perceiving when pointed out to me. For faults often escape our eyes; but infirmity of judgment consists in not being able to perceive them when another reveals them to us. Knowledge and truth can lodge in us without judgment, and judgment also without them; indeed the recognition of ignorance is one of the fairest and surest testimonies of judgment that I find.

I have no other marshal but fortune to arrange my bits. As my fancies present themselves, I pile them up; now they come pressing in a crowd, now dragging single file. I want people to see my natural and ordinary pace, however off the track it is. I let myself go as I am. Besides, these are not matters of which we are forbidden to be ignorant and to speak casually and at random.

I should certainly like to have a more perfect knowledge of things, but I do not want to buy it as dear as it costs. My intention is to pass pleasantly, and not laboriously, what life I have left. There is nothing for which I want to rack my brain, not even knowledge, however great its value.

I seek in books only to give myself pleasure by honest amusement; or if I study, I seek only the learning that treats of the knowledge of myself and instructs me in how to die well and live well:

> This is the goal toward which my sweating horse should strain.
> (Propertius)

If I encounter difficulties in reading, I do not gnaw my nails over them; I leave them there, after making one or two attacks on them. If I planted myself in them, I would lose both myself and time; for I have an impulsive mind. What I do not see at the first attack, I see less by persisting. I do nothing without gaiety; continuation and too strong contention dazes, depresses, and wearies my judgment. My sight becomes confused and dispersed. I have to withdraw it and apply it again by starts, just as in order to judge the luster of a scarlet fabric, they tell us to pass our eyes over it several times, catching it in various quickly renewed and repeated glimpses.

If this book wearies me, I take up another; and I apply myself to it only at the moments when the boredom of doing nothing begins to grip me. I do not take much to modern books, because the ancient ones seem to me fuller and stronger; nor to those in Greek, because my judgment cannot do its work with a childish and apprentice understanding.

Among the books that are simply entertaining, I find, of the moderns, the *Decameron* of Boccaccio, Rabelais, and *The Kisses* of Johannes Secundus, if they may be placed under this heading, worth reading for amusement. As for the Amadises and writings of that sort, they did not have the authority to detain even my childhood. I will also say this, whether boldly or rashly, that this heavy old soul of mine no longer lets itself be tickled, not merely by Ariosto, but even by the good Ovid: his facility and inventions, which once enchanted me, hardly entertain me at all now.

I speak my mind freely on all things, even on those which perhaps exceed my capacity and which I by no means hold to be within my jurisdiction. And so the opinion I give of them is to declare the measure of my sight, not the measure of things. When I feel a distaste for Plato's *Axiochus* as a work without power considering such an author, my judgment does not trust itself: it is not so stupid as to oppose itself to the authority of so many other famous ancient judgments, which it considers its tutors and masters, and with which it is rather content to err. It blames and condemns itself either for stopping at the outer bark, not being able to penetrate to the heart, or for looking at the thing by some false light. It is content with simply securing itself from confusion and disorder; as for its weakness, it readily recognizes and admits it. It thinks it gives a correct interpretation to the appearances that its conception presents to it; but these are weak and imperfect.

Most of Aesop's Fables have many meanings and interpretations. Those who take them allegorically choose some aspect that squares with the fable, but for the most part this is only the first and superficial aspect; there are others more living, more essential and internal, to which they have not known how to penetrate; this is how I read them.

But, to pursue my path, it has always seemed to me that in poetry Virgil, Lucretius, Catullus, and Horace hold the first rank by very far, and especially Virgil in his *Georgics*, which I consider the most accomplished work in poetry; in comparison with it one can easily recognize that there are passages in the *Aeneid* which the author would have brushed up still a little more if he had had the chance. And the fifth book of the *Aeneid* seems to me the most perfect. I also love Lucan and enjoy his company, not so much for his style as for his own worth and the truth of his opinions and judgments. As for the good Terence, the very refinement and charm of the Latin language, I find him admirable at representing to the life the movements of the soul and the state of our characters; at every moment our actions throw me back to him. I cannot read him so often as not to find in him some new beauty and grace.

Those who lived near Virgil's time used to complain that some compared Lucretius to him. I am of the opinion that this is in truth an unequal comparison; but I have much to do to confirm myself in this belief when I find myself fixed on one of the beautiful passages in Lucretius. If they were stung by this comparison, what would they say of the barbarous brutishness and stupidity of those who nowadays compare Ariosto to him? And what would Ariosto himself say?

> O foolish and dull-witted age!
> (Catullus)

I think the ancients had still more reason to complain of those who compared Plautus to Terence (the latter savors much more of the gentleman) than of those who compared Lucretius to Virgil. It does much for the esteem and preference of Terence that the father of Roman eloquence[1] has him, and him alone of his class, so often in his mouth; and also the verdict that the first judge among the Roman poets[2] gives of his fellow.

It has often struck my mind how in our time those who set themselves to write comedies (like the Italians, who are rather happy at it) use three or four plots from Terence or Plautus to make one of their own. They pile up in a single comedy five or six stories from Boccaccio. What makes them so load themselves with material is the distrust they have of being able to sustain themselves by their own graces; they have to find a body to lean on; and not having enough of their own to detain us, they want the story to amuse us. It is quite the contrary with my author: the perfections and beauties of his style of expression make us lose our appetite for his subject. His distinction and elegance hold us throughout; he is everywhere so delightful,

> Clear flowing and most like a crystal stream,
> (Horace)

and so fills our soul with his charms, that we forget those of his plot.

This same consideration draws me on further. I observe that the good ancient poets avoided the affectation and the quest, not only of the fantastic Spanish and Petrarchian flights, but even of the milder and more restrained conceits that are the adornment of all the poetic works of the succeeding centuries. Yet there is no good judge who misses them in those ancients, and who does not admire incomparably more the even polish and that perpetual sweetness and flowering beauty of Catullus' epigrams than all the stings with which Martial sharpens the tails of his. This is for the same reason that I was stating just now, as Martial says of himself: *he had less need for the labor of wit, since his subject matter took the place of wit.* The former, without getting excited and without goading themselves, make themselves sufficiently felt: they have matter enough for laughter everywhere, they don't have to tickle themselves. The latter need outside help: the less wit they have, the more body they need. They mount on horseback because they are not strong enough on their legs.

Just as at our balls these men of low condition who keep dancing schools, not being able to imitate the bearing and fitness of our nobility, seek to recommend themselves by perilous leaps and other strange mountebank's antics. And the ladies can more cheaply show off their carriage in the dances where there are various contortions and twistings of the body, than in certain other formal dances where they need only walk with a natural step and display a natural bearing and their ordinary grace. As I have also seen excellent clowns, in their ordinary dress and usual face, give us all the pleasure that can be derived from their art, while the apprentices and those who are not so highly skilled need to flour their faces, dress up, and counterfeit wild movements and grimaces in order to make us laugh.

This idea of mine is easier to recognize in the comparison of the *Aeneid* and the *Orlando Furioso* than anywhere else. We see the former on outspread wings in lofty and sustained flight always pursuing his point; the latter fluttering and hopping from tale to tale as from branch to branch, not trusting his wings except for a very short hop, and alighting at every turn for fear his breath and strength should fail:

> He tries his wings in short excursions.
> (Virgil)

These, then, in this sort of subjects, are the authors I like best.

As for my other reading, which mingles a little more profit with the pleasure, and by which I learn to arrange my humors and my ways, the books that serve me for this are Plutarch, since he exists in French, and Seneca. They both have this notable advantage for my humor, that the knowledge I seek is there treated in detached pieces that do not demand the obligation of long labor, of which I am incapable. Such are the *Moral Essays* of Plutarch and the *Epistles* of Seneca, which are the finest part of his writings, and the most profitable. I need no great enterprise to get at them, and I leave them whenever I like. For they have no continuity from one to the other.

These authors agree in most of the opinions that are useful and true; and so were their fortunes similar: they were born at about the same time, each tutored a Roman Emperor, both came from foreign countries, both were rich and powerful. Their teaching is the cream of philosophy, and presented in simple and pertinent fashion. Plutarch is more uniform and constant, Seneca more undulating and diverse. The latter labors, strains, and tenses himself to arm virtue against weakness, fear, and vicious appetites; the other seems not to esteem their power so much, and to disdain to hurry his step or stand on guard for them. Plutarch's opinions are Platonic, mild, and accommodated to civil society; the other's are Stoic and Epicurean, more remote from common use, but in my opinion more suitable for private life and more sturdy. In Seneca it seems that he concedes a little to the tyranny of the emperors of his time, for I hold it for certain that it is by a forced judgment that he condemns the cause of those high-minded murderers of Caesar; Plutarch is free throughout. Seneca is full of witty points and sallies, Plutarch of things. The former heats you and moves you more; the latter contents you more and pays you better. He guides us, the other pushes us.

As for Cicero, the works of his that can best serve my purpose are those that treat of philosophy, especially moral. But to confess the truth boldly (for once you have crossed over the barriers of impudence there is no more curb), his way of writing, and every other similar way, seems to me boring. For his prefaces, definitions, partitions, etymologies, consume the greater part of his work; what life and marrow there is, is smothered by his long-winded preparations. If I have spent an hour in reading him, which is a lot for me, and I remember what juice and substance I have derived, most of the time I find nothing but wind; for he has not yet come to the arguments that serve his purpose and the reasons that properly touch on the crux, which I am looking for.

For me, who ask only to become wiser, not more learned or eloquent, these logical and Aristotelian arrangements are not to the point. I want a man to begin with the conclusion. I understand well enough what death and pleasure are; let him not waste his time anatomizing them. I look for good solid reasons from the start, which will instruct me in how to sustain their attack. Neither grammatical subtleties nor an ingenious contexture of words and argumentations are any use for that. I want reasonings that drive their first attack into the stronghold of the doubt; his languish around the pot. They are good for the school, for the bar, and for the sermon, where we have leisure to nap and are still in time a quarter of an hour later to pick up the thread of the discourse. It is necessary to speak thus to judges, whom we want to win over rightly or wrongly, to children, and to the common herd, to whom we have to say everything to see what will carry.

I do not want a man to use his strength making me attentive and to shout at me fifty times "*Or oyez!*" in the manner of our heralds. The Romans used to say in their religion "*Hoc age,*" as we say in ours "*Sursum corda*":[3] these are so many words lost on me. I come fully prepared from my house; I need no allurement or sauce; I can perfectly well eat my meat quite raw; and instead of whetting my appetite by these preparations and preliminaries, they pall and weary it.

Will the license of the times excuse my sacrilegious audacity in considering that even Plato's dialogues drag and stifle his substance too much, and in lamenting the time put into these long vain preliminary interlocutions by a man who had so many better things to say? My ignorance will excuse me better in that I have no perception of the beauty of his language. In general I ask for books that make use of learning, not those that build it up.

The first two, and Pliny, and their like, have no *Hoc age*; they want to have to do with men who themselves have told themselves this; or if they have one, it is a substantial *Hoc age* that has a body of its own.

I also like to read the *Letters to Atticus*,[4] not only because they contain a very ample education in the history and affairs of his time, but much more because in them I discover his personal humors. For I have a singular curiosity, as I have said elsewhere, to know the soul and the natural judgments of my authors. We must indeed judge their capacity, but not their character nor themselves, by that display of their writings that they expose on the stage of the world. I have regretted a thousand times that we have lost the book that Brutus had written on virtue: for it is a fine thing to learn the theory from those who well know the practice. But since the preachings are one thing and the preacher another, I am as glad to see Brutus in Plutarch as in a book of his own. I would rather choose to know truly the conversation he held in his tent with some one of his intimate friends on the eve of a battle than the speech he made the next day to his army; and what he was doing in his study and his chamber than what he was doing in the public square and in the Senate.

As for Cicero, I am of the common opinion, that except for learning there was not much excellence in his soul. He was a good citizen, of an affable nature, as all fat jesting men, such as he was, are apt to be; but of softness and ambitious vanity he had in truth a great deal. And moreover I do not know how to excuse him for having considered his poetry worth being published. It is not a great imperfection to write verses badly; but it is a lack of judgment in him not to have felt how unworthy they were of the glory of his name. As for his eloquence, it is entirely beyond comparison; I believe that no man will ever equal him.

The younger Cicero, who resembled his father only in name, while commanding in Asia, had several strangers at his table one day, and among others Cestius, seated at the lower end, as people often push in to the open tables of the great. Cicero inquired who he was of one of his men, who told him his name. But like a man whose thoughts were elsewhere and who kept forgetting what they answered him, he asked him that again two or three more times. The servant, in order not to have the trouble of repeating the same thing so often to him, and to make him know him by some circumstance, said to him: "It is that Cestius of whom you were told that he sets no great store by your father's eloquence in comparison with his own." Cicero, suddenly stung by this, ordered them to lay hold of this poor Cestius and had him very soundly whipped in his presence. That was a discourteous host!

Even among those who, all things considered, esteemed this eloquence of his as incomparable, there were some who did not fail to note some faults in it; thus the great Brutus, his friend, used to say that it was a broken and weak-loined eloquence, *fractam et elumbem*. The orators who lived near his time also reprehended in him his sedulous care for a certain long cadence at the end of his periods, and noted the words *esse videatur*[5] which he uses so often. As for me, I prefer a cadence that falls shorter, cut into iambics. To be sure, he does sometimes mix up his rhythms quite roughly, but rarely. My ears have noted this passage: "Ego vero me minus diu senem esse mallem, quam esse senem, antequam essem."[6]

The historians come right to my forehand. They are pleasant and easy; and at the same time, man in general, the knowledge of whom I seek, appears in them more alive and entire than in any other place—the diversity and truth of his inner qualities in the mass and in detail, the variety of the ways he is put together, and the accidents that threaten him. Now those who write biographies, since they spend more time on plans than on events, more on what comes from within than on what happens without, are most suited to me. That is why in every way Plutarch is my man. I am very sorry that we do not have a dozen Laertiuses, or that he is not either more receptive or more perceptive. For I consider no less curiously the fortunes and the lives of these great teachers of the world than the diversity of their doctrines and fancies.

In this kind of study of history we must leaf without distinction through all sorts of authors, both old and new, both gibberish and French, in order to learn in them the things of which they variously treat. But it seems to me that Caesar singularly deserves to be studied, not only for the knowledge of history, but for himself, so much perfection and excellence he has above all the others, although Sallust is one of their number. Indeed I read this author with a little more reverence and respect than one reads human works: now considering him in himself by his actions and the miracle of his greatness, now the purity and inimitable polish of his language, which surpassed not only all the historians, as Cicero says, but perhaps Cicero himself. With so much sincerity in his judgments when speaking of his enemies, that except for the false colors with which he tries to cover his evil cause and the filthiness of his pestilential ambition, I think the only fault that can be found in him is that he has been too sparing in speaking of himself. For so many great things cannot have been performed by him without much more of himself having gone into them than he sets down.

I like historians who are either very simple or outstanding. The simple, who have not the wherewithal to mix in anything of their own, and who bring to it only the care and diligence to collect all that comes to their attention and to record everything faithfully without choice or discrimination, leave our judgment intact to discern the truth. Such, for example, among others, is the good Froissart, who has gone along in his undertaking with such frank simplicity that having made a mistake he is not at all afraid to recognize it and correct it at the spot where he has been made aware of it; and who presents to us even the diversity of the rumors that were current and the different reports that were made to him. This is the material of history, naked and unformed; each man can make his profit of it according to his understanding.

The really outstanding ones have the capacity to choose what is worth knowing; they can pick out of two reports the one that is more likely. From the nature and humors of princes they infer their intentions and attribute appropriate words to them. They are right to assume the authority to regulate our belief by their own; but certainly this privilege belongs to very few people.

Those in between (which are the commonest sort) spoil everything for us. They want to chew our morsels for us; they give themselves the right to judge, and consequently to slant history to their fancy; for once the judgment leans to one side, one cannot help turning and twisting the narrative to that bias. They undertake to choose the things worth knowing, and often conceal from us a given word, a given private action, that would instruct us better; they omit as incredible the things they do not understand, and perhaps also some things because they do not know how to say them in good Latin or French. Let them boldly display their eloquence and their reasonings, let them judge all they like; but let them also leave us the wherewithal to judge after them, and not alter or arrange by their abridgments and selection anything of the substance of the matter, but pass it on to us pure and entire in all its dimensions.

Most of the time, especially in these days, people are selected for this work from among the common herd for the sole consideration of knowing how to speak well; as if here we were trying to learn grammar! And having been hired only for that and having put on sale only their babble, they are right accordingly to care chiefly only about that part. Thus with many fine words they go and cook up a fine concoction of the rumors they pick up in the city squares.

The only good histories are those that have been written by the very men who were in command in the affairs, or who were participants in the conduct of them, or who at least have had the fortune to conduct others of the same sort. Such are almost all the Greek and Roman histories. For when several eyewitnesses have written about the same subject (as it happened in those days that greatness and learning usually met), if there is a mistake, it must be very slight, and on a very doubtful incident. What can you expect of a doctor discussing war, or a schoolboy discussing the intentions of princes? If we want to note the scruples the Romans had in this, we need only this example. Asinius Pollio found in the histories even of Caesar some mistake into which he had fallen through not having been able to keep his eyes on every part of his army and having believed individuals who often reported to him things insufficiently verified; or else through not having been carefully enough informed by his lieutenants about what they had done in his absence. We can see by this example whether this quest of truth is delicate, when we cannot trust the commander's knowledge of a battle his soldiers have fought, or the soldiers' knowledge of what happened near them, unless, in the manner of a judicial inquiry, we confront the witnesses and hear the objections about the evidence in the slightest details of each incident. Truly, the knowledge we have of our own affairs is much looser. But this has been sufficiently treated by Bodin, and according to my way of thinking.

To compensate a little for the treachery and weakness of my memory, so extreme that it has happened to me more than once to pick up again, as recent and unknown to me, books which I had read carefully a few years before and scribbled over with my notes, I have adopted the habit for some time now of adding at the end of each book (I mean of those that I intend to use only once) the time I finished reading it and the judgment I have derived of it as a whole, so that this may represent to me at least the sense and general idea I had conceived of the author in reading it. I want to transcribe here some of these annotations.

Here is what I put some ten years ago in my Guicciardini (for whatever language my books speak, I speak to them in my own): "He is a diligent historiographer from whom, in my opinion, one can learn the truth about the affairs of his time as exactly as from any other: and indeed in most of them he was an actor himself, and of honorable rank. There is no appearance that through hatred, favor, or vanity, he disguised things; which is attested by the free judgments he gives of the great, and especially of those by whom he had been advanced and employed in responsibilities, like Pope Clement VII. As for the part he seems to want to make most of, which is his digressions and discourses, there are some good ones and enriched with fine traits, but he is too fond of them. For by not wanting to leave anything unsaid, having a subject so full and ample and almost infinite, he becomes diffuse and smacking a bit of scholastic prattle. I have also noted this, that of so many souls and actions that he judges, so many motives and plans, he never refers a single one to virtue, religion, and conscience, as if these qualities were wholly extinct in the world; and of all actions, however fair in appearance they may be of themselves, he throws the cause back onto some vicious motive or some profit. It is impossible to imagine that among the infinite number of actions that he judges there was not a single one produced by the way of reason. No corruption can have seized men so universally that someone would not escape the contagion. This makes me fear that his taste was a bit corrupted; and it may have happened that he judged others by himself."

In my Philippe de Commines there is this: "Here you will find the language pleasant and agreeable, of a natural simplicity; the narrative pure, and the author's good faith showing through it clearly, free from vanity in speaking of himself, and of partiality or envy in speaking of others; his ideas and exhortations accompanied more by good zeal and truth than by any exquisite capacity; and, throughout, authority and gravity, representing the man of good background and brought up in great affairs."

On the *Memoirs* of Monsieur du Bellay:[7] "It is always a pleasure to see things written by people who have experienced how they should be conducted; but it cannot be denied that there is clearly revealed in these two lords a great falling off from the frankness and freedom of writing that shine forth in the ancients of their class, such as the sire de Joinville, intimate friend of Saint Louis; Eginhard, chancellor of Charlemagne; and, of more recent memory,

Philippe de Commines. This is rather a plea for King Francis against the Emperor Charles V, than a history. I will not believe that they have changed anything in the main facts; but as for turning the judgment of events to our advantage, often contrary to reason, and omitting everything that is ticklish in the life of their master, they make a practice of it: witness the disgrace of Messieurs de Montmorency and de Brion, which are forgotten; indeed the very name of Madame d'Etampes is not to be found. One may cover up secret actions; but to be silent about what all the world knows, and about things that have led to public results of such consequence, is an inexcusable defect. In short, to get a complete knowledge of King Francis and the events of his time, a man should turn elsewhere, if he takes my advice. The profit one can make here is from the detailed narrative of the battles and exploits of war at which these gentlemen were present; some private words and actions of certain princes of their time; and the dealings and negotiations carried on by the seigneur de Langey, in which there are plenty of things worth knowing, and ideas above the ordinary."

NOTES

1. Cicero.
2. Horace.
3. "*Or oyez*"—"Now listen." "*Hoc age*"—"Give heed." "*Sursum corda*"—"Lift up your hearts."
4. By Cicero.
5. "It would seem to be."
6. "For my part, in truth, I would rather be old less long than be old before I am old."
7. These *Memoirs*, which cover the years 1513–47 and were first published in 1569, are presented by Martin du Bellay but include three books (out of ten) by his brother Guillaume du Bellay, Seigneur de Langey. This explains Montaigne's reference to "these two lords."

"E.K."

The Dedicatory Epistle to *The Shepheard's Calender* (*In Praise of the New Poet*) was most probably authored by Edward Kirke (1553–1613), a Cambridge friend of both Edmund Spenser and Gabriel Harvey. It is the first critical introduction in the English language, and it represents a remarkable attempt at editing and critical commentary, an adaption of the marginal notes (the *scholia*) of the ancient grammarians on classical texts. The commentary supplies explanations of unfamiliar or archaic words as well as of classical allusions.

The *Epistle* itself, which is reprinted here, is primarily a defense of Spenser's innovations such as his use of archaic and dialect forms. He praises Spenser for the effort "to restore, as to their rightful heritage, such good and natural English words as have been long time out of use and almost clean disherited." Spenser, according to E.K., is the poet of the "mother tongue" who will rescue the language from becoming "a gallimaufray or hodge-podge" of Latin, French or Italian.

In Praise of the New Poet is taken from *Elizabethan Critical Essays*, edited by G. Gregory Smith (Oxford University Press, 1904).

IN PRAISE OF THE NEW POET

To the Most Excellent and Learned, Both Orator and Poete, Mayster Gabriell Harvey, His Verie Special and Singular Good Frend E. K. Commendeth the Good Lyking of This His Labour, and the Patronage of the New Poete.

Uncovthe, vnkiste, sayde the old famous Poete Chaucer: whom, for his excellencie and wonderfull skil in making, his scholler Lidgate, a worthy scholler of so excellent a maister, calleth the Loadestarre of our Language, and whom our Colin Clout in his Æglogue calleth Tityrus the God of shepheards, comparing hym to the worthines of the Roman Tityrus, Virgile. Which prouerbe, myne owne good friend Ma. Haruey, as in that good old Poete it serued well Pandares purpose for the bolstering of his baudy brocage, so very well taketh place in this our new Poete, who for that he is vncouthe (as said Chaucer) is vnkist, and vnknown to most men is regarded but of few. But I dout not, so soone as his name shall come into the knowledg of men, and his worthines be sounded in the tromp of fame, but that he shall be not onely kiste, but also beloued of all, embraced of the most, and wondred at of the best. No lesse, I thinke, deserueth his wittinesse in deuising, his pithinesse in vttering, his complaints of loue so louely, his discourses of pleasure so pleasantly, his pastoral rudenesse, his morall wisenesse, his dewe obseruing of Decorum euerye where, in personages, in seasons, in matter, in speach; and generally, in al seemely simplycitie of handeling his matter and framing his words: the which, of many thinges which in him be straunge, I know will seeme the straungest, the words them selues being so aunciant, the knitting of them so short and intricate, and the whole Periode and compasse of speache so delightsome for the roundnesse, and so graue for the straungenesse. And firste of the wordes to speake, I graunt they be something hard, and of most men vnused, yet both English, and also vsed of most excellent Authors and most famous Poetes. In whom, whenas this our Poet hath bene much traueiled and throughly redd, how could it be (as that worthy Oratour sayde) but that walking in the sonne, although for other cause he walked, yet needes he mought be sunburnt; and, hauing the sound of those auncient Poetes still ringing in his eares, he mought needes, in singing, hit out some of theyr tunes. But whether he vseth them by such casualtye and custome, or of set purpose and choyse, as thinking them fittest for such rusticall rudenesse of shepheards, eyther for that theyr rough sounde would make his rymes more ragged and rustical, or els because such olde and obsolete wordes are most vsed of country folke, sure I think, and think I think not amisse, that they bring great grace, and, as one would say, auctoritie to the verse. For albe, amongst many other faultes, it specially be obiected of Valla against Liuie, and of other against Saluste, that with ouer much studie they affect antiquitie, as coueting thereby credence and honor of elder yeeres, yet I am of opinion, and eke the best learned are of the lyke, that those aunsient solemne wordes are a great ornament, both in the one and in the other; the one labouring to set forth in hys worke an eternall image of antiquitie, and the other carefully discoursing matters of grauitie and importaunce. For, if my memory faile not, Tullie, in that booke wherein he endeuoureth to set forth the paterne of a perfect Oratour, sayth that ofttimes an aunsient worde maketh the style seeme graue, and as it were reuerend, no otherwise then we honour and reuerence gray heares, for a certein religious regard which we haue of old age. Yet nether euery where must old words be stuffed in, nor the common Dialecte and maner of speaking so corrupted therby, that, as in old buildings, it seme disorderly and ruinous. But all as in most exquisite pictures they vse to blaze and portraict not onely the daintie lineaments of beautye, but also rounde about it to shadow the rude thickets and craggy clifts, that, by the basenesse of such parts, more excellency may accrew to the principall; for oftimes we fynde ourselues, I knowe not how, singularly delighted with the shewe of such naturall rudenesse, and take great pleasure in that disorderly order. Euen so doe those rough and harsh termes enlumine, and make more clearly to appeare, the brightnesse of braue and glorious words. So oftentimes a dischorde in Musick maketh a comely concordaunce: so great delight tooke the worthy Poete Alceus to behold a blemish in the ioynt of a wel shaped body. But if any will rashly blame such his purpose in choyse of old and vnwonted words, him may I more iustly blame and condemne, or of witlesse headinesse in iudging or of heedelesse hardinesse in condemning; for, not marking the compasse of hys bent, he wil iudge of the length of his cast: for in my opinion it is one special prayse of many whych are dew to this Poete, that he hath laboured to restore, as to theyr rightfull heritage, such good and naturall English words as haue ben long time out of vse and almost cleane disherited. Which is the onely cause that our Mother tonge, which truely of it self is both ful enough for prose and stately enough for verse, hath long time ben counted most bare and barrein of both. Which default when as some endeuoured to salue and recure, they patched up the holes with peces and rags of other languages, borrowing here of the French, there of the Italian, every where of the Latine; not weighing how il those tongues accorde with themselues, but much worse with ours: So now they haue made our English tongue a gallimaufray or hodgepodge of al other speches. Other some, no[t] so wel sene in the English tonge as perhaps in other languages, if they happen to here an olde word, albeit very naturall and significant, crye out streightway that we speak no English, but gibbrish, or rather such as in old time Euanders mother spake: whose first shame is, that they are not ashamed, in their own mother tonge, straungers to be counted and alienes. The second shame, no lesse then the first, that what so they vnderstand not they streight way deeme to be sencelesse and not at al to be vnderstode. Much like to the Mole in Æsopes fable, that, being blynd her selfe, would in no wise be perswaded that any beast could see. The last, more shameful then both, that of their owne country and natural speach, which together with their Nources milk they sucked, they haue so base regard and bastard iudgement that they will not onely themselues not labor to garnish and beautifie it, but also repine that of other it shold be embellished. Like to the dogge in the maunger, that him selfe can eate no hay, and yet barketh at the hungry bullock that so faine would feede: whose currish kind, though it cannot be kept from barking, yet I conne them thanke that they refrain from byting.

Now, for the knitting of sentences, whych they call the ioynts and members therof, and for al the compasse of the speach, it is round without roughnesse, and learned wythout hardnes, such indeede as may be perceiued of the leaste, vnderstoode of the moste, but iudged onely of the learned. For what in most English wryters vseth to be loose, and as it were vngyrt, in this Authour is well grounded, finely framed, and strongly trussed up together. In regard wherof, I scorne and spue out the rakehellye route of our ragged rymers (for so themselues vse to hunt the letter) which without learning boste, without iudgement iangle, without reason rage and fome, as if some instinct of Poeticall spirite had newly rauished them aboue the meanenesse of commen capacitie. And being in the middest of all theyr brauery, sodenly, eyther for want of matter or of ryme, or hauing forgotten theyr former conceipt, they seeme to be so pained and traueiled in theyr remembrance, as it were a woman in childebirth, or as that same Pythia when the traunce came vpon her: *Os rabidum fera corda domans*, &c.

Nethelesse, let them a Gods name feede on theyr owne folly, so they seeke not to darken the beames of others glory. As for Colin, vnder whose person the Authour selfe is shadowed, how furre he is from such vaunted titles and glorious showes, both him selfe sheweth, where he sayth,

> Of Muses, Hobbin[ol], I conne no skill,

and

> Enough is me to paint out my vnrest, &c:

And also appeareth by the basenesse of the name, wherein it semeth he chose rather to vnfold great matter of argument couertly then, professing it, not suffice thereto accordingly. Which moued him rather in Æglogues then other wise to write, doubting perhaps his habilitie, which he little needed, or mynding to furnish our tongue with this kinde wherein it faulteth; or following the example of the best and most aunctient Poetes, which deuised this kind of wryting, being both so base for the matter and homely for the manner, at the first to trye theyr habilities, and, as young birdes that be newly crept out of the nest, by little first to proue theyr tender wyngs before they make a greater flyght. So flew Theocritus, as you may perceiue he was all ready full fledged. So flew Virgile, as not yet well feeling his winges. So flew Mantuane, as not being full somd. So Petrarque. So Boccace. So Marot, Sanazarus, and also diuers other excellent both Italian and French Poetes, whose foting this Author euery where followeth; yet so as few, but they be wel sented, can trace him out. So finally flyeth this our new Poete as a birde whose principals be scarce growen out, but yet as [one] that in time shall be hable to keepe wing with the best.

Now, as touching the generall dryft and purpose of his Æglogues, I mind not to say much, him selfe labouring to conceale it. Onely this appeareth, that his vnstayed yougth had long wandred in the common Labyrinth of Loue, in which time to mitigate and allay the heate of his passion, or els to warne (as he sayth) the young shepheards, of his equalls and companions, of his vnfortunate folly, he compiled these xij Æglogues, which, for that they be proportioned to the state of the xij monethes, he termeth the SHEPHEARDS CALENDAR, applying an olde name to a new worke. Hereunto haue I added a certain Glosse or scholion, for thexposition of old wordes and harder phrases; which maner of glosing and commenting, well I wote, wil seeme straunge and rare in our tongue: yet, for so much as I knew many excellent and proper deuises, both in wordes and matter, would passe in the speedy course of reading, either as vnknowen or as not marked, and that in this kind, as in other, we might be equal to the learned of other nations, I thought good to take the paines vpon me, the rather for that by meanes of some familiar acquaintaunce I was made priuie to his counsell and secret meaning in them, as also in sundry other works of his, which albeit I know he nothing so much hateth as to promulgate, yet thus much haue I aduentured vpon his frendship, him selfe being for long time furre estraunged, hoping that this will the rather occasion him to put forth diuers other excellent works of his which slepe in silence, as his *Dreames*, his *Legendes*, his *Court of Cupide*, and sondry others, whose commendations to set out were verye vaine, the thinges though worthy of many yet being knowen to few. These my present paynes, if to any they be pleasurable or profitable, be you iudge, mine own good Maister Haruey, to whom I haue, both in respect of your worthinesse generally and otherwyse vpon some particular and special considerations, voued this my labour and the maydenhead of this our commen frends Poetrie; himselfe hauing already in the beginning dedicated it to the Noble and worthy Gentleman, the right worshipfull Ma. Phi. Sidney, a special fauourer and maintainer of all kind of learning. Whose cause, I pray you, Sir, yf Enuie shall stur vp any wrongful accusasion, defend with your mighty Rhetorick and other your rare gifts of learning, as you can, and shield with your good wil, as you ought, against the malice and outrage of so many enemies, as I know wilbe set on fire with the sparks of his kindled glory. And thus recommending the Author vnto you, as vnto his most special good frend, and my selfe vnto you both, as one making singuler account of two so very good and so choise frends, I bid you both most hartely farwel, and commit you and your most commendable studies to the tuicion of the greatest.

Your owne assuredly to be commaunded,

E. K.

Postscript

Now I trust, M. Haruey, that vpon sight of your speciall frends and fellow Poets doings, or els for enuie of so many vnworthy Quidams which catch at the garlond which to you alone is dewe, you will be perswaded to pluck out of the hateful darknesse those so many excellent English poemes of yours which lye hid, and bring them forth to eternall light. Trust me, you doe both them great wrong, in depriuing them of the desired sonne, and also your selfe, in smoothering your deserued prayses, and all men generally, in withholding from them so diuine pleasures, which they might conceiue of your gallant English verses, as they haue already doen of your Latine Poemes, which, in my opinion, both for inuention and Elocution are very delicate and superexcellent. And thus againe I take my leaue of my good Mayster Haruey: from my lodging at London thys 10. of Aprill, 1579.

Sir Philip Sidney
1554–1586

In Sir Philip Sidney we are presented with a figure who—much in the same manner as Dr. Johnson—is remembered more on account of his personality than his deeds. The very embodiment of the Elizabethan ideal, Sidney's contribution to Renaissance literary criticism was immense, but the full weight of this fact has often been obscured by the almost legendary temper of Sidney's life and career.

The son of a gentleman and diplomat (his father served several terms as Lord Deputy of Ireland), Sidney was born on November 30, 1554 in Kent. Philip II of Spain was his godfather. He was destined from an early age for a career in diplomacy and public life, and pursued this ambition actively, first at Christ Church, Oxford, then by means of an extended tour of the Continent, where he refined his language skills and was introduced to influential statesmen.

His early diplomatic assignments met with failure, however, and Sidney found himself for several years out of favor at Court. Partly out of boredom, and partly because he saw it as a way to win influence, Sidney embarked on a literary career. In 1578, he composed a play, *The Lady of May,* as a present for the Queen. His great prose romance, the *Arcadia,* was written sometime prior to 1580, although it was not published until after his death. A collection of sonnets, *Astrophel and Stella,* was written in 1582 for the Lady Rich; it is often considered the finest collection of Elizabethan sonnets after Shakespeare's, and remains popular and well read to this day.

An Apology For Poetry, Sidney's great summary of critical theory and development, was written in the early 1580's. Strongly influenced by the Italian critics, the *Apology* introduced many Continental ideas into England. Taking the Platonic view that poetry is largely a work of imitation, Sidney argues that poetry well conceived is more real than, and superior to, the object it imitates. Thus Aeneas, for example, who exists solely as a creation of Virgil's imagination, is a man superior to those found in the world of reality. Imitation sharpens rather than dulls reality.

Like Plato, then, Sidney views poetry as a moral and magisterial agent. Plato's objection to verse troubles him, but he concludes that when Plato attacks verse as calumnious and fantastic, he is in reality attacking only the corrupt and meretricious forms to which poetry may descend. Interestingly, Sidney did not share the views of many of his contemporaries concerning the "corruption" of medieval verse, and speaks respectfully of Chaucer.

The *Apology* was circulated privately, and enjoyed a moderate popularity within Court circles. In 1585 Sidney finally gained preferment, and was given command of a troop of cavalry. Sent to the Netherlands to fight against Spain, Sidney exhibited great bravery in the face of superior enemy forces and met a hero's end on October 17, 1586 at Arnhem. The public reaction to his death—at all levels of English society, and in the academic community throughout Europe—was overwhelming.

Sidney's influence as a literary figure came mainly after his death. His studied nonchalance in regard to his accomplishments—he referred to the *Arcadia* as a "trifle"—kept him from publishing anything during his lifetime. Although his involvement in public life occupied much of his time, it does not seem likely that he would have written a great deal more had he been at greater liberty. Sidney's creative efforts went into his life as much as his work, and in a sense his success was greater there: at the time of his death, he was the universally accepted example of the ideal Elizabethan gentleman. The irony is, of course, that his fame today rests not so much on his obscure (and consistently unsuccessful) political maneuvers, but on the very "trifles" for which he affected scorn.

An Apology for Poetry is reprinted by permission of the Bobbs-Merrill Company, Inc. from *An Apology for Poetry*, edited by Forrest G. Robinson (Indianapolis: Bobbs-Merrill Educational Publishing, 1970). © 1970 by the Bobbs-Merrill Company, Inc.

An Apology for Poetry

When the right virtuous Edward Wotton and I were at the Emperor's Court together, we gave ourselves to learn horsemanship of John Pietro Pugliano, one that with great commendation had the place of an esquire[1] in his stable. And he, according to the fertileness of the Italian wit, did not only afford us the demonstration of his practice, but sought to enrich our minds with the contemplations therein, which he thought most precious. But with none I remember mine ears were at any time more loaden, than when (either angered with slow payment, or moved with our learner-like admiration) he exercised his speech in the praise of his faculty. He said soldiers were the noblest estate of mankind, and horsemen the noblest of soldiers. He said they were the masters of war and ornaments of peace, speedy goers and strong abiders, triumphers both in camps and courts. Nay, to so unbelieved a point he proceeded, as that no earthly thing bred such wonder to a prince as to be a good horseman. Skill of government was but a *pedanteria*[2] in comparison. Then would he add certain praises by telling what a peerless beast a horse was; the only serviceable courtier without flattery, the beast of most beauty, faithfulness, courage, and such more, that if I had not been a piece of a logician before I came to him, I think he would have persuaded me to have wished myself a horse. But thus much at least with his no few words he drave into me, that self-love is better than any gilding to make that seem gorgeous wherein ourselves are parties. Wherein, if Pugliano his strong affection and weak arguments will not satisfy you, I will give you a nearer example of myself, who (I know not by what mischance), in these my not old years and idlest times, having slipped into the title of a poet,[3] am provoked to say something unto you in the defence of that my unelected vocation, which if I handle with more good will than good reasons, bear with me, sith the scholar is to be pardoned that followeth the steps of his master. And yet I must say that, as I have just cause to make a pitiful defence of poor poetry, which from almost the highest estimation of learning is fallen to be the laughing-stock of children, so have I need to bring some more available[4] proofs, sith the former is by no man barred of his deserved credit, the silly[5] latter hath had even the names of philosophers used to the defacing of it, with great danger of civil war among the Muses.

And first, truly, to all them that, professing learning, inveigh against poetry, may justly be objected that they go very near to ungratefulness to seek to deface that which, in the noblest nations and languages that are known, hath been the first lightgiver to ignorance, and first nurse, whose milk by little and little enabled them to feed afterwards of tougher knowledges.[6] And will they now play the hedgehog that, being received into the den, drave out his host? Or rather the vipers, that with their birth kill their parents? Let learned Greece, in any of her manifold sciences, be able to show me one book before Musaeus,[7] Homer, and

Hesiod, all three nothing else but poets. Nay, let any history be brought that can say any writers were there before them, if they were not men of the same skill as Orpheus, Linus, and some other are named, who, having been the first of that country that made pens deliverers of their knowledge to their posterity, may justly challenge to be called their fathers in learning: for not only in time they had this priority (although in itself antiquity be venerable), but went before them, as causes to draw with their charming sweetness the wild untamed wits to an admiration of knowledge. So as Amphion[8] was said to move stones with his poetry to build Thebes, and Orpheus to be listened to by beasts, indeed stony and beastly people, so among the Romans were Livius Andronicus and Ennius. So in the Italian language, the first that made it aspire to be a treasure-house of science were the poets Dante, Boccaccio, and Petrarch. So in our English were Gower and Chaucer, after whom, encouraged and delighted with their excellent fore-going, others have followed to beautify our mother tongue, as well in the same kind as in other arts.

This did so notably show itself, that the philosophers of Greece durst not a long time appear to the world but under the masks of poets. So Thales, Empedocles, and Parmenides sang their natural philosophy in verses; so did Pythagoras and Phocylides their moral counsels; so did Tyrtaeus in war matters and Solon in matters of policy: or rather, they being poets, did exercise their delightful vein in those points of highest knowledge which before them lay hid to the world. For that wise Solon was directly a poet, it is manifest, having written in verse the notable fable of the Atlantic Island, which was continued by Plato.[9]

And truly, even Plato, whosoever well considereth shall find that in the body of his work, though the inside and strength were philosophy, the skin as it were and beauty depended most of poetry,[10] for all standeth upon dialogues, wherein he feigneth many honest burgesses of Athens to speak of such matters, that if they had been set on the rack they would never have confessed them; besides his poetical describing the circumstances of their meetings, as the well ordering of a banquet, the delicacy of a walk, with interlacing mere tales, as Gyges' ring, and others, which who knoweth not to be flowers of poetry did never walk into Apollo's garden.[11]

And even historiographers (although their lips sound of things done, and verity be written in their foreheads) have been glad to borrow both fashion and perchance weight of poets. So Herodotus entitled his *History* by the name of the nine Muses, and both he and all the rest that followed him either stole or usurped of poetry their passionate describing of passions, the many particularities of battles, which no man could affirm; or, if that be denied me, long orations put in the mouths of great kings and captains, which it is certain they never pronounced. So that truly, neither philosopher nor historiographer could at the first have entered into the gates of popular judgments if they had not taken a great passport of poetry, which, in all nations at this day where learning flourisheth not, is plain to be seen; in all which they have some feeling of poetry.

In Turkey, besides their law-giving divines, they have no other writers but poets. In our neighbor country Ireland, where truly learning goeth very bare, yet are their poets held in a devout reverence. Even among the most barbarous and simple Indians where no writing is, yet have they their poets, who make and sing songs which they call *areytos*,[12] both of their ancestors' deeds and praises of their gods; a sufficient probability that, if ever learning come among them, it must be by having their hard dull wits softened and sharpened with the sweet delights of poetry. For until they find a pleasure in the exercises of the mind, great promises of much knowledge will little persuade them that know not the fruits of knowledge. In Wales, the true remnant of the ancient Britons,[13] as there are good authorities to show the long time they had poets which they called *bards*, so through all the conquests of Romans, Saxons, Danes, and Normans, some of whom did seek to ruin all memory of learning from among them, yet do their poets even to this day last, so as it is not more notable in soon beginning than in long continuing.

But since the authors of most of our sciences were the Romans, and before them the Greeks, let us a little stand upon their authorities, but even so far as to see what names they have given unto this now scorned skill. Among the Romans a poet was called *vates*, which is as much as a diviner, foreseer, or prophet, as by his conjoined words *vaticinium* and *vaticinari* is manifest; so heavenly a title did that excellent people bestow upon this heart-ravishing knowledge. And so far were they carried into the admiration thereof, that they thought in the chanceable hitting upon any such verses great fore-tokens of their following fortunes were placed. Whereupon grew the word of *Sortes Virgilianae*, when by sudden opening Virgil's book they lighted upon any verse of his making, whereof the Histories of the Emperors' Lives are full: as of Albinus, the governor of our island, who in his childhood met with this verse,

Arma amens capio nec sat rationis in armis,

and in his age performed it; which, although it were a very vain and godless superstition, as also it was to think that spirits were commanded by such verses—whereupon this word charms, derived of *carmina*,[14] cometh—so yet serveth it to show the great reverence those wits were held in. And altogether not without ground, since both the oracles of Delphos and Sibylla's prophecies were wholly delivered in verses. For that same exquisite observing of number and measure in words, and that high flying liberty of conceit[15] proper to the poet, did seem to have some divine force in it.

And may not I presume a little further, to show the reasonableness of this word *vates*, and say that the holy David's Psalms are a divine poem? If I do, I shall not do it without the testimony of great learned men, both ancient and modern. But even the name Psalms will speak for me, which being interpreted is nothing but songs; then, that it is fully written in meter, as all learned hebricians agree, although the rules be not yet fully found; lastly and principally, his handling his prophecy, which is merely poetical. For what else is the awaking his musical instruments, the often and free changing of persons, his notable *prosopopoeias*,[16] when he maketh you, as it were, see God coming in His majesty, his telling of the beasts' joyfulness, and hills leaping, but a heavenly poesy,[17] wherein almost he showeth himself a passionate lover of that unspeakable and everlasting beauty to be seen by the eyes of the mind, only cleared by faith? But truly, now having named him, I fear me I seem to profane that holy name, applying it to poetry, which is among us thrown down to so ridiculous an estimation. But they that with quiet judgments will look a little deeper into it, shall find the end and working of it such, as being rightly applied, deserveth not to be scourged out of the Church of God.

But now let us see how the Greeks named it and how they deemed of it. The Greeks called him a poet, which name hath, as the most excellent, gone through other languages. It cometh of this word *poiein*, which is, to make, wherein I know not whether by luck or wisdom we Englishmen have met with the Greeks in calling him a maker: which name, how high and incomparable a title it is, I had rather were known by marking the scope of other sciences than by my partial allegation.

There is no art delivered to mankind that hath not the works of nature for his principal object, without which they could not consist, and on which they so depend, as they become actors and players, as it were, of what nature will have set forth. So doth the astronomer look upon the stars, and by that he seeth, setteth down what order nature hath taken therein. So do the geometrician and arithmetician in their diverse sorts of quantities. So doth the musician in times tell you which by nature agree, which not. The natural philosopher thereon hath his name, and the moral philosopher standeth upon the natural virtues, vices, and passions of man, and follow nature (saith he) therein, and thou shalt not err.[18] The lawyer saith what men have determined; the historian what men have done. The grammarian speaketh only of the rules of speech, and the rhetorician and logician, considering what in nature will soonest prove and persuade, thereon give artificial[19] rules, which still are compassed within the circle of a question, according to the proposed matter.[20] The physician weigheth the nature of a man's body, and the nature of things helpful or hurtful unto it. And the metaphysic, though it be in the second and abstract notions, and therefore be counted supernatural, yet doth he indeed build upon the depth of nature. Only the poet, disdaining to be tied to any such subjection, lifted up with the vigor of his own invention, doth grow in effect another nature, in making things either better than nature bringeth forth, or quite anew, forms such as never were in nature, as the Heroes, Demigods, Cyclops, Chimeras, Furies, and such like; so as he goeth hand in hand with nature, not enclosed within the narrow warrant of her gifts, but freely ranging only within the zodiac of his own wit.

Nature never set forth the earth in so rich tapestry as divers poets have done, neither with pleasant rivers, fruitful trees, sweet smelling flowers, nor whatsoever else may make the too much loved earth more lovely. Her world is brazen, the poets only deliver a golden.

But let those things alone and go to man, for whom as the other things are, so it seemeth in him her uttermost cunning is employed, and know whether she have brought forth so true a lover as Theagenes, so constant a friend as Pylades, so valiant a man as Orlando, so right a prince as Xenophon's Cyrus, so excellent a man every way as Virgil's Aeneas. Neither let this be jestingly conceived, because the works of the one be essential, the other in imitation or fiction; for any understanding knoweth the skill of the artificer standeth in that *Idea* or fore-conceit of the work, and not in the work itself. And that the poet hath that *Idea* is manifest by delivering them forth in such excellency as he hath imagined them. Which delivering forth also is not wholly imaginative, as we are wont to say by them that build castles in the air, but so far substantially it worketh, not only to make a Cyrus, which had been but a particular excellency, as nature might have done, but to bestow a Cyrus upon the world to make many Cyruses, if they will learn aright why and how that maker made him.

Neither let it be deemed too saucy a comparison to balance the highest point of man's wit with the efficacy of nature, but rather give right honor to the heavenly Maker of that maker, who having made man to His own likeness, set him beyond and over all the works of that second nature, which in nothing he showeth so much as in poetry, when with the force of a divine breath he bringeth things forth far surpassing her doings, with no small argument to the incredulous to that first accursed fall of Adam: sith our erected wit maketh us know what perfection is, and yet our infected will keepeth us from reaching unto it. But these arguments will by few be understood, and by fewer granted. Thus much (I hope) will be given me, that the Greeks with some probability of reason gave him the name above all names of learning.

Now let us go to a more ordinary opening of him, that the truth may be more palpable: and so I hope, though we get not so unmatched a praise as the etymology of his names will grant, yet his very description, which no man will deny, shall not justly be barred from a principal commendation.

Poesy therefore is an art of imitation, for so Aristotle termeth it in this word *mimesis*, that is to say, a representing, counterfeiting, or figuring forth—to speak metaphorically, a speaking picture—with this end, to teach and delight.[21] Of this have been three several kinds.

The chief both in antiquity and excellency were they that did imitate the inconceivable excellencies of God. Such were David in his Psalms, Solomon in his Song of Songs, in his Ecclesiastes and Proverbs, Moses and Deborah in their Hymns, and the writer of Job; which, beside other, the learned Emanuel Tremellius and Franciscus Junius do entitle the poetical part of the Scripture. Against these none will speak that hath the Holy Ghost in due holy reverence. In this kind, though in a full wrong divinity, were Orpheus, Amphion, Homer in his Hymns,[22] and many other, both Greeks and Romans. And this poesy must be used by whosoever will follow St. James[23] his counsel in singing psalms when they are merry, and I know is used with the fruit of comfort by some, when in sorrowful pangs of their death-bringing sins, they find the consolation of the never-leaving goodness.

The second kind is of them that deal with matters philosophical: either moral, as Tyrtaeus, Phocylides, and Cato; or natural, as Lucretius, and Virgil's *Georgics*; or astronomical, as Manilius and Pontanus; or historical, as Lucan: which who mislike, the fault is in their judgments quite out of taste, and not in the sweet food of sweetly uttered knowledge.

But because this second sort is wrapped within the fold of the proposed subject, and takes not the course of his own invention, whether they properly be poets or no let grammarians dispute,[24] and go to the third, indeed right poets, of whom chiefly this question ariseth. Betwixt whom and these second is such a kind of difference as betwixt the meaner sort of painters (who counterfeit only such faces as are set before them), and the more excellent, who having no law but wit, bestow that in colors upon you which is fittest for the eye to see: as the constant though lamenting look of Lucretia[25] when she punished in herself another's fault. Wherein he painteth not Lucretia whom he never saw, but painteth the outward beauty of such a virtue. For these third be they which most properly do imitate to teach and delight, and to imitate borrow nothing of what is, hath been, or shall be, but range only reined with learned discretion into the divine consideration of what may be and should be.[26] These be they that, as the first and most noble sort, may justly be termed *vates*, so these are waited on in the excellentest languages and best understandings with the fore-described name of poets. For these indeed do merely make to imitate, and imitate both to delight and teach, and delight to move men to take that goodness in hand which without delight they would fly as from a stranger, and teach, to make them know that goodness whereunto they are moved: which being the noblest scope to which ever any learning was directed, yet want there not idle tongues to bark at them.[27]

These be subdivided into sundry more special denominations. The most notable be the Heroic, Lyric, Tragic, Comic, Satiric, Iambic, Elegiac, Pastoral, and certain others, some of these being termed according to the matter they deal with, some by the sorts of verses they liked best to write in. For indeed the greatest part of poets have apparelled their poetical inventions in that numbrous[28] kind of writing which is called verse; indeed but apparelled, verse being but an ornament and no cause to poetry, sith there have been many most excellent poets that never versified, and now swarm many versifers that need never answer to the name of poets.[29] For Xenophon, who did imitate so excellently as to give us *effigiem justi imperii*, the portraiture of a just empire, under the name of Cyrus (as Cicero saith of him[30]), made therein an absolute heroical poem. So did Heliodorus in his sugared invention of that picture of love in Theagenes and Cariclea, and yet both these writ in prose: which I speak to show, that it is not rhyming and versing that maketh a poet, no more than a long gown maketh an advocate, who though he pleaded in armor should be an advocate and no soldier. But it is that feigning notable images of virtues, vices, or what else, with that delightful teaching, which must be the right describing note to know a poet by: although indeed the senate of poets hath chosen verse as their fittest raiments, meaning, as in matter they passed all in all, so in manner to go beyond them, not speaking (table talk fashion, or like men in a dream) words as they chanceably fall from the mouth, but peizing[31] each syllable of each word by just proportion according to the dignity of the subject.

Now therefore it shall not be amiss first to weigh this latter sort of poetry by his works, and then by his parts, and if in neither of these anatomies he be condemnable, I hope we shall obtain a more favorable sentence. This purifying of wit, this enriching of memory, enabling of judgment, and enlarging of conceit, which commonly we call learning, under what name soever it come forth, or to what immediate end soever it be directed, the final end is to lead and draw us to as high a perfection as our degenerate souls, made worse by their clayey lodgings, can be capable of. This, according to the inclination of the man, bred many formed impressions.[32] For some that thought this felicity principally to be gotten by knowledge, and no knowledge to be so high and heavenly as acquaintance with the stars, gave themselves to astronomy; others, persuading themselves to be demi-gods if they knew the causes of things,[33] became natural and supernatural philosophers; some an admirable delight drew to music; and some, the certainty of demonstration, to the mathematics. But all, one and other, having this scope, to know, and by knowledge to lift up the mind from the dungeon of the body to the enjoying his own divine essence. But when by the balance of experience it was found that the astronomer, looking to the stars, might fall into a ditch,[34] that the inquiring philosopher might be blind in himself, and the mathematician might draw forth a straight line with a crooked heart, then lo did proof, the overruler of opinions, make manifest that all these are but serving sciences,[35] which, as they have each a private end in themselves, so yet are they all directed to the highest end of the mistress knowledge, by the Greeks called *architectonike*, which stands (as I think) in the knowledge of a man's self, in the ethic and politic consideration, with the end of well doing and not of well knowing only: even as the saddler's next end is to make a good saddle, but his farther end, to serve a nobler faculty, which is horsemanship; so the horseman's to soldiery, and the soldier not only to have the skill, but to perform the practice of a soldier. So that, the ending end of all earthly learning, being virtuous action, those skills that most serve to bring forth that have a most just title to be princes over all the rest.

Wherein if we can show the poet's nobleness by setting him before his other competitors, among whom as principal challengers step forth the moral philosophers, whom, me thinketh, I see coming towards me with a sullen gravity, as though they could not abide vice by daylight, rudely clothed for to witness outwardly their contempt of outward things, with books in their hands against glory,[36] whereto they set their names, sophistically speaking against subtlety, and angry with any man in whom they see the foul fault of anger. These men casting largesse as they go of definitions, divisions, and distinctions, with a scornful interrogative do soberly ask whether it be possible to find any path so ready to lead a man to virtue as that which teacheth what virtue is; and teacheth it not only by delivering forth his very being, his causes and effects, but also by making known his enemy vice, which must be destroyed, and his cumbersome servant passion, which must be mastered, by showing the generalities that containeth it, and the specialities that are derived from it; lastly, by plain setting down, how it extendeth itself out of the limits of a man's own little world to the government of families, and maintaining of public societies.

The historian scarcely giveth leisure to the moralist to say so much, but that he, loaden with old mouse-eaten records, authorizing himself (for the most part) upon other histories, whose greatest authorities are built upon the notable foundation of hearsay, having much ado to accord differing writers, and to pick truth out of partiality, better acquainted with a thousand years ago than with the present age, and yet better knowing how this world goeth than how his own wit runneth, curious for antiquities and inquisitive of novelties, a wonder to young folks and a tyrant in table talk, denieth in a great chafe that any man, for teaching of virtue and virtuous actions, is comparable to him. I am *testis temporum, lux veritatis, vita memoriae, magistra vitae, nuncia vetustatis.*[37] The philosopher (saith he) teacheth a disputative virtue,[38] but I do an active; his virtue is excellent in the dangerless Academy of Plato, but mine showeth forth her honorable face in the battles of Marathon, Pharsalia, Poitiers, and Agincourt. He teacheth virtue by certain abstract considerations, but I only bid you follow the footing of them that have gone before you. Old-aged experience goeth beyond the fine-witted philosopher, but I give the experience of many ages. Lastly, if he make the song-book, I put the learner's hand to the lute; and if he be the guide, I am the light.

Then would he allege you innumerable examples, confirming story by story, how much the wisest senators and princes have been directed by the credit of history, as Brutus, Alphonsus of Aragon, and who not, if need be? At length the long line of their disputation maketh a point in this, that the one giveth the precept, and the other the example.

Now whom shall we find (sith the question standeth for the highest form[39] in the school of learning) to be moderator? Truely, as me seemeth, the poet; and if not a moderator, even the man that ought to carry the title from them both, and much more from all other serving sciences. Therefore compare we the poet with the historian and with the moral philosopher, and if he go beyond them both, no other human skill can match him. For as for the divine, with all reverence it is ever to be excepted, not only for having his scope as far beyond any of these as eternity exceedeth a moment, but even for passing each of these in themselves.[40] And for the lawyer, though *jus* be the daughter of justice, and justice the chief of virtues, yet because he seeketh to make men good rather *formidine poenae* than *virtutis amore*, or to say righter, doth not endeavor to make men good, but that their evil hurt not others, having no care so he be a good citizen, how bad a man he be; therefore as our wickedness maketh him necessary, and necessity maketh him honorable, so is he not in the deepest truth to stand in rank with these who all endeavor to take naughtiness away, and plant goodness even in the secretest cabinet of our souls. And these four are all that any way deal in that consideration of men's manners, which being the supreme knowledge, they that best breed it deserve the best commendation.

The philosopher therefore and the historian are they which would win the goal, the one by precept, the other by example. But both, not having both, do both halt. For the philosopher, setting down with thorny argument the bare rule, is so hard of utterance and so misty to be conceived, that one that hath no other guide but him shall wade in him till he be old before he shall find sufficient cause to be honest. For his knowledge standeth so upon the abstract and general that happy is that man who may understand him, and more happy that can apply what he doth understand.

On the other side, the historian, wanting the precept, is so tied, not to what should be but to what is, to the particular truth of things and not to the general reason of things, that his example draweth no necessary consequence, and therefore a less fruitful doctrine.

Now doth the peerless poet perform both: for whatsoever the philosopher saith should be done, he giveth a perfect picture of it in someone by whom he presupposeth it was done, so as he coupleth the general notion with the particular example. A perfect picture I say, for he yieldeth to the powers of the mind an image of that whereof the philosopher bestoweth but a wordish description, which doth neither strike, pierce, nor possess the sight of the soul so much as that other doth. For as in outward things, to a man that had never seen an elephant or a rhinoceros, who should tell him most exquisitely all their shapes, color, bigness, and particular marks; or of a gorgeous palace, the architecture, with declaring the full beauties, might well make the hearer able to repeat, as it were by rote, all he had heard, yet should never satisfy his inward conceits with being witness to itself of a true lively knowledge. But the same man, as soon as he might see those beasts well painted, or the house well in model, should straightways grow without need of any description, to a judicial comprehending of them. So no doubt the philosopher, with his learned definition,[41] be it of virtue, vices, matters of public policy or private government, replenisheth the memory with many infallible grounds of wisdom, which, notwithstanding, lie dark before the imaginative and judging power if they be not illuminated or figured forth by the speaking picture of poesy.

Tully taketh much pains and many times not without poetical helps to make us know the force love of our country hath in us. Let us but hear old Anchises speaking in the midst of Troy's flames, or see Ulysses in the fulness of all Calypso's delights bewail his absence from barren and beggarly Ithaca. Anger, the Stoics say, was a short madness: let but Sophocles bring you Ajax on a stage, killing and whipping sheep and oxen, thinking them the army of Greeks with their chieftains Agamemnon and Menelaus, and tell me if you have not a more familiar insight into anger than finding in the schoolmen his genus and difference. See whether wisdom and temperance in Ulysses and Diomedes, valor in Achilles, friendship in Nisus and Euryalus, even to an ignorant man, carry not an apparent shining; and contrarily, the remorse of conscience in Oedipus, the soon repenting pride in Agamemnon, the self-devouring cruelty in his father Atreus, the violence of ambition in the two Theban brothers, the sour-sweetness of revenge in Medea; and to fall lower, the Terentian Gnatho and our Chaucer's Pandar, so expressed that we now use their names to signify their trades; and finally, all virtues, vices, and passions so in their own natural seats laid to the view that we seem not to hear of them, but clearly to see through them.

But even in the most excellent determination of goodness, what philosopher's counsel can so readily direct a prince as the feigned Cyrus in Xenophon, or a virtuous man in all fortunes, as Aeneas in Virgil, or a whole commonwealth, as the way of Sir Thomas More's *Utopia*? I say the way, because where Sir Thomas More erred, it was the fault of the man and not of the poet, for that way of patterning a commonwealth was most absolute, though he perchance hath not so absolutely performed it.[42] For the question is, whether the feigned image of poesy or the regular instruction of philosophy hath the more force in teaching: wherein if the philosophers have more rightly showed themselves philosophers than the poets have obtained to the high top of their profession, as in truth,

Mediocribus esse poetis,
Non dii, non homines, non concessere columnae;[43]

it is, I say again, not the fault of the art, but that by few men that art can be accomplished.

Certainly, even our Saviour Christ could as well have given the moral commonplaces of uncharitableness and humbleness as the divine narration of Dives and Lazarus;[44] or of disobedience and mercy, as that heavenly discourse of the lost child and the gracious father;[45] but that His through-searching wisdom knew the estate of Dives burning in hell, and of Lazarus being in Abraham's bosom, would more constantly (as it were) inhabit both the memory and judgment. Truly, for myself, me seems I see before my eyes the lost child's disdainful prodigality, turned to envy a swine's dinner: which by the learned divines are thought not historical acts, but instructing parables.[46] For conclusion, I say the philosopher teacheth, but he teacheth obscurely, so as the learned only can understand him; that is to say, he teacheth them that are already taught. But the poet is the food for the tenderest stomachs, the poet is indeed the right popular philosopher, whereof Aesop's tales give good proof; whose pretty allegories, stealing under the formal tales of beasts, make many more beastly than beasts begin to hear the sound of virtue from these dumb speakers.

But now may it be alleged that if this imagining of matters be so fit for the imagination, then must the historian needs surpass, who bringeth you images of true matters, such as indeed were done, and not such as fantastically or falsely may be suggested to have been done. Truly, Aristole himself, in his discourse of poesy, plainly determineth this question, saying that poetry is *philosophoteron* and *spoudaioteron*, that is to say, it is more philosophical and more studiously serious than history. His reason is, because poesy dealeth with *katholou*, that is to say, with the universal consideration, and the history with *kathekaston*, the particular: now, saith he, the universal weighs what is fit to be said or done, either in likelihood or necessity (which the poesy considereth in his imposed names), and the particular only marks whether Alcibiades did or suffered this or that. Thus far Aristotle, which reason of his (as all his) is most full of reason.

For indeed, if the question were whether it were better to have a particular act truly or falsely set down, there is no doubt which is to be chosen, no more than whether you had rather have Vespasian's picture right as he was, or at the painter's pleasure, nothing resembling. But if the question be for your own use and learning, whether it be better to have it set down as it should be or as it was, then certainly is more doctrinable the feigned Cyrus in Xenophon than the true Cyrus in Justin, and the feigned Aeneas in Virgil than the right Aeneas in Dares Phrygius. As to a lady that desired to fashion her countenance to the best grace, a painter should more benefit her to portrait a most sweet face, writing Canidia upon it, than to paint Canidia as she was, who Horace sweareth was foul and ill favored.

If the poet do his part aright, he will show you in Tantalus, Atreus, and such like, nothing that is not to be shunned; in Cyrus, Aeneas, Ulysses, each thing to be followed; where the historian, bound to tell things as things were, cannot be liberal (without he will be poetical) of a perfect pattern,[47] but as in Alexander or Scipio himself, show doings, some to be liked, some to be misliked. And then how will you discern what to follow but by your own discretion, which you had without reading Quintus Curtius? And whereas a man may say, though in universal consideration of doctrine the poet prevaileth, yet that the history, in his saying such a thing was done, doth warrant a man more in that he shall follow. The answer is manifest, that if he stand upon that was, as if he should argue, because it rained yesterday, therefore it should rain today, then indeed it hath some advantage to a gross conceit.[48] But if he know an example only informs a conjectured likelihood, and so go by reason, the poet doth so far exceed him, as he is to frame his example to that which is most reasonable, be it in warlike, politic, or private matters; where the historian in his bare was hath many times that which we call fortune to overrule the best wisdom. Many times he[49] must tell events whereof he can yield no cause; or if he do, it must be poetical.

For that a feigned example hath as much force to teach as a true example (for as for to move, it is clear, sith the feigned may be tuned to the highest key of passion, let us take one example wherein a poet and a historian do concur. Herodotus and Justin do testify that Zopyrus, King Darius' faithful servant, seeing his master long resisted by the rebellious Babylonians, feigned himself in extreme disgrace of his king, for verifying of which he caused his own nose and ears to be cut off: and so flying to the Babylonians, was received, and for his known valor so far credited that he did find means to deliver them over to Darius. Much like matter doth Livy record of Tarquinius and his son. Xenophon excellently feigneth such another strategem performed by Abradatas in Cyrus' behalf. Now would I fain know, if occasion be presented unto you to serve your prince by such an honest dissimulation, why you do not as well learn it of Xenophon's fiction as of the other's verity? And truly so much the better, as you shall save your nose by the bargain, for Abadatas did not counterfeit so far. So then the best of the historian is subject to the poet; for whatsoever action or faction, whatsoever counsel, policy, or war stratagem the historian is bound to recite, that may the poet (if he list) with his imitation make his own, beautifying it both for further teaching and more delighting, as it pleaseth him: having all, from Dante his heaven to his hell,[50] under the authority of his pen. Which if I be asked what poets have done so, as I might well name some, yet say I, and say again, I speak of the art and not of the artificer.

Now, to that which commonly is attributed to the praise of histories, in respect of the notable learning is gotten by marking the success, as though therein a man should see virtue exalted and vice punished; truly that commendation is peculiar to poetry, and far off from history. For indeed poetry ever setteth virtue so out in her best colors, making fortune her well-waiting handmaid, that one must needs be enamored of her. Well may you see Ulysses in a storm and in other hard plights, but they are but exercises of patience and magnanimity, to make them shine the more in the near-following prosperity. And of the contrary part, if evil men come to the stage, they ever go out (as the tragedy writer answered to one that misliked the show of such persons) so manacled as they little animate folks to follow them. But the historian, being captived to the truth of a foolish world, is many times a terror from well doing, and an encouragement to unbridled wickedness. For see we not valiant Miltiades rot in his fetters; the just Phocion and the accomplished Socrates put to death like traitors; the cruel Severus live prosperously; the excellent Severus miserably murdered; Sylla and Marius dying in their beds; Pompey and Cicero slain then, when they would have thought exile a happiness? See we not virtuous Cato driven to kill himself, and rebel Caesar so advanced that his name yet after 1600 years lasteth in the highest honor? And mark but even Caesar's own words of the fore-named Sylla (who in that only did honestly, to put down his dishonest tyranny), *literas nescivit*,[51] as if want of learning caused him to do well. He meant it not by poetry, which not content with earthly plagues, deviseth new punishments in hell for tyrants, nor yet by philosophy, which teacheth *occidendos esse*;[52] but no doubt by skill in history, for that indeed can afford you Cypselus, Periander, Phalaris, Dionysius, and I know not how many more of the same kennel, that speed well enough in their abominable unjustice or usurpation. I conclude therefore, that he excelleth history, not only in furnishing the mind with knowledge, but in setting it forward to that which deserveth to be called and accounted good: which setting forward and moving to well doing indeed setteth the laurel crown upon the poet as victorious, not only of the historian, but over the philosopher, howsoever in teaching it may be questionable.

For suppose it be granted (that which I suppose with great reason may be denied) that the philosopher, in respect of his methodical proceeding, doth teach more perfectly than the poet: yet do I think that no man is so much *philophilosophos*[53] as to compare the philosopher in moving with the poet. And that moving is of a higher degree than teaching, it may by this appear: that it is well nigh the cause and the effect of teaching. For who will be taught if he be not moved with desire to be taught; and what so much good doth that teaching bring forth (I speak still of moral doctrine) as that it moveth one to do that which it doth teach? For as Aristotle saith, it is not *gnosis* but *praxis* must be the fruit. And how *praxis* can be, without being moved to practice, is no hard matter to consider.

The philosopher showeth you the way, he informeth you of the particularities, as well of the tediousness of the way, as of the pleasant lodging you shall have when your journey is ended, as of the many by-turnings that may divert you from your way. But this is to no man but to him that will read him, and read him with attentive studious painfulness; which constant desire, whosoever hath in him, hath already passed half the hardness of the way, and therefore is beholding to the philosopher but for the other half. Nay truly, learned men have learnedly thought that where once reason hath so much overmastered passion as that the mind hath a free desire to do well, the inward light each mind hath in itself is as good as a philosopher's book; seeing in nature we know it is well to do well, and what is well and what is evil, although not in the words of art[55] which philosophers bestow upon us; for out of natural conceit[56] the philosophers drew it. But to be moved to do that which we know, or to be moved with desire to know, *hoc opus, hic labor est*.[57]

Now therein of all sciences (I speak still of human, and according to the human conceits) is our poet the monarch. For he doth not only show the way, but giveth so sweet a prospect into the way, as will entice any man to enter into it. Nay, he doth as if your journey should lie through a fair vineyard, at the first give you a cluster of grapes, that full of that taste, you may long to pass further. He beginneth not with obscure definitions which must blur the margent with interpretations and load the memory with doubtfulness, but he cometh to you with words set in delightful proportion, either accompanied with, or prepared for, the well enchanting skill of music; and with a tale forsooth he cometh unto you, with a tale which holdeth children from play and old men from the chimney corner. And pretending no more,[58] doth intend the winning of the mind from wickedness to virtue, even as the child is often brought to take most wholesome things by hiding them in such other as have a pleasant taste: which, if one should begin to tell them the nature of aloes or rhubarb[59] they should receive, would sooner take their physic at their ears than at their mouth. So is it in men (most of which are childish in the best things till they be cradled in their graves), glad they will be to hear the tales of Hercules, Achilles, Cyrus, and Aeneas; and hearing them, must needs hear the right description of wisdom, valor, and justice; which, if they had been barely, that is to say, philosophically set out, they would swear they be brought to school again.

That imitation whereof poetry is, hath the most conveniency to nature of all other, insomuch that, as Aristotle saith, those things which in themselves are horrible, as cruel battles, unnatural monsters, are made in poetical imitation delightful. Truly, I have known men that, even with reading *Amadis de Gaule* (which God knoweth wanteth much of a perfect poesy), have found their hearts moved to the exercise of courtesy, liberality, and especially courage. Who readeth Aeneas carrying old Anchises on his back that wisheth not it were his fortune to perform so excellent an act? Whom do not the words of Turnus move (the tale of Turnus having planted his image in the imagination)?

Fugientem haec terra videbit,
Usque adeone mori miserum est?[60]

Where the philosphers, as they scorn to delight, so must they be content little to move, saving wrangling whether virtue be the chief or the only good, whether the contemplative or the active life do excel: which Plato and Boethius well knew, and therefore made mistress philosophy very often borrow the masking raiment of poesy. For even those hard-hearted evil men who think virtue a school name, and know no other good but *indulgere genio*,[61] and therefore despise the austere admonitions of the philosopher, and feel not the inward reason they stand upon, yet will be content to be delighted, which is all the good fellow poet seemeth to promise, and so steal to see the form of goodness (which seen they cannot but love) ere themselves be aware, as if they took a medicine of cherries.

Infinite proofs of the strange effects of this poetical invention might be alleged; only two shall serve, which are so often remembered as I think all men know them. The one of Menenius Agrippa, who, when the whole people of Rome had resolutely divided themselves from the Senate, with apparent show of utter ruin, though he were (for that time) an excellent orator, came not among them upon trust of figurative speeches or cunning insinuations, and much less with far fet maxims of philosophy, which (especially if they were Platonic) they must have learned geometry before they could well have conceived; but forsooth he behaves himself like a homely[62] and familiar poet. He telleth them a tale, that there was a time when all the parts of the body made a mutinous conspiracy against the belly, which they thought devoured the fruits of each other's labor: they concluded they would let so unprofitable a spender starve. In the end, to be short (for the tale is notorious, and as notorious that it was a tale), with punishing the belly they plagued themselves. This applied by him wrought such effect in the people, as I never read that ever words brought forth but then so sudden and so good an alteration; for upon reasonable conditions a perfect reconcilement ensued. The other is of Nathan the prophet, who when the holy David had so far forsaken God as to confirm adultery with murder, when he was to do the tenderest office of a friend, in laying his own shame before his eyes, sent by God to call again so chosen a servant, how doth he it but by telling of a man whose beloved lamb was ungratefully taken from his bosom?—the application most divinely true, but the discourse itself feigned; which made David (I speak of the second and instrumental cause[63]), as in a glass, to see his own filthiness, as that heavenly psalm of mercy[64] well testifieth.

By these therefore examples and reasons I think it may be manifest that the poet, with that same hand of delight, doth draw the mind more effectually than any other art doth. And so a conclusion not unfitly ensueth, that as virtue is the most excellent resting place for all worldly learning to make his end of, so poetry, being the most familiar to teach it, and most princely to move towards it, in the most excellent work is the most excellent workman.

But I am content not only to decipher him by his works (although works in commendation or dispraise must ever hold an high authority), but more narrowly will examine his parts, so that (as in a man), though all together may carry a presence full of majesty and beauty, perchance in some one defectious piece we may find a blemish. Now in his parts, kinds, or species (as you list to term them), it is to be noted that some poesies have coupled together two or three kinds, as tragical and comical, whereupon is risen the tragi-comical. Some, in the like manner, have mingled prose and verse, as Sannazzaro and Boethius. Some have mingled matters heroical and pastoral. But that cometh all to one in this question, for if severed they be good, the conjunction cannot be hurtful. Therefore, perchance forgetting some, and leaving some as needless to be remembered, it shall not be amiss in a word to cite the special kinds, to see what faults may be found in the right use of them.

Is it then the pastoral poem which is misliked (for perchance where the hedge is lowest they will soonest leap over)? Is the poor pipe disdained which sometime out of Meliboeus' mouth can show the misery of people under hard lords or ravening soldiers? And again, by Tityrus, what blessedness is derived to them that lie lowest from the goodness of them that sit highest? sometimes, under the pretty tales of wolves and sheep, can include the whole considerations of wrong doing and patience; sometimes show that contention for trifles can get but a trifling victory; where perchance a man may see that even Alexander and Darius, when they strave who should be cock of this world's dunghill, the benefit they got was that the afterlivers may say,

> *Haec memini et victum frustra contendere Thirsin:*
> *Ex illo Corydon, Corydon est tempore nobis.*[65]

Or is it the lamenting elegiac?[66] which in a kind heart would move rather pity than blame, who bewails with the great philosopher Heraclitus the weakness of mankind and the wretchedness of the world; who surely is to be praised, either for compassionate accompanying just causes of lamentation, or for rightly painting out how weak be the passions of woefulness. Is it the bitter but wholesome iambic?[67] which rubs the galled mind in making shame the trumpet of villainy with bold and open crying out against naughtiness. Or the satiric? who

> *Omne vafer vitium, ridenti tangit amico;*

who sportingly never leaveth until he make a man laugh at folly, and at length ashamed to laugh at himself, which he cannot avoid, without avoiding the folly; who, while

> *Circum praecordia ludit,*[68]

giveth us to feel how many head-aches a passionate life bringeth us to; how, when all is done,

> *Est Ulubris, animus si nos non deficit aequus.*[69]

No, perchance it is the comic, whom naughty play-makers and stage-keepers have justly made odious. To the argument of abuse I will answer after. Only thus much now is to be said, that the comedy is an imitation of the common errors of our life, which he representeth in the most ridiculous and scornful sort that may be, so as it is impossible that any beholder can be content to be such a one.

Now, as in geometry the oblique must be known as well as the right, and in arithmetic the odd as well as the even, so in the actions of our life who seeth not the filthiness of evil wanteth a great foil to perceive the beauty of virtue. This doth the comedy handle so in our private and domestical matters, as with hearing it we get as it were an experience what is to be looked for of a niggardly Demea, of a crafty Davus, of a flattering Gnatho, of a vainglorious Thraso; and not only to know what effects are to be expected, but to know who be such by the signifying badge given them by the comedian. And little reason hath any man to say that men learn evil by seeing it so set out, sith, as I said before, there is no man living but, by the force truth hath in nature, no sooner seeth these men play their parts, but wisheth them *in pistrinum*;[70] although perchance the sack of his own faults lie so behind his back that he seeth not himself dance the same measure; whereto yet nothing can more open his eyes than to find his own actions contemptibly set forth. So that the right use of comedy will (I think) by nobody be blamed, and much less of the high and excellent tragedy, that openeth the greatest wounds and showeth forth the ulcers that are covered with tissue; that maketh kings fear to be tyrants, and tyrants manifest their tyrannical humors; that with stirring the affects[71] of admiration and commiseration teacheth the uncertainty of this world, and upon how weak foundations gilden roofs are builded; that maketh us know,

> *Qui sceptra saevus duro imperio regit,*
> *Timet timentes, metus in auctorem redit.*[72]

But how much it can move, Plutarch yieldeth a notable testimony of the abominable tyrant Alexander Pheraeus, from whose eyes a tragedy well made and represented drew abundance of tears; who without all pity had murdered infinite numbers, and some of his own blood, so as he that was not ashamed to make matters for tragedies, yet could not resist the sweet violence of a tragedy. And if it wrought no further good in him, it was that he, in despite of himself, withdrew himself from hearkening to that which might mollify his hardened heart. But it is not the tragedy they do mislike; for it were too absurd to cast out so excellent a representation of whatsoever is most worthy to be learned.

Is it the lyric that most displeaseth? who with his tuned lyre and well accorded voice giveth praise, the reward of virtue, to virtuous acts; who gives moral precepts and natural problems; who sometimes raiseth up his voice to the height of the heavens in singing the lauds of the immortal God. Certainly, I must confess my own barbarousness, I never heard the old song of Percy and Douglas that I found not my heart moved more than with a trumpet; and yet is it sung but by some blind crowder[73] with no rougher voice than rude style; which, being so evil apparelled in the dust and cobwebs of that uncivil age, what would it work, trimmed in the gorgeous eloquence of Pindar? In Hungary I have seen it the manner at all feasts, and other such meetings, to have songs of their ancestors' valor, which that right soldier-like nation think the chiefest kindlers of brave courage. The incomparable Lacedemonians did not only carry that kind of music ever with them to the field, but even at home, as such songs were made, so were they all content to be the singers of them; when the lusty men were to tell what they did, the old men what they had done, and the young men what they would do. And where a man may say that Pindar many times praiseth highly victories of small moment, matters rather of sport than virtue; as it may be answered, it was the fault of the poet, and not of the poetry, so indeed the chief fault was in the time and custom of the Greeks, who set those toys at so high a price that Philip of Macedon reckoned a horserace won at Olympus among his three fearful felicities.[74] But as the unimitable Pindar often did, so is that kind most capable and most fit to awake the thoughts from the sleep of idleness to embrace honorable enterprises.

These rests the heroical, whose very name (I think) should daunt all back-biters; for by what conceit can a tongue be directed to speak evil of that which draweth with it no less champions than Achilles, Cyrus, Aeneas, Turnus, Tydeus, and Rinaldo? who doth not only teach and move to a truth, but teacheth and moveth to the most high and excellent truth; who maketh magnanimity and justice shine throughout all misty fearfulness and foggy desires; who, if the saying of Plato and Tully be true, that who could see virtue would be wonderfully ravished with the love of her beauty, this man sets her out to make her more lovely in her holiday apparel, to the eye of any that will deign not to disdain until they understand. But if anything be already said in the defence of sweet poetry, all concurreth to the maintaining the heroical, which is not only a kind, but the best and most accomplished kind of poetry. For as the image of each action stirreth and instructeth the mind, so the lofty image of such worthies most inflameth the mind with desire to be worthy, and informs with counsel how to be worthy. Only let Aeneas be worn in the tablet of your memory, how he governeth himself in the ruin of his country; in the preserving his old father and carrying away his religious ceremonies;[75] in obeying the god's commandment to leave Dido, though not only all passionate kindness, but even the human consideration of virtuous gratefulness, would have craved other of him; how in storms, how in sports, how in war, how in peace, how a fugitive, how victorious, how besieged, how besieging, how to strangers, how to allies, how to enemies, how to his own; lastly, how in his inward self, and how in his outward government. And, I think, in a mind not prejudiced with a prejudicating humor, he will be found in excellency fruitful; yea, even as Horace saith,

melius Chrysippo et Crantore.[76]

But truly I imagine it falleth out with these poet-whippers, as with some good women, who often are sick, but in faith they cannot tell where. So the name of poetry is odious to them, but neither his cause nor effects, neither the sum that contains him nor the particularities descending from him, give any fast handle to their carping dispraise.

Sith then poetry is of all human learning the most ancient and of most fatherly antiquity, as from whence other learnings have taken their beginnings; sith it is so universal that no learned nation doth despise it, nor no barbarous nation is without it; sith both Roman and Greek gave divine names unto it, the one of prophesying, the other of making, and that indeed, that name of making is fit for him, considering that whereas other arts retain themselves within their subject and receive, as it were, their being from it, the poet only bringeth his own stuff, and doth not learn a conceit out of a matter, but maketh matter for a conceit;[77] sith neither his description nor his end containeth any evil, the thing described cannot be evil; sith his effects be so good as to teach goodness and to delight the learners; sith therein (namely in moral doctrine, the chief of all knowledges) he doth not only far pass the historian, but for instructing is well nigh comparable to the philosopher, and for moving, leaves him behind him; sith the Holy Scripture (wherein there is no uncleanness) hath whole parts in it poetical, and that even our Saviour Christ vouchsafed to use the flowers of it, sith all his kinds are not only in their united forms, but in their severed dissections, fully commendable; I think (and think I think rightly) the laurel crown appointed for triumphing captains doth worthily (of all other learnings) honor the poet's triumph.

But because we have ears as well as tongues, and that the lightest reasons that may be will seem to weigh greatly if nothing be put in the counter-balance, let us hear, and, as well as we can, ponder, what objections may be made against this art, which may be worthy either of yielding or answering.

First, truly, I note not only in these *mysomousoi*, poet-haters, but in all that kind of people who seek a praise by dispraising others, that they do prodigally spend a great many wandering words in quips and scoffs, carping and taunting at each thing which, by stirring the spleen[78] may stay the brain from a thorough beholding the worthiness of the subject. Those kind of objections, as they are full of very idle easiness, sith there is nothing of so sacred a majesty but that an itching tongue may rub itself upon it, so deserve they no other answer, but instead of laughing at the jest, to laugh at the jester. We know a playing wit can praise the discretion of an ass, the comfortableness of being in debt, and the jolly commodity of being sick of the plague. So of the contrary side, if we will turn Ovid's verse,

Ut lateat virtus proximitate mali,[79]

that good lie hid in nearness of the evil, Agrippa will be as merry in showing the vanity of science as Erasmus was in commending of folly. Neither shall any man or matter escape some touch of these smiling railers. But for Erasmus and Agrippa, they had another foundation than the superficial part would promise. Marry, these other pleasant fault-finders, who will correct the verb before they understand the noun, and confute others' knowledge before they confirm their own, I would have them only remember that scoffing cometh not of wisdom.[80] So as the best title in true English they get with their merriments is to be called good fools, for so have our grave forefathers ever termed that humorous kind of jesters.

But that which giveth greatest scope to their scorning humors is rhyming and versing. It is already said (and, as I think, truly said), it is not rhyming and versing that maketh poesy. One may be a poet without versing, and a versifier without poetry. But yet presuppose it were inseparable (as indeed it seemeth Scaliger judgeth), truly it were an inseparable commendation. For if *oratio* next to *ratio*, speech next to reason, be the greatest gift bestowed upon mortality, that cannot be praiseless which doth most polish that blessing of speech, which considers each word not only (as a man may say) by his forcible quality,[81] but by his best measured quantity, carrying even in themselves a harmony (without [perchance] number, measure, order, proportion be in our time grown odious). But lay aside the just praise it hath, by being the only fit speech for music (music, I say, the most divine striker of the senses), thus much is undoubtedly true, that if reading be foolish without remembering, memory being the only treasurer of knowledge, those words which are fittest for memory are likewise most convenient for knowledge.

Now, that verse far exceedeth prose in the knitting up of the memory, the reason is manifest. The words (besides their delight, which hath a great affinity to memory) being so set as one word cannot be lost but the whole work fails; which accuseth itself, calleth the remembrance back to itself, and so most strongly confirmeth it. Besides, one word so, as it were, begetting another, as be it in rhyme or measured verse, by the former a man shall have a near guess to the follower. Lastly, even they that have taught the art of memory have showed nothing so apt for it as a certain room divided into many places, well and thoroughly known. Now that hath the verse in effect perfectly, every word having his natural seat, which seat must needs make the words remembered. But what needeth more in a thing so known to all men? Who is it that ever was a scholar that doth not carry away some verses of Virgil, Horace, or Cato, which in his youth he learned, and even to his old age serve him for hourly lessons? as

Percontatorem fugito, nam garrulus idem est.[82]

Dum sibi quisque placet, credula turba sumus.[83]

But the fitness it hath for memory is notably proved by all delivery of arts: wherein for the most part, from grammar to logic, mathematic, physic, and the rest, the rules chiefly necessary to be borne away are compiled in verses. Sothat verse, being in itself sweet and orderly, and being best for memory, the only handle of knowledge, it must be in jest that any man can speak against it.

Now then go we to the most important imputations laid to the poor poets. For aught I can yet learn, they are these. First, that there being many other more fruitful knowledges, a man might better spend his time in them than in this. Secondly, that it is the mother of lies. Thirdly, that it is the nurse of abuse, infecting us with many pestilent desires, with a siren's sweetness drawing the mind to the serpent's tail of sinful fancy. And herein especially comedies give the largest field to ear,[84] as Chaucer saith;[85] how both in other nations and in ours, before poets did soften us, we were full of courage, given to martial exercises, the pillars of manlike liberty, and not lulled asleep in shady idleness with poets' pastimes. And lastly, and chiefly, they cry out with an open mouth, as if they had outshot Robin Hood, that Plato banished them out of his commonwealth. Truly, this is much, if there be much truth in it.

First, to the first, that a man might better spend his time is a reason indeed; but it doth (as they say) but *petere principium*:[86] for if it be, as I affirm, that no learning is so good as that which teacheth and moveth to virtue, and that none can both teach and move thereto so much as poetry, then is the conclusion manifest that ink and paper cannot be to a more profitable purpose employed. And certainly, though a man should grant their first assumption, it should follow (methinks) very unwillingly, that good is not good because better is better. But

I still and utterly deny that there is sprung out of earth a more fruitful knowledge.

To the second therefore, that they should be the principal liars, I answer paradoxically, but truly, I think truly, that of all writers under the sun the poet is the least liar, and, though he would, as a poet can scarcely be a liar. The astronomer, with his cousin the geometrician, can hardly escape, when they take upon them to measure the height of the stars. How often, think you, do the physicians lie when they aver things good for sickness, which afterwards send Charon a great number of souls drowned in a potion before they come to his ferry? And no less of the rest, which take upon them to affirm. Now for the poet, he nothing affirms, and therefore never lieth. For, as I take it, to lie is to affirm that to be true which is false; so as the other artists, and especially the historian, affirming many things, can, in the cloudy knowledge of mankind, hardly escape from many lies. But the poet (as I said before) never affirmeth. The poet never maketh any circles about your imagination[87] to conjure you to believe for true what he writes. He citeth not authorities of other histories, but even for his entry calleth the sweet Muses to inspire into him a good invention; in troth, not laboring to tell you what is or is not, but what should or should not be. And therefore, though he recount things not true, yet because he telleth them not for true, he lieth not, without we will say that Nathan lied in his speech before alleged to David; which, as a wicked man durst scarce say, so think I none so simple would say that Aesop lied in the tales of his beasts; for who thinks that Aseop writ it for actually true were well worthy to have his name chronicled among the beasts he writeth of. What child is there that, coming to a play, and seeing Thebes written in great letters upon an old door, doth believe that it is Thebes? If then a man can arrive at that child's age to know that the poet's persons and doings are but pictures what should be, and not stories what have been, they will never give the lie to things not affirmatively but allegorically and figuratively written. And therefore, as in history looking for truth, they go away full fraught with falsehood, so in poesy looking for fiction, they shall use the narration but as an imaginative ground-plot of a profitable invention.

But hereto is replied that the poets gives names to men they write of, which argueth a conceit of an actual truth, and so, not being true, proves a falsehood. And doth the lawyer lie then, when under the names of John a Stile and John a Noakes[88] he puts his case? But that is easily answered. Their naming of men is but to make their picture the more lively, and not to build any history: painting men, they cannot leave men nameless. We see we cannot play at chess but that we must give names to our chessmen; and yet, methinks, he were a very partial champion of truth that would say we lied for giving a piece of wood the reverend title of a Bishop. The poet nameth Cyrus or Aeneas no other way than to show what men of their fames, fortunes, and estates should do.

Their third is, how much it abuseth men's wit, training it to wanton sinfulness and lustful love: for indeed that is the principal, if not the only, abuse I can hear alleged. They say the comedies rather teach than reprehend amorous conceits. They say the lyric is larded with passionate sonnets, the elegiac weeps the want of his mistress, and that even to the heroical Cupid hath ambitiously climbed. Alas, Love, I would thou couldst as well defend thyself as thou canst offend others. I would those on whom thou dost attend could either put thee away, or yield good reason why they keep thee. But grant love of beauty to be a beastly fault (although it be very hard, sith only man, and no beast, hath that gift to discern beauty); grant that lovely name of love to deserve all hateful reproaches (although even some of my masters the philosophers spent a good deal of their lamp-oil in setting forth the excellency of it); grant, I say, whatsoever they will have granted, that not only love, but lust, but vanity, but (if they list) scurrility, possesseth many leaves of the poet's books; yet think I, when this is granted they will find their sentence may with good manners put the last words foremost, and not say that poetry abuseth man's wit, but that man's wit abuseth poetry.

For I will not deny but that man's wit may make poesy (which should be *eikastike*,[89] which some learned have defined, figuring forth good things) to be *phantastike*,[89] which doth contrariwise infect the fancy with unworthy objects; as the painter, that should give to the eye either some excellent perspective, or some fine picture fit for building or fortification, or containing in it some notable example, as Abraham sacrificing his son Isaac, Judith killing Holofernes, David fighting with Goliath, may leave those, and please an ill-pleased eye with wanton shows of better hidden matters. But what, shall the abuse of a thing make the right use odious? Nay truly, though I yield that poesy may not only be abused, but that being abused, by the reason of his sweet charming force it can do more hurt than any other army of words, yet shall it be so far from concluding that the abuse should give reproach to the abused, that contrariwise it is a good reason that whatsoever being abused doth most harm, being rightly used (and upon the right use each thing conceiveth his title) doth most good.

Do we not see the skill of physic[90] (the best rampire[91] to our often-assaulted bodies), being abused, teach poison the most violent destroyer? Doth not knowledge of law, whose end is to even and right all things, being abused, grow the crooked fosterer of horrible injuries? Doth not (to go to the highest) God's word abused breed heresy, and His name abused become blasphemy? Truly a needle cannot do much hurt, and as truly (with leave of ladies be it spoken) it cannot do much good. With a sword thou mayest kill thy father, and with a sword thou mayest defend thy prince and country. So that, as in their calling poets the fathers of lies they say nothing, so in this their argument of abuse they prove the commendation.

They allege herewith that before poets began to be in price our nation hath set their hearts' delight upon action, and not upon imagination, rather doing things worthy to be written than writing things fit to be done. What that before time was, I think scarcely Sphinx can tell, sith no memory is so ancient that hath the precedence of poetry. And certain it is that, in our plainest homeliness, yet never was the Albion[92] nation without poetry. Marry, this argument, though it be levelled against poetry, yet is it indeed a chain-shot against all learning, or bookishness, as they commonly term it. Of such mind were certain Goths, of whom it is written that, having in the spoil of a famous city taken a fair library, one hangman (belike fit to execute the fruits of their wits) who had murdered a great number of bodies, would have set fire on it. No, said another very gravely, take heed what you do, for while they are busy about these toys, we shall with more leisure conquer their countries. This indeed is the ordinary doctrine of ignorance, and many words sometimes I have heard spent in it; but because this reason is generally against all learning as well as poetry, or rather all learning but poetry; because it were too large a digression to handle, or at least too superfluous (sith it is manifest that all government of action is to be gotten by knowledge, and knowledge best by gathering many knowledges, which is reading), I only, with Horace, to him that is of that opinion,

Jubeo stultum esse libenter;[93]

for as for poetry itself, it is the freest from this objection.

For poetry is the companion of camps. I dare undertake *Orlando Furioso* or honest King Arthur, will never displease a soldier: but the quiddity of *ens* and *prima materia* will hardly agree with a corselet.[94] And therefore, as I said in the beginning, even Turks and Tartars are delighted with poets. Homer, a Greek, flourished before Greece flourished. And if to a slight conjecture a conjecture may be opposed, truly it may seem that, as by him their learned men took almost their first light of knowledge, so their active men received their first motions of courage. Only Alexander's example may serve, who by Plutarch is accounted of such virtue that fortune was not his guide,[95] but his foot-stool; whose acts speak for him, though Plutarch did not, indeed the phoenix of warlike princes. This Alexander left his schoolmaster, living Aristotle, behind him, but took dead Homer with him.[97] He put the philosopher Callisthenes to death for his seeming philosophical, indeed mutinous, stubbornness; but the chief thing he ever was heard to wish for was that Homer had been alive. He well found he received more bravery of mind by the pattern of Achilles than by hearing the definition of fortitude. And therefore, if Cato misliked Fulvius for carrying Ennius with him to the field, it may be answered that if Cato misliked it, the noble Fulvius liked it, or else he had not done it: for it was not the excellent Cato Uticensis (whose authority I would much more have reverenced), but it was the former, in truth a bitter punisher of faults, but else a man that had never well sacrificed to the Graces.[98] He misliked and cried out upon all Greek learning, and yet, being eighty years old, began to learn it, belike fearing that Pluto understood not Latin. Indeed, the Roman laws allowed no person to be carried to the wars but he that was in the soldier's roll, and therefore, though Cato misliked his unmustered[99] person, he misliked not his work. And if he had, Scipio Nasica, judged by common consent the best Roman, loved him. Both the other Scipio brothers, who had by their virtues no less surnames than of Asia and Afric, so loved him that they caused his body to be buried in their sepulcher. So as Cato, his authority being but against his person, and that answered with so far greater than himself, is herein of no validity.

But now indeed my burden is great; now Plato his name is laid upon me, whom I must confess, of all philosophers I have ever esteemed most worthy of reverence, and with great reason, sith of all philosophers he is the most poetical. Yet if he will defile the fountain out of which his flowing streams have proceeded, let us boldly examine with what reasons he did it. First, truly a man might maliciously object that Plato, being a philosopher, was a natural enemy of poets: for indeed, after the philosophers had picked out of the sweet mysteries of poetry the right discerning true points of knowledge, they forthwith putting it in method, and making a school-art of that which the poets did only teach by a divine delightfulness, beginning to spurn at their guides like ungrateful prentices, were not content to set up shops for themselves but sought by all means to discredit their masters; which, by the force of delight being barred them, the less they could overthrow them, the more they hated them. For indeed, they found for Homer seven cities, and strave who should have him for their citizen; where many cities banished philosophers as not fit members to live among them. For only repeating certain of Euripides' verses, many Athenians had their lives saved of the Syracusans, when the Athenians themselves thought many philosophers unworthy to live. Certain poets, as Simonides and Pindar, had so prevailed with Hiero the First, that of a tyrant they made him a just king, where Plato could do so little with Dionysius, that he himself of a philosopher was made a slave. But who should do thus, I confess, should requite the objections made against poets with like cavillation against philosophers; as likewise one should do that should bid one read *Phaedrus* or *Symposium*[100] in Plato, or the discourse of love in Plutarch,[101] and see whether any poet do authorize abominable filthiness, as they do. Again, a man might ask out of what commonwealth Plato did banish them. In sooth, thence where he himself alloweth community of women. So as belike this banishment grew not for effeminate wantonness, sith little should poetical sonnets be hurtful when a man might have what woman he listed. But I honor philosophical instructions, and bless the wits which bred them, so as they be not abused, which is likewise stretched to poetry.

Saint Paul himself (who yet for the credit of poets allegeth twice two poets, and one of them by the name of prophet)[102] setteth a watchword upon philosophy, indeed upon the abuse; so doth Plato, upon the abuse, not upon poetry. Plato found fault that the poets of his time filled the world with wrong opinions of the gods, making light tales of that unspotted essence, and therefore would not have the youth depraved with such opinions. Herein may much be said; let this suffice: the poets did not induce such opinions, but did imitate those opinions already induced. For all the Greek stories can well testify that the very religion of that time stood upon many and many-fashioned gods, not taught so by the poets, but followed according to their nature of imitation. Who list may read in Plutarch the discourses of Isis and Osiris, of the cause why oracles ceased, of the divine providence, and see whether the theology of that nation stood not upon such dreams, which the poets indeed superstitiously observed, and truly (sith they had not the light of Christ) did much better in it than the philosophers, who, shaking off superstition, brought in atheism. Plato therefore (whose authority I had much rather justly construe than unjustly resist) meant not in general of poets, in those words of which Julius Scaliger saith, *Qua authoritate barbari quidam atque hispidi abuti velint ad poetas e republica exigendos;*[103] but only meant to drive out those wrong opinions of the Deity (whereof now, without further law, Christianity hath taken away all the hurtful belief), perchance (as he thought) nourished by the then esteemed poets. And a man need go no further than to Plato himself to know his meaning: who, in his dialogue called *Ion*, giveth high and rightly divine commendation to poetry. So as Plato, banishing the abuse, not the thing, not banishing it, but giving due honor unto it, shall be our patron and not our adversary. For indeed, I had much rather (sith truly I may do it) show their mistaking of Plato (under whose lion's skin they would make an ass-like braying against poesy) than go about to overthrow his authority; whom, the wiser a man is, the more just cause he shall find to have in admiration; especially sith he attributeth unto poesy more than myself do, namely, to be a very inspiring of a divine force, far above man's wit, as in the afore-named dialogue[104] is apparent.

Of the other side, who would show the honors have been by the best sort of judgments granted them, a whole sea of examples would present themselves: Alexanders, Caesars, Scipios, all favorers of poets; Laelius, called the Roman Socrates, himself a poet, so as part of *Heautontimorumenos* in Terence was supposed to be made by him. And even the Greek Socrates, whom Apollo confirmed to be the only wise man, is said to have spent part of his old time in putting Aesop's fables into verses. And therefore full evil should it become his scholar Plato to put such words in his master's mouth against poets. But what need more? Aristotle writes the Art of Poesy; and why, if it should not be written? Plutarch teacheth the use to be gathered of them, and how if they should not be read? And who reads Plutarch's either history or philosophy, shall find he trimmeth both their garments with guards of poesy. But I list not to defend poesy with the help of her underling historiography. Let it suffice that it is a fit soil for praise to dwell upon; and what disparise may set upon it, is either easily overcome, or transformed into just commendation.

So that, sith the excellencies of it may be so easily and so justly confirmed, and the low-creeping objections so soon trodden down, it not being an art of lies, but of true doctrine; not of effeminateness, but of notable stirring of courage; not of abusing man's wit, but of strengthening man's wit; not banished, but honored by Plato; let us rather plant more laurels for to engarland our poets' heads (which honor of being laureate, as besides them only triumphant captains wear, is a sufficient authority to show the price they ought to be had in), than suffer the ill-favoring breath of such wrong-speakers once to blow upon the clear springs of poesy.

But sith I have run so long a career in this matter, methinks before I give my pen a full stop it shall be but a little more lost time to inquire why England (the mother of excellent minds) should be grown so hard a step-mother to poets, who certainly in wit ought to pass all other, sith all only proceedeth from their wit, being indeed makers of themselves, not takers of others. How can I but exclaim

Musa, mihi causas memora, quo numine laeso?[105]

Sweet poesy, that hath anciently had kings, emperors, senators, great captains, such as, besides a thousand others, David, Adrian, Sophocles, Germanicus, not only to favor poets, but to be poets. And of our nearer times can present for her patrons a Robert, king of Sicily, the great King Francis of France, King James of Scotland; such cardinals as Bembus and Bibbiena; such famous preachers and teachers as Beza and Melanchthon; so learned philosophers as Fracastorius and Scaliger; so great orators as Pontanus and Muretus; so piercing wits as George Buchanan; so grave counselors as, besides many, but before all, that Hospital of France, than whom (I think) that realm never brought forth a more accomplished judgment, more firmly builded upon virtue—I say these, with numbers of others, not only to read others' poesies, but to poetise for others' reading—that poesy, thus embraced in all other places, should only find in our time a hard welcome in England, I think the very earth lamenteth it, and therefore decketh our soil with fewer laurels than it was accustomed. For heretofore poets have in England also flourished, and, which is to be noted, even in those times when the trumpet of Mars did sound loudest. And now that an over-faint quietness should seem to strew the house for poets, they are almost in as good reputation as the mountebanks at Venice.[106] Truly even that, as of the one side it giveth great praise to poesy, which like Venus (but to better purpose) had rather be troubled in the net with Mars than enjoy the homely quiet of Vulcan; so serves it for a piece of a reason why they are less grateful to idle England, which now can scarce endure the pain of a pen. Upon this necessarily followeth that base men with servile wits undertake it, who think it enough if they can be rewarded of the printer. And so as Epaminondas is said, with the honor of his virtue to have made an office, by his exercising it which before was contemptible, to become highly respected; so these, no more but setting their names to it, by their own disgracefulness disgrace the most graceful poesy. For now, as if all the Muses were got with child to bring forth bastard poets, without any commission they do post over the banks of Helicon, till they make the readers more weary than post-horses; while in the meantime they,

Queis meliore luto finxit praecordia Titan,[107]

are better content to suppress the out-flowing of their wit than, by publishing them, to be accounted knights of the same order.

But I, that before ever I durst aspire unto the dignity, am admitted into the company of the paper-blurrers, do find the very true cause of our wanting estimation is want of desert, taking upon us to be poets in despite of Pallas.[108] Now wherein we want desert were a thank-worthy labor to express; but if I knew, I should have mended myself. But I, as I never desired the title, so have I neglected the means to come by it. Only, over-mastered by some thoughts, I yielded an inky tribute unto them. Marry, they that delight in poesy itself should seek to know what they do, and how they do, and especially look themselves in an unflattering glass of reason, if they be inclinable unto it. For poesy must not be drawn by the ears; it must be gently led, or rather it must lead; which was partly the cause that made the ancient-learned affirm it was a divine gift, and no human skill; sith all other knowledges lie ready for any that hath strength of wit;

a poet no industry can make, if his own genius be not carried unto it; and therefore is it an old proverb, *orator fit, poeta nascitur.*[109] Yet confess I always that as the fertilest ground must be manured, so must the highest flying wit have a Daedalus to guide him. That Daedalus, they say, both in this and in other, hath three wings to bear itself up into the air of due commendation: that is, Art, Imitation, and Exercise. But these, neither artificial rules[110] nor imitative patterns,[111] we much cumber ourselves withal. Exercise indeed we do, but that very fore-backwardly: for where we should exercise to know, we exercise as having known; and so is our brain delivered of much matter which never was begotten by knowledge. For there being two principal parts, matter to be expressed by words, and words to express the matter; in neither we use Art or Imitation rightly. Our matter is *quodlibet*[112] indeed, though wrongly performing Ovid's verse,

Quicquid conabor dicere, versus erit:[113]

never marshalling it into an assured rank, that almost the readers cannot tell where to find themselves.

Chaucer undoubtedly did excellently in his *Troilus and Criseyde*, of whom truly I know not whether to marvel more, either that he in that misty time could see so clearly, or that we in this clear age walk so stumblingly after him. Yet had he great wants, fit to be forgiven in so reverent antiquity. I account the *Mirror of Magistrates* meetly furnished of beautiful parts, and in the Earl of Surrey's lyrics many things tasting of a noble birth, and worthy of a noble mind. *The Shepherd's Calendar* hath much poetry in his eclogues, indeed worthy the reading if I be not deceived. That same framing of his style to an old rustic language I dare not allow, sith neither Theocritus in Greek, Virgil in Latin, nor Sannazzaro in Italian, did affect it. Besides these, do I not remember to have seen but few (to speak boldly) printed that have poetical sinews in them: for proof whereof, let but most of the verses be put in prose, and then ask the meaning, and it will be found that one verse did but beget another, without ordering at the first what should be at the last; which becomes a confused mass of words with a tingling sound of rhyme, barely accompanied with reason.

Our tragedies and comedies (not without cause cried out against), observing rules neither of honest civility nor of skillful poetry, excepting *Gorboduc* (again I say, of those that I have seen), which notwithstanding, as it is full of stately speeches and well sounding phrases, climbing to the height of Seneca his style,[114] and as full of notable morality, which it doth most delightfully teach, and so obtain the very end of poesy; yet in troth it is very defectious in the circumstances, which grieveth me, because it might not remain as an exact model of all tragedies. For it is faulty both in place and time, the two necessary companions of all corporal actions. For where the stage should always represent but one place, and the uttermost time presupposed in it should be, both by Aristotle's precept and common reason, but one day, there is both many days and many places inartificially[115] imagined.

But if it be so in *Gorboduc*, how much more in all the rest? where you shall have Asia of the one side, and Afric of the other, and so many other under-kingdoms, that the player, when he cometh in, must ever begin with telling where he is, or else the tale will not be conceived. Now ye shall have three ladies walk to gather flowers, and then we must believe the stage to be a garden. By and by we hear news of shipwreck in the same place, and then we are to blame if we accept it not for a rock. Upon the back of that comes out a hideous monster with fire and smoke, and then the miserable beholders are bound to take it for a cave. While in the meantime two armies fly in, represented with four swords and bucklers, and then what hard heart will not receive it for a pitched field?

Now of time they are much more liberal, for ordinary it is that two young princes fall in love. After many traverses, she is got with child, delivered of a fair boy, he is lost, groweth a man, falls in love, and is ready to get another child, and all this in two hours' space: which, how absurd it is in sense, even sense may imagine, and art hath taught, and all ancient examples justified, and at this day, the ordinary players in Italy will not err in. Yet will some bring in an example of *Eunuchus* in Terence, that containeth matter of two days, yet far short of twenty years. True it is, and so was it to be played in two days, and so fitted to the time it set forth. And though Plautus hath in one place done amiss, let us hit with him, and not miss with him. But they will say, how then shall we set forth a story which containeth both many places and many times? And do they not know that a tragedy is tied to the laws of poesy, and not of history, not bound to follow the story, but having liberty, either to feign a quite new matter, or to frame the history to the most tragical conveniency? Again, many things may be told which cannot be showed, if they know the difference betwixt reporting and representing. As for example, I may speak (though I am here) of Peru, and in speech digress from that to the description of Calicut; but in action I cannot represent it without Pacolet's horse. And so was the manner the ancients took, by some *nuncius*[116] to recount things done in former time or other place.

Lastly, if they will represent an history, they must not (as Horace saith) begin *ab ovo*,[117] but they must come to the principal point of that one action which they will represent. By example this will be best expressed. I have a story[118] of young Polydorus, delivered for safety's sake, with great riches, by his father Priam, to Polymnestor, king of Thrace, in the Trojan war time. He, after some years, hearing the overthrow of Priam, for to make the treasure his own, murdereth the child. The body of the child is taken up by Hecuba. She, the same day, findeth a sleight to be revenged most cruelly of the tyrant. Where now would one of our tragedy writers begin, but with the delivery of the child? Then should he sail over into Thrace, and so spend I know not how many years, and travel numbers of places. But where doth Euripides? Even with the finding of the body, leaving the rest to be told by the spirit of Polydorus. This need no further to be enlarged; the dullest wit may conceive it.

But besides these gross absurdities, how all their plays be neither right tragedies, nor right comedies, mingling kings and clowns not because the matter so carrieth it, but thrust in clowns by head and shoulders, to play a part in majestical matters, with neither decency nor discretion, so as neither the admiration and commiseration, nor the right sportfulness,[119] is by their mongrel tragi-comedy[120] obtained. I know Apuleius did somewhat so, but that is a thing recounted with space of time, not represented in one moment: and I know the ancients have one or two examples of tragi-comedies, as Plautus hath *Amphitrio*. But if we mark them well, we shall find that they never, or very daintily, match horn-pipes and funerals. So falleth it out, that having indeed no right comedy, in that comical part of our tragedy we have nothing but scurrility, unworthy of any chaste ears, or some extreme show of doltishness, indeed fit to lift up a loud laughter, and nothing else: where the whole tract of a comedy should be full of delight, as the tragedy should be still maintained in a well raised admiration.

But our comedians think there is no delight without laughter; which is very wrong, for though laughter may come with delight, yet cometh it not of delight, as though delight should be the cause of laughter; but well may one thing breed both together: nay, rather in themselves they have, as it were, a kind of contrariety; for delight we scarcely do, but in things that have a conveniency to ourselves, or to the general nature; laughter almost ever cometh of things most disproportioned to ourselves and nature. Delight hath a joy in it, either permanent or present. Laughter hath only a scornful tickling. For example, we are ravished with delight to see a fair woman, and yet are far from being moved to laughter. We laugh at deformed creatures, wherein certainly we cannot delight. We delight in good chances, we laugh at mischances; we delight to hear the happiness of our friends or country, at which he were worthy to be laughed at that would laugh; we shall contrarily laugh sometimes to find a matter quite mistaken and go down the hill against the bias,[121] in the mouth of some such men, as for the respect of them one shall be heartily sorry, yet he cannot choose but laugh; and so is rather pained than delighted with laughter. Yet deny I not but that they may go well together; for as in Alexander's picture well set out, we delight without laughter, and in twenty mad antics we laugh without delight, so in Hercules, painted with his great beard and furious countenance, in a woman's attire, spinning at Omphale's commandment, it breedeth both delight and laughter. For the representing of so strange a power in love procureth delight, and the scornfulness of the action stirreth laughter.

But I speak to this purpose, that all the end of the comical part be not upon such scornful matters as stirreth laughter only, but, mixed with it, that delightful teaching which is the end of poesy. And the great fault even in that point of laughter, and forbidden plainly by Aristotle,[122] is that they stir laughter in sinful things, which are rather execrable than ridiculous: or in miserable, which are rather to be pitied than scorned. For what is it to make folks gape at a wretched beggar or a beggarly clown; or against law of hospitality, to jest at strangers because they speak not English so well as we do? What do we learn? sith it is certain

> *Nil habet infelix paupertas durius in se,*
> *Quam quod ridiculos homines facit.*[123]

But rather a busy loving courtier; a heartless threatening Thraso; a self-wise-seeming schoolmaster; an awry-transformed traveler: these, if we saw walk in stage names, which we play naturally, therein were delightful laughter, and teaching delightfulness: as in the other, the tragedies of Buchanan do justly bring forth a divine admiration. But I have lavished out too many words of this play matter. I do it becuase, as they are excelling parts of poesy, so is there none so much used in England, and none can be more pitifully abused; which, like an unmannerly daughter, showing a bad education, causeth her mother poesy's honesty to be called in question.

Other sorts of poetry almost have we none, but that lyrical kind of songs and sonnets: which, Lord, if He gave us so good minds, how well it might be employed, and with how heavenly fruit, both private and public, in singing the praises of the immortal beauty, the immortal goodness of that God who giveth us hands to write and wits to conceive; of which we might well want words, but never matter; of which we could turn our eyes to nothing but we should ever have new budding occasions. But truly many of such writings as come under the banner of unresistable love,[124] if I were a mistress, would never persuade me they were in love; so coldly they apply fiery speeches, as men that had rather read lovers' writings, and so caught up certain swelling phrases, which hang together, like a man which once told me the wind was at north-west and by south, because he would be sure to name winds enough, than that in truth they feel these passions, which easily (as I think) may be bewrayed by that same forcibleness or *energia*[125] (as the Greeks call it) of the writer. But let this be a sufficient though short note, that we miss the right use of the material point of poesy.

Now, for the outside of it, which is words, or (as I may term it) diction, it is even well worse. So is that honey-flowing matron eloquence apparelled, or rather disguised, in a courtesan-like painted affectation: one time with so far fet words, that may seem monsters, but must seem strangers to any poor Englishman; another time, with coursing of a letter, as if they were bound to follow the method of a dictionary; another time, with figures and flowers, extremely winter-starved. But I would this fault were only peculiar to versifiers, and had not as large possession among prose-printers; and (which is to be marvelled) among many scholars; and (which is to be pitied) among some preachers. Truly I could wish, if at least I might be so bold to wish in a thing beyond the reach of my capacity, the diligent imitators of Tully and Demosthenes (most worthy to be imitated) did not so much keep Nizolian paper-books[126] of their figures and phrases, as by attentive translation (as it were) devour them whole, and make them wholly theirs.[127] For now they cast sugar and spice upon every dish that is served to the table, like those Indians, not content to wear earrings at the fit and natural place of the ears, but they will thrust jewels through their nose and lips because they will be sure to be fine.

Tully, when he was to drive out Catiline, as it were with a thunderbolt of eloquence, often used that figure of repetition, *Vivit. Vivit? Imo vero etiam in senatum venit,*[128] &c. Indeed, inflamed with a well-grounded rage, he would have his words (as it were) double out of his mouth, and so do that artificially which we see men do in choler naturally. And we, having noted the grace of those words, hale them in sometime to a familiar epistle, when it were too too much choler[129] to be choleric. How well store of *similiter cadences*[130] doth sound with the gravity of the pulpit, I would but invoke Demosthenes' soul to tell, who with a rare daintiness useth them. Truly they have made me think of the sophister[131] that with too much subtlety would prove two eggs three, and though he might be counted a sophister, had none for his labor. So these men, bringing in such a kind of eloquence, well may they obtain an opinion of a seeming fineness, but persuade few, which should be the end of their fineness.

Now for similitudes in certain printed discourses, I think all herbarists, all stories of beasts, fowls, and fishes are rifled up, that they come in multitudes to wait upon any of our conceits; which certainly is as absurd a surfeit to the ears as is possible: for the force of a similitude not being to prove anything to a contrary disputer, but only to explain to a willing hearer; when that is done, the rest is a most tedious prattling, rather over-swaying the memory from the purpose whereto they were applied, than any whit informing the judgment, already either satisfied, or by similitudes not to be satisfied.[132] For my part, I do not doubt, when Antonius and Crassus, the great forefathers of Cicero in eloquence, the one (as Cicero testifieth of them[133]) pretended not to know art, the other not to set by it, because with a plain sensibleness they might win credit of popular ears; which credit is the nearest step to persuasion; which persuasion is the chief mark of oratory;[134] I do not doubt (I say) but that they used these knacks very sparingly; which, who doth generally use, any man may see doth dance to his own music, and so be noted by the audience more careful to speak curiously[135] than to speak truly.

Undoubtedly (at least to my opinion undoubtedly) I have found in divers smally[136] learned courtiers a more sound style than in some professors of learning; of which I can guess no other cause but that the courtier, following that which by practice he findeth fittest to nature, therein (though he know it not) doth according to art, though not by art: where the other, using art to show art, and not to hide art (as in these cases he should do), flieth from nature, and indeed abuseth art.

But what? methinks I deserve to be pounded[137] for straying from poetry to oratory: but both have such an affinity in this wordish consideration, that I think this digression will make my meaning receive the fuller understanding; which is not to take upon me to teach poets how they should do, but only, finding myself sick among the rest, to show some one or two spots of the common infection grown among the most part of writers; that, acknowledging ourselves somewhat awry, we may bend to the right use both of matter and manner; whereto our language giveth us great occasion, being indeed capable of any excellent exercising of it. I know some will say it is a mingled language.[138] And why not so much the better, taking the best of both the other? Another will say it wanteth grammar. Nay truly, it hath that praise, that it wanteth not grammar: for grammar it might have, but it needs it not; being so easy of itself, and so void of those cumbersome differences of cases, genders, moods, and tenses, which I think was a piece of the Tower of Babylon's curse, that a man should be put to school to learn his mother-tongue. But for the uttering sweetly and properly the conceits of the mind, which is the end of speech, that hath it equally with any other tongue in the world; and is particularly happy in compositions[139] of two or

AN APOLOGY FOR POETRY

three words together, near the Greek, far beyond the Latin, which is one of the greatest beauties can be in a language.

Now of versifying there are two sorts, the one ancient, the other modern: the ancient marked the quantity of each syllable, and according to that framed his verse; the modern, observing only number (with some regard of the accent), the chief life of it standeth in that like sounding of the words which we call rhyme. Whether of these be the more excellent would bear many speeches: the ancient (no doubt) more fit for music, both words and tune observing quantity, and more fit lively to express divers passions, by the low and lofty sound of the well-weighed syllable. The latter likewise, with his rhyme, striketh a certain music to the ear; and, in fine, sith it doth delight though by another way, it obtains the same purpose: there being in either sweetness, and wanting in neither majesty. Truly the English, before any other vulgar language I know, is fit for both sorts: for, for the ancient, the Italian is so full of vowels that it must ever be cumbered with elisions; the Dutch, so of the other side with consonants, that they cannot yield the sweet sliding fit for a verse; the French in his whole language hath not one word that hath his accent in the last syllable saving two, called *antepenultima*; and little more hath the Spanish, and therefore very gracelessly may they use dactyls.[140] The English is subject to none of these defects.

Now for the rhyme, though we do not observe quantity, yet we observe the accent very precisely, which other languages either cannot do, or will not do so absolutely. That *caesura*, or breathing place in the midst of the verse, neither Italian nor Spanish have; the French and we never almost fail of. Lastly, even the very rhyme itself, the Italian cannot put in the last syllable, by the French named the masculine rhyme, but still in the next to the last, which the French call the female, or the next before that, which the Italians term *sdrucciola*. The example of the former is *buono, suono*; of the *sdrucciola*[141] is *femina, semina*. The French, of the other side, hath both the male, as *bon, son*, and the female, as *plaise, taise*. But the *sdrucciola* he hath not: where the English hath all three, as *due, true; father, rather; motion, potion*;[142] with much more which might be said, but that I find already the triflingness of this discourse is much too much enlarged.

So that sith the ever-praiseworthy poesy is full of virtue-breeding delightfulness, and void of no gift that ought to be in the noble name of learning; sith the blames laid against it are either false or feeble; sith the cause why it is not esteemed in England is the fault of poet-apes, not poets; sith, lastly, our tongue is most fit to honor poesy, and to be honored by poesy; I conjure you all that have had the evil luck to read this ink-wasting toy of mine, even in the name of the nine Muses, no more to scorn the sacred mysteries of poesy, no more to laugh at the name of poets, as though they were next inheritors to fools, no more to jest at the reverent title of a rhymer; but to believe with Aristotle that they were the ancient treasurers of the Grecians' divinity; to believe with Bembus that they were first bringers-in of all civility; to believe with Scaliger that no philosopher's precepts can sooner make you an honest man than the reading of Virgil; to believe with Clauserus, the translator of Cornutus, that it pleased the heavenly

Deity, by Hesiod and Homer, under the veil of fables, to give us all knowledge, logic, rhetoric, philosophy natural and moral, and *quid non*?[143] to believe with me that there are many mysteries contained in poetry, which of purpose were written darkly, lest by profane wits it should be abused; to believe with Landino that they are so beloved of the gods, that whatsoever they write proceeds of a divine fury; lastly, to believe themselves when they tell you they will make you immortal by their verses.

Thus doing, your name shall flourish in the printers' shops; thus doing, you shall be of kin to many a poetical preface; thus doing, you shall be most fair, most rich, most wise, most all, you shall dwell upon superlatives. Thus doing, though you be *libertino patre natus*,[144] you shall suddenly grow *Hurculea proles*,[145]

Si quid mea carmina possunt.[146]

Thus doing, your soul shall be placed with Dante's Beatrix, or Virgil's Anchises. But if (fie of such a but) you be born so near the dull-making cataract of Nilus that you cannot hear the planet-like music of poetry, if you have so earth-creeping a mind that it cannot lift itself up to look to the sky of poetry, or rather, by a certain rustical disdain, will become such a mome[147] as to be a Momus[148] of poetry; then, though I will not wish unto you the ass's ears of Midas, nor to be driven by a poet's verses (as Bubonax was) to hang himself, nor to be rhymed to death, as it is said to be done in Ireland;[149] yet thus much curse I must send you in the behalf of all poets, that while you live, you live in love, and never get favor for lacking skill of a sonnet; and when you die, your memory die from the earth for want of an epitaph.

FINIS.

NOTES

1. An esquire, or equerry, was an officer in charge of the horses and stables of a noble personage.
2. Italian for pedantry.
3. Sidney is probably referring to the original *Arcadia*, which he completed during the year or so that preceded the composition of the *Apology*.
4. Capable of producing a desired result.
5. Here used with an affectionate rather than pejorative connotation.
6. The notion that poets were the first philosophers and the founders of learning had great currency during the Renaissance, though the idea was also common in antiquity. Boccaccio, for example, extrapolating from Aristotle, argues that the earliest Greek poets were also theologians (*The Life of Dante*). Sidney may have been following the lead of Sir Thomas Elyot, who wrote (*The Governor*): "I feare me to be longe from noble Homere: from whom as from a fountaine proceded all eloquence and lernyng." See also Puttenham (*Arte of English Poetry*).
7. Musaeus, a mythical singer of antiquity, was often associated with Orpheus. Plato (*Republic*, II, 364) speaks of Musaeus and Orpheus as the descendants of the Muses

and the Moon. Julius Scaliger, in his *Poetices* (I, 2), ranks Musaeus with Orpheus and Linus as poets of the second period of poetry, singers of religion and mysteries.

8. Amphion was the son of Zeus and Antiope. The association of Amphion and Orpheus in this passage suggests that Sidney's source was Horace (*Ars Poetica*, 390 ff.), who relates that the two singers were able to tame beasts and control inanimate objects through the magic of their music. (See n. 7, above.) Scaliger (*Poetices*, I, 2), probably following Horace, remarks that Amphion and Orpheus were religious poets with divine powers over the inanimate.

9. For the story of the lost continent of Atlantis see Plato's *Timaeus*.

10. The notion that Plato was a poet was a commonplace among Renaissance humanists, and had some currency even in classical antiquity.

11. Have no sense of what it is that constitutes true poetry.

12. This was a ceremonial dance accompanied by songs, common among the Indians in the Americas. Sidney's information was apparently derived from Peter Martyr's *Decades*, which appeared in Richard Eden's *Hystorie of the West Indies* (1555).

13. The popular notion that Brutus (the great-grandson of Aeneas) was the founder of the British race was still current in the sixteenth century. Geoffrey of Monmouth (ca. 1100–ca. 1155) initiated the legend in his Latin *History of the Kings of Britain*, claiming a secret book as his source. Geoffrey's fanciful historiography became a fertile authority for the medieval romance writers and was the source of Spenser's chronicle of British kings in *The Faerie Queene*. Hideous giants ruled the countryside

> Until that Brutus, anciently deriv'd
> From roiall stocke of old Assaracs line,
> Driven by fatall error here arriv'd,
> And them of their unjust possession depriv'd (II, x, 9).

The same story appears in Michael Drayton's *Poly-Olbion*, I, 312 ff.

14. Nominative plural of the Latin *carmen*, a song, poem, or incantation.

15. A concept.

16. This is a Greek term, perhaps best rendered "personification," in which an inanimate object or abstraction is endowed with human attributes.

17. Sidney is generally careful to distinguish between "poetry," the finished product of the poet's art, and "poesy," the craft or technique of writing. A somewhat similar distinction appears in Scaliger's Poetices (I, 2).

18. A very common Stoic prescription. Cf. Cicero, *De Officiis*, I, xxviii, 97–98.

19. Part of an established discipline or art. The usage here bears none of the pejorative connotations ("fictitious," "unnatural") current today.

20. The rhetorician and logician, unlike the poet, must limit themselves to the terms and issues of the topic under consideration ("the circle of a question"). Sidney's confusion of logic and rhetoric, whether or not intended, is probably a result of his acquaintance with Ramism. Traditionally, logic was the art of making true statements in syllogisms, while rhetoric had persuasion rather than demonstration as its end, and employed enthymemes (arguments based on probable premises) rather than full-scale syllogisms. Classical rhetoric was divided into five parts: invention, disposition, elocution, memory, and pronunciation. In the Ramist system, however, rhetoric was limited to elocution and pronunciation, memory was dropped altogether, and invention and disposition were placed in the domain of logic. But the result of this division between logic and rhetoric was more nominal than real, for Ramist rhetoric was contingent upon the effective use of logic. Before statements of any kind could be made it was necessary, in

theory at least, to invent and dispose the materials that the statements would articulate. Where classical rhetoric could be distinguished from logic, Ramist rhetoric was useless in the absence of logic. As a result it was almost inevitable that the two would overlap, as they do here in Sidney's discourse.

21. "Imitation" is misleading in this context, for it can be understood to mean the exact duplication of external objects. This confusion is intensified by Sidney's allusion to the doctrine of *ut pictura poesis*, which suggests that poetry and painting are sister arts, alike in their rendering of natural things. By "speaking picture," however, Sidney means that a poem is a general or universal concept (a "picture" seen in the mind) presented through the medium of language ("speaking"). The poet imitates his own "Idea or fore-conceit," not the brazen world of "second nature."

For further discussion see Rensselaer W. Lee, "*Ut Pictura Poesis:* The Humanistic Theory of Painting," *The Art Bulletin*, XXII (1940), 197–269 (republished in book form in 1967). There are numerous precedents for the "as painting, so poetry" doctrine, though Horace (*Ars Poetica*, 360 ll.) and Plutarch (*Moralia, How to Study Poetry*, 3) are the most important.

22. The Homeric Hymns are of unknown authorship, and consist of preludes to epics and Greek legends. They were translated by George Chapman in the early seventeenth century.

23. "Is any among you afflicted? let him pray. Is any merry? let him sing psalms" (James 5:13).

24. The "philosophical" poet, like the rhetorician and logician (see n. 20, above), is limited to the specific materials of the subject under discussion.

25. In legend Lucretia was the wife of Tarquinius Collatinus, who vindicated her honor by committing suicide after having been raped by Sextus Tarquinius.

26. The most important classical precedent for Sidney's argument occurs in Aristotle's *Poetics*, XXV, where the poet, like the portrait painter, is instructed to preserve the type, and yet make it more noble. Fracastoro echoes this position in *Naugerius* (trans. Kelso, p. 60), though he adds the qualification that painters "imitate the particular," while "the poet imitates not the particular but the simple idea clothed in its own beauties, which Aristotle calls the universal." Like Fracastoro, Sidney distinguishes between pictorial representations of individual external objects, and the conceptual image of the universal, pictures "of what may be and should be."

27. Sidney concurs with the Horatian dictum that poetry should be both profitable and pleasurable (*Ars Poetica*, 333 ff.), but adds that it should also "move" the reader. Knowledge, particularly for those of a Calvinistic inclination, was considered an insufficient basis for moral action; for although "our erected wit maketh us know what perfection is . . . our infected will keepeth us from reaching unto it."

28. Adhering to certain meters.

29. Sidney is clearly more concerned with the content of poetry than with its form. His distinction is identical to Elyot's (*The Governor*): "They that make verses, expressynge therby none other lernynge but the craft of versifyeng, be nat of auncient writers named poetes, but onely called versifyers."

30. See Cicero's *Epistles to His Brother Quintus*, I, viii, 23 ff.

31. Weighing.

32. Each man, according to the disposition of his faculties, is drawn to one or another of the arts and sciences.

33. Cf. Virgil, *Georgics*, II, 490–91.

34. Although the story of the stumbling astronomer was a commonplace, the classical original appears in Plato's *Theaetetus* (174), where Socrates relates that Thales

tumbled into a well while gazing at the stars. Sidney uses the same story in *Astrophil and Stella*, XIX.

35. Like logic and rhetoric (see n. 20, above), the "serving sciences" have certain fixed boundaries.

36. The moral philosophers carry books which argue against the pursuit of personal glory. Cf. Cicero, *Tusculan Disputations*, I, xv, 34.

37. "The witness of time, the light of truth, the life of memory, the directress of life, the herald of antiquity." This allusion to Cicero's *De Oratore*, II, ix, 36 would have been familiar to many of Sidney's readers. The Latin quotation is from Ponsonby. Olney's text reads (incorrectly): *"lux vitae, temporum magistra, vita memoriae, nuncia vetustatis, &c."* Norwich is almost identical to Olney.

38. Philosophers debate over the definitions of virtues and vices, but care little for their practical application.

39. A form is a class in school.

40. Poetry, like the rest of the arts and sciences, teaches through an appeal to human reason. Matters of divinity, however, are "to be excepted" because they fall beyond the reach of the rational faculties.

41. The "wordish description."

42. Sidney's portrait of "the whole Arte of governement" in Evarchus is evidence that he would not have agreed with the communistic political ideal presented in *Utopia*.

43. "Neither gods, nor men, nor booksellers, tolerate mediocrity in poets" (Horace, *Ars Poetica*, 372–73).

44. Luke 16:20–31.

45. Sidney is referring to the parable of the prodigal son, in Luke 15:11–32.

46. The notion that the methods of the Bible and of poetry were similar was not uncommon among writers before and during the Renaissance.

47. Limited to relating things as they actually happened, the historian cannot ennoble his materials ("cannot be liberal") through the use of the universal ("a perfect pattern") without becoming "poetical."

48. Someone easily convinced.

49. The historian.

50. *The Divine Comedy*, with its tripartite division between *Inferno, Purgatorio*, and *Paradiso*, quite literally fulfills Sidney's description.

51. "He was ignorant of letters."

52. "They are to be killed." Plato's intense hatred of despotism is well illustrated in *The Republic*, VIII–IX. Cicero (*De Officiis*, III, vi, 32 and III, xxi, 83) contends that tyrannicide is justified because the tyrant destroys the natural bond between men in society. An even more extreme view is taken by More's Utopians. See Robert P. Adams, *The Better Part of Valor* (1962), pp. 155–57.

53. "Lover of philosophers."

54. *Gnosis* is "knowledge"; *praxis* is "practice" or "action." The reference is to Aristotle's *Nicomachean Ethics*, I, 3.

55. "Words of art" refers to the elaborate technical vocabulary of the scholastic philosophers.

56. By "natural conceit" Sidney means concepts derived from nature as they appear in the mind. The distinction here is between concepts in their natural form, seen in the mind, and concepts artificially set forth in words.

57. "This is the task, this is the labor" (*Aeneid*, VI, 129).

58. Making no greater claim than to be a tale.

59. Aloes and rhubarb are generic names for plants notable for their bitterness which were often used as purgatives during the period in which Sidney lived.

60. "Shall this land see Turnus in flight? Is it such a terrible thing to die?" (*Aeneid*, XII, 645–46).

61. "Indulge your desires" (Persius, *Satires*, V, 151).

62. "Homely" here means "natural."

63. The second cause is the parable itself, while the first cause of David's repentance is the will of God.

64. Psalm 50, in which David prays for the remission of his sins.

65. "These things I remember, that the conquered Thyrsis contended in vain. Henceforth Corydon, Corydon is ours" (Virgil, *Eclogues*, VII, 69–70).

66. Although the Latin elegy was defined by its special meter, elegiac poets very often wrote on amorous themes (as in Ovid's *Amores*). In English poetry the metrical distinction was lost, the association with love was partially retained (as in Donne's *Elegies*), though the limits of the genre were expanded to include any serious poem on love or death.

67. Aristotle (*Poetics*, IV) associates verse in iambic meters with lower types of poetry, particularly with satire and invective. By "wholesome" Sidney means "usefully corrective."

68. This quotation is adapted from Persius' description (*Satires*, I, 116–17) of Horace's satirical method: Horace, "the rascal, probes his friend's every fault while making him laugh; once inside he toys with his most secret feelings."

69. With a firm and even mind one can achieve happiness even in an out-of-the-way town like Ulubrae" (rendered freely) (Horace, *Epistles*, I, xi, 30).

70. "In the mill," where recalcitrant slaves were punished with hard labor.

71. Passions or affections.

72. "The cruel tyrant who rules with harsh authority fears those who fear him, and fear returns upon its author" (slightly misquoted from Seneca, *Oedipus*, III, 705–6).

73. A fiddler. The crowd is an ancient Welsh stringed instrument.

74. According ot Plutarch (*Life of Alexander*, III), Philip of Macedon received news of a victory in battle, a winner at the race track in Olympia, and the birth of Alexander, all on the same day.

75. *Aeneid*, II, 705 ff. By "ceremonies" Sidney means religious objects.

76. "Better than Chrysippus and Crantor" (Horace, *Epistles*, I, ii, 4).

77. The poet does not simply derive his concepts from external nature ("matter"); rather, he generates ideal conceptions in his own mind and then sets them forth in concrete characters and events of his own invention.

78. Spleen was regarded during the Renaissance as the physiological basis for whimsical or capricious feelings, variously interpreted as the source of laughter, melancholy, or ill temper.

79. Adapted from Ovid, *Ars Amatoria*, II, 662. Sidney's Latin and his English translation ("that good lie hid in nearness of the evil") invert Ovid's original: *Et lateat vitium proximitate boni* ("And let its proximity to a virtue disguise a fault"). For a particularly humorous, if also vicious, application of the Ovidian tag, see Donne's *Elegy*, II, "The Anagram."

80. "A scorner seeketh wisdom, and findeth it not" (Proverbs 14:6).

81. Accent.

82. "Shun the inquisitive man, for he is a talker" (Horace, *Epistles*, I, xviii, 69).

83. "While each of us pleases himself, we are a credulous crew" (Ovid, *Remedium Amoris*, 686).

84. To plough.
85. *The Knight's Tale*, 1. 28. Sidney is alluding to the words, but not the sense, of Chaucer's phrase.
86. "To beg the question."
87. The poet never uses magic to charm his readers into accepting falsehoods. Fulke Greville (*Caelica*, LXXVII, 9) speaks of "Circles to enthrall Mens hearts."
88. These are fictitious names equivalent to our John Doe.
89. *Eikastike* ("imitative," the creation of a perfect likeness) and *phantastike* ("fanciful," the creation of a semblance) are terms which appear in Plato's *Sophist*, 235–36. The distinction between likenesses and mere semblances leads to the conclusion that artists and sophists do not create perfect images of things, but deal with fanciful illusions, at two removes from the truth. In Sidney's usage, however, the terms are not used to explain the proximity of images to their models, but to make a moral distinction between "figuring forth good things" and presenting "unworthy objects."
90. Medicine.
91. Rampart or fortification.
92. Albion was an ancient name for Britain.
93. "I readily bid him to be a fool" (adapted from Horace, *Satires*, I, i, 63).
94. A piece of armor designed to protect the torso.
95. This is a reference to Plutarch, *Moralia* (*On The Fortune or The Virtue of Alexander*), where Alexander's virtues, and not his good fortune, determine the course of events.
96. Even if Plutarch had not spoken for him.
97. Plutarch, in his *Life of Alexander*, VII–VIII, relates that Philip of Macedon gave Aristotle a good wage to tutor his son, Alexander. Plutarch adds that Alexander was very fond of Homer's *Iliad*, and considered the book a useful guide to military discipline.
98. The three Graces, personifying grace and beauty, are usually described as the daughters of Zeus. Sidney is making reference to Cato's reputed indifference to the fine arts.
99. Not enlisted in the army.
100. Sidney is referring to the alleged homosexuality in these works. Scaliger (*Poetices*, I, 2) makes the same charge.
101. This is probably an allusion to Plutarch's *Amatorius*, a discussion of erotic love which concludes in favor of heterosexuality.
102. Paul's clearest reference to poets occurs in his description of God to the Athenians (Acts 17:28): "For in him we live, and move, and have our being; as certain also of your own poets have said." Thomas Lodge points out that Paul had read Aratus of Cilicia (ca. 315–240 B.C.), whose astronomical poem, *Phaenomena*, was very popular in antiquity, and may be the subject of Paul's allusion. Lodge adds that Paul was also familiar with Epimenides, a poet and prophet of Crete, one of whose verses appears in Titus 1:12. Cook notes (p. 109) that the fourth poet is the dramatist Menander (342–291 B.C.), whose aphorism, "Evil communications corrupt good manners," appears in I Corinthians 15:33.
103. "Whose authority some barbarous and insensitive men wish to misuse in order to expel the poets from the state" (*Poetices*, I, 2). Scaliger is discussing the arguments against poets in Plato's *Republic*.
104. Sidney is referring to *Ion*. In his conclusion that Plato did not banish the poets from the state, Sidney is certainly wrong. He may be making the most of a difficult problem, or, as Gilbert suggests, he may be misinformed. For a modern treatment of the question, see Eric A. Havelock, *Preface to Plato* (1963).
105. "O Muse, remind me of the causes, what deity has been offended" (*Aeneid*, I,

8). Sidney is using the line in his own context, asking what the causes are for the present state of poetry in England.

106. A mountebank (literally "mount-on-bench") was an Italian variety of the quack doctor who regaled his audience with tricks and jests before peddling his medicines. In Ben Jonson's *Volpone*, which is situated in Venice, the dupe, Sir Politick Would-Be, describes the mountebanks as "the only knowing men of Europe" (II, ii, 9). In the same scene the treacherous Volpone impersonates a mountebank.

107. "Whose heart Titan has fashioned with finer earth" (adapted from Juvenal, *Satires*, XIV, 35).

108. Without wisdom. Pallas Athena was thought to be the personification of Wisdom.

109. "The orator is made, the poet born" (a tag of uncertain origin).

110. The laws that define a discipline or art.

111. The things imitated in any art.

112. Literally, "what it pleases"; any philosophical or theological question proposed for an exercise in disputation. The term is generally associated with scholastic philosophy.

113. "Whatever I try to say will turn into verse" (adapted from Ovid's *Tristia*, IV, x, 26).

114. Note the pun on "style."

115. Artlessly.

116. "Messenger." Most Renaissance critics thought of the role of the messenger as a device for reporting horrible events without actually portraying them on stage.

117. "From the egg" (Horace, *Ars Poetica*, 147).

118. Sidney is about to outline the plot of Euripides' *Hecuba*.

119. The end of comedy.

120. Tragi-comedy is a term usually applied to the type of play developed by Beaumont and Fletcher in the first decade of the seventeenth century. Fletcher, in his preface to *The Faithful Shepherdess* (ca. 1610), states that "A tragie-comedie is not so called in respect of mirth and killing, but in respect it wants deaths, which is inough to make it no tragedie, yet brings some neere it, which is inough to make it no comedie."

121. This is an allusion to the game of bowls. The balls used in bowls are not perfectly round, but have a bias which causes them to curve as they roll.

122. *Poetics*, V; and *Nicomachean Ethics*, IV, 8.

123. "Luckless poverty involves nothing more regrettable than that it makes men ridiculous" (Juvenal, *Satires*, III, 152–53).

124. Cf. The Song of Solomon 2:4.

125. *Energia* is a very specific kind of "energy." Aristotle (*Rhetoric*, III, 10 ff.) and Scaliger (*Poetices*, III, 26) both emphasize that *energia* (*efficacia* in Scaliger) is that quality in language which makes concepts or ideas clear. Puttenham compares *energia* with *enargia*. *Enargia* gives "glosse onely to a language"; it exploits those qualities in words which have auditory appeal. *Energia*, on the other hand, is designed to give "efficacie by sence"; it serves "the conceit onely." In other words, *energia* is conceptual clarity in language; a clarity which can result only from the poet's precise apprehension of his own "fore-conceit."

126. Nizolian paper-books were named after Marius Nizolius, an Italian lexicographer of the sixteenth century whose Ciceronian lexicon was widely known. Sidney's contempt for collecting and copying phrases from other authors, a process described and encouraged by Ascham, results from his conviction that poetry should express unique personal feelings.

127. Poets should read Cicero and Demosthenes for their wisdom and learning, and

not simply in order to collect elegant "figures and phrases." The slavish imitation of Cicero's style was common in the Renaissance, and earned the name of "Ciceronianism." Sidney's views on the matter are clear enough in a letter to his brother (*Works*, III, 132): "I never require great study in Ciceronianisme the chiefe abuse of Oxford."

128. "The man lives. He lives? Indeed, and he even comes into the Senate" (adapted from Cicero, *In Catilinam*, I, i, 2).

129. "Anger," with a possible pun on "collar."

130. From the Latin *similiter cadentia*, "similar cadences." The term describes the rhythmic effect achieved when consecutive sentences or phrases terminate with the same cadence (e.g., "he who works heartily, works worthily"). It can also mean "rhyme."

131. A deceiver; one who makes use of fallacious arguments.

132. Similes and comparisons add nothing to the substance of an argument, but simply make the ideas of the argument accessible. Accordingly, when a statement is already clear, the addition of "similitudes" is unwarranted.

133. *De Oratore*, II, i, 1 ff.

134. Sidney's argument derives from Aristotle, *Rhetoric*, II, 1.

135. Elaborately.

136. Slightly.

137. Impounded, as a stray animal.

138. "Mingled language" is a combination of two or more distinct langauges. It was a common objection among the Elizabethans that the mother tongue was inadequate; either because the native vocabulary made clarity, or eloquence, impossible, or because grammar and spelling were insufficiently standardized.

139. Compounds. Joseph Hall, *Vergidemiarum*, VI, i, 255–56, suggests that Sidney was copying the French in his habit of compounding words (e.g., "well-grounded"), though there was an equally strong classical precedent.

140. A dactyl, composed of an accented and two unaccented syllables (e.g., fórmŭlăte), is obviously easier to produce in languages abundant with words that have accented antepenultimate ("the last saving two") syllables.

141. "Slippery," referring to trisyllabic rhyme, as in *Old Arcadia*, VII

> Come *Dorus*, come, let songs thy sorrowes signifie:
> And if for want of use thy minde ashamed is,
> That verie shame with Love's high title dignifie.

142. "Motion" and "potion" are pronounced as trisyllables.

143. "What not?"

144. "The son of a freedman" (Horace, *Satires*, I, vi, 6).

145. "Descendant of Hercules" (of doubtful origin).

146. "If aught my songs can do" (Virgil, *Aeneid*, IX, 446).

147. A dolt.

148. Momus was the ancient god of mockery and censure.

149. It was commonly believed that Irish sorcerers used charms to exterminate rats. Cf. Shakespeare, *As You Like It*, III, ii, 185.

Jacopo Mazzoni
1548–1598

The controversy concerning the merits of Dante's *Divine Comedy* was one of the great literary quarrels of the sixteenth century in Italy, illustrating in a very practical manner the extent to which Italian critics labored in the thrall of a rigid Aristotelianism. Dante's *Comedy* was attacked for its supposed divergences from Aristotelian precepts, even though those precepts had originally been formulated with regard to tragedy. Jacopo Mazzoni's *On the Defense of the "Comedy" of Dante* stands as the most important of the defenses of Dante's works.

Mazzoni was a humanist and teacher of philosophy at Macerata, Pisa and Rome, and he took a superficial interest in the reform of the church. He composed his *Defense* in response to the work of Ridolfo Castravilla, who charged that Dante's work was not dramatic and that it lacked unity, clarity, and simplicity, as well as other Aristotelian virtues. Mazzoni's response consisted of an introduction, which is the theory of poetry for which he is primarily known, as well as specific rebuttals of Castravilla's charges.

In setting out a theory of poetry, Mazzoni is most concerned with its truth value, making much use of Plato's distinction between icastic and fantastic imitation. The icastic is simply an imitation of reality while the fantastic poet imitates in Mazzoni's words "according to the whim of his imagination." Mazzoni, in fact, constructs a classification of poetry in which these modes of imitation play a great role: dramatic-fantastic, narrative-fantastic, dramatic-icastic, and narrative-icastic. Mazzoni privileges the dramatic-fantastic as the "purest" form of imitation; he claims that the fantastic is proper to poetry. In doing so, he attempts to free poetry from the kind of naive emphasis upon "realism" which engendered so many of the attacks upon Dante. The object of poetry, says Mazzoni, is to create an "idol," which is credible and verisimilar but not necessarily an accurate reflection of reality. In this respect, Mazzoni is almost Neoplatonic in his concern with a "higher" poetic truth. At the same time, Mazzoni sufficiently broadens the notion of imitation in order to include narrative and lyric poems as imitative modes. Mazzoni is also conscious of the moral problems raised by poetry, and he insists upon what he calls the "civil faculty" of poetry.

The selections from *On the Defense of the* Comedy *of Dante*, translated by R.L. Montgomery, are reprinted by permission of Harcourt Brace Jovanovich, Inc. from *Critical Theory Since Plato*, edited by Hazard Adams

(New York: Harcourt Brace Jovanovich, 1971). © 1971 by Harcourt Brace Jovanovich, Inc.

ON THE DEFENSE OF THE COMEDY OF DANTE

FROM

INTRODUCTION AND SUMMARY

It is the common view of the philosophic schools that the arts and sciences have come to be distinct and different by means of individual and particular objects and subjects.... Some have supposed ... that the objects of the arts and sciences differ according to differences among things insofar as they are things. And from this they are constrained to admit two very extraordinary conclusions. The first is that metaphysics is a total science, that which considers, so to speak, universal being, and that the other arts and sciences are a part of it, because each one of these is a part of universal being. The other conclusion is that each particular art and science must have something for a subject which could not be the subject of another art or science.... Both these conclusions are false.... Following the Peripatetics,[1] I say, as they believe, that the arts and sciences derive their true and real distinctiveness from their objects, not insofar as they are things but insofar as they are knowable things, supposing that things can be said to be capable of being devised.... In the same way, the division of the objects of the senses is not apprehended through a classification of their qualities as such but by a classification of sensible things insofar as they are sensible.... By means of this discourse we can establish two firm conclusions. The first is that metaphysics is not a total science ... that is, it does not totally comprehend other sciences as its parts. But we can say that it is a special science distinct from all others by virtue of having an object quite different, in its mode of being known, from the objects of the other sciences. A nice corollary derives from this first conclusion, which is that the definition of poetics given by Mirandola and his followers—that poetics is that part of philosophy which deals with human actions insofar as they are imitable in verse, number, and harmony—is false and perhaps ridiculous. The second conclusion is that since the division of knowable things (and not of things) separates the sciences, it necessarily follows that the same things can be treated in diverse sciences under diverse modes of knowledge and consideration.... Therefore, just as the sciences are differentiated by their objects, not insofar as they are things but insofar as they are knowable, so the arts, of whatever sort they may be, are classified not by their objects insofar as they are things, but by their objects insofar as they are (I cannot say it otherwise if I wish to speak accurately) capable of being devised.

And because of this subject I find no doctrine more copious or sound than that taught by Plato in the tenth book of the *Republic,* therefore following his lead I say that there are three types of object and that they have three types of artifice, which as a result constitute three species of art. . . . They are "idea," "work," and "idol." The idea is the object of the ruling, or we might say governing arts. The work is the object of the fabricating arts. And the idol is the object of the imitative arts. Therefore the modes of the objects of the arts insofar as they are capable of being treated by artifice are three: the observable, the fabricable, the imitable. The arts which only contemplate things pertinent to some object are the ruling arts, and they are founded in the idea. Such is the art of horsemanship when it deals with the bridle. For the art of horsemanship does not consist in making the bridle but is concerned solely with the idea of how it must work and then prescribes to the rider the rules by which he must hold the bridle so as to guide the horse. The art which makes the bridle (which was first conceived by the ruling art) is that which has the work as object. So it is bridlemaking which fashions the work of the bridle, and that is all it does. The imitative arts are so named because they deal with the object only insofar as it is imitable; hence Plato said that they have the idol as object, which means a simulacrum or image of some other thing. Since, therefore, the same thing can be treated by different sciences under different modes of the knowable, then also the same thing can be submitted to different arts by different modes of artifice. And we have a clear example in the bridle which belongs to the art of horsemanship when considered in its idea, to the art of bridlemaking when made as a work, and to painting when imitated as an idol.

But there may be doubt as to the importance of distinguishing the imitative arts from the others. For it would seem that the fabricating arts also deserve the name of imitation, since each one imitates with its work the model of the idea conceived by the ruling art. As, for example, the art of bridlemaking conforms to the idea conceived by horsemanship. . . . I reply (as I said before) that the distinction between arts derives from their objects insofar as they are variously capable of being devised. Now the artifice of the work consists not only in representing the idea of the ruling art, but also serves other ends. And so we can say that bridlemaking forms the bridle in accordance with the idea conceived by horsemanship, but yet this bridle is not made in order to represent the similitude of the idea, but rather so that it can be used in the various ways of managing horses. Hence we see that the artifice of the fabricating arts takes its direction from another art whose sole aim is to represent and resemble; therefore I say that the fabricating arts cannot be called imitative. But those arts which have the idol as object, have an object with no other end in its artifice than to represent and resemble; hence they are justly called imitative. And just as philosophy has called the logical faculty rational, not because it uses reason—for in this sense all the arts and faculties are rational—but because it has an object which takes all its being from reason and in reason; so I say that the imitative arts are so named not because they use imitation—for in this sense all the arts are more or less some kind of imitation—but because they have objects which have no other existence or use except by reason of imitation or in imitation. This I believe is what Plato wished to show in the second book of the *Laws* where he said, "The rightness of an imitation consists in this, as we said, that it is made of such a nature and size that the imitation expresses the nature and size of the object itself."[2]. . .

In this way, therefore, the idol is the object of the imitative arts. . . . The idol . . . is an image and similitude of some other thing, and it can come into being, as Plato has taught us in the *Sophist* and in the sixth book of the *Republic*, either with or without our agency. And that which comes into being without human agency has its origin either in material things or in spiritual. Those which originate in material things are understood to be in that portion of visible being which Plato in the sixth book of the *Republic* calls obscure. And so that everyone may understand what I mean it must be remembered that Plato divides existing things into two species: one he called intelligible; the other, visible. And again he wished to subdivide both species into two parts, the clear and the obscure. Now he calls that portion of visible things clear which includes plants, animals, the heavens, the elements, and all complex and simple things. But about the obscure portion of the visible he has reasoned as follows: "A portion of the visible kind contains images, for I call images first shadows, then simulacra, which appear in water and in solid bodies as denseness, lightness, etc."[3]. . . I believe idols are of this species. . . .

Now coming to our proposition I say that when I earlier concluded that idols are the objects of the imitative arts, I did not refer to the sort of idols which originate without human artifice . . . but to those which do originate by our artifice, which are born only in our imagination and our intellect by means of our choice and will, as idols in painting, sculpture, and similar things. I conclude, then, that this species of idol is that which is a suitable object of human imitation and that when Aristotle says in the first chapter of the *Poetics* that all the species of poetry are imitation, he means that imitation which has for its object idols which derive totally from human artifice.[4] . . . But it appears that the words of Suidas are contrary to this proposition; he believes that idols which derive from human artifice are not suitable objects for the imitative arts, but that idols joined to a different thing, which he calls similitudes, are. Here are his words: "Idols are effigies of things which do not subsist, such as Tritons, Sphinxes, Centaurs. But similitudes are the images of things which do subsist, such as beasts and men."[5] According to this statement of Suidas, we have two sorts of imitation. One represents the true, as a painter does when he depicts with colors the effigy of a man who is known; and the other represents the caprice of the imitator, as the painter when he depicts according to the whim of his imagination; and we see at the same time that the idol is the object of this second sort of imitation and that the similitude is the object of the first. Therefore it is not true that the idol which derives from human artifice is a suitable object for every imitation.

I reply that that view of Suidas about idols is too restricted and also contrary to that held by other writers. . . . In addition, Plato in the *Sophist* has left a statement that there are two species of imitation, one of which he calls icastic, representing things which are truly found to exist, or at least have been found to exist; the other he calls fantastic, of which we have examples in paintings which are made according to the caprice of the artist. And moreover he himself says in the tenth book of the *Republic* that the idol is the object of every imitation.[6] Therefore, the idol is also common to fantastic imitation. . . . Now I add that under this sort of imitative art, or under this imitation, poetry ought to be placed, as a species under its genus. . . .

As for Aristotle, I believe that he establishes poetic imitation as an analogous genus which contains within itself four species. The first and most important is the dramatic-fantastic, which is imitation because it necessarily contains within itself two sorts of idol and image. One is that of the person represented [i.e., the actor]. The other is the false but verisimilar image which the actor represents, since he does not represent the literally true but the verisimilar; he therefore represents the idol or simulacrum of the true. The second species is dramatic-icastic imitation, which always necessarily contains the idol of a real person. The third species is narrative-fantastic imitation, which doubtless always includes the idol and simulacrum of the true, and may also have another feature, always found in narrative-icastic imitation, which we will consider now. The fourth and last species is narrative-icastic poetry which contains those idols and images consisting in particularization.[7] . . . I add that even if Aristotle has indeed called all four species of poetry imitation, nevertheless when he compares dramatic and narrative imitation, he considers dramatic more worthy of the name of imitation, to the extent that he sometimes calls narrative the otiose part of the poem and not imitation; but this must always be understood to hold in [the context of] comparison with dramatic poetry, and not absolutely. . . .

Now coming to Plato I say that he also has in some places denied that narrative poetry is imitation. . . . Yet he also has maintained that narrative poetry is not imitation when compared with dramatic representation, but one ought not to conclude from this that speaking absolutely he believes that poetic narration is not imitation. And moreover I say that he himself in the *Sophist* has said that narrative is imitation.[8] . . .

As for narrative-icastic poetry, I say that the poet is also obliged to imitate, which he does rightly if he sets out to describe anything in a most particular manner. Therefore in this fashion also idols and images are made suitable to narrative. . . . I conclude therefore that poetic narration is also the icastic form of idols and images and is consequently imitation by means of particularization. . . . I believe it is likely that when Plato differentiated narrative poetry from imitation, he meant that compared to dramatic representation it did not merit the name of imitation. . . . But we ought not, because of that, assert that speaking absolutely poetic narration is not in some fashion imitative, also according to the concept of Plato. It can therefore be understood as a firm and fixed conclusion that the genus of poetry is imitation and so consequently all species of poetry make idols and images in the way already mentioned. And because the rightness of imitation . . . consists in the precise representation of things, it then follows that a fundamental error in poetics would be to represent by distortion or dissimilarity. . . . For this reason it seems that Plato in the second book of the *Republic* thinks that Homer erred fundamentally in his imitation by representing many most ugly vices of the gods and heroes when he ought to have done just the opposite by representing with proper imitation the divine and heroic natures.[9] ... It is also a fact that Proclus has justified the distortions through which poets ascribe many vices to the gods on the grounds that they were writing allegories.[10] ...

We can now discuss the subject and material proper to poetry. In the opinion of many they are falsehood and lies, but that when these are verisimilar they are an adequate subject for poetry. And they let themselves be persuaded to believe this because they think that the true poet is he who derives his poem from his own invention, adding that whoever takes his subject from somewhere other than his own invention does not deserve the name of a true poet. They also believe that this was Aristotle's view when he called Empedocles more a natural philosopher than a poet because he sought to expound the truth of natural things in verse, rather than to expound his own invention.[11] ... It also seems that Plato supported this view in the *Phaedo* when he said, "He who hopes to be a poet ought not only to put together words, but also to compose." Plutarch, in the little book where he asks whether the Athenians have acquired greater glory through arms or letters, writes as follows:

> They say also that one of the friends of Menander said to him, "The feasts of Bacchus are approaching; have you not made a comedy?" And Menander replied, "I have made a comedy, for I have discovered the fable and given it its order. All that remains is to add the verse." For poets believe the fable to be more essential than the words. Corinna said to Pindar when he was still young and boldly using his eloquence, that he was ignorant of poetics because he put no fables in his writings, which is the proper work of a poet.

And Plutarch adds, "It is certain also that Plato himself wrote that the occupation of poetry is the composition of fables."[12]

On the basis of all these authorities and many others, one could easily fall in with the view of those who say that poetry has no other subject but the fabulous and false, though joined to the verisimilar, since according to the rule of Aristotle, verisimilitude is required in the fables of poets. Nevertheless I say that this opinion is not correct for many reasons, some of which I shall select as they come to mind. ... Consider first that the false verisimilar occurs in some other arts which are different from poetry, as in rhetoric. ... And in this respect I recall having read a very fine dialogue by Signor Camillo Paleotti ... in which he ... shows ... that the false verisimilar is greatly abused by the corrupt world in that it is a nearly universal subject of the arts, sciences, and education. Therefore it cannot be concluded that it is a fit and adequate subject of the poet's art. For if this were the true subject of poetry, it would mean that poetry could not in any way be capable of truth, and yet Plato writes, and Aristotle confirms, and reason convinces us, that quite the contrary is so. Therefore Plato in the *Republic* and the *Laws*, having approved that kind of poetry that deals with the gods in accordance with the truth, showed that as a consequence the truth is not alien to poetry.[13] Likewise Aristotle has confirmed this conclusion in three places in the *Poetics*.[14] ... In all three places, and especially in the last, we see plainly that Aristotle concedes that poetry sometimes has the true for its subject, and we see that because of all that has been said above, the idols of icastic imitation are, according to Aristotle, poetic idols.

But besides the authority of Plato and Aristotle, there is also reason which proves that the poet sometimes speaks the truth, for in narrating the wanderings of certain heroes, he often could not help but describe the location of cities. When the poet adheres to geographical truth, it must be said that either he forfeits the name of poet for the time being (which is completely ridiculous) or we must confess that sometimes the true can be a poetic subject. And we have already shown that idols and images can be made from true things, both narratively and dramatically. According to all these considerations we ought to affirm two conclusions as true. The first is that the false is not always necessarily the subject of poetry. The second is that, since the subject of poetry is sometimes the true and sometimes the false, it is therefore necessary to establish a poetic subject that in itself can be sometimes true and sometimes false.[15]

Therefore it seems that we ought to reject that point of view which seemed to prove that poetic subjects are always false. . . .

Now if we remove the false and accept the true in its place, we do not thereby destroy poetry, since we have already said that it can tolerate the true. The same can be said of the possible, because if in poetry we put the impossible in its place, it does not by this become either improved or deficient. But if the credible is removed and the incredible put in its place, the nature of poetry is totally destroyed. And on the other hand whoever takes the credible and totally removes the possible, nevertheless has a poetic subject, as Aristotle has clearly testified: "For in what belongs to poetry the credible impossible is preferable to the incredible and possible."[16] Therefore it should be said that among all the subjects for poetry there is none more proper than the credible, and all the more because by its nature the credible contains both the true and the false, since many times not only the true but also the false is credible.[17] . . . And therefore I think that the credible is a subject correlative to belief, that is, to persuasion or faith. And belief, generally speaking, is an aspect of conclusions, as are opinion and knowledge. But knowledge derives from necessary causes, which cannot be said of opinion or of faith, which have contingent causes. Therefore it is plain that all the difficulty lies in knowing how to recognize the difference between opinion and belief. . . .

First I say that pesuasion concentrates on the particular as its instrument and means for proving its conclusions. And therefore it makes use of enthymemes and examples, both of which are lacking in universal propositions. . . . The means of proving conclusions are particulars, and they are ordinarily drawn from sensible objects. . . . And please note that I am speaking of belief and faith which originate in human arguments and not those founded in divine revelation. Hence we see that persuasion and belief concern the particular. But opinion always concerns the universal. This refers to the way of proving a conclusion rather than to the conclusion itself, for I am quite well aware that opinion can be about the conclusion of some particular emotion which is involved in some particular subject. But still I say that the means by which one attempts to prove a conclusion are universal. . . . Persuasion derives from those things which can move not just the intellect but also the appetite. This is to say that persuasion, deriving from particular and sensible means, therefore derives from things which can also move the appetite; but opinion, deriving from universal types, therefore derives from things which do not have the power to move the appetite. . . . In infinite questions, in which natural things are treated in a persuasive way, there is produced in the human mind conviction alone without any stirring of the appetite. But whenever moral matters are involved in the same infinite questions and are primarily under the jurisdiction of good and bad, one cannot convince the human intellect without some stirring of the appetite, as the following example illustrates: As to whether one ought to choose a beautiful or an ugly wife, it is clear that many things could be said on both sides of the question which would have the power to stir the appetite, even if by its nature the question is infinite.[18] Therefore, when Cicero says that infinite questions have as their end a conviction which must be chosen, he means that in all inifinite questions treated in a persuasive manner there is always this end. But he does not absolutely deny that sometimes in infinite questions the stirring of the soul has a place. With these considerations in mind, it can be concluded that the second difference, that between opinion and persuasion, is that persuasion can be derived from things which have the power to move the appetite. I say "can be derived" because it is not always so, as is seen in infinite questions about natural things which are treated in a persuasive way that is with sensible and particular means. But opinion derives from things which cannot ever stir the appetite, for they are universals. Therefore the credible is the object of the kind of persuasion I have just now discussed.

And because we have already concluded, with the authority of Aristotle, that the credible is the subject of the poet's art, it seems that from what has been said we can establish three conclusions. The first is that because the poet always deals with the credible, he ought as a consequence to treat everything in a way consistent with credibility, that is, he ought always necessarily to use individual and sensible means to represent the things about which he writes, whatever they may be. And when he treats things pertinent to contemplative doctrine, he ought to make every effort to represent them with idols and sensible simulacra, which Empedocles did not do.[19] He was therefore said to be a physicist more often than a poet. But in this respect Dante is certainly magnificent, as I will show more fully in the fifth book. For now we can be content with this single example in which, speaking of the holy and ineffable Trinity, he writes:

> In the profound and clear being of the exalted light there appeared to me three turning wheels of three colors and a single extent. And the one seemed reflected from the other, as rainbow from rainbow, and the third seemed a flame breathing equally from the one and from the other.[20]

And for this reason it happens that the poet frequently uses comparison and long, distinct parables. And whoever asks why the poet is at least obligated to use this mode of the credible in his narrative must be satisfied with the following answer: the poet must speak to the people, among whom are many vulgar and ill-educated men, and therefore if he should present knowledge in a fashion suited to the sciences, they would not understand him. For this reason he treats things in a credible fashion, that is, he teaches them by means of comparisons and similitudes taken from sensible things. And the people, who know that truth resides in sensible things as they are treated by the poet, easily believe that the same is true of intelligible things.

From this we can conclude that the poet is not forbidden to deal with things pertinent to the sciences and to the speculative intellect if he deals with them in credible manner, fashioning poetic idols and images, as Dante with most marvelous and noble art has presented the whole of intellectual being and the intelligible world itself to the eyes of everyone by means of idols and most beautiful images. I recall that in the *Phaedrus* Plato, exalting his own invention, wrote thus: "But none of the poets has ever treated or ever will treat the place above the heavens as it should be treated." But if he had seen the third canticle of Dante, he would doubtless have acknowledged the inferiority of his own invention and given the palm to Dante, and therefore to the poets for knowing how to make idols and images appropriate to bringing the people to understand the quality of the supercelestial world. . . .

The second conclusion is that since the poet's subject is the credible, he ought therefore to place the credible in opposition to the true, the false, the possible, and the impossible; that is to say, he ought to rely more on the credible than on any of the others mentioned. Hence if by chance two things should be available to him, one false but credible and the other true but incredible (or at least scarcely credible), then the poet ought entirely to leave the true aside and follow the credible.

The third and last conclusion, which is almost a corollary to the two preceding, is that poetry, by relying more on the credible than on the true, ought to be classified under the rational faculty, which the ancients called sophistic. And to entirely understand this truth, which, if I am not mistaken, has up to now remained obscure, it must be known that the poetic art can be regarded as two modes: according as it concerns the laws of the poetic idol or according as it makes and forms the idol.

I say that the first mode ought to be called poetic and the second "poetry." According to the first mode, poetic is an art which governs the idol and uses it and is part of the civil faculty,[21] as we will show presently.

According to the second mode the poetic art is that which forms and fabricates the idol and is a species of the rational faculty; and, as I have said, it is to be classified under sophistic, since it disregards the truth. But I recognize that I have offended the poets by giving their art, which until now has been considered divine, the title of sophistic, which is considered ugly and infamous. Therefore to console them some, I wish to pause a bit over the art of the sophists and at the same time show where it possesses good and where evil views. . . . Sophistic was that which treated all things rhetorically, that is credibly, and which certainly argued somewhat boastfully about its propositions and chose feigned subjects, such as Orestes or Alcmaeon, imitating them both together and representing them by means of idols. That this representation by idols and images was proper to the sophistic art is clearly shown by Plato in the *Sophist* where he uses the term *eidōlopoiētikēn*, or fabricator of images, as that which represents what appears to be true. This is also confirmed by Alexander Aphrodisias in his commentary on the *Elenches* of Aristotle. Philostratus . . . wishing to prove that Prodicus of Ceos was also a sophist shows that he made a book in which he dealt with one thing pertinent to moral philosophy by means of idols and images, that is, the appetites for virtue and vice which in the young man struggle for supremacy.

> And for this reason Prodicus of Ceos wrote a pleasant speech in which virtue and vice appeared to Hercules in feminine form. Vice was adorned and variously colored and Virtue was as chance found her. They made obvious offers to the young Hercules. Vice offered ease and softness and Virtue hardship and fatigue.[22]

It seems to me then that it is reasonable to say that poetry should be classified under the ancient form of sophistic, since it also treats things credibly and speaks with such audacity that it claims by means of the Muse and Apollo to know all things. Certainly Hesiod as a poet has the lofty arrogance to suggest that in an instant he learned all things past, present, and future; for this reason I am delighted with the opinion of a very learned commentator on the *Poetics* who believes that it is entirely inappropriate for the poet to use words or ways of speaking in any fashion that might cast doubt on the things he says. For since he professes credibility above all, he ought to recount everything with great assurance and boldness. For this reason as well the poet deserves the name of sophist. But even more he deserves it because he is a maker of idols and images. . . .

Philostratus also says that the old sophists spoke freely of the gods and heroes, a subject firmly considered proper to poets. Therefore by this also we can conclude that poetry is a species of old sophistic. But to understand perfectly everything pertinent to this subject it is necessary to know all the other kinds of sophistic and then to see which are appropriate to poetry and which are not. . . . Old sophistic was not essentially different from the second sophistic, except that the old used fictitious names and the second used real names. Hence it can be said that icastic poetry is a species of the second sophistic and fantastic poetry a species of old sophistic. Now I believe that everyone is capable of understanding that Philostratus thought that the sophistic art set aside the true to concern itself with the credible and that he thought it worthy and noble, not vile and infamous, as Boethius preferred to label it, and perhaps also Plato and Aristotle. But in order to reconcile those authors who censure and those who praise sophistic, it must be understood that sophistic was assumed to deviate in some way from the rules of genuine philosophy. Now genuine philosophy is accustomed to direct the intellect by means of truth and the will by means of the good. Therefore sophistic, which is totally the opposite of genuine philosophy, is accustomed to mislead the intellect by means of the false and the will by means of evil. This was the sort of sophistic censured by Plato, Aristotle, and all their followers, and it appears that Plato sought to include the poetry of Homer in this species of sophistic, as that which misled the intellect by representing falsehoods about the gods and heroes and which misled the will by the variety of its imitation and by stirring up our passions immoderately. . . . And therefore it can be said that any other poetry similar to Homer's may be classified under the sophistic censured by that philosopher. . . .

Therefore one species of sophistic censured by the philosophers is that which misleads the intellect by the false and the will by injustice. Likewise under that sophistic they classify that sort of poetry which produces the same disorders and which does not truly deserve the name of poetry since it does not form its idols in conformity with the laws of poetry for governing and using idols.

The other species of sophistic is that which Philostratus called the old sophistic and which, thought it does offer feigned things to the intellect, does not mislead the will, but wholly and in every way tries to make it conform to what is just. And this species of sophistic was not censured by the ancients. And if it should seem to anyone that it deserved blame for misleading the intellect by some falsehood, I say it must be understood that the ancient philosophers (in this respect they were out of step with the truth of sacred theology) praised this distortion in certain instances when it was directed to an honest end. So Plato allowed his magistrates to lie to his citizens for the purpose of some public good. I leave out the fact that this kind of sophistic almost always contained some truth under the surface of first appearances. Now I say that fantastic poetry regulated by proper rules is part of the old sophistic, since it also submits feigned things to our intellect to control the appetite and many times contains the truth of many noble concepts under the surface of the fiction.

The third species of sophistic is what Philostratus called the second sophistic which does not propose feigned names or business, but true names and real events, upon which it discourses according to the laws of justice. . . . And this species is also called sophistic because even though it dealt with truth for the sake of justice, it nevertheless dealt with it in a credible way; hence it sometimes departed from truth when it recognized that falsehood was a more credible or a more effective instrument in pesuading. . . . In my judgment icastic poetry ought to be classified under this third species of sophistic, for it represents true actions and people, though always in a credible way.

Therefore according to everything I have said about sophistic I believe that everyone can understand fundamentals of the view that poetry is a rational faculty and that among the rational faculties it ought not to be classified with that which seeks to teach the truth and which opposes the truth to all other things, but under that which exerts its full force to seek out credible appearances and which opposes them to the truth. . . .

I conclude then with assurance that poetry is a sophistic art: because of imitation, which is its proper genus; because of the credible, which is its subject; and because of delight, which is its end. Also, because it is under that genus, because it has that subject, and because it concentrates on that end, poetry is many times forced to find a place for the false. . . . And therefore the credible is the subject of poetry. But because it is also the subject of rhetoric, it is still necessary to see in what mode the credible can become suitable to poetry and in what mode suitable to rhetoric, since we do not wish to fall into the error of those who prefer the verisimilar and false. I say, then, that the credible, insofar as it is marvelous, is the subject of poetry, because the poet must not only utter credible things but also marvelous things. Thus, when he can do so credibly, he falsifies human and natural history and passes on to impossibilities.[23] . . . If there were presented to the poet two things equally credible, but one more marvelous than the other, even though it were false, but not impossible, that is what the poet ought to choose, rejecting the other.

But perhaps there is some doubt that the credible and marvelous can be found together with the true. And perhaps it can be thought that it was poorly expressed above, that poetry is sometimes capable of truth. I reply that there are some truths which are sometimes more marvelous than the false, not only in the natural world . . . but also in human history. . . . On this topic there remains only to deal with those authorities who seem to prove that the false, insofar as it is verisimilar, is the subject of poetry. I say then in the first place that it is true that Aristotle remarked that Empedocles was more a physicist than a poet.[24] And this was confirmed by Plutarch in his book on listening to poetry in these words: "We do not know of any poetry without fables and fictions. For the verses of Empedocles and Parmenides, the *Theriaca* of Nicander, and the sayings of Theognis are more often treatises which to avoid the baseness of prose took on the grandeur and rhythm of poetry as vehicles."[25] Now as for Aristotle, there are two ways of responding. The first is that he did say that Empedocles was more a physicist than a poet, but he did not say absolutely that Empedocles was not a poet, and thus, in affirming that he was more physicist than poet, he was in some way a poet, since, as the grammarians say, the comparative supports the positive.

The second way of responding to Aristotle is that it can be said . . . that Empedocles did not deserve the name of poet, not because he dealt with truth (for it has already been shown that poetry is capable of the truth) but because he dealt scientifically with things pertaining to the sciences, where he would be obliged, were he a poet, to treat them credibly, that is by making idols and images and joining to them a way of instructing the sensitive powers more often than the intellect. As for Plutarch, I say that he speaks either of the true and perfect poet who (as I have said) ought sooner to be placed under fantastic rather than icastic imitation; or, truly, what is apparently opposite to the views of Aristotle and Plato, that is that poetry has nothing at all to do with the truth. . . . To the text of Aristotle, in which he writes that the history of Herodotus spread out in verse would always be history and thus unworthy of the name of poetry, we reply that it is true: but it does not follow that history cannot in some way be a poem when it represents the marvelous as credible by means of idols and particularized images. But when it narrates in a way suited to history without making idols and images, even if displayed in verse, it always remains history. . . . Also the true can be improved by narrating it in conformity with the credible and by making idols and images of it. And for this reason I believe that icastic poetry, which takes its truth from history, can nevertheless on that account make many things its own by rendering that history in exact particulars.

As for the authority of Plato in the *Phaedo*, I say that he has written of fantastic poetry which always has a fabulous subject or creates a fictitious one or falsifies true history. And therefore he says that the poet merits his name more for inventing his fable than for inventing his verses. Or it could be said that he finds a fable at the heart of each invention which is suited to poems and calls it a fable because thereby these subjects are more like the false and fabulous. But it ought to be said because of this that Plato does not believe that the true can be a poetic subject since in many other places he says quite the contrary. . . .

Summing up then what has been said above about the subject of poetry: it ought to be credible and at the same time marvelous; and linking this subject to the form which has already been made manifest, we can now say that poetry is an imitation made with harmony, rhythm, and verse joined to or accompanied by the credible and marvelous. . . .

To discover a cause peculiar to poetry with some assurance, I believe that there is no more certain way than to consider what that art is that reveals the use of poetry, because this, if I am not mistaken, will show us the origin and end of poetry. Hence I believe that the civil faculty is that which shows not only the use of poetry, but next considers the standards and rules for the poetic idol. I am drawn to this view by the following consideration, namely, that all natural forces and arts which derive from human reason are usually directed towards contrary objects, as for example medicine, which not only deals with health and health-giving potions but also with sickness and deadly potions. And so we can say that the legal profession also is one which comprehends not only justice but also injustice.

Now given these considerations, I say that the civil faculty professes to understand not only the propriety of human actions but also the propriety of the cessation of these actions, which is opposite to the first propriety, as deprivation is to habit. But because someone might suspect that the habits of our intellect and of human arts are concerned only with positive contrariety, and not the negative, I therefore suggest that the positive and the negative are always the concern of the same art. As, for example, the natural philosopher not only considers the contrariety of motion insofar as it is positive, that is, the contrariety which is found in motion according to which it moves either upwards or downwards; but also he considers the negative contrariety which is implied in motion, and is its cessation, that is, stasis. Also zoology deals not only with the contrariety of difference which makes different species, but also with negative contrarieties, such as life and death. . . . But the cessation of activity . . . ought to dispose and prepare men so that they are more apt and eager for renewed acitvity. Therefore the same faculty will provide the law of activity and of its cessation. And please note that I do not take cessation as total negation but as cessation of important and difficult activities. And so in the above meaning of cessation we include activities of pleasure and amusement which we engage in for recreation and entertainment. Thus it can be said that the contrariety either of activity or of cessation is not just negative . . . but also positive. It is negative insofar as cessation means an absence of important activity. It is positive insofar as the cessation of important activity contains some pleasant activity apt to restore the spirits tired out by some more serious business. . . .

Thus it seems to me that it can be firmly stated that, since this contrariety of cessation and activity is both negative and positive, it ought to be considered as part of one art and by one faculty. But the civil faculty is that which is concerned with the propriety of activity; therefore it ought also to be concerned with the propriety of cessation. In this are contained, as I have said, all activities done for amusement, that is, everything which gives pleasure. Therefore consideration of the legitimacy of pleasures will no doubt be pertinent in some way to the civil faculty and to moral philosophy. But of all the pleasures there is none more worthy, more noble, or more primary than that given by the works of poets. Therefore the civil faculty should take care to consider the norm and legitimacy of the pleasure of poetry first before all others. Now the fact that poetry was thought a pleasure by the ancients is shown . . . by the authority of Virgil, Horace, Timocles the comic poet, Plato in the tenth book of the *Republic*, and in the fifth book of the *Laws*, and Eusebius of Caesarea in the twelfth book of his *Evangelical Preparations*. . . .

All these considerations, it seems to me, make it reasonable to say that the civil faculty ought to be divided into two main parts, one of which deals with the principles of activity and has been given the general name of politics, or civil affairs. The other deals with the principles of cessation, or the law of recreation, and has been called poetics. And for this reason I believe that the *Poetics* is the ninth book of the *Politics*, and this belief of mine seems to me all the more reasonable because Aristotle in the eighth book of the *Politics* already begins to discuss music and the first principles of poetry so that step by step he may come to discuss the management of the civil faculty. So I can say that the first seven books of the *Politics* deal with the civil faculty in action and the last two (so to speak) deal with the civil faculty at rest, which we have just named poetics.

And therefore poetic is part of the civil faculty and is that which prescribes the norms, the rules, and the laws of the poetic idol for poetry. So that one may say that poetic deals with the concept of the idol, and poetry makes the idol. Hence in its genus poetic is the art governing and using the idol made by poets. . . . And poetry in its genus is the fabricating art of the idol which then is used by poetics and the civil faculty. Therefore we can add the efficient cause to what was written above relative to the definition of poetry and say: Poetry is an imitation made with harmony, number, and verses accompanied by and joined with credible or marvelous things which have been discovered by the civil faculty. . . .

I say then that many people would find it most unusual (and with good reason) if one should ask writers whether delight or utility were the end of poetry. For if it is true that poetry is an imitative art, and that each imitative art has the idol as its object, and that idol . . . is of value only through representing and resembling, then it appears to me that one must say that poetry has no other aim than to represent and resemble. Therefore it is not reasonable to inquire whether the aim of poetry is to be useful or delightful. I suggest that if the aim of poetry were to be useful or delightful, it would not be an imitative art. . . .

Now it ought to be known that, as Aristotle has said in the tenth book of the *Ethics*, delight is an accident belonging to some activities, and among others it is no doubt quite natural to imitation, since it appears to be joined to imitation in such a way that no kind of imitation can be found that does not also give delight and pleasure.[26]. . . Since, then imitation is always allied to delight, it has therefore happened that those who have wished to devise entertainments and amusements have created some sort of imitation. . . . We can cite the game of primero in which is represented the image of an ochlochracy, that is, the kind of republic in which the common people are more powerful than the nobles. For as in this sort of republic the nobles are weak and the common people are strong, so in the game the noblest cards, commonly called court cards, are the least valuable and of smaller worth than the other cards which because of their ignobility the common people have come to call *cartaccie* ["waste paper"]. Now since in this game imitation can be considered for its own sake and in this case has no other purpose than to represent the image of an ochlochracy, and since entertainments and amusements can be considered in such a way that we recognize no other ends for them than delight and pleasure; so I say that poetry can likewise be thought of as an imitative art, and as amusement and entertainment. In the first instance it has as its aim the precision of the idol, that is, that things be imitated properly. But in the second instance it concentrates on the aims of delight and pleasure which are joined to good and perfect imitation. I conclude, therefore, that poetry as an imitative art has the precision of the idol for its aim, but as a thing to be used for amusement and recreation and to effect some cessation of more serious and strict business, it proposes delight as its aim, which derives from suitable imitation. Now this delight which poetry effects can be considered in two modes, tht is, either for itself alone, free and without laws; or insofar as it is subordinate to and regulated by the civil faculty. In the first mode is the aim of that sort of poetry which was gathered under sophistic and is worthy of blame since it is such that it disorders the appetite with immoderate pleasure and makes it in every way rebellious to reason and also causes damage and harm to virtuous living.

This is the sort of poetry which Plato drove out of his republic. . . .

If, then, we are to reason about the aim of this sort of poetry, we can certainly say that as an imitative art it should have the precision of the idol as its aim, but that as amusement it has only pleasure as its aim. But if this delight is considered insofar as it is regulated and given its quality by the civil faculty, it is necessary to say that it should be directed towards the useful. Consequently that kind of poetry which was classified under praiseworthy sophistic (this is, the sort which regulates the appetite and subordinates it to reason) would be considered as amusement qualified by the civil faculty and would have the useful for its end. . . .

Now without any doubt I believe that, as regards the aim of poetry, this is true: that perfect poetry considers delight for the purpose of utility. . . . I say then that true poetry is amusement and receives its quality from the civil faculty and insofar as it is amusement it has delight for its aim. But insofar as it receives its quality from and, so to speak, is given its character by moral philosophy, it places delight first and gives us profit afterwards. . . . .

But now to come to the end of this definition, I think that it would be well to assemble in a brief epilogue everything mentioned above concerning the final cause of poetry. I say therefore that since the tongue is always an instrument of the concupiscible power and has gratification as its aim, but that nevertheless when it is considered as an instrument of the irascible power, its end is the defense of the animal soul, and that when it is considered as an instrument of the rational power, its aim is speech; so in the same way poetry is always an imitative art, and as such its end is always to represent the images of things directly. But nevertheless considered as recreation deriving its quality from the civil faculty, its aim is delight, but directed towards utility. From this premise it seems to me that we can conclude that poetry will admit of three definitions, according as it is thought of in three ways: as imitation, as pure enjoyment, or as enjoyment deriving its quality from the civil faculty.

In the first mode perhaps it can be defined thus: Poetry is an imitative art made with verses, number, and harmony accompanied with or joined to the credible marvelous and devised by the human intellect for the suitable representation of the images of things.

In the second mode perhaps this second definition will serve: Poetry is an imitative recreation made with verses, number, and harmony accompanied by or joined with the credible marvelous and devised by the human intellect for delight. . . .

The third mode perhaps amidst of this last definition: Poetry is an imitative recreation made with verses, number, and harmony accompanied by or joined to the credible marvelous and devised by the civil faculty to delight the people usefully. . . .

From these three definitions follow necessarily four corollaries. The first is that poetry understood in the first mode is not regulated or governed by the civil faculty. The second corollary is that only poetry understood in the third mode is that which is regulated and governed by moral philosophy and the civil faculty. The third corollary is that poetic, which considers the idol belonging to the first mode and at the same time considers the idol of the second mode, ought not in any way to be called a part of moral philosophy. The fourth and last corollary is that only the poetic which deals with the idol of the third mode of poetry is that which is worthy to be named part of the civil faculty, according to the rules of which each good poet ought to fashion his poem, as indeed Dante has done better than all the others. . . .

FROM

BOOK I

I say, then, that the fantasy is the power of the soul common to dreams and to poetic verisimilitude. But because my opponents do not doubt of what I too believe, that the fantasy is the power upon which the dream is founded (which

Aristotle said many times and which has been repeated more often by his followers), it is therefore well to explain that poetic verisimilitude is also based on the same power. The verisimilitude which is sought by the poet is of such a nature that it is feigned by poets according to their own will. Therefore it is necessary that it should be fashioned by that power which has the virtue of forming concepts in accordance with the will. Now this power cannot in any way be intellectual, for the intellectual power is necessary in producing concepts in accordance with the nature of objects. Hence the subtle Scotus in many places in his *Sentences* says that the intellect is a capacity more natural than free. Therefore it is necessary that the power fitted to generate verisimilar concepts dependent upon the will be the power of the phantasy, called by the Latins *imaginative*. And all that we have said was stated first by Aristotle in the second book of *De Anima*:

> It is in our power to imagine not only things which can be, but also those which cannot, such as men with three heads and three bodies, as Geryon in the fables is supposed to have been, and as men with wings, like Zetes and Calais the sons of Boreas, and the Centaurs and Scylla and Charybdis. For in whatever way a painter may depict an animal of any form, so it is possible to create it in the mind. In addition when we think that some formidable and fearful calamity may occur, we immediately dismiss our courage and our whole body trembles, we shake, and we grow pale.... But when we build these things in our mind (as when we imagine terrifying earthquakes and the fierce aspects of wild beasts), we are not affected at all, no consternation follows, and just as paintings do not affect us, neither do visions nor those figments which we willfully gather together. From this we can distinguish imagination from opinion and apprehension.[27]

Therefore if I am not mistaken we can clearly see that the fantasy is the proper power of the poetic fable, since it alone is capable of those fictions which we ourselves are able to create. From this it follows necessarily that poetry is composed of feigned and imagined things, because it is based in the fantasy.

NOTES

1. Followers of Aristotle.
2. *Laws*, II. 668. Jowett translates this passage: "And the truth of an imitation consists, as we were saying, in rendering the thing imitated according to quantity and quality."
3. Plato, *Republic*, VI. 509–10. See also *Sophist*, 253–36.
4. Mazzoni expands his concept of the idol in Book III, the main body of his *Defense*: "[564] I say therefore that anyone who with words expounds some true concept in a certain fashion creates idols by means of his speaking, since each concept is a similitude and image of the thing to which it corresponds, and likewise names appear, according to

Plato and also Aristotle, to be like idols and imitations of things. In this way not only history, but also natural philosophy and every one of the other arts which teaches something or deals with truth, makes quasi-idols with its languages and imitates things with concepts and names."

5. Suidas is the supposed compiler of the *Suda Lexicon* (c. 1000), a combined dictionary and encyclopedia gathered from a wide variety of sources.

6. See Plato, *Sophist*, and *Republic*. The drift of Mazzoni's understanding of the difference between icastic and fantastic imagery may be gathered from the following remarks in Book III of his *Defense*: "[580] it can probably be said that fantastic and icastic imitation are determined by the true and the false, not insofar as they are in themselves true and false, but insofar as they are considered true and false in the mind of the poet. . . . That poet who creates his own invention as a consequence produces it by the living power of his own imagination, even if by chance it conforms to what has happened in history. And thus not only, according to his belief, does he have the false as an object, but also its form and structure are in his imagination. It thus seems reasonable that these suit the title of fantastic imitator."

7. Mazzoni argues in Book III that "narration" has a special virtue in addition to those it shares with rhetoric: "[974] And that virtue is particularity, through which the poet should extend and display the parts of his concept because in this way he will be apt to imitate and make resemblances of everything he may have occasion to discuss."

8. Plato does not say this directly; rather he suggests that all image-making is imitation. See *Sophist*.

9. See *Republic*.

10. Mazzoni expands on this traditional idea in portions of Book III, "[807–08] each time poets have sought to follow the marvelous on the literal level they have uttered incredible things. . . . The license has sometimes been conceded to poets to feign the impossible in the literal sense while following the credible in the allegorical sense." These propositions are liberally illustrated with examples from classical literature and commentaries, chiefly Homer and Proclus.

11. See *Poetics*, I. 8.

12. "Were the Athenians More Famous in War or in Wisdom?" *Moralia* (Loeb edition, Vol. IV, p. 507).

13. See *Republic*, and *Laws*. Mazzoni is reading Plato in his own way. In both passages cited Plato asserts that only poetry containing acceptable doctrine belongs in the state, and in the passage from the *Republic* he says flatly that poetry "is not to be regarded seriously as attaining to the truth."

14. See *Poetics*, IX. 1–4, and XXV. 1 and 5–8.

15. For Mazzoni this involves the purpose for which idols and images are used. In Book III he argues to this point: "[564–65] But yet I say that the language of history and the arts and sciences does not use poetic imitation, and that the poet who treats either of history or of the arts or sciences will use poetic imitation, which we have above called similitudinousness (*similitudinaria*). According to the understanding of those who ought to know . . . the idol is that which has no other use in itself but to represent and resemble. And because the concepts of philosophy are not true and perfect idols (since they are not made solely to represent but to instruct and to disclose the truth of things), therefore we can say that history, and whatever else teaches things that are true, even if by means of its concepts it forms idols, does not form them insofar as they are idols, that is, it does not form them for the sole purpose of representing and resembling something else. Rather it moves to another mode and another cause of the object, that is, to recount the truth of what has happened or to teach some doctrine. But the imitator fabricates the perfect idol,

that is, the idol insofar as it is an idol, which means . . . the idol insofar as it represents and resembles something else. So we can conclude that the historian and the poet who has history for the subject of his poem are different in that the historian will recount things in order to leave behind a memory of the truth, but the poet will write to imitate and leave behind a simulacrum, insofar as it is a simulacrum, of the truth. And the poet will be constrained to write with greater diligence than the historian and to ornament his writing with many poetic lights and colors so that the simulacrum which he wishes to form may be better seen and understood by everyone who reads his poem."

16. *Poetics*, XXIV. 10.

17. See n. 10, above.

18. Mazzoni is referring to Cicero's dialogue *Of the Classification of Rhetoric* (Loeb edition, p. 357): "Questions . . . are of two kinds; one kind is limited by its referring to *particular* (*finitum*) occasions and persons, and this I call a cause, and the other is *unlimited* (*infinitum*), that is, marked by no persons or occasions, and this I designate a thesis." In this treatise Cicero generally assigns finite questions a role in moving the feelings and infinite questions the task of persuading the judgment in more general matters.

19. See Aristotle, *Poetics*, I. 8.

20. *The Divine Comedy*, "Paradise," XXXIII. 115–20.

21. Rational principles for understanding the proper organization and functions of human society.

22. Philostratus, *Lives of the Sophists*, 481 (Loeb edition, p. 9).

23. Mazzoni explores this point at some length in Book III: "[584] The true and perfect poet, then, prefers that sort of fable which has, among others, three conditions: novelty, credibility, and the marvelous. And if we wish to consider seriously these three conditions, we will discover that the fable in fantastic poetry is always the impossible credible, because the fantastic poet always presents the audience of his poem with an action which either has not taken place or has not taken place in the fashion imitated by the poet. Now what is above all impossible is an event which either has not taken place or has not taken place in the way revealed by the poet, since it would be impossible that past events would occur in a manner other than that in which they did occur. In any case, the clever poet unfolds his actions so as to make them credible to the people who listen to him."

24. See *Poetics*, I. 8.

25. "How a Young Man Ought to Study Poetry," *Moralia* (Loeb edition, Vol. I, pp. 83–85).

26. See *Nichomachean Ethics*, X. iv.

27. This quotation is not from Aristotle, whose remarks on the imagination are more cursory, but from the commentary of Themistius, philosopher and rhetorician of the fourth century A.D.

George Puttenham
c. 1529–1590

George Puttenham, despite his current obscurity, deserves to be remembered as one of the earliest organizers of the English language. Baxter Hathaway has compared Puttenham's systematization of English rhetoric and poetry to the simultaneous effort throughout the Continent to impose classical order upon vernacular traditions:

> Puttenham, like the Pléiade poets and the Italian vernacular humanists, was willing to survey the terrain around him, and accept, inductively, forms and styles that imposed discipline and stabilizing restraint upon what he took to be the utter chaos of the unstudied English language.

Puttenham was the nephew of Sir Thomas Elyot. He matriculated at Cambridge in 1546, moving to the Inner Temple in 1556. His marriage to Lady Elizabeth Windsor enhanced his connections at court, but did not prevent his being thrown into jail in 1569, when he was charged with conspiring to murder the Calvinist Bishop of London. He was jailed again in 1570 for his criticism of the Queen's counselors. He was later rewarded, however, for writing *A Justification of Queen Elizabeth in Relation to the Affair of Mary Queen of Scots*, which he undertook at the Queen's own request.

Puttenham is universally accepted as the author of *The Art of English Poetry* (1589), although it was published anonymously. It is almost an encyclopedia of Renaissance attitudes toward poetry and language. Hathaway writes that the *Art* is "an organized exhibition of tested ideas and attitudes, techniques and forms, social stances, cultural rivalries." One recognizes, for instance, much in the first book, "Of Poets and Poetry," that is reminiscent of Sidney's *Apology*. Like Sidney, Puttenham adopts an essentially Neoplatonic theory of poetry, mixing it with a sense of the poet's tremendous power: "It is therefore of poets thus to be conceived, that if they be able to devise and make all these things of themselves, without any subject of verity, that they be (by manner of speech) as creating gods."

Puttenham is probably most important as an organizer and systematizer of classical rhetorical and poetic theory for the English language. He insists upon the necessity of recognizing a Standard English, settling upon the dialect of London and its vicinity because of its courtly connection. He is remembered for his translation of classical rhetorical terms into plain English: "hyperbole" becomes "the loud liar or over-reacher," paradox "the wonderer," rhyme "the like-loose," metaphor the "figure of transport," metonymy the "figure of abuse," allegory the "figure of false semblant," irony "the dry mock," and so forth.

The selections from *The Art of English Poetry* are taken from *Elizabethan Critical Essays,* edited by G. Gregory Smith (Oxford University Press, 1904).

FROM

THE ART OF ENGLISH POETRY

Book I

Chapter I

A Poet is as much to say as a maker. And our English name well conformes with the Greeke word, for of *poiein*, to make, they call a maker *Poeta*. Such as (by way of resemblance and reuerently) we may say of God; who without any trauell to his diuine imagination made all the world of nought, nor also by any paterne or mould, as the Platonicks with their Ideas do phantastically suppose. Euen so the very Poet makes and contriues out of his owne braine both the verse and matter of his poeme, and not by any foreine copie or example, as doth the translator, who therefore may well be sayd a versifier, but not a Poet. The premises considered, it giueth to the name and profession no smal dignitie and preheminence, aboue all other artificers, Scientificke or Mechanicall. And neuerthelesse, without any repugnancie at all, a Poet may in some sort be said a follower or imitator, because he can express the true and liuely of euery thing is set before him, and which he taketh in hand to describe: and so in that respect is both a maker and a counterfaitor: and Poesie an art not only of making, but also of imitation. And this science in his perfection can not grow but by some diuine instinct—the Platonicks call it furor; or by excellencie of nature and complexion; or by great subtiltie of the spirits & wit; or by much experience and obseruation of the world, and course of kinde; or, peraduenture, by all or most part of them. Otherwise, how was it possible that Homer, being but a poore priuate man, and, as some say, in his later age blind, should so exactly set foorth and describe, as if he had bene a most excellent Captaine or Generall, the order and array of battels, the conduct of whole armies, the sieges and assaults of cities and townes? or, as some great Princes maiordome and perfect Surueyour in Court, the order, sumptuousnesse, and magnificence of royal bankets, feasts, weddings, and enteruewes? or, as a Polititian very prudent and much inured with the priuat and publique affaires, so grauely examine the lawes and ordinances Ciuill, or so profoundly discourse in matters of estate and formes of all politique regiment? Finally, how could he so naturally paint out the speeches, countenance, and maners of Princely persons and priuate, to wit, the wrath of Achilles, the magnanimitie of Agamemnon, the prudence of Menelaus, the prowesse of Hector, the maiestie of king Priamus, the grauitie of Nestor, the pollicies and eloquence of Vlysses, the calamities of the distressed Queenes, and valiance of all the Captaines and aduenturous knights in those lamentable warres of Troy? It is therefore of Poets thus to be conceiued, that if they be able to deuise and make all these things of them selues, without any subiect of veritie, that they be (by maner of speech) as creating gods. If they do it by instinct diuine or naturall, then surely much fauoured from aboue; if by their experience, then no doubt very wise men; if by any president or paterne layd before them, then truly the most excellent imitators & counterfaitors of all others. But you (Madame) my most Honored and Gracious, if I should seeme to offer you this my deuise for a discipline and not a delight, I might well be reputed of all others the most arrogant and iniurious, your selfe being alreadie, of any that I know in our time, the most excellent Poet; forsooth by your Princely purse, fauours, and countenance, making in maner what ye list, the poore man rich, the lewd well learned, the coward couragious, and vile both noble and valiant: then for imitation no lesse, your person as a most cunning counterfaitor liuely representing Venus in countenance, in life Diana, Pallas for gouernement, and Iuno in all honour and regall magnificence.

Chapter III

The profession and vse of Poesie is most ancient from the beginning, and not, as manie erroniously suppose, after, but before, any ciuil society was among men. For it is written that Poesie was th'originall cause and occasion of their first assemblies, when before the people remained in the woods and mountains, vagarant and dispersed like the wild beasts, lawlesse and naked, or verie ill clad, and of all good and necessarie prouision for harbour or sustenance vtterly vnfurnished, so as they litle diffred for their maner of life from the very brute beasts of the field. Whereupon it is fayned that Amphion and Orpheus, two Poets of the first ages, one of them, to wit Amphion, builded vp cities, and reared walles with the stones that came in heapes to the sound of his harpe, figuring thereby the mollifying of hard and stonie hearts by his sweete and eloquent perswasion. And Orpheus assembled the wilde beasts to come in heards to harken to his musicke, and by that meanes made them tame, implying thereby, how by his discreete and wholsome lesons vttered in harmonie and with melodious instruments he brought the rude and sauage people to a more ciuill and orderly life, nothing, as it seemeth, more preuailing or fit to redresse and edifie the cruell and sturdie courage of man then it. And as these two Poets, and Linus before them, and Museus also and Hesiodus in Greece and Archadia, so by all likelihood had mo Poets done in other places and in other ages before them, though there be no remembrance left of them, by reason of the Recordes by some accident of time perished and failing. Poets therfore are of great antiquitie. Then forasmuch as they were the first that entended to the obseruation of nature and her works, and specially of the Celestiall courses, by reason of the continuall motion of the heauens, searching after the first mouer, and from thence by degrees comming to know and consider of the substances separate & abstract, which we call the diuine intelligences or good Angels (*Demones*), they were the first that instituted sacrifices of placation, with inuocations and worship to them, as to Gods; and inuented and stablished all the rest of the obseruances and ceremonies of religion, and so were the first Priests and ministers of the holy misteries. And because for the better execution of that high charge and function it behoued them to liue chast, and in all holines of life, and in continuall studie and contemplation, they came by instinct diuine, and by deepe meditation, and much abstinence (the same assubtiling and refining their spirits) to be made apt to receaue visions, both waking and sleeping, which made them vtter prophesies and foretell things to come. So also were they the first Prophetes or seears, *Videntes*, for so the Scripture tearmeth them in Latine after the Hebrue word, and all the oracles and answers of the gods were giuen in meeter or verse, and published to the people by their direction. And for that they were aged and graue men, and of much wisedome and experience in th'affaires of the world, they were the first lawmakers to the people, and the first polititiens, deuising all expedient meanes for th'establishment of Common wealth, to hold and containe the people in order and duety by force and vertue of good and wholesome lawes, made for the preseruation of the publique peace and tranquillitie: the same peraduenture not purposely intended, but greatly furthered by the aw of their gods and such scruple of conscience as the terrors of their late inuented religion had led them into.

Chapter IV

Vtterance also and language is giuen by nature to man for perswasion of others and aide of them selues, I meane the first abilite to speake. For speech it selfe is artificiall and made by man, and the more pleasing it is, the more it preuaileth to such purpose as it is intended for: but speech by meeter is a kind of vtterance more cleanly couched and more delicate to the eare then prose is, because it is more currant and slipper vpon the tongue, and withal tunable and melodious, as a kind of Musicke, and therfore may be tearmed a musicall speech or vtterance, which cannot but please the hearer very well. Another cause is, for that is briefer & more compendious, and easier to beare away and be retained in memorie, then that which is contained in multitude of words and full of tedious ambage and long periods. It is beside a maner of vtterance more eloquent and rethoricall then the ordinarie prose which we vse in our daily talke, because it is decked and set out with all maner of fresh colours and figures, which maketh that it sooner inueigleth the iudgement of man, and carieth his opinion this way and that, whither soeuer the heart by impression of the eare shalbe most affectionatly bent and directed. The vtterance in prose is not of so great efficacie, because not only it is dayly vsed, and by that occasion the eare is ouerglutted with it, but is also not so voluble and slipper vpon the tong, being wide and lose, and nothing numerous, nor contriued into measures and sounded with so gallant and harmonical accents, nor, in fine, alowed that figuratiue conueyance nor so great licence in choise of words and phrases as meeter is. So as the Poets were also from the beginning the best perswaders, and their eloquence the first Rethoricke of the world, euen so it became that the high mysteries of the gods should be reuealed & taught by a maner of vtterance and language of extraordinarie phrase, and briefe and compendious, and aboue al others sweet and ciuill as the Metricall is. The same also was meetest to register the liues and noble gests of Princes, and of the great Monarkes of the world, and all other the memorable accidents of time: so as the Poet was also the first historiographer. Then forasmuch as they were the first obseruers of all naturall causes & effects in the things generable and corruptible, and from thence mounted vp to search after the celestiall courses and influences, & yet penetrated further to know the diuine essences and substances separate, as is sayd before, they were the first Astronomers and Philosophists and Metaphisicks. Finally, because they did altogether endeuor them selues to reduce the life of man to a certaine method of good maners, and made the first differences betweene vertue and vice, and then tempered all these knowledges and skilles with the exercise of a delectable Musicke by melodious instruments, which withall serued them to delight their hearers, & to call the people together by admiration to a plausible and vertuous conuersation, therefore were they the first Philosophers Ethick, & the first artificial Musiciens of the world. Such was Linus, Orpheus, Amphion, & Museus, the most ancient Poets and Philosophers of whom there is left any memorie by the prophane writers. King Dauid also & Salomon his sonne and many other of the holy Prophets wrate in meeters, and vsed to sing them to the harpe, although to many of vs, ignorant of the Hebrue language and phrase, and not obseruing it, the same seeme but a prose. It can not bee therefore that anie scorne or indignitie should iustly be offred to so noble, profitable, ancient, and diuine a science as Poesie is.

Chapter V

And the Greeke and Latine Poesie was by verse numerous and metricall, running vpon pleasant feete, sometimes swift, sometime slow (their words very aptly seruing that purpose) but without any rime or tunable concord in th'end of their verses, as we and all other nations now vse. But the Hebrues & Chaldees, who were more ancient then the Greekes, did not only vse a metricall Poesie, but also with the same a maner of rime, as hath bene of late obserued by learned men. Wherby it appeareth that our vulgar running Poesie was common to all the nations of the world besides, whom the Latines and Greekes in speciall called barbarous. So as it was, notwithstanding, the first and most ancient Poesie, and the most vniuersall; which two points do otherwise giue to all humane inuentions and affaires no small credit. This is proued by certificate of marchants and trauellers, who by late nauigations haue surueyed the whole world, and discouered large countries and strange peoples wild and sauage, affirming that the American, the Perusine, and the very Canniball do sing and also say their highest and holiest matters in certaine riming versicles, and not in prose, which proues also that our maner of vulgar Poesie is more ancient then the artificiall of the Greeks and Latines, ours comming by instinct of nature, which was before Art or obseruation, and vsed with the sauage and vnciuill, who were before all science or ciuilitie, euen as the naked by prioritie of time is before the clothed, and the ignorant before the learned. The naturall Poesie therefore, being aided and amended by Art, and not vtterly altered or obscured, but some signe left of it (as the Greekes and Latines haue left none), is no lesse to be allowed and commended then theirs.

Chapter VI

But it came to passe, when fortune fled farre from the Greekes and Latines, & that their townes florished no more in traficke, nor their Vniuersities in learning as they had done continuing those Monarchies, the barbarous conquerers inuading them with innumerable swarmes of strange nations, the Poesie metricall of the Grecians and Latines came to be much corrupted and altered, in so much as there were times that the very Greekes and Latines themselues tooke pleasure in Riming verses, and vsed it as a rare and gallant thing. Yea, their Oratours proses nor the Doctors Sermons were acceptable to Princes nor yet to the common people, vnlesse it went in manner of tunable rime or metricall sentences, as appeares by many of the auncient writers about that time and since. And the great Princes, and Popes, and Sultans would one salute and greet an other sometime in frendship and sport, sometime in earnest and enmitie, by ryming verses, & nothing seemed clerkly done, but must be done in ryme. Whereof we finde diuers examples from the time of th'Emperours Gracian & Valentinian downwardes: For then aboutes began the declination of the Romain Empire, by the notable inundations of the Hunnes and Vandalles in Europe, vnder the conduict of Totila & Atila and other their generalles. This brought the ryming Poesie in grace, and made it preuaile in Italie and Greece (their owne long time cast aside, and almost neglected), till after many yeares that the peace of Italie and of th'Empire Occidentall reuiued new clerkes, who, recouering and perusing the bookes and studies of the ciuiler ages, restored all maner of arts, and that of the Greeke and Latine Poesie withall, into their former puritie and netnes. Which neuerthelesse did not so preuaile but that the ryming Poesie of the Barbarians remained still in his reputation, that one in the schole, this other in Courts of Princes more ordinary and allowable.

Chapter IX

Wherefore, the Nobilitie and dignitie of the Art considered aswell by vniuersalitie as antiquitie and the naturall excellence of it selfe, Poesie ought not to be abased and imployed vpon any vnworthy matter & subiect, nor vsed to vaine purposes; which neuerthelesse is dayly seene, and that is to vtter conceits infamous & vicious, or ridiculous and foolish, or of no good example & doctrine. Albeit in merry matters (not vnhonest) being vsed for mans solace and recreation it may be well allowed, for, as I said before, Poesie is a pleasant maner of vtteraunce, varying from the ordinarie of purpose to refresh the mynde by the eares delight. Poesie also is not onely laudable, because I said it was a metricall speach vsed by the first men, but because it is a metricall speach corrected and reformed by discreet iudgements, and with no lesse cunning and curiositie then the Greeke and Latine Poesie, and by Art bewtified & adorned & brought far from the primitiue rudenesse of the first inuentors: otherwise it may be sayd to me that Adam and Eues apernes were the gayest garmentes, because they were the first, and the shepheardes tente or pauillion the best housing, because it was the most auncient & most vniuersall; which I would not haue so taken, for it is not my meaning but that Art & cunning concurring with nature, antiquitie, & vniuersalitie, in things indifferent, and not euill, doe make them more laudable. And right so our vulgar riming Poesie, being by good wittes brought to that perfection, we see is worthily to be preferred before any other maner of vtterance in prose, for such vse and to such purpose as it is ordained, and shall hereafter be set downe more particularly.

Chapter XI

As the matter of Poesie is diuers, so was the forme of their poemes & maner of writing, for all of them wrote not in one sort, euen as all of them wrote not vpon one matter. Neither was euery Poet alike cunning in all, as in some one kinde of Poesie, nor vttered with like felicitie. But wherein any one most excelled, thereof he tooke a surname, as to be called a Poet Heroick, Lyrick, Elegiack, Epigrammatist, or otherwise. Such therefore as gaue themselues to write long histories of the noble gests of kings & great Princes entermedling the dealings of the gods, halfe gods, or Heroes of the gentiles, & the great & waighty consequences of peace and warre, they called Poets Heroick, whereof Homer was chief and most auncient among the Greeks, Virgill among the Latines: Others who more delighted to write songs or ballads of pleasure, to be song with the voice, and to the harpe, lute, or citheron, & such other musical instruments, they were called melodious Poets (*melici*), or, by a more common name, Lirique Poets: of which sort was Pindarus, Anacreon, and Callimachus, with others among the Greeks, Horace and Catullus among the Latines. There were an other sort, who sought the fauor of faire Ladies, and coueted to bemone their estates at large & the perplexities of loue in a certain pitious verse called Elegie, and thence were called Elegiack: such among the Latines were Ouid, Tibullus, & Propertius. There were also Poets that wrote onely for the stage, I meane plays and interludes, to recreate the people with matters of disporte, and to that intent did set forth in shewes [&] pageants, accompanied with speach, the common behauiours and maner of life of priuate persons, and such as were the meaner sort of men, and they were called Comicall Poets: of whom among the Greekes Menander and Aristophanes were most excellent, with the Latines Terence and Plautus. Besides those Poets Comick there were other who serued also the stage, but medled not with so base matters, for they set forth the dolefull falles of infortunate & afflicted Princes, & were called Poets Tragicall: such were Euripides and Sophocles with the Greeks, Seneca among the Latines. There were yet others who mounted nothing so high as any of them both, but, in base and humble stile by maner of Dialogue, vttered the priuate and familiar talke of the meanest sort of men, as shepheards, heywards, and such like: such was among the Greekes Theocritus, and Virgill among the Latines; their poems were named Eglogues or shepheardly talke. There was yet another kind of Poet, who intended to taxe the common abuses and vice of the people in rough and bitter speaches, and their inuectiues were called Satyres, and them selues Satyricques: such were Lucilius, Iuuenall, and Persius among the Latines, & with vs he that wrote the booke called Piers plowman. Others of a more fine and pleasant head were giuen wholly to taunting and scoffing at vndecent things, and in short poemes vttered pretie merry conceits, and these men were called Epigrammatistes. There were others that for the peoples good instruction, and triall of their owne witts, vsed in places of great assembly to say by rote nombers of short and sententious meetres, very pithie and of good edification, and thereupon were called Poets Mimistes, as who would say, imitable and meet to be followed for their wise and graue lessons. There was another kind of poeme, inuented onely to make sport & to refresh the company with a maner of buffonry or counterfaiting of merry speaches, conuerting all that which they had hard spoken before to a certaine derision by a quite contrary sence, and this was done when Comedies or Tragedies were playing, & that betweene the actes when the players went to make ready for another, there was great silence, and the people waxt weary, then came in these maner of conterfaite vices; they were called *Pantomimi*, and all that had before bene sayd, or great part of it, they gaue a crosse construction to it very ridiculously. Thus haue you how the names of the Poets were giuen them by the formes of their poemes and maner of writing.

Chapter XII

The gods of the Gentiles were honoured by their Poetes in hymnes, which is an extraordinarie and diuine praise, extolling and magnifying them for their great powers and excellencie of nature in the highest degree of laude; and yet therein their Poets were after a sort restrained, so as they could not with their credit vntruly praise their owne gods, or vse in their lauds any maner of grosse adulation or vnueritable report. For in any writer vntruth and flatterie are counted most great reproches. Wherfore to praise the gods of the Gentiles, for that by authoritie of their owne fabulous records they had fathers and mothers, and kinred and allies, and wiues and concubines, the Poets first commended them by their genealogies or pedegrees, their mariages and aliances, their notable exploits in the world for the behoofe of mankind, and yet, as I sayd before, none otherwise then the truth of their owne memorials might beare, and in such sort as it might be well auouched by their old written reports, though in very deede they were not from the beginning all historically true, and many of them verie fictions,and such of them as were true were grounded vpon some part of an historie or matter of veritie, the rest altogether figuratiue & misticall, couertly applied to some morall or natural sense, as Cicero setteth it foorth in his bookes *de natura deorum*. For to say that Iupiter was sonne to Saturne, and that he maried his owne sister Iuno, might be true, for such was the guise of all great Princes in the Orientall part of the world both at those dayes and now is. Againe, that he loued Danae, Europa, Leda, Callisto, & other faire Ladies, daughters to kings, besides many meaner women, it is likely enough, because he was reported to be a very incontinent person and giuen ouer to his lustes, as are for the most part all the greatest Princes; but that he should be the highest god in heauen, or that he should thunder and lighten, and do manie other things very vnnaturally and absurdly, also that Saturnus should geld his father Coelus, to th'intent to make him vnable to get any moe children, and other such matters as are reported by them, it seemeth to be some wittie deuise and fiction made for a purpose, or a very no[ta]ble and impudent lye, which could not be reasonably suspected by the Poets, who were otherwise descreete and graue men, and teachers of wisedome to others. Therefore either to transgresse the rules of their primitiue records or to seeke to giue their gods honour by belying them (otherwise then in that sence which I haue alledged) had bene a signe not onely of an vnskilfull Poet but also of a very impudent and leude man. For vntrue praise neuer giueth any true reputation. But with vs Christians, who be better disciplined, and do acknowledge but one God Almightie, euerlasting, and in euery respect selfe suffizant, *autharcos*, reposed in all perfect rest and soueraigne blisse, nor needing or exacting any forreine helpe or good, to him we can not exhibit ouermuch praise, nor belye him any wayes, vnlesse it be in abasing his excellencie by scarsitie of praise, or by misconceauing his diuine nature, weening to praise him if we impute to him such vaine delights and peeuish affections as commonly the frailest men are reproued for: namely, to make him ambitious of honour, iealous and difficult in his worships, terrible, angrie, vindicatiue, a louer, a hater, a pitier, and indigent of mans worships, finally, so passionate as in effect he shold be altogether *Anthropopathis*. To the gods of the Gentiles they might well attribute these infirmities, for they were but the children of men, great Princes and famous in the world, and not for any other respect diuine then by some resemblance of vertue they had to do good and to benefite many. So as to the God of the Christians such diuine praise might be verified; to th'other gods none, but figuratiuely or in misticall sense, as hath bene said. In which sort the ancient Poets did in deede giue them great honors & praises, and made to them sacrifices, and offred them oblations of sundry sortes, euen as the people were taught and perswaded by such placations and worships to receaue any helpe, comfort, or benefite to them selues, their wiues, children, possessions, or goods. For if that opinion were not, who would acknowledge any God? the verie Etimologie of the name with vs of the North partes of the world declaring plainely the nature of the attribute, which is all one as if we sayd good, *bonus*, or a giuer of good things. Therfore the Gentiles prayed for peace to the goddesse Pallas; for warre (such as thriued by it) to the god Mars; for honor and empire to the god Iupiter; for riches & wealth to Pluto; for eloquence and gayne to Mercurie; for safe nauigation to Neptune; for faire weather and prosperous windes to Eolus; for skill in musick and leechcraft to Apollo; for free life & chastitie to Diana; for bewtie and good grace, as also for issue & prosperitie in loue, to Venus; for plenty of crop and corne to Ceres; for seasonable vintage to Bacchus; and for other things to others. So many things as they could imagine good and desirable, and to so many gods as they supposed to be authors thereof, in so much as Fortune was made a goddesse, & the feuer quartaine had her aulters: such blindnes & ignorance raigned in the harts of men at that time, and whereof it first proceeded and grew, besides th'opinion hath bene giuen, appeareth more at large in our bookes of Ierotekni, the matter being of another consideration then to be treated of in this worke. And these hymnes to the gods was the first forme of Poesie and the highest & the stateliest, & they were song by the Poets as priests, and by the people or whole congregation, as we sing in our Churches the Psalmes of Dauid, but they did it commonly in some shadie groues of tall tymber trees: In which places they reared aulters of green turfe, and bestrewed them all ouer with flowers, and vpon them offred their oblations and made their bloudy sacrifices (for no kinde of gift can be dearer then life) of such quick cattaille, as euery god was in their conceit most delighted in, or in some other respect most fit for the misterie: temples or churches or other chappels then these they had none at those dayes.

Chapter XIII

Some perchance would thinke that next after the praise and honoring of their gods should commence the worshippings and praise of good men, and specially of great Princes and gouernours of the earth in soueraignety and function next vnto the gods. But it is not so, for before that came to passe the Poets or holy Priests chiefly studied the rebuke of vice, and to carpe at the common abuses, such as were most offensiue to the publique and priuate, for as yet for lacke of good ciuility and wholesome doctrines there was greater store of lewde lourdaines then of wise and learned Lords or of noble and vertuous Princes and gouernours. So as next after the honours exhibited to their gods, the Poets, finding in man generally much to reproue & litle to praise, made certaine poems in plaine meetres, more like to sermons or preachings then otherwise, and when the people were assembled togither in those hallowed places dedicate to their gods, because they had yet no large halles or places of conuenticle, nor had any other correction of their faults, but such as rested onely in rebukes of wise and graue men, such as at these dayes make the people ashamed rather then afeard, the said aunctient Poets vsed for that purpose three kinds of poems reprehensiue, to wit, the Satyre, the Comedie, and the Tragedie. And the first and most bitter inuectiue against vice and vicious men was the *Satyre*: which, to th'intent their bitternesse should breede none ill will, either to the Poets, or to the recitours (which could not haue bene chosen if they had bene openly knowen), and besides to make their admonitions and reproofs seeme grauer and of more efficacie, they made wise as if the gods of the woods, whom they called Satyres or Siluanes, should appeare and recite those verses of rebuke, whereas in deede they were but disguised persons vnder the shape of Satyres, as who would say, these terrene and base gods, being conuersant with mans affaires, and spiers out of all their secret faults, had some great care ouer man, & desired by good admonitions to reforme the euill of their life, and to bring the bad to amendment by those kinde of preachings; whereupon the Poets inuentours of the deuise were called Satyristes.

Chapter XIV

But when these maner of solitary speaches and recitals of rebuke, vttered by the rurall gods out of bushes and briers, seemed not to the finer heads sufficiently perswasiue, nor so popular as if it were reduced into action of many persons, or by many voyces liuely represented to the eare and eye, so as a man might thinke it were euen now a doing, the Poets deuised to haue many parts played at once by two or three or foure persons, that debated the matters of the world, sometimes of their owne priuate affaires, sometimes of their neighbours, but neuer medling with any Princes matters nor such high personages, but commonly of marchants, souldiers, artificers, good honest housholders, and also of vnthrifty youthes, yong damsels, old nurses, bawds, brokers, ruffians, and parasites, with such like, in whose behauiors lyeth in effect the whole course and trade of mans life, and therefore tended altogither to the good amendment of man by discipline and example. It was also much for the solace & recreation of the common people by reason of the pageants and shewes. And this kind of poeme was called Comedy, and followed next after the Satyre, & by that occasion was somwhat sharpe and bitter after the nature of the Satyre, openly & by expresse names taxing men more maliciously and impudently then became, so as they were enforced for feare of quarell & blame to disguise their players with strange apparell, and by colouring their faces and carying hatts & capps of diuerse fashions to make them selues lesse knowen. But as time & experience do reforme euery thing that is amisse, so, this bitter poeme called the old Comedy being disused and taken away, the new Comedy came in place, more ciuill and pleasant a great deale, and not touching any man by name, but in a certaine generalitie glancing at euery abuse, so as from thenceforth fearing none illwill or enmitie at any bodies hands they left aside their disguisings and played bare face, till one Roscius Gallus, the most excellent player among the Romaines, brought vp these vizards which we see at this day vsed, partly to supply the want of players, when there were moe parts than there were persons, or that it was not thought meet to trouble & pester princes chambers with too many folkes. Now by the chaunge of a vizard one man might play the king and the carter, the old nurse & the yong damsell, the marchant and the souldier, or any other part he listed very conueniently. There be that say Roscius did it for another purpose, for being him selfe the best Histrien or buffon that was in his dayes to be found, insomuch as Cicero said Roscius contended with him by varietie of liuely gestures to surmount the copy of his speach, yet because he was squint eyed and had a very vnpleasant countenance, and lookes which made him ridiculous or rather odious to the presence, he deuised these vizards to hide his owne ilfauored face. And thus much touching the Comedy.

Chapter XV

But because in those dayes when the Poets first taxed by Satyre and Comedy there was no great store of Kings or Emperors or such high estats (al men being yet for the most part rude, & in a maner popularly egall), they could not say of them or of their behauiours any thing to the purpose, which cases of Princes are sithens taken for the highest and greatest matters of all. But after that some men among the moe became mighty and famous in the world, soueraignetie and dominion hauing learned them all maner of lusts and licentiousnes of life, by which occasions also their high estates and felicities fell many times into most lowe and lamentable fortunes: whereas before in their great prosperities they were both feared and reuerenced in the highest degree, after their deathes, when the posteritie stood no more in dread of them, their infamous life and tyrannies were layd open to all the world, their wickednes reproched, their follies and extreme insolencies derided, and their miserable ends painted out in playes and pageants, to shew the mutabilitie of fortune, and the iust punishment of God in reuenge of a vicious and euill life. These matters were also handled by the Poets, and represented by action as that of the Comedies: but because the matter was higher then that of the Comedies, the Poets stile was also higher and more loftie, the prouision greater, the place more magnificent; for which purpose also the players garments were made more rich & costly and solemne, and euery other thing apperteining, according to that rate: So as where the Satyre was pronounced by rusticall and naked Syluanes speaking out of a bush, & the common players of interludes called *Planipedes* played barefoote vpon the floore, the later Comedies vpon scaffolds, and by men well and cleanely hosed and shod. These matters of great Princes were played vpon lofty stages, & the actors thereof ware vpon their legges buskins of leather called *Cothurni*, and other solemne habits, & for a speciall preheminence did walke vpon those high corked shoes or pantofles, which now they call in Spaine and Italy *Shoppini*. And because those buskins and high shoes were commonly made of goats skinnes very finely tanned, and dyed into colours, or for that, as some say, the best players reward was a goate to be giuen him, or for that, as other thinke, a goate was the peculiar sacrifice of the god Pan, king of all the gods of the woodes—forasmuch as a goate in Greeke is called *Tragos*, therfore these stately playes were called Tragedies. And thus haue ye foure sundry formes of Poesie Drammatick reprehensiue, & put in execution by the feate and dexteritie of mans body, to wit, the Satyre, old Comedie, new Comedie, and Tragedie, whereas all other kinde of poems, except Eglogue, whereof shalbe entreated hereafter, were onely recited by mouth or song with the voyce to some melodious instrument.

Chapter XVIII

Some be of opinion, and the chiefe of those who haue written in this Art among the Latines, that the pastorall Poesie which we commonly call by the name of Eglogue and Bucolick, a tearme brought in by the Sicilian Poets, should be the first of any other, and before the Satyre, Comedie, or Tragedie, because, say they, the shepheards and haywards assemblies & meetings when they kept their cattell and heards in the common fields and forests was the first familiar conuersation, and their babble and talk vnder bushes and shadie trees the first disputation and contentious reasoning, and their fleshly heates growing of ease the first idle wooings, and their songs made to their mates or paramours either vpon sorrow or iolity of courage the first amorous musicks; sometime also they sang and played on their pipes for wagers, striuing who should get the best game and be counted cunningest. All this I do agree vnto, for no doubt the shepheards life was the first example of honest felowship, their trade the first art of lawfull acquisition or purchase, for at those daies robbery was a manner of purchase. So saith Aristotle in his bookes of the Politiques; and that pasturage was before tillage, or fishing, or fowling, or any other predatory art or cheuisance. And all this may be true, for before there was a shepheard keeper of his owne or of some other bodies flocke, there was none owner in the world, quick cattel being the first property of any forreine possession. I say forreine, because alway men claimed property in their apparell and armour, and other like things made by their owne trauel and industry, nor thereby was there yet any good towne, or city, or Kings palace, where pageants and pompes might be shewed by Comedies or Tragedies. But for all this, I do deny that the *Eglogue* should be the first and most auncient forme of artificiall Poesie, being perswaded that the Poet deuised the Eglogue long after the other dramatick poems, not of purpose to counterfait or represent the rusticall manner of loues and communication, but vnder the vaile of homely persons and in rude speeches to insinuate and glaunce at greater matters, and such as perchance had not bene safe to haue beene disclosed in any other sort, which may be perceiued by the Eglogues of Virgill, in which are treated by figure matters of greater importance then the loues of Titirus and Corydon. These Eglogues came after to containe and enforme morall discipline, for the amendment of mans behauiour, as be those of Mantuan and other moderne Poets.

Chapter XIX

There is nothing in man of all the potential parts of his mind (reason and will except) more noble or more necessary to the actiue life then memory; because it maketh most to a sound iudgement and perfect worldly wisedome, examining and comparing the times past with the present, and, by them both considering the time to come, concludeth with a stedfast resolution what is the best course to be taken in all his actions and aduices in this world. It came, vpon this reason, experience to be so highly commended in all consultations of importance, and preferred before any learning or science, and yet experience is no more than a masse of memories assembled, that is, such trials as man hath made in time before. Right so no kinde of argument in all the Oratorie craft doth better perswade and more vniuersally satisfie then example, which is but the representation of old memories, and like successes happened in times past. For these regards the Poesie historicall is of all other next the diuine most honorable and worthy, as well for the common benefit as for the speciall comfort euery man receiueth by it: no one thing in the world with more delectation reuiuing our spirits then to behold as it were in a glasse the liuely image of our deare forefathers, their noble and vertuous maner of life, with other things autentike, which because we are not able otherwise to attaine to the knowledge of by any of our sences, we apprehend them by memory, whereas the present time and things so swiftly passe away, as they giue vs no leasure almost to looke into them, and much lesse to know & consider of them throughly. The things future, being also euents very vncertaine, and such as can not possibly be knowne because they be not yet, can not be vsed for example nor for delight otherwise then by hope; though many promise the contrary, by vaine and deceitfull arts taking vpon them to reueale the truth of accidents to come, which, if it were so as they surmise, are yet but sciences meerely coniecturall, and not of any benefit to man or to the common wealth where they be vsed or professed. Therefore the good and exemplarie things and actions of the former ages were reserued only to the historicall reportes of wise and graue men: those of the present time left to the fruition and iudgement of our sences: the future, as hazards and incertaine euentes vtterly neglected and layd aside for Magicians and mockers to get their liuings by, such manner of men as by negligence of Magistrates and remiss[n]es of lawes euery countrie breedeth great store of. These historical men neuerthelesse vsed not the matter so precisely to wish that al they wrote should be accounted true, for that was not needeful nor expedient to the purpose, namely to be vsed either for example or for pleasure: considering that many times it is seene a fained matter or altogether fabulous, besides that it maketh more mirth than any other, works no lesse good conclusions for example then the most true and veritable, but often times more, because the Poet hath the handling of them to fashion at his pleasure, but not so of th'other, which must go according to their veritie, and none otherwise, without the writers great blame. Againe, as ye know, mo and more excellent examples may be fained in one day by a good wit then many ages through mans frailtie are able to put in vre; which made the learned and wittie men of those times to deuise many historicall matters of no veritie at all, but with purpose to do good and no hurt, as vsing them for a maner of discipline and president of commendable life. Such was the common wealth of Plato, and Sir Thomas Moores *Vtopia*, resting all in deuise, but neuer put in execution, and easier to be wished then to be performed. And you shall perceiue that histories were of three sortes, wholly true, and wholly false, and a third holding part of either, but for honest recreation and good example they were all of them. And this may be apparant to vs not onely by the Poeticall histories but also by those that be written in prose: for as Homer wrate a fabulous or mixt report of the siege of Troy and another of Ulisses errors or wandrings, so did Museus compile a true treatise of the life & loues of Leander and Hero, both of them Heroick, and to none ill edification. Also, as Theucidides wrate a worthy and veritable historie of the warres betwixt the Athenians and the Peloponeses, so did Zenophon, a most graue Philosopher and well trained courtier and counsellour, make another (but fained and vntrue) of the childhood of Cyrus, king of Persia; neuertheless both to one effect, that is for example and good information of the posteritie. Now because the actions of meane & base personages tend in very few cases to any great good example; for who passeth to follow the steps and maner of life of a craftes man, shepheard, or sailer, though he were his father or dearest frend? yea how almost is it possible that such maner of men should be of any vertue other then their profession requireth? therefore was nothing committed to historie but matters of great and excellent persons & things, that the same by irritation of good courages (such as emulation causeth) might worke more effectually, which occasioned the story writer to chuse an higher stile fit for his subiect, the Prosaicke in prose, the Poet in meetre, and the Poets was by verse exameter for his grauitie and statelinesse most allowable: neither would they intermingle him with any other shorter measure, vnlesse it were in matters of such qualitie as became best to be song with the voyce and to some musicall instrument, as were with the Greeks all your Hymnes & Encomia of Pindarus & Callimachus, not very histories, but a maner of historicall reportes; in which cases they made those poemes in variable measures, & coupled a short verse with a long to serue that purpose the better. And we our selues who compiled this treatise haue written for pleasure a litle brief Romance or historicall ditty in the English tong, of the Isle of great Britaine, in short and long meetres, and by breaches or diuisions to be more commodiously song to the harpe in places of assembly, where the company shalbe desirous to heare of old aduentures & valiaunces of noble knights in times past, as are those of king Arthur and his knights of the round table, Sir Beuys of Southampton, Guy of Warwicke, and others like. Such as haue not premonition hereof, and consideration of the causes alledged, would peraduenture reproue and disgrace euery Romance or short historicall ditty for that they be not written in long meeters or verses Alexandrins, according to the nature and stile of large histories; wherein they should do wrong, for they be sundry formes of poems, and not all one.

Chapter XXIII

Pleasure is the chiefe parte of mans felicity in this world, and also (as our Theologians say) in the world to come. Therefore, while we may (yea alwaies if it coulde be), to reioyce and take our pleasures in vertuous and honest sort, it is not only allowable but also necessary and very naturall to man. And many be the ioyes and consolations of the hart, but none greater than such as he may vtter and discouer by some convenient meanes: euen as to suppresse and hide a mans mirth, and not to haue therein a partaker, or at least wise a witnes, is no little griefe and infelicity. Therfore nature and ciuility haue ordained (besides the priuate solaces) publike reioisings for the comfort and recreation of many. And they be of diuerse sorts and vpon diuerse occasions growne. One & the chiefe was for the publike peace of a countrie, the greatest of any other ciuill good; and wherein your Maiestie (my most gracious Soueraigne) haue shewed your selfe to all the world, for this one and thirty yeares space of your glorious raigne, aboue all other Princes of Christendome, not onely fortunate, but also most sufficient, vertuous, and worthy of Empire. An other is for iust & honourable victory atchieued against the forraine enemy. A third at solemne feasts and pompes of coronations and enstallments of honourable orders. An other for iollity at weddings and marriages. An other at the births of Princes children. An other for priuate entertainments in Court, or other secret disports in chamber, and such solitary places. And as these reioysings tend to diuers effects, so do they also carry diuerse formes and nominations; for those of victorie and peace are called Triumphall, whereof we our selues haue heretofore giuen some example by our Triumphals, written in honour of her Maiesties long peace. And they were vsed by the aunciencts in like manner as we do our generall processions or Letanies, with bankets and bonefires and all manner of ioyes. Those that were to honour the persons of great Princes or to solemnise the pompes of any installment were called Encomia; we may call them carols of honour. Those to celebrate marriages were called songs nuptiall or Epithalamies, but in a certaine misticall sense, as shall be said hereafter. Others for magnificence at the natiuities of Princes children, or by custome vsed yearely vpon the same dayes, are called songs natall, or Genethliaca. Others for secret recreation and pastime in chambers with company or alone were the ordinary Musickes amorous, such as might be song with voice or to the Lute, Citheron, or Harpe, or daunced by measures, as the Italian Pauan and galliard are at these daies in Princes Courts and other places of honourable or ciuill assembly; and of all these we will speake in order and very briefly.

Chapter XXIV

Lamenting is altogether contrary to reioising; euery man saith so, and yet is it a peece of ioy to be able to lament with ease, and freely to poure forth a mans inward sorrowes and the greefs wherewith his minde is surcharged. This was a very necessary deuise of the Poet and a fine, besides his poetrie to play also the Phisitian, and not onely by applying a medicine to the ordinary sicknes of mankind, but by making the very greef it selfe (in part) cure of the disease. Nowe are the causes of mans sorrowes many: the death of his parents, frends, allies, and children (though many of the barbarous nations do reioyce at their burials and sorrow at their birthes), the ouerthrowes and discomforts in battell, the subuersions of townes and cities, the desolations of countreis, the losse of goods and worldly promotions, honour and good renowne, finally, the trauails and torments of loue forlorne or ill bestowed, either by disgrace, deniall, delay, and twenty other wayes, that well experienced louers could recite. Such of these greefs as might be refrained or holpen by wisedome and the parties owne good endeuour, the Poet gaue none order to sorrow them. For first, as to the good renowne, it is lost for the more part by some default of the owner, and may be by his well doings recouered againe. And if it be vniustly taken away, as by vntrue and famous libels, the offenders recantation may suffise for his amends: so did the Poet Stesichorus, as it is written of him in his *Pallinodie* vpon the disprayse of Helena, and recouered his eye sight. Also, for worldly goods, they come and go, as things not long proprietary to any body, and are not yet subiect vnto fortunes dominion so but that we our selues are in great part accessarie to our own losses and hinderaunces by ouersight & misguiding of our selues and our things; therefore, why should we bewaile our such voluntary detriment? But death, the irrecouerable losse, death, the dolefull departure of frendes, that can neuer be recontinued by any other meeting or new acquaintance—besides our vncertaintie and suspition of their estates and welfare in the places of their new abode—seemeth to carry a reasonable pretext of iust sorrow. Likewise, the great ouerthrowes in battell and desolations of countreys by warres, aswell for the losse of many liues and much libertie as for that it toucheth the whole state, and euery priuate man hath his portion in the damage. Finally, for loue, there is no frailtie in flesh and bloud so excusable as it, no comfort or discomfort greater then the good and bad successe thereof, nothing more naturall to man, nothing of more force to vanquish his will and to inuegle his iudgement. Therefore of death and burials, of th'aduersities by warres, and of true loue lost or ill bestowed are th'onely sorrowes that the noble Poets sought by their arte to remoue or appease, not with any medicament of a contrary temper, as the Galenistes vse to cure *contraria contrariis*, but as the Paracelsians, who cure *similia similibus*, making one dolour to expell another, and, in this case, one short sorrowing the remedie of a long and grieuous sorrow. And the lamenting of deathes was chiefly at the very burialls of the dead, also at monethes mindes and longer times, by custome continued yearely, when as they vsed many offices of seruice and loue towardes the dead, and thereupon are called Obsequies in our vulgare; which was done not onely by cladding the mourners their friendes and seruauntes in blacke vestures, of shape dolefull and sad, but also by wofull countenaunces and voyces, and besides by Poeticall mournings in verse. Such funerall songs were called *Epicedia* if they were song by many, and *Monodia* if they were vttered by one alone, and this was vsed at the enterment of Princes and others of great accompt, and it was reckoned a great ciuilitie to vse such ceremonies, as at this day is also in some countrey vsed. In Rome they accustomed to make orations funerall and commendatorie of the dead parties in the publique place called *Pro rostris*: and our Theologians in stead thereof vse to make sermons, both teaching the people some good learning and also saying well of the departed. Those songs of the dolorous discomfits in battaile and other desolations in warre, or of townes saccaged and subuerted, were song by the remnant of the army ouerthrowen, with great skrikings and outcries, holding the wrong end of their weapon vpwards in signe of sorrow and dispaire. The cities also made generall mournings & offred sacrifices with Poeticall songs to appease the wrath of the martiall gods & goddesses. The third sorrowing was of loues, by long lamentation in Elegie: so was their song called, and it was in a pitious maner of meetre, placing a limping Pentameter after a lusty Exameter, which made it go dolourously, more then any other meeter.

Chapter XXVII

But all the world could not keepe, nor any ciuill ordinance to the contrary so preuaile, but that men would and must needs vtter their splenes in all ordinarie matters also, or else it seemed their bowels would burst: therefore the poet deuised a prety fashioned poeme short and sweete (as we are wont to say) and called it *Epigramma*, in which euery mery conceited man might, without any long studie or tedious ambage, make his frend sport, and anger his foe, and giue a prettie nip, or shew a sharpe conceit in few verses: for this Epigramme is but an inscription or writting made as it were vpon a table, or in a windowe, or vpon the wall or mantell of a chimney in some place of common resort, where it was allowed euery man might come, or be sitting to chat and prate, as now in our tauernes and common tabling houses, where many merry heades meete, and scrible with ynke, with chalke, or with a cole, such matters as they would euery man should know & descant vpon. Afterward the same came to be put in paper and in bookes and vsed as ordinarie missiues, some of frendship, some of defiaunce, or as other messages of mirth. Martiall was the cheife of this skil among the Latines, & at these days the best Epigrammes we finde, & of the sharpest conceit, are those that haue bene gathered among the reliques of the two muet Satyres in Rome, Pasquill and Marphorius, which in time of *Sede vacante*, when merry conceited men listed to gibe & iest at the dead Pope or any of his Cardinales, they fastened them vpon those Images which now lie in the open streets, and were tollerated, but after that terme expired they were inhibited againe. These inscriptions or Epigrammes at their begining had no certaine author that would auouch them, some for feare of blame, if they were ouer saucy or sharpe, others for modestie of the writer, as was that *disticke* of Virgil which he set vpon the pallace gate of the emperour Augustus, which I will recite for the breifnes and quicknes of it, and also for another euente that fell out vpon the mater worthy to be remembred. These were the verses:

> *Nocte pluit tota, redeunt spectacula mane;*
> *Diuisum imperium cum Ioue Caesar habet.*

Which I haue thus Englished:

> It raines all night, early the shewes returne;
> God and Caesar do raigne and rule by turne.

As much to say, God sheweth his power by the night raines, Caesar his magnificence by the pompes of the day.

These two verses were very well liked, and brought to th'Emperours Maiestie, who tooke great pleasure in them, & willed the author should be knowen. A sausie courtier profered him selfe to be the man, and had a good reward giuen him, for the Emperour him self was not only learned, but of much munificence toward all learned men: whereupon Virgill, seing him self by his ouermuch modestie defrauded of the reward, that an impudent had gotten by abuse of his merit, came the next night, and fastened vpon the same place this halfe metre, foure times iterated. Thus:

> *Sic vos non vobis*
> *Sic vos non vobis*
> *Sic vos non vobis*
> *Sic vos non vobis*

And there it remained a great while because no man wist what it meant, till Virgill opened the whole fraude by this deuise. He wrote aboue the same halfe metres this whole verse *Exameter*:

> *Hos ego versiculos feci: tulit alter honores.*

And then finished the foure half metres, thus:

> *Sic vos non vobis*   nidificatis aues.
> *Sic vos non vobis*   vellera fertis oues.
> *Sic vos non vobis*   mellificatis apes.
> *Sic vos non vobis*   fertis aratra boues.

And put to his name Publius Virgilius Maro. This matter came by and by to Th'emperours eare, who, taking great pleasure in the deuise, called for Virgill, and gaue him not onely a present reward, with a good allowance of dyet, a bouche in court as we vse to call it, but also held him for euer after, vpon larger triall he had made of his learning and vertue, in so great reputation as he vouchsafed to giue him the name of a frend (*amicus*), which among the Romanes was so great an honour and speciall fauour as all such persons were allowed to the Emperours table, or to the Senatours who had receiued them (as frendes), and they were the only men that came ordinarily to their boords, & solaced with them in their chambers and gardins when none other could be admitted.

Chapter XXVIII

An Epitaph is but a kind of Epigram only applied to the report of the dead persons estate and degree, or of his other good or bad partes, to his commendation or reproch, and is an inscription such as a man may commodiously write or engraue vpon a tombe in few verses, pithie, quicke, and sententious, for the passer-by to peruse and iudge vpon without any long tariaunce. So as if it exceede the measure of an Epigram, it is then (if the verse be correspondent) rather an Elegie then an Epitaph, which errour many of these bastard rimers commit, because they be not learned, nor (as we are wont to say) craftes masters, for they make long and tedious discourses and write them in large tables to be hanged vp in Churches and chauncells ouer the tombes of great men and others, which be so exceeding long as one must haue halfe a dayes leasure to reade one of them, & must be called away before he come halfe to the end, or else be locked into the Church by the Sexten, as I my selfe was once serued reading an Epitaph in a certain cathedrall Church of England. They be ignorant of poesie that call such long tales by the name of Epitaphes; they might better call them Elegies, as I said before, and then ought neither to be engrauen nor hanged vp in tables. I haue seene them neuertheles vpon many honorable tombes of these late times erected, which doe rather disgrace then honour either the matter or maker.

Chapter XXIX

As frendes be a rich and ioyfull possession, so be foes a continual torment and canker to the minde of man; and yet there is no possible meane to auoide this inconuenience, for the best of vs all, he that thinketh he liues most blamelesse, liues not without enemies, that enuy him for his good parts, or hate him for his euill. There be wise men, and of them the great learned man Plutarch tooke vpon them to perswade the benefite that men receiue by their enemies, which though it may be true in manner of Paradoxe, yet I finde mans frailtie to be naturally such, and alwayes hath beene, that he cannot conceiue it in his owne case, nor shew that patience and moderation in such greifs, as becommeth the man perfite and accomplisht in all vertue: but either in deede or by word he will seeke reuenge against them that malice him, or practise his harmes, specially such foes as oppose themselues to a mans loues. This made the aunciet Poetes to inuent a meane to rid the gall of all such Vindicatiue men: so as they might be awrecked of their wrong, & neuer bely their enemie with slaunderous vntruthes. And this was done by a maner of imprecation, or as we call it by cursing and banning of the parties, and wishing all euill to alight vpon them, and, though it neuer the sooner happened, yet was it great easment to the boiling stomacke. They were called *Dirae*, such as Virgill made aginst Battarus, and Ouide, against Ibis: we Christians are forbidden to vse such vncharitable fashions, and willed to referre all our reuenges to God alone.

Chapter XXX

There be also other like Epigrammes that were sent vsually for new yeares giftes, or to be Printed or put vpon their banketting dishes of suger plate or of march paines, & such other dainty meates as by the curtesie & custome euery gest might carry from a common feast home with him to his owne house, & were made for the nonce. They were called *Nenia* or *apophoreta*, and neuer contained aboue one verse, or two at the most, but the shorter the better; we call them Posies, and do paint them now a dayes vpon the backe sides of our fruite trenchers of wood, or vse them as deuises in rings and armes and about such courtly purposes.

So haue we remembred and set forth to your Maiestie very briefly all the commended fourmes of the auncient Poesie, which we in our vulgare makings do imitate and vse vnder these common names: enterlude, song, ballade, carroll, and ditty; borrowing them also from the French, al sauing this word "song" which is our naturall Saxon English word: the rest, such as time and vsurpation by custome haue allowed vs out of the primitiue Greeke & Latine, as Comedie, Tragedie, Ode, Epitaphe, Elegie, Epigramme, and other moe. And we haue purposely omitted all nice or scholasticall curiosities not meete for your Maiesties contemplation in this our vulgare arte, and what we haue written of the auncient formes of Poemes we haue taken from the best clerks writing in the same arte. The part that next followeth, to wit of proportion, because the Greeks nor Latines neuer had it in vse nor made any obseruation, no more then we doe of their feete, we may truly affirme to haue bene the first deuisers thereof our selues, as *autodidaktoi*, and not to haue borrowed it of any other by learning or imitation, and thereby trusting to be holden the more excusable if any thing in this our labours happen either to mislike or to come short of th'authors purpose, because commonly the first attempt in any arte or engine artificiall is amendable, & in time by often experiences reformed. And so no doubt may this deuise of ours be, by others that shall take the penne in hand after vs.

Chapter XXXI

It appeareth by sundry records of bookes both printed & written that many of our countreymen haue painfully trauelled in this part: of whose works some appeare to be but bare translations, other some matters of their owne inuention and very commendable, whereof some recitall shall be made in this place, to th'intent chiefly that their names should not be defrauded of such honour as seemeth due to them for hauing by their thankefull studies so much beautified our English tong as at this day it will be found our nation is in nothing inferior to the French or Italian for copie of language, subtiltie of deuice, good method and proportion in any forme of poeme, but that they may compare with the most, and perchance passe a great many of them. And I will not reach aboue the time of king Edward the third and Richard the second for any that wrote in English meeter, because before their times, by reason of the late Normane conquest, which had brought into this Realme much alteration both of our langage and lawes, and there withall a certain martiall barbarousnes, whereby the study of all good learning was so much decayd as long time after no man or very few entended to write in any laudable science: so as beyond that time there is little or nothing worth commendation to be founde written in this arte. And those of the first age were Chaucer and Gower, both of them, as I suppose, Knightes. After whom followed Iohn Lydgate, the monke of Bury, & that nameles, who wrote the Satyre called Piers Plowman; next him followed Harding, the Chronicler; then, in king Henry th'eights time, Skelton, (I wot not for what great worthines) surnamed the Poet Laureat. In the latter end of the same kings raigne sprong vp a new company of courtly makers, of whom Sir Thomas Wyat th'elder & Henry Earle of Surrey were the two chieftaines, who hauing trauailed into Italie, and there tasted the sweete and stately measures and stile of the Italian Poesie, as nouices newly crept out of the schooles of Dante, Arioste, and Petrarch, they greatly pollished our rude & homely maner of vulgar Poesie from that it had bene before, and for that cause may iustly be sayd the first reformers of our English meetre and stile. In the same time, or not long after, was the Lord Nicholas Vaux, a man of much facilitie in vulgar makings. Afterward, in King Edward the sixths time, came to be in reputation for the same facultie Thomas Sternehold, who first translated into English certaine Psalmes of Dauid, and Iohn Heywood, the Epigrammatist, who for the myrth and quicknesse of his conceits more then for any good learning was in him came to be well benefited by the king. But the principall man in this profession at the same time was Maister Edward Ferrys, a man of no lesse mirth & felicitie that way, but of much more skil & magnificence in his meeter, and therefore wrate for the most part to the stage, in Tragedie and sometimes in Comedie or Enterlude, wherein he gaue the king so much good recreation as he had thereby many good rewardes. In Queenes Maries time florished aboue any other Doctour Phaer, one that was well learned & excellently well translated into English verse Heroicall certaine bookes of Virgils *Æneidos*. Since him followed Maister Arthure Golding, who with no lesse commendation turned into English meetre the Metamorphosis of Ouide, and that other Doctour, who made the supplement to those bookes of Virgils *Æneidos* which Maister Phaer left vndone. And in her Maiesties time that now is are sprong vp an other crew of Courtly makers, Noble men and Gentlemen of her Maiesties owne seruauntes, who haue written excellently well, as it would appeare if their doings could be found out and made publicke with the rest; of which number is first that noble Gentlemen Edward Earle of Oxford, Thomas Lord of Bukhurst, when he was young, Henry Lord Paget, Sir Philip Sydney, Sir Walter Rawleigh, Master Edward Dyar, Maister Fulke Greuell, Gascon, Britton, Turberuille, and a great many other learned Gentlemen, whose names I do not omit for enuie, but to auoyde tediousnesse, and who haue deserued no little commendation. But of them all particularly, this is myne opinion, that Chaucer, with Gower, Lidgat, and Harding, for their antiquitie ought to haue the first place, and Chaucer, as the most renowmed of them all, for the much learning appeareth to be in him, aboue any of the rest. And though many of his bookes be but bare translations out of the Latin & French, yet are they wel handled, as his bookes of *Troilus* and *Cresseid*, and the Romant of the Rose, whereof he translated but one halfe,—the deuice was Iohn de Mehunes, a French Poet: the Canterbury tales were Chaucers owne inuention, as I suppose, and where he sheweth more the naturall of his pleasant wit then in any other of his workes; his similitudes, comparisons, and all other descriptions are such as can not be amended. His meetre Heroicall of *Troilus* and *Cresseid* is very graue and stately, keeping the staffe of seuen and the verse of ten; his other verses of the Canterbury tales be but riding ryme, neuerthelesse very well becomming the matter of that pleasaunt pilgrimage, in which euery mans part is playd with much decency. Gower, sauing for his good and graue moralities, had nothing in him highly to be commended, for his verse was homely and without good measure, his wordes strained much deale out of the French writers, his ryme wrested, and in his inuentions small subtillitie: the applications of his moralities are the best in him, and yet those many times very grossely bestowed; neither doth the substance of his workes sufficently aunswere the subtilitie of his titles. Lydgat, a translatour onely, and no deuiser of that which he wrate, but one that wrate in good verse. Harding, a Poet Epick or Historicall, handled himselfe well according to the time and maner of his subiect. He that wrote the Satyr of Piers Ploughman seemed to haue bene a malcontent of that time, and therefore bent himselfe wholy to taxe the disorders of that age, and specially the pride of the Romane Clergy, of whose fall he seemeth to be a very true Prophet; his verse is but loose meetre, and his termes hard and obscure, so as in them is litle pleasure to be taken. Skelton, a sharpe Satirist, but with more rayling and scoffery then became a Poet Lawreat: such among the Greekes were called *Pantomimi*, with vs Buffons, altogether applying their wits to Scurrillities & other ridiculous matters. Henry Earle of Surrey and Sir Thomas Wyat, betweene whom I finde very litle difference, I repute them (as before) for the two chief lanternes of light to all others that haue since employed their pennes vpon English Poesie: their conceits were loftie, their stiles stately, their conueyance cleanely, their termes proper, their meetre sweete and well proportioned, in all imitating very naturally and studiously their Maister Francis Petrarcha. The Lord Vaux his commendation lyeth chiefly in the facillitie of his meetre, and the aptnesse of his descriptions such as he taketh vpon him to make, namely in sundry of his Songs, wherein he sheweth the counterfait action very liuely & pleasantly. Of the later sort I thinke thus. That for Tragedie, the Lord of Buckhurst & Maister Edward Ferrys, for such doings as I haue sene of theirs, do deserue the hyest price: Th'Earle of Oxford and Maister Edwardes of her Maiesties Chappell for Comedy and Enterlude. For Eglogue and pastorall Poesie, Sir Philip Sydney and Maister Challenner, and that other Gentleman who wrate the late shepheardes Callender. For dittie and amourous Ode I finde Sir Walter Rawleyghs vayne most loftie, insolent, and passionate. Maister Edward Dyar, for Elegie most sweete, solempne, and of high conceit. Gascon, for a good meeter and for a plentifull vayne. Phaer and Golding, for a learned and well corrected verse, specially in translation cleare and very faithfully answering their authours intent. Others haue also written with much facillitie, but more commendably perchance if they had not written so much nor so popularly. But last in recitall and first in degree is the Queene our soueraigne Lady, whose learned, delicate, noble Muse easily surmounteth all the rest that haue written before her time or since, for sence, sweetnesse, and subtillitie, be it in Ode, Elegie, Epigram, or any other kinde of poeme Heroick or Lyricke wherein it shall please her Maiestie to employ her penne, euen by as much oddes as her owne excellent estate and degree exceedeth all the rest of her most humble vassalls.

Thomas Nashe
1567–c. 1601

Gabriel Harvey
c. 1550–1630

Elizabethan England was entertained in the 1590s by a series of "flytings," (personal invectives) launched by Gabriel Harvey and Thomas Nashe, in which Harvey represented an academic traditionalism and Nashe the brashness of the younger Elizabethans.

Gabriel Harvey was educated at Christ's College, Cambridge, and became a fellow of Pembroke Hall in 1574. He was an intimate friend of Edmund Spenser and appeared as the character Hobbinol in *The Shepheard's Calender* (1579). He was generally regarded as a pedantic teacher, and the students at Trinity College once staged a Latin comedy, *Pedantus*, which satirized him (in Nashe's words) as "the concise and firking finicaldo fine schoolmaster." After he failed to be elected Master of Trinity, he became a doctor of civil law at Oxford.

Thomas Nashe was the type of eccentric peculiar to the Elizabethan era. He was a writer who possessed formidable powers of sarcasm and abuse: C.S. Lewis called him "the supreme master of literary *sansculottisme*." His rambling style is also filled with colloquial diction and idiosyncratic compounds. He was a keen judge of contemporary literature, championing many of the greatest writers of the period. He wrote a preface to an unauthorized edition of Sidney's *Astrophel and Stella* as well as completing and publishing Marlowe's unfinished work, *The Tragedy of Dido*.

Nashe studied at St. John's College, Cambridge, beginning in 1581 or 1582. He went to London around 1588 and became associated with Robert Greene and Christopher Marlowe. His early works—a preface to Greene's *Menaphon* entitled *To the Gentlemen Students of Both Universities* as well as *The Anatomy of Absurdity* (both 1589)—are attacks upon the contemporary state of English poetry, written in a style popularized by John Lyly. The preface recommends, in a somewhat contradictory fashion, the realistic expression of ordinary life. The plain man, says Nashe, is "often more judicial in matters of conceit than our quadrant crepundios" (academic chatterboxes). He also attacks the Puritans, who "in a senseless stoical austerity accounted poetry and wit folly." Nashe was an apologist for the episcopacy in the Marprelate controversy, a Puritan attack upon church government. He also wrote a novel, *The Unfortunate Traveler, or, The Life of Jack Wilton* (1954), and a masque, *Summer's Last Will and Testament* (1592). He was the author of "a grossly indecent poem" entitled "The Choosing of Valentines," and he admitted that financial considerations forced him to pen such work for "new-fangled Galiardos and senior Fantasticos."

Nashe's friend Robert Greene had long quarrelled with Gabriel and Richard Harvey. Nashe himself contributed an attack on Richard Harvey in his digression to his *Pierce Peniless his supplication to the Divell* (1592). After Greene's death, Gabriel Harvey published *Four Letters and Certain Sonnets* (1592), which mercilessly detailed Greene's pathetic death and attacked Nashe. Nashe entered the fray in the same year with his *Strange Newes*.

Harvey objected to Nashe's colorful use of language, calling him "the brave Columbus of terms" and one who by his "ruffian rhetoric" surpassed even Arentino, who was "a mere hyperbole incarnate." Nashe, on the other hand, attacked Harvey's Latinized diction and argued for a personal style "of his own begetting, calling no man father in England." J.W.H. Atkins writes of Nashe's polemics: "It was thus a notable plea for the development of originality in style and for the free expression of personality, as against the fixed and formal precepts of the rhetoricians."

The "flyting" continued for some time, at least partially to satisfy the financial demands of London booksellers: Thomas Middleton termed it "but the running a tilt of wits in booksellers shops on both sides of John of Paul's churchyard." The Archbishop of Canterbury terminated the publication of pamphlets on the controversy in 1599.

A General Censure, A Commendation of Sidney, and the selections from *Four Letters* and *Strange News* are all taken from *Elizabethan Critical Essays,* edited by G. Gregory Smith (Oxford University Press, 1904).

A General Censure

TO THE GENTLEMEN STUDENTS OF BOTH UNIVERSITIES

Cvrteovs and wise, whose iudgements (not entangled with enuie) enlarge the deserts of the Learned by your liberall censures, vouchsafe to welcome your schollerlike Shepheard with such Vniuersitie entertainement as either the nature of your bountie or the custome of your common ciuilitie may affoord. To you he appeales that knew him *ab extrema pueritia*, whose *placet* he accounts the *plaudite* of his paines; thinking his daie labour was not altogether lauisht *sine linea*, if there be anie thing of all in it that doth *olere atticum* in your estimate. I am not ignorant how eloquent our gowned age is growen of late, so that euerie mœchanicall mate abhorres the english he was borne too, and plucks with a solemne periphrasis his *vt vales* from the inkhorne: which I impute not so much to the perfection of arts as to the seruile imitation of vainglorious tragœdians, who contend not so seriouslie to excell in action as to embowell the clowdes in a speach of comparison; thinking themselues more than initiated in poets immortalitie if they but once get Boreas by the beard, and the heauenlie bull by the deaw-lap. But herein I cannot so fully bequeath them to follie, as their idiote art-masters, that intrude themselues to our eares as the alcumists of eloquence, who (mounted on the stage of arrogance) think to outbraue better pens with the swelling bumbast of a bragging blanke verse. Indeed, it may be the ingrafted ouerflow of some kilcow conceipt, that ouer-cloieth their imagination with a more than drunken resolution, beeing not extemporall in the inuention of anie other meanes to vent their manhood, commits the digestion of their cholerick incumbrances to the spacious volubilitie of a drumming decasillabon. Mongst this kinde of men that repose eternitie in the mouth of a player, I can but ingrosse some deepe read Grammarians, who, hauing no more learning in their scull than will serue to take vp a commoditie, nor Arte in their brain than was nourished in a seruing mans idlenesse, will take vpon them to be the ironicall censors of all, when God and Poetrie doth know they are the simplest of all.

To leaue these to the mercie of their mother tongue, that feed on nought but the crummes that fal from the translators trencher, I come (sweet friend) to thy *Arcadian Menaphon*, whose attire, though not so statelie, yet comelie, dooth entitle thee aboue all other to that *temperatum dicendi genus* which Tullie in his *Orator* tearmeth true eloquence. Let other men (as they please) praise the mountaine that in seauen yeares brings foorth a mouse, or the Italianate pen that of a packet of pilfries affoordeth the presse a pamphlet or two in an age, and then in disguised arraie vaunts Ouids and Plutarchs plumes as their owne; but giue me the man whose extemporall vaine in anie humor will excell our greatest Art-masters deliberate thoughts, whose inuention, quicker than his eye, will challenge the proudest Rethoritian to the contention of like perfection with like expedition. What is he amongst Students so simple that cannot bring forth (*tandem aliquando*) some or other thing singular, sleeping betwixt euerie sentence? Was it not Maros xij. years toyle that so famed his xij. *Æneidos*? Or Peter Ramus xvj. yeares paines that so praised his pettie Logique? Howe is it, then, our drowping wits should so wonder at an exquisite line that was his masters day labour? Indeede, I must needes say the descending years from the Philosophers Athens haue not been supplied with such present Orators as were able in anie English vaine to be eloquent of their owne, but either they must borrow inuention of Ariosto and his Countreymen, take vp choyce of words by exchange in Tullies *Tusculane* and the Latine Historiographers store-houses, similitudes, nay whole sheetes and tractacts *verbatim*, from the plentie of Plutarch and Plinie, and, to conclude, their whole methode of writing from the libertie of Comical fictions that haue succeeded to our Rethoritians by a second imitation: so that well may the Adage, *Nil dictum quod non dictum prius*, bee the most iudiciall estimate of our latter Writers.

But the hunger of our vnsatiate humorists, beeing such as it is, readie to swallowe all draffe without indifference, that insinuates it selfe to their senses vnder the name of delight, imployes oft times manie thred bare witts to emptie their inuention of their Apish deuices, and talke most superficiallie of Pollicie, as those that neuer ware gowne in the Vniuersitie; wherein they reuiue the olde saide Adage, *Sus Mineruam*, & cause the wiser to quippe them with *Asinus ad Lyram*. Would Gentlemen & riper iudgements admit my motion of moderation in a matter of follie, I wold perswade them to phisicke their faculties of seeing & hearing, as the Sabœans doo their dulled senses with smelling; who (as Strabo reporteth), ouer-cloyed with such odoriferous sauours as the naturall encrease of their Countrey (Balsamum, Amomum, with Myrrhe and Frankencense) sends foorth, refresh their nosthrills with the vnsauorie sent of the pitchie slime that Euphrates casts vp, and the contagious fumes of Goates beardes burnt; so woulde I haue them, beeing surfetted vnawares with the sweete satietie of eloquence which the lauish of our copious Language maie procure, to vse the remedie of contraries, and recreate their rebated witts not, as they did, with the senting of slyme or Goates beardes burnt, but with the ouer-seeing of that *sublime dicendi genus*, which walkes abroad for wast paper in each seruing mans pocket, and the otherwhile perusing of our Gothamists barbarisme; so shoulde the opposite comparison of Puritie expell the infection of absurditie, and their ouer-rackte Rhethorique bee the Ironicall recreation of the Reader. But so farre discrepant is the idle vsage of our vnexperienst punies from this prescription, that a tale of Ihon a Brainfords will and the vnluckie furmentie wilbe as soon interteined into their libraries as the best poeme that euer Tasso eternisht: which, being the effect of an vndescerning iudgement, makes drosse as valuable as gold, and losse as welcome as gaine, the Glowworme mentioned in Æsops fables, namelie the apes follie, to be mistaken for fire, when, as God wot, poore soules, they haue nought but their toyle for their heate, their paines for their sweate, and (to bring it to our english prouerbe) their labour for their trauaile. Wherin I can but resemble them to the Panther, who is so greedie of mens excrements that, if they be hangd vp in a vessell higher than his reach, he sooner killeth himselfe with the ouer-stretching of his windlesse bodie than he wil cease from his intended enterprise. Oft haue I obserued what I now set downe; a secular wit, that hath liued all daies of his life by what doo you lacke, to bee more iudiciall in matters of conceit than our quadrant crepundios that spit *ergo* in the mouth of euerie one they meete: yet those & these are so affectionate to dogged detracting, as the most poysonous Pasquil anie durtie mouthed Martin or Momus euer composed is gathered vp with greedinesse before it fall to the ground, and bought at the deerest, though they smell of the friplers lauander half a yeere after: for I know not how the minde of the meanest is fedde with this follie, that they impute singularitie to him that slanders priuelie, and count it a great peece of arte in an inkhorne man, in anie tapsterlie tearmes whatsoeuer, to oppose his superiours to enuie. I will not denie but in scholler-like matters of controuersie a quicker stile may passe as commendable, and that a quippe to an asse is as good as a goad to an oxe; but when an irregular idiot, that was vp to the eares in diuinitie before euer he met with *probabile* in the Vniuersitie, shall leaue *pro & contra* before he can scarcely pronounce it, and come to correct Common weales, that neuer heard of the name of Magistrate before he came to Cambridge, it is no meruaile if euery alehouse vaunt the table of the world turned vpside down; since the childe beats his father, & the asse whippes his master. But least I might seeme with these night crowes *Nimis curiosus in aliena republica*, I'le turne backe to my first text, of studies of delight, and talke a little in friendship with a few of our triuiall translators.

It is a common practise now a daies amongst a sort of shifting companions, that runne through euery arte and thriue by none, to leaue the trade of *Nouerint*, whereto they were borne, and busie themselues with the indeuors of Art, that could scarcelie latinize their necke-verse if they should haue neede; yet English Seneca read by candle light yeeldes manie good sentences, as *Bloud is a begger*, and so foorth; and, if you intreate him faire in a frostie morning, he will affoord you whole Hamlets, I should say handfulls of tragical speaches. But O griefe! *tempus edax rerum*, what's that will last alwaies? The sea exhaled by droppes will in continuance be drie, and Seneca let bloud line by line and page by page at length must needes die to our stage: which makes his famisht followers to imitate the Kidde in Æsop, who, enamored with the Foxes newfangles, forsooke all hopes of life to leape into a new occupation, and these men, renowncing all possibilities of credit or estimation, to intermeddle with Italian translations: wherein how poorelie they haue plodded (as those that are neither prouenzall men nor are able to distinguish of Articles), let all indifferent Gentlemen that haue trauailed in that tongue discerne by their twopenie pamphlets: & no meruaile though their home-born mediocritie be such in this matter, for what can be hoped of those that thrust Elisium into hell, and haue not learned, so long as they haue liued in the spheares, the iust measure of the Horizon without an hexameter. Sufficeth them to bodge vp a blanke verse with iffs and ands, & other while for recreation after their candle stuffe, hauing starched their beardes most curiouslie, to make a peripateticall path into the inner parts of the Citie, & spend two or three howers in turning ouer French Doudie, where they attract more infection in one minute than they can do eloquence all dayes of their life by conuersing with anie Authors of like argument.

But least in this declamatorie vaine I should condemne all & commend none, I will propound to your learned imitation those men of import that haue laboured with credit in this laudable kinde of Translation. In the forefront of whom I cannot but place that aged Father Erasmus, that inuested most of our Greeke Writers in the roabes of the aunclent Romaines; in whose traces Philip Melancthon, Sadolet, Plantine, and manie other reuerent Germaines insisting haue reedified the ruines of our decayed Libraries, and merueilouslie inriched the Latine tongue with the expence of their toyle. Not long after, their emulation beeing transported into England, euerie priuate Scholler, William Turner and who not, beganne to vaunt their smattering of Latine in English Impressions. But amongst others in that Age, Sir Thomas Eliots elegance did seuer it selfe from all equalls, although Sir Thomas Moore with his Comicall wit at that instant was not altogether idle: yet was not Knowledge fullie confirmed in hir Monarchie amongst vs till that most famous and fortunate Nurse of all learning, Saint Iohns in Cambridge, that at that time was as an Vniuersitie within it selfe—shining so farre aboue all other Houses, Halls, and Hospitalls whatsoeuer, that no Colledge in the Towne was able to compare with the tythe of her Students; hauing (as I haue hearde graue men of credite report) more candles light in it euerie Winter Morning before fowre of the clocke than the fowre of clocke bell gaue stroakes—till Shee (I saie), as a pittying Mother, put too her helping hande, and sent from her fruitefull wombe sufficient Schollers, both to support her owne weale as also to supplie all other inferiour foundations defects, and namelie that royall erection of Trinitie Colledge, which the Vniuersitie Orator, in an Epistle to the Duke of Somerset, aptlie tearmed *Colona diducta* from the Suburbes of Saint Iohns: In which echequer of eloquence Sir Iohn Cheeke, a man of men, supernaturally traded in al tongues, Sir John Mason, Doctor Watson, Redman, Aschame, Grindall, Leuer, Pilkington, all which haue, either by their priuate readings or publique workes, repurged the errors of Arts expelde from their puritie, and set before our eyes a more perfect Methode of Studie.

But howe ill their preceptes haue prospered with our idle Age, that leaue the fountaines of sciences, to follow the riuers of Knowledge, their ouer-fraught Studies with trifling Compendiaries maie testifie: for I knowe not howe it comes to passe by the doating practise of our Diuinitie dunces, that striue to make their Pupills pulpet men before they are reconciled to Priscian, but those yeares which shoulde bee employed in Aristotle are expired in Epitomes; and well too they maye haue so much Catechisme vacation to rake vp a little refuse Philosophie. And heere could I enter into a large fielde of inuectiue against our abiect abbreuiations of Artes, were it not growen to a newe fashion amongst our Nation to vaunt the pride of contraction in euerie manuarie action: in so much, that the *Pater noster*, which was woont to fill a sheete of paper, is written in the compasse of a pennie; whereupon one merelie affirmed that prouerb to be deriued, *No pennie, no pater noster*; which their nice curtailing puts me in mind of the custome of the Scythians, who, if they be at any time distressed with famin, take in their girdles shorter & swaddle themselues streighter, to the intent, no vacuum beeing left in their intrayles, hunger should not so much tirannize ouer their stomacks; euen so these men, opprest with a greater penurie of Art, do pound their capacitie in barren Compendiums, and bound their base humors in the beggerly straites of a hungry Analysis, least, longing after that *infinitum* which the pouertie of their conceit cannot compasse, they sooner yeeld vp their youth to destinie than their heart to vnderstanding. How is it, then, such bungling practitioners in principles shuld euer profite the Common wealth by their negligent paines, who haue no more cunning in Logique or Dialogue Latine than appertains to the literall construction of either: neuerthelesse, it is daily apparant to our domesticall eyes that there is none so forward to publish their imperfections, either in the trade of glose or translations, as those that are more vnlearned than ignorance and lesse conceiuing than infants. Yet dare I not impute absurditie to all of that societie, though some of them haue set their names to their simplicitie. Who euer my priuate opinion condemneth as faultie, Master Gascoigne is not to bee abridged of his deserued esteeme, who first beate the path to that perfection which our best Poets haue aspired too since his departure; whereto he did ascend by comparing the Italian with the English, as Tullie did *Græca cum Latinis*. Neither was Master Turberuile the worst of his time, although in translating he attributed too much to the necessitie of rime. And, in this page of praise, I cannot omit aged Arthur Golding, for his industrious toile in Englishing Ouids *Metamorphosis*, besides manie other exquisite editions of Diuinitie, turned by him out of the French tongue into our own. Master Phaer likewise is not to be forgot in regard of his famous Virgil, whose heauenly verse had it not bin blemisht by his hautie thoghts, England might haue long insulted in his wit, and *corrigat qui potest* haue been subscribed to his workes. But fortune, the Mistres of change, with a pitying compassion respecting Master Stanihursts praise, would that Phaer shoulde fall that hee might rise, whose heroicall Poetrie, infired, I should say inspired, with an hexameter furie, recalled to life whateuer hissed barbarisme hath bin buried this hundred yeare, and reuiued by his ragged quill such carterlie varietie as no hodge plowman in a countrie but would haue held as the extremitie of clownerie; a patterne whereof I will propounde to your iudgements, as neere as I can, being parte of one of his descriptions of a tempest, which is thus:

> Then did he make heauens vault to rebounde, with rounce robble hobble
> Of ruffe raffe roaring, with thwick thwack thurley bouncing.

Which strange language of the firmament, neuer subiect before to our common phrase, makes vs, that are not vsed to terminate heauens moueings in the accents of any voice, esteeme of their triobulare interpreter as of some Thrasonical huffe snuffe, for so terrible was his stile to all milde eares, as would haue affrighted our peaceable Poets from intermedling hereafter with that quarrelling kinde of verse, had not sweete Master France, by his excellent translation of Master Thomas Watsons sugred *Amintas*, animated their dulled spirits to such high witted endeuors. But I knowe not how their ouer timerous cowardise hath stoode in awe of enuie, that no man since him durst imitate any of the worste of those Romane wonders in english, which makes me thinke that either the louers of medocritie are verie many or that the number of good Poets are very small: and in trueth, Master Watson except (whom I mentioned before), I knowe not almost any of late dayes that hath shewed himselfe singular in any speciall Latin Poëm, whose *Amintas* and translated *Antigone* may march in equipage of honour with any of our ancient Poets. I will not say but wee had a Haddon whose pen would haue challenged the Lawrell from Homer, together with Carre, that came as nere him as Virgil to Theocritus. But Tho. Newton with his *Leyland*, and Gabriell Haruey, with two or three other, is almost all the store that is left vs at this hower. Epitaphers and position Poets haue wee more than a good many, that swarme like Crowes to a dead carcas, but flie, like Swallows in the Winter, from any continuate subiect of witte. The efficient whereof I imagine to issue from the vpstart discipline of our reformatorie Churchmen, who account wit vanitie, and poetrie impietie; whose error, although the necessitie of Philosophie might confute, which lies couched most closely vnder darke fables profounditie, yet I had rather referre it as a disputatiue plea to diuines than set it downe as a determinate position, in my vnexperienst opinion. But how euer their dissentious iudgements should decree in their afternoone sessions of *an sit*, the priuat trueth of my discouered Creede in this controuersie is this, that as that beast was thought scarce worthie to bee sacrifised to the Ægiptian Epaphus, who had not some or other blacke spotte on his skinne, so I deeme him farre vnworthie of the name of scholler, & so, consequentlie, to sacrifice his endeuors to art, that is not a Poet, either in whole or in a parte. And here, peraduenture, some desperate quipper will canuaze my proposed comparison *plus vltra*, reconciling the allusion of the blacke spot to the blacke pot; which makes our Poets vndermeale Muses so mutinous, as euerie stanzo they pen after dinner is full poynted with a stabbe. Which their dagger drunkennesse, although it might be excused with *Tam Marti quam Mercurio*, yet will I couer it as well as I may with that prouerbial *fœcundi calices*, that might wel haue been doore keeper to the kanne of Silenus, when, nodding on his Asse trapt with iuie, hee made his moist nosecloth the pausing intermedium twixt euerie nappe. Let frugale scholares and fine fingerd nouices take their drinke by the ownce and their wine by the halpe-worthes, but it is for a Poet to examine the pottle pottes and gage the bottome of whole gallons; *qui bene vult poiein, debet ante pinein*. A pot of blew burning ale, with a fierie flaming tost, is as good as Pallas with the nine Muses on Parnassus top: without the which, in vaine may they crie, "O thou, my muse, inspire mee with some pen," when they want certaine liquid sacrifice to rouze her foorth her denne. Pardon me, Gentlemen, though somewhat merely I glaunce at their imoderate follie, who affirme that no man can write with conceit, except he takes counsell of the cup: nor would I haue you thinke that *Theonino dente* I arme my stile against all, since I doo knowe the moderation of many Gentlemen of that studie to be so farre from infamie as their verse from equalitie: whose sufficiencie, were it as well seene into, by those of higher place, as it wanders abroade vnrewarded in the mouthes of vngratefull monsters, no doubt but the remembrance of Mœcenas liberalitie extended to Maro, and men of like qualitie, would haue lefte no memorie to that prouerb of pouertie, *Si nihil attuleris, ibis Homere foras.* "Tut," saies our English Italians, "the finest witts our Climate sends foorth are but drie braind doltes, in comparison of other countries": whome if you interrupt with *redde rationem*, they will tell you of Petrarche, Tasso, Celiano, with an infinite number of others; to whome if I should oppose Chaucer, Lidgate, Gower, with such like, that liued vnder the tirranie of ignorance, I do think their best louers would bee much discontented with the collation of contraries, if I should write ouer al their heads, Haile fellow well met. One thing I am sure of, that each of these three haue vaunted their meeters with as much admiration in English as euer the proudest Ariosto did his verse in Italian. What should I come to our court, where the otherwhile vacations of our grauer Nobilitie are prodigall of more pompous wit and choyce of words than euer tragick Tasso could attaine too? But, as for pastorall Poemes, I will not make the comparison, least our countrimens credit should bee discountenanst by the contention, who, although they cannot fare with such inferior facilitie, yet I knowe would carrie the bucklers full easilie from all forreine brauers, if their *subiectum circa quod* should sauor of any thing haughtie: and, should the challenge of deepe conceit be intruded by an forreiner to bring our english wits to the tutchstone of Arte, I would preferre diuine Master Spencer, the miracle of wit, to bandie line for line for my life in the honor of England, gainst Spaine, France, Italie, and all the worlde. Neither is he the only swallow of our summer (although Apollo, if his Tripos were vp again, would pronounce him his Socrates), but, he being forborne, there are extant about London many most able men to reuiue Poetrie, although it were executed ten thousand times, as in Platos, so in Puritanes common wealth; as for example Mathew Roydon, Thomas Atchelow, and George Peele, the first of whome, as hee hath shewed himselfe singular in the immortall Epitaph of his beloued Astrophel, besides many other most absolute comicke inuentions (made more publique by euerie mans praise than they can bee by my speache), so the second hath more than once or twise manifested his deepe witted schollership in places of credit, and for the last, thogh not the least of them all, I dare commend him to all that know him as the chiefe supporter of pleasance nowe liuing, the Atlas of Poetrie and *primus verborum Artifex*, whose first encrease, the Arraignement of Paris, might plead to your opinions his pregnant dexteritie of wit and manifold varietie of inuention, wherein (*me iudice*) hee goeth a step beyond all that write. Sundrie other sweete Gentlemen I know, that haue vaunted their pens in priuate deuices, and trickt vp a companie of taffata fooles with their feathers, whose beautie if our Poets had not peecte with the supply of their periwigs, they might haue antickt it vntill this time vp and downe the countrey with the King of Fairies, and dined euerie daie at the pease porredge ordinarie with Delphrigus. But Tolossa hath forgot that it was sometime sackt, and beggers that euer they caried their fardles on footback: and in truth no meruaile, when as the deserued reputation of one Roscius is of force to inrich a rabble of counterfets; yet let subiects for all their insolence dedicate a *De profundis* euerie morning to the preseruation of their Cæsar, least their encreasing indignities returne them ere long to their iuggling to mediocrity, and they bewaile in weeping blankes the wane of their Monarchie.

As Poetrie hath beene honoured in those her forenamed professours, so it hath not beene any whit disparaged by William Warners absolute Albions. And heere Authoritie hath made a full point: in whose reuerence insisting I cease to expose to your sport the picture of those Pamphleters and Poets, that make a patrimonie of *In speech*, and more than a younger brothers inheritance of their *Abcie*. Reade fauourably, to incourage me in the firstlings of my folly, and perswade your selues I will persecute those idiots and their heires vnto the third generation, that haue made Art bankerout of her ornaments, and sent Poetry a begging vp and downe the Countrey. It may be my Anatomie of Absurdities may acquaint you ere long with my skill in surgery, wherein the diseases of Art more merrily discouered may make our maimed Poets put together their blankes vnto the building of an Hospitall.

If you chance to meete it in Paules, shaped in a new suite of similitudes, as if, like the eloquent apprentice of Plutarch, it were propped at seuen yeares end in double apparell, thinke his master hath fulfilled couenants, and onely cancelled the Indentures of dutie. If I please, I will thinke my ignorance indebted vnto you that applaud it: if not, what rests but that I be excluded from your curtesie, like Apocrypha from your Bibles?

How euer, yours euer,
Thomas Nashe.

A Commendation of Sidney

Tempus adest plausus; aurea pompa venit: so endes the Sceane of Idiots, and enter Astrophel in pompe. Gentlemen, that haue seene a thousand lines of folly, drawn forth *ex vno puncto umpudentiae*, & two famous Mountains to goe to the conception of one Mouse, that haue had your eares defned with the eccho of Fames brasen towres when only they haue been toucht with a leaden pen, that haue seene Pan sitting in his bower of delights & a number of Midasses to admire his miserable hornepipes, let not your surfeted sight, new come from such puppet play, think scorne to turn aside into this Theater of pleasure, for here you shal find a paper stage streud with pearle, an artificial heau'n to ouershadow the fair frame, & christal wals to encounter your curious eyes, while the tragicommody of loue is performed by starlight. The chiefe Actor here is Melpomene, whose dusky robes, dipt in the ynke of teares, as yet seeme to drop when I view them neere. The argument cruell chastitie, the Prologue hope, the Epilogue dispaire; *videte, quaeso, et linguis animisque fauete*. And here, peraduenture, my witles youth may be taxt with a margent note of presumption for offering to put vp any motion of applause in the behalfe of so excellent a Poet (the least sillable of whose name sounded in the eares of iudgment is able to giue the meanest line he writes a dowry of immortality); yet those that obserue how iewels oftentimes com to their hands that know not their value, & that the cockcombes of our days, like Esop's Cock, had rather haue a Barly kernell wrapt vp in a Ballet then they wil dig for the welth of wit in any ground that they know not, I hope wil also hold me excused though I open the gate to his glory & inuite idle eares to the admiration of his melancholy.

Quid petitur sacris nisi tantum fama poetis?

Which although it be oftentimes imprisoned in Ladyes casks & the president bookes of such as cannot see without another man's spectacles, yet at length it breakes foorth in spight of his keepers, and vseth some priuate penne (in steed of a picklock) to procure his violent enlargement. The Sunne for a time may maske his golden head in a cloud, yet in the end the thicke vaile doth vanish, and his embellished blandishment appeares. Long hath Astrophel (Englands Sunne) withheld the beames of his spirite from the common view of our darke sence, and night hath houered ouer the gardens of the nine Sisters, while *Ignis fatuus* and grosse fatty flames (such as commonly arise out of Dunghilles) haue tooke occasion, in the middest eclipse of his shining perfections, to wander a broade with a wispe of paper at their tailes like Hobgoblins, and leade men vp and downe in a circle of absurditie a whole weeke, and neuer know where they are. But now that cloude of sorrow is dissolued which fierie Loue exhaled from his dewie haire, and affection hath vnburthened the labouring streames of her wombe in the lowe cesterne of his Graue; the night hath resigned her iettie throne vnto Lucifer, and cleere daylight possesseth the skie that was dimmed; wherfore breake off your daunce, you Fayries and Elues, and from the fieldes with the torne carcases of your Timbrils, for your kingdome is expired. Put out your rush candles, you Poets and Rimers, and bequeath your crazed quaterzayns to the Chaundlers; for loe, here he cometh that hath broke your legs. Apollo hath resigned his Iuory Harp vnto Astrophel, & he, like Mercury, must lull you a sleep with his musicke. Sleepe Argus, sleep Ignorance, sleep Impudence, for Mercury hath Io, & onely Io Pœan belongeth to Astrophel. Deare Astrophel, that in the ashes of thy Loue liuest againe like the Phœnix, O might in the ashes of thy bodie (as thy name) live againe likewise here amongst vs! but the earth, the mother of mortalitie, hath snacht thee too soone into her chilled colde armes, and will not let thee by any meanes be drawne from her deadly imbrace; and thy diuine Soule, carried on an Angel's wings to heauen, is installed in Hermes place, sole prolocutor to the Gods. Therefore mayest thou neuer returne from the Elisian fieldes like Orpheus; therefore must we euer mourne for our Orpheus.

Fayne would a seconde spring of passion heere spend it selfe on his sweet remembrance; but Religion, that rebuketh prophane lamentation, drinkes in the riuers of those dispaireful teares which languorous ruth hath outwelled, & bids me looke back to the house of honor, where from one and the selfe same root of renowne I shal find many goodly branches deriued, & such as, with the spreading increase of their vertues, may somewhat ouershadow the Griefe of his los. Amongst the which, fayre sister of Phœbus, and eloquent secretary to the Muses, most rare Countesse of Pembroke, thou art not to be omitted, whom Artes doe adore as a second Minerua, and our Poets extoll as the Patronesse of their inuention; for in thee the Lesbian Sappho with her lirick Harpe is disgraced, and the Laurel Garlande which thy Brother so brauely aduaunst on his Launce is still kept greene in the Temple of Pallas. Thou only sacrificest thy soule to contemplation, thou only entertainest emptie handed Homer, & keepest the springs of Castalia from being dryed vp. Learning, wisedom, beautie, and all other ornaments of Nobilitie whatsoeuer seeke to approue themselues in thy sight and get a further seale of felicity from the smiles of thy fauour:

O Joue digna viro ni Joue nata fores.

I feare I shall be counted a mercenary flatterer for mixing my thoughts with such figuratiue admiration, but generall report that surpasseth my praise condemneth my rhetoricke of dulnesse for so colde a commendation. Indeede, to say the truth, my stile is somewhat heauie gated, and cannot daunce, trip, and goe so liuely, with "oh! my loue, ah! my loue, all my loues gone," as other Sheepheards that haue been fooles in the Morris time out of minde; nor hath my prose any skill to imitate the Almond leape verse, or sit tabring fiue yeres together nothing but "to bee, to hee," on a paper drum. Onely I can keepe pace with Grauesend barge, and care not if I haue water enough to lande my ship of fooles with the Tearme (the tyde I shoulde say). Now euery man is not of that minde; for some, to goe the lighter away, will take in their fraught of spangled feathers, golden Peebles, Straw, Reedes, Bulrushes, or anything, and then they beare out their sayles as proudly as if they were balisted with Bulbiefe. Others are so hardly bested for loading that they are faine to retaile the cinders of Troy, and the shiuers of broken trunchions, to fill vp their boate that else should goe empty; and if they haue but a pound weight of good Merchandise, it shall be placed at the poope, or pluckt in a thousand peeces to credit their carriage. For my part, euery man as he likes, *mens cuiusque is est quisque*. 'Tis as good to goe in cut-fingerd Pumps as corke shooes, if one were Cornish diamonds on his toes. To explain it by a more familiar example, an Asse is no great statesman in the beastes common-wealth, though he weare his eares *vpseuant muffe*, after the Muscouy fashion, & hange the lip like a Capcase halfe open, or look as demurely as a sixpenny browne loafe, for he hath some imperfections that do keepe him from the common Councel; yet of many he is deemed a very vertuous member, and one of the honestest sort of men that are. So that our opinion (as Sextus Empiricus affirmeth) giues the name of good or ill to euery thing. Out of whose works (latelie translated into English for the benefit of vnlearned writers) a man might collect a whole booke of this argument, which no doubt woulde proue a worthy commonwealth matter, and far better than wits waxe karnell: much good worship haue the Author.

Such is this golden age wherein we liue, and so replenisht with golden asses of all sortes, that, if learning had lost it selfe in a groue of Genealogies, wee neede doe no more but sette an olde goose ouer halfe a dozen pottle pots (which are as it were the egges of inuention), and wee shall haue such a breede of bookes within a little while after, as will fill all the world with the wilde fowle of good wits. I can tell you this is a harder thing then making golde of quick siluer, and will trouble you more then the Morrall of Æsop's Glow-worme hath troubled our English Apes, who, striuing to warme themselues with the flame of the Philosopher's stone, haue spent all their wealth in buying bellowes to blowe this false fyre. Gentlemen, I feare I haue too much presumed on your idle leysure, and beene too bold to stand talking all this while in an other mans doore; but now I will leaue you to suruey the pleasures of Paphos, and offer your smiles on the Aulters of Venus.

    Yours in all desire to please,
                    Tho: Nashe.

Four Letters

FROM
THE THIRD LETTER

It were pittie but wonderous wits (giue enemies their due) shoulde become more woonderous by comparison; conference maketh excellent things appeare more admirable: & I am so far from being a Saturnist by nature, or a Stoick by discipline, that I can easily frame a certaine pleasurable delight vnto my selfe, by ministring some matter vnto them that now are faine to make something of nothing, and wittily to plaie with their own shadowes. It goeth somewhat hard in my harsh Legend, when the father of Musicke must be mocked—not Tubulcain, as he mistearmeth him, but Tuball, whom Genesis voutsafeth honourable mention—and the Hexameter verse flouted: whereof neither Homer in Greeke, nor Virgill in Latine (how valorous Autors!), nor Alexander in conquest, nor Augustus in maiesty (how puissant Princes!) were ashamed, but accompted it the onely gallant trompet of braue and Heroicall Actes. And I wis the English is nothing too good to imitat the Greeke, or Latine, or other eloquent Languages that honour the Hexameter as the soueraigne of verses and the high Controwler of Rimes. If I neuer deserue anye better remembraunce, let mee rather be epitaphed, The Inuentour of the English Hecellent Sir Phillip Sidney disdained not to follow in his Arcadia & elsewhere—then be chronicled, The greene maister of the Blacke Arte, or the founder of vgly oathes, or the father of misbegotten *Infortunatus*, or the Scriuener of Crosbiters, or, as one of his owne sectaries termed him, the Patriarch of shifters. Happy man I, if these two be my hainousest crimes and deadliest sinnes: To bee the Inuentour of the English Hexameter, and to bee orderlie clapt in the Fleete for the foresaide Letters; where he that sawe me sawe me at Constantinople. . . .

I will not condemne or censure his [Greene's] works, which I neuer did so much as superficially ouer-runne, but as some fewe of them occursiuly presented themselues in Stationers shops and some other houses of my acquaintaunce. But I pray God they haue not done more harme by corruption of manners then good by quickening of witte: and I would some Buyers had either more Reason to discerne, or lesse Appetite to desire such Nouels. The world is full inough of fooleries, though the humor be not feasted with such luxurious and riotous Pamphlets. Howe vnlike Tullies sweete Offices; or Isocrates pithy instructions; or Plutarches holesome Morrals; or the delicate Dialogues of Xenophon and Plato; or the sage Tragedies of Sophocles and Euripides; or the fine Comedies of the dainetiest Atticke wittes; or other excellent monumentes of antiquity, neuer sufficientlie perused! Yet the one as stale as oldest fashions; and what more freshly current for awhile then the other? Euen Guicciardines siluer Historie and Ariostos golden Cantoes grow out of request, & the Countesse of Pembrookes Arcadia is not greene inough for queasie stomackes; but they must haue Greenes Arcadia, and, I beleeue, most eagerlie longed for Greenes Faerie Queene. . . .

Great and small things may in some proportion be compared together: and beholde as miserable a spectacle in their kinde. Flourishing Mr. Greene is most wofully faded: and whilest I am bemoaning his ouer-pittious decay, & discoursing the vsuall successe of such ranke wittes, Loe, all on the suddaine, his sworne brother, M. Pierce Pennie-lesse (still more paltery; but what remedy? we are already ouer shoes and must now goe through), Loe his inwardest companion, that tasted of the fatall herringe, cruelly pinched with want, vexed with discredite, tormented with other mens felicitie, and ouerwhelmed with his owne misery, in a raving and franticke moode most desperately exhibiteth his supplication to the Diuell. A strange title, an od wit, and a mad hooreson I warrant him: doubtles it wil proue some dainty deuise, queintly contriued by way of humble Supplication To the high and mighty Prince of Darkenesse; not Dunsically botched-vp, but right-formally conueied, according to the stile and tenour of Tarletons president, his famous play of the seauen Deadly sinnes. Which most dea[d]ly, but most liuely, playe I might haue seene in London, and was verie gently inuited thereunto at Oxford by Tarleton himselfe. Of whome I merrily demaunding which of the seauen was his owne deadlie sinne, he bluntly aunswered after this manner, "By God, the sinne of other Gentlemen, Lechery." "Oh but that, M. Tarleton, is not your part vpon the stage; you are too blame that dissemble with the world & haue one part for your frends pleasure, an other for your owne." "I am somewhat of Doctor Pernes religion," quoth he; and abruptlie tooke his leaue. Surely it must needes bee current in matter, and autentical in forme, that had first such a learned president, and is now pleasantlie interlaced with diuers new-founde phrases of the Tauerne, and patheticallie intermiperience. For the poore Tennement of his Purse (quoth himselfe, grammercy, good Tarleton) hath bene the Diuels Dauncing schoole, anie time this halfe yeare; and I pray God (quoth another) the poore Tennement of his Heart hath not also beene the Diuels Fencing Schoole twise as long. Particulars and Circumstances are tedious, especially in sorrowfull and forlorne causes. The summe of summes is, he tost his imagination a thousand waies, and, I beleeue, searched euery corner of his Grammer-schoole witte (for his margine is as deepelie learned as *Fauste precor gelida*) to see if he coulde finde anie meanes to relieue his estate; but all his thoughtes and marginal notes consorted to his conclusion that the worlde was vncharitable, and he ordained to be miserable. It were cruelty to ad affliction to affliction: what flinty Heart would not sigh, or rather melt, to heare the bewailefull moane of that sobbing and groning Muse, the daughter of most pregnant, but most wretched, Niobe?

> Why ist damnation to despaire, and die,
> When Life is my true happines disease?

And a little after:

> Diuines and dying men may talke of Hell:
> But in my Heart her seueral tormentes dwell.

And so foorth, most hideouslie, for the Text is much more dolefull then the Glosse. And who woulde not be moued with more pittifull compunction to heare the lamentable Farewell,

> England, adieu! the soile that brought me foorth:
> Adieu vnkinde! where Skill is nothing worth:

then to read that profound Quotation,

> *Hei mihi, quam paucos haec mea dicta mouent?*

Which was thought Patheticall out of crie.

> Forgiue him God, although he curse his Birth,
> Since Miserie hath dawnted all his Mirth.

. . . Good sweete Oratour, be a deuine Poet indeede; and vse heauenly Eloquence indeede; and employ thy golden talent with amounting vsance indeede; and with heroicall Cantoes honour right Vertue, & braue valour indeede; as noble Sir Philip Sidney and gentle Maister Spencer haue done, with immortall Fame; and I will bestow more complements of rare amplifications vpon thee then euer any bestowed vppon them, or this Tounge euer affoorded, or any Aretinish mountaine of huge exaggerations can bring foorth. Right artificiality (whereat I once aimed to the vttermost power of my slender capacity) is not mad-brained, or ridiculous, or absurd, or blasphemous, or monstrous, but deepe conceited, but pleasurable, but delicate, but exquisite, but gratious, but admirable; not according to the fantasticall mould of Aretine or Rabelays, but according to the fine modell of Orpheus, Homer, Pindarus, & the excellentest wittes of Greece, and of the Lande that floweth with milke and hony. For what Festiuall Hymnes so diuinely dainty as the sweete Psalmes of King Dauid, royally translated by Buchanan? or what sage Gnomes so profoundly pithy as the wise Prouerbes of King Salomon, notably also translated. But how few Buchanans? Such liuely springes of streaming Eloquence & such right-Olympicall hilles of amountinge witte I cordially recommend to the deere Louers of the Muses; and namely to the professed Sonnes of the same, Edmond Spencer, Richard Stanihurst, Abraham France, Thomas Watson, Samuell Daniell, Thomas Nash, and the rest; whome I affectionately thancke for their studious endeuours, commendably employed in enriching & polishing their natiue Tongue, neuer so furnished or embellished as of late. For I dare not name the Honorabler Sonnes & Nobler Daughters of the sweetest & diuinest Muses that euer sang in English or other language, for feare of suspition of that which I abhorre; and their owne most delectable and delicious Exercises (the fine handy worke of excellent Nature and excellenter Arte combined) speake incomparably more then I am able briefly to insinuate. Gentle mindes and flourishing wittes were infinitely to blame, if they should not also for curious imitation propose vnto themselues such faire Types of refined and engraced Eloquence. The right Noouice of pregnante and aspiring conceit wil not ouerskippe any precious gemme of Inuention or any beautifull floure of Elocution that may richly adorne or gallantly bedecke the trimme garland of his budding stile. I speake generally to euery springing wit, but more specially to a few, and at this instante singularly to one, whom I salute with a hundred blessings, and entreate with as many prayers, to loue them that loue all good wittes, and hate none but the Diuell, and his incarnate Impes, notoriously professed. I protest it was not thy person that I any way disliked, but thy rash and desperate proceeding against thy well-willers; which in some had bene vnsufferable; in an youth was more excusable; in a reformed youth is pardonable, and rather matter of concordance then of aggrieuance.

FROM
THE FOURTH LETTER

Pregnant Rules auail much, but visible Examples amount incredibly: Experience, the onely life of perfection, & onely perfection of life. Whatsoeuer occasion causeth me to be mistaken, as ouer-much addicted to Theory, without respect of action (for that is one of the especiallest points, which I am importuned to resolue), I neuer made account of any study, meditation, conference, or Exercise that importeth not effectual vse, & that aymeth not altogether at action, as the singuler marke, whereat euery Arte & euery vertue is to leuell. I loue Method, but honour Practise: must I shew the difference? Either Arte is obscure, or the quickest capacity dull and needeth Methode, as it were the bright Moone, to illuminate the darkesome night: but Practise is the bright Sun that shineth in the day, & the soueraigne Planet that gouerneth the world: as elsewhere I haue copiously declared. To excell, ther is no way but one: to marry studious Arte to diligent Exercise: but where they must be vnmarried, or diuorced, geue me rather Exercise without Arte then Arte without Exercise. Perfect vse worketh masteries, and disgraceth vnexperienced Arte. Examples are infinite, and dayly display themselues. A world without a Sunne; a Boddy without a Soule; Nature without Arte; Arte without Exercise—sory creatures. Singular practise the only singuler and admirable woorkeman of the world.

Must I dispatch the rest that is exacted? It is no fit place; and the least little wil seme too much. As in other thinges, so in Artes; formality doth well, but materiality worketh the feat. Were Artists as skillfull as Artes are powerfull, wonders might be atchieued by Arte emprooued; but they that vnderstand little write much; and they that know much write little. The vayne Peacocke with his gay coullours, and the prattling Parrat with his ignorant discourses (I am not to offend any but the Peacocke and the Parrat) haue garishly disguised the worthiest Artes, and deepely discredited the profoundest Artistes, to the pitifull defacement of the one and the shamefull preiudice of the other. Rodolph Agricola, Philip Melancthon, Ludouike Viues, Peter Ramus, and diuers excellent schollers haue earnestly complaned of Artes corrupted, and notably reformed many absurdities: but still corruption ingendreth one vermine or other, and still that pretious Trainement is miserably abused which should be the fountaine of skill, the roote of vertue, the seminary of gouernment, the foundation of all priuate and publike good.

The Methodist & Discourser might be more materiall; the Theorist and Practitioner more formall: all fower more effectuall: or how cometh it to passe that much more is professed but much lesse perfourmed then in former ages? especially in the mathematikes, and in naturall Magic, which being cunningly and extensiuely imployed (after the manner of Archimedes, Archytas, Apollonius, Regiomontanus, Bacon, Cardan, and such like industrious Philosophers, the Secretaries of Art and Nature) might wonderfully bestead the Commonwealth with many puissant engins and other commodious devises for warre and peace. In actuall Experimentes and Polymechany, nothing too profound: a superficiall slightnesse may seeme fine for sheetes, but proueth good for nothinge: as in other businesse, so in learninge, as good neuer a whit, according to the Prouerbe, as neuer the better: one perfect Mechanician worth ten vnperfect Philosophers: an ignorant man lesse shameth himselfe, lesse beguileth his frend, lesse disableth the Common-wealth, then a putatiue Artiste: a whole naturall wit more seruiceable, and more sufficient, then a Demi-scholler, who presuming on that which he hath not abateth the force of that which he hath. He must not dreame of perfection that emproueth not the perfectest Art with most perfec industrie. A snatch and away, with Neoptolemus and the common sort of studentes, may please a little, but profiteth nothing. It is the Body, not the shadow, that dispatcheth the businesse. The flower delighteth to-day, and fadeth to-morrow: the fruite edifieth and endureth: the visard, the painted sheath, and such terrible braueries, can best report their owne entertainment: the peacock and the parrat haue good leaue to prancke vppe themselues, and leysure inough to reuiue and repolish their expired workes. "What can last allwayes?" quote the neat Tayler, when his fine seames began to cracke their credite at the first drawing-on. I appeale to Poules Churchyard, whether lines be like vnto seames: and whether the Deft writer be as sure a workman as the neat Tayler. There may be a fault in the Reader, aswell as in the weauer: but euery manne contente himselfe to beare the burthen of his owne faultes; and, good sweete Autors, infourme your selues before you vndertake to instruct other . . .

God helpe, when Ignorance and want of Experience, vsurping the chayre of scrupulous and rigorous Iudgement, will in a fantasticall Imagination, or percase in a melancholy moode, presume farther, by infinite degrees, then the learnedest men in a ciuill Common-wealth, or the sagest counsellours in a Princes Court. Our new-new writers, the Loadstones of the Presse, are wonderfully beholdinge to the Asse; in a manner the only Autor, which they alledge. The world was euer full inough of fools, but neuer so full of Asses in print; the very Elephant, a great Asse; the Camell, a huge Asse; the Beare, a monstrous Asse; the Horse, an absurd Asse; the Fox himselfe, a little Asse, or, for variety, an Ape: who not an Asse or an Ape in good plaine English, that chanceth to come in the wise Asse-makers & mighty Ape-dubbers way? They are fine men, & haue many sweete phrases: it is my simplicity that I am so slenderly acquainted with that dainty stile, the only new fashion of current Eloquence in Esse, far surpassing the stale vein of Demosthenes or Tully, Iewel or Harding, Whitgift or Cartwright, Sidney or Spencer. But I could wish Ignorance would fauour it selfe: & it were not amisse that want of Experience should be content to be a little modest or somewhat quiet: & both enforce les occasion to be termed, as they will needes notoriously proclaime themselues, as it were, with a publike "Oh-is," or a generall *Nouerint vniuersi per praesentes*. For if any thing indeede be a right Asse in print, it is the one; and if any thing indeede be a right Calfe in print, it is the other: Ignorance, the famousest Asse; and want of Experience, the notablest Calfe in the world.

FROM
Strange News

or, Four Letters Confuted

O Heathenists and Pagan Hexamiters, come thy waies down from thy Doctourship, & learne thy Primer of Poetry ouer again; for certainly thy pen is in state of a Reprobate with all men of iudgement and reckoning. . . .

The tickling and stirring inuectiue vaine, the puffing and swelling Satiricall spirit came vpon him, as it came on Coppinger and Arthington, when they mounted into the pease-cart in Cheapeside and preacht. Needes hee must cast vp certayne crude humours of English Hexameter Verses that lay vppon his stomacke; a Noble-man stoode in his way as he was vomiting, and from top to toe he all to berayd him with Tuscanisme. . . .

Tubalcan, alias Tuball, first founder of Farriers Hall, heere is a great complaint made, that *Vtriusque Academiae* Robertus Greene hath mockt thee, because hee saide that as thou wert the first inuenter of Musicke, so Gabriell Howliglasse was the first inuenter of English Hexameter verses. *Quid respondes*? canst thou brooke it; yea or no? Is it any treason to thy well tuned hammers to say they begat so renowmed a childe as Musicke? Neither thy hammers nor thou I knowe, if they were put to their booke oaths, will euer say it.

The Hexamiter verse I graunt to be a Gentleman of an aunciant house (so is many an english begger); yet this Clyme of ours hee cannot thriue in. Our speech is too craggy for him to set his plough in; hee goes twitching and hopping in our language like a man running vpon quagmiers, vp the hill in one Syllable, and downe the dale in another, retaining no part of that stately smooth gate which he vaunts himselfe with amongst the Greeks and Latins.

Homer and Virgil, two valorous Authors, yet were they neuer knighted, they wrote in Hexameter Verses: *Ergo*, Chaucer and Spencer, the Homer and Virgil of England, were farre ouerseene that they wrote not all their Poems in Hexamiter verses also. In many Countries veluet and Satten is a commoner weare than cloth amongst vs: *Ergo* wee must leaue wearing of cloth, and goe euerie one in veluet and satten, because other Countries vse so.

The Text will not beare it, good Gilgilis Hobberdehoy. Our english tongue is nothing too good, but too bad to imitate the Greeke and Latine.

Master Stannyhurst (though otherwise learned) trod a foule, lumbring, boystrous, wallowing, measure in his translation of Virgil. He had neuer been praisd by Gabriel for his labour, if therein hee had not bin so famously absurd. . . .

Let Maister Butler of Cambridge his testimoniall end this controuersie, who at that time that thy ioyes were in the Fleeting, and thou crying for the Lords sake out at an iron window, in a lane not farre from Ludgate hill, questiond some of his companions verie inquisitiuelie that were newlie come from London, what nouelties they brought home with them. Amongst the rest he broke into this Hep Knowne to the world for a foole, and clapt in the Fleete for a Rimer?

> But ah! what newes do you heare of that good Gabriel huffe snuffe,
> Knowne to the world for a foole, and clapt in the Fleete for a Rimer?

. . . Thy Hexameter Verses, or thy hue and cry after a person as cleare as Christall, I do not so deeply commend, for al Maister Spencer *long* since imbrast it with an ouerlouing sonnet.

Why should friends dissemble one with another: they are very vgly and artlesse. You will neuer leaue your olde trickes of drawing M. Spencer into euerie pybald thing you do. If euer he praisd thee, it was because he had pickt a fine vaine foole out of thee, and he would keepe thee still by flattring thee, til such time as he had brought thee into that extreame loue with thy selfe, that thou shouldst run mad with the conceit, and so be scorned of all men. . . .

As for *Flores Poetarum*, they are flowers that yet I neuer smelt too. Ile pawne my hand to a halfepenny, I haue readd more good Poets thorough than thou euer hardst off.

The floures of your *Foure Letters* it may be I haue ouerlookt more narrowlie, and done my best deuoire to assemble them together into patheticall posie, which I will here present to Maister Orator Edge for a Newyeares gift, leauing them to his wordie discretion to be censured whether they be currant in inkehornisme or no: Conscious mind; canicular tales; egregious an argument—when as egregious is neuer vsed in English but in the extreame ill part; Ingenuitie; Iouiall mind; valorous Authors; inckehorne aduentures; inckehorne pads; putatiue opinions; putatiue artists; energeticall persuasions; Rascallitie; materiallitie; artificiallitie; Fantasticallitie; diuine Entelechy; loud mentery; deceitfull perfidy; addicted to Theory; the worlds great Incendiarie; sirenized furies; soueraigntie immense; abundant Cauteles; cautelous and aduentrous; cordiall liquor; Catilinaries and Phillipicks; perfunctorie discourses; Dauids sweetnes olimpique; The Idee; high and deepe Abisse of excellence; the only Vnicorne of the Muses; the Aretinish mountaine of huge exaggerations; the gratious law of Amnesty; amicable termes; amicable end; effectuate; addoulce his melodie; Mag[ic] polimechany; extensiuely emploid; precious Traynment; Nouellets; Notorietie; negotiation; mechanician.

Nor are these all, for euerie third line hath some of this ouer-rackt absonisme. Nor do I altogether scum off all these as the new ingendred fome of the English, but allowe some of them for a neede to fill vp a verse; as *Traynment*, and one or two wordes more, which the libertie of prose might well haue spar'd. In a verse, when a worde of three sillables cannot thrust in but sidelings, to ioynt him euen, we are oftentimes faine to borrowe some lesser quarry of elocution from the Latine, alwaies retaining this for a principle, that a leake of indesinence, as a leake in a shippe, must needly bee stopt with what matter soeuer.

Chaucers authoritie I am certaine shal be alleadgd for a many of these balductums. Had Chaucer liu'd to this age, I am verily perswaded hee would haue discarded the tone halfe of the harsher sort of them.

They were the Oouse which ouerflowing barbarisme, withdrawne to her

Scottish Northren chanell, had left behind her. Art, like yong grasse in the spring of Chaucers florishing, was glad to peepe vp through any slime of corruption, to be beholding to she car'd not whome for apparaile, trauailing in those colde countries. There is no reason that shee, a banisht Queene into this barraine soile, hauing monarchizd it so long amongst the Greeks and Romanes, should (although warres furie had humbled her to some extremitie) still be constrained, when she had recouerd her state, to weare the robes of aduersitie [&] iet it in her old rags, when she is wedded to new prosperitie. *Vtere moribus praeteritis*, saith Caius Caesar in *Aulus Gellius, loquere verbis praesentibus*. . . .

Wherein I haue borrowed from Greene or Tarlton, that I should thanke them for all I haue? Is my stile like Greenes, or my ieasts like Tarltons? Do I talke of any counterfeit birds, or hearbs, or stones, or rake vp any new-found poetry from vnder the wals of Troy? If I do, trip mee with it; but I doe not, therefore Ile be so saucy as trip you with the grand lie. Ware stumbling of whetstones in the darke there, my maisters.

This I will proudly boast (yet am I nothing a kindred to the three brothers) that the vaine which I haue (be it a median vaine, or a madde vaine) is of my owne begetting, and cals no man father in England but my selfe, neyther Euphues, nor Tarlton, nor Greene. Not Tarlton nor Greene but haue beene contented to let my simple iudgement ouerrule them in some matters of wit. Euphues I readd when I was a little ape in Cambridge, and then I thought it was *Ipse ille*; it may be excellent good still for ought I know, for I lookt not on it this ten yeare: but to imitate it I abhorre, otherwise than it imitates Plutarch, Ouid, and the choisest Latine Authors.

If you be auisde I tooke shortest vowels and longest mutes in the beginning of my books as suspitious of being accessarie to the making of a Sonnet wherto Maister Christopher Birds name is set, there I saide that you mute forth many such phrases in the course of your booke which I would point at as I past by. Heere I am as good as my word, for I note that thou, beeing afraide of beraying thy selfe with writing, wouldest faine bee a mute, when it is too late to repent. Againe, thou reuiest on vs, and saist that mutes are coursed and vowels haunted. Thou art no mute, yet shalt thou be haunted and coursed to the full. I will neuer leaue thee as long as I am able to lift a pen.

Whether I seeke to bee counted a terrible bulbegger or no, Ile baite thee worse than a bull, so that the[n] thou shalt desire some body on thy knees to helpe thee with letters of commendation to Bull the hangman, that he may dispatch thee out of the way before more affliction come vpon thee.

Sir John Harington
1560–1612

Sir John Harington, the first English translator of Ariosto's *Orlando Furioso,* was one of the more colorful characters of a distinctly colorful age. The son of a minor courtier and an illegitimate daughter of Henry VIII, Harington was schooled at Eton, Cambridge, and Lincoln's Inn before he moved to Court and became famous as the "saucy godson" of Elizabeth on account of his barbed wit. He was banished from Court several times, once for translating and circulating among the ladies-in-waiting a lascivious tale from Ariosto. As condition for his return, Elizabeth demanded that he translate the entire *Orlando Furioso,* which he did in 1591.

Along with his literary achievements, Harington is remembered as the inventor of the flush toilet (he installed one at the Royal Palace at Richmond). In *The Metamorphosis of Ajax,* published in 1596 ("Ajax" or "jakes" being Elizabethan slang for privy), he describes his invention in terms more Rabelaisian than mechanical. *The Metamorphosis* won him his second banishment, this time for an innuendo about the Earl of Leicester. After Elizabeth's death, Harington found the new Court of James I unamused by his wit, so he retired to end his days in the pursuit of a legacy from his mother-in-law.

The first part of Harington's *Brief Apology for Poetry,* which is appended to his translation, repeats many arguments which were fast becoming commonplace. In fact, Harington says that he doubts whether poetry any longer requires a defense since it is no longer challenged, save by a weak faction. Yet, he says, "every blind corner hath a squint-eyed Zoilus that can look aright on no man's doings." His fundamental argument for poetry is that it serves as a preparation for greater studies, claiming that heroic poetry "with her sweet stateliness doth erect the mind and lift it up to the consideration of the highest matters," an argument that finds its precedent in Plutarch. He also repeats the Renaissance *topos* [commonplace] of poetry as the "gilded pill," the sweetened medicine or "honest fraud" which leads one to divine truths. In considering whether the gift for poetry is learned or innate, he takes a shot at Puttenham (Ignoto), as one who "laboreth greatly to prove, or rather to make poetry an art," while his own poetry proves that poetry "is a gift and not an art."

The second part of the *Apology,* in which Harington specifically defends the *Orlando Furioso,* is perhaps more interesting because it is the first critical discussion of the epic in English. In response to the charges that Ariosto does not follow the precepts of Aristotle and the example of

Vergil, Harington demonstrates Ariosto's affinity with Vergil. But he also declares that "that which was commendable in him to write in that age, the times being changed, would be thought otherwise now," making himself something of a "modernist" despite his attempt to tie Ariosto to Vergil. J.W.H. Atkins has praised the *Apology* for its steps toward a "mature" critical methodology:

> In it a maturing of the critical spirit becomes visible, not only in the discriminating treatment of stock arguments or in the tentative use made of comparative and historical methods, but also, and above all, in the claim for the recognition of relative standards in poetry and in the freedom with which Aristotle, Puttenham, and others are discussed.

A Brief Apology for Poetry is taken from *Elizabethan Critical Essays*, edited by G. Gregory Smith (Oxford University Press, 1904).

A Brief Apology for Poetry

The learned Plutarch in his Laconicall Apothegmes tels of a Sophister that made a long and tedious Oration in praise of Hercules, and expecting at the end thereof for some great thanks and applause of the hearers, a certaine Lacedemonian demanded him who had dispraised Hercules. Me thinkes the like may be now said to me, taking vpon me the defence of Poesie, for surely if learning in generall were of that account among vs, as it ought to be among all men, and is among wise men, then should this my Apologie of Poesie (the verie first nurse and ancient grandmother of all learning) be as vaine and superfluous as was that Sophisters, because it might then be aunswered, and truly answered, that no man disgraced it. But sith we liue in such a time, in which nothing can escape the enuious tooth and backbiting tongue of an impure mouth, and wherein euerie blind corner hath a squint eyed Zoilus that can looke a right vpon no mans doings, (yea sure there be some that will not sticke to call Hercules himselfe a dastard, because forsooth he fought with a club and not at the rapyer and dagger), therefore I thinke no man of iudgement will iudge this my labour needlesse, in seeking to remoue away those slaunders that either the malice of those that loue it not, or the folly of those that vnderstand it not, hath deuised against it; for indeed as the old saying is, *Scientia non habet inimicum praeter ignorantem*, Knowledge hath no foe but the ignorant. But now because I make account I haue to deale with three sundrie kindes of reproouers, one of those that condemne all Poetrie, which (how strong head soeuer they haue) I count but a verie weake faction; another of those that allow Poetrie, but not this particular Poem, of which kind sure there cannot be manie; a third of those that can beare with the art, & like of the worke, but will finde fault with my not well handling of it, which they may not onely probably, but I doubt too truely do, being a thing as commonly done as said, that where the hedge is lowest, there doth euery man go ouer: therfore against these three I must arme me with the best defensiue weapons I can, and if I happen to giue a blow now and then in mine owne defence, and as good fensers vse to ward & strike at once, I must craue pardon of course, seing our law allowes that is done *se defendendo* and the law of nature teacheth *vim vi repellere*.

First therfore of Poetrie it selfe, for those few that generally disallow it might be sufficient to alledge those many that generally approue it, of which I could bring in such an army, not of souldiers, but of famous kings & captaines, as not only the sight, but the verie sound of them were able to vanquish and dismay the final forces of our aduersaries. For who would once dare to oppose himselfe against so many Alexanders, Cæsars, Scipios (to omit infinite other princes, both of former and later ages, and of forraine and nearer countries), that with fauour, with studie, with practise, with example, with honor, with giftes, with preferments, with great and magnificent cost, haue encoraged and aduanced Poets and Poetry? as witnes the huge Theaters and Amphitheaters, monuments of stupendious charge, made onely for Tragedies and Comedies, the workes of Poets, to be represented on: but all these aids and defences I leaue as superfluous. My cause I count so good, and the euidence so open, that I neither neede to vse the countenance of any great state to boulster it, nor the cunning of anie little lawyer to enforce it: my meaning is plainly and *bona fide*, confessing all the abuses that can truely be objected against some kind of Poets, to shew you what good vse there is of Poetrie. Neither do I suppose it to be greatly behoofull for this purpose to trouble you with the curious definitions of a Poet and Poesie, & with the subtill distinctions of their sundrie kinds; nor to dispute how high and supernatural the name of a Maker is, so christned in English by that vnknowne God-father that this last yeare saue one, viz. 1589, set forth a booke called the Art of English Poetrie: and least of all do I purpose to bestow any long time to argue whether Plato, Zenophon, and Erasmus writing fictions and Dialogues in prose may iustly be called Poets, or whether Lucan writing a story in verse be an historiographer, or whether Master Faire translating Virgil, Master Golding translating Ouids Metamorphosis, and my selfe in this worke that you see, be any more then versifiers, as the same Ignoto termeth all translators: for as for all, or the most part of such questions, I will refer you to Sir Philip Sidneys Apologie, who doth handle them right learnedly, or to the forenamed treatise where they are discoursed more largely, and where, as it were, a whole receit of Poetrie is prescribed, with so manie new named figures as would put me in great hope in this age to come would breed manie excellent Poets—saue for one obseruation that I gather out of the verie same book. For though the poore gentleman laboreth greatly to proue, or rather to make Poetrie an art, and reciteth as you may see, in the plurall number, some pluralities of patterns and parcels of his owne Poetrie, with diuerse pieces of Partheniads and hymnes in praise of the most praisworthy, yet whatsoeuer he would proue by all these, sure in my poore opinion he doth proue nothing more plainly then that which M. Sidney and all the learneder sort that haue written of it do pronounce, namely that it is a gift and not an art. I say he proueth it, because making himselfe and manie others so cunning in the art, yet he sheweth himselfe so slender a gift in it, deseruing to be commended as Martiall praiseth one that he compares to Tully.

> *Carmina quod scribis musis & Apolline nullo*
> *Laudari debes: hoc Ciceronis habes.*

But to come to the purpose, and to speake after the phrase of the common sort that terme all that is written in verse Poetrie, and, rather in scorne then in praise, bestow the name of a Poet on euerie base rymer and balladmaker, this I say of it, and I thinke I say truly, that there are many good lessons to be learned out of it, many good examples to be found in it, many good vses to be had of it, and that therfore it is not nor ought not to be despised by the wiser sort, but so to be studied and imployed as was intended by the first writers and deuisers thereof, which is to soften and polish the hard and rough dispositions of men, and make them capable of vertue and good discipline.

I cannot denie but to vs that are Christians, in respect of the high end of all, which is the health of our soules, not only Poetrie but al other studies of Philosophy are in a manner vaine and superfluous, yea (as the wise man saith) whatsoeuer is under the sunne is vanitie of vanities, and nothing but vanitie. But sith we liue with men & not with saints, and because few men can embrace this strict and stoicall diuinitie, or rather, indeed, for that the holy scriptures, in which those high mysteries of our saluation are contained, are a deepe & profound studie and not subiect to euerie weake capacitie, no nor to the highest wits and iudgments, except they be first illuminat by Gods spirit or instructed by his teachers and preachers: therefore we do first read some other authors, making them as it were a looking glasse to the eyes of our minde, and then after we haue gathered more strength, we enter into profounder studies of higher mysteries, hauing first as it were enabled our eyes by long beholding the sunne in a bason of water at last to looke vpon the sunne it selfe. So we read how that great Moses, whose learning and sanctitie is so renowned ouer all nations, was first instructed in the learning of the Egyptians before he came to that high contemplation of God and familiaritie (as I may so terme it) with God. So the notable Prophet Daniel was brought vp in the learning of the Chaldeans, & made that the first step of his higher vocation to be a Prophet. If then we may by the example of two such special seruants of God spend some of our young yeares in studies of humanitie, what better and more meete studie is there for a young man then Poetrie? specially Heroicall Poesie, that with her sweet statelinesse doth erect the mind & lift it vp to the consideration of the highest matters, and allureth them that of themselues would otherwise loth them to take and swallow & digest the holsome precepts of Philosophie, and many times even of the true diuinitie. Wherefore Plutarch, hauing written a whole treatise of the praise of Homers workes, and another of reading Poets, doth begin this latter with this comparison, that as men that are sickly and haue weake stomakes or daintie tastes do many times thinke that flesh most delicate to eate that is not flesh, and those fishes that be not fish, so young men (saith he) do like best that Philosophy that is not Philosophie, or that is not deliuered as Philosophie, and such are the pleasant writings of learned Poets, that are the popular Philosophers and the popular diuines. Likewise Tasso in his excellent worke of Jerusalem *Liberata* likeneth Poetrie to the Phisicke that men giue vnto little children when they are sick; his verse is this in Italian, speaking to God with a pretie Prosopopeia,

> Sai, che là corre il mondo, oue più versi
> Di sue dolcezze il lusinghier Parnaso,
> E che 'l vero condito in molli versi
> I più schiui allettando hà persuaso.
> Così à l'egro fanciul porgiamo aspersi
> Di soaue licor gli orli del vaso:
> Succhi amari ingannato intanto ei beue,
> E da l'inganno suo vita riceue.

Thou knowst, the wanton worldlings euer runne
To sweete Parnassus fruites, how otherwhile
The truth well saw'st with pleasant verse hath wonne

> Most squeamish stomakes with the sugred stile:
> So the sicke child that Pocions all doth shunne
> With comfets and with sugar we begile,
> And cause him take a holsome sowre receit:
> He drinkes, and saues his life with such deceit.

This is then that honest fraud in which (as Plutarch saith) he that is deceiued is wiser than he that is not deceiued, & he that doth deceiue is honester than he that doth not deceiue.

But briefly to answere to the chiefe objections: Cornelius Agrippa, a man of learning & authoritie not to be despised, maketh a bitter inuectiue against Poets and Poesie, and the summe of his reproofe of it is this (which is al that can with any probability be said against it), that it is a nurse of lies, a pleaser of fooles, a breeder of dangerous errors, and an inticer to wantonnes. I might here warne those that wil vrge this mans authoritie to the disgrace of Poetrie, to take heed (of what calling so euer they be) least with the same weapon that they thinke to giue Poetrie a blow they giue themselues a maime. For Agrippa taketh his pleasure of greater matters then Poetrie; I maruel how he durst do it, saue that I see he hath done it; he hath spared neither myters nor scepters. The courts of Princes where vertue is rewarded, iustice maintained, oppressions relieued, he cals them a Colledge of Giants, of Tyrants, of oppressors, warriors: the most noble sort of noble men he termeth cursed, bloodie, wicked, and sacrilegious persons. Noble men (and vs poore Gentlemen) that thinke to borrow praise of our auncestors deserts and good fame, he affirmed to be a race of the sturdier sort of knaues and lycencious liuers. Treasurers & other great officers of the common welth, with graue counsellors whose wise heads are the pillers of the state, he affirmeth generally to be robbers and peelers of the realme, and priuie traitors that sell their princes fauours and rob weldeseruing seruitors of their reward. I omit, as his *peccadilia*, how he nicknameth priests, saying for the most part they are hypocrites, lawyers, saying they are all theeues, phisicians, saying they are manie of them murtherers: so as I thinke it were a good motion, and would easily passe by the consent of the three estates, that this mans authoritie should be vtterly adnihilated, that dealeth so hardly and vniustly with all sorts of professions. But for the reiecting of his writings, I refer it to others that haue powre to do it, and to condemne him for a generall libeller; but for that he writeth against Poetrie, I meane to speake a word or two in refuting thereof.

And first for lying, I might if I list excuse it by the rule of *Poetica licentia*, and claime a priuiledge giuen to Poet[s], whose art is but an imitation (as Aristotle calleth it), & therefore are allowed to faine what they list, according to that old verse,

> *Iuridicis, Erebo, fisco, fas viuere [r]apto;*
> *Militibus, medicis, tortori, occidere ludo est;*
> *Mentiri astronomis, pictoribus atque poetis,*

which, because I count it without reason, I will English without rime.

> Lawyers, Hell, and the Checquer are allowed to liue on spoile;
> Souldiers, Phisicians, and Hangmen make a sport of murther;
> Astronomers, Painters, and Poets may lye by authoritie.

Thus you see that Poets may lye if they list *Cum priuelegio*. But what if they lye least of all other men? what if they lye not at all? then I thinke that great slaunder is verie vniustly raised upon them. For in my opinion they are said properly to lye that affirme that to be true that is false: and how other arts can free themselues from this blame, let them look that professe them: but Poets neuer affirming any for true, but presenting them to vs as fables and imitations, cannot lye though they would: and because this obiection of lyes is the chief, and that vpon which the rest be grounded, I wil stand the longer vpon the clearing thereof.

The ancient Poets haue indeed wrapped as it were in their writings diuers and sundry meanings, which they call the senses or mysteries thereof. First of all for the litterall sence (as it were the vtmost barke or ryne) they set downe in manner of an historie the acts and notable exploits of some persons worthy memorie: then in the same fiction, as a second rine and somewhat more fine, as it were nearer to the pith and marrow, they place the Morall sence profitable for the actiue life of man, approuing vertuous actions and condemning the contrarie. Manie times also vnder the selfesame words they comprehend some true vnderstanding of naturall Philosophie, or somtimes of politike gouernement, and now and then of diuinitie: and these same sences that comprehend so excellent knowledge we call the Allegorie, which Plutarch defineth to be when one thing is told, and by that another is vnderstood. Now let any man iudge if it be a matter of meane art or wit to containe in one historicall narration, either true or fained, so many, so diuerse, and so deepe conceits: but for making the matter more plaine I will alledge an example thereof.

Perseus sonne of Iupiter is fained by the Poets to haue slaine Gorgon, and, after that conquest atchieued, to haue flown vp to heauen. The Historicall sence is this, Perseus the sonne of Iupiter, by the participation of Iupiters vertues which were in him, or rather comming of the stock of one of the kings of Creet, or Athens so called, slew Gorgon, a tyrant in that countrey (Gorgon in Greeke signifieth earth), and was for his vertuous parts exalted by men vp vnto heauen. Morally it signifieth this much: Perseus a wise man, sonne of Iupiter, endewed with vertue from aboue, slayeth sinne and vice, a thing base & earthly signified by Gorgon, and so mounteth vp to the skie of vertue. It signifies in one kind of Allegorie thus much: the mind of man being gotten by God, and so the childe of God killing and vanquishing the earthlinesse of this Gorgonicall nature, ascendeth vp to the vnderstanding of heauenly things, of high things, of eternal things, in which contemplacion consisteth the perfection of man: this is the natural allegory, because man [is] one of the chiefe works of nature. It hath also a more high and heauenly Allegorie, that the heauenly nature, daughter of Iupiter, procuring with her continuall motion corruption and mortality in the inferiour bodies, seuered it selfe at last from these earthly bodies, and flew vp on high, and there remaineth for euer. It hath also another Theological Allegorie:

that the angelicall nature, daughter of the most high God the creator of all things, killing & ouercomming all bodily substance, signified by Gorgon, ascended into heauen. The like infinite Allegories I could pike out of other Poeticall fictions, saue that I would auoid tediousnes. It sufficeth me therefore to note this, that the men of greatest learning and highest wit in the auncient times did of purpose conceale these deepe mysteries of learning, and, as it were, couer them with the vaile of fables and verse for sundrie causes: one cause was that they might not be rashly abused by prophane wits, in whom science is corrupted, like good wine in a bad vessell; another cause why they wrote in verse was conseruation of the memorie of their precepts, as we see yet the generall rules almost of euerie art, not so much as husbandrie, but they are oftner recited and better remembered in verse then in prose; another, and a principall cause of all, is to be able with one kinde of meate and one dish (as I may so call it) to feed diuers tastes. For the weaker capacities will feede themselues with the pleasantnes of the historie and sweetnes of the verse, some that haue stronger stomackes will as it were take a further taste of the Morall sence, a third sort, more high conceited then they, will digest the Allegorie: so as indeed it hath bene thought by men of verie good iudgement, such manner of Poeticall writing was an excellent way to preserue all kinde of learning from that corruption which now it is come to since they left that mysticall writing of verse. Now though I know the example and authoritie of Aristotle and Plato be still vrged against this, who took to themselues another manner of writing, first I may say indeed that lawes were made for poore men and not for Princes, for these two great Princes of Philosophie brake that former allowed manner of writing, yet Plato still preserued the fable, but refuseth the verse. Aristotle, though reiecting both, yet retained still a kind of obscuritie, in so much he aunswered Alexander, who reproued him in a sort for publishing the sacred secrets of Philosophie, that he had set forth his bookes in a sort, and yet not set them forth, meaning that they were so obscure that they would be vnderstood of few, except they came to him for instructions, or else without they were of verie good capacitie and studious of Philosophie. But (as I say) Plato howsoeuer men would make him an enimie of Poetrie (because he found indeed iust fault with the abuses of some comicall Poets of his time, or some that sought to set vp new and strange religions), yet you see he kept still that principall part of Poetrie, which is fiction and imitation; and as for the other part of Poetrie which is verse, though he vsed it not, yet his master Socrates euen in his old age wrote certaine verses, as Plutarke testifieth.

But because I haue named the two parts of Poetrie, namely inuention or fiction and verse, let vs see how well we can authorise the vse of both these. First for fiction, against which, as I told before, many inueigh, calling it by the foul name of lying, though notwithstanding, as I then said, it is farthest from it. Demosthenes, the famous and renowned Orator, when he would persuade the Athenians to warre against Philip, told them a solemne tale how the wolues on a time sent Ambassadors to the sheepe, offering them peace if they would deliuer vp the dogs that kept their folds, with al that long circumstance (needlesse to be repeated), by which he perswaded them far more strongly then if he should haue told them in plain termes that Philip sought to bereaue them of their chief bulwarks & defences, to haue the better abilitie to ouerthrow them. But what need we fetch an authority so far of from heathen authors, that haue many neerer hand both in time & in place? Bishop Fisher, a stout Prelate (though I do not praise his Religion), when he was assaied by king Henrie the eight for his good will and assent for the suppression of Abbeys, the king alledging that he would but take away their superfluities and let the substance stand still, or at least see it be conuerted to better and more godly vses, the graue Bishop answered it in this kind of Poeticall parable. He said there was an axe that, wanting a helue, came to a thicke and huge ouergrowne wood, & besought some of the great okes in that wood to spare him so much timber as to make him a handle or helue, promising that if he might finde that fauour he would in recompence thereof haue great regard in preseruing that wood, in pruning the braunches, in cutting away the vnprofitable and superfluous boughes, in paring away the bryers and thornes that were combersome to the fayre trees, and make it in fine a groue of great delight and pleasure: but when this same axe had obtained his suit, he so laid about him, & so pared away both timber and top and lop, that in short space of a woodland he made it a champion, and made her liberalitie the instrument of her ouerthrow.

Now though this Bishop had no very good success with his parable, yet it was so farre from being counted a lye, that it was plainly seen soone after that the same axe did both hew down those woods by the roots & pared off him by the head, and was a peece of Prophecie as well as a peece of Poetrie: and indeed Prophets and Poets haue been thought to haue a great affinitie, as the name *Vates* in Latin doth testifie. But to come again to this maner of fiction or parable, the Prophet Nathan, reprouing King Dauid for his great sinne of adulterie and murther, doth he not come to him with a pretie parable of a poore man and his lambe that lay in his bosome and eate of his bread, and the rich man, that had whole flocks of his own, would needs take it from him? in which, as it is euident, it was but a parable, so it were vnreuerent and almost blasphemous to say it was a lye. But to goe higher, did not our Sauiour himselfe speake in parables? as that diuine parable of the sower, that comfortable parable of the Prodigall sonne, that dreadfull parable of Diues and Lazarus, though I know of this last many of the fathers hold that it is a storie indeed and no parable. But in the rest it is manifest that he was all holinesse, all wisedome, all truth, vsed parables, and euen such as discreet Poets vse, where a good and honest and wholesome Allegorie is hidden in a pleasaunt and pretie fiction; and therefore for that part of Poetry of Imitation, I thinke no body will make any question but it is not onely allowable, but godly and commendable, if the Poets ill handling of it doe not marre and peruert the good vse of it.

The other part of Poetrie, which is Verse, as it were the clothing or ornament of it, hath many good vses. Of the helpe of memorie I spake somewhat before; for the words being couched together in due order, measure, and number, one doth as it were bring on another, as my selfe haue often proued, & so I thinke do many beside (though for my own part I can rather bost of the marring a good memorie then of hauing one), yet I have euer found that Verse is easier to learne and farre better to preserue in memorie then is prose. An other speciall grace in Verse is the forcible manner of phrase, in which, if it be well made, it farre excelleth loose speech or prose. A third is the pleasure and sweetnesse to the eare which makes the discourse pleasaunt vnto vs often time when the matter it selfe is harsh and vnacceptable: for myne owne part I was neuer yet so good a husband to take any delight to heare one of my ploughmen tell how an acre of wheat must be fallowd and twyfallowed, and how cold land should be burned, and how fruitfull land must be well harrowed; but when I heare one read Virgill, where he saith,

> *Saepe etiam steriles incendere profuit agros,*
> *Atque leuem stipulam crepitantibus vrere flammis.*
> *Siue inde occultas vires & pabula terrae*
> *Pinguia concipiunt: siue illis omne per ignem*
> *Excoquitur vitium, atque exsudat inutilis humor, &c.,*

and after,

> *Multum adeo, rastris glebas qui frangit inertes,*
> *Vimineasque trahit crates iuuat arua;*

with many other lessons of homly husbandrie, but deliuered in so good Verse that me thinkes all that while I could find in my hart to driue the plough. But now for the authoritie of Verse, if it be not sufficient to say for them that the greatest Philosophers and grauest Senatours that euer were haue vsed them both in their speeches and in their writings, that precepts of all Arts haue been deliuered in them, that verse is as aunceint a writing as prose, and indeed more auncient in respect that the oldest workes extant be verse, as Orpheus, Linus, Hesiodus, & others beyond memory of man or mention almost of history; if none of these will serue for the credit of it, yet let this serue that some part of the Scripture was written in verse, as the Psalmes of Dauid, & certain other songs of Deborah, of Salomon, & others, which the learnedest diuines do affirme to be verse and find that they are in meeter, though the rule of the Hebrew verse they agree not on. Suffiseth it me only to proue that by the authoritie of sacred Scriptures both parts of Poesie, inuention or imitation and verse, are allowable, & consequently that great obiection of lying is quite taken away & refuted.

Now the second obiection is pleasing of fooles. I haue already showed how it displeaseth not wise men. Now if it haue this vertue to, to please the fooles and ignorant, I would thinke this an article of prayse not of rebuke: wherefore I confesse that it pleaseth fooles, and so pleaseth them that, if they marke it and obserue it well, it will in time make them wise, for in verse is both goodnesse and sweetnesse, Rubarb and Sugercandie, the pleasaunt and the profitable. Wherefore, as Horace sayth, *Omne tulit punctum qui miscuit vtile dulci*, he that can mingle the sweete and the wholesome, the pleasaunt & the profitable, he is indeed an absolute good writer: and such be Poets, if any be such; they present vnto vs a pretie tale, able to keepe a childe from play, and an old man from the chimnie corner; Or, as the same Horace sayth to a couetous man,

A BRIEF APOLOGY FOR POETRY

Tantalus a labris sitiens fugientia captat
Flumina. Quid rides? mutato nomine de te
Fabula narratur.

One tels a couetous man a tale of Tantalus that sits vp to the chinne in water, and yet is plagued with thirst. This signifies the selfe same man to whom the tale is told, that wallows in plentie, and yet his miserable minde barres him the vse of it: As my selfe knew, and I am sure many remember, Iustice Randall of London, a man passing impotent in body but much more in mind, that, leauing behind him a thousand pounds of gold in a chest ful of old boots & shoes, yet was so miserable that at my Lord Maiors dinner they say he would put vp a widgen for his supper, & many a good meale he did take of his franke neighbour the widdow Penne. But to come to the matter, this same great sinne that is layd to Poetrie of pleasing fooles is sufficiently answered if it be worth the answering.

Now for the breeding of errours which is the third Obiection, I see not why it should breed any when none is bound to beleeue that they write, nor they looke not to haue their fictions belieued in the litterall sence; and therefore he that well examines whence errours spring shall finde the writers of prose & not of verse the authors and maintainers of them; and this point I count so manifest as it needes no proofe.

The last reproofe is lightnes & wantonnes. This is indeed an Obiection of some importaunce, sith, as Sir Philip Sidney confesseth, Cupido is crept euen into the Heroicall Poemes, & consequently makes that also subiect to this reproofe. I promised in the beginning not partially to prayse Poesie, but plainly and honestly to confesse that that might truely be obiected against it, and, if any thing may be, sure it is this lasciuiousnesse: yet this I will say, that of all kinde of Poesie the Heroicall is least infected therewith. The other kindes I will rather excuse then defende, though of all the kindes of Poesie it may bee sayd where any scurrilitie and lewdnesse is founde, there Poetry doth not abuse vs, but writers haue abused Poetrie.

And brieflie to examine all the kindes. First, the Tragicall is meerly free from it, as representing onely the cruell & lawlesse proceedings of Princes, mouing nothing but pitie or detestation. The Comicall, whatsoeuer foolish playmakers make it offend in this kind, yet being rightly vsed, it represents them so as to make the vice scorned and not embraced. The Satyrike is meerly free from it, as being wholly occupied in mannerly & couertly reprouing of all vices. The Elegie is still mourning. As for the Pastorall with the Sonnet or Epigramme, though many times they sauour of wantonnes and loue and toying, and, now and then breaking the rules of Poetry, go into plaine scurrilitie, yet euen the worst of them may be not ill applied, and are, I must confesse, too delightfull, in so much as Martiall saith,

Laudant illa, sed ista legunt,

and in another place,

Erubuit posuitque meum Lucrecia librum,
Sed coram Bruto; Brute recede; leget.

Lucrecia (by which he signifies any chast matron) will blush and be ashamed to read a lasciuious booke. But how? not except Brutus be by, that is if any graue man should see her read it. But if Brutus turne his backe, she will go to it agayne and read it all.

But to end this part of my Apologie, as I count and conclude Heroicall Poesie allowable and to be read and studied without all exception, so I may as boldly say that Tragedies well handled be a most worthy kinde of Poesie, that Comedies may make men see and shame at their owne faults, that the rest may be so written and so read as much pleasure and some profite may be gathered out of them. And for myne owne part, as Scaliger writeth of Virgill, so I beleeue that the reading of a good Heroicall Poeme may make a man both wiser and honester. And for Tragedies, to omit other famous Tragedies, that that was played at S. Iohns in Cambridge, of Richard the 3, would moue (I thinke) Phalaris the tyraunt, and terrifie all tyrannous minded men from following their foolish ambitious humors, seeing how his ambition made him kill his brother, his nephews, his wife, beside infinit others, and, last of all, after a short and troublesome raigne, to end his miserable life, and to haue his body harried after his death. Then, for Comedies, how full of harmeless myrth is our Cambridge *Pedantius*? and the Oxford *Bellum Grammaticale*? or, to speake of a London Comedie, how much good matter, yea and matter of state, is there in that Comedie cald the play of the Cards, in which it is showed how foure Parasiticall knaues robbe the foure principall vocations of the Realme, *videl.* the vocation of Souldiers, Schollers, Marchants, and Husbandmen? Of which Comedie I cannot forget the saying of a notable wise counseller that is now dead, who when some (to sing *Placebo*) aduised that it should be forbidden, because it was somewhat too plaine, and indeed as the old saying is, *sooth boord is no boord*, yet he would haue it allowed, adding it was fit that *They which doe that they should not should heare that they would not*. Finally, if Comedies may be so made as the beholders may be bettered by them, without all doubt all other sortes of Poetrie may bring their profit as they do bring delight, and if all, then much more the chiefe of all, which by all mens consent is the Heroicall. And thus much be sayd for Poesie.

Now for this Poeme of *Orlando Furioso*, which, as I haue heard, hath been disliked by some (though by few of any wit or iudgement), it followes that I say somewhat in defence thereof, which I will do the more moderately and coldly; by how much the paynes I haue taken, it (rising as you may see to a good volume) may make me seeme a more partiall prayser. Wherefore I will make choise of some other Poeme that is allowed and approued by all men, and a litle compare them together. And what worke can serue this turne so fitly as Virgils Æneados, whom aboue all other it seemeth my authour doth follow, as appeares both by his beginning and ending? The tone begins,

Arma virumque cano.

The tother,

Le donne, i cauallier, l'arme, gli amori,
Le cortesie, l'audaci imprese io canto.

Virgill endes with the death of Turnus,

> *Vitaque cum gemitu fugit indignata sub vmbras.*

Ariosto ends with the death of Rodomont,

> *Bestemmiando fuggfì l'alma sdegnosa,*
> *Che fu sì altera al mondo, e sì orgogliosa.*

Virgill extolled Æneas to please Augustus, of whose race he was thought to come; Ariosto prayeth Rogero to the honour of the house of Este: Æneas hath his Dido that retaineth him; Rogero hath his Alcina: finally, least I should note euery part, there is nothing of any speciall obseruation in Virgill but my author hath with great felicitie imitated it, so as whosoeuer wil allow Virgil must *ipso facto* (as they say) admit Ariosto. Now of what account Virgil is reckned, & worthily reckned, for aunceint times witnesseth August. C. verse of him:

> *Ergone supremis potuit vox improba verbis*
> *Tam dirum mandare nefas?* &c.,

concluding thus,

> *Laudetur, placeat, vigeat, relegatur, ametur.*

This is a great prayse comming from so great a Prince. For later times, to omit Scaliger, whom I recited before, that affirmeth the reading of Virgill may make a man honest and vertuous, that excellent Italian Poet Dant professeth plainly that when he wandred out of the right way, meaning thereby when he liued fondly and looslie, Virgill was the first that made him looke into himselfe and reclaime himselfe from that same daungerous and lewd course. But what need we further witnes, do we not make our children read it commonly before they can vnderstand it, as a testimonie that we do generally approue it? And yet we see old men study it, as a proofe that they do specially admire it: so as one writes very pretily, that children do wade in Virgill, and yet strong men do swim in it.

Now to apply this to the prayse of myne author, as I sayd before so I say still, whatsoeuer is prayseworthy in Virgill is plentifully to be found in Ariosto, and some things that Virgill could not haue, for the ignoraunce of the age he liued in, you finde in my author, sprinckled ouer all his worke, as I will very briefly note and referre you for the rest to the booke it selfe. The deuout and Christen demeanor of Charlemayne in the 14 booke, with his prayer,

> *Non uoglia tua bontà per mio fallire,*
> *Che 'l tuo popol fedele habbia à patire.* &c.

And in the beginning of the xvii booke, that would beseeme any pulpit,

> *Il giusto Dio, quando i peccati nostri.*

But, aboue all, that in the xli. booke of the conuersion of Rogero to the Christen Religion, where the Hermit speaketh to him, contayning in effect a full instruction against presumption and dispaire, which I haue set downe thus in English,

> Now (as I sayd), this wise that Hermit spoke,
> And part doth comfort him, and part doth checke;
> He blameth him that in that pleasaunt yoke
> He had so long defer'd to put his necke,
> But did to wrath his maker still prouoke,
> And did not come at his first call and becke,
> But still did hide himselfe away from God
> Vntill he saw him comming with his rod;
> Then did he comfort him and make him know
> That grace is near denyde to such as aske,
> As do the workemen in the Gospell show
> Receauing pay alike for diuers taske.

And so after, concluding,

> How to Christ he must impute
> The pardon of his sinnes, yet near the later
> He told him he must be baptisde in water.

These and infinit places full of Christen exhortation, doctrine, & example I could quote out of the booke, saue that I hasten to an ende, and it would be needles to those that will not read them in the booke it selfe, and superfluous to those that will: but most manifest it is & not to be denyed, that in this point my author is to be preferred before all the aunceint Poets, in which are mentioned so many false Gods, and of them so many fowle deeds, their contentions, their adulteries, their incest, as were both obscenous in recitall and hurtful in example: though indeed those whom they termed Gods were certaine great Princes that committed such enormous faults, as great Princes in late ages (that loue still to be cald Gods of the earth) do often commit. But now it may be & is by some obiected that although he write Christianly in some places, yet in other some he is too lasciuious, as in that of the baudy Frier, in Alcina and Rogeros copulation, in Anselmus his Giptian, in Richardetto his metamorphosis, in mine hosts tale of Astolfo, & some few places beside. Alas, if this be a fault, pardon him this one fault, though I doubt too many of you (gentle readers) wil be to exorable in this point: yea, me thinks, I see some of you searching already for these places of the booke, and you are halfe offended that I haue not made some directions that you might finde out and read them immediatly. But I beseech you stay a while, and as the Italian sayth *Pian piano,* fayre and softly, & take this caueat with you, to read them as my author ment them, to breed detestation and not delectation. Remember, when you read of the old lecherous Frier, that a fornicator is one of the things that God hateth; when you read of Alcina, thinke how Joseph fled from his intising mistres; when you light on Anselmus tale, learne to loth bestly couetousnes; when on Richardetto, know that sweet meate wil haue sowre sawce; when on mine hostes tale, (if you will follow my counsell) turne ouer the leafe and let it alone, although euen that lewd tale may bring some men profit, and I haue heard that it is already (and perhaps not vnfitly) termed the comfort of cuckolds. But as I say, if this be a fault, then Virgill committed the same fault in *Dido* and Æneas intertainement, and if some will say he tels that mannerly and couertly, how will they excuse that where Vulcan was intreated by Venus to make an armour for Æneas?

> *Dixerat, & niueis hinc atque hinc diua lacertis*
> *Cunctantem amplexu molli fouet: ille repente*
> *Accepit solitam flammam, notusque per artus*
> *Intrauit calor.*

And a little after:

> *Ea verba locutus*
> *Optatos dedit amplexus, placitumque petiuit*
> *Coniugis infusus gremio per membra soporem.*

I hope they that vnderstand Latin will confesse this is plaine enough, & yet with modest words & no obscenous phrase: and so I dare take vpon me that in all Ariosto (and yet I thinke is as much as three *Æneades,*) there is not a word of ribaldry or obscenousness; farther there is so meet a decorum in the persons of those that speake lasciuiously, as any of iudgement must needs allow. And therfore, though I rather craue pardon then prayse for him in this point, yet me thinkes I can smile at the finesse of some that will condemne him, and yet not onely allow but admire our Chawcer, who both in words & sence incurreth far more the reprehension of flat scurrilitie, as I could recite many places, not onely in his millers tale, but in the good wife of Bathes tale, & many more, in which onely the decorum he keepes is that that excuseth it and maketh it more tolerable.

But now whereas some will say Ariosto wanteth art, reducing all heroicall Poems vnto the methode of Homer and certain precepts of Aristotle, for Homer I say that that which was commendable in him to write in that age, the times being changed, would be thought otherwise now, as we see both in phrase & in fashions the world growes more curious each day then other. Ouid gaue precepts of making loue, and one was that one should spill wine on the boord & write his mistresse name therewith. This was a quaynt cast in that age; but he that should make loue so now, his loue would mocke him for his labour, and count him but a slouenly sutor. And if it be thus chaunged since Ouids time, much more since Homers time. And yet for Ariostos tales that many thinke vnartificially brought in, Homer him selfe hath the like: as in the Iliads the conference of Glaucus with Diomedes vpon some acts of Bellerophon, & in his Odysse as the discourse of the hog with Vlysses.

Further, for the name of the booke, which some carpe at because he called it *Orlando Furioso* rather than *Rogero*, in that he may also be defended by example of Homer, who, professing to write of Achilles, calleth his book Iliade of Troy, and not Achillide.

As for Aristotles rules, I take it he hath followed them verie strictly.

Briefly, Aristotle and the best censurers of Poesie would haue the *Epopeia*, that is the heroicall Poem, should ground on some historie, and take some short time in the same to bewtifie with his Poetrie: so doth mine Author take the storie of k. Charls the great, and doth not exceed a yeare or therabout in his whole work. Secondly, they hold that nothing should be fayned vtterly incredible. And sure Ariosto neither in his inchantments exceedeth credit (for who knowes not how strong the illusions of the deuill are?) neither in the miracles that Altolfo by the power of S. Iohn is fayned to do, since the Church holdeth that Prophetes both aliue and dead haue done mightie great miracles. Thirdly, they would haue an heroicall Poem (aswell as a Tragedie) to be full of *Peripet[e]ia*, which I interpret an agnition of some vnlooked for fortune either good or bad, and a sudden change thereof: of this what store there be the reader shall quickly find. As for apt similitudes, for passions well expressed of loue, of pitie, of hate, of wrath, a blind man may see, if he can but heare, that this worke is full of them.

There follows only two reproofs, which I rather interpret two peculiar praises of this writer aboue all that wrate before him in this kind. One, that he breaks off narrations verie abruptly, so as indeed a loose vnattentiue reader will hardly carrie away any part of the storie: but this doubtlesse is a point of great art, to draw a man with a continuall thirst to reade out the whole worke, and toward the end of the booke to close vp the diuerse matters briefly and clenly. If S. Philip Sidney had counted this a fault, he would not haue done so himselfe in his Arcadia. Another fault is, that he speaketh so much in his own person by digression, which they say also is against the rules of Poetrie, because neither Homer nor Virgill did it. Me thinks it is a sufficient defence to say, Ariosto doth it. Sure I am it is both delightfull and verie profitable, and an excellent breathing place for the reader, and euen as if a man walked in a faire long alley, to haue a seat or resting place here and there is easie and commodious: but if at the same seat were planted some excellent tree, that not onely with the shade shoulde keepe vs from the heat, but with some pleasant and right wholsom fruite should allay our thirst and comfort our stomacke, we would thinke it for the time a litle paradice. So are Ariostos morals and pretie digressions sprinkled through his long worke to the no lesse pleasure then profit of the reader. And thus much be spoken for defence of mine Author, which was the second part of my Apologie.

Now remaines the third part of it, in which I promised to speake somwhat for my selfe, which part, though it haue most need of an Apologie both large & substantiall, yet I will runne it ouer both shortly & slightly, because indeed the nature of the thing it self is such that the more one doth say, the lesse he shall seeme to say; and men are willinger to praise that in another man which himselfe shall debase then that which he shall seeme to maintaine. Certainly if I shold confesse or rather professe that my verse is vnartificiall, the stile rude, the phrase barbarous, the meeter vnpleasant, many more would beleeue it to be so, then would imagine that I thought them so: for this same *philautia* or self pleasing is so common a thing, as the more a man protests himself to be free from it, the more we wil charge him with it. Wherfore let me take thus much vpon me that admit it haue many of the fornamed imperfections, & many not named, yet as writing goes now a dayes it may passe among the rest; and as I haue heard a friend of mine (one verie iudicious in the bewtie of a woman) say of a Ladie whom he meant to praise, that she had a low forhead, a great nose, a wide mouth, a long visage, and yet all these put together she seemed to him a verie well fauoured woman, so I hope and I find alreadie some of my partiall friends that what seuerall imperfections soeuer they find in this translation, yet taking all together they allow it, or at least wise they reade it, which is a great argument of their liking.

Sir Thomas Moore, a man of great wisdome & learning, but yet a litle enclined (as good wits are many times) to scoffing, when one had brought him a booke of some shallow discourse, and preassed him very hard to haue his opinion of it, aduised the partie to put it into verse. The plaine meaning man in the best maner he could did so, and a twelue-month after at the least came with it to Sir Thomas, who, slightly perusing it, gaue it this encomium, that now there was rime in it, but afore it had neither rime nor reason. If any man had ment to serue me so, yet I haue preuented him; for sure I am he shall find rime in mine, and, if he be not voyd of reason, he shall find reason to. Though for the matter I can challenge no praise, hauing but borowed it; & for the verse I do challenge none, being a thing that euery body that neuer scarce bayted their horse at the Vniuersitie take vpon them to make. It is possible that, if I would haue employed that time that I haue done vpon this vpon some inuention of mine owne, I could haue by this made it haue risen to a iust volume, &, if I wold, haue done, as many spare not to do, flowne very high with stolen fethers. But I had rather men should see and know that I borrow all then that I steale any: and I would wish to be called rather one of the worst translators then one of the meaner makers, specially with the Earle of Surrey and Sir Thomas Wiat, that are yet called the first refiners of the English tong, were both translators out of Italian. Now for those that count it such a contemptible and trifling matter to translate, I wil but say to them as M. Bartholomew Clarke, an excellent learned man, and a right good translator, saith in maner of a pretie challenge, in his Preface (as I remember) vpon the Courtier, which booke he translated out of Italian into Latin. "You," saith he, "that thinke it such a toy, lay aside my booke, and take my author in your hand, and trie a leafe or such a matter, and compare it with mine." If I should say so, there would be inow that would quickly put me down perhaps: but doubtlesse he might boldly say it, for I thinke none could haue mended him. But as our English prouerb saith, many talke of Robin Hood that neuer shot in his bow, and some correct *Magnificat* that know not *quid significat*.

For my part I will thanke them that will mend any thing that I haue done amisse, nor I haue no such great conceipt of that I haue done but that I thinke much in it is to be mended; & hauing dealt plainly with some of my plaine dealing frends, to tell me frankly what they heard spoken of it (for indeed I suffred some part of the printed copies to go among my frends, & some more perhaps went against my will), I was told these in effect were the faults were found with it. Some graue men misliked that I should spend so much good time on such a trifling worke as they deemed a Poeme to be. Some more nicely found fault with so many two sillabled and three sillabled rimes. Some (not vndeseruedly) reproued the fantasticalnes of my notes, in which they say I haue strained my selfe to make mention of some of my kindred and frends that might very well be left out. And one fault more there is which I will tell my selfe, though many would neuer find it, and that is, I haue cut short some of his Cantos, in leauing out many staues of them, and sometimes put the matter of two or three staues into one. To these reproofes I shall pray you gentle and noble Readers with patience heare my defence, and then I will end.

For the first reproofe, either it is alreadie excused or it will neuer be excused; for I haue I thinke sufficiently proued both the art to be allowable and this worke to be commendable. Yet I will tell you an accident that happened vnto my selfe. When I was entred a pretie way into the translation, about the seuenth booke, comming to write that where Melissa, in the person of Rogeros Tutor, comes and reproues Rogero in the 4 staffe,

> Was it for this that I in youth thee fed
> With marrow?

and againe,

> Is this a meanes or readie way you trow,
> That other worthie men haue trod before,
> A Cæsar or a Scipio to grow?

straight I began to thinke that my Tutor, a graue and learned man, and one of a verie austere life, might say to me in like sort, "was it for this that I read Aristotle and Plato to you, and instructed you so carefully both in Greek & Latin, to haue you now become a translator of Italian toyes?" But while I thought thus, I was aware that it was no toy that could put such an honest and seriouse consideration into my mind.

Now for them that find fault with polysyllable meeter, me thinke they are like those that blame men for putting suger in their wine, and chide to bad about it, and say they marre all, but yet end with Gods blessing on their hearts. For indeed if I had knowne their diets, I could haue saued some of my cost, at least some of my paine: for when a verse ended with *ciuillitie*, I could easier, after the aunceient maner of rime, haue made *see*, or *flee*, or *decree* to aunswer it, leauing the accent vpon the last syllable, then hunt after three syllabled words to answere it with *facillitie, gentillitie, tranquillitie, hostillitie, scurillitie, debillitie, agillitie, fragillitie, nobillitie, mobillitie*, which who mislike may tast lamp oyle with their eares. And as for two syllabled meeters, they be so approued in other languages, that the French call them the feminine rime, as the sweeter, & the one syllable the masculin. But in a word to answer this, & to make them for euer hold their peaces of this point, Sir Philip Sidney, not only vseth them, but affecteth them—*signifie, dignifie, shamed is, named is, blamed is, hide away, bide away*. Thogh if my many blotted papers that I haue made in this kind might affoord me authoritie to giue a rule of it, I would say that to part them with a one syllable meeter between them wold giue it best grace. For as men vse to sow with the hand and not with the whole sacke, so I would haue the eare fed but not cloyed with these pleasing and sweet falling meeters.

For the third reproofe about the notes, sure they were a worke (as I may so call it) of supererogation, and I would wish sometimes they had bin left out, & the rather if I be in such faire possibilitie to be thought a foole or fantasticall for my labour. True it is I added some notes to the end of euery canto, euen as if some of my frends and my selfe reading it together (and so it fell out indeed many times) had after debated vpon them what had bene most worthie consideration in them, and so oftimes immediatly I set it downe. And wheras I make mention here & there of some of mine owne frends & kin, I did it the rather because Plutarke in one place speaking of Homer, partly lamenteth, and partly blameth him, that writing so much as he did, yet in none of his works there was any mention made, or so much as inkling to be gathered, of what stocke he was, of what kindred, of what towne, nor, saue for his language, of what countrey. Excuse me then if I in a worke that may perhaps last longer then a better thing, and being not ashamed of my kindred, name them here and there to no mans offence, though I meant not to make euery body so far of my counsell why I did it, till I was told that some person of some reckening noted me of a litle vanitie for it: and thus much for that point.

For my omitting and abreuiating some things, either in matters impertinent to vs, or in some to tediouse flatteries of persons that we neuer heard of, if I haue done ill I craue pardon: for sure I did it for the best. But if anie being studious of the Italian would for his vnderstanding compare them, the first six bookes, saue a litle of the third, will stand him in steed. But yet I would not haue any man except that I should obserue his phrase so strictly as an interpreter, nor the matter so carefully as if it had bene a storie, in which to varie were as great a sinne as it were simplicitie in this to go word for word.

But now to conclude, I shall pray you all that haue troubled yourselues to read this my triple apologie to accept my labors and to excuse my erors, if with no other thing, at least with the name of youth (which commonly hath need of excuses); and so presuming this pardon to be graunted, we shall part good frends. Only let me intreate you in reading the booke ensuing not to do me that iniurie that a Potter did to Ariosto.

Torquato Tasso
1544–1595

Torquato Tasso was one of the major literary figures of the Italian Renaissance, and he remains in the constellation of the great Italian poets along with Dante, Petrarch and Ariosto. At the same time, his literary career reflects the course of literary criticism in the latter half of the sixteenth century as well as its tremendous power in shaping the cultural ideology of the period since, as Allan Gilbert points out, "perhaps no poet of a high order has ever been more concerned with criticism or more susceptible to the influence of critical opinion than Tasso." In Tasso's career the tensions between the development of a specifically Renaissance genre such as the romance and the demands of the neo-Aristotelian criticism of the period find their grandest expression. Tasso labored the last years of his life upon a revision of his chief work, *Jerusalem Delivered,* in order to adapt it to the dictates of the Italian critics as well as religious orthodoxy. The result, *Jerusalem Conquered,* has not proved the stronger version; it is the original version which is widely circulated.

Tasso was born in Sorrento, but he shared the political exile of his father, wandering throughout Italy. He studied at the universities in Padua and Bologna, producing the chivalric poem *Rinaldo* at the age of eighteen. The Cardinal Luigi d'Este became his patron in 1565. Tasso published the pastoral drama *Aminta* in 1573; it remained the most popular of his works during his own lifetime. He completed *Jerusalem Delivered* in 1575, but it remained unpublished until 1581 because of Tasso's dissatisfaction with it (it was published only after a pirated version appeared). He began to consult both literary scholars and religious authorities in order to revise his poem. While working upon his revision, he was imprisoned in 1577 for a paranoid display of violence in the presence of Lucrezia d'Este. After another outburst, in which he vilified his patron the Cardinal, he was shut up in a hospital for seven years (1579–86). In the years after his release, Tasso accepted the hospitality of religious orders, academies, and even Pope Clement VIII in wandering throughout Italy. *Jerusalem Conquered* was published in 1593, two years before his death.

Discourses on the Heroic Poem (1594) is an expanded version of his *Discourses on the Art of Poetry,* which Tasso had written for the academy at Ferrara while he was in his twenties. In it, one can discern in crystalized form the theory which underlies Tasso's need to rewrite his own poem. The *Discourses* is related to the debates of the 1580's between Tasso's followers and Lionardo Salviati and his followers concerning the relative merits of

Tasso and Ariosto, in which Ariosto was thought of as the representative fantastic poet and Tasso the representative historical realist. Tasso insists that "the subject of a heroic poem should . . .be derived from true history and from religion that is not false." While insisting upon truth and verisimilitude, however, Tasso manages to allow for the marvelous in poetry—attempting to reconcile the sixteenth century debate over the relationship of poetry to truth—as a representation of the miracles allowed for in Christian orthodoxy and therefore a representation of reality. Tasso comes down strongly on the side of the "ancients," the literary theorists who insisted that contemporary poetry must adhere to the rules formulated by Aristotle and Horace. This is particularly true of those sections in which Tasso deals with the question of unity versus variety in modern poetry. Taking the side of the neo-Aristotelian critics, Tasso asserts the immutability and universality of Aristotle's laws. At the same time, however, Tasso does allow the poet to "season" his poetry with the "spice of variety." The *Discourse* also reflects Tasso's determination to bring poetry closer to Christian truth, and the work heavily emphasizes the role of religion and ethics in the formation of literature.

Tasso's *Minturno, or On Beauty* is an aesthetic rather than specifically literary work, and it is unusual for the period in its Platonic rather than Aristotelian framework. It is in many ways a Neoplatonic document which attempts to persuade the reader to see beyond a merely material beauty and "enter the *sancta sanctorum*" where one may recognize the soul's beauty.

The selections from *Discourses on the Heroic Poem*, translated by Allan H. Gilbert, are reprinted with his permission from *Literary Criticism: Plato to Dryden*, edited by Allan H. Gilbert (Detroit: Wayne State University Press, 1962). © 1962 by Allan H. Gilbert. *Minturno, or On Beauty*, translated by Carnes Lord and Dain A. Trafton, is reprinted by permission of the University of California Press from *Tasso's Dialogues*, edited by Carnes Lord and Dain A. Trafton (Berkeley: University of California Press, 1982). © 1982 by The Regents of the University of California.

Discourses on the Heroic Poem

FROM
Book I

Poetry Defined

Since each definition should have in view the best, in defining poetry we should set before ourselves a most excellent end; and that is to give profit to men through the example of human actions, because the example of the animals cannot be of equal profit and that of divine beings is not fitted to us. . . . Poetry, then, is an imitation of human actions, produced for giving instruction on life. And because every act is performed with some reason and some choice, character and thought, which the Greeks call *dianoia*,[1] must accordingly be treated. And though when this imitation is made it produces the greatest delight, it cannot be said that there are two ends, one that of delight, the other that of profit, as it appears that Horace indicates in that verse

> The poets aim either to profit or to delight.[2]

A single art cannot have two ends unless one is subordinate to the other, but it should either lay aside the profit that comes from admonition and advice (as Isocrates says)[3] and following the example of Homer and the tragic poets direct all the force of its words toward delight; or if profit is to be retained, the pleasure should be directed to this end. And perhaps delight is the end of poetry, and an end arranged with a view to profit. Hence we read in the second oration of the same Isocrates that the ancient poets left us a heritage of teaching about life, through which men might become better,[4] and in the Panathenaic oration that poetry diverts us from many sins.[5] Hence no other employment is better fitted to youth.

Pleasure and Profit

But profit is considered chiefly with respect to that art which is as it were architect of all others. Therefore, it is the statesman's duty to consider what poetry and what delight should be prohibited, since pleasure, which should correspond to that honey with which the lip of the cup is smeared when medicine is given to children, should not produce the effect of injurious poison and should not keep the mind occupied in vain reading. The poet should not, then, set for himself pleasure as his end, as Eratosthenes seems to have thought, for he is rebuked by Strabo, who defended Homer from such imputations.[6] But profit should be the poet's end, because poetry, as the same author thinks, following the opinions of the ancients, is a first philosophy which even from early youth instructs us in morals and in the truths of life. But later authors are of the opinion that the poet should merely be wise. At least it should be believed that not every pleasure is the end of poetry but only the pleasure which is joined with goodness; because just as the delight that rises from reading of inhuman and disgraceful acts is unworthy of the good poet, so the pleasure of learning many things, joined with goodness, is suitable to him. Hence it may be that this end is not so much to be despised as appears to Fracastoro in his *Dialogue on Poetry*;[7] rather, if compared to the useful, pleasure is the nobler end, for pleasure is desired for itself and other things are desired because of it. In this respect it is so like felicity, which is the end of man in society, that nothing can be found more similar. In addition, pleasure is the friend of virtue, because it makes the nature of man magnificent, as may be read in Athenaeus;[8] therefore, those who love pleasure are likely to become both magnanimous and splendid. But the useful is not sought for itself alone, but for some other reason. Therefore, it is a less noble end than pleasure and has less similarity with the final end. If the poet then in so far as he is poet has this end, he will not widely miss that mark to which he should direct all his thoughts as an archer does his arrows. But in so far as he is a man in society and part of a city, or at least in so far as his art is subordinate to that which is queen of the others, profit is proposed as an end, as something that is rather decorous than useful. Of the two ends, then, that a poet sets for himself, one is especially that of his own art, the other that of the superior art. But when he is intent on that which is especially his own, he should guard against the opposite excess, because virtuous pleasures are contrary to dishonorable ones. For this reason they merit no praise who have described amorous embracings in such a way as Ariosto does those of Ruggiero with Alcina, or of Ricciardetto with Fiordispina.[9] . . .

Imitation

Anyone who, in defining the poet, makes him a good man and a good imitator of the actions and habits of men for the purpose of giving profit by means of delight will not perhaps offer a definition that fits all poets; yet he will define the best and most excellent poet. Then if the poet is an imitator of human actions and habits, poetry will be an imitation of the same thing, and if the poet is a good imitator, his poetry will be an imitation equally well done. But some have thought the poet should consider not so much the goodness as the beauty of his subjects. Among these is Fracastoro, who in the *Naugerius* proves that the end of the poet should be to concern himself with the idea of the beautiful.[10]

Poetry and Philosophy

Now it does not appear to me that the opinion of Maximus Tyrius ought to be despised; he thought that philosophy and poetry were one thing, double in name but single in essence, as is the light with respect to the sun, and therefore he defines poetry as a philosophy of ancient standing, metrical in sound, in subject fabulous.[11] But philosophy is, it seems to him, poetry that is younger and more independent of meter, and more obvious in its reasoning. But I think its method of considering things makes one different from the other, for poetry considers things so far as they are beautiful, and philosophy considers them so far as they are good, as the same author points out in another place,[12] saying that Homer had two things to do, one of them pertaining to philosophy, the other to poetry; in the first he had virtue to consider, in the other the figures set forth by the plot. Poetry is then a searcher for and as it were a lover of beauty, and in two ways seeks to show it and to put it before our eyes; one way is narration, the other representation; both methods are included under imitation, as under its genus, but sometimes it gets its name from a particular kind of imitation. Those then who have defined poetry as the narration of a human action that is memorable and possible have not given a definition appropriate to all the species of poetry, but merely to the epic poem, or the heroic as we wish to call it, and have excluded comedy and tragedy.

Profit and Delight

I say that a heroic poem is an imitation of illustrious actions, grand and perfect, composed in narrative form in the loftiest verse, having as its end to profit by delighting, that is, delight is the cause why no one fails to obtain benefit, because delight induces him to read the more gladly. But to profit through delight is perhaps the end of all poetry, for tragedy profits by delighting, and so does comedy. . . .The epic, however, ought to produce its special kind of delight with its own special method of working, and this perhaps is to move the reader to wonder; yet this does not seem wholly confined to the epic, for tragedy also moves to wonder, as may be gathered from those words of Isocrates which I not long ago referred to. . . .

FROM
Book II

The Matter of Poetry

No forest was ever so crowded with a great variety of trees as poetry is with a great diversity of subjects. The matter of poetry then appears more varied than that of any other subject, for it includes things high and low, serious and comic, sad and laughable, public and private, the unknown and known, modern and ancient, native and foreign, sacred and secular, civilized and primitive, human and divine; hence its boundaries are not the mountains or seas that separate Italy from Spain; not the Taurus, not Atlas, not Bactria, not Thule, not the south or the north or the east or the west, but the sky and the earth, indeed the highest part of the sky and the deepest of the heavier elements, for Dante, ascending from the center, rose above all the fixed stars and above all the circles of the heavens,[13] and Vergil and Homer described not merely the things beneath the earth but also those the intellect can scarcely comprehend, but they covered them with a charming veil of allegory. The variety then of the things treated by them and by the others who have written before and after them is very great; and great too is the diversity of opinions, or rather the contrariety of judgments, the mutations of words, of customs, of laws, of ceremonies, of republics, of kingdoms, of emperors, and as it were of the world itself, which appears to have changed its appearance and to be represented to us as though in another form and under another aspect. Therefore if anyone is able to select, among such a multitude of things doubtful and uncertain, the best and what is most fitted to receive ornament and beauty, he will show art and wisdom above all others; for art should not be dissociated from wisdom, but, as some think, is wisdom itself, since its activities are not carried on and its judgments made without choice and the advice of others, though some have thought the taking of advice has no place in the most exact arts. But I write these things as a man who utters his opinion and asks for that of others, as though wishing to kindle a great light from the many sparks that light up the shades that darken the immense forest of poetic matter. . . .

Truth and Feigning

Though we read in the *Poetics* of Aristotle that feigned stories please because of their novelty, as among the ancients the *Flower* of Agathon and among the modern Tuscans the heroic stories of Boiardo and Ariosto and the tragedies of some still more recent poets,[14] we should not allow ourselves to be persuaded that any feigned story is worthy of greater commendation, for the contrary has already been established by many proofs; two of the most important may be cited here. One of them is by Aristotle himself, to the effect that those things are credible that can be done, but if we are not sure they have been done we think them hardly possible.[15] The last is, as it were, a fruit of the same seed, sprung, I say, from his opinion that the novelty of the poem does not consist chiefly in the falsity of the subject that has not been heard of before, but in the clever entanglement and in the solution of the story.[16] The subjects of Thyestes, Medea, and Oedipus were treated by various ancients in Greek and in Latin, but by a different weaving of the threads they made something specific of what was general and something new of what was old. Therefore, Robertello is badly deceived when he assigns the false as the material of a poem, for the reason that the false, in the judgment of Plato and Aristotle, is the matter of the sophist, who labors on that which does not exist. The poet, however, bases his work on some true action and considers it as like the truth. Hence his matter is something having verisimilitude that can be true or false, though it tends to be true, since it is not at all reasonable that what possesses verisimilitude should tend toward the false, for the probable is very unlike the false, because where there is dissimilitude there cannot be identity, so to speak; but similar things can be the same, if not in substance at least in quality. Hence Monsignor Alessandro Piccolomini was little less wrong in holding the opinion that the subject of a poem should be false rather than true. . . .[17]

Poetry and Logic

I cannot concede that poetry is to be placed among the arts of the sophists or that the most excellent species of poetry is the phantastic. Though I concede that poetry is a maker of images, as is sophistry, and not merely of idols but of gods (since it is necessary to the highest renown of the poets that they deify just and valorous princes and place them in the number of the immortals and consecrate their memory to endless ages), yet I do not concede that the art of the sophists and that of the poets is the same. I say then that without doubt poetry is to be classified under dialectic with rhetoric, which, as Aristotle says, is the other scion of the dialectic power, to which appertains the consideration not of the false but the probable; hence rhetoric treats the false not in so far as it is false but in so far as it is probable; but the probable in so far as it has verisimilitude pertains to the poet. The poet, however, uses proof less efficiently than does the dialectician; indeed the imitation and the example and the comparison are the weakest kinds of proof, as Boethius teaches in his *Topics*.[18] . . . Since the poet, like the dialectician, differs from the sophist rather through choice than through faculty, it thence results that the good poet ought to labor more gladly than any other on subjects probable in themselves, as Homer did, who in the person of Hector wished to show it was a very laudable thing to defend one's native land, and in that of Achilles that vengeance was very laudable and the act of a magnanimous man and consequently just and approved by the gods. These opinions, being certainly probable in themselves, have verisimilitude, and because of the art of Homer become very probable or certain and very like to the truth. Or I should say that poetry is not a subdivision of dialectic but rather of logic, which contains three parts, the demonstrative, the probable, and the apparently probable, which is the sophistic; hence, in some things the poet demonstrates, as did Parmenides and Empedocles among the ancient Greeks, Lucretius and Boethius among the Latins, Dante among the Tuscans;[19] in some other matters the poet gives probable syllogisms, and this he does more often, because in doing so he attends properly to his own function; in some matters he uses a paralogism, and this he does more rarely. If I am right, the latitude of poetry is as great as that of logic, and it has three parts subordinate and correspondent with the three superior parts of logic, sometimes demonstrating with philosophers and using the philosopheme, at other times following verisimilitude and making use of the example and the enthymeme, as did Homer and Vergil, and at other times, like the sophist, the poet applies himself to the apparently probable, and with equivocation and other sorts of fallacious arguments, which consist in words and things, he captivates his auditors at his pleasure. This sophistic artifice was first used by the Tuscan poets in the poetry of love more than in any other, and perhaps many of them were not conscious of it. Nevertheless the most nearly perfect imitation or the best species of poetry does not rest on sophistry, whether new or old, but on dialectic.

Phantasy

Much less is true what is said by Mazzoni,[20] that the best poetry is the phantastic imitation, for such an imitation is of things that are not and never were, but the best poetry imitates the things that are, that were, and that can be, such as the war at Troy, the wrath of Achilles, the piety of Aeneas, the battles between the Trojans and the Latins, and other things that were or can be done. But the Centaurs, the Harpies, and the Cyclopes are not the adequate or principal subject of poetry, nor the flying horses and the other monsters that fill the romances.[21] But because the poet, according to the opinion of Aristotle, imitates things either as they are or as it is possible for them to be, or as report makes them, or as they are believed to be, the principal subject of poetry is what is, or what can be, or what is believed to be, or what is told of; or as Aristotle held,[22] all of these together, since they can be imitated by the poet, furnish matter fit for poetry according to this requirement of verisimilitude. One of the classes mentioned is not, then, the sole subject fitted for poetry, as Mazzoni thinks, nor does he present a conclusive argument, namely, "poetry is a maker of idols, sophistic is a maker of idols, therefore poetry is sophistic."[23] The argument does not hold, not merely because in the second figure of the syllogism the two affirmative propositions are unsound, but also because the term *idols* has various meanings, and as it is variously defined the making of idols pertains either to the poet or to the sophist. Favorinus, as Mazzoni himself says, defines an idol as a shadowy similitude or a thing feigned that truly is not, a form that has no substance, like the forms that appear in water and in mirrors. . . . But idols, as Suidas defines them, are effigies of things that do not subsist, as Tritons, Sphinxes, and Centaurs; and the similitudes are images of existing things, as animals and men.[24] Hesychius, giving with another word the meanings of the word *idol*, says: "An idol is an image, and a similitude, and a sign,"[25] as though it might be of the things that are and those that are not, as appears also to Ammonius and to Plato himself. When we say, then, that the sophist is a maker of idols, we refer to the idols that are images of things that do not subsist, for the subject of the sophist is that which is not, and in this meaning Saint Paul says: "An idol is nothing."[26] But when we affirm that the poet is a maker of idols, we do not mean merely the idols of things not subsisting, for the poet imitates things that subsist and chiefly produces a resemblance of them.

Poetry and Theology

Then in so far as the poet is a maker of idols, this should not be understood in the same sense in which it is said that the sophist is a maker of idols; but we ought rather to say that he is a maker of images in the guise of a speaking picture,[27] and in this like to the divine theologian who forms the ideas of things and commands that they be realized, and if dialectic and metaphysic, which were the divine philosophy of the Gentiles, have such conformity that they were by the ancients thought of as the same, it is not strange that the poet should be almost the same as the theologian and the dialectician. But divine philosophy, or theology as we prefer to call it, has two parts, and each of them is adapted and fitted to one part of our mind, which is composed of the divisible and the indivisible, not merely according to the opinion of Plato and of Aristotle, but of the Areopagite, who wrote in the epistles to Pope Titus in the *Mystic Theology*, and elsewhere, that that part of occult theology that is contained in the signs, and has the power of making one perfect, is fitting to the indivisible part of our soul, which is the intellect at its purest.[28] The other, eager for wisdom, which brings proofs, he attributes to the divisible part of the soul, much less noble than the indivisible. Thence it leads to the contemplation of divine things; and to move readers in this way with images, as do the mystic theologian and the poet, is a much more noble work than to teach by means of demonstrations, which is the function of the scholastic theologian. The mystic theologian and the poet, then, are far more noble than any of the others, even though Saint Thomas in the first part of the *Summa* put poetry in the lowest order of teaching,[29] but he is dealing with those parts of poetry that teach with weak proofs, such as examples and comparisons used for demonstrations; and yet he does not class it with the art of the sophists, which is not a genuine branch of learning but a deceitful appearance and an art like that of the jugglers. Then the poet as a maker of images is not a phantastic imitator, as appears to Mazzoni. . . .[30]

Images

But if the images are of subsisting things, this imitation pertains to the icastic imitator. But what sort of things shall we say subsist? Are they the intelligible or the visible? Certainly they are the intelligible, and this is the judgment of Plato, who puts things visible in the genus of not-being, and puts the intelligible only in the genus of being. Then the images of the angels, described by Dionysius,[31] are of things superior to all the human subsistances, and the winged lion too, and the eagle, and the ox, and the angel, which are the images of the Evangelists, do not then pertain chiefly to phantasy and are not its special object, because the phantasy is in the divisible part of the soul, and not in the indivisible, which is the intellect in its purest form, if indeed besides the phantasy which is a capacity of the sensitive soul there is not also another which is the capacity of the intellective. This appears likely enough, because phantasy among the Greeks had its name from the light (this may be read in the book *On the Dogmas of the Philosophers* by Plutarch)[32] as being that power which is similar to light in making things plain and in revealing itself; this is wholly fitting to the intellectual phantasy. Yet this power, though it is posited by our theologians who concede the intellective memory and by the Platonic philosophers, was not recognized and admitted by Aristotle nor by Plato in the *Sophist*; otherwise he would not distinguish icastic from phantastic imagination, since the icastic can also fit with the intellectual imagination. Perhaps Dante had this in mind when he wrote:

> To my lofty phantasy here power failed,
>
> (*Paradiso*, XXXIII, 142)

and elsewhere:

> Next rained down within my deep phantasy one crucified, despiteful and proud in his visage.
>
> (*Purgatory*, XVII 25–7)

The poet, then, though he is a maker of images, is like the dialectician and the theologian rather than the sophist, though not only among the ancients, according to the opinion of Aristotle, were poets and theologians the same, as Linus, Orpheus, and Musaeus, but also among the moderns, as Boccaccio writes in the *Life of Dante*.[33] Therefore the poet's imitation is icastic rather than phantastic; if it was merely an operation of the phantasy, an intellectual imagination would be understood, but this cannot be distinguished from the icastic.

Poetry and Truth

We can give another proof that the subject of the poem is rather the true than the false; it is derived from the teaching of Saint Thomas in his *Summa* and in his other works. He says that the good and the true and the one are convertible, and that the true is the good of the intellect.[34] Besides this, he thinks that evil is not a natural being.[35] Hence if it is not in any natural being, it is founded on something good, or on some good thing, for there is nothing wholly evil and bad. In this same way every multitude is based on unity, nor is there any multitude that does not participate in unity,[36] and every falsehood is founded on the truth. Hence what is wholly false cannot be the subject of poetry; indeed it does not exist. Hesiod, an old Greek poet, in his *Genealogy of the Gods* writes that the Muses know how to utter lies similar to the truth, and also know how to speak the truth, if they so desire, but absolutely he calls them daughters of Jove and tellers of the truth.[37] Hence I conclude that poetry is an art or faculty of speaking what is true or what is false, but chiefly what is true. Among the theologians, Athanasius holds an opinion not unlike what I think the best, for, writing against the Gentiles, who thought it was the function of the poet to feign what does not exist, he shows the opposite and proves it with the example of poets who uttered lies, but more about the gods than about men, for when writing of human actions they were not deceivers in everything; and he brings forward the authority of Homer himself, who if he had written falsely of everything, would have attributed timidity to Achilles and courage to Thersites.[38] Then the poet is in some ways a friend of the truth, which he renders splendid and beautiful with new colors and, so to speak, makes it new instead of old and antique. . . .[39]

The Marvelous

However that may be, the argument of the best epic should be founded on history. But history is concerned either with false religion or with true, nor do I think the actions of pagans give us a very fitting subject on which to base an epic poem, for in such poems we determine either to have recourse to the deities that were adored by the pagans or we decide not to do so. If we do not do so, the marvelous will be lacking; if we do have recourse to the same ones as were invoked by the ancients, by that plan we are deprived of the probable and the credible. . . . I speak of the enchanted rings, the flying horses, the ships turned into nymphs, the ghosts that interpose in battles, the burning sword, the garland of flowers, the forbidden chamber . . . and other inventions that please even in prose and are gladly read and reread without the charm of verse. But if these miracles, or prodigies rather, cannot be brought about by the power of nature, it is necessary that the cause be some supernatural force or some diabolical power, and if we turn to the deities of the pagans, we for the most part give up the lifelike and the probable, or rather I would say the credible. . . . How wholly without probability, without verisimilitude, without credibility, without charm, and without authority is the marvelous that Joves and Apollos give rise to, anyone of moderate judgment can easily see on reading the modern authors, but in the ancient poets these things should be read in another frame of mind and with another taste, as it were, not merely as things received by the people but as those approved by their religion. Therefore Robertello has no reason for blaming that beauteous story and learned allegory of the branch of gold, yet he condemns it as a thing impossible.[40] If what is impossible to nature were also impossible to the gods, . . . the opinion of Robertello would be sound, but if nothing is impossible to the gods, this marvel should not be thought more nearly impossible than the others, nor does it merit more censure than the fleece of gold and the apples of gold, whose stories are told in so many poems with so much praise for the storytellers and so much delight for the readers. These things would be thought impossible by students of physics, but since to the theologians of the pagans they did not appear so, to the poets was granted this daring and free range in feigning. In fact the theologians and the ancient poets were the same, as Aristotle says in his *Metaphysics*,[41] which Robertello does not pay much attention to, for there he could have read what the theologians might write of ambrosia and other things censured by him; yet he does not censure them as a Christian theologian, whom alone this office would befit, but as a critic of the pagan poets. . . .

Truth and the Marvelous

But now let us go on with our inquiry into how what is true to life can be joined with the marvelous, without relying on the grace and the charm of verses, which are as it were enticements to persuade the ear. The natures of these two things, the marvelous and the lifelike, are very different, and different in such a way that they are like contraries, yet both of them are necessary in a poem, though the art of an excellent poet is required to couple them. The fact has, however, been performed by many, though, so far as I know, no one has taught how it is to be done. Some men of great learning, seeing the mutual repugnance of these two kinds of things, have judged that the lifelike parts of poems cannot be marvelous, and the marvelous cannot be lifelike; but since both are necessary, one should give attention part of the time to what is true to fact, part of the time to the marvelous, in such a manner that one will not yield to the other, but the one may be tempered by the other. But I do not approve this opinion, nor do I think there should be any part of the poem that does not represent the truth. The reason that moves me to this belief is as follows: Poetry is nothing else than imitation; this cannot be called in question; imitation cannot be separated from verisimilitude, for imitation is nothing else than giving a resemblance; no part, then, of poetry can be other than true to fact. In short, truth is not one of the conditions demanded from poetry for its greater beauty and ornament, but it is intrinsic to its very essence and in every part is necessary above anything else. But though I hold the epic poet to a perpetual obligation to keep to the truth, I do not therefore exclude the other quality, that is, the marvelous; rather I hold that the same action can be both marvelous and true. I believe there are many modes of joining these discordant qualities; so . . . we shall speak here of what is most important for this matter. Some actions which greatly exceed the power of men the poet attributes to God, to his angels, to devils, or to those to whom God or the devils have conceded this power, such as the saints, magicians, and fairies. These actions, if they are considered of themselves, appear marvelous; in fact, they are called miracles in ordinary speech. If one regards the virtue and power of the doer, these same things will be judged true to life, because the men of the present age drank in this opinion with their milk when they were in their swaddling clothes and were confirmed in it by the teachers of our holy faith, namely that God and his ministers, and by his permission the demons and the magicians, are able to do wondrous things exceeding the force of nature; by reading and observation they seem every day to get new instances; therefore not merely what they believe is possible but what they think has often happened and can happen many times again will not seem beyond the limits of verisimilitude, just as the ancients who lived in the error of their vain religion saw no improbability in the miracles that not the poets alone but the historians as well fabled of their gods. But if learned men give us little credit, the opinion of the multitude is enough for the poet in this as in many other things, and leaving the exact truth, he does and should attend to it. The same action, then, can be both marvelous and according to verisimilitude, marvelous when thought of for itself and circumscribed within the limits of nature, true to life when considered apart from those limits and with respect to its cause, which is a force, supernatural, powerful, and accustomed to bring about similar marvels. But this method of joining the true with the marvelous is not open to those poems in which the deities of the pagans are introduced, as the *Ercole* of Giraldi,[42] and the *Costante* of Bolognetto. . . .[43]

Good Examples

And in addition if anyone wishes to form the idea of a perfect knight, I do not see that we can by any means deny him the right to praise piety and religion; for this purpose I should greatly prefer the person of Charles or Arthur[44] to that of Theseus or Jason. Finally, since the poet should be much concerned for the profit of his readers, he can much better set on fire the souls of our knights with the example of Christians than of infidels, since the authority of those like ourselves is always more influential than that of those unlike us, and that of those we know than of strangers. . . . The subject of a heroic poem should then be derived from true history and from religion that is not false. But histories and writings are sacred or not sacred, and of the sacred some have greater authority, if it is permitted to say so, for all spiritual things are sacred, as it appears to Saint Thomas, but not all sacred things are spiritual; the others without doubt have less authority. The poet hardly dares put his hand to histories of the first quality; but they can be left in pure and simple truth, for there is no labor in obtaining the subject, and it appears that feigning is hardly to be allowed in this matter; and he who may not feign and may not imitate, since he is tied down to the exact particulars that are contained there, would not be a poet but rather a historian. In these same histories another distinction can be made, namely, that they contain events of our days or of very remote times or else things neither very new or very old. In some ways the history of an age or a nation very distant from us appears a subject well-suited for a heroic poem, because, since those things are so buried in antiquity that there scarcely remains a weak and obscure memory of them, the poet is able to change them and change them again and tell of them as he pleases.[45]

Anachronism

But this convenience is perhaps accompanied by an inconvenience and not a small one, for with the antiquity of time it is almost necessary that antiquity of manners be introduced into the poem, but the manner of carrying on war used by the ancients, their banquets, ceremonies, and other usages of a remote age sometimes seem to our contemporaries tedious and distasteful rather than not, as happens to some persons of little education who read the divine works of Homer translated into another language. The cause of a good part of this is the antiquity of the customs, which, to those whose taste is accustomed to the refinement and propriety of the present time, are despised as old fashioned and obsolete. But one who determined to combine ancient times with modern customs would perhaps sometimes appear similar to a painter of little judgment who presents a figure of Cato or Cincinnatus clothed according to the fashions of the young men of Milan or Naples, or takes away from Hercules his club and lion's skin and equips him with a doublet and helmet, as Giraldi did in his poem,[46] though not without an important precedent, for long ago Hesiod described the arms and the shield of Hercules as though competing with Homer and told of his combat with Cycnus the son of Mars.[47] Modern histories are very convenient and easy for a poet in this matter of customs and usages, but they deprive him almost wholly of the opportunity for feigning and imitating, which is indispensable to poets, especially epic poets. Besides this, it appears that Aristotle for another reason denies to the tragic poet a subject taken from modern times, because tragedy is the imitation of men more excellent than are the moderns, and for this reason events in the present or those that happened but a short time ago should not be the subject of a heroic poem. . . .

Tragedy and Epic

If the epic and the tragic actions were of the same nature, they would produce the same effects, for from the same causes the same effects are derived, but since they produce diverse passions it follows that they are diverse in nature. Tragic actions excite horror and compassion, and if the piteous and the horrifying are lacking the tragic no longer remains. But epics do not generally in the same way produce a feeling of sadness nor is it a necessity of their nature that they should. Aristotle says that the taking of pleasure in the suffering of the wicked, though pleasing to the spectators, is not of the essence of the tragic plot, but in the heroic poem it is certainly praiseworthy. If sometimes in heroic poems there is seen something horrible or worthy of pity, horror or compassion is not sought for in all the weaving of the plot, in which we take pleasure in the victory of friends and the overthrow of enemies, but for enemies, since they are barbarians or infidels, we should not have the same pity. Nor do the actions of the tragedy and the epic present high matters in the same fashion; for their concern with great affairs is diverse in nature and form. In tragedy it appears in an unexpected and sudden change of fortune, and in the greatness of the happenings that produce pity and terror, but the splendid action of the heroic poem is founded on lofty military virtue and on a magnanimous resolution to die, on piety, on religion, and on actions in which these virtues are resplendent, which are in harmony with the nature of the epic and not fitting in a tragedy. Thence it comes about that the persons introduced in the two types of poem are not of the same nature, though both types deal with kings and great princes. Tragedy demands persons neither good nor wicked, but of a middle sort; such as Orestes, Electra, Jocasta, Eteocles, and Oedipus, who were judged by Aristotle very suitable for a tragic plot. The epic poet, on the contrary, requires the highest degree of virtue; therefore the persons are heroic, as their virtue is. In Aeneas is found the excellence of piety, in Achilles that of military courage, in Ulysses that of prudence. And if sometimes the tragic and the epic poet both take the same person as their subject, he is considered diversely by them and from different points of view. The epic writer considers in Hercules, Theseus, Agamemnon, Ajax, and Pyrrhus their valor and ability in arms; the tragedian is concerned with them in so far as they have fallen into infelicity through some error. Epic poets, however, run much less risk than tragedians do in taking as their subject not only the highest attainment of virtue in the persons described by them but the utmost of vice as well. Such are Mezentius, Busiris, Procrustes,

Diomede, Thersites, and others of the sort; of the same kind, or not much different, are the Cyclops and the Laestrygonians, in whom savagery stands in the place of vice, though it is much more terrible than vice and more horrifying. . . .

Love as a Poetic Subject

Some are of the opinion that love is not suitable material for the heroic or the tragic poet and say that in his two poems, the *Iliad* and the *Odyssey*, Homer scarcely speaks of love. . . .They assign love rather to comedy. But I have ever been of the contrary opinion, since it seems to me that the most beautiful things are well adapted to heroic poetry, and love is very beautiful, as Phaedrus thought, according to Plato.[48] But if it is neither beautiful nor ugly, as on the other hand Diotima thought,[49] it is not therefore fitting to comedies, which delight their audiences with ugly things and those that move to laughter. For this reason the old comedy ought perchance to be more praised, as Maggi believed,[50] for the new comedy has many times presented to us love as so beautiful that it could hardly be described with more colors in heroic poetry. But it cannot be denied that love is a passion suitable to heroes. . . .If love is not merely a passion and a movement of the sensitive appetite but also a noble habit of the will, as Saint Thomas thought, love will be praiseworthy in heroes and consequently in the heroic poem. The ancients did not know this love, or did not wish to describe it in heroes. But if they did not honor love as a human virtue, they adored it as divine; therefore they should have esteemed no other virtue more fitting to heroes. Hence those actions resulting from love, in addition to the others, could appear to them heroic. But modern poets, if they do not wish to describe the divinity of love in those who exposed their lives for Christ, are yet able in creating a knight to describe love as a constant habit of the will; and so, more clearly than any of the others, those Spanish authors have formed it who write in their own mother tongue without any necessity for rhyme, and with so little ambition that the name of scarcely one of them has come down to posterity. But whoever he was who described to us Amadigi the lover of Oriana, he merits more fame than any of the French writers, and I do not make an exception of Arnaut Daniel, who wrote of Lancelot, though Dante says of him:

> All verses of love and prose of romance he excelled; and let the fools talk who believe that he of Limoges surpasses him.[51]

But if he had read *Amadis of Gaul*, or *Amadis of Greece*, or *Primaleón*,[52] perhaps he would have changed his opinion, for loves are described by Spanish poets more nobly and with greater constancy than by the French, except that *Girone il Cortese* merits to be excepted from this number,[53] because it so severely punishes the hero's amorous incontinence at the fountain, but certainly it deserves greater praise to have produced such a disposition in the soul that no passion is able to take up arms against the reason. Hence the friendship of Girone with Danaino would have been more perfect if it had not been disturbed by love. Yet the fault of Girone is rather less serious than that of Odorico of

Biscay in the *Orlando Furioso*,[54] or rather no comparison can be made between them, and if Girone had not been so near to committing a fault, his virtue doubtless would appear greater to us, but the poem would not seem so pleasing in that portion. But the virtue of Leone in the *Orlando Furioso* surpasses all the other instances that I have read of.[55] It appears to me, however, that the dispute over which is the more courteous, Leone or Ruggiero, is a foolish one, for that is not courtesy that is done against honor and justice. But it was not honest for Ruggiero to deceive Bradamante.[56] Ruggiero therefore did not show courtesy; hence his courtesy cannot vie with that of Leone, the Greek prince. . . . In short, love and friendship form a most fitting subject for a heroic poem, and if we wish to give the name of friendship to the attachment of Achilles and Patroclus, no other theme can give matter for writing in a more heroic strain. But the opinion of Dante should not be neglected, for his authority in this tongue, which is not small, can be used as the foundation of our opinion. He says in his book *On the Vulgar Tongue* that there are three things that should be sung in the most elevated style: salvation, love, and virtue,[57] salvation because it is profitable, love because it is delightful, virtue because it is noble. But if the highest style is the tragic in so far as it is the same as the epic or in so far as it includes it, there is no doubt that love should be sung in the heroic poem. But such a poem considers love delightful, and love can also be considered as noble, or as a knightly virtue, that is, as a habit of the will. Let it be admitted, then, that a heroic poem can be formed with an amorous subject, such as the love of Leander and Hero, of which Musaeus,[58] a very ancient Greek poet, wrote, and that of Jason and Medea, of which Apollonius wrote among the Greeks and Valerius Flaccus among the Latins,[59] . . . and the loves of Theagenes and Chariclea, and of Leucippe and Clitophon, which were written of in the same language by Heliodorus[60] and Achilles Tatius;[61] or the others of Arcite and Palamon, and of Florio and Biancofiore, of whom Boccaccio wrote poems in our language,[62] or the adventures of Pyramus and Thisbe, who gave matter for a little poem by Tasso my father;[63] or the madness of Narcissus, from which Alamanni took a subject.[64]

The Noble Action

But in this idea of the perfect poem that we now go searching for, it is needful for us to consider nobility and excellence more than everything else. Therefore we should select actions in which there is the greatest possible amount of nobility, as in the undertaking of the Argonauts who went for the golden fleece, of which first Orpheus[65] and then Apollonius[66] wrote their poems. This requirement is equally satisfied by the Trojan war and the wanderings of Ulysses sung by Homer, the siege of Thebes and the youth of Achilles written by Statius,[67] the *Civil War* put in verse by Lucan, and the second African war versified by Silius Italicus[68] and Petrarch, who in the loves of Massinissa surpassed the first by a great distance.[69] But an action noble beyond all the others is the coming of Aeneas into Italy, because the subject is in itself great and splendid, and yet more great and splendid because the Roman Empire took origin from it, as in the beginning of the *Aeneid* the divine poet writes:

> So great a labor was it to lay the foundations of the Roman people.

Such was the liberation of Italy from the Goths, which furnished material for the poem of Trissino;[70] such are those enterprises for the confirmation of the Christian faith or for the exaltation of the Church and the Empire that were fortunately and gloriously accomplished.[71] These actions in themselves win over the souls of the readers and produce expectation and marvelous pleasure, and when the art of an able poet is added there is nothing they cannot accomplish in our souls.

The Perfect Subject

The poet should then avoid feigned subjects, especially if it is feigned that something has come about in a land near at hand and well known and among a friendly people, for among distant peoples and in unknown countries we can easily feign many things without taking away authority from the story.[72] Therefore from the land of the Goths and from Norway and Sweden and Iceland or from the East Indies or the countries recently discovered in the vast ocean beyond the pillars of Hercules, the subjects of such poems should be taken.[73] The poet should not touch those subjects that cannot be treated poetically and in which there is no place for fiction and artistry, and he should reject subjects too rude, to which he cannot add splendor, and should remember that precept of Horace:

> Abandon a subject if you fear you cannot make it splendid by your treatment.[74]

He should reject what is badly arranged as though it were a stick of timber too crooked to be good for building; he should refuse materials too dry and arid, which do not give much scope to the ability and art of the poet, and above all those that are unpleasant and annoying, and those that end unhappily, as the death of the Paladins and the defeat at Roncesvalles.[75] . . . The poet should not become fascinated with material too subtle, and fitted for the schools of the theologians and the philosophers rather than the palaces of princes and the theaters, and he should not show himself ambitious in the questions of nature and theology,[76] and should not forget what Horace says in praise of Homer, putting him higher than many philosophers who have written of virtue and nobility, as may be read in the second epistle to Lollius (ll. 1–4):

> While you, Lollius Maximus, declaim at Rome, I have been reading afresh at Praeneste the writer of the Trojan War; who tells us what is fair, what is foul, what is helpful, what is not, more plainly and better than Chrysippus or Crantor.

Nor should the poet show himself too curious in the knowledge of antiquity that is obscure and as it were forgotten, when the obscurity is not that of things that are very great and worthy of knowledge; he should despise trifles rather than not; in the witty he should be magnificent, in the hidden he should be clear, and in all he should excite wonder; he should not be too lengthy in describing sacred or secular ceremonies; in games he should be ornate, and vigorous, and put events before our eyes, and not describe all that is done, but the more famous and splendid, and those that are imitations of war or warlike exercises, as Homer and Vergil did, one in the obsequies of Patroclus, the other in the burial of Anchises. But now the place of games has been taken by tournaments and jousts, which have been splendidly described by our poets, as by Ariosto that of Damascus and by Tasso that of Cornwall with more propriety,[77] for in England they were accustomed to conduct them but it was not the custom of the Turks and Saracens to joust; hence Gemma, the brother of Bajazet II, when he was a prisoner in Rome was in the habit of saying that there was too much play and too little reality. The poet should also have in mind the glory of the nation, the origin of cities, famous families, and princes of kingdoms and empires, as did Vergil beyond all the others. But he should not be too free in feigning things that are impossible, monstrous, supernatural, and unfitting, as did the man who wished to imitate the fable of Tiresias, who struck the serpents twice and was first transformed from a man to a woman and then from a woman to a man, for it was not a happy thought to transform Rinaldo into a woman. The author should consider the power of the magic art and of nature itself, as though inclosed within certain limits and confined by certain laws, and ancient and forgotten prodigies, and the occasions of marvels and miracles and monstrous events, and the diversity of religions, and the dignity of the persons, and should seek as much as he can to increase faith in the marvel without diminishing the pleasure. He should therefore not reject incantations or hunting scenes, though they show the pursuit of terrible animals such as have seldom been seen. . . . In this matter we may follow the authority of the ancients in the hunt of the boar killed by Atalanta, which supplied the cause for the unhappiness of Meleager, celebrated by the Greek and Latin poets, and in that of the bull overcome by Theseus, and of the serpents killed by Hercules. He describes tempests, great fires, voyages, countries and particular places; he takes pleasure in the description of battles by land and by sea, of assaults on cities, of the drawing up of an army, and of the method of encamping it. But in this he avoids excess and tempers the unpleasantness of too detailed instruction. . . . The poet should be similarly careful in his descriptions of hunger, thirst, sickness, the sunrise, the sunset, midday, midnight, the seasons of the year, the quality of the months or of the days, whether rainy, or clear, or calm, or stormy. But in councils and assemblies he can confidently write at greater length with the authority of the ancient poets. And in describing arms, impresses,[78] horses, ships, temples, pavilions, tents, paintings, and statues and other similar things, he should always have in mind what is fitting, and avoid the irritation that too great length always causes. In deaths he should seek for variety, effectiveness, pathos; in encounters with the lance, and in blows with the sword, for verisimilitude, not passing too far beyond what has come about or can come about or is believed or told of. In menaces he should be lofty and bitter, in laments short and full of feeling, in jests playful and gracious. He should not conceal things that are true in antiquity and as though in the clouds; he should not show feigned things in the light of the sun, but rather in the darkness, like goods that in that way are more easily sold. Of the ages between our times and high antiquity he should select those removed from our memory a convenient distance, like a painter who does not put his picture close before our faces nor yet so distant that it cannot be made out, but suitably disposes it in the light in a high place. He chooses the most beautiful among beautiful things, the grandest among the grand, the most marvelous among the marvelous, and to the most marvelous he seeks to add novelty and greatness. Necessary things, such as eating and preparing food, he leaves out or describes briefly, as Vergil describes them in the following passage:

> They gird themselves to deal with the game, their forthcoming meal; strip the hide from the ribs, and lay bare the flesh—some cut it into pieces and impale it yet quivering on spits, others set up the caldrons on the beach, and supply them with flame. Then with food they recall their strength, and, stretched along the turf, feast on old wine and fat venison to their hearts' content.[79]

But such descriptions are pleasing in proportion as they are more distant from us in place and their methods are different from ours. Our poet should also disdain all low things, all that are popular, all that are indecent, like the story of Fiametta and that of the Doctor.[80] Things not on a high level he should elevate; to the obscure he should give the effect of being generally known and illustrious, he should supply art to the simple, ornament to the true, authority to the false. If he sometimes makes use of shepherds, goatherds, swineherds, and other persons of that sort, he should have regard not merely to fitness of person but also to that of the poem, and show them as they are in royal palaces and on occasions of ceremony.[81]

Summary

Here are the conditions that the judicious poet should seek in his matter. Briefly summarizing what has already been said, they are the authority of history, the truth of religion, opportunity to feign new stories, attention to the nature of the times, and greatness in the events represented.

FROM

Book III

The Divinity of Art

Let us go on to consider the idea of things formed by art, for the operations of art appear to us as though divine and in imitation of God, the first artist. . . .

The Universal

When the poet has selected material in itself capable of every perfection, there remains to him the other still more difficult task of giving it poetic form and disposition; this is a procedure on which, as its most appropriate object, art expends its utmost strength. Because what chiefly constitutes the nature of poetry and makes it different from history is not verse, as Aristotle says,[82] . . . but is the consideration of things not as they are but as they ought to be—with regard rather to the universal than to the truth of particulars—the poet before anything else should consider whether in the matter he is to treat there is any event which, if it happened otherwise, would be more marvelous, or more true to life, or for any other reason would cause greater delight. Everything he can find of that sort, that is, anything that would have been better if it had happened in some other way, he may, without any regard to truth or history, alter and change as he wishes, arranging, rearranging, and modifying the circumstances as he thinks best, and mingling the false with the true, but in such a way that the true will be the foundation of the plot. . . . Vergil in the wanderings of Aeneas and in the war fought between him and Latinus did not write merely things he thought true, but what he judged better and more excellent, for not merely are the love and death of Dido false, and the story of Polyphemus and the descent of Aeneas to the lower world fabulous, but the battles between Aeneas and the people of Latium are described otherwise than as they truly came about. . . . And in the story of Dido he makes great confusion in the order of time by means of that figure the Greeks call anachronism, or rather with that license first used by Plato and the Greek poets who introduce as speaking together men who lived in different ages, as Athenaeus notes in the *Banquet of the Deipnosophists*.[83] This license was likewise used by Ovid in his *Metamorphoses*, at the end of which Pythagoras, an Italian philosopher, gives instruction to Numa, king of the Romans, though it is certain that Pythagoras was born some hundreds of years later than Numa. The same theory or the same artistic practice of mingling the true with the false or with the feigned can be learned from Horace[84] and from Plutarch at the beginning of his *Life of Theseus*[85] . . . and from Plato himself, and by Xenophon in his *Cyropaedia*, and though the last was not a poet, but a philosopher and a historian, yet, in his outlook on the universal and the ideal, he was more like the poets than like the historians. . . . With this authority of old and new writers Vergil can be defended, but he perhaps sought occasion for mingling with the severity of other matters some pleasant discourses of love, though the death of Dido, a terrible and unhappy event, might follow; or rather he wished to assign a noble and inherited cause to the enmity between Romans and Carthaginians. . . .

Poetic License

The license of the poet should not extend so far that he dares to change the outcome of the actions he undertakes to treat, or to narrate anything contrary to the issue of some of the principal and best-known events which are accepted as true by the opinion of the world. . . . Our epic poet, then, should retain, with little or no change, the truth about the origin and the end of the action and the other things best known and accepted in common report; he may change, if it appears well to him, the means and the circumstances, and may confuse the temporal connections and the relations of the other things, and in short may show himself a poet, working artistically, rather than a veracious historian, keeping ever in mind what was said by Plutarch in his book *On the Fortune of the Romans*, that is, that the man who conceals falsehood in the antiquity of the ages is like him who escapes from brightly lighted places into those that are dark and shady.[86]

Poetry and Fact

But if in the material he has chosen there are some actions that happened just as the poet wishes, what shall he do? Can he relate them in his poem? Most certainly, if his narrative is poetical, and he does not despoil himself of the person of the poet to put on that of the historian, for at times it can happen that one man as poet, another as historian may deal with the same matter, though they will look at it differently, for the historian narrates it as true, the poet imitates it as like the truth. . . . If Lucan is not a poet, this is because he is in bondage to the truth of particulars rather than attending to the universal, and, as it seems to Quintilian,[87] is more like an orator than a poet. In addition, the order followed by Lucan is not the order appropriate to the poet but the true and natural order in which are narrated things that have already happened; he has this in common with the historian.[88]

Suspense

But in the artistic order, which Castelvetro calls the perturbed order,[89] some of the early events should be first narrated, and others postponed, others should be passed over for the present and reserved for a better time, as Horace teaches.[90] The author should give first those without which there would be no knowledge of the present state of affairs, but if possible should remain silent about many, for to tell them would diminish the expectation and the astonishment of the reader, who should always be kept in suspense and desirous of reading further.

Unity

Unity is the topic which has given to our times occasion for various and long contests among those "whom the fury of letters leads into war." Some have judged unity necessary; others, on the contrary, have thought a multitude of actions more suitable for heroic poetry, and "each one considers himself a great judge." The defendes of unity, making a shield of the authority of Aristotle and the majesty of the ancient Greek and Latin poets, and not lacking the arms that are given by reason, have as adversaries the habit of the present age, the universal agreement of ladies, knights, and courts, and, as it seems, experience as well, an infallible touchstone of the truth. It is evident that Ariosto, who, leaving the path trod by the ancient writers and the rules of Aristotle, has included in his poem many and diverse actions, is read and reread by persons of all ages and by both sexes, is known to speakers of all languages, pleases all, is praised by all, lives, and ever renews the youth of his fame, and flies in glory over the tongues of mortals. Yet Trissino, on the contrary, who determined to imitate religiously the poems of Homer and to observe the precepts of Aristotle, is named by few, and read by very few, is mute in the theater of the world and dead to the light,[91] and can hardly be found buried in the libraries and in the study of some scholar. Nor are there lacking in favor of this plan, in addition to experience, solid and striking arguments, since some men both learned and ingenious, either because they truly think so or merely to show the force of their ability and to make themselves acceptable to the world, which flatters this universal agreement as though it were a tyrant (for such it truly is), have found new and subtle reasons with which they have confirmed it and made it stronger. . . .

Unity a General Law

But against this virtual law of poetry, that of unity (which was accepted as good by Horace when he said: Let what is treated be simple and one),[92] various men have directed opposition supported with various reasons, excluding unity of plot from those heroic poems that are called romances, not merely as unnecessary but even as damaging.[93] [He then proceeds to show that the romance is of the same kind as the epic.] If then the romance and the epic are of the same species, they should be confined by the same bonds of law, especially when these laws are absolutely necessary not merely to the heroic poem, but to every poem. Such a law is unity of plot, which Aristotle prescribes for every species of poem, not more for the heroic than for the tragic and the comic.[94] Therefore if what is said of the romance is true [that it differs from the epic] it would not therefore follow that unity of plot would not according to the idea of Aristotle be necessary to it. . . .

The second reason was that every tongue has some individual quality, and that a number of actions is appropriate to Tuscan poetry, as is unity to Greek and Latin poetry. I do not deny that each language has some forms peculiar to itself. . . . But what is the particular property of one language is either a matter of speech, and not of importance in this matter, since we are speaking of actions, not of words, or we should make the peculiar property of a language these matters that are better treated by it than by any other, as is war by the Latin language and love by the Tuscan. But it is plain that if the Tuscan speech is fitted to set forth many amorous happenings, it is equally fitted to set forth one, and if the Latin tongue is fitted to deal with one warlike event, it will be equally fitted to deal with many. So for my part I cannot understand the reason why unity of action is appropriate for Latin poems and multiplicity of action for those in the vulgar tongue. . . .

Unity and Nature

It is not more difficult to deal with the third reason, which was that those poems are most excellent that are most approved in practice; the romance would therefore be more excellent than the epic, being more approved in practice. Wishing to contradict this reason, it is necessary that for greater intelligibility and clearness of the truth I should derive my reasoning from a remote beginning. Some things in their nature are neither good nor bad, but, since they depend on custom, are good or bad as custom determines. Such is clothing, which is commendable in proportion as it is accepted by custom. . . . There are other things the quality of which is determined by their nature; that is, they are either good or evil in themselves and custom has no rule or authority over them. Of this sort are vice and virtue; vice is evil in itself; virtue is admirable in itself; virtuous and vicious actions are in themselves commendable and blameworthy. And what has this characteristic in itself, though customs may vary, always has this characteristic. Hence the eating of human flesh will always be reputed savage, though it was practiced by some nations. Chastity always has been and always will be a virtue, though the Spartan women were not esteemed chaste. If at any time the man deserved praise who refused the gold of the Samnites, or that man who bound himself when he was alive and released his father who was dead, they will never be blamed for such noble acts. Of the same kind are the acts of nature, for in spite of the instability of custom, what was once excellent will always be excellent. Nature is very stable in its operations and ever proceeds with a certain and perpetual tenor, even if it sometimes seems to vary because of the weakness and inconstancy of the matter it works on, for, directed by a light and guide that are infallible, it considers always the good and the perfect; and since the good and the perfect are always the same, it is needful that its mode of working always be the same. Beauty is a work of nature, and since it consists in a certain proportion of limb with a fitting size and beautiful and pleasing coloring,[95] these conditions that once were beautiful in themselves will ever be beautiful, nor can custom bring about that they will appear otherwise; as on the contrary custom cannot bring about that pointed heads and goitres will appear beautiful even among those nations where they are seen in the majority of men and women. But if such in themselves are the works of nature, such must needs be the works of that art which without any intermediary is an imitator of nature. Thence it is reasonable for Cicero in his *Topics*[96] to enumerate nature and art among the causes that are unchangeable, for their effects are invariable, as Boethius says in his commentary on that passage. And to linger over the example that has been given, if the proportion of the members in itself is beautiful, it will be in itself beautiful when imitated by the painter and the sculptor, and if something in nature is worthy of admiration, the artificial thing that is similar to the natural will also be admirable. Thence it happens that those statues by Praxiteles and Phidias that have survived the attacks of envious Time appear as beautiful in our eyes as they did in those of the ancients, nor has the flight of so many ages or the alterations of so many customs been able to lessen their dignity. Having made this distinction, I can easily answer the argument that those poets are most excellent who are most approved in practice, for every piece of poetry is composed of words and things. In respect to the words it may be conceded (since they have nothing to do with our contention) they are the best that are most approved by practice, for in themselves they are neither beautiful nor ugly, but they appear such as custom makes them, so that some words that were highly regarded by the Emperor Frederick and King Enzio and other old writers have in our ears I do not know what that is displeasing. Things then that depend on custom, as the manner of jousting, the customs of sacrifices and banquets, ceremonies, the decorum and dignity of persons can, I believe, be arranged as befits the customs that exist and rule the world today. It would therefore be unfitting to the majesty of our times that the daughter of a king, with her maiden companions, should go to wash clothes in the river, yet in the time of Nausicaa, told of by Homer, it was not deserving of reprehension.[97] Equally he who instead of jousts should describe combats with chariots would merit little praise. But the things that in themselves are good do not have any regard for custom nor does the tyranny of convention extend over them in any respect. Such is unity of plot, which carries in its nature goodness and perfection for the poem, as in every age, past and future, it has carried and will carry it. Such are human traits, not those that are called by the name of customs, but those by which we may form the habits that can be put among constant causes. . . . Of them Horace speaks in these verses:

> The child who now knows how to speak and to walk with a firm step delights in play with other children, and easily gets angry and easily forgets his anger, and changes from one hour to the other.[98]

And Aristotle at length in the *Rhetoric*.[99] Any of these characteristics of the boy, the old man, the rich man, the powerful man, the noble and ignoble man that are suitable in one age will be suitable in every age. Were this not so, Aristotle would not have spoken of it, for he professes to teach only those things that fall within the realm of art, and since art is fixed and determined, nothing can be comprehended within its rules which, being dependent on the instability of custom, is mutable and uncertain. Similarly he would not have discussed unity of plot if he had not thought it necessary in every age. But while some wish to found a new art on new custom, they destroy the nature of art and show that they do not know that of custom. . . .

Variety

The last reason against unity remains, which was that since the end of poetry is delight, those poems are most excellent which most nearly attain this end, but the romance arrives nearer to it than does the epic, as experience shows. Let us concede what we could deny, namely, that delight is the end of poetry. I concede also what experience shows us, to wit, that greater delight is given to men of our day by the *Orlando Furioso* than by the *Italy Liberated*[100] or even by the *Iliad* or the *Odyssey*. But I deny that the concession is of great importance or applies at all to our argument, that is, that a number of actions are more fitted to delight than unity; for the opposite can be proved on the authority of Aristotle and with the proof he gives in the *Problems*.[101] And though the *Orlando Furioso*, which contains a number of plots, is more delightful than any other Tuscan poem, or even than the poems of Homer, that is not the result of unity or of number, but of two reasons that have no application to our theme. The one is that in the *Furioso* one can read of loves, knighthood, adventure, and incantations, and in short, inventions very delightful and well suited to our ears; the other is that in the propriety of action and in the decorum of persons Ariosto is more excellent than any of the others. These causes are accidental to the multiplicity and the unity of the plot, and not in such a fashion fitted to the one type that they are not fitted to the other as well. Thence it should not be concluded that multiplicity is more pleasing than unity. But perhaps it can be proved by another reason, for, since our humanity is composed of natural qualities rather different among themselves, it is necessary that it should not always be delighted by one and the same thing, but by means of diversity should contrive to satisfy now one, now another of its parts. Since then variety is very delightful to our nature, it can be said that much greater delight is found in multiplicity than in unity of plot. I do not deny that variety gives pleasure, for the denial would contradict experience and our perceptions, since we see that things displeasing in themselves through their variety become pleasant to us, and that the sight of deserts and the roughness and severity of the mountains please us after the softness of lakes and gardens. I say that variety is pleasing just so long as it does not pass over into confusion, and unity is quite capable of variety up to that point, for to unity . . . multiplicity is accidental, and if such diversity is not seen in a poem of one action, we can believe it comes rather from the lack of skill of the artists than from a defect inherent in art itself, for artists, perhaps to excuse their own insufficiency, attribute their own faults to art. Perhaps this variety was less necessary in the times of Vergil and Homer,[102] since the men of that age were less sated in their tastes; at any rate they did not attain so much, though more is found in Vergil than in Homer. Variety is especially pleasing to our times,[103] and therefore our poets have to season their poems with this spice of variety if they wish not to be rejected by our delicate palates, and if some of them do not attempt to introduce it, either they do not understand the need for it or they despair of it as impossible. I too think it very pleasant in a heroic poem and possible of introduction there, for in this admirable realm of God called the world, the sky is seen to be scattered over and beautified with a great variety of stars, and descending lower from region to region, the air and the sea are full of birds and fishes, and the earth harbors many animals both fierce and gentle, and in it we can see many streams, fountains, lakes, fields, plains, forests, and mountains, here fruits and flowers, there ice and snow, here dwellings and cultivation, there solitude and wild places. Yet for all that, the world, which includes in its bosom so many and so diverse things, is one, one in its form and essence, one the knot with which its parts are joined and bound together in discordant concord; and while there is nothing lacking in it, yet there is nothing there that does not serve either for necessity or ornament. I judge that in the same way the great poet (who is called divine for no other reason but that, because he resembles in his works the supreme architect, he comes to participate in his divinity) is able to form a poem in which as in a little world can be read in one passage how armies are drawn up, and in various others there are battles by land and sea, attacks on cities, skirmishes, duels, jousts, descriptions of hunger and thirst, tempests, conflagrations, prodigies; there are a variety of celestial and infernal councils, and the reader encounters seditions, discords, wanderings, adventures, incantations, works of cruelty, audacity, courtesy, and generosity, and actions of love, now unhappy, now happy, now pleasing, now causing compassion. Yet in spite of all, the poem that contains so great variety of matter is one, one is its form and its soul; and all these things are put together in such a way that one has relation to the other, one corresponds to the other, the one necessarily or apparently so depends on the other that if one part is taken away or changed in position the whole is destroyed. And if this is true, the art of composing a poem is like the nature of the universe, which is composed of contraries, such as appear in the law of music, for if there were no multiplicity there would be no whole, and no law, as Plotinus says.

Unity Difficult

But this variety will be so much the more marvelous in proportion as it carries with it more difficulty and as it were impossibility, for contrary qualities cannot be found together except in ascending order, as in the heavens, or at least abated as in the elements. In a poem then in which tragedy is joined with comedy, laughter should not be laughter except blunted. It surely is an easy thing to bring it about that in many and separate actions there should be a variety of events, but that the same variety should be furnished by one sole action, *hoc opus, hic labor est*.[104] In that variety which arises from the multitude of the plots in themselves, no art or ingenuity of the poet is to be observed, and it is common to both learned and ignorant. Variety in the unified plot depends on the skill of the poet, and when it is attained is recognized as the result of his skill and as not to be achieved by any moderate capacities. The multiple plot will delight the less in proportion as it is more confused and less intelligible; the unified plot because of its arrangement and the binding together of its parts will not merely be more clear and distinct but will appear much more novel and marvelous. The plot and the form should then be one in every sort of poem, including those that treat of arms and the loves of heroes and of errant knights, which generally are called heroic poems. . . .

Qualities of Heroic Poetry

The heroic style is not remote from the gravity of tragic style nor from the beauty of lyric style, but it exceeds both the one and the other in the splendor of its wonderful majesty. Yet it is not inappropriate to the epic poet that issuing sometimes from the limits of his splendid magnificence, he should cause his style to approach the gravity of the tragic writer, as he often does; at other times, though more rarely, he can cause it to approach the flowery ornament of lyric style. But the style of a tragedy, though it describes glorious events and royal personages, for two reasons should be less sublime than the heroic. The first is that it normally deals with matter of a more passionate sort, and passion demands purity and simplicity, for it is likely that in that manner a person would speak who is full of anxiety, fear, pity, or some similar disturbance. The other cause is that in a tragedy the poet never speaks, but only those who carry on the action of the play, to whom should be assigned a manner of speaking less strange and less unlike that of ordinary life than epic diction. But the chorus perhaps should speak more loftily, for, as Aristotle says in the *Problems*,[105] it is a sort of guardian that is additional and separate, and for the same reason the poet speaks more loftily in his own person and discourses as though with another tongue, like one who feigns to be rapt out of himself by divine inspiration. . . .

FROM

Book VI

Comedy

Many have thought the delight that springs from things full of grace is the same as laughter; therefore they have sought to move this delight everywhere, and all their writings are full of their attempt to do it; they have wished to sprinkle as it were with this salt their stories, letters, orations, satires and other burlesque poems, comedies, heroic poetry, and even tragedy itself, which gladly receives grace but is the enemy of laughter, as Demetrius of Phalerum says.[106] And according to my opinion heroic poetry is of the same nature, though it may move a terrible laugh by means of the Cyclops; but in the same way the tragedy of Euripides called by that name can move laughter, if indeed it is a tragedy, and not a satyr drama as some have believed; yet if it is a tragic poem it is of the less perfect sort, for laughter would probably have no place in the more perfect, as it does not have in the heroic poem, except in the manner that has been mentioned, full of bitterness and terror and far from the immodest; indeed this is not properly laughter, for laughter arises from ugly things without pain. The words, then, that put ugliness before our eyes can move us to laughter, for they, being as it were images of ugly things, are ugly words. But beautiful words are the cause of that gracious delight that is fitting for the heroic and the lyric poet beyond all others, and is also fitting to tragedy, but less so. Laughter and the gracious, then, arise from two opposite causes, that is, one from the beautiful and one from the ugly, and they are as different as are Thersites and Cupid. But both of them arise with astonishment, because astonishment is in the habit of accompanying both. Therefore we marvel at dwarfs and at an ugly old woman who has the face of a monkey as did Gabrina,[107] and we marvel also at the beauty of a girl; for that reason Laura was called a monster by her gentle poet:

> O proud and rare monster among ladies.[108]

But though astonishment arises from either kind of poetry, that is, from that which imitates ugly things and from that which resembles beautiful things, yet it is not so suited to one as to the other, for astonishment rapidly disappears from ugly things, which as they lost their novelty lose the power to astonish us, but our astonishment at beautiful things is more durable and of higher value. And beautiful beyond all other poems is the heroic; hence this delight is its peculiar property. The heroic is also the most magnificent of poems; this is another reason why such astonishment is appropriate to it. . . .

Teaching by Example

There are two modes of teaching by example, one that of inciting to good works by showing the reward of the noblest virtue and of well-nigh divine valor, the other that of frightening us from evil with a punishment. The first is that of the epic, the second that of tragedy, which for that reason is less beneficial and also causes less delight, for man is not of so fierce and wicked a nature as to put his greatest pleasure in sorrow and in the unhappiness of those who through some human error have fallen into misery.

NOTES

1. Aristotle, *Poetics*, XIX, 56a33.
2. *Art of Poetry*, 3.
3. "This much, however, is clear, that those who aim to write anything in verse or prose which will make a popular appeal should seek out, not the most profitable discourses, but those which most abound in fictions; for the ear delights in these just as the eye delights in games and contests. Wherefore we may well admire the poet Homer and the first inventors of tragedy, seeing that they, with true insight into human nature, have embodied both kinds of pleasure in their poetry; for Homer has dressed the contests and battles of the demigods in myths, while the tragic poets have rendered the myths in the form of contests and action, so that they are presented, not to our ears alone, but to our eyes as well. With such models, then, before us, it is evident that those who desire to command the attention of their hearers must abstain from admonition and advice, and must say the kind of things which they see are most pleasing to the crowd" (Isocrates, *To Nicocles*, 48–9, trans. by George Norlin [New York, 1928].
4. *To Nicocles*, 43.
5. Apparently an error by Tasso. In the *Panathenaicus* (35) there is a promise to discuss poetry, but it is not kept.
6. "Eratosthenes is wrong in his contention that the aim of every poet is to entertain, not to instruct; indeed the wisest of the writers on poetry say, on the contrary, that poetry is a kind of elementary philosophy" (Strabo, *Geography*, I, 1, 10, trans. by H. I. Jones [New

York, 1917]). See also I, 2, 3. The earlier part of Strabo's work is an expansion of this assertion by means of examples from the geographical knowledge of Homer.

7. Girolamo Fracastoro, *Naugerius sive de poetica dialogus*, University of Illinois Press, 1924, with translation by Ruth Kelso: "Teaching is in a measure the concern of the poet, but not in his peculiar capacity" (p. 56).

8. *The Deipnosophists*, XII, 512.

9. *Orlando Furioso*, VII, 23–29; XXV, 50–70.

10. "The aim of the poet is to please and to instruct, by imitating in every individual object the most excellent and most beautiful elements, in a style which is appropriate and simply beautiful" (*Naugerius*, concluding par.).

11. Near the beginning of the essay entitled "Whether the Poets or the Philosophers Treat Better of the Gods."

12. In the essay on "What Homer Chose to Do."

13. Sidney, *Defense of Poetry*, sect. 24: "the poet . . . having all, from Dante's Heaven to his Hell, under the authority of his pen." Cf. also Vauquelin de la Fresnaye, *Art poétique*, Bk. I.

14. Perhaps Giraldi Cinthio is one of the tragic poets.

15. *Poetics*, IX, 51a36.

16. *Poetics*, XVIII, first par.

17. "It is not then necessary that a poetic imitation in itself should deal with what is false or with what is true, but it is necessary that a thing should be imitated according to verisimilitude; from this follows that as not merely the false but the true as well can be combined with what is suitable and has verisimilitude, so equally it can come about by accident that not merely the false but the true as well can become the subject and the matter for poetry, but this comes to pass, as I have said, by accident. For it must be admitted that nature and art seldom reach the height of their powers, because of the various impediments that are opposed to them; and so likewise man in his acts and passions and habits is infrequently able to rise to the greatest heights. If, for example, anyone, as enraged, or envious, or fearful, or strong, or pious, or avaricious, or prodigal, or as under the sway of any other habit or desire, should perform some action, it will rarely happen that his actions will result from these habits or desires in their most extreme form. That is, very rarely will be found in him wrath, envy, timidity, fortitude, piety, prodigality, avarice, or any other passion or habit in the greatest force or in the greatest excess that is possible. Consequently, the actions resulting from such false habits and passions will usually not be so intense and so full as according to verisimilitude they ought to be if they were derived from and issued out of such habits or feelings on the highest level. This is the reason why human actions that actually are performed by one individual or another are far different from those that the poets attribute to them, since the poets view the actions of men, and with them their habits and their feelings, in their universal aspect, and not in accord with their exact truth, except in the cases we have alluded to when the exact truth is accidentally united with the universal. Thence it comes about that the false is more often found in poetic imitation than is the true, not because falsehood is the matter most suitable for poetry, but because though not merely the false but the true as well can by accident be joined with the universal and with what has verisimilitude, yet the false is more often joined with it than is the true" (Alessandro Piccolomini, *Annotationi nel libro della poetica d'Aristotele* [Venice, 1575], sig. †† 6 recto).

Tasso refers also to Mazzoni, *On the Defense of the "Comedy,"* Introduction, sect. 4.

18. Such use of logic in literary criticism is frequent in the sixteenth century. See, for example, Bernardino Parthenio, *Della imitatione poetica* (Vinega, 1560), pp. 34, 78, 82, and the last note in the selections from Minturno, above. In France the union of logic

and rhetoric appears in the *Logic* of Peter Ramus (1515–72). Ramus had great influence in England, as on Sir Philip Sidney and Milton. The latter issued in 1672 a *Logic* based on that of Ramus and reproducing his quotations from the poets. For text and translation see the *Works* of Milton, Columbia University Press, XI.

19. Mazzoni in his *Discourse in Defense of Dante* points out Dante's use of logic in the following passage: "He cannot be absolved who does not repent, and it is not possible at once to repent and to wish to sin, because of the contradiction that does not allow it" (*Inferno*, XXVII, 118–20).

For a discussion of contradictories in logic, with examples from Latin literature, see Milton's *Art of Logic*, 1, 16 (ed. cit., pp. 136 ff.). In this chapter Milton quotes from the *Topics* of Boethius, mentioned by Tasso just above.

20. *On the Defense of the "Comedy,"* Introduction, sect. 3.
21. Cf. Sidney's apparently opposed opinion, *Defense*, sect. 9.
22. *Poetics*, XXV, 60b32.
23. *On the Defense of the "Comedy,"* Introduction, sect. 6.
24. Suidas, *Lexicon*, s.v. *eidōlon*.
25. Hesychius of Alexandria, author of a Greek lexicon; an edition was issued in 1514. See *eidōlon*.
26. I Corinthians 8, 4.
27. Cf. Sidney, *Defense*, sect. 12.
28. Dionysius the Areopagite, *Epistle* IX, sect. 1 (in Migne, *Patrologia Graeca*, III, 1107).
29. Part I, q. 1, art. 9: "It is objected that sacred teaching should not use metaphors. . . . But to proceed by various similitudes and representations is proper to poetry, which is the humblest branch of knowledge. . . . I answer that it is proper for Sacred Scripture to set forth in metaphors divine and spiritual things under the similitude of corporeal things."
30. *On the Defense of the "Comedy,"* Introduction, sect. 1.
31. Dionysius the Areopagite (see Acts 17, 34), formerly supposed to be the author of the work on the celestial hierarchies from which was derived much of the Renaissance theory of angels.
32. *De plac. phil.* IV, 12.
33. See the end of the selection from Boccaccio, above.
34. A simplification of the teaching of Aquinas, perhaps founded on *Summa theologica*, I, 16, *De veritate* (Of Truth). Cf. Dante, *Inferno*, III, 18.
35. *Summa*, I, 48, 1. *Utrum malum sit natura quaedam* (Is Evil an Existing Thing?).
36. *Summa*, I, 11, 2.
37. Hesiod, *Theogony*, 26–9.
38. *Iliad*, II, 243–77.
39. Cf. Shelley: "Poetry lifts the veil from the hidden beauty of the world, and makes familiar objects be as if they were not familiar." And some pages further: "It reproduces the common universe of which we are portions and percipients, and it purges from our inward sight the film of familiarity which obscures from us the wonder of our being" (*Defense of Poetry*). Wordsworth also wrote: "The principal object, then, proposed in these poems was to choose incidents and situations from common life, and . . . to throw over them a certain coloring of imagination, whereby ordinary things should be presented to the mind in an unusual aspect" (Preface to the second edition of *Lyrical Ballads*).
40. Robertello or Robortelli, Italian commentator on Aristotle's *Poetics* (1548)

and editor of Longinus, *On the Sublime*. For the branch of gold, see *Aeneid*, VI, 137.

41. Bk. III, chap. 4.

42. An epic on the life of Hercules.

43. Francesco Bolognetti published his *Costante*, on the heroic adventures of the great-grandfather of Constantine the Great, in 1565–6.

44. Charlemagne appears in the *Orlando Furioso* and in many other romances. King Arthur and his knights, well known to English readers, appear also in continental romances.

45. See also sect. 20, below.

46. The *Ercole*. For Giraldi's theory on the subject see *On the Composition of Romances*, sect. 57.

47. Hesiod, *Shield of Hercules*, 57–end.

48. See Plato's *Symposium*, 178–80.

49. *Ibid.*, 202.

50. Author, with Lombardi, of a commentary on the *Poetics* of Aristotle (1550).

51. *Purgatorio*, XXVI, 118–20. He of Limoges is Gerard of Borneuil.

52. *Amadis of Gaul* was one of the romances saved from the bonfire described in *Don Quixote*, I, 6; *Amadis of Greece* was burned. *Primaleón*, or *La historia de Primaleón Polendos*, was first published in 1548, a romance following that of *Palmerin de Oliva*, and dealing with the sons of Palmerin.

53. A poem of chivalry by Luigi Alamanni, first published in 1548. The reference is to Bk. V.

54. XIII, 12 ff.

55. *Orlando Furioso*, XLV, 41 ff. Leone resigned Bradamante, whom he hoped to marry, to his friend Ruggiero.

56. By disguising himself to fight in Leone's interests.

57. Dante, *On the Vulgar Tongue*, II, 4.

58. Musaeus (sixth century B.C.), *Hero and Leander*.

59. Apollonius Rhodius, *Argonautica*, Bks. III and IV. Valerius Flaccus, *Argonautica*, Bks. V–VIII.

60. The *Aethiopica* of Heliodorus, the most famous of Greek romances, tells of the loves of Theagenes and Chariclea. A Latin translation appeared in 1552.

61. Achilles Tatius, *Leucippe and Clitophon*, a Greek romance of the fifth or sixth century. A Latin translation appeared in 1554.

62. Boccaccio (1313–75) in the *Teseide*, or poem on Theseus, presents Palamon and Arcite. Chaucer retold their story in "The Knight's Tale." The *Filocolo* gives the story of Florio and Biancofiore.

63. Bernardo Tasso, *The Story of Pyramus and Thisbe*.

64. Alamanni, *The Fable of Narcissus*, published in 1532.

65. To him was attributed an epic poem, called *Argonautica*, on his own exploits during the voyage of the Argonauts.

66. Apollonius Rhodius, *Argonautica*, a Greek epic composed in the third century B. C.

67. Statius, *The Thebaid*, the story of the strife at Thebes between the children of Oedipus; *The Achilleid*.

68. Lucan (first century A.D.), *The Pharsalia*. Silius Italicus (died in 102 A.D.). *Punica*.

69. Petrarch (1304–73) left unfinished the *Africa*, an epic poem in Latin on the second Punic war.

70. The *Italy Liberated from the Goths*.

71. Apparently a reference to the Crusades, the first of which Tasso dealt with in his epic of *Jerusalem Delivered*.

72. On this subject cf. Mazzoni, *On the Defense of the "Comedy,"* Bk. III, chap. VI.

73. The *Lusiad* of Camoens, the national epic of Portugal, deals with the East Indies, and *La Araucana*, by Alonso de Ercilla, with South America. Both authors were contemporaries of Tasso. The curate in *Don Quixote* pronounced the *Araucana* one of the three best heroic poems in Spanish, able to compete with the most famous of Italy (*Don Quixote* I, 6).

74. Modified from Horace, *Art of Poetry*, 149–50.

75. The defeat of part of Charlemagne's army on its retirement from Spain is the subject of *The Song of Roland*. Tasso looked on it as an overthrow of Christians by pagans.

76. Cf. Castelvetro on *Poetics*, I, sect. 29, 10 ff.

77. For Damascus, see Ariosto, *Orlando Furioso*, XVIII, 132. But these jousts are not fully described; we are merely told that they were held and that Sansonetto won the prize. Bernardo Tasso tells of jousts in Cornwall in his *Amadigi*.

78. Individual symbolic devices worn on the shield and elsewhere. Sidney describes a number in the *Arcadia*, e.g., III, II. Milton declared he was "not sedulous by nature . . . to describe impresses quaint" (*Paradise Lost*, IX, 27–35).

79. *Aeneid*, I, 210–15, trans. by Conington. Tasso quotes also the similar passages I, 637–42; 701–6.

80. *Orlando Furioso*, XXVIII, 57–74; XLIII, 72–144.

81. This whole section may be illustrated by the practice of Tasso in his *Jerusalem Delivered*, for example, a battle VII, 106–21; an army arrayed XX, 8–10; a city assaulted XVIII, 68–105; sunrise III, 1; IX, 74; XVIII, 12; assemblies I, 20–34; IV, 4–17; a helmet IX, 25; an impress VIII, 49; decorated doors XVI, 2–7; deaths IX, 32–8; XIX, 26; blows with the sword IX, 31–9; IX, 68–70; XX, 120. Similar examples canced be found in Spenser's *Faerie Queene*. Milton, according to a reference in his tractate *Of Education*, had read Tasso's advice and perhaps profited by it, as in the description of the council in *Paradise Lost*, II, 1–506 of a battle in VI, 189–866, of dawn in V, 1–2, of an army in *Paradise Regained*, III, 299–336.

82. *Poetics*, I.

83. Bk. V, 216c.

84. *Art of Poetry*, 119–30, 240–3.

85. "Let us hope that fable may, in what shall follow, so submit to the purifying processes of reason as to take the character of exact history. In any case, however, where it shall be found contumaciously slighting credibility, and refusing to be reduced to anything like probable fact, we shall beg that we may meet with candid readers, and such as will receive with indulgence the stories of antiquity" (Dryden and Clough's trans. [Boston, 1916]).

86. Sect. 2.

87. X, 1, 90.

88. In his letter to Sir Walter Raleigh (above) Spenser explains that in the *Faerie Queene* he does not follow the chronological order, as would a "historiographer."

89. *Commentary* on the *Poetics* of Aristotle, 156, 19 ff.

90. *Art of Poetry*, 148.

91. Cf. Lope de Vega, *New Art of Making Comedies*, sect. 1.

92. *Art of Poetry*, 23.

93. For Giraldi's opinion see his *Discourse on the Romances*, sect. 44.

94. Cf. Castelvetro on *Poetics*, VIII, 178, 39.

95. Cf. Aristotle, *Poetics*, VII, 50b34.
96. Sect. 16.
97. *Odyssey*, VI.
98. *Art of Poetry*, 158–60.
99. Bk. II, chaps. 12–17.
100. By Trissino. Cf. Tasso's remarks in sect. 19.
101. *Problems*, XVIII, 9: "Why do we take more pleasure in listening to narratives in which the attention is concentrated on a single point than in hearing those concerned with many subjects?"
102. Cf. Giraldi's presentation of the variety of Vergil especially (*On the Romances*, sect. 42).
103. Julius Caesar Scaliger writes: "Variety, which we have so often advised, is the greatest of all poetic virtues" (*Poetice*, IV, 48, near the end, p. 212D2; see also III, 25, p. 113D1; III, 27, p. 116D2; III, 28 is devoted to variety in the *Aeneid*).
104. Vergil, *Aeneid*, VI, 129: "this the task, this the labor." Cf. Castelvetro on *Poetics*, VIII, 179, 14.
105. The chorus "takes no active part" (Problems, trans. by E. S. Forster [Oxford, 1927], XIX, 48, 922b26). But in 922b20, Aristotle says that a quiet musical mode is suited to the chorus.
106. "There is, indeed, one place in which the arts of laughter and of charm are found together, in the satyric drama and in comedy. It is different, however, with tragedy, which often welcomes charm, but finds in laughter a sworn foe" (*On Style*, trans. by Rhys Roberts [New York, 1927], sect. 169).
107. *Orlando Furioso*, XX, 120.
108. Petrarch, *Donna, che lieta col principio nostro*.

Minturno, or On Beauty[1]

Interlocutors:
Antonio Minturno, Geronimo Ruscelli[2]

A.M. It is not often that we have the privilege of seeing you in this delightful land of ours,[3] noble and most learned Signor Geronimo.

G.R. Only rarely do I have the leisure to come here. The business of my lord the marquis used to take up the greater part of my time, and now I am almost always employed in matters concerning the majesty and glory of the emperor,[4] and no one treats of peace or war or an alliance, no army is equipped, no expedition assembled, no city fortified, without my having a say in it. This is why I have been coming less often to this shore and to these hills, where I used to find my amusements.

A.M. Here too one recognizes that prudence which separates you from the vulgar and from the schools of boys and places you among men of state, elevating you to a knowledge of the things of the world and of princes, or even to a familiarity with kings and emperors. And I cannot understand why it is that Aretino, Dolce, Clario, Franco, Muzio, Fortunio, Domenichi, Flavio, Corso, Atanagi, and so many others of our friends who in this age have acquired fame as men of letters have been unwilling to imitate you.[5]

G.R. If I'm not mistaken, the reason is a weakness of mind which has made them unable to deal at once with public and private matters and to win glory at the same time in action and in contemplation. Even Ariosto himself, who was frequently employed by his princes and was able to acquire experience equal to his knowledge, was more often than not unsuccessful in the actions of the world; yielding finally to his own timidity, he withdrew from the service of his cardinal, a man of great spirit who was the ornament and glory of that age.[6]

A.M. If Ariosto were to come back to life, then, perhaps he would be mocked by us, as a new Daedalus would have been by the sculptors who succeeded him, men who ridiculed works which in his time had seemed marvelous and had won him immortal glory.

G.R. That would certainly happen, Signor Minturno. But it is my practice always and on every occasion to set the men of former times before modern men, so as to avoid both the envy of the living and the indignation of the dead.

A.M. Your view is certainly a good one, and your words carry conviction and authority, and if my testimony can confirm them, I can truthfully state that I have known Bonfadio, Flaminio, and many others in this city who left it, if not loaded with gifts, at any rate honored by the wealth of the nobility of Naples.[7] And yet it seemed to me that their knowledge and intelligence could not be compared with the keenness and the shrewd understanding of some of those of more recent times, and you beyond all others, most charming Signor Ruscelli, to whom it would be impossible to give so much that you would not merit more.

G.R. Up to now I have been richer in favor and friendship than in means. And, apart from those ornaments which create respect for a man's person and house, there are few things that I can use, or rather that I need.

A.M. It is surely a great misfortune for these times, or rather for our poetic and humane literature, that it is granted no other reward than glory, while lawyers, doctors, architects, sculptors, and painters usually manage to make money and even to become rich, as in our own time has happened to Raphael, Michelangelo, and the noble Paciotto.[8]

G.R. The poets are paid in the same currency—glory—which at any rate ought to resemble that currency of leather which is used in times of necessity and in better fortune is redeemed for gold and silver. As for myself, though inferior to some in composing poems, I will yield to none in the judging of them, and I have been well received by audiences in Rome, Tuscany, Venice, Naples, and Sicily and have everywhere gained honor and glory, and sometimes considerable profit.

A.M. Most noble Signor Ruscelli, it is apparent that your wisdom suits this obliging and courtly age. In earlier times, men of letters were of a rougher cast, and knew little how to accommodate themselves to the opinions of princes and of the world. But where was this talent of yours most honored? Perhaps in Rome?

G.R. Far from it; in fact, almost anything is better received in Rome than the subjects I profess. When I spoke of arms and emblems[9] and of the beauty of our language and our poets, or even of courtesy and matters pertaining to courts and courtiership, what I had to say was sometimes well received, but the reward was merely praise for a man of talent. As for the more recondite arts—alchemy, for example—no one was prepared to believe me; in matters of state, most of them disagreed with my opinion, and few joined the imperial party out of respect for my judgment. But the greatest honors were given to those who would argue the question of whether the pope has authority over the council, or whether the residence of bishops is theirs by divine right.[10] I was rather dissatisfied with myself for not having paid attention to weightier subjects, and I left the city and returned to Naples.

A.M. In this city, surely, your talent was given a more courteous reception.

G.R. True, but I found that musicians and singers were held in higher esteem, and even wrestlers, fencers, and riding Masters. And so I was forced to go to Venice, where for a short time I gave my attention to the improvement of printing and succeeded in printing books that were more beautiful and more legible than any others. But I was called back to this kingdom by the courtesy of the marquis, for whom I had made some emblems which were quite beautiful and were to be sculpted in the trophies of Charles V. And while I was acting as secretary in his service, though giving my attention mostly to matters of state—it was then that I acquired a thorough knowledge of kingdoms, republics, customs, laws, and their various mutations—I never lost my concern for literature, or indeed for all beautiful things, or the love I have for beauty. And this is why, when someone is planning to raise an army or send a fleet to sea, I usually think not only of the number and quality of the soldiers, horses, ships, and the arms and instruments that are necessary for war on sea and land, but also of uniforms, standards, the emblems of princes and lords, and above all of making a good appearance and beautiful display. I consider it a great part of the victory when a man displays himself so as to appear worthy of the exercise of arms.

A.M. You would prefer to conquer, then, by the beauty rather than by the virtue of your soldiers. But perhaps this is impossible. Rich coats, plumes, pavilions, and the other baggage of an army are more often the spoils of the enemy than a terror to him.

G.R. That is not always true; there are many times when the beauty of the arms and emblems causes fear. I would like to see our armies resemble those of the Cimbrians, who—as one may read in Plutarch[11]—used to carry shields decorated with bears, wolves, lions, boars, and other wild animals, which made them look like an army of beasts equipped by nature itself to be a terror to the enemy. So great is the importance, in my judgment, of the fear caused by arms together with beauty.

A.M. I imagined you would have sought that beauty of which you are so fond, not among armies and in the glitter of steel and in the smoke and crash of artillery, but in gardens and in villas adorned with marble and paintings, of the sort one sees along this fertile shore and in these delightful hills, where there are perhaps no images so well sculpted or painted as those which nature itself has formed.

G.R. And nature has been kind enough to supply its paradise with angels. For it would hardly be proper if in this country, which the moon-like crescent of its bay makes almost an image of heaven, the nature of the inhabitants were anything other than celestial and angelic. But if what some of our theologians say is true, that God is always creating new angels, it seems to me that these miracles of his are better attested here than in any other part of the world. But I was seeking beauty and in many things, and I believed I had found it in the camps and amid the emblems of nobles.

A.M. Perhaps you were seeking it in arms rather than in love when you wrote your book on the beauties of the *Furioso*.[12]

G.R. I really sought it in everything, though I may have failed to recognize it.

A.M. You recognized it even in the madness of Orlando, when he appears before his companions in a condition so foul and ugly, so horrible and terrifying to look at that they barely recognize him.[13]

G.R. The conceit is certainly very beautiful.

A.M. What about Rodomonte, when he is completely covered with blood and then swims in the river Seine?[14] Did you think you saw beauty there too?

G.R. I thought so—and even before he goes to the river. Still, there were many times when I doubted whether I had found it.

A.M. If beauty exists or is to be found among the things of the world, who would be better able to find it than you?

G.R. Possibly no one seeks it more than I do, but it has often happened that what I judged beautiful was not considered to be so by others, or not by everyone, as the *Furioso* is.

A.M. Is there some way we can be sure of this? It seems to me that just as wise men are wise by wisdom, and just men by justice, so beautiful men, or all beautiful things, are beautiful by beauty, and that beauty—or the beautiful, as we may call it—is that which makes them what they are. With this observation and rule, as it were, let us try to recognize beauty in such a way that no other thing could be mistaken for it—if indeed it is some other thing that makes horrible and monstrous figures appear beautiful, as with the serpents or devils painted by Raphael or Michelangelo, or the fables of the Cyclops and the Orc.[15]

G.R. It is the beauty of poetic genius which allows us to recognize with certainty what is terrible or marvelous in these things. Still, I'm more inclined to seek it in Marfisa, Bradamante, and Olimpia, whose beauties Ariosto has described with such felicity of language and thought, and if I were forced to say what beauty is, I would say it is a beautiful woman resembling Olimpia, at the moment when, without any robe or veil, she shows herself naked to the eyes of her beholders.[16]

A.M. If you remove the veil from beauty, it will perhaps be found to exist only in souls separated from bodies, for bodies are, so to speak, a veil covering the beauty of the soul. But when Ariosto describes the beauty of Angelica and Olimpia, he resembles that Daedalus you mentioned earlier—or rather he is less artful, for while Daedalus gave movement to statues, Ariosto takes it away from living persons. As he says of Angelica:

> And had so far in sorrow gone
> She seemed turned to senseless stone.[17]

And of the same person:

> A statue would Ruggiero have thought her
>   Made of marble or of alabaster,
>   And to that rock so closely bound
>   By art of sculptors far renowned,
>   Had he not seen her tears distinct
>   Past roses white and whiter lily sink
>   To streak with drew her ripening breast,
>   And breezes move her golden tress.[18]

G.R. It seems to me that no more art is required to give movement to inanimate things than to take it away from living things, and Ariosto, in his Olimpia, shows no less marvelous an art than Daedalus.

A.M. All the same, I did not ask you for a statue of beauty; I asked what that beauty is which is able to make beautiful what is not beautiful in itself, such as the whale[19] and the Orc.

G.R. Beauty is the beautiful virgin who makes beautiful the thoughts and conceits of a poem; who makes beautiful the sighs, tears, sorrows, and passions of love, and even death and the wounds received in her behalf; who makes beautiful the air, the earth, rivers, springs, gardens, woods, valleys, mountains, caves, and everything around her, and, like the sun, illuminates them with her light.

A.M. You have almost described the daughter of your marquis. But as there are two daughters, and the choice between them is not easy, there must be two beauties, but we are seeking a beauty which makes both of them beautiful as well as every young girl who participates in it, and which is not lost with virginity. Otherwise, beauty would be too short-lived a flower—like the rose described by the same poet, which loses its glory as the season advances.[20] But beauty, if I'm not mistaken, can also make a mature woman beautiful. Consider the marchesa, the mother of these girls: in her dignified appearance there is a certain radiance, a marvelous and divine quality which never ceases to please and indeed to amaze.

G.R. That is quite true. Still, in the beauty of a beautiful young girl there is nothing that is lacking or that one could add, and so I would say that the marchesa is beautiful insofar as she is the mother of this girl.

A.M. It is through participating in beauty that other things become beautiful and dear, but children participate in the beauty of the father and mother, and not the other way around. By this argument, then, beauty would be more present in the mother than in the daughter.

G.R. I consider beauty, like love, the proper possession of youth.

A.M. If love came into being before the beginning of the world, as the poets say,[21] it must be very old indeed, and the same argument applies to beauty, for love is the desire for beauty. But leaving this aside, tell me, if you will: this lady, whom you consider beauty itself—do her clothes also seem beautiful to you?

G.R. Extremely beautiful.

A.M. Through the art of the tailor or embroiderer or of some other artisan?

G.R. Everything she wears is beautiful—she adds beauty to whatever she happens to be wearing.

A.M. Are her horse and carriage also beautiful?

G.R. As beautiful as the chariot of the sun.

A.M. But what would we say of the same things if they belonged to someone else?

G.R. Perhaps they would be beautiful, perhaps not.

A.M. Because they might belong to someone they were not suited to, or for some other reason?

G.R. For the reason you mention.

A.M. Then it is the suitable, or the fitting, which makes every ornament beautiful. The same clothes would not be suitable if worn by a Grabina,[22] and hence not beautiful, and it was because gold is not a beautiful color for eyes that Phidias made his statue of Minerva with eyes of ivory and pupils of precious stone.[23]

G.R. So it seems.

A.M. And Omphale's clothes were not beautiful when Hercules wore them, nor his lion's skin when worn by Omphale, because in both cases the other's clothes were unsuitable.[24]

G.R. What you are saying seems to me very true.

A.M. In your opinion, then, the fitting and the beautiful are the same thing, since the fitting is what makes everything beautiful.

G.R. Certainly.

A.M. But the clothes of a shepherdess would not be beautiful if worn by your lady, for they would not suit her as well as the clothes of royalty.

G.R. No, all kinds of clothing are beautiful on her. For she makes everything beautiful, and she would look beautiful not only in the form of a queen but in that of a shepherdess, a nymph, or a huntress—the form in which Venus appeared to her own son.[25]

A.M. Your lady is then not only beauty itself but fittingness itself, for she makes all things seem beautiful and suitable even if they might not be so in themselves.

G.R. There is no doubt about it.

A.M. All the same, I wonder about two things, and in the first place whether her case is like that of the very wise man who, as Heraclitus thought, is little better than an ape when compared to the gods.[26] In the same way, the most beautiful woman would appear ugly in comparison with the beauty of the angels.

G.R. I said some time ago that in the opinion of certain theologians God makes new angels when he creates human souls that resemble the angelic nature.

A.M. Let's leave this opinion aside—even though it differs from the opinion of Evagrius, which was condemned as heretical[27]—and allow the poets to speak of

> A new angel, welcomed in its flight,[28]

or

> An angel newly made, it flies to heaven,
>   Its proper home, and leaves the earth
>   Deprived of earth's most valued prize.[29]

But, if you don't mind, help me resolve the other question I was wondering about. If it is really true that the fitting makes things appear beautiful when they are not, then the fitting would not be the beautiful but rather an illusion of the beautiful—for the beautiful makes things beautiful, but the fitting makes them appear to be such. The difference between the fitting and the beautiful is, therefore, the same as that between the true and the false and between being and appearing. Accordingly, if your lady makes everything appear beautiful, I would have to call her an illusionist or rather an enchantress, and someone you ought to beware of no less than of any form of deception.

G.R. There is no illusion or deception in the beauty of this most noble lady. As the light of the sun scatters the illusions created by the shadows of night and reveals the various forms and diverse colors of things, so the illumination of her beauty only makes apparent that charm of manners and those marvelous virtues which would otherwise remain hidden. And so I cannot agree that the fitting is an illusion of beauty; it is rather an illumination of beauty, through which beauty becomes clearly apparent. Between the fitting and illusion there is, then, the same difference as between night and day, shadows and brilliance.

A.M. Most learned Signor Ruscelli, I am glad to hear from you that the fitting does not create the appearance of beauty but rather makes beauty apparent. One may infer that if any beauty is joined with the fitting, it cannot remain hidden, and conversely, that what is hidden cannot possess beauty. And yet if the beauty of wisdom—intelligible beauty—is hidden, it follows that it lacks the fitting. But this is a difficult and harsh thing to affirm, at least if, as Socrates thought, the fitting is not the same as illusion.[30] For the opinion of Plotinus, that it is a kind of brilliance through which the virtues become apparent,[31] is perhaps exposed to the objection we have made regarding those kinds of beauty which are not apparent to the human senses.

G.R. I would not agree at all that beauty or the fitting is a silent illusion, as Theophrastus thought,[32] or that the fitting is the illusion of beauty, as Hippias believed.[33] But it seems to me that beauty is rather a violence of nature which forces the spirit to love in such a way that it is unable to defend itself or to offer any resistance, and the person who called beauty a short-lived tyranny understood its nature very well.[34] Nor can I recall ever having read or heard a better definition than this, for the beautiful resemble tyrants and want to be feared and worshipped in just the same way. And there was never a king of Memphis or Babylonia who was made so arrogant by the extent of his empire as are the beautiful by the force of their beauty, which constrains, compels, seizes, enchains, kindles, and consumes, and, like a fire, transmutes the spirit into a substance of another nature. I would therefore say that beauty is a power and a pleasing violence and a graceful tyranny of nature, as Socrates thought,[35] or the rule of a single king, as Carneades believed,[36] for beauty does not want to share its rule, but rules alone, like love. Ugliness, on the other hand, I would call lack of power, weakness, natural servitude, for if anyone is a servant by nature, it is more fitting for an ugly man to serve than for anyone else. And as the Ethiopians and the Indians chose as their kings the most beautiful men, it is reasonable that the ugliest ought to be the servants of servants.

A.M. Would you also prefer your lady to have ugly servants, or ugly waiting-maids?

G.R. You force me to yield and abandon my opinion, for she would deserve to be waited on by the Graces and Loves, as if she were a new goddess. But I define the ugly and beautiful by comparison and relatively: her waiting-maids, who in respect to others are very beautiful, are more nearly ugly in comparison with her.

A.M. You place the beautiful, like the good, in the category of relation, and suppose that there is the same relation between the ugly and the beautiful as there is between the father and the son, but perhaps Hippocrates was wrong in placing the good in the category of relative things. If the beautiful has the force and the violence that you say it has, it must necessarily be a substance and a quality of very great power.[37] And yet how can it be both violent and natural, if everything violent is contrary to nature? And if beauty were violence, how could there be any voluntary or freely chosen love? In any event, we know that there are many who not only wish to love but freely choose to love, and this deliberation is strengthened by judgments formed over a period of time. For this reason I would say that beauty is neither tyranny nor violence nor the rule of a single king, for it belongs to the beautiful as to the good to give of itself to many.

G.R. But who can deny it is a power? To be powerful in a kingdom or a republic is a very beautiful thing, but in the kingdom of Love—if, as is generally believed, Love has a kingdom—the most beautiful is the most powerful. What power can equal that of Cleopatra, who conquered Caesar, the conqueror of the world, and, as it were, triumphed over him? For we read that

> The one who first came to try the powers
>   Of Egypt's proud queen was Caesar:
>   Cleopatra bound him in chains of flowers.
> Now she has her triumph, and it is fair,
>   If he who won the world is by another won,
>   That the conquered glory in his conqueror.[38]

A.M. Does this power lead then only to good deeds, whether in the kingdom you call the kingdom of Love or in others, or to vicious and criminal deeds as well? In my opinion it was an evil power by which Cleopatra compelled first Caesar and then Mark Antony to deeds unworthy of Roman virtue, and finally to shameful flight, and nothing is so unworthy of one who desires to rule. But it seems to me that beauty cannot be the cause of things that are not good. And so it is not the same as that power which, as we have already said, gives rise to wrong actions and to things yet worse—to arson, exile, plunder, murder, war, and the destruction of cities and empires.

G.R. If that were true, Helen would not have been beautiful, for she incited Asia and Europe to war, and she was the fire and ruin of the ancient kingdom of Troy, and if plundering and the carrying off of women is not good, then the cause of it could not have been her beauty—which compelled Theseus and Alexander to act as they did. But I recall having read just the contrary, that Helen was judged worthy of eternal glory on account of her beauty, first by Theseus, then by Alexander, who was able to judge not only of human but of divine beauty as well.[39]

A.M. I could perhaps reply that the carrying off of women is not always something bad, as for example that of the Sabine women, through which the generation of the Romans increased and multiplied.[40] But I would reply instead that beauty by itself is not the cause of the carrying off of women, but rather of honoring and revering them. As one may read:

> She who to love and reverence trains,
>   Who wants desire and kindled hope made tame
>   By check of reason, reverence and shame,
>   Our passion in her heart disdains.[41]

But the incontinence of men and women's lack of chastity can give rise to the carrying off of women and to war, and if Helen was not chaste, she was perhaps not beautiful, for beauty is always joined with decency, and the Greek word *to kalon* signifies both the beautiful and the decent. If this is true, one could affirm that the beautiful is the advantageous and that which is useful, and that the beautiful is related to the good as a father, as it were, for the beautiful would be in the nature of a cause, the good of an effect. It is for this reason that we are accustomed to consider prudence and wisdom a beautiful thing, for they are the cause of much that is useful in the life of men. What do you say to this, Signor Geronimo?

G.R. This opinion seems very good to me.

A.M. But if it is indeed true, then that other opinion, which is accepted by everyone, is not true—namely, that the beautiful is the good and the good the beautiful. For the father is not the son nor the son the father, nor can the one be changed into the other by a change that is simply relative to them, as would be the case with a change of position, where the one on the right could become the one on the left, and the one on the left the one on the right. In addition to this, beauty is one of those things that are loved for their own sakes, but the things that are useful and advantageous are not loved for themselves. What, Signor Geronimo, are we then to say is beauty? Since it is not a beautiful young girl, it is not the fitting, as it seemed to Hippias; it is not an illusion, as Theophrastus thought; it is not tyranny, as Socrates said; it is not violence or power, as was the opinion of the same sophist, and of many Platonists as well; it is not the rule of a single king, as Carneades believed; it is not what is advantageous, as Socrates seemed to believe in arguing with Hippias—but then Socrates was not constant in his opinion.[42]

G.R. Let's say that the beautiful is what pleases.

A.M. Then the beautiful will be pleasing, and conversely, the pleasing will be beautiful.

G.R. Without a doubt.

A.M. But what pleases one person rarely pleases others, for some praise as the mark of elegance in a woman

> A pallor of the shade of the violet and love,[43]

while others praise a coloring of white and vermilion; some are enamoured of blue eyes, others are more pleased by black; many are charmed by severity, many by complaisance. Nor is everyone equally pleased by pride or humility, and indeed the same man may be pleased by pride or humility, and indeed the same man may be pleased by different things at different times. As the poet says:

> It gladdens me still in a lady who loves
> That she walk disdainful and proud,
> Though not arrogant, not cold.[44]

And elsewhere he gives greater praise to obliging manners and to courtesy, as in these verses:

> She lowered her pretty and obliging glance

> And spoke silently, as it seemed to me:
> Who takes from me my faithful friend?[45]

and in the ones preceding them. And so the beautiful will be changeable, and like a chameleon will take on different colors, different forms, and different images and appearances. But I should rather believe that the beautiful appears beautiful to everyone and makes everything beautiful, for I am not looking for what is beautiful according to some usage or convention—though that too can be most delightful—but for what is beautiful in itself.

G.R. Let's say then that the beautiful is what pleases everyone, just as the good is what everyone desires.

A.M. But what kind of pleasure do we mean, that which pleases all the senses, or that which pleases only sight and hearing? For if what pleases taste and touch and smell is beautiful, as Aristotle seems to argue in his *Problems* and Nifo in his book on beauty,[46] then sweet things will be beautiful by the fact that they are sweet, and bitter things by the fact that they are bitter, and the smell of amber and musk and the smoke of incense will be beautiful.

G.R. I would certainly have thought so.

A.M. And perhaps you would not have found displeasing the view of Aristotle, who states in the same part of the *Problems* that what is smoothest to the touch usually seems beautiful, and that liquids seem beautiful to one who is thirsty on account of the smoothness anticipated in drinking.

G.R. It is certainly not displeasing to me.

A.M. And possibly it is not a false opinion, if it is understood of those things that are beautiful according to some usage. And yet to be subordinate to usage is a property of useful things, not of things beautiful or pleasing, and we are looking for what is beautiful in itself, without regard to the manner in which it can be used or abused. And because beauty is truly something divine, it seems to me very unfitting to make it subject to the judgment of the material senses of taste and touch; indeed, it can barely be judged by the more spiritual senses, sight and hearing, which reserve the full judgment of beauty for the intellect—a judgment exercised in the contemplation of forms which are separate from this mixture and residue, as it were, of matter.

G.R. The beautiful will then be a part of the pleasing, for as that which gives delight is the object of all the senses, only that small part of it deserves to be called beautiful which is judged to be so by the nobler senses. Not only, therefore, will colors and lights and the various images of things be beautiful, but also songs and the music of instruments, which provide a most beautiful harmony for ears that are suitably refined. But it seems to me that to these senses belongs as well everything that has been written of customs, laws, and the sciences—things which yield many marvelous beauties.

A.M. What you say is undoubtedly true. Still, the senses judge in one way of color and sound, and in another way of proportions or the things that belong to the sciences, for of the latter the senses are unable to make a judgment that is true, and act instead as ministers or messengers to the intellect, bringing to the mind what they learn from the world outside. And so it seems that the beauty we are in the process of seeking is not one and the same, for the objects of the material senses must of necessity be corruptible, as must the senses themselves, but the mind, which is divine and immortal, judges only of those things that resemble it. The genus of beauty is not, then, one or univocal, as the philosophers say and as Nifo believed, but just as the light of the glowworm or of rotting mushrooms appearing at night differs from the light of the stars or the sun, so the beauty of the things of this world is very different from that beauty which may be contemplated in the eternal and divine forms. If this is true, that which is beautiful in itself will not be pleasing to the senses, for they will not be able to judge of it.

G.R. If the beautiful is not what is pleasing to the senses of hearing and sight, what other definition can we find that is equally satisfactory?

A.M. Let's not abandon the search for one.

G.R. I have often read that beauty is a proportion between parts that are well arranged. This opinion, which many have shared, is not easy to dismiss.[47]

A.M. There is proportion only where there are dissimilar parts. But if beauty were a proportion between parts that do not resemble each other, there would be no beauty in simple things, but gold and silver are beautiful, in the judgment of miserable mortals, as well as diamonds, rubies, and other precious stones; colors are beautiful, and light, in which there is no proportion at all, is very beautiful indeed. Besides, there are times when the proportion between the parts remains—as in bodies grown old and feeble—but not beauty, which is lost with the flower of youth. For these reasons I am not satisfied with this definition either.

G.R. I do not know if I can produce any other that will satisfy you more. But you must recall the definitions of Plutarch and Plotinus. The first is that beauty is an ornament or glory of the soul which irradiates the body, the other that is a victory of form over matter.[48] To these one could add another: that beauty is an appearance or an image of the good, as ugliness is a darkened face of evil.

A.M. I remember having read something of these things and heard them spoken about, but I find myself with the same doubts. For if beauty is an ornament of the soul imparted to the body or a victory of form over matter, then it must exist in bodily and material things, in which there is perhaps no beauty at all, or not the kind we are seeking. And I wonder at Nifo and the other Peripatetics, who have located beauty in the body and in matter, because by its nature matter is ugly and deformed in the extreme, or rather is ugliness itself, so that the beautiful would be found to exist in the ugly as its proper medium, which is not at all fitting, for the beautiful should issue from the beautiful as flower issues from flower. Besides, if the opinion of those who have defined it in this way is true, the angels would not be beautiful, since in the angelic nature matter is not overcome by form, and there is no body to which the soul's quality can be imparted. Let us leave to low and earthly things, then, this victory of form—to things in which rebellious matter makes a thousand changes of appearance, stripping away the old forms and clothing itself in new ones, and in which there remains always a perpetual desire to change every form for another, like a badly ordered city or republic which makes a thousand changes, altering its laws, governments, and customs. But in celestial things, where matter is obedient to form and never rebellious or contrary, or in those things where there is no matter at all, what kind of victory of form or of divine art could there be? None, unless I am mistaken. Accordingly—if you are of the same opinion—we shall say that beauty exists in those things in which, there being neither war nor discord, there is no need of victory, and in the future we shall seek beauty not in the discords and the arms of kings and emperors, but rather, if we are to find it anywhere, in the peaceful study of the sciences. What is your view of this, Signor Ruscelli?

G.R. I do not know how to seek it except through the guidance of the senses, by which I can raise myself to the contemplation of the sun and the stars and their order, which is beautiful beyond anything else.

A.M. Tell me, if you will: do you think that beauty, if it is to be found anywhere, exists in false things or rather in true things?

G.R. In true things.

A.M. But which seem to you true—those that change, or those that remain always in the same state? I think there can be no doubt that what is unstable and inconstant resembles a lie. The man who makes a thousand changes of appearance, of manners, of age, is not a true man, nor is the child a true child, the youth a true youth, or the old man a true old man. Man is rather an image and a phantasm of the human essence, as Mercury Trismegistus says,[49] and a very great lie. Only that is true which never changes or varies or increases or diminishes, but remains always within itself and identical to itself. Accordingly, all things subject to generation and corruption are false, and the sun, of which our poet said

> That the sun is false,
> Who would dare say?[50]

contains in itself, on account of the changes it undergoes, a certain lying element, and the same is true of the other celestial bodies.

G.R. Man, then, is an image and a lie, and the heavens and planets are liars for the most part.

A.M. So it seems one can conclude from this argument. And it is from this that one can recognize not only how vain and illusory are the judgments of the astrologers, but also how deceptive is the appearance of those things that are judged beautiful by miserable mortals. And, in particular, those we call feminine beauties are fraudulent illusions of natural things, shadows of light, masks and simulations of beauty—in short, a complete and manifest lie, and something that a blind man would be hard put to recognize.

G.R. Beauty does not exist, then, in the sun and the stars and the celestial spheres, since they contain some element of falsity, and much less in things that are transitory and mortal.

A.M. It does not. But where then would it be? Perhaps, Signor Geronimo, in the angelic nature, or even in the human soul?

G.R. In both, in my opinion.

A.M. But if, as has been written, the soul is composed of that which is indivisible and that which can be divided,[51] the divisible part is subject to changes and alterations and in consequence is much less capable of beauty. The other, the part that cannot be divided, is indeed very beautiful, but its beauty is not a tyranny; not a kingdom; not illusion, violence, proportion, or measure; not a victory over matter; not a quality imparted to the body; and though I would not deny that it is something eternal and divine, I do not for that reason know what it is. For if it could be defined, it would have a limit, but perhaps it is impossible to describe or circumscribe the beauty of the soul in place, time, matter, or in words, and to seek more than this is perhaps too daring and presumptuous, or a sign of too audacious a faith, as with those who go beyond the curtain in a temple and enter the *sancta sanctorum*. There one may recognize the soul's beauty and there contemplate it; there only may one know what it is. But those of us on the outside of the curtain walk about admiring the columns and the beams of cedar and scented cypress, the arches, the vault, the capitals and the statues that support them, and call beautiful whatever we see, or rather what seems beautiful to us and flatters our senses. So you were not mistaken, Signor Geronimo, in consecrating your *Temple* to the immortal glory of the Lady Giovanna of Aragon, since there is nothing that resembles beauty so much as a temple.[52]

G.R. I was indeed the architect of that marvelous enterprise. But so many were the statues, so many the painters and sculptors of every nation who there demonstrated their talents and their art, that I had a lesser share both in the work itself and in the honor.

A.M. It was glorious for you and for the poets who had the opportunity to celebrate her, for in praising her they were like those who sing the praises of God, but she who made you share in her glory is glorious beyond all the others. And I would say she is most beautiful as she is described by Nifo[53]—if I were to speak and reason in these matters as a Peripatetic.

G.R. At any rate her soul is most beautiful—and yet a long life has not robbed her body of its grace and majesty.

A.M. This is certainly everyone's belief, though the veil of humanity prevents the contemplation of it. But in what way, Signor Girolamo, do we believe the soul becomes beautiful?

G.R. That can better be learned from an imitation of this lady than through any other art or reasoning.

A.M. Then we shall liken her intellect itself to a sculptor who, wishing to make a beautiful statue, cuts away a part, planes and scrapes off more, and polishes and rubs away still more, until there appears in the statue a beautiful face fashioned by his art. In this way others too can occupy themselves with their own statues, removing what is superfluous, planing what appears crooked and distorted, illuminating what is dark, and not ceasing until they radiate a divine light of virtue, with which temperance is seen to sit in majesty.[54]

G.R. They are marvelous sculptresses who have polished statues of eternal beauty on the columns of their own nobility.

A.M. They also say that the soul does not become beautiful through the acquisition of anything external to it, but by purifying itself as the fire is purified in the flame, and the human virtues, which seem so beautiful, are nothing other than a purgation of the impurity which has fastened onto them as a result of their being accompanied by the body. The virtues are then natural to the soul, just as beauty is native to it, but ugliness is foreign, and derived from contact with the body. And it is certainly the case that those who seek beauty in these earthly limbs judge very foolishly: they seem to me to resemble those who admire images and shadows in a pool, as Narcissus is supposed to have done in the fable, and while embracing the water and the fleeting images manage to drown themselves while being scarcely aware of what they are doing. And so someone might cry out to us: "Friends, come away from those springs and those deceiving pools, and let us return to our own country. But what point is there in fleeing? By what path shall we flee the charms and spells of Circe? The fable of Ulysses shows us, though perhaps obscurely, the way of flight—in the avoiding of those things that please and as it were welcome us and engage our senses. But we must return to our country, to the country we left. Where then is our flight? Where the army to escort us? It is too late to flee on foot, for our feet will carry us to another land far away, nor ought we to provide ourselves with horses to ride or ships for sailing. All these things must be abandoned; we must not even think of them, and should avoid them with the eyes of the body. We must use instead the eyes of the mind, which all men have but few use."[55] And that young poet of ours, or rather that youth, of whom many foretell a high and marvelous future—please God that unhappy fortune may not mar a happy talent—spoke very wisely. Have you heard these verses?

> I, who saw on earth an earthly form,
> Shut my eyes and said: To look
> On her is foolish daring. But
> I never sensed the greater harm.
> Through the ears my heart was struck:
> Words went where a glance did not.[56]

G.R. If I'm not mistaken, the verses belong to Torquato Tasso, Signor Bernardo's son, who at an early age has shown much promise.

A.M. The young man's insight, his warning to flee with the ears shut as well as the eyes, is certainly fine, but he is not about to flee himself, being caught in the toils of love and a target for its arrows.

G.R. I am fairly well along in age, but I have not yet become suspicious of beautiful and pleasing things. On the contrary, there are times I wish I had a thousand eyes and a thousand ears in order to see and hear fully the beauty and the harmony of my lady, who like the sun shows us an oblique path by which to ascend to heaven and return to ourselves.[57] But you, Signor Minturno, are too severe in your opinions and thoughts, as if you had forgotten your loves or indeed your "Love in Love."[58] As for me, I am inclined to the belief of those who understand beauty as a proportion or measure of things that have dissimilar parts, so that neither earth, water, air, fire, nor heaven itself is beautiful, for it does not have parts dissimilar in shape or nature, even though it is sculpted and adorned—for this is why, if we are to believe Pliny, it is called *caelum*.[59] I will not speak of the angels and of God, who in the opinion of some is neither beautiful nor perfect because He is not made,[60] but if the angels are beautiful in heaven, nothing on earth is more beautiful than my lady, who in her manners and nature is truly angelic.

A.M. I do not want to prolong our dispute about this. Believe, then, as your own judgment dictates, so long as you are not deprived of it by this courtly opinion of yours, which is fixed in your head

> By nails stronger than another's speech,[61]

by, that is, the liberality of her father the marquis, in whom prudence, courage, and all the civil and military arts are virtues of great beauty and worthy of immortal praise.

NOTES

1. Although there is no direct evidence as to the date of its composition, the *Minturno* is now generally agreed to have been written toward the end of Tasso's life, in 1593 or 1594. See *Dialoghi* 1:59–63. The notes that follow are indebted to those of Mazzali.

2. Antonio Sebastiani (?–1579), called Minturno from the name of his native town, pursued a career in the Church, eventually becoming bishop of Crotone in southern Italy. He was the author of two influential treatises on literary theory, *De poeta* (Venice, 1559) and *Arte poetica* (Venice, 1564), and is said to have studied philosophy under Agostino Nifo. For a brief account of him see Croce, *Poeti e scrittori del pieno e del tardo Rinascimento*, 3 vols. (Bari: Laterza, 1952–58), 2:85–102. Much of the career of Geronimo (or Girolamo) Ruscelli (?–1566) is presented in the *Minturno* itself. Ruscelli was or had been at various times an editor, translator, printer, poet, and critic; patronized by a Neapolitan aristocrat active in the service of Spain, Ruscelli increasingly flourished in the role of courtier and eventually attached himself to the emperor, Charles V. Tasso's portrait of him appears to draw particularly on a work entitled *Lettura di Girolamo Ruscelli sopra un sonnetto dell' illustriss, signor marchese della Terza alla divina signora marchesa del Vasto* (Venice, 1552). The dramatic date of the *Minturno* would appear to fall between the death of Ruscelli's patron Alfonso d'Avalos in 1546 and the abdication of Charles V some ten years later (see n. 4 below).

3. Naples.

4. Alfonso d'Avalos, marquis of Vasto (1502–46), a Neapolitan noble of Aragonese descent, held a number of important political and military posts in Italy under the Emperor Charles V; he was also a patron of artists and men of letters, including such figures as Titian and Pietro Aretino.

5. Pietro Aretino, Lodovico Dolce, Isidoro Clario, Niccolo Franco, Girolamo Muzio, Gianfrancesco Fortunio, Lodovico Domenichi, Rinaldo Corso, and Dionigi Atanagi (the identity of Flavio is uncertain) were contemporary men of letters, many of them friends of Tasso or his father. Aretino and Domenichi had written works attacking courts and courtiers.

6. Ludovico Ariosto (1474–1533), the author of *Orlando Furioso*, was secretary to Cardinal Ippolito d'Este from 1503 to 1517, when he was discharged for refusing to accompany the cardinal to Hungary after d'Este had been made bishop of Buda. Ariosto subsequently entered the service of the cardinal's brother Alfonso, duke of Ferrara, eventually becoming governor of a district of Ferrara before retiring to devote himself entirely to poetry.

7. Iacopo Bonfadio had been secretary to some important ecclesiastical figures in Rome and Naples during the 1530s; later professor of philosophy and the official historian of Genoa, he was executed by the Genoese in 1550 on suspicion of religious heterodoxy. Marcantonio Flaminio (1498–1550) was an important poet of Latin verse and author of commentaries on parts of the Bible and the Aristotelian corpus. During their stay in Naples both men had frequented the reformist religious and literary circle of Juan de Valdes, which also included Alfonso d'Avalos, his wife Maria of Aragon, and her sister Giovanna.

8. Francesco Paciotto of Urbino (1521–91), a famous military architect.

9. Emblems (*imprese*) were the personal symbols—usually composed of a picture accompanied by a motto—that were popular among the nobility of sixteenth-century Italy. Tasso devotes a dialogue to this subject (*The Count, or On Emblems*); Ruscelli had written a treatise on it (*Discorso intorno all' invenzioni delle imprese, dell' insegne, de' motti e delle livree* [Venice, 1556]).

10. The movement for a general council of the Church had gained in strength with the rise of Protestantism and resulted in the convening of the Council of Trent in 1545. Those who held the view that the residences of bishops belong to them by divine right denied that the pope had authority over the bishops in council; this was the position particularly of the Spanish bishops.

11. Plutarch *Life of Marius* 25. 10.

12. *Le Bellezze del Furioso*, originally intended as an introduction to Ruscelli's edition of *Orlando Furioso*, was in fact never published. See the preface to that edition (Venice, 1556) as well as Ruscelli's *Del modo di comporre in versi nella lingua italiana* (Venice, 1558), p. xix.

13. Ariosto *Orlande Furioso* 39. 36–38, 44–47.

14. Ariosto *Orlando Furioso* 18. 18–25.

15. The Orc is the sea monster killed by Orlando, *Orlando Furioso* 11. 28–45. In his *Arte poetica*, Minturno argues that Ariosto's genius "makes what is barbaric in its nature and devoid of grace seem beautiful by his style" (Naples, 1725, p. 30).

16. Ariosto *Orlando Furioso* 11. 67–69.

17. "Ed in quel suo dolor tanto penetra / che par cangiata in insensibil pietra." The reference is evidently to *Orlando Furioso* 1. 39, where Ariosto says of Sacripante, who is being observed by Angelica: "Ed in un gran pensier tanto penetra / che par cangiato in insensibil pietra" ("And had so far in thought gone / He seemed turned to senseless stone").

18. Ariosto *Orlando Furioso* 10. 96.

19. Ariosto *Orlando Furioso* 6. 37.

20. Ariosto *Orlando Furioso* 1. 42.

21. See particularly Hesiod *Theogony* 116–22 (cf. Plato *Symposium* 178a–c).

22. A reference to the character Gabrina (the name is misspelled in the text); see Ariosto *Orlando Furioso* 20. 115–16.

23. Cf. Plato *Hippias major* 290a–d.

24. See Ovid *Heroides* 9. 54 ff.

25. See Virgil *Aeneid* 1. 314–20.

26. Heraclitus fr. B83 (Diels-Kranz; cf. Plato *Hippias major* 289a–b).

27. Evagrius Ponticus, a Greek theologian of the fourth century, was anathematized by the early ecumenical councils as a follower of Origen. The writings of Evagrius and Origen on angels have not survived, but they evidently argued that angels or angelic souls have been sent by God to inhabit human bodies as punishment for their sins—a view which the orthodox seem to have regarded as a relic of Platonism (see, for example, St. Jerome *Epistles* 124). The view advanced by Ruscelli seems to lack theological authority of any kind.

28. Petrarch *Rime* 106. 1. The text of Petrarch has *accorta* ("*observant*") *for accolta* ("welcomed"); the reference is to Petrarch's Laura.

29. Giovanni della Casa *Rime* 37. 9–11. The poem is an elegy addressed to Venice on the death of Pietro Bembo, the "new angel" being Bembo's soul.

30. Plato *Hippias major* 294b–c.

31. Plotinus *Enneads* 1. 6. 3–4.

32. Diogenes Laertius *Lives of the Philosophers* 5. 19.

33. Plato *Hippias major* 293e–94a and ff.

34. The remark is attributed to Socrates by Diogenes Laertius (*Lives of the Philosophers* 5. 19). A similar saying was associated with the philosopher Bion (Plutarch *Amatorius* 770b, Stobaeus *Anthology* 4. 21. 23).

35. The definition or definitions attributed to Socrates appear to represent a combination of Diogenes Laertius *Lives of the Philosophers* 5. 19 with Plato *Phaedrus* 250d–52a. Tasso's immediate source is evidently Agostino Nifo, *De pulchro* (Rome, 1531), Sections 14 and 20.

36. Diogenes Laertius *Lives of the Philosophers* 5. 19. Instead of "rule of a single king" (*regno solitario*) Diogenes' text actually has "kingdom without bodyguards": the point of Carneades' remark is that beauty brings voluntary obedience. According to Stobaeus *Anthology* 4. 21. 15 (cf. Diogenes Laertius *Lives of the Philosophers* 6. 63), Diogenes the Cynic "called beautiful courtesans queens, because there are many who do what they command."

37. "Relation," one of Aristotle's ten categories or modes of being, describes terms whose meaning can only be stated with reference to something else, like "father" or "half" (see, for example, *Metaphysics* 1020b26–1021b11). Minturno's point is that Ruscelli treats beauty as something entirely relative rather than as an inherent quality or a substance. The reference to Hippocrates is perhaps to the beginning of the treatise *On Breaths*.

38. Petrarch *Trionfo d'Amore* 1. 88–93.

39. Alexander (Paris) is supposed to have been appointed by Zeus to judge a beauty contest between Aphrodite, Athena, and Hera, which Aphrodite won by promising to deliver Helen to him. Many legends also connected Helen with Theseus, king of Athens.

40. An account of this event of early Roman history may be found in Livy *History of Early Rome* 1. 9–10.

41. Petrarch *Rime* 140. 5–8. But the first line of Petrarch's text reads: "Quella ch' amare e sofferir ne 'nsegna" ("She who to love and its suffering trains").

42. Plato *Hippias major* 303e; cf. 296e–297c.

43. Petrarch *Rime* 224. 8. In Petrarch's poem, the phrase describes a despairing lover.

44. Petrarch *Rime* 105. 8–10.

45. Petrarch *Rime* 123. 12–14.

46. [Aristotle] *Problems* 10. 52. 896b10–28; Nifo *De pulchro* 28, 39–40, 63.

47. It was the opinion of the Stoics in particular. See Plotinus *Enneads* 1. 6. 1, Nifo *De pulchro* 19.

48. The definition ascribed to Plutarch is a combination of two remarks attributed to him by Stobaeus, 4. 21. 12 and 13 (cf. also 22). For Plotinus's definition see *Enneads* 1. 6. 3–4.

49. Probably a reference to the Hermetic treatise *Pimander* (*Corpus Hermeticum* 1) 14.

50. Virgil *Georgics* 1. 463–64.

51. Aristotle *On the Soul* 430a26–b31.

52. Cf. Plotinus *Enneads* 1. 6. 7. Minturno is alluding to a work edited by Ruscelli, *Il tempio alla divina signora donna Giovanna d'Aragona fabricato da tutti i piu gentili spirti e in tutte le lingue principali del mondo* (Venice, 1565), a poetic anthology honoring Giovanna of Aragon (1502–75), the sister-in-law of Alfonso d'Avalos.

53. Nifo's treatise is dedicated to Giovanna and gives a very full description of her physical beauty (*De pulchro* 5, 18).

54. Cf. Plotinus *Enneads* 1. 6. 9.

55. This passage largely derives from Plotinus *Enneads* 1. 6. 6 and 8.

56. Tasso *Rime d'Amore* 3. 9–14.

57. Ruscelli had once argued that women are "capable of separating and cleansing us from earthly things and lifting us to the way of heaven, and from them we derive the fullest contentment and happiness in this world" (*Lettura*, p. 30r).

58. An allusion to Minturno's *Amore innamorató*, a composition in prose and verse in celebration of love, published in his *Rime et prose* (Venice, 1559) with a dedication by Ruscelli.

59. Pliny *Natural History* 2. 3. 8.

60. Consider Nifo *De pulchro* 37.

61. Dante *Purgatorio* 8. 138.

Giambattista Guarini

1538–1612

Giambattista Guarini is remembered as the Italian poet who wrote the play *Il Pastor Fido* (*The Faithful Shepherd*), published in 1590. He was a native of Ferrara who taught rhetoric there before serving in the Este court where the young Torquato Tasso was court poet. Guarini was jealous of the younger poet and composed his drama at least partly in order to challenge Tasso's *Aminta*. In fact, Guarini replaced Tasso as the court poet after the latter's disgrace. He left the Este court twice, however, after quarrels with Alfonso II, Duke of Ferrara, and he spent the last years of his contentious life in litigation and family quarrels.

Even before it was printed, *Il Pastor Fido* elicited controversy among the Italian critics, primarily because of Guarini's claim to have invented a new genre of drama which he christened "pastoral tragicomedy." Such a claim, of course, deeply offended Aristotelian critics who did not allow for any sort of drama not discussed by the master himself. This controversy was essentially a version of the ongoing battle between the "ancients" and the "moderns" over the question of whether the contemporary poet is allowed to break with the forms of poetry discussed and utilized in ancient Greece and Rome. Guarini's most important opponent was Giasone di Nores, who published his objections to the drama in 1587. Guarini replied in 1590 and again in 1593. His two replies were revised to appear in 1601 as the *Compendium of Tragicomic Poetry*.

Guarini adeptly cites classical sources, particularly the comedies of Terence, in order to justify his own stance. He also demonstrates a great knowledge of Aristotle and, says Allan Gilbert:

> he sets out to show that what he has done is countenanced by the very letter of the *Poetics,* or at least that his methods follow directly in the course of development from hints in the exposition of the Greek philosopher.

Guarini demonstrates to his own satisfaction that the tragicomedy is an entirely distinct species of drama, comparing it to the mule, which is a distinct species even though it is sired by a horse and an ass. Because it is a distinct species, its laws do not contradict the laws formulated by Aristotle for the tragedy and the comedy. Attempting to reconcile the novelty of his position to the Aristotelian tradition, Guarini speaks of the works of Dante and Petrarch as "new forms of writing poetry derived from the springs of poetic nature marked out to us by the Philosopher."

It is perhaps most interesting to read Guarini's defense in the light of the Elizabethan drama simultaneously developing in England. It is there that one discovers the fullest flowering of the techniques advocated by Guarini. "Here's *Pastor Fido*," says a character in Ben Jonson's *Volpone* (1607), "all our English writers, I mean such as are happy in the Italian, will deign to steal out of this author."

The selections from *The Compendium of Tragicomic Poetry*, translated by Allan H. Gilbert, are reprinted with his permission from *Literary Criticism: Plato to Dryden*, edited by Allan H. Gilbert (Detroit: Wayne State University Press, 1962). © 1962 by Allan H. Gilbert.

FROM

THE COMPENDIUM OF TRAGICOMIC POETRY

Imitation

To poetry alone the name of imitator is especially appropriate, as that which for the most part does not, like other objects of man's attention, present concepts, thoughts, or forms, but human activities which are highly valued by all. And truly what is making something resemble the truth if it is not imitation? Is it not strange that this marvelous and truly divine activity is so delightful and highly valued, because there is nothing of any sort in this world subject to perception and alteration which does not participate in some way in this rare gift of imitation. Beginning with the creation of the world, does it not appear that when the divine workman produced it he wished in some sense to imitate? and not merely because he produced it in conformity with the divine idea that had been in his breast from all eternity, but because in the celestial production he made it in the semblance of eternity, in that it could not be injured or altered; this condition is the sign of a nature that does not perish. Hence it is not strange if Aristotle, seeing the world to be of such a nature, deceived himself by thinking it eternal. Then in forming man as a little world,[1] the divine voice of the same divine artist indicated that he was pleased with the work of imitation, saying: Let us make man in our image, after our own likeness. And further, he was so desirous to see imitation carried on that he wished man to obtain nothing except by imitation. What teaches us to speak? Imitation. What to live well? Imitation. How is human felicity acquired? By making oneself like to God. When sciences discuss the truth, what else do they do than show the way to set forth and imitate, with the intellect and the tongue, the thing that has been learned, by retracing the true form of it like a picture either on paper or by the voice? Finally, everything that is active and directs itself toward its natural and true perfection in some mode partakes in imitation, whether more or less. It is no wonder, then, that imitation is so delightful, when through it man learns to know what is the first desire of human nature, its dearest delight, and the thing most fitted to it. In addition, imitation is a sort of producing what is new—an operation in itself very dear to nature, who avails herself of it to preserve herself in her species, every day supplying all that has been lost. Now poetry, among all the arts that give their effort to imitation, succeeds marvelously, not merely because she imitates human actions—for in that she is not alone—but because she imitates with speech. In this she is a unique imitator, because all the others carry on imitation with other means and other instruments, but no other art with speech, which is peculiar to poetry. . . .

Types of Plot

There are two ways in which it can be said that the precept of unity is not preserved in the poem[2] of the *Pastor Fido*: one is that it contains two forms, the tragic and the comic; the other is that it has more than one subject, like almost all the plays of Terence. In order that we may make our discourse more convenient and clear, we shall call the first of these by the usual name of mixed and the second "grafted." As to the first, it must be considered that tragicomedy is not made up of two entire plots, one of which is a perfect tragedy and the other a perfect comedy, connected in such a way that they can be disjoined without doing injury to either. Nor should anyone think that it is a tragic story vitiated with the lowliness of comedy or a comic fable contaminated with the deaths of tragedy, for neither of these would be a proper component; for he who makes a tragicomedy does not intend to compose separately either a tragedy or a comedy, but from the two a third thing that will be perfect of its kind and may take from the others the parts that with most verisimilitude can stand together. Therefore, in judging it, one does not need to confound the terms *mixed* and *double*, as do those of little understanding who do not realize that nothing can be mixed if it is not one and if its parts are not so mingled that one cannot be independently recognized or separated from the other. . . .

Components Common to Tragedy and Comedy

Let us consider the parts of these two poems that are both opposed and in harmony with each other, in order to see that the mixed tragicomic is reasonable. Tragedy shares with comedy presentation on the stage, and all the rest of the apparatus, rhythm, harmony, limited time, dramatic plot, probability, recognition, and reversal. I mean that each makes use of the same things, though in the method of use there is some difference between them. Other qualities are then peculiar to one and to the other, and these qualities not only vary in their use, as do the other things that have been mentioned, but they diversify the species in such a way that they become differences between them. And I have no doubt that he who would think of making one of these pass entire into the confines of the other, and of using in tragedy what belongs to comedy alone, or *vice versa*, would produce an unseemly and monstrous story. But the point is that one should see whether these specific differences cause so much opposition that it is in no way possible to form a third species that can be a legitimate and reasonable poem.

Comic Characters in Tragedy

In tragedy these differences are the character of high rank, the serious action, terror and commiseration. In comedy they are private character and affairs, laughter, and witty speeches. As to the first, I confess, and admit it is the doctrine of Aristotle, that characters of high rank are fitting to tragedy, and those of humble station are suited to comedy;[3] but I deny that it is contrary to nature and to poetic art in general that persons great and those not great should be introduced into one plot. What tragedy has there ever been that did not have many more servants and other persons of similar station than men of great consequence? Who unfastens the admirably tied knot in the *Oedipus* of Sophocles? Not the king, not the queen, not Creon, not Tiresias, but two servants, guardians of herds. Then it is not contrary to the nature of the stage that there should be united in a play persons of high rank and those of low station, not merely under the name of a mixed poem, such as is tragicomedy, but also under that of pure tragedy, and comedy as well, if Aristophanes is alluded to, who mixes men and gods, citizens and countrymen, and even brings in beasts and clouds to speak in his plays.

Grave and Light Are to Be Reconciled

With respect to actions that are great and not great, I cannot see for what reason it is unfitting that they should appear in one same plot, not entirely tragic, if they are inserted with judgment. Can it not be that amusing events intervene between serious actions? Are they not many times the cause of bringing perils to a happy conclusion? But then, do princes always act majestically? Do they not at times deal with private affairs? Assuredly they do. Why, then, cannot a character of high importance be presented on the stage at a time when he is not dealing with important matters? Certainly Euripides did this in his *Cyclops*, where he mixed grave danger for the life of Odysseus, a tragic character, with the drunkenness of the Cyclops, which is a comic action. And among the Latins, Plautus did the same thing in the *Amphitryo*, mingling the laugher and the jests of Mercury with persons of importance, not merely Amphitryo, but the king of the gods. It is, then, not unreasonable that in one story for the stage there can be at the same time persons of high rank and those not of high rank.

Pity and Laughter Not Inharmonious

The same can be said of commiseration and laughter, qualities of which one is tragic and the other comic. And indeed to me they do not appear so completely opposite that the same story cannot include them under diverse occasions and persons. On reading in Terence the fate of Menedemus,[4] who willingly mortified himself because of the severity he adopted toward his son, what man is not moved to pity, and does not with Chremes, who does not restrain his tears, weep over it? And in the same play there is laughter at the art with which the astute Syrus mocks and deceives Chremes. I do not say that there can be happiness and sorrow in the same story, but there can be pity with laughter. Thus all the sum of this contradiction is seen to be reduced to a single difference, that is, the terrible, which can never occur except in a tragic plot, nor can any comedy ever be mixed with it, since terror is never introduced except by means of serious and mournful dramas; where it is found, there is never any room for laughter and sport.

Are Tragedy and Comedy Too Diverse for Union?

All the things I have said above can be brought forward in defense of tragicomic poetry. But I do wish to avail myself of them, and am content to hand over to tragedy kings, serious actions, the terrible, and the piteous; to comedy I assign private affairs, laughter, and jests; in these things are the specific differences between the two. I wish for the present to concede that one may not enter into the jurisdiction of the other. Will it follow from this that, since they are of diverse species, they cannot be united to make up a third poem? Certainly it cannot be said that this is in opposition to the practice of nature, and much less to that of art.

Nature Joins Diverse Things

Speaking first of nature, are not the horse and the ass two distinct species? Certainly, and yet of the two is made a third, the mule, which is neither one nor the other. . . . But perhaps it will be said that these third natures spring from the mixture of seeds and not of bodies, and that they are works of nature and not of art, though we are treating of works of art. Therefore, we may pass to the arts and to their mixtures, made of bodies that are solid and diverse by nature. Bronze is made of copper and tin, and the body of both of them enters into the mixture, and they and their natures are so well mingled that the third which results from them is neither tin nor copper. Into gunpowder enter sulphur and nitre and as a third carbon, all complete bodies and wholly different in their characteristics; the powder is not any one of them. But someone may say that these examples are not appropriate, for the mixture is brought about by means of fire, which alters the qualities of bodies in such a way that nature can be said to have a part in the process; but this is not true of poetic mixtures, which are dependent on the skill of the worker, without any intervention of the work of nature.

Painting and Music Unite Diversities

We may concede this and speak of painting, which is blood-cousin to poetry; does not painting make various mixtures of her colors without the employment of any other means? The same can be said of music, born at the same birth with poetry. Does it not mix the diatonic with the chromatic, and the chromatic with the enharmonic, and does it not mix what the Philosopher calls harmonies? And it is indeed a single work of music. But anyone who still wishes to contradict would be able to say in reply that the painter manages colors and the musician sounds, but the poet sets in motion human deeds and persons. Yet this may be made good and in the end a mixture may be found so similar to poetry that there will be no difference between them except that between the true and the feigned. This is so fitting to our condition that the figure is as it were the same thing as that which it sets forth, since poetry is nothing other than the verisimilar imitated.

Contraries in Politics

Has it not been said before that poetry employs actions and persons? We may give, then, an example of them. Do not Marcus Tullius and Horace say comedy is the mirror of human relations?[5]

We may give an example from human relations. Does not Aristotle say that tragedy is made up of persons of high rank and comedy of men of the people? Let us give an example of men of rank and men of the people. The republic is such a thing. I do not say this in respect to its material, for every city is of necessity composed of nobles and those who are not noble, of rich and poor, and, as the Philosopher himself says, of greater and less; but I speak of the forms that spring from the diversity of these two, that is, the power of the few and the power of the masses. Are not these two species of government very different among themselves? If we believe Aristotle, or even pure reason, there is no doubt of it; yet the Philosopher puts them together and makes of them the mixture of the republic. But in the republic are not the citizens human persons and the acts of government human operations? If these, that work practically, can be mixed, cannot the art of poetry do it in those things that are done for sport? In an oligarchy do not the few alone govern? Are not these contraries? Yet they join in a single mixed form. Is not tragedy an imitation of the great and comedy an imitation of the humble? Are not the humble opposite to the great? Why cannot poetry make the mixture if politics can do it?. . . .

Tragic and Comic Elements That Cohere

He who composes tragicomedy takes from tragedy its great persons but not its great action, its verisimilar plot but not its true one, its movement of the feelings but not its disturbance of them, its pleasure but not its sadness, its danger but not its death; from comedy it takes laughter that is not excessive, modest amusement, feigned difficulty, happy reversal, and above all the comic order, of which we shall speak in its place. These components, thus managed, can stand together in a single story, especially when they are handled in a way in accord with their nature and the kind of manners that pertains to them. We conclude, then, that the ability of the tragic poet, naturally fitted to produce tragedy, will not produce either comedy or tragicomedy when the parts other than I have mentioned appear in their vigor and entirety, but only when they are not all present. And if instead of tragic components we speak of those of comedy, the comic power will never work toward the formation of a tragic poem; on the contrary the contest between the tragic parts and the comic will render that power very weak and destroy its capacity for being put into practice. . . .

Selection by Art

Art observes that tragedy and comedy are composed of heterogeneous parts, and that therefore if an entire tragedy and an entire comedy should be mixed, they would not be able to function properly together as in a natural mixture, because they do not have a single intrinsic natural principle, and it would then follow that in a single subject two forms contrary to each other would be included. But art, a most prudent imitator of nature, plays the part of the intrinsic principle, and while nature alters the parts after they are united, art alters them before they are joined in order that they may be able to exist together and, though mixed, produce a single form.

Tragicomedy the Highest Form

But it would be possible here to raise a new question, namely, what actually is such a mixture as tragicomedy? I answer that it is the mingling of tragic and comic pleasure, which does not allow hearers to fall into excessive tragic melancholy or comic relaxation. From this results a poem of the most excellent form and composition, not merely fully corresponding to the mixture of the human body, which consists entirely in the tempering of the four humors,[6] but much more noble than simple tragedy or simple comedy, as that which does not inflict on us atrocious events and horrible and inhumane sights, such as blood and deaths, and which, on the other hand, does not cause us to be so relaxed in laughter that we sin against the modesty and decorum of a well-bred man. And truly if today men understood well how to compose tragicomedy (for it is not an easy thing to do), no other drama should be put on the stage, for tragicomedy is able to include all the good qualities of dramatic poetry and to reject all the bad ones; it can delight all dispositions, all ages, and all tastes—something that is not true of the other two, tragedy and comedy, which are at fault because they go to excess.[7] For this reason one of them is today abhorred by many great and wise men, and the other is little regarded.

The End of Tragicomedy

But I should not appear to have completed my task if, after I have made known the parts or forms, as it were, that tragicomedy ought to have as a good and legitimate poem, I should fail to prove the same thing of its end. Someone, perhaps, may wish to know what its end is, whether tragic or comic or mixed, as it seems that he might ask its function, since it is a mixed story. This cannot be explained without much difficulty, for each art has its end, toward which it is directed as it works; and if it has two of them, one of them is dependent on the other, in such a way that one thing alone is the chief end toward which the art is directed. Now if we concede that tragicomedy is a reasonable mixture, what does it attempt to do? what end has it? does it wish laughter or tears? for the two cannot be done at once. Then what does it do first? what next? what is of less importance? what of chief importance? what is subaltern? To such questions one can hardly give answers without first determining what the end of tragedy is and what the end of comedy. To understand those matters one must realize that each art, in addition to the principal end of which we have spoken before, has another end. One of them is that by means of which the artist as he works introduces into the matter which he has in hand the form that is the end of the work. The other is that for the good and advantage of which he labors at the work he wishes to carry to its end. In that sense Aristotle says that man is the end of all things. We call one of these ends instrumental, and the other, using Aristotle's own word, architectonic. Both of these appear in both tragic and comic art.

The Ends of Comedy

Beginning with comedy, its instrumental end is to imitate those actions of private men which by their deficiency move us to laughter; this is Aristotle's notion.[8] But the architectonic end is not mentioned in his extant writings, for we lack the discussion of comedy in that treatise of his called the *Poetics*, though it may be supposed that there he gave an end for comedy as he did for tragedy. But from the instrumental end we are able to conjecture what he would assign as the architectonic end, since this is the exemplar which the artist sets before himself. Hence, if we consider that the Bacchic songs, all full of drunkenness and phallic license, gave rise to comedy, and, besides this, seeing that the same Aristotle distinguishes it from tragedy by means of its plebeian persons, assigning laughter to it as its specific difference, it appears to me that it can have no end other than that of purging men's minds of those passions that are caused in us by labors both private and public. It purges melancholy, an emotion so injurious that often it leads a man to grow mad and to inflict death on himself, in the same way as, according to Aristotle's teaching, melody purges the feeling the Greeks call enthusiasm; the Sacred Scriptures in dealing with it say that David, with the harmony of his music, drove away the evil spirits from Saul, the first king of the Hebrews. And just as one part of music, as the Scriptures teach us, is necessary to recreate us and enable us to gain that restoration of which human life has so great need, so comedy, with its gay and ridiculous presentations, refreshes our spirit. As a breeze is wont to drive away the thickened air, comedy by moving us to laughter shakes off that gloomy and foggy humor, generated in us by too much mental concentration, which often renders us slow and obtuse in our activities. For this reason comedy represents only private persons, with defects evoking laughter, mocks, sports, intrigues of little importance, covering but a short time and ending happily. Such is the architectonic end of comedy.

The Ends of Tragedy

But tragedy, on the other hand, calls back the relaxed and wandering soul; it has, therefore, ends wholly diverse, both of them demonstrated by Aristotle in the *Poetics*, where he defines tragedy, more fortunate in this matter than comedy. One end is the imitation of some horrible and pitiable action, and this is the instrumental; the other is the purgation of terror and compassion, the architectonic end. It is very necessary to understand how this purgation is carried on if one wishes to lay one's hand on what is sought after. I know that the passage on the catharsis is one of the most difficult in all the *Poetics* of

Aristotle.[9] For that reason I intend to treat it with great modesty toward those who have been the first men of their time, who, in my opinion, have rather obscured it than made it clear. Everything in it that raises serious doubt can, in my opinion, be reduced to two points.

Why Is Compassion to Be Purged Away?

One point, required by Aristotle, is that a man should be freed from compassion, a feeling, as Boccaccio says, altogether human. And in fact that terror should be purged, as a disordered feeling that corrupts the virtue of fortitude, is much more reasonable or, to put it better, more necessary. But to rid ourselves of pity, who can do it without ridding himself of humanity? For this alone tragedy would deserve to be abhorred as a savage and offensive spectacle.

Do Terrors Purge Fear?

The other point is how it can be that terrible things purge fear, since it does not appear that choleric matters purge anger but rather make it worse, and so with the phlegmatic and other humors. Therefore, by means of the sight of things horrible and alarming there would rather come fear to a person who is by nature easily frightened. Yet some say that habituation to the sight of horrible things, as blood, wounds, and deaths, renders the spirit intrepid, and from the example of the soldier they conclude that in such a fashion tragedy purges terror.[10] This perhaps could be conceded if tragedy presented gladiators or assassins. But tragedy is so far from this that even the deaths that appear in it rarely occur before the eyes of the spectators, but are narrated, though sometimes the dead bodies are produced on the stage, as Euripides did in the *Phoenician Women*. It is altogether certain that Sophocles never did it, as some say who have thought that the death of Ajax happened in the sight of the audience, but anyone who understands the passage and considers it well knows that that is not so. Tragedy, then, cannot wish to purge in this fashion, since scenes of ferocity surely make men more cruel but not more brave. Nor can the courage of the soldier, when it comes from the habit of seeing dead bodies, be called virtue, and he who is not brave in some other way is improperly called brave, as even the virtue of the sailor, since he is habituated to storms at sea, cannot according to the teaching of Aristotle be called true courage.[11] If a man sees death often, it gives him assurance in working where death is, and for this reason executioners and, in times of pestilence, gravediggers, who are persons of the lowest sort, are more intrepid in their duties than are others; but the sight of death does not make the spirits valiant or purge away the fear of death. And this is true, for even though soldiers see blood every day, yet there are few of them who will stand in firm order of battle and not turn their backs when the peril of death is no longer in the hands of Fortune but in those of a strong enemy, and they see themselves overcome. And the few who do resist and forge ahead are not strong through the habit of seeing terrifying and horrid sights, but because they are fixed upon an honored, virtuous, and praiseworthy object.

To Lose Compassion is to Lose Humanity

Now I come to compassion, of which I can say that the continual sight of actions that arouse compassion would cause the destruction of the feeling. But I do not see how anyone can be divested of this feeling without divesting himself of humanity, that is, by making himself cruel; nor do I see how Aristotle could have meant it, since he teaches in the *Ethics* that he who has a friend must sympathize with his afflictions.[12] Now these are the difficulties which one must first resolve if he wishes to understand correctly the way in which the tragic poem purges.

The Word Purge Has Two Senses

First of all, it must be realized that the word *purge* has two meanings. One means *to blot out completely*; in this sense Boccaccio uses it, in the passage where he writes: "The sins which you have committed up to the hour of repentance will all be purged." The other meaning is *to purify and cleanse*; in this sense Petrarch says: "Virgin, I consecrate and purge to your name both thought and ability and style." Yet here he does not mean to blot out his own ability, as Boccaccio meant to blot out the sins, but to rid it of all vileness and make it perfect in its nature. In this second sense is to be taken the *purge* of tragedy, as also the physicians take it; when, for example, they wish to purge bile, they do not have the intention of blotting it out or eradicating it wholly from the human body, for that would be to wish not to heal but to kill by completely depriving nature of a humor she uses to keep the proper proportion among the others; to purge is merely to take away the parts which by passing their natural bounds corrupt the symmetry of life and so cause disease. A tragic poem, then, does not purge the affections in stoic fashion, by removing them totally from our hearts, but by moderating and reducing them to that proper consistency which can contribute to a virtuous habit. It rather avails itself of one affection as medicine for the other, since it is so far from true that all fears are vicious that rather there are some of them which naturally kindle virtue, as for example fear of infamy. Equally pity is not all good, because, if the proper modes are not preserved, it passes into softness and effeminacy which deprive the spirits of their proper strength.

Purgation Correctly Explained

These two feelings then need to be purged, that is, reduced to a proper mixture,[13] and this is done by tragedy. But if purging is considered as the effect of the thing that purges, we shall say these feelings are purged in the first meaning, for good has as its purpose to blot out and entirely uproot the bad. If then fear and compassion purge feelings similar to themselves, and some fears and some feelings of pity are good and others not, it must needs be that we see what things in tragedy are purging and what are purged; thence it will appear that it is not contradictory to their nature to purge and be purged. And beginning at the beginning, I say that as man has two lives, one of the intellect and the other of the senses, so he can fear two deaths, on which, according to Aristotle,[14] the terrible for the most part depends. What is, then, the purging terror of tragedy? It is terror of internal death, which, excited in the spirit of the spectator by the image of what is represented, interprets the injurious evil tendency as a calamity because of the likeness that one fear has with another. Then reason, which is the nature and first principle of the life of the spirit, abhorring the bad tendency as its capital enemy and opponent, drives it out, leaving behind only the beneficial fear of infamy and of internal death, which is the foundation of virtue. When then terror purges terror, it is not as though wrath were joined to wrath, but the terror acts like rhubarb, which, though it has an occult likeness to the humor that it purges,[15] yet in respect to its end is wholly opposed, for one heals and the other corrupts. Thus terror purges terror, since no way can be found more valid nor more certain of not fearing death than to give vigor and spirit to the life of the spirit, which is the perception of reason. All the other arguments are less effective, for, if of the two lives the internal is the more appropriate to man, there is no doubt that he who perceives it as active in himself will prefer not to exist rather than to be wicked. In this, then, consists all the business of tragedy, which, presenting before us the terrible as it may appear in the death of the spirit, teaches us to have no fear of that of the body, and makes us perceive within ourselves the force of justice, because of which we see that the persons of tragedy, when they are tormented in spirit, are unaware of the torments of the body and have no fear of death. For this reason the wicked have no place in tragedy, for they have completely killed the internal perceptions of reason. But let us come to examples. For what does Oedipus sorrow in the *Tyrannus* of Sophocles, the queen and exemplar of tragedies? For what, I say, does that unhappy king sorrow after the recognition of the parricide and incest he has committed? Is it that he is going to be deprived of his kingdom? of his native land? that he has fallen from his royal estate and been made a beggar instead of a king? No. And yet these are the greatest and heaviest blows that can come on one who is nobly born. But he does not feel this, but prays that as soon as possible he may be led out of the city, leaving the kingdom to Creon by a death that is legal rather than natural. Nothing torments him but his parricide and his incest, for he sees that he has fallen into a sin so horrible and so greatly abhorred that, according to internal justice, he preferred to die rather than commit it. This horror, this infamy occupies him so much that he forgets every other evil; this sorrow he so lays to heart that he does not perceive the loss of his eyes nor of his native land nor of his regal scepter, and speaks of his internal pains as if he perceived no external pain or loss. This is a spectacle that makes us consider and repent of our sins and makes those who fear to die realize clearly that there is something more terrible to human nature than death, for if death is to be feared at all, only that of the spirit should be feared, since in comparison with it that of the body becomes as it were unfelt. Sophocles gives us the same teaching in the *Ajax*, where the hero is tormented by infamy alone, into which he appears to have fallen by a madness that is the death of the spirit; this infamy drives him to take his own life, since he does not wish to live in the flesh when he is dead to honor. . . .

The Function of Tragedy: To Purge, Not to Teach

But at this point can arise a question that should be dealt with, since in his discussion of courage Aristotle does not accept suicide as a virtuous action;[16] this permits us to think that tragedy, teaching us to fall into sin, would not purge our spirits, but rather would corrupt them. Answer can be made in two ways. One is that the Philosopher does not rebuke those who are brought to kill themselves to flee infamy or because they have knowledge of their sin, but those who do it because they cannot bear poverty or other bodily annoyance. And though our holy and true religion teaches that it is always a sin when a man brings about his own death, yet paganism, which did not have this light, judged it a noble deed to commit suicide, as did Cato, Brutus, and others, and above all Lucretia, who not for glory but to prove her chastity inflicted death on herself. The other answer is that tragedy is not brought about by the voluntary action of a man who kills himself to imitate a virtuous act, but exists to show that so great is the sorrow of the spirit that he who kills himself does not perceive the suffering of the body, and that our humanity suffers things which are more grievous and terrible than death, and finally that a tragedy is a story and does not have as its function the teaching of virtue, but that its function is to purge—so far as a story can—those two perturbations of the spirit which are an obstacle to fortitude, which in all human actions is so noble and necessary a virtue.

Compassion

Now let us go on to the other feeling, that of compassion, which is nothing other than sorrow for the affliction of someone else. But this evil can be of two sorts, either of the body or of the spirit; thence spring the two kinds of compassion, good and ill; the good kind is present when we are sorrowful for someone who is afflicted in spirit because he has had too great pleasure in the body; and the bad kind is present when we feel sorrowful for someone who injures his body that he may have peace in his spirit. In this consists the true understanding of this feeling, which is most useful, indeed necessary, to all human life; for there is no other difference between the continent and the incontinent, who can be called the soldiers of virtue, except that one does not have pity for his body and afflicts it that he may not have torment in his spirit, while the other is so tender of his body that he permits himself to fall into an offense of the spirit, which causes him the anxiety of repentance. Thence comes the proverb that the compassionate physician makes a wound maggoty, for if he used the knife and did not have such foolish pity that he is unwilling to pain the injured man, he would save him from death by giving him a little pain. The same is true of the soldier, who, if he is too careful of himself, flies fatigues and perils, whence it easily comes about that by leaving the ranks or turning his back or doing something else unworthy of him, he falls into infamy and then suffers and is worthy of true compassion. . . .

Two Kinds of Compassion

It is not necessary, then, to have compassion for any pain of body when it is just, but rather for a fault which when known and perceived by the sinner becomes pain for his sin. The first weakens the spirit of him who has compassion and the second strengthens it; the first disintegrates it and the second unites it; the first relaxes it and the second makes it firm. There is no doubt that without suffering and hardening himself against the flatteries and injuries of the body, by abstaining and enduring, man cannot follow the virtuous course suitable to his nature. Whoever suffers in this way disposes himself to suffer in body in order not to have anxiety of mind. What then is the compassion that purges and what is that which ought to be purged can be understood from what has been said. Not to give up the celebrated example of Oedipus, consider his troubles, which were of two sorts, some of the body and some of the reason. On seeing that king, once so great but now deprived of rank, blind, and banished—ills that he had not foreseen but rather that he had guarded against—who is there who would not have more compassion for the internal cause of that blindness and that sad fortune than for its external effect? Who does not see the same thing in the *Ajax*, and in the *Iphigenia* of Euripides and, contemplating the fortitude of that maiden in preparing herself to die for the benefit of the public, does not purge his spirit of that softness and baseness which excites selfishness? Who does not learn to expose his life to the perils of death for the sake of virtue and of great and striking works? In proportion, then, as a story has more of the terrible and the piteous it will be the more tragic.

Varying Tragic Quality

For this reason, if to be tragic is a quality that can be altered and increased and diminished, as may be gathered from the words of Aristotle, it will be in the hand of the poet to make the story more and less tragic, according as he endows it with more and less of terror and compassion. Stories that are exceedingly tragic will have great characters, true names, a serious action, and magnificent manners, stage appliances, decorum, language and ideas; there will be a recognition, a change of fortune, and a calamitous end. Such is the *Oedipus Tyrannus* of Sophocles. Less tragic plays do not have either recognition or change of fortune; those much less tragic lack an unhappy conclusion; the least perfect are the double, of which I shall speak in their proper place, the episodic, and those that are not true. Hence the terrible and the piteous, in various degrees of purgative power, determine the classes of tragedy.

The Difficulty Solved

If, as has been said, tragic quality can be raised and lowered in degree, there is no doubt it can also be injured and diluted in such a way it will no longer be tragic, but will pass into another species. Therefore, if in its changes it receives anything which is not repugnant to the feelings of the terrible and the miserable, it will continue to be tragic, though more and less so. But if with the two qualities that have been named are mingled those repugnant and contrary to them, such as laughter, corruption of the species will result, and when the end is changed the form will also be changed, since where laughter is desired there can be neither pity nor terror, for the feelings are opposite, and one destroys the other. If then laughter corrupts tragic form, when laughter is found in a subject that is not vile and plebeian, and that possesses those parts of tragedy that are not repugnant to the ridiculous, what sort of poem shall we have? Not tragedy, because the tragic form is destroyed by reason of the laughter; and not comedy either, which does not receive a noble subject and does nothing but represent to us the defects of men who are vile and deserve to be laughed at. What will the poem be if not a third sort participating in those qualities both tragic and comic that can be united? But what end will it have? We have come to the solution of that difficulty that has moved us to so long a discourse.

Tragicomedy Does Not Purge Pity and Terror

Though tragicomedy, like the others, has two ends, the instrumental, which is the form resulting from the imitation of tragic and comic affairs mixed together, and the architectonic, which is to purge the mind from the evil affection of melancholy, an end which is wholly comic and wholly simple, yet I say that tragicomedy can be connected in no way with tragedy. The effects of the purging in the two types are truly opposite; one gladdens and the other saddens, one relaxes and the other constrains; these are mutually repellent motions of the spirit, since one goes from the center to the circumference, the other travels in the opposite direction; these are the ends that in a drama can be called contradictory. But the instrumental end can be a mixed one, since tragedy has many parts which, when the terrible is removed, have with the other comic parts the power of producing comic pleasure. Therefore, since Aristotle concedes pleasure in tragedy, pleasure is easily reconciled with pleasure. And what is tragic pleasure? The imitation of serious actions of persons of rank with new and unexpected accidents. Now if terror is removed and the work is reduced to pleasure alone, a new story and new names may be feigned and all may be made harmonious with laughter; the delight in the imitation will remain, which will be tragic in possibility but not in fact, and only the outside of it will remain, but not the tendency for purging that resides in the terrible; purgation can be produced only by means of all the tragic parts; if it could be done otherwise the story would still be a tragedy. There is a great difference between the two types; for one, with its simple narrative, does not wish to purge; but the other, with its gravity, and its stage setting, with harmony, numbers, magnificent and sumptuous diction and other tragic sights and devices, wishes to excite the terrible and the piteous, in order to purge them. This is the reason why, when Aristotle says that stories with sad endings are especially tragic, he thinks it well to add "when they are well handled,"[17] meaning that all dramas do not produce a tragic effect, but merely those accompanied by all the other parts that belong with them. Tragic pleasure consists, then, in the imitation of horrible and pitiable actions, which in itself, according to Aristotle,[18] is delightful. But that is not enough; it is also necessary that the other parts also be of a similar sort, if the end of purging is to be attained; otherwise it will be a tragedy only equivocally, that is, outside the terms of the definition given by the Philosopher. If a poet wishes to make use of any subject in such a way as not to purge terror, he must temper it with laughter and other comic qualities in such a manner that, though it is by nature terrible and pitiable, yet it has not the power of producing either terror or compassion, and much less of purging them, but remains with the single virtue of delighting by imitating. And just as every terrible action is not fit to purge terror (something that is proved in pictures, though they may be horrible and terrifying, and in things of similar quality which are merely narrated without any dramatic art), so every imitation of the terrible does not produce tragedy, if it is not united with other parts that agree with it. . . .

Purgation No Longer Needed

If then tragedy delights, it does it by imitating, and does it in the way in which men deceive a child who dislikes medicine, by smearing the edge of the glass, as Lucretius says, with some sweet thing to make easy for him the drinking of the medicine.[19] Tragic sights delight, but when they leave at the end a great sadness in the spirit, and that is what has a purgative effect. Hence, to many the tragic poem is not pleasing in nature, since all do not have need of what purges. And just as the age changes, habits change. . . . And to come to our age, what need have we today to purge terror and pity with tragic sights, since we have the precepts of our most holy religion, which teaches us with the word of the gospel? Hence these horrible and savage spectacles are superfluous, nor does it seem to me that today we should introduce a tragic action for any other reason than to get delight from it.

The Decay of Comedy

On the other side comedy has come to be so tedious and is so little valued that if she is not accompanied with the marvels of the intermezzi, there is today no one who can endure her. This is because of mercenary and sordid persons who have contaminated her and reduced her to a vile state, carrying here and there for vile pay that excellent poem which was once accustomed to crown its makers with glory. In order to raise comic poetry from such a state of disgrace, that it may be able to please the unwilling ears of a modern audience, the makers of tragicomedy—following the steps of Menander and Terence, who raised it to dignity graver and more entitled to respect—have undertaken to mingle with the pleasing parts of comedy those parts of tragedy that can suitably accompany comic scenes to such an extent that they strive for the purgation of sadness. They defend themselves, and not badly, by explaining that as the ancient Romans, according to the testimony of Horace,[20] introduced satyrs, who were ridiculous persons, into the severity of the tragic poem, as will be shown below, for no other reason than the solace and recreation of their hearers, so, in order to remove the dislike and distaste which the world today has for simple and ordinary comedies, we should be permitted to temper them with such tragic gravity as is not repugnant to the architectonic end of purging sadness.

Description of Tragicomedy

But to conclude once for all that which it was my first intention to show, I say that to a question on the end of tragicomedy I shall answer that it is to imitate with the resources of the stage an action that is feigned and in which are mingled all the tragic and comic parts that can coexist in verisimilitude and decorum, properly arranged in a single dramatic form, with the end of purging with pleasure the sadness of the hearers. This is done in such a way that the imitation, which is the instrumental end, is that which is mixed, and represents a mingling of both tragic and comic events. But the purging, which is the architectonic end, exists only as a single principle, which unites two qualities in one purpose, that of freeing the hearers from melancholy. And as in mixed bodies found in nature, though in these all four of the elements are found in an abated state,[21] as has been said, yet each of them retains a peculiar quality of either one or another of the elements that is dominant and surpasses the others and toward which especially that which is most like it is directed, so in the mixed form of which I speak, though its parts are altogether tragic and comic, it is still not impossible for the plot to have more of one quality than of another, according to the wish of him who composes it, if only he will remain within the bounds that have been mentioned above. The *Amphitryo* of Plautus has more of the comic, the *Cyclops* of Euripides more of the tragic. Yet it is not true that the first or the second is not a tragicomedy, since neither of them has as its end the purging of terror and compassion, for this purgation cannot exist where there is laughter, which disposes the spirits to expand, and not to restrain themselves. . . . No one has described tragicomedy better than has Horace in his poetic *Epistle to the Pisos*. . . . [22]

The Style of Tragicomedy

Now having sufficiently proved that the mixed tragicomedy is reasonable in its parts and its end, it remains that this should also be proved of the style, which, since it should be suited to the story, must if that is mixed also be mixed, in order to be a unit. And as Demetrius of Phalerum,[23] a complete master of styles, teaches us that the two forms he calls humble and magnificent cannot mix, so he affirms that the other two, the polished and the dignified, can mingle, even when accompanied by one or other of those first mentioned; hence the composer of tragicomedy, though he may grant that the first two do not mix, would be unable to deny that the other two properly can. The normal and chief style of tragicomedy is the magnificent, which, when accompanied with the grave, becomes the norm of tragedy, but when mingled with the polished, makes the combination fitting to tragicomic poetry. Since it deals with great persons and heroes, humble diction is unfitting, and since it is not concerned with the terrible and the horrible, but rather avoids it, it abandons the grave and employs the sweet, which modifies the greatness and sublimity that is proper to pure tragedy. So Donatus praised the judgment and art of Terence,[24] because he so well understood to take a middle course between these two forms that are so completely contrary. Still further, the styles are not like bells, which beyond the ordinary, crude tone the artificer gave them, are unfitted to make any sound more or less sharp than they have always done; but styles are like the sensitive and pliant cords of a musical instrument, which, though they all have their proper tone, still are normally more or less intense or relaxed according as it pleases the musician. The *ipate*[25] certainly will never be the *nete*,[26] nor will the second ever be deep or the first sharp. Either one sounds more or less deep or sharp as is necessary, yet in these pleasing alterations they never issue from their bounds to such an extent that the *ipate* is not always a chord of the deep and the *nete* of the sharp. In the same way the styles are handled, nor because the magnificent is relaxed will it cease therefore to be magnificent, nor because the humble becomes more strong will it therefore pass into the confines of the grand. And as the deep and sharp chords in their greater and lesser extensions run through grades which are called tones, so the styles pass through some parts of a composition which receive them and modify them. These parts are the sentence, the method, the figure, the locution, the texture, and the number.[27] From these parts the styles emerge in the same way as from the forehead, the eyes, the mouth, the chin, and the other parts of the human face emerges an expression that in one man is virile and severe, in another soft, delicate, and humble, and in another temperate. Now how does the tragicomic poet proceed in giving the right effect to his style? Certainly he will not compose a sentence or a figure in the sublime manner, and a locution and a number in the humble style, but, moderating the gravity of the sentence with those methods that normally make it humble, and in other ways sustaining the humility of some person or subject of which he treats, and using a little of that nobility of speech that is proper to the magnificent style, he proceeds to turn out an idea in harmony with his subject matter, not so grand that it rises to the tragic nor so humble that it approaches the comic. And so in dealing with the other parts he will proceed pleasingly to temper their texture with the contrary quality. This is not my doctrine but that of Hermogenes, the famous artist in ideas.[28] Speaking of the attractive and beautiful mixture that Demosthenes and Xenophon and Plato knew how to produce, he says that the styles are mixed in the same way as colors, and as of black and white, which are wholly contrary, there is formed a third that is called gloomy, so from the opposite forms of speech spring the mixed forms, which render discourse beautiful and striking. It may be added that it is no wonder if one idea touches another at some point and in some other does not harmonize with it; an example is that of man, who as a whole is very different from the other animals, yet in being mortal is similar to many of them, and in having intellect has something in common with the gods. This mixture, then, so much praised by two famous Greek rhetoricians, ought not to be unsuitable to tragicomic poetry, since, according to the testimony of Hermogenes, the most famous tongues and the best chosen pens of all Greece have used it with such pleasure. . . .

New Poetry Truly Aristotelian

Up to this point we have proved with the precepts of the Aristotelian art in general that even though it may be conceded that in the *Poetics* of Aristotle there is found no particular poem like the tragicomedy, nevertheless, since it is composed according to those rules of nature on which the Philosopher has based the other poems, it is not to be called a phantastic poem; this is confirmed by the example of the *Comedy* of Dante, the *Triumphs* of Petrarch, and the romances of our times, which are all new forms of writing poetry derived from the springs of poetic nature marked out to us by the Philosopher.[29] It now remains to be proved, if I am not to omit anything bearing on the perfection of such a poem, that poetry mingled of tragic and comic parts is composed not merely according to the universal rules of Aristotle, but is so like one of the particular species he mentions that tragicomedy is not merely its daughter, as we have proved, but its legitimate daughter. [He then attempts to show that the tragedy with a double conclusion, happy for the good and unhappy for the bad (*Poetics*, XIII, end, above), is the mother of tragicomedy.]

No Punishment in Tragicomedy

Punishment, which in the double form of tragedy comes upon the malefactors, is unfitting to tragicomic poetry, in which according to comic custom, the bad characters are not chastised. . . .[30] Comedy ordinarily desires to give a prosperous end to its worst characters. . . .

Terence and the Double Plot

I will first tell what cause moved Terence to graft one story into another and then I will defend him, to the confusion of those who have been forward in blaming him, and to the consolation of those who, following him, have written or think to write in this genus. That man of genius, that judicious poet, says that simple comedy was rather a poor thing. . . . And because episodes are needed in all stories, he thought to make essential parts not of speeches and persons outside the theme, but of the action and subject itself. He reasoned well, as follows: Since the principal duty of the poet and the delight of poetry are founded in the representation of the deeds and performances of men, no episode can be joined to comedy that is more fitting and more delightful and more artistic than that which contains not words alone, but actions, which are handled and knit together with such art and judgment that the unity of the subject is not impaired, and—that which is all-important and cannot come from other episodes—the story is more firmly knotted and in consequence is made more beautiful and more delightful. These were the causes of the comedy in which one plot is grafted on another, and this its origin. But such grafting of secondary stories is unsuitable to a tragic poem, as something that would tend directly to injure the parts of it that are most its own and most necessary.

The Sub-Plot of the Andria

It now remains to defend this grafting in of subordinate stories. In order to do this I shall consider four agents indispensable to the plot of the *Andria*, the first, not merely in date but in beauty, of the comedies of Terence: Pamphilus the first, Glycerium the second, Philumena the third, and Charinus the fourth; the love of Pamphilus and Glycerium is the chief thing, and that of Charinus and Philumena is episodic and grafted to the other. That this is so, he who has but a little understanding of the dramatic art cannot doubt, since all the difficulties arise because of Pamphilus and Glycerium. With the person of Glycerium is concerned the recognition through which the plot is turned in an opposite direction, and in her marriage it has its happy end. Concerning the marriage of Charinus there is but a little sport at the end, and that with admirable artistry. Hence the principal subject is nothing else than the love of Pamphilus and Glycerium, not interrupted by that of Charinus, but greatly aided. And if that love alone had been represented, with the pregnancy of Glycerium and the displeasure of Simo, the father of Pamphilus, how insipid the story would have been! A young man fallen under the displeasure of his father because he has married a woman of no standing, who at last, when she is discovered to be a free woman, is given to him as his wife—what is there in that to make a plot? The plot might indeed have been pathetic and have displayed character, but there would have been no activity, which is the strength of the dramatic art. How would the plot have come to a crisis? From the indignation of the father and the love of the son strong feelings could have resulted, but not intrigues. The knot is tied by the marriage that Simo arranges, for it causes Pamphilus a great deal of trouble in his need for escaping it, since he has pledged his faith to Glycerium that he will take her as his wife, and causes the astute Davos to set about his clever plans. If this marriage then is so necessary that without it the drama would have little or no action, how can the person of Philumena be passed over? Pamphilus would not have believed his father when he said that he wished that day, all of a sudden, to give him a wife, if the wife had not been selected, named, and known by Pamphilus, and if the marriage had not a little before been negotiated. So the necessity of the third agent is obvious. Now that girl who was going to be that day a wife and who had been announced as such in the house of her father, was she then to remain disappointed because of the marriage of Glycerium? Was she to be all that day in the belief and hope of being a wife and then to be left high and dry? It would be very unwise and unfitted to a comic poem that, whenever there is introduced a person so necessary to tying the knot and to such an extent an accessory in untying it, no account should be made of her at the end of the story and she should not share in the common rejoicing. Hence it was necessary to prepare her a husband and to make him her lover, that he might be dearer to her and the end of the story might be more joyous, and—

what is still more important—that there might be more intrigue and continual enrichment of the subject with new incidents. This makes clear the necessity of the fourth agent and the second love. It is false then that the action of Charinus and Philumena does not depend on that of Pamphilus and Glycerium, and that the dependence is not necessary; consequently it is also true to life. On the defense of the *Andria* necessarily follows that of the *Pastor Fido*. . . . [31]

The Pastoral

Now having fully and sufficiently proved that the *Pastor Fido*, in so far as it is a story in which tragic and comic parts are mixed, and in so far as it contains two subjects grafted together in the manner of Terence, is a poem reasonable, properly proportioned, and capable of every artifice that pertains to a well-knit story, and finally that it is a true son of the art and legitimate according to the rules of Aristotle, it remains for us to make clear the scope of a pastoral drama and the word *pastoral*, which appears on the title page of the work. This word, either not being well understood or not very plainly interpreted, was the cause of scandal to some and to its defenders a cause of much praise, since they had an occasion and field sufficiently large to enable them to gather such new and curious things about life, nobility, and pastoral poetry that to neglect them will be a great fault, considering our labor and the end we have in view.

Pastoral Characters

In order to understand better, one must know that the ancient shepherds, in that first age the poets call golden, were not distinguished from persons of rank by the distinction which exists today between countrymen and citizens, since all were surely shepherds, but, as happens in the classes of society in a city, some were important, some poor, some rich, and, to speak in the manner of Aristotle, some better and others worse. Neither were they all servants of the citizens, for in that age there were no cities, but they ruled themselves and he who was of most worth was governor; but not for that reason was he who governed any the less a shepherd than was some other man who obeyed him, nor was it unfitting to say "the shepherd who is master," "the shepherd who rules the others;" nor because he was ruler did he cease to be shepherd, just as in an army he who is called a captain or a colonel does not for that reason cease to be a soldier. And so in all organizations it is found that the importance of one's duties changes the name but not the profession. In the same way in those early times the pastoral life was conducted; they were all shepherds, but some of them governed and others were governed; some took the flocks afield and others did not. [The author continues to develop the dignity possible to shepherds, referring to Aristotle's *Politics*, instancing Moses and King David, and quoting Basil the Great.]

The Pastoral Drama a New Form

It must always be recognized that though, in respect to the persons introduced, pastoral poetry[32] recognizes its origin in the eclogue and the satyr drama of the ancients, yet as to form and method it can be called something modern, since we have from antiquity no example of such a drama in either Greek or Latin. The first of the moderns who had the courage to do it and succeeded was Agostin de' Beccari, a respected citizen of Ferrara, to whom alone the world should assign the happy invention of such a poem. He saw certainly with excellent judgment, that the eclogue is not other than a short, and, as it were, selected discourse by two shepherds, in nothing unlike that scene that the Latins call dialogue, except in being united, independent, with its beginning and end in itself. Moreover Theocritus, a very famous Greek and master of the great Vergil, departing from the general practice of those who speak in compositions of the sort, made one of them not merely of many persons, but also on a subject more dramatic than is usual and notable for length beyond the others, with five interlocutors, some of whom speak without the intervention of the others and the others then enter in and take their parts; above all, he made use of that distinction of times and places and actions that is suitable to the dramatic poem. . . . Examining all these things, Beccari decided that he could much more easily do the same thing with the eclogue, since without doubt it has more conformity with pastoral than comedy and tragedy have with their own weak beginnings, for according to the testimony of Aristotle himself they were nothing else than rude and, as reason persuades us, rather short improvisations.[33] And so occupying this beautiful situation, not yet touched by a Greek or a Latin pen, and arranging many pastoral speeches within the single form of a dramatic story, and separating it into acts, with a beginning, middle, and end sufficient and properly proportioned, with a knot, with a reversal, with its setting, and with the other necessary parts—apart from the chorus, which was added by Tasso—he gave origin to a comedy, except that the persons introduced are shepherds; for this reason he called it a pastoral drama. In this way, if the life of citizens has its drama, which is called comedy, so, through the work of Beccari, pastoral life also has its drama, which is called pastoral alone, though composed in comic form. The invention has been acclaimed by the world with so great applause and so happily received as genuine on Parnassus that the first composers of our age, and especially Torquato Tasso, who undeniably was in his *Aminta* an imitator of Beccari, have had the honor not merely of giving their efforts to it but of obtaining from it, or at least hoping for, great renown and fame in poetry.

What Pastoral Is

Now this epithet of pastoral drama does not mean other than actions by the sort of men who are called shepherds. And since every dramatic action must be either comic or tragic or mixed, there is no doubt that the *Sacrificio* of Beccari is thrown into the form of a comedy, dealing with characters in a private station, causing laughter, and having a knot, a solution, and an end that are wholly comic. Yet he does not wish to call it comedy, but takes the generic rather than the specific name, and says *fable*[34] rather than *comedy* in order not to use the latter name improperly, for though it would be very suitable to the form and other parts of the work, yet because the action is without the city and does not represent citizens, it would be called a comedy with less than the usual reason. And then there is this adjective *pastoral*, which has with time acquired the force and meaning of a substantive, such that when one says *pastoral*, without anything further, drama dealing with shepherds is understood. This word is today so received and understood everywhere when it is alone, as "the pastoral of Beccari," "the pastoral of Tasso." And so too of all the others, though when their authors have joined it to *fable* they have availed themselves of it as an adjective signifying quality and not as a substantive signifying an action distinct from that story. The word *pastoral* can then be taken in two ways, either as an adjunct meaning pastoral quality, or as that particular substantive that today signifies action and story of shepherds, when it stands by itself. The word pastoral applied to the *Pastor Fido* should not be taken for a substantive signifying a fable separated from the tragicomedy, but for an adjective relating to tragicomedy, signifying that it differs from those that represent citizens by being composed of pastoral persons. The word *tragicomedy* shows us the quality of the drama and the word *pastoral* that of the persons who are presented in it, for since they could be citizens the poet wishes to show that they are shepherds. And since some of the shepherds are noble and others are not, the first produce the tragedy and the second the comedy, and both together the tragicomedy, which is pastoral because of the persons represented in it. There are not then in the *Pastor Fido* three dramas, one of private persons who cause a comic action, a second of men of high rank who sustain the tragic part, and a third of shepherds who compose the pastoral action; there is only one drama of pastoral characters, made up of mingled tragedy and comedy, but constructed in comic fashion; this poem is a unit. And truly who is stupid that he does not see that when this word *pastoral* is accompanied by *comedy* or *tragedy* or *tragicomedy*, it refers to a drama of shepherds in a form comic or tragic or tragicomic, and not to a play bringing in both citizens and shepherds? As *tragicomedy* refers to the quality of the story, so *pastoral* adds to it that of the persons, from which issues a single conception of this sort: an action of shepherds, composed of tragic and comic parts mixed together, and not three actions, one of private persons, the second of persons of rank, the third of shepherds; there is one action that at the same time is kingly and private and pastoral. Thus the parts that are kingly, private, and pastoral produce a single subject, just as the reasonable animal, in virtue of his specific differences, forms the single human being, and not an animal and a man distinct by nature and then joined together.

NOTES

1. The microcosm.
2. In England also in the Elizabethan period it was customary to speak of dramas as poems.
3. This is rather the Renaissance Aristotle than the Greek himself; see *Poetics*, II,

end. For example, the Latin grammarian Diomedes (fourth century A.D.) wrote "Comedy differs from tragedy in that heroes, generals, and kings are introduced into tragedy, into comedy humble and private persons" (Keil, *Grammatici Latini*, I, 488). Diomedes was known in the middle ages and there were several editions of his work in the sixteenth century.

4. In the *Heautontimorumenos*.

5. Cicero's saying is given in full by Thomas Heywood, *Apology for Actors*, Bk. III, sect. 3. Horace does not speak of the mirror in this connection; Guarini perhaps has in mind such remarks as that the characteristics of various ages are to be observed (*Art of Poetry*, 158 ff.).

6. The psychology and physiology of the time believed that in a healthy body the four humors—blood, phlegm, black bile, and yellow bile—were mixed in the right proportions.

7. A bold declaration of the superiority of the new Renaissance drama to that of antiquity. Tragicomedy is also defended by Tirso de Molina in *The Orchards of Toledo*. For a translated selection see Barrett H. Clark, *European Theories of the Drama*, p. 94.

8. *Poetics*, v. Guarini gives us a very Renaissance Aristotle, when he changes Aristotle's "men worse than the average" to private citizens as opposed to men of rank.

9. Guarini's words are still true. See *Poetics*, VI, 49b20.

10. Apparently a reference to Castelvetro on *Poetics*, VI, 116, 34.

11. *Ethics*, III, 6.

12. *Ethics*, IX, 10–11.

13. The Italian is "ridotti a vertuoso temperamento," which suggests "to temper and reduce them to just measure" in Milton's preface to the *Samson Agonistes*.

14. Apparently a reference to *poetics*, XIV.

15. Cf. in Milton's preface to *Samson Agonistes*, "sour against sour" etc. Milton and Guarini hold a homeopathic theory.

16. Aristotle discusses courage in *Ethics*, III, 6–9.

17. *Poetics*, XIII, 53a12.

18. *Poetics*, XIV, 53b1.

19. Lucretius, *On the Nature of Things*, IV, 11–17. The figure is used also by Tasso in the *Jerusalem Delivered*, I, 3. It admirably expresses a view of poetry important in the Renaissance. Cf. Sidney, *Defense of Poetry*, sect. 27; and Tasso, *Discourses on the Heroic Poem*, sect 2.

20. *Art of Poetry*, 220–4.

21. The reference is to the four elements, earth, air, fire, and water.

22. He here quotes from the *Art of Poetry*, 221–9.

23. Demetrius's work *On Style*, trans. by Rhys Roberts, may be found in the same volume of the Loeb Classics as Aristotle's *Poetics*. Milton speaks of the work as valuable in his tractate *Of Education*.

24. Donatus was a Latin grammarian of the middle of the fourth century A.D. For his comment on Terence see Thomas Heywood, *Apology for Actors*, sect. 3.

25. The lowest chord or note in the earliest Greek musical scale.

26. The highest note.

27. Giraldi, *Discourse on Tragedy and Comedy*, speaks of a "measured movement of the body that is called number."

28. Hermogenes, a Greek rhetorician of the second century A.D. He is mentioned by Milton in his tractate *Of Education* as one from whom rhetoric is to be learned.

29. The spirit of this passage appears in Milton's question whether he should follow the rules or nature (*Reason of Church Government*, sect. 1).

30. Guarini here abandons the highly moral position usual among Renaissance critics, who expected wickedness to be punished (see Sidney, *Defense of Poetry*, sect. 25).

31. Guarini proceeds to show that his play is constructed on the Terentian model. I feel that the analysis of the *Andria*, more accessible in English translation than the *Pastor Fido*, is sufficient to illustrate the idea. It should be recalled, however, that Guarini's drama, first published in 1590, was very popular in Italy and known in other countries. Perhaps the clearest sign of its influence in England is the *Faithful Shepherdess* of John Fletcher.

32. i.e., pastoral drama.

33. *Poetics*, IV.

34. In the Italian *favola*; the word in this connection, like the Latin *fabula*, means *play* or *drama*.

George Chapman
c. 1559–1634

George Chapman's translation of Homer's works is one of the enduring achievements of the Elizabethan age. Dryden writes of it: "The Earl of Mulgrave and Mr. Waller, two of the best judges of our age, have assured me they could never read over the translation of Chapman without incredible transport." Coleridge said that Chapman's Homer was as truly an original poem as *The Faerie Queen*.

Chapman grew up in a strongly Protestant family. He was perhaps a student at Oxford before going to London in 1585. By 1596 he had a successful comedy, *The Blind Beggar of Alexandria*, in the theatre. His best-known dramatic works are probably *Bussy d'Ambois* (1607) and *The Conspiracy and Tragedy of Charles Duke of Byron* (1608). Chapman maintained a stormy friendship with Ben Jonson, and the two of them were imprisoned in 1605 for *Eastward Ho!*, whose satirical remarks on the Scots reflected on the new King James. This friendship later came to an end, and among Chapman's unpublished manuscripts is a lengthy fragment of a violent invective against Jonson. It has been suggested that Chapman is the rival poet of Shakespeare's *Sonnets* and the character of Holofernes in *Love's Labour's Lost* may be a caricature of Chapman. He suffered throughout his life, it is assumed, from poverty and neglect, and was forced to renounce his claims to his mother's inheritance in 1599 in exchange for ready money.

Chapman uses the two prefaces to his translation of the *Iliad* (1598) to provide a ringing defense of Homer's position of authority in Western literature and to attack "soul-blind" Scaliger for his declaration that Vergil was the superior poet and that even Musaeus' *Hero and Leander* was a better poem. Nowhere, says Chapman, in his "all-countries-exploded filcheries" was Scaliger's "drossy spirit" more clearly revealed. Chapman consistently views poetry as a "divine infusion" and as a symbolic revelation of the profoundest truth. Thus he favors Homer because "Homer's poems were writ from a free fury, an absolute and full soul, Vergil's out of a courtly, laborious, and altogether imitatory spirit." Chapman also endorses the esoteric idea of poetry according to which the obscurity of poetry was necessary to conceal truth from the irreverent, a version of the Christianized Neoplatonism of the period.

On Homer originally appeared as a preface to Chapman's first translation of the *Iliad*. The version reprinted here is taken from *Elizabethan Critical Essays*, edited by G. Gregory Smith (Oxford University Press, 1904).

ON HOMER

To the Reader

I suppose you to be no meare reader, since you intend to reade Homer; and therefore wish I may walke free from their common obiections that can onelie reade. When my disorder is seene, that fower bookes are skipped (as a man would say) and yet the Poem continued according to the Greeke alphabet, viz. that for *Gamma* which is *Eta*, and that for *Delta* which is *Theta*, &c., then comes my knowne condemnation more greeuously then charitie would wish; especially with those that, hauing no eyes to peruse and iudge of the translation and whatsoeuer the maine matter deserues, will be glad to shew they see something, in finding fault with that forme; and peraduenture finde their queasie stomackes turnde at whatsoeuer is merited in the much laborde worke.

But to him that is more than a reader I write; and so consequentlie to him that will disdaine those easie obiections which euery speller may put together. The worth of a skilfull and worthy translator is to obserue the sentences, figures, and formes of speech proposed in his author, his true sence and height, and to adorne them with figures and formes of oration fitted to the originall in the same tongue to which they are translated: and these things I would gladlie haue made the questions of whatsoeuer my labors haue deserued; not slighted with the slight disorder of some bookes, which if I can put in as fit place hereafter without checke to your due vnderstanding and course of the Poet, then is their easie obiection answerde, that, I expect, wilbe drounde in the fome of their eager and emptie spleanes. For likelyhood of which habilitie I haue good authoritie that the bookes were not set together by Homer himselfe: Licurgus first bringing them out of Ionia in Greece as an entire Poeme, before whose time his verses were sung disseuered into many workes, one calde the battaile fought at the fleete, another Doloniades, another Agamemmon's fortitude, another the Catalogue of ships, another Patroclus death, another Hectors redemption, an other the funerall games, &c. All which are the titles of seuerall Iliades: and, if those were ordred by others, why may not I chalenge as much authority, reseruing the right of my president? But to omit what I can say further for reason to my present alteration, in the next edition, when they come out by the dosen, I will reserue the ancient and common receiued forme: in the meane time do me the encouragement to confer that which I haue translated with the same in Homer, and, according to the worth of that, let this first edition passe: so shall you do me but lawfull fauor, and make me take paines to giue you this Emperor of all wisedome (for so Plato will allow him) in your owne language, which will more honor it (if my part bee worthily discharged) then anything else can be translated. In the meane time peruse the pamphlet of errors in the impression, and helpe to point the rest with your iudgement; wherein, and in purchase of the whole seauen, if you be quicke and acceptiue, you shall in the next edition haue the life of

Homer, a table, a prettie comment, true printing, the due praise of your mother tongue aboue all others for Poesie: and such demonstratiue proofe of our english wits aboue beyond sea-muses (if we would vse them), that a proficient wit should be the better to heare it.

To the Most Honored Earle, Earle Marshall

Spondanus, one of the most desertfull Commentars of Homer, cals all sorts of all men learned to be iudicial beholders of this more than Artificiall and no lesse then Diuine Rapture, then which nothing can be imagined more full of soule and humaine extraction: for what is here prefigurde by our miraculous Artist but the vniuersall world, which, being so spatious and almost vnmeasurable, one circlet of a Shield representes and imbraceth? In it heauen turnes, the starres shine, the earth is enflowered, the sea swelles and rageth, Cities are built, one in the happinesse and sweetnesse of peace, the other in open warre & the terrors of ambush, &c.: and all these so liuely proposde, as not without reason many in times past haue belieued that all these thinges haue in them a kind of voluntarie motion, euen as those Tripods of Vulcan and that Dedalian Venus *autokinētos*. Nor can I be resolu'd that their opinions be sufficiently refuted by Aristonicus, for so are all things here described by our diuinest Poet as if they consisted not of hard and solid mettals, but of a truely liuing and mouing soule. The ground of his inuention he shews out of Eustathius, intending by the Orbiguitie of the Shield the roundnesse of the world, by the foure mettalles the foure elementes, viz. by gold fire, by brasse earth, for the hardnes, by Tinne water, for the softnes and inclination to fluxure, by siluer Aire, for the grosnes & obscuritie of the mettal before it be refind. That which he calls *antyga triplaka marmareēn* he vnderstands the Zodiack, which is said to be triple for the latitude it contains, & shining by reason of the perpetual course of the Sun made in that circle, by *argyreon telamōna* the Axletree, about which heauen hath his motion, &c. Nor do I deny (saith Spondanus) Eneas arms to be forged with an exceeding height of wit by Virgil, but comparde with these of Homer they are nothing. And this is it (most honorde) that maketh me thus sodainely translate this Shield of Achilles, for since my publication of the other seuen bookes comparison hath beene made between Virgill and Homer; who can be comparde in nothing with more decysall & cutting of all argument then in these two Shieldes. And whosoeuer shall reade Homer throughly and worthily will know the question comes from a superficiall and too vnripe a reader; for Homers Poems were writ from a free furie, an absolute & full soule, Virgils out of a courtly, laborious, and altogether imitatorie spirit: not a Simile hee hath but is Homers: not an inuention, person, or disposition, but is wholly or originally built vpon Homericall foundations, and in many places hath the verie wordes Homer vseth: besides, where Virgill hath had no more plentifull and liberall a wit then to frame twelue imperfect bookes of the troubles and trauailes of Æneas, Homer hath of as little subiect finisht eight & fortie perfect. And that the triuiall obiection may be answerd, that not the number of bookes but the nature and excellence of the worke commends it—all Homers bookes are such as haue beene presidents euer since of all sortes of Poems; imitating none, nor euer worthily imitated of any. Yet would I not be thought so ill created as to bee a malicious detracter of so admired a Poet as Virgill, but a true iustifer of Homer, who must not bee read for a few lynes with leaues turned ouer caprichiously in dismembred fractions, but throughout, the whole drift, weight, & height of his workes set before the apprensiue eyes of his iudge: the maiestie he enthrones and the spirit he infuseth into the scope of his worke so farre outshining Virgill, that his skirmishes are but meere scramblings of boyes to Homers; the silken body of Virgils muse curiously drest in guilt and embrodered siluer, but Homers in plaine massie and vnaulued gold; not onely all learning, gouernment, and wisedome being deduc't as from a bottomlesse fountaine from him, but all wit, elegancie, disposition, and iudgement. *Homēros prōtos didaskalos kai hēgemōn*, &c,; Homer (saith Plato) was the Prince and maister of all prayses and vertues, the Emperour of wise men, an host of men against any deprauer in any principle he held. All the ancient and lately learned haue had him in equall estimation. And for anie to be now contrarilie affected, it must needes proceed from a meere wantonnesse of witte, an Idle vnthriftie spirit, wilfull because they may choose whether they will think otherwise or not, & haue power and fortune enough to liue like true men without truth; or els they must presume of puritanicall inspiration, to haue that with delicacie & squemishnes, which others with as good means, ten times more time, and ten thousand times more labour could neuer conceiue. But some will conuey their imperfections vnder his Greeke Shield, and from thence bestowe bitter arrowes against the traduction, affirming their want of admiration grows from defect of our language, not able to expresse the coppie and elegancie of the originall. But this easie and traditionall pretext hides them not enough: for how full of height and roundnesse soeuer Greeke be aboue English, yet is there no depth of conceipt triumphing in it, but, as in a meere admirer it may bee imagined, so in a sufficient translator it may be exprest. And Homer that hath his chiefe holinesse of estimation for matter and instruction would scorne to haue his supreame worthinesse glosing in his courtshippe and priuiledge of tongue. And if Italian, French, & Spanish haue not made it daintie, nor thought it any presumption to turne him into their languages, but a fit and honorable labour and (in respect of their countries profit and their poesies credit) almost necessarie, what curious, proud, and poore shamefastnesse should let an English muse to traduce him, when the language she workes withall is more conformable, fluent, and expressiue; which I would your Lordship would commaunde mee to proue against all our whippers of their owne complement in their countries dialect.

O what peeuish ingratitude and most vnreasonable scorne of our selues we commit to bee so extrauagant and forreignely witted to honour and imitate that in a strange tongue which wee condemne and contemne in our natiue! For if the substance of the Poet will be exprest, and his sentence and sence rendred with truth and elocution, hee that takes iudiciall pleasure in him in Greeke cannot beare so rough a browe to him in English, to entombe his acceptance in austeritie.

But thou soule-blind Scalliger, that neuer hadst anything but place, time, and termes to paint thy proficiencie in learning, nor euer writest any thing of thine owne impotent braine but thy onely impalsied diminuation of Homer (which I may sweare was the absolute inspiration of thine owne ridiculous Genius), neuer didst thou more palpably damn thy drossy spirit in al thy all-countries-exploded filcheries, which are so grossely illiterate that no man will vouchsafe their refutation, then in thy sencelesse reprehensions of Homer, whose spirit flew asmuch aboue thy groueling capacitie as heauen moues aboue Barathrum. But as none will vouchsafe repetition nor answere of thy other vnmanly fooleries, no more will I of these, my Epistle being too tedious to your Lo. besides, and no mans iudgement seruing better (if your high affaires could admit their deligent perusall) then your Lo. to refute and reiect him. But alas Homer is not now to bee lift vp by my weake arme, more then he is now deprest by more feeble oppositions. If any feele not their conceiptes so rauisht with the eminent beauties of his ascentiall muse, as the greatest men of all sorts and of all ages haue beene. Their most modest course is (vnlesse they will be powerfully insolent) to ascribe the defect to their apprehension, because they read him but sleightly, not in his surmised frugalitie of obiect, that really and most feastfully powres out himselfe in right diuine occasion. But the chiefe and vnanswerable meane to his generall and iust acceptance must be your Lo. high and of all men expected president, without which hee must, like a poore snayle, pull in his English hornes, that out of all other languages (in regard of the countries affection, and royaltie of his Patrones) hath appeared like an Angell from a clowde, or the world out of Chaos, when no language can make comparison of him with ours if he be worthily conuerted; wherein before he should haue beene borne so lame and defectiue, as the French midwife hath brought him forth, he had neuer made question how your Lo. would accept him: and yet haue two of their Kings embraced him as a wealthy ornament to their studies, and the main battayle of their armies.

If then your bountie would do me but the grace to conferre my vnhappie labours with theirs so successful & commended (your iudgement seruing you much better then your leysure, & yet your leisure in thinges honourable being to bee inforced by your iudgement), no malitious & dishonorable whisperer that comes armed with an army of authority and state against harmeles & armeles vertue could wrest your wonted impression so much from it self to reiect (with imitation of tiranous contempt) any affection so zealous & able in this kind to honor your estate as mine. Onely kings & princes haue been Homers Patrones, amongst whom Ptolomie wold say, he that had sleight handes to entertayne Homer had as sleight braines to rule his common wealth. And an vsuall seueritie he vsed, but a most rationall (how precise and ridiculous soeuer it may seeme to men made of ridiculous matter), that, in reuerence of the pietie and perfect humanitie he taught, whosoeuer writ or committed any proud detraction against Homer (as euen so much a man wanted not his malitious deprauers), hee put him with torments to extreamest death. O high and magically raysed prospect, from whence a true eye may see meanes to the absolute redresse, or much to be wished extenuation, of all the vnmanly degeneracies now tyranysing amongst vs! For if that which teacheth happinesse and hath vnpainefull corosiues in it (being entertayned and obserued) to eate out the hart of that raging vlcer, which like a Lernean Fen of corruption furnaceth the vniuersall sighes and complaintes of this transposed world, were seriously and as with armed garrisons defended and hartned, that which engenders & disperseth that wilfull pestilence would bee purged and extirpate; but that which teacheth being ouerturned, that which is taught is consequently subiect to euersion; and if the honour, happinesse, and perseruation of true humanitie consist in obseruing the lawes fit for mans dignitie, and that the elaborate prescription of those lawes must of necessitie be authorised, fauoured, and defended before any obseruations can succeed, is it vnreasonable to punish the contempt of that mouing prescription with one mans death, when at the heeles of it followes common neglect of obseruation, and in the necke of it an vniuersall ruine? This my Lord I enforce only to interrupt in others that may reade this vnsauorie stuffe, the too open mouthed damnation of royall & vertuous Ptolomies seueritie. For to digest, transforme, and sweat a man's soule into rules and attractions to societie, such as are fashioned and tempered with her exact and long laborde contention of studie, in which she tosseth with her impertiall discourse before her all cause of fantasticall obiections and reproofes, and without which she were as wise as the greatest number of detractors that shall presume to censure her, and yet by their flash and insolent castigations to bee sleighted and turnde ouer their miserably vaine tongues in an instant, is an iniurie worthy no lesse penaltie then Ptolomie inflicted. To take away the heeles of which running prophanation, I hope your Lo. honourable countenance will be as the Vnicorns horne, to leade the way to English Homers yet poysoned fountaine: for till that fauour be vouchsafed, the herde will neuer drinke, since the venemous galles of their fellowes haue infected it, whom alas I pittie. Thus confidently affirming your name and dignities shall neuer bee more honored in a poore booke then in English Homer, I cease to afflict your Lordshippe with my tedious dedicatories, and to still sacred Homers spirit through a language so fitte and so fauourles; humbly presenting your Achilleian vertues with Achilles Shield; wishing as it is much more admirable and diuine, so it were as many times more rich then the Shild the Cardinall pawned at Anwerp.

By him that wisheth all the degrees of iudgement, and honour, to attend your deserts to the highest.

GEORGE CHAPMAN

TO THE UNDERSTANDER

You are not euery bodie; to you (as to one of my very few friends) I may be bold to vtter my minde; nor is it more empaire to an honest and absolute mans sufficiencie to haue few friendes then to an Homericall Poeme to haue few commenders, for neyther doe common dispositions keepe fitte or plausible consort with iudiciall and simple honestie, nor are idle capacities comprehensible of an elaborate Poeme. My Epistle dedicatorie before my seuen bookes is accounted darke and too much laboured: for the darkenes there is nothing good or bad, hard or softe, darke or perspicuous but in respect, & in respect of mens light, sleight, or enuious perusalles (to whose loose capacities any worke worthily composde is knit with a riddle); & that the stile is materiall, flowing & not ranke, it may perhaps seeme darke to ranke riders or readers that haue no more soules then burbolts: but to your comprehension, & in it selfe, I know it is not. For the affected labour bestowed in it, I protest two morninges both ended it and the Readers Epistle: but the truth is, my desire & strange disposition in all thinges I write is to set downe vncommon and most profitable coherents for the time, yet further remoued from abhorde affectation then from the most popular and cold disgestion. And I euer imagine that as Italian & French Poems to our studious linguistes win much of their discountryed affection, as well because the vnderstanding of forreigne tongues is sweete to their apprehension as that the matter & inuention is pleasing, so my farre fetcht and, as it were, beyond sea manner of writing, if they would take as much paines for their poore countrimen as for a proud stranger when they once vnderstand it, should be much more gracious to their choice conceiptes then a discourse that fals naked before them, and hath nothing but what mixeth it selfe with ordinarie table talke. For my varietie of new wordes, I haue none Inckepot I am sure you know, but such as I giue pasport with such authoritie, so significant and not ill sounding, that if my countrey language were an usurer, or a man of this age speaking it, hee would thanke mee for enriching him. Why, alas, will my young mayster the reader affect nothing common, and yet like nothing extraordinarie? Swaggering is a new worde amongst them, and rounde headed custome giues it priuiledge with much imitation, being created as it were by a naturall Prosopopeia without etimologie or deriuation; and why may not an elegancie authentically deriued, & as I may say of the vpper house, bee entertayned as well in their lower consultation with authoritie of Arte as their owne forgeries lickt up by nature? All tongues haue inricht themselues from their originall (onely the Hebrew & Greeke which are not spoken amongst vs) with good neighbourly borrowing, and as with infusion of fresh ayre and nourishment of newe blood in their still growing bodies, & why may not ours? Chaucer (by whom we will needes authorise our true english) had more newe wordes for his time then any man needes to deuise now. And therefore for currant wits to crie from standing braines, like a broode of Frogs from a ditch, to haue the ceaselesse flowing riuer of our tongue turnde into their Frogpoole, is a song farre from their arrogation of sweetnes, & a sin wold soone bring the plague of barbarisme amongst vs; which in faith needes not bee hastned with defences of his ignorant furtherers, since it comes with mealemouth'd toleration too sauagely vpon vs. To be short, since I had the reward of my labours in their consummation, and the chiefe pleasure of them in mine owne profit, no young preiudicate or castigatorie braine hath reason to thinke I stande trembling vnder the ayry stroke of his feuerie censure, or that I did euer expect any flowing applause from his drie fingers; but the satisfaction and delight that might probably redound to euerie true louer of vertue I set in the seat of mine owne profit and contentment; and if there be any one in whome this successe is enflowred, a few sprigges of it shall bee my garland. Since then this neuer equald Poet is to bee vnderstood, and so full of gouernment and direction to all estates, sterne anger and the affrights of warre bearing the mayne face of his subiect, soldiers shall neuer spende their idle howres more profitablie then with his studious and industrious perusall; in whose honors his deserts are infinite. Counsellors haue neuer better oracles then his lines: fathers haue no morales so profitable for their children as his counsailes; nor shal they euer giue them more honord iniunctions then to learne Homer without book, that, being continually conuersant in him, his height may descend to their capacities, and his substance proue their worthiest riches. Husbands, wiues, louers, friends, and allies hauing in him mirrors for all their duties; all sortes of which concourse and societie in other more happy ages haue in steed of sonnets & lasciuious ballades sung his Iliades. Let the length of the verse neuer discourage your endeuours; for talke our quidditicall Italianistes of what proportion soeuer their strooting lips affect, vnlesse it be in these coopplets into which I haue hastely translated this Shield, they shall neuer doe Homer so much right, in any octaues, canzons, canzonets, or with whatsoeuer fustian Epigraphes they shall entitle their measures. Onely the extreame false printing troubles my conscience, for feare of your deserued discouragement in the empaire of our Poets sweetnes; whose generall diuinitie of spirit, clad in my willing labours (enuious of none nor detracting any), I commit to your good nature and solid capacitie.

Francis Meres
1565–1647

Francis Meres was born in Lincolnshire in 1565. Very little is known of his life apart from the facts that he studied at Pembroke College, Cambridge, and subsequently served as rector of Wing Church in Rutland. He is remembered chiefly on the basis of his *Palladis Tamia*, a discursive collection of apothegms which Meres published in 1598. The *Palladis Tamia* (*Wit's Treasury*) is most interesting for Meres' appraisal of English poetry in the section entitled "A Comparative Discourse of our English Poets with the Greek, Latin, and Italian Poets," in which he discovers a corresponding classical poet for each of the English poets. He calls Chaucer, for instance, "the God of English poets" and compares him with Homer. It also contains the earliest recorded praise of Shakespeare as "most excellent in both kings [comedy and tragedy] for the stage" and provides a list of the plays he had produced by 1598. It is thus highly interesting as an example of Elizabethan canon formation.

The selections from the *Palladis Tamia* are taken from *Elizabethan Critical Essays*, edited by G. Gregory Smith (Oxford University Press, 1904).

FROM
PALLADIS TAMIA
POETRY

As in a Vine clusters of grapes are often hidde vnder the broade and spacious leaues: so in deepe conceited and well couched poems, figures and fables, many things verie profitable to be knowne, do passe by a yong scholler. *Plut.*

As, according to Philoxenus, that flesh is most sweete which is no flesh, and those the delectablest fishes which are no fishes: so that Poetrie dooth most delight which is mit with Poetrie. *Plutarchus in Commentario, quomodo adolescens Poetas audire debet.*

As a Bee gathereth the sweetest and mildest honie from the bitterest flowers and sharpest thornes: so some profite may bee extracted out of obscene and wanton Poems and fables. *idem.*

Albeit many be drunke with wine, yet the Vines are not to bee cut downe, as Lycurgus did, but Welles and Fountaines are to be digged neare vnto them: so although many abuse poetrie, yet it is not to bee banished, but discretion is to be vsed, that it may bee made holesome. *idem.*

As Mandrake growing neare Vines doth make the wine more mild: so philosophie bordering vppon poetrie dooth make the knowledge of it more moderate. *idem.*

As poyson mixt with meate is verie deadlie: so lasciuiousnesse and petulancie in poetrie mixt with profitable and pleasing matters is very pestilent. *idem.*

As we are delighted in deformed creatures artificallye painted: so in poetrie, which is a liuely adumbration of things, euil matters ingeniously contriued do delight.

As Phisitians vse for medicine the feete and wings of the flies Cantharides, which flies are deadly poyson: so we may gather out of the same poem that may quell the hurtfull venome of it; for poets do alwaies mingle somewhat in their Poems, whereby they intimate that they condemne what they declare. *idem.*

As our breath doth make a shiller sound being sent through the narrow channell of a Trumpet then if it be diffused abroad into the open aire: so the well knitte and succinct combination of a Poem dooth make our meaning better knowen and discerned then if it were deliuered at random in prose. *Seneca.*

As he that drinkes of the Well Clitorius doth abhorre wine: so they that haue once tasted of poetry cannot away with the study of philosophie. After the same maner holdes the contrarie.

As the Anabaptists abhorre the liberall artes and humane sciences: so puritanes and precisians detest poetrie and poems.

As eloquence hath found many preachers & oratours worthy fauourers of her in the English tongue: so her sister poetry hath found the like welcome and entertainment giuen her by our English poets, which makes our language so gorgeous & delectable among vs.

As Rubarbe and sugarcandie are pleasant & profitable: so in poetry ther is sweetnes and goodness. *M. John Haring.*, in his *Apologie for Poetry* before his translated *Ariosto*.

Many cockney and wanton women ar often sicke, but in faith they cannot tell where: so the name of poetrie is odious to some, but neither his cause nor effects, neither the summe that contains him nor the particularities descending from him, giue any fast handle to their carping dispraise. *Sir Philip Sidney*, in his *Apologie for Poetry*.

POETS

As some do vse an Amethist in compotation agaynst drunkennes: so certain precepts are to be vsed in hearing and reading of poets, least they infect the mind. *Plut. & Plin.* lib. 37. cap. 9.

As in those places where many holsome hearbes doe growe there also growes many poysonfull weedes: so in Poets there are many excellent things and many pestilent matters. *Plut.*

As Simonides sayde that the Thessalians were more blockish then that they could be deceiued of him: so the riper and pregnanter the wit is the sooner it is corrupted of Poets. *idem.*

As Cato when he was a scholler woulde not beleeue his maister, except hee rendered a reason of what he taught him: so wee are not to beleeue Poets in all that they write or say, except they yeelde a reason. *idem.*

As in the same pasture the Bee seaseth on the flower, the Goate grazeth on the shrub, the swine on the root, & Oxen, Kine, & Horses on the grasse: so in Poets one seeketh for historie, an other for ornament of speech, another for proofe, & an other for precepts of good life. *idem.*

As they that come verie suddainlie out of a very darke place are greatly troubled, except by little & little they be accustomed to the light: so, in reading of Poets, the opinions of Phylosophers are to bee sowne in the mindes of young schollers, least many diuersities of doctrines doe afterwardes distract their mindes. *idem.*

As in the portraiture of murder or incest we praise the Art of him that drewe it, but we detest the thing it selfe: so in lasciuious Poets let vs imitate their elocution but execrate their wantonnes. *idem.*

Some thinges that are not excellent of themselues are good for some, bicause they are meet for them: so some things are commended in Poets which are fit and correspondent for the persons they speak of, although in themselues they bee filthy and not to be spoken; As lame Demonides wished that the shoes that were stolne from him might fit his feet that had stoln them. *idem.*

As that ship is endaungered where all leane to one side, but is in safetie one leaning one way and another another way: so the dissensions of Poets among themselues doth make them that they lesse infect their readers. And for this purpose our Satyrists Hall, the Author of *Pigmalion's Image* and *Certaine Satyres*, Rankins, and such others are very profitable.

As a Bee doth gather the iuice of honie from flowres, whereas others are onely delighted with the colour and smel: so a Philosopher findeth that among Poets which is profitable for good life, when as others are tickled only with pleasure. *Plut.*

As wee are delighted in the picture of a viper or a spider artificially enclosed within a precious iewell: so Poets do delight vs in the learned & cunning depainting of vices.

As some are delighted in counterfet wines confected of fruites, not that they refresh the hart but that they make drunke; so some are delighted in Poets only for their obscenity, neuer respecting their eloquence, good grace, or learning.

As Emperors, Kings, & princes haue in their handes authority to dignifie or disgrace their nobles, attendants, subiects, & vassals: so Poets haue the whole power in their handes to make men either immortally famous for their valiant exploites and vertuous exercises, or perpetually infamous for their vicious liues.

As *God giueth* life vnto man: so a Poet giueth ornament vnto it.

As the Greeke and Latine Poets haue wonne immortall credit to their natiue speech, beeing encouraged and graced by liberall patrones and bountifull Benefactors: so our famous and learned Lawreat masters of England would entitle our English to far greater admired excellency if either the Emperor Augustus, or Octauia his sister, or noble Mecænas were aliue to rewarde and countenaunce them; or if our witty Comedians and stately Tragedians (the glorious and goodlie representers of all fine witte, glorified phrase, and queint action) bee still supported and vphelde, by which meanes for lacke of Patrones (O ingratefull and damned age) our Poets are soly or chiefly maintained, countenaunced, and patronized.

In the infancy of Greece they that handled in the audience of the people graue and necessary matters were called wise men or eloquent men, which they ment by Vates: so the rest, which sang of loue matters, or other lighter deuises alluring vnto pleasure and delight, were called Poets or makers.

As the holy Prophets and sanctified apostles could neuer haue foretold nor spoken of such supernaturall matters vnlesse they had bin inspired of God: so Cicero in his Tusculane questions is of that minde, that a Poet cannot expresse verses aboundantly, sufficiently, and fully, neither his eloquence can flow pleasantly, or his wordes sound well and plenteously, without celestiall instruction; which Poets themselues do very often and gladly witnes of themselues, as namely Ouid in 6 Fast.

Est Deus in nobis; agitante calescimus illo. &c.

And our famous English Poet Spenser, who in his Sheepeheards Calender, lamenting the decay of Poetry at these dayes, saith most sweetly to the same,

> 'Then make the wings of thine aspiring wit,
> And whence thou camest fly backe to heauen apace.' &c.

As a long gowne maketh not an Aduocate, although a gowne be a fit ornament for him: so riming nor versing maketh a Poet, albeit the Senate of

Poets hath chosen verse as their fittest rayment; but it is the faining notable images of vertues, vices, or what else, with that delightfull teaching, which must bee the right describing note to knowe a Poet by. *Sir Philip Sidney* in his *Apology for Poetry.*

A COMPARATIVE DISCOURSE OF OUR ENGLISH POETS WITH THE GREEK, LATIN, AND ITALIAN POETS.

As Greece had three poets of great antiquity, Orpheus, Linus, and Musæus, and Italy other three auncient poets, Liuius Andronicus, Ennius, and Plautus: so hath England three auncient poets, Chaucer, Gower, and Lydgate.

As Homer is reputed the Prince of Greek poets, and Petrarch of Italian poets: so Chaucer is accounted the God of English poets.

As Homer was the first that adorned the Greek tongue with true quantity: so *Piers Plowman* was the first that obserued the true quantitie of our verse without the curiositie of rime.

Ouid writ a Chronicle from the beginning of the world to his own time, that is, to the raign of Augustus the Emperor: so hath Harding the Chronicler (after his maner of old harsh riming) from Adam to his time, that is, to the raigne of King Edward the fourth.

As Sotades Maronites, the Iambicke Poet, gaue himself wholy to write impure and lasciuious things: so Skelton (I know not for what great worthines surnamed the Poet Laureat) applied his wit to scurrilities and ridiculous matters; such among the Greeks were called *Pantomimi*, with vs, buffons.

As Consaluo Periz, that excellent learned man, and Secretary to King Philip of Spayne, in translating the 'Ulysses' of Homer out of Greeke into Spanish, hath by good iudgement auoided the faulte of ryming, although not fully hit perfect and true versifying: so hath Henrie Howarde, that true and noble Earle of Surrey, in translating the fourth book of Virgil's *Æneas*; whom Michael Drayton in his *England's heroycall Epistles* hath eternized for an *Epistle to his fair Geraldine.*

As these Neoterickes, Iouianus Pontanus, Politianus, Marullus Tarchaniota, the two Strozæ, the father and the son, Palingenius, Mantuanus, Philelphus, Quintianus Stoa, and Germanus Brixius have obtained renown and good place among the ancient Latine poets: so also these Englishmen, being Latine poets, Gualter Haddon, Nicholas Car, Gabriel Haruey, Christopher Ocland, Thomas Newton with his *Leyland*, Thomas Watson, Thomas Campion, Brunswerd, and Willey haue attained good report and honourable aduancement in the Latin empyre.

As the Greeke tongue is made famous and eloquent by Homer, Hesiod, Euripedes, Æschylus, Sophocles, Pindarus, Phocylides, and Aristophanes; and the Latine tongue by Virgill, Ouid, Horace, Silius Italicus, Lucanus, Lucretius, Ausonius, and Claudianus: so the English tongue is mightily enriched and gorgeously inuested in rare ornaments and resplendent abiliments by Sir Philip

Sydney, Spencer, Daniel, Drayton, Warner, Shakespeare, Marlow, and Chapman.

As Xenophon, who did imitate so excellently as to giue vs *effigiem insti imperii*, 'the portraiture of a iust empyre,' vnder the name of Cyrus (as Cicero saieth of him), made therein an absolute heroicall poem; and as Heliodorus writ in prose his sugred inuention of that picture of Loue in *Theagines and Cariclea*; and yet both excellent admired poets: so Sir Philip Sidney writ his immortal poem, *The Countess of Pembrooke's Arcadia* in Prose; and yet our rarest Poet.

As Sextus Propertius said, *Nescio quid magis nascitur Iliade*: so I say of Spencer's *Fairy Queene*, I knowe not what more excellent or exquisite Poem may be written.

As Achilles had the aduantage of Hector, because it was his fortune to bee extolled and renowned by the heauenly verse of Homer: so Spenser's *Eliza, the Fairy Queen*, hath the aduantage of all the Queenes in the worlde, to be eternized by so diuine a Poet.

As Theocritus is famoused for his *Idyllia* in Greeke, and Virgill for his *Eclogs* in Latine: so Spencer their imitator in his *Shepheardes Calender* is renowned for the like argument, and honoured for fine Poeticall inuention and most exquisit wit.

As Parthenius Nicæus excellently sung the praises of his *Arete*: so Daniel hath diuinely sonetted the matchlesse beauty of his *Delia*.

As euery one mourneth when hee heareth of the lamentable plangors of Thracian Orpheus for his dearest *Euridice*: so euery one passionateth when he readeth the afflicted death of Daniel's distressed *Rosamond*.

As Lucan hath mournefully depainted the ciuil wars of Pompey and Cæsar: so hath Daniel the civill wars of Yorke and Lancaster, and Drayton the civill wars of Edward the second and the Barons.

As Virgil doth imitate Catullus in the like matter of *Ariadne* for his story of Queene *Dido*: so Michael Drayton doth imitate Ouid in his *England's Heroicall Epistles*.

As Sophocles was called a Bee for the sweetnes of his tongue: so in Charles Fitz-Iefferies *Drake* Drayton is termed 'golden-mouth'd' for the purity and pretiousnesse of his stile and phrase.

As Accius, M. Atilius, and Milithus were called *Tragaediographi*, because they writ tragedies: so may wee truly terme Michael Drayton *Tragaediographus* for his passionate penning the downfals of valiant Robert of Normandy, chast Matilda, and great Gaueston.

As Joan. Honterus, in Latine verse, writ three bookes of Cosmography, with geographicall tables: so Michael Drayton is now in penning, in English verse, a Poem called *Poly-olbion*, Geographicall and Hydrographicall of all the forests, woods, mountaines, fountaines, riuers, lakes, flouds, bathes, and springs that be in England.

As Aulus Persius Flaccus is reported among al writers to be of an honest life and vpright conuersation: so Michael Drayton, *quem toties honoris et amoris causa nomino*, among schollers, souldiours, Poets, and all sorts of people is helde for a man of vertuous disposition, honest conuersation, and well gouerned cariage; which is almost miraculous among good wits in these declining and corrupt times, when there is nothing but rogery in villanous man, and when cheating and craftines is counted the cleanest wit, and soundest wisedome.

As Decius Ausonius Gallus, *in libris Fastorum*, penned the occurrences of the world from the first creation of it to his time, that is, to the raigne of the Emperor Gratian: so Warner, in his absolute *Albion's Englande*, hath most admirably penned the historie of his own country from Noah to his time, that is to the raigne of Queen Elizabeth. I haue heard him termd of the best wits of both our Vniversities our English Homer.

As Euripedes is the most sententious among the Greek Poets: so is Warner among our English Poets. As the soule of Euphorbus was thought to liue in Pythagoras: so the sweete wittie soule of Ouid liues in mellifluous and honytongued Shakespeare, witnes his *Venus and Adonis*, his *Lucrece*, his surgred *Sonnets* among his priuate friends, &c.

As Plautus and Seneca are accounted the best for Comedy and Tragedy among the Latines: so Shakespeare among the English is the most excellent in both kinds for the stage. For Comedy, witnes his *Gentlemen of Verona*, his *Errors*, his *Loue Labors Lost*, his *Loue Labours Wonne*, his *Midsummers Night Dreame*, and his *Merchant of Venice*; For Tragedy, his *Richard the 2*, *Richard the 3*, *Henry the 4*, *King Iohn*, *Titus Adronicus*, and his *Romeo and Iuliet*.

As Epius Stolo said that the Muses would speake with Plautus tongue if they would speak Latin: so I say that the Muses would speake with Shakespeares fine filed phrase if they would speak English.

As Musæus, who wrote the loue of Hero and Leander, had two excellent schollers, Thamaras and Hercules: so hath he in England two excellent poets, imitators of him in the same argument and subiect, Christopher Marlow and George Chapman.

As Ouid saith of his work,

> *Iamque opus exegi, quod nec Iouis ira, nec ignis,*
> *Nec poterit ferrum, nec edax abolere vetustas;*

and as Horace saith of his,

> *Exegi monumentum aere perennius*
> *Regalique situ pyramidum altius,*
> *Quod non imber edax, non Aquilo impotens*
> *Possit diruere, aut innumerabilis*
> *Annorum series, et fuga temporum:*

so I say seuerally of Sir Philip Sidney's, Spenser's, Daniel's, Drayton's, Shakespeare's, and Warner's workes,

> *Non Iovis ira, imbres, Mars, ferrum, flamma, senectus,*
> *Hoc opus vnda, lues, turbo, venena ruent.*
> *Et quanquam ad pulcherrimum hoc opus euertendum,*
>   *tres illi Dii conspirabunt, Chronus, Vulcanus, et Pater*

ipse gentis.
Non tamen annorum series, non flamma, nec ensis;
Aeternum potuit hoc abolere Decus.

As Italy had Dante, Boccace, Petrarch, Tasso, Celiano, and Aristo: so England had Matthew Roydon, Thomas Atchelow, Thomas Watson, Thomas Kid, Robert Greene, and George Peele.

As there are eight famous and chiefe languages, Hebrew, Greek, Latine, Syriack, Arabicke, Italian, Spanish, and French: so there are eight notable seuerall kindes of Poets, Heroicke, Lyricke, Tragicke, Comicke, Satiricke, Iambicke, Elegiacke, and Pastoral.

As Homer and Virgil among the Greeks and Latines are the chiefe Heroick Poets: so Spencer and Warner be our chiefe heroicall Makers.

As Pindarus, Anacreon, and Callimachus among the Greekes, and Horace and Catullus among the Latines are the best Lyrick poets: so in this faculty the best among our poets are Spencer (who excelleth in all kinds), Daniel, Drayton, Shakespeare, Bretton.

As these Tragicke Poets flourished in Greece, Æschylus, Euripedes, Sophocles, Alexander Ætolus, Achæus Erithrioeus, Astydamas Atheniensis, Apollodorus Tarsensis, Nicomachus Phrygius, Thespis Atticus, and Timon Apolloniates; and these among the Latines, Accius, M. Atilius, Pompon[i]us Secundus, and Seneca: so these are our best for Tragedie, The Lorde Buckhurst, Doctor Leg of Cambridge, Doctor Edes of Oxford, Master Edward Ferris, the author of the *Mirror for Magistrates*, Marlow, Peele, Watson, Kid, Shakespeare, Drayton, Chapman, Decker, and Beniamin Iohnson.

As M. Anneus Lucanus writ two excellent tragedies, one called *Medea*, the other *De incendio Troiae cum Priami calamitate*: so Doctor Leg hath penned two famous tragedies, the one of *Richard the 3*, the other of *The Destruction of Ierusalem*.

The best Poets of Comedy among the Greeks are these, Menander, Aristophanes, Eupolis Atheniensis, Alexis Terius, Nicostratus, Amipsias Atheniensis, Anaxandrides Rhodius, Aristonymus, Archippus Atheniensis, and Callias Atheniensis; and among the Latines, Plautus, Terence, Næuius, Sextus Turpilius, Licinius Imbrex, and Virgilius Romanus: so the best for Comedy amongst vs bee Edward, Earle of Oxforde, Doctor Gager of Oxforde, Master Rowley, once a rare scholler of learned Pembrooke Hall in Cambridge, Maister Edwardes, one of Her Maiesties Chappell, eloquent and wittie Iohn Lilly, Lodge, Gascoyne, Greene, Shakespeare, Thomas Nash, Thomas Heywood, Anthony Mundye, our best plotter, Chapman, Porter, Wilson, Hathway, and Henry Chettle.

As Horace, Lucilius, Iuuenall, Persius, and Lucullus are the best for Satyre among the Latines: so with vs, in the same faculty, these are chiefe, *Piers Plowman*, Lodge, Hall of Imanuel Colledge in Cambridge, the Author of *Pigmalion's Image* and certain Satyrs, the Author of *Skialetheia*.

Among the Greekes I will name but two for Imabicks, ArchilochusParius and Hipponax Ephesius: so amongst vs I name but two Iambical Poets, Gabriel Haruey and Richard Stanyhurst, bicause I haue seene no mo in this kind.

As these are famous among the Greeks for Elegie, Melanthus, Mymnerus Colophonius, Olympius Mysius, Parthenius Nicæus, Philetas Cous, Theogenes Megarensis, and Pigres Halicarnassæus; and these among the Latines, Mæcenas, Ouid, Tibullus, Properitus, C. Valgius, Cassius Seuerus, and Clodius Sabinus: so these are the most passionate among vs to bewaile and bemoane the perplexities of loue, Henrie Howard, Earle of Surrey, Sir Thomas Wyat the elder, Sir Francis Brain, Sir Philip Sidney, Sir Walter Rawley, Sir Edward Dyer, Spencer, Daniel, Drayton, Shakespeare, Whetstone, Gascoyne, Samuell Page, sometimes Fellowe of Corpus Christi Colledge in Oxford, Churchyard, Bretton.

As Theocritus in Greek, Virgil and Mantuan in Latine, Sanazar in Italian, and the Authour of *Amintæ Gaudia* and *Walsingham's Melibœus* are the best for Pastorall: so amongst vs the best in this kind are Sir Philip Sidney, Master Challener, Spencer, Stephen Gosson, Abraham Fraunce, and Barnefield.

These and many other Epigrammatists the Latin tongue hath, Q. Catulus, Porcius Licinius, Quintus Cornificius, Martial, Cnœus Getulicus, and wittie Sir Thomas Moore: so in English we have these, Heywood, Drante, Kendal, Bastard, Dauies.

As noble Mæcenas, that sprang from the Hetruscan Kinges, not onely graced Poets by his bounty but also by beeing a Poet himself; and as Iames the 6, nowe King of Scotland, is not only a fauorer of Poets but a Poet, as my friend Master Richard Barnefielde hath in this disticke passing well recorded,

> The King of Scots now liuing is a Poet,
> As his Lepanto and his Furies show it:

so Elizabeth, our dread Souereign and gracious Queene, is not only a liberal Patrone vnto Poets, but an excellent Poet herselfe, whose learned, delicate, and noble Muse surmounteth, be it in Ode, Elegy, Epigram, or in any other kind of poem, Heroicke or Lyricke.

Octauia, sister unto Augustus the Emperour, was exceeding bountifull vnto Virgil, who gaue him for making 26 verses, 1,137 pounds, to wit, tenne *sestertiæ* for euerie verse (which amounted to aboue 43 pounds for euery verse): so learned Mary, the honourable Countesse of Pembrook, the noble sister of immortall Sir Philip Sidney, is very liberall vnto Poets; besides, shee is a most delicate Poet, of whome I may say, as Antipater Sidonius writeth of Sappho,

> *Dulcia Mnemosyne demirans carmina Sapphus,*
> *Quaesiuit decima Pieris vnde foret.*

Among others, in times past, Poets had these fauourers, Augustus, Mæcenas, Sophocles, Germanicus, an Emperor, a Nobleman, a Senatour, and a Captaine: so of later times Poets haue these patrones, Robert, King of Sicil, the great King Francis of France, King Iames of Scotland, and Queene Elizabeth of England.

As in former times two great Cardinals, Bembus and [Bib]biena, did countenance Poets: so of late yeares two great preachers haue giuen them their right hands in fellowship, Beza and Melancthon.

As the learned philosophers Fracastorius and Scaliger haue highly prized them: so haue the eloquent Orators Pontanus and Muretus very gloriously estimated them.

As Georgius Buchananus' *Iepthœ* amongst all moderne Tragedies is able to abide the touch of Aristotle's precepts and Euripedes's examples: so is Bishop Watson's *Absalon*.

As Terence for his translations out of Apollodorus and Menander, and Aquilius for his translation out of Menander, and C. Germanicus Augustus for his out of Aratus, and Ausonius for his translated *Epigrams* out of Greeke, and Doctor Iohnson for his *Frogge-fight* out of Homer, and Watson for his *Antigone* out of Sophocles, have got good commendations: so these versifers for their learned translations are of good note among vs, Phaer for Virgil's *Æneads*, Golding for Ouid's *Metamorphosis*, Harington for his *Orlando Furioso*, the Translators of Seneca's *Tragedies*, Barnabe Googe for Palingenius, Turberuile for Ouid's *Epistles* and Mantuan, and Chapman for his inchoate Homer.

As the Latines haue these Emblematists, Andreas Alciatus, Reusnerus, and Sambucus: so we haue these, Geffrey Whitney, Andrew Willet, and Thomas Combe.

As Nonnus Panapolyta writ the *Gospell* of Saint Iohn in Greeke hexameters: so Iervis Markham hath written Salomon's *Canticles* in English verse.

As C. Plinius writ the life of Pompon[i]us Secundus: so young Charles Fitz-Ieffrey, that high touring Falcon, hath most gloriously penned *The honourable Life and Death of worthy Sir Francis Drake*.

As Hesiod writ learnedly of husbandry in Greeke: so hath Tusser very wittily and experimentally written of it in English.

As Antipater Sidonius was famous for ex temporall verse in Greeke, and Ouid for his *Quicquid conabar dicere versus erat*: so was our Tarleton, of whome Doctor Case, that learned physitian, thus speaketh in the Seuenth Booke and seuenteenth chapter of his *Politikes: Aristoteles suum Theodoretum laudauit quendam peritum Tragaediarum actorem, Cicero suum Roscium: nos Angli Tarletonum, in cuius voce et vultu omnes iocosi affectus, in cuius cerebroso capite lepidae facetiae habitant*. And so is now our wittie Wilson, who for learning and extemporall witte in this facultie is without compare or compeere, as, to his great and eternall commendations, he manifested in his challenge at the *Swanne* on the Banke Side.

As Achilles tortured the deade bodie of Hector, and as Antonius and his wife Fuluia tormented the liuelesse corps of Cicero: so Gabriell Haruey hath shewed the same inhumanitie to Greene, that lies full low in his graue.

As Eupolis of Athens vsed great libertie in taxing the vices of men: so doth Thomas Nash, witnesse the broode of the Harueys!

As Actæon was wooried of his owne hounds: so is Tom Nash of his *Isle of Dogs*. Dogges were the death of Euripedes; but bee not disconsolate, gallant young Iuuenall, Linus, the sonne of Apollo, died the same death. Yet God forbid that so braue a witte should so basely perish! Thine are but paper dogges, neither is thy banishment like Ouid's, eternally to conuerse with the barbarous

Getæ. Therefore comfort thyselfe, sweete Tom, with Cicero's glorious return to Rome, and with the counsel Æneas giues to his seabeaten soldiers, *Lib. I, Æneid.*

> Pluck vp thine heart, and driue from thence both feare and care away!
> To thinke on this may pleasure be perhaps another day.
> *Durate et temet rebus seruate secundis.*

As Anacreon died by the pot: so George Peele by the pox.

As Archesilaus Prytanœus perished by wine at a drunken feast, as Hermippus testifieth in *Diogenes*: so Robert Greene died of a surfet taken at pickeld herrings and Rhenish wine, as witnesseth Thomas Nash, who was at the fatall banquet.

As Iodelle, a French tragical poet, beeing an epicure and an atheist, made a pitifull end: so our tragicall poet Marlow for his Epicurisme and Atheisme had a tragical death. You may read of this Marlow more at large in the *Theatre of God's judgments*, in the 25th chapter entreating of *Epicures and Atheists.*

As the poet Lycophron was shot to death by a certain riual of his: so Christopher Marlow was stabd to death by a bawdy Servingman, a riual of his in his lewde loue.

Thomas Campion
1567–1620

More of a musician and composer than a literary figure, Campion's fame today rests on what he would have considered his peripheral interests. Born on February 12, 1567 to the son of a Court clerk, Campion studied at Peterhouse, Cambridge, and subsequently entered Gray's Inn. He seems never to have been called to the bar, however. There is evidence that he served as a soldier in the Earl of Essex's Normandy campaign of 1591, and it is probable that he studied medicine abroad sometime after this period, since he set up a medical practice in London around 1605.

Campion's literary interest was primarily lyric verse, and in 1601 he published (jointly with Philip Rosseter) *A Book of Airs,* for which he composed the music and perhaps some of the lyrics as well. Throughout most of his career, Campion sought to strengthen the concept of poetry as a musical form—an ancient idea which still exerted great influence among Campion's contemporaries, but which was nonetheless on the wane.

This attempt received fuller treatment the following year, when Campion wrote *Observations in the Art of English Poetry.* A work of considerable power, it is remembered (perhaps unfortunately) chiefly for its scornful view of medieval verse (extreme even by Elizabethan standards) and its condemnation of rhyme (which inspired Samuel Daniel to write his famous rebuttal).

Campion's view in the *Observations* is that of the Renaissance humanist *par excellence*—the poets of antiquity are for him the touchstone against which true verse is to be measured. Consequently, he advocates "quantitative" meters (based on the duration of sound), rather than "accentual" meters, which are measured by the stress placed on individual syllables. The accentual meter, of course, lends itself very easily to rhyme, and is associated with traditional English verse. Campion's view of this as a corruption is a harking back to an idealized classical age.

Whether as a reform or a retrogression, Campion's prescriptions on rhyme and meter were largely ignored. Campion's own verse is written almost entirely in accentual meter ("Rose Cheek'd Laura" being the great exception), and quantitative meter became increasingly rare. However, the *Observations* ought not to be dismissed on this account. Campion's emphasis upon the importance of timing in verse structure is admirable, and he was possessed of a keen enough ear to discern and pinpoint the unworkability of many Elizabethan poetic styles (notably the dactylic hexameter). It is unfortunate that, in his only major contribution to literary theory, Campion should have allowed his neoclassical prejudices concerning rhyme to overshadow a highly useful and informative work.

Campion practiced medicine throughout his adult life, and occupied himself in composing music, airs, and Latin verse (most of which is entirely forgotten today). He died on March 1, 1620.

Observations in the Art of English Poetry is taken from *Elizabethan Critical Essays*, edited by G. Gregory Smith (Oxford University Press, 1904).

OBSERVATIONS IN THE ART OF ENGLISH POETRY

Chapter I

There is no writing too breefe that, without obscuritie, comprehends the intent of the writer. These my late obseruations in English Poesy I haue thus briefely gathered, that they might proue the lesse troublesome in perusing, and the more apt to be retayn'd in memorie. And I will first generally handle the nature of Numbers. Number is *discreta quantitas*: so that when we speake simply of number, we intend only the disseruer'd quantity; but when we speake of a Poeme written in number, we consider not only the distinct number of the sillables, but also their value, which is contained in the length or shortnes of their sound. As in Musick we do not say a straine of so many notes, but so many sem'briefes (though sometimes there are no more notes then sem'briefes), so in a verse the numeration of the sillables is not so much to be obserued as their waite and due proportion. In ioyning of words to harmony there is nothing more offensiue to the eare then to place a long sillable with a short note, or a short sillable with a long note, though in the last the vowell often beares it out. The world is made by Simmetry and proportion, and is in that respect compared to Musick, and Musick to Poetry: for Terence saith, speaking of Poets, *artem qui tractant musicam*, confounding Musick and Poesy together. What musick can there be where there is no proportion obserued? Learning first flourished in Greece; from thence it was deriued vnto the Romaines, both diligent obseruers of the number and quantity of sillables, not in their verses only but likewise in their prose. Learning, after the declining of the Romaine Empire and the pollution of their language through the conquest of the Barbarians, lay most pitifully deformed till the time of Erasmus, Rewcline, Sir Thomas More, and other learned men of that age, who brought the Latine toong again to light, redeeming it with much labour out of the hands of the illiterate Monks and Friers: as a scoffing booke, entituled *Epistolae obscurorum virorum*, may sufficiently testifie. In those lack-learning times, and in barbarized Italy, began that vulgar and easie kind of Poesie which is now in vse throughout most parts of Christendome, which we abusiuely call Rime and Meeter, of *Rithmus* and *Metrum*, of which I will now discourse.

Chapter II

I am not ignorant that whosoeuer shall by way of reprehension examine the imperfections of Rime must encounter with many glorious enemies, and those very expert and ready at their weapon, that can if neede be extempore (as they say) rime a man to death. Besides there is growne a kind of prescription in the vse of Rime, to forestall the right of true numbers, as also the consent of many nations, against all which it may seeme a thing almost impossible and vaine to contend. All this and more can not yet deterre me from a lawful defence of perfection, or make me any whit the sooner adheare to that which is lame and vnbeseeming. For custome I alleage that ill vses are to be abolisht, and that things naturally imperfect can not be perfected by vse. Old customes, if they be better, why should they not be recald, as the yet flourishing custome of numerous poesy vsed among the Romanes and Grecians? But the vnaptnes of our toongs and the difficultie of imitation dishartens vs: againe, the facilitie and popularitie of Rime creates as many Poets as a hot sommer flies.

But let me now examine the nature of that which we call Rime. By Rime is vnderstoode that which ends in the like sound, so that verses in such maner composed yeeld but a continual repetition of that Rhetoricall figure which we tearme *similiter desinentia*, and that, being but *figura verbi*, ought (as Tully and all other Rhetoritians haue iudicially obseru'd) sparingly to be vs'd, least it should offend the eare with tedious affectation. Such was that absurd following of the letter amongst our English so much of late affected, but now hist out of Paules Churchyard: which foolish figuratiue repetition crept also into the Latine Toong, as it is manifest in the booke of P[s] called *praelia porcorum*, and another pamphlet all of F[s] which I haue seene imprinted; but I will leaue these follies to their owne ruine, and returne to the matter intended. The eare is a rationall sence and a chiefe iudge of proportion; but in our kind of riming what proportion is there kept where there remaines such a confused inequalitie of sillables? Iambick and Trochaick feete, which are opposed by nature, are by all Rimers confounded; nay, oftentimes they place instead of an Iambick the foot Pyrrchius, consisting of two short sillables, curtailling their verse, which they supply in reading with a ridiculous and vnapt drawing of their speech. As for example:

> Was it my desteny, or dismall chaunce?

In this verse the two last sillables of the word *Desteny*, being both short, and standing for a whole foote in the verse, cause the line to fall out shorter then it ought by nature. The like impure errors haue in time of rudenesse bene vsed in the Latine toong, as the *Carmina prouerbialia* can witnesse, and many other such reuerend bables. But the noble Grecians and Romaines, whose skilfull monuments outliue barbarisme, tyed themselues to the strict obseruation of poeticall numbers, so abandoning the childish titillation of riming that it was imputed a great error to Ouid for setting forth this one riming verse,

> *Quot caelum stellas tot habet tua Roma puellas.*

For the establishing of this argument, what better confirmation can be had then that of Sir Thomas Moore in his booke of Epigrams, where he makes two sundry Epitaphs vpon the death of a singing-man at Westminister, the one in learned numbers and dislik't, the other in rude rime and highly extold: so that he concludes, *tales lactucas talia labra petunt*, like lips like lettuce.

But there is yet another fault in Rime altogether intollerable, which is, that it inforceth a man oftentimes to abiure his matter and extend a short conceit beyond all bounds of arte; for in Quatorzens, methinks, the poet handles his subiect as tyrannically as Procrustes the thiefe his prisoners, whom, when he had taken, he vsed to cast vpon a bed, which if they were too short to fill, he would stretch them longer, if too long, he would cut them shorter. Bring before me now any the most self-lou'd Rimer, and let me see if without blushing he be able to reade his lame halting rimes. Is there not a curse of Nature laid vpon such rude Poesie, when the Writer is himself asham'd of it, and the hearers in contempt call it Riming and Ballating? What Deuine in his Sermon, or graue Counsellor in his Oration will alleage the testimonie of a rime? But the deuinity[1] of the Romaines and Gretians was all written in verse; and Aristotle, Galene, and the bookes of all the excellent Philosphers are full of the testimonies of the old Poets. By them was laid the foundation of all humane wisdome, and from them the knowledge of all antiquitie is deriued. I will propound but one question, and so conclude this point. If the Italians, Frenchmen, and Spanyards, that with commendation have written in Rime, were demaunded whether they had rather the bookes they haue publisht (if their toong would beare it) should remaine as they are in Rime or be translated into the auncient numbers of the Greekes and Romaines, would they not answere into numbers? What honour were it then for our English language to be the first that after so many yeares of barbarisme could second the perfection of the industrious Greekes and Romaines? which how it may be effected I will now proceede to demonstrate.

Chapter III

There are but three feete which generally distinguish the Greeke and Latine verses, the Dactil, consisting of one sillable and two short, as *vĭuĕrĕ*; the Trochy, of one long and one short, as *vītă*; and the Iambick of one short and one long, as *ămōr*. The Spondee of two long, the Tribrach of three short, the Anapœstick of two short and a long, are but as seruants to the first. Diuers other feete I know are by the Grammarians cited, but to little purpose. The Heroicall verse that is distinguisht by the Dactile hath bene oftentimes attempted in our English toong, but with passing pitifull successe; and no wonder, seeing it is an attempt altogether against the nature of our language. For both the concurse of our monasillables make our verses vnapt to slide, and also, if we examine our polysillables, we shall finde few of them, by reason of their heauinesse, willing to serue in place of a Dactile. Thence it is that the writers of English heroicks do so often repeate Amyntas, Olympus, Auernus, Erinnis, and suchlike borrowed words, to supply the defect of our hardly intreated Dactile. I could in this place set downe many ridiculous kinds of Dactils which they vse, but that it is not my purpose here to incite men to laughter. If we therefore reiect the Dactil as vnfit for our vse which of necessity we are enforst to do), there remayne only the Iambick foote, of which the Iambick verse is fram'd, and the Trochee, from which the Trochaick numbers haue their originall. Let vs now then examine the property of these two feete, and try if they consent with the nature of our English sillables. And first for the Iambicks, they fall out so naturally in our toong, that, if we examine our owne writers, we shall find they vnawares hit oftentimes vpon the true Iambick numbers, but alwayes ayme at them as far as their eare without the guidance of arte can attain vnto, as it shall hereafter more euidently appeare. The Trochaick foote, which is but an Iambick turn'd ouer and ouer, must of force in like manner accord in proportion with our Brittish sillables, and so produce an English Trochaicall verse. Then hauing these two principall kinds of verses, we may easily out of them deriue other formes, as the Latines and Greekes before vs haue done: whereof I will make plaine demonstration, beginning at the Iambick verse.

Chapter IV

I haue obserued, and so may any one that is either practis'd in singing, or hath a naturall eare able to time a song, that the Latine verses of sixe feete, as the Heroick and Iambick, or of fiue feete, as the Trochaick are in nature all of the same length of sound with our English verses of fiue feet; for either of them being tim'd with the hand, *quinque perficiunt tempora*, they fill vp the quantity (as it were) of fiue sem'briefs; as for example, if any man will proue to time these verses with his hand.

A pure Iambick:
>*Suis et ipsa Roma viribus ruit.*

A licentiate Iambick:
>*Ducunt volentes fata, nolentes trahunt.*

An Heroick verse:
>*Tityre, tu patulae recubans sub tegmine fagi.*

A Trochaick verse:
>*Nox est perpetua vna dormienda.*

English Iambicks pure:
>The more secure, the more the stroke we feele

THE ART OF ENGLISH POETRY

> Of vnpreuented harms; so gloomy stormes
> Appeare the sterner, if the day be cleere.

Th' English Iambick licentiate:

> Harke how these winds do murmur at thy flight.

The English Trochee:

> Still where Enuy leaues, remorse doth enter.

The cause why these verses differing in feete yeeld the same length of sound, is by reason of some rests which either the necessity of the numbers or the heauiness of the sillables do beget. For we find in musick that oftentimes the straines of a song cannot be reduct to true number without some rests prefixt in the beginning and middle, as also at the close if need requires. Besides, our English monasillables enforce many breathings which no doubt greatly lengthen a verse, so that it is no wonder if for these reasons our English verses of fiue feete hold pace with the Latines of sixe. The pure Iambick in English needes small demonstration, because it consists simply of Iambick feete; but our Iambick licentiate offers itselfe to a farther consideration, for in the third and fift place we must of force hold the Iambick foote, in the first, second, and fourth place we may vse a Spondee or Iambick and sometime a Tribrack or Dactile, but rarely an Anapestick foote, and that in the second or fourth place. But why an Iambick in the third place? I answere, that the forepart of the verse may the gentlier slide into his Dimeter, as, for example sake, deuide this verse:

> Harke how these winds do murmure at thy flight.

Harke how these winds, there the voice naturally affects a rest; then *murmur at thy flight*, that is of itselfe a perfect number, as I will declare in the next Chapter; and therefore the other odde sillable betweene them ought to be short, least the verse should hang too much betweene the naturall pause of the verse and the Dimeter following; the which Dimeter though it be naturally Trochaical, yet it seemes to haue his originall out of the Iambick verse. But the better to confirme and expresse these rules, I will set downe a short Poeme in Licentiate Iambicks, which may giue more light to them that shall hereafter imitate these numbers.

> Goe, numbers, boldly passe, stay not for ayde
> Of shifting rime, that easie flatterer,
> Whose witchcraft can the ruder eares beguile.
> Let your smooth feete, enur'd to purer arte,
> True measures tread.   What if your pace be slow,
> And hops not like the Grecian elegies?
> It is yet gracefull, and well fits the state
> Of words ill-breathed and not shap't to runne.
> Goe then, but slowly, till your steps be firme;
> Tell them that pitty or peruersely skorne
> Poore English poesie as the slaue to rime,

> You are those loftie numbers that reuiue
> Triumphs of Princes and sterne tragedies:
> And learne henceforth t'attend those happy sprights
> Whose bounding fury height and waight affects.
> Assist their labour, and sit close to them,
> Neuer to part away till for desert
> Their browes with great Apollos bayes are hid.
> He first taught number and true harmonye;
> Nor is the lawrell his for rime bequeath'd.
> Call him with numerous accents paisd by arte,
> He'le turne his glory from the sunny clymes
> The North-bred wits alone to patronise.
> Let France their Bartas, Italy Tasso prayse;
> Phœbus shuns none but in their flight from him.

Though, as I said before, the naturall breathing-place of our English Iambick verse is in the last sillable of the second foote, as our Trochy after the manner of the Latine Heroick and Iambick rests naturally in the first of the third foote, yet no man is tyed altogether to obserue this rule, but he may alter it, after the iudgment of his eare, which Poets, Orators, and Musitions of all men ought to haue most excellent. Againe, though I said peremtorily before that the third and fift place of our licentiate Iambick must alwayes hold an Iambick foote, yet I will shew you example in both places where a Tribrack may be very formally taken, and first in the third place:

> Some trade in Barbary, some in Turky trade.

An other example:

> Men that do fall to misery, quickly fall.

If you doubt whether the first of *misery* be naturally short or no, you may iudge it by the easy sliding of these two verses following. The first:

> Whome misery cannot alter, time deuours.

The second:

> What more vnhappy life, what misery more?

Example of the Tribrack in the fift place, as you may perceiue in the last foote of the fourth verse:

> Some from the starry throne his fame deriues,
> Some from the mynes beneath, from trees or herbs:
> Each hath his glory, each his sundry gift,
> Renown'd in e'ry art there liues not any.

To proceede farther, I see no reason why the English Iambick in his first place may not as well borrow a foote of the Trochy as our Trochy, or the Latine Hendicasillable, may in the like case make bold with the Iambick: but it must be done euer with this caueat, which is, that a Sponde, Dactile, or Tribrack do supply the next place; for an Iambick beginning with a single short sillable, and the other ending before with the like, would too much drinke vp the verse if they came immediatly together.

The example of the Sponde after the Trochy:

> As the faire sonne the lightsome heau'n adorns.

The example of the Dactil:

> Noble, ingenious, and discreetly wise.

The example of the Tribrack:

> Beauty to ielousie brings ioy, sorrow, feare.

Though I haue set downe these second licenses as good and ayreable enough, yet for the most part my first rules are generall.

These are those numbers which Nature in our English destinates to the Tragick and Heroik Poeme: for the subiect of them both being all one, I see no impediment why one verse may not serue for them both, as it appeares more plainly in the old comparison of the two Greeke writers, when they say, *Homerus est Sophocles heroicus*, and againe *Sophocles est Homerus tragicus*, intimating that both Sophocles and Homer are the same in height and subiect, and differ onely in the kinde of their numbers.

The Iambick verse in like manner being yet made a little more licentiate, that it may thereby the neerer imitate our common talke, will excellently serue for Comedies; and then may we vse a Sponde in the fift place, and in the third place any foote except a Trochy, which neuer enters into our Iambick verse but in the first place, and then with his caueat of the other feete which must of necessitie follow.

Chapter V

The Dimeter (so called in the former Chapter) I intend next of all to handle, because it seems to be a part of the Iambick, which is our most naturall and ancient English verse. We may terme this our English march, because the verse answers our warlick forme of march in similitude of number. But call it what you please, for I will not wrangle about names, only intending to set down the nature of it and true structure. It consists of two feete and one odde sillable. The first foote may be made either a Trochy, or a Spondee, or an Iambick, at the pleasure of the composer, though most naturally that place affects a Trochy or Spondee; yet, by the example of Catullus in his Hendicasillables, I adde in the first place sometimes an Iambick foote. In the second place we must euer insert a Trochy or Tribrack, and so leaue the last sillable (as in the end of a verse it is alwaies held) common. Of this kinde I will subscribe three examples, the first being a peece of Chorus in a Tragedy.

> Rauing warre, begot
> In the thirstye sands
> Of the Lybian Iles,
> Wasts our emptye fields;
> What the greedye rage
> Of fell wintrye stormes
> Could not turne to spoile,
> Fierce Bellona now
> Hath laid desolate,
> Voyd of fruit, or hope.
> Th' eger thriftye hinde,
> Whose rude toyle reuiu'd
> Our skie-blasted earth,
> Himselfe is but earth,
> Left a skorne to fate
> Through seditious armes:
> And that soile, alive
> Which he duly nurst,
> Which him duly fed,
> Dead his body feeds:
> Yet not all the glebe
> His tuffe hands manur'd
> Now one turfe affords
> His poore funerall.
> Thus still needy liues,
> Thus still needy dyes
> Th' vnknowne multitude.

An example Lyrical:

> Greatest in thy wars,
> Greater in thy peace,
> Dread *Elizabeth*;
> Our muse only Truth,
> Figments cannot vse,
> Thy ritch name to deck
> That itselfe adorns:
> But should now this age
> Let all poesye fayne,
> Fayning poesy could
> Nothing faine at all
> Worthy halfe thy fame.

An Example Epigrammaticall:

> Kind in euery kinde
> This, deare Ned, resolue.
> Neuer of thy prayse
> Be too prodigall;
> He that prayseth all
> Can praise truly none.

Chapter VI

Next in course to be intreated of is the English Trochaick, being a verse simple, and of itselfe depending. It consists, as the Latine Trochaick, of fiue feete, the first whereof may be a Trochy, a Spondee, or an Iambick, the other foure of necessity all Trochyes; still holding this rule authenticall, that the last sillable of a verse is always common. The spirit of this verse most of all delights in Epigrams, but it may be diuersely vsed, as shall hereafter be declared. I haue written diuers light Poems in this kinde, which for the better satisfaction of the reader I thought conuenient here in way of example to publish. In which though sometimes vnder a knowne name I haue shadowed a fain'd conceit, yet it is done without reference or offence to any person, and only to make the stile appeare the more English.

The first Epigramme:

> Lockly spits apace, the rhewme he cals it,
> But no drop (though often urgd) he straineth
> From his thirstie iawes, yet all the morning
> And all day he spits, in eu'ry corner;
> At his meales he spits, at eu'ry meeting;
> At the barre he spits before the Fathers;
> In the Court he spits before the Graces;
> In the Church he spits, thus all prophaning
> With that rude disease, that empty spitting:
> Yet no cost he spares, he sees the Doctors,
> Keeps a strickt diet, precisely vseth
> Drinks and bathes drying, yet all preuailes not.
> 'Tis not China (Lockly), *Salsa Guacum*,
> Nor dry Sassafras can help, or ease thee;
> 'Tis no humor hurts, it is thy humor.

The second Epigramme:

> Cease, fond wretch, to loue, so oft deluded,
> Still made ritch with hopes, still vnrelieued.
> Now fly her delaies; she that debateth
> Feeles not true desire; he that, deferred,

Others times attends, his owne betrayeth:
Learne t'affect thy self; thy cheekes deformed
With pale care reuiue by timely pleasure,
Or with skarlet heate them, or by paintings
Make thee louely; for such arte she vseth
Whome in vayne so long thy folly loued.

The third Epigramme:

Kate can fancy only berdles husbands,
Thats the cause she shakes off eu'ry suter,
Thats the cause she liues so stale a virgin,
For, before her heart can heate her answer,
Her smooth youths she finds all hugely berded.

The fourth Epigramme:

All in sattin Oteny will be suted,
Beaten sattin (as by chaunce he cals it);
Oteny sure will haue the bastinado.

The fift Epigramme:

Tosts as snakes or as the mortall Henbane
Hunks detests when huffcap ale he tipples,
Yet the bread he graunts the fumes abateth;
Therefore apt in ale, true, and he graunts it;
But it drinks vp ale, that Hunks detesteth.

The sixt Epigramme:

What though Harry braggs, let him be noble;
Noble Harry hath not half a noble.

The seauenth Epigramme:

Phœbe all the rights Elisa claymeth,
Mighty riuall, in this only diff'ring
That shees only true, thou only fayned.

The eight Epigramme:

Barnzy stiffly vows that hees no Cuckold;
Yet the vulgar eu'rywhere salutes him,
With strange signes of hornes, from eu'ry corner;
Wheresoere he commes, a sundry Cucco
Still frequents his eares; yet he's no Cuccold.
But this Barnzy knowes that his Matilda,
Skorning him, with Haruy playes the wanton.
Knowes it? nay desires it, and by prayers
Dayly begs of heau'n, that it for euer
May stand firme for him; yet hees no Cuccold.

> And 'tis true, for Haruy keeps Matilda,
> Fosters Barnzy, and relieues his houshold,
> Buyes the Cradle, and begets the children,
> Payes the Nurces, eu'ry charge defraying,
> And thus truly playes Matilda's husband:
> So that Barnzy now becomes a cypher,
> And himselfe th' adultrer of Matilda.
> Mock not him with hornes, the case is alterd;
> Haruy beares the wrong, *he* proues the Cuccold.

The ninth Epigramme:

> Buffe loues fat vians, fat ale, fat all things.
> Keepes fat whores, fat offices, yet all men
> Him fat only wish to feast the gallous.

The tenth Epigramme:

> Smith, by sute diuorst, the knowne adultres
> Freshly weds againe; what ayles the mad-cap
> By this fury? euen so theeues by frailty
> Of their hemp reseru'd, againe the dismal
> Tree embrace, againe the fatall halter.

The eleuenth Epigramme:

> His late losse the Wiueless Higs in order
> Eu'rywhere bewailes to friends, to strangers;
> Tels them how by night a yongster armed
> Saught his Wife (as hand in hand he held her)
> With drawne sword to force; she cryed; he mainely
> Roring ran for ayde, but (ah) returning
> Fled was with with the prize the beawty-forcer,
> Whome in vain he seeks, he threats, he followes.
> Chang'd is Hellen, Hellen hugs the stranger,
> Safe as Paris in the Greeke triumphing.
> Therewith his reports to teares he truneth,
> Peirst through with the louely Dames remembrance;
> Straight he sighes, he raues, his haire he teareth,
> Forcing pitty still by fresh lamenting.
> Cease vnworthy, worthy of thy fortunes,
> Thou that couldst so faire a prize deliuer,
> For feare vnregarded, vndefended,
> Hadst no heart I thinke, I know no liuer.

The twelfth Epigramme:

> Why droopst thou, Trefeild? Will Hurst the Banker
> Make dice of thy bones? By heau'n he cannot.

> Cannot?   What's the reason?   Ile declare it:
> Th'ar all growne so pockie and so rotten.

Chapter VII

The Elegeick verses challenge the next place, as being of all compound verses the simplest. They are deriu'd out of our own naturall numbers as neere the imitation of the Greekes and Latines as our heauy sillables will permit. The first verse is a meere licentiate Iambick; the second is fram'd of two vnited Dimeters. In the first Dimeter we are tyed to make the first foote either a Trochy or a Spondee, the second a Trochy, and the odde sillable of it alwaies long. The second Dimeter consists of two Trochyes (because it requires more swiftnes than the first) and an odde sillable, which, being last, is euer common. I will giue you example both of Elegye and Epigramme, in this kinde.

An Elegy:

> Constant to none, but euer false to me,
>   Traiter still to loue through thy faint desires,
> Not hope of pittie now nor vaine redresse
>   Turns my griefs to teares and renu'd laments.
> Too well thy empty vowes and hollow thoughts
>   Witnes both thy wrongs and remorseles hart.
> Rue not my sorrow, but blush at my name;
>   Let thy bloudy cheeks guilty thoughts betray.
> My flames did truly burne, thine made a shew,
>   As fires painted are which no heate retayne,
> Or as the glossy Pirop faines to blaze,
>   But toucht cold appeares, and an earthy stone.
> True cullours deck thy cheeks, false foiles thy brest,
>   Frailer then thy light beawty is thy minde.
> None canst thou long refuse, nor long affect,
>   But turn'st feare with hopes, sorrow with delight,
> Delaying, and deluding eu'ry way
>   Those whose eyes are once with thy beawty chain'd.
> Thrice happy man that entring first thy loue
>   Can so guide the straight raynes of his desires,
> That both he can regard thee and refraine:
>   If grac't, firme he stands, if not, easely falls.

Example of Epigrams, in Elegeick verse. The first Epigramme:

> Arthure brooks only those that brooke not him,
>   Those he most regards, and deuoutly serues:
> But them that grace him his great brau'ry skornes,

> Counting kindnesse all duty, not desert:
> Arthure wants forty pounds, tyres eu'ry friend,
> But finds none that holds twenty due for him.

The second Epigramme:

> If fancy can not erre which vertue guides,
> In thee, Laura, then fancy can not erre.

The third Epigramme:

> Drue feasts no Puritans; the churles, he saith,
> Thanke no men, but eate, praise God, and depart.

The fourth Epigramme:

> A wiseman wary liues, yet most secure,
> Sorrowes moue not him greatly, nor delights:
> Fortune and death he skorning, only makes
> Th' earth his sober Inne, but still heau'n his home.

The fifth Epigramme:

> Thou tel'st me, Barnzy, Dawson hath a wife:
> Thine he hath, I graunt; Dawson hath a wife.

The sixt Epigramme:

> Drue giues thee money, yet thou thank'st not him,
> But thankst God for him, like a godly man.
> Suppose, rude Puritan, thou begst of him,
> And he saith God help, who's the godly man?

The seauenth Epigramme:

> All wonders Barnzy speakes, all grosely faind:
> Speake some wonder once, Barnzy, speake the truth.

The eight Epigramme:

> None then should through thy beawty, Lawra, pine,
> Might sweet words alone ease a loue-sick heart:
> But your sweet words alone, that quit so well
> Hope of friendly deeds, kill the loue-sick heart.

The ninth Epigramme:

> At all thou frankly throwst, while, Frank, thy wife,
> Bars not Luke the mayn; Oteny barre the bye.

Chapter VIII

To descend orderly from the more simple numbers to them that are more compounded, it is now time to handle such verses as are fit for Ditties or Odes; which we may call Lyricall, because they are apt to be soong to an instrument, if they were adorn'd with conuenient notes. Of that kind I will demonstrate three in this Chapter, and in the first we will proceede after the manner of the Saphick, which is a Trochaicall verse as well as the Hendicasillable in Latine. The first three verses therefore in our English Saphick are meerely those Trochaicks which I handled in the sixt Chapter, excepting only that the first foote of either of them must euer of necessity be a Spondee, to make the number more graue. The fourth and last closing verse is compounded of three Trochyes together, to giue a more smooth farewell, as you may easily obserue in this Poeme made vpon a Triumph at Whitehall, whose glory was dasht with an vnwelcome showre, hindring the people from the desired sight of her Majestie.

The English Sapphick:

> Faiths pure shield, the Christian Diana,
> Englands glory crownd with all deuinenesse,
> Liue long with triumphs to blesse thy people
>   At thy sight triumphing.
>
> Loe, they sound; the Knights in order armed
> Entring threat the list, adrest to combat
> For their courtly loues; he, hees the wonder
>   Whome Eliza graceth.
>
> Their plum'd pomp the vulgar heaps detaineth,
> And rough steeds; let vs the still deuices
> Close obserue, the speeches and the musicks
>   Peacefull arms adorning.
>
> But whence showres so fast this angry tempest,
> Clowding dimme the place? Behold, Eliza
> This day shines not here; this heard, the launces
>   And thick heads do vanish.

The second kinde consists of Dimeter, whose first foote may either be a Sponde or a Trochy. The two verses following are both of them Trochaical, and consist of foure feete, the first of either of them being a Spondee or Trochy, the other three only Trochyes. The fourth and last verse is made of two Trochyes. The number is voluble, and fit to expresse any amorous conceit. The Example:

> Rose-cheekt Lawra, come
> Sing thou smoothly with thy beawtie's
> Silent musick, either other
>   Sweetely gracing.

THE ART OF ENGLISH POETRY

>   Louely formes do flowe
> From concent deuinely framed;
> Heau'n is musick, and thy beawtie's
>   Birth is heauenly.
>
>   These dull notes we sing
> Discords neede for helps to grace them;
> Only beawty purely louing
>   Knowes no discord,
>
>   But still moues delight,
> Like cleare springs renu'd by flowing,
> Euer perfet, euer in them-
>   selues eternall.

The third kind begins as the second kind ended, with a verse consisting of two Trochy feete, and then as the second kind had in the middle two Trochaick verses of foure feete, so this hath three of the same nature, and ends in a Dimeter as the second began. The Dimeter may allow in the first place a Trochy or a Spondee, but no Iambick. The Example.

>   Iust beguiler,
> Kindest loue, yet only chastest,
> Royall in thy smooth denyals,
> Frowning or demurely smiling,
>   Still my pure delight.
>
>   Let me view thee
> With thoughts and with eyes affected,
> And if then the flames do murmur,
> Quench them with thy vertue, charme them
>   With thy stormy browes.
>
>   Heau'n so cheerefull
> Laughs not euer, hory winter
> Knowes his season, euen the freshest
> Sommer mornes from angry thunder
>   Iet not still secure.

Chapter IX

If any shall demaund the reason why this number, being in itselfe simple, is plac't after so many compounded numbers, I answere, because I hold it a number to licentiate for a higher place, and in respect of the rest imperfect; yet is it passing gracefull in our English toong, and will excellently fit the subiect of a Madrigall, or any other lofty or tragicall matter. It consists of two feete: the first may be either a Sponde or Trochy, the other must euer represent the nature of a Trochy, as for example:

> Follow, followe,
> Though with mischiefe
> Arm'd, like whirlewind
> Now she flyes thee;
> Time can conquer
> Loues vnkindnes;
> Loue can alter
> Times disgraces;
> Till death faint not
> Then but followe.
> Could I catch that
> Nimble trayter,
> Skornefull Lawra,
> Swift foote Lawra,
> Soone then would I
> Seeke auengement.
> Whats th'auengement?
> Euen submissely
> Prostrate then to
> Beg for mercye.

Thus haue I briefely described eight seueral kinds of English numbers simple or compound. The first was our Iambick pure and licentiate. The second, that which I call our Dimeter, being deriued either from the end of our Iambick or from the beginning of our Trochaick. The third which I deliuered was our English Trochaick verse. The fourth our English Elegeick. The fift, sixt, and seauenth were our English Sapphick, and two other Lyricall numbers, the one beginning with that verse which I call our Dimeter, the other ending with the same. The eight and last was a kind of Anacreontick verse, handled in this Chapter. These numbers which by my long obseruation I have found agreeable with the nature of our sillables, I haue set forth for the benefit of our language, which I presume the learned will not only imitate but also polish and amplifie with their owne inuentions. Some eares accustomed altogether to the fatnes of rime may perhaps except against the cadences of these numbers; but let any man iudicially examine them, and he shall finde they close of themselues so perfectly that the help of rime were not only in them superfluous but also absurd. Moreouer, that they agree with the nature of our English it is manifest, because they entertaine so willingly our owne British names, which the writers in English Heroicks could neuer aspire vnto, and euen our rimers themselues haue rather delighted in borrowed names than in their owne, though much more apt and necessary. But it is now time that I proceede to the censure of our sillables, and that I set such lawes vpon them as by imitation, reason, or experience I can confirme. Yet before I enter into that discourse, I will briefely recite and dispose in order all such feete as are necessary for composition of the verses before described. They are sixe in number, three whereof consist of two sillables, and as many of three.

Feete of two sillables.

Iambick:		rĕuēnge
Trochaick:	as	bēawtie
Sponde:		cōnstānt

Feete of three sillables.

Tribrack:		mĭsĕrie
Anapestick:	as	mĭsĕrīes
Dactile:		dēstenie

Chapter X

The Greekes in the quantity of their sillables were farre more licentious than the Latines, as Martiall in his Epigramme of Earinon witnesseth, saying, *qui Musas colimus seueriores*. But the English may very well challenge much more licence than either of them, by reason it stands chiefely vpon monasillables, which, in expressing with the voyce, are of a heauy cariage, and for that cause the Dactil, Trybrack, and Anapestick are not greatly mist in our verses. But aboue all the accent of our words is diligently to be obseru'd, for chiefly by the accent in any language the true value of the sillables is to be measured. Neither can I remember any impediment except position that can alter the accent of any sillable in our English verse. For though we accent the second of Trumpington short, yet is it naturally long, and so of necessity must be held of euery composer. Wherefore the first rule that is to be obserued is the nature of the accent, which we must euer follow.

The next rule is position, which makes euery sillable long, whether the position happens in one or in two words, according to the manner of the Latines, wherein is to be noted that *h* is no letter.

Position is when a vowell comes before two consonants, either in one or two words. In one, as in *best*, *e* before *st* makes the word *best* long by position. In two words, as in *setled loue*, *e* before *d* in the last sillable of the first word and *l* in the beginning of the second makes *led* in *seltēd* long by position.

A vowell before a vowell is alwaies short, as *flīīng, dīīng, gŏīng*, vnlesse the accent alter it, in *dĕnīing*.

The diphthong in the midst of a word is alwaies long, as *plaīing, deceīving*.

The Synalœphas or Elisions, in our toong are either necessary to auoid the hollowness and gaping in our verse, as *to* and *the, t'inchaunt, th' inchaunter*, or may be vsd at pleasure, as for *let vs* to say *let's*; for *we will, wee'l*; for *euery, eu'ry*; for *they are, th'ar*; for *he is, hee's*; for *admired, admir'd*; and such like.

Also, because our English Orthography (as the French) differs from our common pronunciation, we must esteeme our sillables as we speake, not as we write; for the sound of them in a verse is to be valued, and not their letters, as for *follow* we pronounce *follo*; for *perfect, perfet*; for *little, littel*; for *loue-sick, loue-sik*; for *honour, honor*; for *money, mony*; for *dangerous, dangerus*; for *raunsome, raunsum*; for *though, tho*; and their like.

Deriuatiues hold the quantities of their primitiues, as *dĕvōut, dĕvōutelie*; *prŏphāne, prŏphānelie*; and so do the compositiues, as *dĕsēru'd, ūndĕsēru'd*.

In words of two sillables, if the last haue a full and rising accent that sticks long vpon the voyce, the first sillable is always short, vnlesse position, or the diphthong, doth make it long, as *dĕsīre, prĕsērue, dĕfīne, prōphāne, rĕgārd, mănūre*, and such like.

If the like dissillables at the beginning haue double consonants of the same kind, we may vse the first sillable as common, but more naturally short, because in their pronunciation we touch but one of those double letters, as *ătēnd, ăpēare, ŏpōse*. The like we may say when silent and melting consonants meete together, as *ădrēst, rĕdrēst, ōprēst, rĕprēst, rĕtrīu'd*, and such like.

Words of two sillables that in their last sillable mayntayne a flat or falling accent, ought to hold their first sillable long, as *rīgŏr, glōrie, spīrĭt, fūrie, lābŏur* and the like: *ăny, măny, prĕty, hŏly*, and their like are excepted.

One obseruation which leades me to iudge of the difference of these dissillables whereof I last spake, I take from the originall monasillable; which if it be graue, as *shāde*, I hold that the first of *shādie* must be long; so *trūe, trūlie, hāue, hāuĭng; tīre, tīrĭng*.

Words of three sillables for the most part are deriued from words of two sillables, and from them take the quantity of their first sillable, as *flōrĭsh, flōrĭshĭng* long; *hŏlie, hŏlĭnes* short,; but *mi* in *mīser* being long hinders not the first of *mĭsery* to be short, because the sound of the *i* is a little altred.

De, di, and *pro* in trisillables (the second being short) are long, as *dēsŏlāte, dīlĭgēnt, prōdĭgāll*.

Re is euer short, as *rĕmĕdie, rĕfĕrēnce, rĕdŏlēnt, rĕuĕrēnd*.

Likewise the first of these trisillables is short, as the first of *bĕnĕfit, gĕnĕall, hĭdĕous, mĕmŏrie, nŭmĕrous, pĕnĕtrāte, sĕpărat, tĭmĕrous, vărĭant, vărĭous*; and so may we esteeme of all that yeeld the like quicknes of sound.

In words of three sillables the quantity of the middle sillable is lightly taken from the last sillable of the originall dissillable, as the last of *dĕuīne*, ending in a graue or long accent, makes the second of *dĕuīnĭng* also long, and so *ēspīe, ēspīĭng, dĕnīe, dĕnīĭng*: contrarywise it falles out if the last of the dissillable beares a flat or falling accent, as *glōrĭe, glŏrīĭng, ēnvīĭng*, and so forth.

Words of more sillables are eyther borrowed and hold their owne nature, or are likewise deriu'd and so follow the quantity of their primatiues, or are knowne by their proper accents, or may be easily censured by a iudiciall eare.

All words of two or more sillables ending with a falling accent in *y* or *ye*, as *faīrelĭe, dĕmurelĭe, beawtĭe, pīttĭe*, or in *ue*, as *vertuĕ, rēscuĕ*, or in *ow*, as *fŏllŏw, hŏllŏw*, or in *e*, as *parlĕ, Daphnĕ*, or in *a* as *Mannă*, are naturally short in their last sillables: neither let any man cauill at this licentiate abbreuiating of sillables, contrary to the custome of the Latines, which made all their last sillables that ended in *u* long, but let him consider that our verse of fiue feete, and for the most part but of ten sillables, must equall theirs of sixe feete and of many sillables, and therefore may with sufficient reason aduenture vpon this allowance. Besides, euery man may obserue what an infinite number of sillables both among the Greekes and Romaines are held as common. But words of two sillables ending with a rising accent in *y* or *ye*, as *denye, descrye*, or in *ue*, as *ensue*, or in *ee*, as *foresee*, or in *oe*, as *forgoe*, are long in their last sillables, vnlesse a vowell begins the next word.

All monasillables that end in a graue accent are euer long, as *wrāth, hāth, thēse, thōse, tōoth, sōoth, thrōugh, dāy, plāy, feāte, speēde, strīfe, flōw, grōw, shēw*.

The like rule is to be obserued in the last of dissillables bearing a graue rising sound, as *deuine, delaie, retire, refuse, manure*, or a graue falling sound, as *fortune, pleasure, vampire*.

All such as haue a double consonant lengthning them, as *wārre, bārre, stārre, fūrre, mūrre*, appear to me rather long then any way short.

These are of these kinds other, but of a lighter sound, that, if the word following do begin with a vowell, are short, as *doth, though, thou, now, they, too, flye, dye, true, due, see, are, far, you, thee*, and the like.

These monasillables are always short, as *ă, thĕ, thĭ, shĕ, wĕ, bĕ, hĕ, nŏ, tŏ, gŏ, sŏ, dŏ*, and the like.

But if *i* or *y* are ioyn'd at the beginning of a word with any vowell, it is not then held as a vowell, but as a consonant, as *ielosy, iewce, iade, ioy, Iudas, ye, yet, yel, youth, yoke*. The like is to be obseru'd in *w*, as *winde, wide, wood*: and in all words that begin with *va, ve, vi, vo*, or *vu*, as *vacant, vew, vine, voide*, and *vulture*.

All Monasillables or Polysillables that end in single consonants, either written or sounded with single consonants, hauing a sharp liuely accent and standing without position of the word following, are short in their last sillable, as *scăb, flĕd, pārtĕd, Gŏd, ŏf, ĭf, bāndŏg, ănguĭsh, sĭck, quĭck, rīuăl, wĭll, pēoplĕ, sīmplĕ, comĕ, somĕ, hĭm, thĕm, frŏm, sūmmŏn, thĕn, prŏp, prōspĕr, hŏnoŭr, lābŏur, thĭs, hĭs, spēchĕs, gōddĕsse, pērfĕct, bŭt, whăt, thăt*, and their like.

The last sillable of all words in the plurall number that haue two or more vowels before *s* are long, as *vertūes, dutīes, miserīes, fellowēs*.

These rules concerning the quantity of our English sillables I haue disposed as they came next into my memory; others more methodicall, time and practise may produce. In the meane season, as the Grammarians leaue many sillables to the authority of the Poets, so do I likewise leaue many to their iudgments; and withall thus conclude, that there is no Art begun and perfected at one enterprise.

Samuel Daniel
c. 1562–1619

Like so many of his contemporaries, Samuel Daniel was primarily a courtier who used his modest literary facility as a means of social advancement. His poetry, largely forgotten today, contains many fine examples of Elizabethan style, but never approached the level achieved by Spenser or Sidney. His criticism—the product of public controversy—is perhaps of greater interest to the modern reader.

Daniel studied at Magdalen College, Oxford, and thereafter sought a diplomatic career for himself. He served in various capacities in Europe and travelled extensively before returning to England in 1592. After working as tutor in several noble households, he sought preferment at Court, where he received the patronage of Queen Anne and was commissioned to write a number of masques for ceremonial occasions.

In 1592, Daniel published *The Complaint of Rosamund,* containing the "Delia" sonnets written in honor of the Countess of Pembroke; the volume attracted both attention and praise. Between 1595 and 1609, Daniel wrote the epic drama *The Civil Wars,* a history of the War of the Roses, which was to influence Shakespeare when he composed *Richard II* and *Henry IV.* Daniel's greatest poetic work, however, was the "Musophilus," a "defense" of poetry written in verse and published in *Poetical Essays* in 1599.

The Defence of Rhyme, written in 1603, was a response to Thomas Campion's *Observations in the Art of English Poetry,* published the previous year. Daniel's tone is calm and polite throughout (indeed, he never mentions Campion or his work by name), but the effect of the piece was devastating nonetheless. He points out, among other things, the fact that Campion does not follow his own rules of composition, that many of the respected poets of the classical era did not follow them, that Campion's views concerning the "barbarism" of the Middle Ages are unfounded and absurd, and that rhyme serves a useful and pleasant function within poetry.

The most important aspect of Daniel's *Defence,* however, is to be found in his declaration that it is futile and impossible to lay down rules which poetry must follow as a first principle. Poetic custom, according to Daniel, not only takes precedence over artistic conventions: it defines them. This simple idea was to exert a mighty influence in subsequent years, particularly upon the Romantics, who would elevate it to the level of a manifesto. While Daniel did not, by any means, invent this concept, he was one of the first to pronounce it, and did so in a work of much influence and weight.

Daniel stayed on at Court a number of years, writing plays, masques, and poetry, and cultivating friends and influence. There is some evidence that he fell into disfavor towards the end of his life, and he retired to Beckington, in Wiltshire, where he died on October 14, 1619.

A Defence of Rhyme is taken from *Elizabethan Critical Essays*, edited by G. Gregory Smith (Oxford University Press, 1904).

A Defence of Rhyme

To All the Worthie Louers and Learned Professors of Ryme Within His Maiesties Dominions

Worthie Gentlemen, about a yeare since, vpon the great reproach giuen to the Professors of Rime and the vse thereof, I wrote a priuate letter, as a defence of mine owne vndertakings in that kinde, to a learned Gentleman, a great friend of mine, then in Court. Which I did rather to confirm my selfe in mine owne courses, and to hold him from being wonne from vs, then with any desire to publish the same to the world.

But now, seeing the times to promise a more regarde to the present condition of our writings, in respect of our Soueraignes happy inclination this way, whereby wee are rather to expect an incoragement to go on with what we do then that any innouation should checke vs with a shew of what it would do in an other kinde, and yet doe nothing but depraue, I haue now giuen a greater body to the same Argument, and here present it to your view, vnder the patronage of a noble Earle, who in bloud and nature is interessed to take our parte in this cause with others, who cannot, I know, but holde deare the monuments that haue beene left vnto the world in this manner of composition, and who I trust will take in good parte this my Defence, if not as it is my particular, yet in respect of the cause I vndertake, which I heere inuoke you all to protect.

Sa. D.

To William Herbert, Erle of Pembrooke

The Generall Custome and vse of Ryme in this kingdome, Noble Lord, hauing beene so long (as if from a Graunt of Nature) held vnquestionable, made me to imagine that it lay altogither out of the way of contradiction, and was become so natural, as we should neuer haue had a thought to cast it off into reproch, or be made to thinke that it ill-became our language. But now I see, when there is opposition made to all things in the world by wordes, wee must nowe at length likewise fall to contend for words themselues, and make a question whether they be right or not. For we are tolde how that our measures goe wrong, all Ryming is grosse, vulgare, barbarous; which if it be so, we haue lost much labour to no purpose; and, for mine owne particular, I cannot but blame the fortune of the times and mine owne Genius, that cast me vppon so wrong a course, drawne with the current of custome and an vnexamined example. Hauing beene first incourag'd or fram'd thereunto by your most Worthy and Honorable Mother, and receiuing the first notion for the formall ordering of those compositions at Wilton, which I must euer acknowledge to haue beene my best Schoole, and thereof alwayes am to hold a feeling and gratefull Memory; afterward drawne farther on by the well liking and approbation of my worthy Lord, the fosterer of mee and my Muse; I aduentured to bestow all my whole powers therein, perceiuing it agreed so well, both with the complexion of the times and mine owne constitution, as I found not wherein I might better imploy me. But yet now, vpon the great discouery of these new measures, threatning to ouerthrow the whole state of Ryme in this kingdom, I must either stand out to defend, or els be forced to forsake my selfe and giue ouer all. And though irresolution and a selfe distrust be the most apparent faults of my nature, and that the least checke of reprehension, if it sauour of reason, will as easily shake my resolution as any man's liuing, yet in this case I know not how I am growne more resolued, and, before I sinke, willing to examine what those powers of iudgement are that must beare me downe and beat me off from the station of my profession, which by the law of Nature I am set to defend: and the rather for that this detractor (whose commendable Rymes, albeit now himselfe an enemy to ryme, haue giuen heretofore to the world the best notice of his worth) is a man of faire parts and good reputation; and therefore the reproach forcibly cast from such a hand may throw downe more at once then the labors of many shall in long time build vp againe, specially vpon the slippery foundation of opinion, and the world's inconstancy, which knowes not well what it would haue, and

> *Discit enim citius meminitque libentius illud*
> *Quod quis deridet, quam quod probat et veneratur.*

And he who is thus become our vnkinde aduersarie must pardon vs if we be as iealous of our fame and reputation as hee is desirous of credite by his new-old arte, and must consider that we cannot, in a thing that concernes vs so neere, but haue a feeling of the wrong done, wherein euery Rymer in this vniuersall Iland, as well as myselfe, stands interressed. So that if his charitie had equally drawne with his learning, hee would haue forborne to procure the enuie of so powerfull a number vpon him, from whom he can not but expect the returne of a like measure of blame, and onely haue made way to his owne grace by the proofe of his abilitie, without the disparaging of vs, who would haue bin glad to haue stood quietly by him, and perhaps commended his aduenture, seeing that euermore of one science an other may be borne, and that these Salies made out of the quarter of our set knowledges are the gallant proffers onely of attemptiue spirits, and commendable, though they worke no other effect than make a Brauado: and I know it were *Indecens et morosum nimis alienae industriae modum ponere.*

We could well haue allowed of his numbers, had he not disgraced our Ryme, which both Custome and Nature doth most powerfully defend: Custome that is before all Law, Nature that is aboue all Arte. Euery language hath her proper number or measure fitted to vse and delight, which Custome, intertaininge by the allowance of the Eare, doth indenize and make naturall. All verse is but a frame of wordes confined within certaine measure, differing from the ordinarie speach, and introduced, the better to expresse mens conceipts, both for delight and memorie. Which frame of words consisting of *Rithmus* or *Metrum*, Number or measure, are disposed into diuers fashions, according to the humour of the Composer and the set of the time. And these *Rhythmi*, as Aristotle saith, are familiar amongst all Nations, and *e naturali et sponte fusa compositione*: and they fall as naturally already in our language as euer Art can make them, being such as the Eare of it selfe doth marshall in their proper roomes; and they of themselues will not willingly be put out of their ranke, and that in such a verse as best comports with the nature of our language. And for our Ryme (which is an excellencie added to this worke of measure, and a Harmonie farre happier than any proportion Antiquitie could euer shew vs) dooth adde more grace, and hath more of delight then euer bare numbers, howsoeuer they can be forced to runne in our slow language, can possibly yeeld. Which, whether it be deriu'd of *Rhythmus* or of Romance, which were songs the Bards and Druydes about Rymes vsed, and therof were called *Remensi*, as some Italians holde, or howsoeuer, it is likewise number and harmonie of words, consisting of an agreeing sound in the last sillables of seuerall verses, giuing both to the Eare an Echo of a delightful report, and to the Memorie a deeper impression of what is deliuered therein. For as Greeke and Latine verse consists of the number and quantitie of sillables, so doth the English verse of measure and accent. And though it doth not strictly obserue long and short sillables, yet it most religiously respects the accent; and as the short and the long make number, so the acute and graue accent yeelde harmonie. And harmonie is likewise number; so that the English verse then hath number, measure, and harmonie in the best proportion of Musicke. Which, being more certain and more resounding, works that effect of motion with as happy successe as either the Greek or Latin. And so naturall a melody is it, and so vniuersall, as it seems to be generally borne with al the Nations of the world as an hereditary eloquence proper to all mankind. The vniuersalitie argues the generall power of it: for if the Barbarian vse it, then it shewes that it swais th' affection of the Barbarian: if ciuil nations practise it, it proues that it works vpon the harts of ciuil nations: if all, then that it hath a power in nature on all. *Georgieuez de Turcarum moribus* hath an example of the Turkish Rymes iust of the measure of our verse of eleuen sillables, in feminine Ryme; neuer begotten I am perswaded by any example in Europe, but borne no doubt in Scythia, and brought over Caucasus and Mount Taurus. The Sclauonian and Arabian tongs acquaint a great part of Asia and Affrique with it; the Moscouite, Polacke, Hungarian, German, Italian, French, and Spaniard vse no other harmonie of words. The Irish, Briton, Scot, Dane, Saxon, English, and all the Inhabiters of this Iland either haue hither brought or here found the same in vse. And such a force hath it in nature, or so made by nature, as the Latine numbers, notwithstanding their excellencie, seemed not sufficient to satisfie the eare of the world thereunto accustomed, without this Harmonicall cadence: which made the most learned of all nations labour with exceeding trauaile to bring those numbers likewise vnto it: which many did with that happinesse as neither their puritie of tongue nor their materiall contemplations are thereby any way disgraced, but rather deserue to be reuerenced of all grateful posteritie, with the due regard of their worth. And for *Schola Salerna*, and those *Carmina*

Prouerbialia, who finds not therein more precepts for vse, concerning diet, health, and conuersation, then Cato, Theognis, or all the Greekes and Latines can shew vs in that kinde of teaching? and that in so few words, both for delight to the eare and the hold of memorie, as they are to be imbraced of all modest readers that studie to know and not to depraue.

Me thinkes it is a strange imperfection that men should thus ouer-runne the estimation of good things with so violent a censure, as though it must please none else because it likes not them: whereas *Oportet arbitratores esse non contradictores eos qui verum indicaturi sunt*, saith Arist, though he could not obserue it himselfe. And milde charitie tells vs:

> ——— *Non ego paucis*
> *Offendar maculis quas aut incuria fudit*
> *Aut humana parum cauit natura.*

For all men haue their errours, and we must take the best of their powers, and leaue the rest as not apperteining vnto vs.

'Ill customes are to be left.' I graunt it; but I see not howe that can be taken for an ill custome which nature hath thus ratified, all nations receiued, time so long confirmed, the effects such as it performes those offices of motion for which it is imployed; delighting the eare, stirring the heart, and satisfying the iudgement in such sort as I doubt whether euer single numbers will doe in our Climate, if they shew no more worke of wonder than yet we see. And if euer they prooue to become anything, it must be by the approbation of many ages that must giue them their strength for any operation, as before the world will feele where the pulse, life, and enargie lies; which now we are sure where to haue in our Rymes, whose knowne frame hath those due staies for the minde, those incounters of touch, as makes the motion certaine, though the varietie be infinite.

Nor will the Generall sorte for whom we write (the wise being aboue books) taste these laboured measures but as an orderly prose when wee haue all done. For this kinde acquaintance and continuall familaritie euer had betwixt our eare and this cadence is growne to so intimate a friendship, as it will nowe hardly euer be brought to misse it. For be the verse neuer so good, neuer so full, it seemes not to satisfie nor breede that delight, as when it is met and combined with a like sounding accent: which seemes as the iointure without which it hangs loose, and cannot subsist, but runnes wildely on, like a tedious fancie without a close. Suffer then the world to inioy that which it knowes, and what it likes: Seeing that whatsoeuer force of words doth mooue, delight, and sway the affections of men, in what Scythian sorte soeuer it be disposed or vttered, that is true number, measure, eloquence, and the perfection of speach: which I said hath as many shapes as there be tongues or nations in the world, nor can with all the tyrannicall Rules of idle Rhetorique be gouerned otherwise then custome and present obseruation will allow. And being now the trym and fashion of the times, to sute a man otherwise cannot but giue a touch of singularity; for when hee hath all done, hee hath but found other clothes to the same body, and peraduenture not so fitting as the former. But could our Aduersary hereby set vp the musicke of our times to a higher note of iudgement and discretion, or could these new lawes of words better our imperfections, it were a happy attempt; but when hereby we shall but as it were change prison, and put off these fetters to receiue others, what haue we gained? As good still to vse ryme and a little reason as neither ryme nor reason, for no doubt, as idle wits will write in that kinde, as do now in this, imitation wil after, though it breake her necke. *Scribimus indocti doctique poemata passim.* And this multitude of idle Writers can be no disgrace to the good; for the same fortune in one proportion or other is proper in a like season to all States in their turne; and the same vnmeasurable confluence of Scriblers hapned when measures were most in vse among the Romanes, as we finde by this reprehension,

> *Mutauit mentem populus leuis, et calet vno*
> *Scribendi studio; pueri[que] patresque seueri*
> *Fronde comas vincti cenant et carmina dictant.*

So that their plentie seemes to haue bred the same waste and contempt as ours doth now, though it had not power to disualew what was worthy of posteritie, nor keep backe the reputation of excellencies destined to continue for many ages. For seeing it is matter that satisfies the iudiciall, appeare it in what habite it will, all these pretended proportions of words, howsoeuer placed, can be but words, and peraduenture serue but to embroyle our vnderstanding; whilst seeking to please our eare, we enthrall our iudgement; to delight an exterior sense, wee smooth vp a weake confused sense, affecting sound to be vnsound, and all to seeme *Servum pecus*, onely to imitate Greekes and Latines, whose felicitie in this kinde might be something to themselues, to whome their owne *idioma* was naturall; but to vs it can yeeld no other commoditie then a sound. We admire them not for their smooth-gliding words, nor their measures, but for their inuentions; which treasure if it were to be found in Welch and Irish, we should hold those languages in the same estimation; and they may thanke their sword that made their tongues so famous and vniuersall as they are. For to say truth, their Verse is many times but a confused deliuerer of their excellent conceits, whose scattered limbs we are faine to looke out and ioyne together, to discerne the image of what they represent vnto vs. And euen the Latines, who professe not to be so licentious as the Greekes, shew vs many times examples, but of strange crueltie in torturing and dismembering of words in the middest, or disioyning such as naturally should be married and march together, by setting them as farre asunder as they can possibly stand: that sometimes, vnlesse the kind reader out of his owne good nature wil stay them vp by their measure, they will fall downe into flatte prose, and sometimes are no other indeede in their naturall sound: and then againe, when you finde them disobedient to their owne Lawes, you must hold it to be *licentia poetica*, and so dispensable. The striuing to shew their changable measures in the varietie of their Odes haue been verie painefull no doubt vnto them, and forced them thus to disturbe the quiet streame of their words, which by a naturall succession otherwise desire to follow in their due course.

But such affliction doth laboursome curiositie still lay vpon our best delights (which euer must be made strange and variable), as if Art were ordained to afflict Nature, and that we could not goe but in fetters. Euery science, euery profession, must be so wrapt vp in vnnecessary intrications, as if it were not to fashion but to confound the vnderstanding: which makes me much to distrust man, and feare that our presumption goes beyond our abilitie, and our Curiositie is more then our Iudgement; laboring euer to seeme to be more then we are, or laying greater burthens vpon our mindes then they are well able to beare, because we would not appeare like other men.

And indeed I haue wished that there were not that multiplicitie of Rymes as is vsed by many in Sonets, which yet we see in some so happily to succeed, and hath beene so farre from hindering their inuentions, as it hath begot conceit beyond expectation, and comparable to the best inuentions of the world: for sure in an eminent spirit, whome Nature hath fitted for that mysterie, Ryme is no impediment to his conceit, but rather giues him wings to mount, and carries him, not out of his course, but as it were beyond his power to a farre happier flight. Al excellencies being sold vs at the hard price of labour, it followes, where we bestow most thereof we buy the best successe: and Ryme, being farre more laborious than loose measures (whatsoeuer is obiected), must needs, meeting with wit and industry, breed greater and worthier effects in our language. So that if our labours haue wrought out a manumission from bondage, and that wee goe at libertie, notwithstanding these ties, wee are no longer the slaues of Ryme, but we make it a most excellent instrument to serue vs. Nor is this certaine limit obserued in Sonnets, any tyrannicall bounding of the conceit, but rather reducing it in *girum* and a iust forme, neither too long for the shortest proiect, nor too short for the longest, being but onely imployed for a present passion. For the body of our imagination being as an vnformed Chaos without fashion, without day, if by the diuine power of the spirit it be wrought into an Orbe of order and forme, is it not more pleasing to Nature, that desires a certaintie and comports not with that which is infinite, to haue these clozes, rather than not to know where to end, or how farre to goe, especially seeing our passions are often without measure? and wee finde the best of the Latines many times either not concluding or els otherwise in the end then they began. Besides, is it not most delightfull to see much excellentlie ordred in a small roome, or little gallantly disposed and made to fill vp a space of like capacitie, in such sort that the one would not appeare so beautifull in a larger circuite, nor the other do well in a lesse? which often we find to be so, according to the powers of nature in the workman. And these limited proportions and rests of stanzes, consisting of six, seuen, or eight lines, are of that happines both for the disposition of the matter, the apt planting the sentence where it may best stand to hit, the certaine close of delight with the full bodie of a iust period well carried, is such as neither the Greekes or Latines euer attained vnto. For their boundlesse running on often so confounds the Reader, that, hauing once lost himselfe, must either giue off vnsatisfied, or vncertainely cast backe to retriue the escaped sence, and to find way againe into this matter.

Me thinkes we should not so soone yeeld our consents captiue to the authoritie of Antiquitie, vnlesse we saw more reason; all our vnderstandings are not to be built by the square of Greece and Italie. We are the children of nature as well as they; we are not so placed out of the way of iudgement but that the same Sunne of Discretion shineth vppon vs; we haue our portion of the same virtues as well as of the same vices: *Et Catilinam quocunque in populo videas, quocunque sub axe.* Time and the turne of things bring about these faculties according to the present estimation: and *Res temporibus non tempora rebus seruire oportet.* So that we must neuer rebell against vse: *Quem penes arbitrium est et vis et norma loquendi.* It is not the obseruing of *Trochaicques* nor their *Iambicques* that wil make our writings ought the wiser. All their Poesie, all their Philosophie is nothing, vnlesse we bring the discerning light of conceipt with vs to apply it to vse. It is not bookes, but onely that great booke of the world and the all-ouerspreading grace of heauen that makes men truly iudiciall. Nor can it be but a touch of arrogant ignorance to hold this or that nation Barbarous, these or those times grosse, considering how this manifold creature man, wheresoeuer hee stand in the world, hath alwayes some disposition of worth, intertaines the order of societie, affects that which is most in vse, and is eminent in some one thing or other that fits his humour and the times. The Grecians held all other nations barbarous but themselues; yet Pirrhus when he saw the well ordered marching of the Romanes, which made them see their presumptuous errour, could say it was no barbarous manner of proceeding. The Gothes, Vandales, and Longobards, whose comming downe like an inundation ouerwhelmed, as they say, al the glory of learning in Europe, haue yet left vs stil their lawes and customes as the originalls of most of the prouinciall constitutions of Christendome, which well considered with their other courses of gouernement may serue to cleare them from this imputation of ignorance. And though the vanquished neuer yet spake well of the Conquerour, yet even thorow the vnsound couerings of malidiction appeare those monuments of trueth as argue wel their worth and proues them not without iudgement, though without Greeke and Latine.

Will not experience confute vs, if wee shoulde say the state of China, which neuer heard of Anapestiques, Trochies, and Tribracques, were grosse, barbarous, and vnciuille? And is it not a most apparant ignorance, both of the succession of learning in Europe, and the generall course of things, to say 'that all lay pittifully deformed in those lacke-learning times from the declining of the Romane Empire till the light of the Latine tongue was reuiued by Rewcline, Erasmus, and Moore'? when for three hundred yeeres before them, about the comming downe of Tamburlaine into Europe, Franciscus Petrarcha (who then no doubt likewise found whom to imitate) shewed all the best notions of learning, in that degree of excellencie both in Latine, Prose and Verse, and in the vulgare Italian, as all the wittes of posteritie haue not yet much ouer-matched him in all kindes to this day: his great Volumes in Moral Philosophie shew his infinite reading and most happy power of disposition: his twelue Æglogues, his *Affrica*, containing nine Bookes of the last Punicke warre, with his three bookes of Epistles in Latine verse shew all the transformations of wit and inuention that a Spirite naturally borne to the inheritance of Poetrie and iudiciall knowledge could expresse: all which notwithstanding wrought him not that glory and fame with his owne Nation as did his Poems in Italian, which they esteeme aboue al whatsoeuer wit could haue inuented in any other forme then wherein it is: which questionles they wil not change with the best measures Greeks or Latins can shew them, howsoeuer our Aduersary imagines. Nor could this very same innouation in Verse, begun amongst them by C. Tolomœi, but die in the attempt, and was buried as soone as it came borne, neglected as a prodigious and vnnaturall issue amongst them: nor could it neuer induce Tasso, the wonder of Italy, to write that admirable Poem of *Ierusalem*, comparable to the best of the ancients, in any other forme than the accustomed verse. And with Petrarch liued his scholar Boccacius, and neere about the same time Iohannis Rauenensis, and from these, *tanquam ex equo Troiano*, seemes to haue issued all those famous Italian Writers, Leonardus Aretinus, Laurentius Valla, Poggius, Biondus, and many others. Then Emanuel Chrysolaras, a Constantinopolitan gentleman, renowmed for his learning and vertue, being imployed by Iohn Paleologus, Emperour of the East, to implore the ayde of Christian Princes for the succouring of perishing Greece, and vnderstanding in the meane time how Baiazeth was taken prisoner by Tamburlan, and his country freed from danger, stayed still at Venice, and there taught the Greeke tongue, discontinued before in these parts the space of seauen hundred yeeres. Him followed Bessarion, George Trapezuntius, Theodorus Gaza, and others, transporting Philosophie, beaten by the Turke out of Greece, into christendome. Hereupon came that mightie confluence of Learning in these parts, which, returning as it were *per postliminium*, and heere meeting then with the new inuented stampe of Printing, spread it selfe indeed in a more vniuersall sorte then the world euer heertofore had it; when Pomponius Laetus, Aeneas Syluius, Angelus Politianus, Hermolaus Barbarus, Iohannes Picus de Mirandula, the miracle and Phœnix of the world, adorned Italie, and wakened other Nations likewise with this desire of glory, long before it brought foorth Rewclen, Erasmus, and Moore, worthy men, I confesse, and the last a great ornament to this land, and a Rymer.

And yet long before all these, and likewise with these, was not our Nation behinde in her portion of spirite and worthinesse, but concurrent with the best of all this lettered world; witnesse venerable Bede, that flourished aboue a thousand yeeres since; Aldelmus Durotelmus, that liued in the yeere 739, of whom we finde this commendation registred: *Omnium Poetarum sui temporis facile primus, tantae eloquentiae, maiestatis, et eruditionis homo fuit, vt nunquam satis admirari possim vnde illi in tam barbara ac rudi aetate facundia accreuerit, vsque adeo omnibus numeris tersa, elegans, et rotunda, versus edidit cum antiquitate de palma contendentes.* Witnesse Iosephus Deuonius, who wrote *de bello Trioano* in so excellent a manner, and so neere resembling Antiquitie, as Printing his Worke beyond the seas they haue ascribed it to Cornelius Nepos, one of the Ancients. What should I name Walterus Mape, Gulielmus Nigellus, Geruasius Tilburiensis, Bracton, Bacon, Ockam, and an infinite Catalogue of excellent men, most of them liuing about foure hundred yeeres since, and haue left behinde them monuments of most profound iudgement and learning in all sciences! So that it is but the clowds gathered about our owne iudgement that makes vs thinke all other ages wrapt vp in mists, and the great distance betwixt vs that causes vs to image men so farre off to be so little in respect of our selues.

We must not looke vpon the immense course of times past as men ouerlooke spacious and wide countries from off high Mountaines, and are neuer the neere to iudge of the true Nature of the soyle or the particular syte and face of those territories they see. Nor must we thinke, viewing the superficiall figure of a region in a Mappe, that wee know strait the fashion and place as it is. Or reading an Historie (which is but a Mappe of Men, and dooth no otherwise acquaint vs with the true Substance of Circumstances then a superficiall Card dooth the Seaman with a Coast neuer seene, which alwayes prooues other to the eye than the imagination forecast it), that presently wee know all the world, and can distinctly iudge of times, men, and manners, iust as they were: When the best measure of man is to be taken by his owne foote bearing euer the meerest proportion to himselfe, and is neuer so farre different and vnequall in his powers, that he hath all in perfection at one time, and nothing at another. The distribution of giftes are vniuersall, and all seasons haue them in some sort. We must not thinke but that there were Scipioes, Cæsars, Catoes, and Pompeies borne elsewhere then at Rome; the rest of the world hath euer had them in the same degree of nature, though not of state. And it is our weaknesse that makes vs mistake or misconcieue in these deliniations of men the true figure of their worth. And our passion and beliefe is so apt to leade vs beyond truth, that vnlesse we try them by the iust compasse of humanitie, and as they were men, we shall cast their figures in the ayre, when we should make their models vpon Earth. It is not the contexture of words, but the effects of Action, that giues glory to the times: we find they had *mercurium in pectore*, though not in *lingua*; and in all ages, though they were not Ciceronians, they knew the Art of men, which onely is *Ars Artium*, the great gift of heauen, and the chiefe grace and glory on earth; they had the learning of Gouernement, and ordring their State; Eloquence inough to shew their iudgements. And it seemes the best times followed Lycurgus councell; *Literas ad vsum saltem discebant, reliqua omnis disciplina erat vt pulchre pararent vt labores preferrent, &c.* Had not vnlearned Rome laide the better foundation, and built the stronger frame of an admirable state, eloquent Rome had confounded it vtterly, which we saw ranne the way of all confusion, the plaine course of dissolution, in her greatest skill: and though she had not power to vndoe herselfe, yet wrought she so that she cast herselfe quite away from the glory of a commonwealth, and fell vpon the forme of state she euer most feared and abhorred of all other: and then scarse was there seene any shadowe of pollicie vnder her first Emperours, but the most horrible and grosse confusion that could be conceued; notwithstanding it still indured, preseruing not onely a Monarchie, locked vp in her own limits, but therewithall held vnder her obedience so many Nations so farre distant, so ill affected, so disorderly commanded and vniustly conquered, as it is not to be attributed to any other fate but to the first frame of that commonwealth; which was so strongly ioynted, and with such infinite combinations interlinckt as one naile or other euer held vp the Maiestie thereof. There is but one learning, which *omnes gentes habent scriptum in cordibus suis*, one and the selfe-same spirit that worketh in all. We haue but one bodie of Iustice, one bodie of Wisdome thorowout the whole world; which is but apparelled according to the fashion of euery nation.

Eloquence and gay wordes are not of the substance of wit; it is but the garnish of a nice time, the Ornaments that doe but decke the house of a State, and *imitatur publicos mores*: Hunger is as well satisfied with meat serued in pewter as siluer. Discretion is the best measure, the rightest foote in what habit soeuer it runne. Erasmus, Rewcline, and More brought no more wisdome into the world with all their new reuiued wordes then we finde was before; it bred not a profounder Diuine then S. Thomas, a greater Lawyer then Bartolus, a more acute Logician then Scotus; nor are the effects of all this great amasse of eloquence so admirable or of that consequence, but that *impexa illa antiquitas* can yet compare with them.

Let vs go no further but looke vpon the wonderfull Architecture of this state of England, and see whether they were deformed times that could giue it such a forme: Where there is no one the least piller of Maiestie but was set with most profound iudgement, and borne vp with the iust conueniencie of Prince and people: no Court of iustice but laide by the Rule and Square of Nature, and the best of the best commonwealths that euer were in the world: so strong and substantial as it hath stood against al the storms of factions, both of beliefe and ambition, which so powerfully beat vpon it, and all the tempestuous alterations of humorous times whatsoeuer: being continually in all ages furnisht with spirites fitte to maintaine the maiestie of her owne greatnes, and to match in an equall concurrencie all other kingdomes round about her with whome it had to incounter.

But this innouation, like a Viper, must euer make way into the world's opinion, thorow the bowelles of her owne breeding, and is alwayes borne with reproch in her mouth; the disgracing others is the best grace it can put on, to winne reputation of wit; and yet it is neuer so wise as it would seeme, nor doth the world euer get so much by it as it imagineth; which being so often deceiued, and seeing it neuer performes so much as it promises, me thinkes men should neuer giue more credite vnto it. For, let vs change neuer so often, wee can not change man; our imperfections must still runne on with vs. And therefore the wiser Nations haue taught menne alwayes to vse, *Moribus legibusque praesentibus etiamsi deteriores sint.* The Lacedæmonians, when a Musitian, thincking to winne himselfe credite by his new inuention and be before his fellowes, had added one string more to his Crowde, brake his fiddle and banished him the Citie, holding the Innouator, though in the least things, dangerous to a publike societie. It is but a fantastike giddinesse to forsake the way of other men, especially where it lies tolerable: *Vbi nunc est respublica, ibi simus potius quam dum illam veterem sequimur simus in nulla.*

But shal we not tend to perfection? Yes: and that euer best by going on in the course we are in, where we haue aduantage, being so farre onward, of him that is but now setting forth. For we shall neuer proceede, if wee be euer beginning, nor arriue at any certayne Porte, sayling with all windes that blowe— *non conualescit planta quae saepius transfertur*—and therefore let vs hold on in the course wee haue vndertaken, and not still be wandring. Perfection is not the portion of man; and if it were, why may wee not as well get to it this way as another, and suspect those great vndertakers, lest they have conspired with enuy to betray our proceedings, and put vs by the honour of our attempts, with casting vs backe vpon another course, of purpose to ouerthrow the whole action of glory when we lay the fairest for it, and were so neere our hopes? I thanke God that I am none of these great Schollers, if thus their hie knowledges doe but giue them more eyes to looke out into vncertaintie and confusion, accounting my selfe rather beholding to my ignorance that hath set me in so lowe an vnderroome of conceipt with other men, and hath giuen me as much distrust, as it hath done hope, daring not aduenture to goe alone, but plodding on the plaine tract I finde beaten by Custome and the Time, contenting me with what I see in vse.

And surely mee thinkes these great wittes should rather seeke to adorne than to disgrace the present; bring something to it, without taking from it what it hath. But it is euer the misfortune of Learning to be wounded by her owne hand. *Stimulos dat emula virtus*, and where there is not abilitie to match what is, malice will finde out ingines, either to disgrace or ruine it, with a peruerse incounter of some new impression; and, which is the greatest misery, it must euer proceed from the powers of the best reputation, as if the greatest spirites were ordained to indanger the worlde, as the grosse are to dishonour it, and that we were to expect *ab optimis periculum, a pessimis dedecus publicum*. Emulation, the strongest pulse that beats in high mindes, is oftentimes a winde, but of the worst effect; for whilst the soule comes disappoynted of the obiect it wrought on, it presently forges another, and euen cozins it selfe, and crosses all the world, rather than it will stay to be vnder her desires, falling out with all it hath, to flatter and make faire that which it would haue.

So that it is the ill successe of our longings that with Xerxes makes vs to whippe the sea, and send a cartel of defiance to Mount Athos: and the fault laide vpon others weakenesse is but a presumptuous opinion of our owne strength, who must not seeme to be maistered. But had our Aduersary taught vs by his owne proceedings this way of perfection, and therein fram'd vs a Poeme of that excellencie as should haue put downe all, and beene the maisterpeece of these times, we should all haue admired him. But to depraue the present forme of writing, and to bring vs nothing but a few loose and vncharitable Epigrammes, and yet would make vs belieue those numbers were come to raise the glory of our language, giueth vs cause to suspect the performance, and to examine whether this new Arte *constat sibi*, or *aliquid sit dictum quod non sit dictum prius*.

First, we must heere imitate the Greekes and Latines, and yet we are heere shewed to disobey them, euen in their owne numbers and quantities; taught to produce what they make short, and make short what they produce; made beleeue to be shewd measures in that forme we haue not seene, and no such matter; tolde that heere is the perfect Art of versifying, which in conclusion is yet confessed to be vnperfect, as if our Aduersary, to be opposite to vs, were become vnfaithfull to himselfe, and, seeking to leade vs out of the way of reputation, hath aduentured to intricate and confound him in his owne courses, running vpon most vneuen groundes, with imperfect rules, weake proofs, and vnlawful lawes. Whereunto the world, I am perswaded, is not so vnreasonable as to subscribe, considering the vniust authoritie of the Lawgiuer: for who hath constituted him to be the Radamanthus, thus to torture sillables and adiudge them their perpetuall doome, setting his Theta or marke of condemnation vppon them, to indure the appoynted sentence of his crueltie, as hee shall dispose? As though there were that disobedience in our wordes, as they would not be ruled or stand in order without so many intricate Lawes; which would argue a great peruersenesse amongst them, according to that *in pessima republica plurimae leges*, or that they were so farre gone from the quiet freedome of nature that they must thus be brought backe againe by force. And now in what case were this poore state of words, if in like sorte another tyrant the next yeere should arise and abrogate these lawes and ordaine others cleane contrary according to his humor, and say that they were onely right, the others vniust? what disturbance were there here, to whome should we obey? Were it not farre better to holde vs fast to our olde custome than to stand thus distracted with vncertaine Lawes, wherein right shall haue as many faces as it pleases Passion to make it, that wheresoeuer mens affections stand, it shall still looke that way? What trifles doth our vnconstant curiositie cal vp to contend for? what colours are there laid vpon indifferent things to make them seeme other then they are, as if it were but only to intertaine contestation amongst men, who, standing according to the prospectiue of their owne humour, seeme to see the selfe same things to appeare otherwise to them than either they doe to other, or are indeede in them selues, being but all one in nature? For what adoe haue we heere? what strange precepts of Arte about the framing of an Iambique verse in our language? which, when all is done, reaches not by a foote, but falleth out to be the plaine ancient verse, consisting of ten sillables or fiue feete, which hath euer beene vsed amongest vs time out of minde, and, for all this cunning and counterfeit name, can or will [not] be any other in nature then it hath beene euer heretofore: and this new Dimeter is but the halfe of this verse diuided in two, and no other then the Caesura or breathing place in the middest thereof, and therefore it had bene as good to haue put two lines in one, but only to make them seeme diuerse. Nay, it had beene much better for the true English reading and pronouncing thereof, without violating the accent, which now our Aduersarie hath heerein most vnkindely doone: for, being as wee are to sound it, according to our English March, we must make a rest, and raise the last sillable, which falles out very vnnaturall in *Desolate, Funerall, Elizabeth, Prodigall*, and in all the rest, sauing the Monosillables. Then followes the English Trochaicke, which is saide to bee a simple verse, and so indeede it is, being without Ryme: hauing here no other grace then that in sound it runnes like the knowne measure of our former ancient Verse, ending (as we terme it according to the French) in a feminine foote, sauing that it is shorter by one sillable at the beginning, which is not much missed, by reason it falles full at the last. Next comes the Elegiacke, being the fourth kinde, and that likewise is no other then our old accustomed measure of fiue feet: if there be any difference, it must be made in the reading, and therein wee must stand bound to stay where often we would not, and sometimes either breake the accent or the due course of the word. And now for the other foure kinds of numbers, which are to be employed for Odes, they are either of the same measure, or such as haue euer beene familiarly vsed amongst vs.

So that of all these eight seuerall kindes of new promised numbers, you see what we haue: Onely what was our owne before, and the same but apparelled in forraine Titles; which had they come in their kinde and naturall attire of Ryme, wee should neuer haue suspected that they had affected to be other, or sought to degenerate into strange manners, which now we see was the cause why they were turnd out of their proper habite, and brought in as Aliens, onely to induce men to admire them as farre commers. But see the power of Nature; it is not all the artificiall couerings of wit that can hide their natiue and originall condition, which breakes out thorow the strongest bandes of affectation, and will be it selfe, doe Singularitie what it can. And as for those imagined quantities of sillables, which haue bin euer held free and indifferent in our language, who can inforce vs to take knowledge of them, being *in nullius verba iurati*, and owing fealty to no forraine inuention? especially in such a case where there is no necessitie in Nature, or that it imports either the matter or forme, whether it be so or otherwise. But euery Versifier that wel obserues his worke findes in our language, without all these vnnecessary precepts, what numbers best fitte the Nature of her Idiome, and the proper places destined to such accents as she will not let in to any other roomes then in those for which they were borne. As for example, you cannot make this fall into the right sound of a verse—

> None thinkes reward rendred worthy his worth,

vnlesse you thus misplace the accent vpon *Rendrèd* and *Worthìe*, contrary to the nature of these wordes: which sheweth that two feminine numbers (or Trochies, if so you wil call them) will not succeede in the third and fourth place of the Verse. And so likewise in this case,

> Though Death doth consume, yet Vertue preserues,

it wil not be a Verse, though it hath the iust sillables, without the same number in the second, and the altering of the fourth place in this sorte,

> Though Death doth ruine, Virtue yet preserues.

Againe, who knowes not that we can not kindely answere a feminine number with a masculine Ryme, or (if you will so terme it) a Trochei with a Sponde, as *Weaknes* with *Confesse*, *Nature* and *Indure*, onely for that thereby wee shall wrong the accent, the chiefe Lord and graue Gouernour of Numbers? Also you cannot in a verse of foure feet place a Trochei in the first, without the like offence, as, *Yearely out of his watry Cell*; for so you shall sound it Yearelìe, which is vnnaturall. And other such like obseruations vsually occurre, which Nature and a iudiciall eare of themselues teach vs readily to auoyde.

But now for whom hath our Aduersary taken all this paines? For the Learned, or for the Ignorant, or for himselfe, to shew his owne skill? If for the

Learned, it was to no purpose, for euerie Grammarian in this land hath learned his Prosodia, and alreadie knowes all this Arte of numbers: if for the Ignorant, it was vaine, for if they become Versifiers, wee are like to haue leane Numbers instead of fat Ryme; and if Tully would haue his Orator skilld in all the knowledges appertaining to God and man, what should they haue who would be a degree aboue Orators? Why then it was to shew his owne skill, and what himselfe had obserued; so he might well haue done without doing wrong to the fame of the liuing, and wrong to England, in seeking to lay reproach vpon her natiue ornaments, and to turne the faire streame and full course of her accents into the shallow current of a lesse vncertaintie, cleane out of the way of her knowne delight. And I had thought it could neuer haue proceeded from the pen of a Scholler (who sees no profession free from the impure mouth of the scorner) to say the reproach of others idle tongues is the curse of Nature vpon vs, when it is rather her curse vpon him, that knowes not how to vse his tongue. What, doth he think himselfe is now gotten so farre out of the way of contempt, that his numbers are gone beyond the reach of obloquie, and that, how friuolous or idle soeuer they shall runne, they shall be protected from disgrace? as though that light rymes and light numbers did not weigh all alike in the graue opinion of the wise. And that is not Ryme but our ydle Arguments that hath brought downe to so base a reckning the price and estimation of writing in this kinde; when the few good things of this age, by comming together in one throng and presse with the many bad, are not discerned from them, but ouerlooked with them, and all taken to be alike. But when after-times shall make a quest of inquirie, to examine the best of this Age, peraduenture there will be found in the now contemned recordes of Ryme matter not vnfitting the grauest Diuine and seuerest Lawyer in this kingdome. But these things must haue the date of Antiquitie to make them reuerend and authentical. For euer in the collation of Writers men rather weigh their age then their merite, and *legunt priscos cum reuerentia, quando coaetaneos non possunt sine inuidia.* And let no writer in Ryme be any way discouraged in his endeuour by this braue allarum, but rather animated to bring vp all the best of their powers, and charge with all the strength of nature and industrie vpon contempt, that the shew of their reall forces may turne backe insolencie into her owne holde. For be sure that innouation neuer works any ouerthrow, but vpon the aduantage of a carelesse idlenesse. And let this make vs looke the better to our feete, the better to our matter, better to our maners. Let the Aduersary that thought to hurt vs bring more profit and honor by being against vs then if he had stoode still on our side. For that (next to the awe of heauen) the best reine, the strongest hand to make men keepe their way, is that which their enemy beares vpon them: and let this be the benefite wee make by being oppugned, and the meanes to redeeme backe the good opinion vanitie and idlenesse haue suffered to be wonne from vs; which nothing but substance and matter can effect. For *Scribendi recte sapere est et principium et fons.*

When we heare Musicke, we must be in our eare in the vtter-roome of sense, but when we intertaine iudgement, we retire into the cabinet and innermost withdrawing chamber of the soule: And it is but as Musicke for the eare *Verba sequi fidibus modulanda Latinis*; but it is a worke of power for the soule *Numerosque modosque ediscere vitae*. The most iudiciall and worthy spirites of this Land are not so delicate, or will owe so much to their eare, as to rest vppon the outside of wordes, and be intertained with sound; seeing that both Number, Measure, and Ryme is but as the ground or seate, whereupon is raised the work that commends it, and which may be easilie at the first found out by any shallow conceipt: as wee see some fantasticke to beginne a fashion, which afterward grauity itselfe is faine to put on, because it will not be out of the weare of other men, and *Recti apud nos locum tenet error vbi publicus factus est*. And power and strength that can plant it selfe any where hauing built within this compasse, and reard it of so high a respect, wee now imbrace it as the fittest dwelling for our inuention, and haue thereon bestowed all the substance of our vnderstanding to furnish it as it is. And therefore heere I stand foorth, onelie to make good the place we haue thus taken vp, and to defend the sacred monuments erected therein, which containe the honour of the dead, the fame of the liuing, the glory of peace, and the best power of our speach, and wherein so many honourable spirits haue sacrificed to Memorie their dearest passions, shewing by what diuine influence they haue beene moued, and vnder what starres they liued.

But yet notwithstanding all this which I haue heare deliuered in the defence of Ryme, I am not so farre in loue with mine owne mysterie, or will seeme so froward, as to bee against the reformation and the better setling these measures of ours. Wherein there be many things I could wish were more certaine and better ordered, though my selfe dare not take vpon me to be a teacher therein, hauing so much neede to learne of others. And I must confesse that to mine owne eare those continuall cadences of couplets vsed in long and continued Poemes are verie tyresome and vnpleasing, by reason that still, me thinks, they run on with a sound of one nature, and a kinde of certaintie which stuffs the delight rather then intertaines it. But yet, notwithstanding, I must not out of mine owne daintinesse condemne this kinde of writing, which peraduenture to another may seeme most delightfull; and many worthy compositions we see to haue passed with commendation in that kinde. Besides, me thinkes, sometimes to beguile the eare with a running out, and passing ouer the Ryme, as no bound to stay vs in the line where the violence of the matter will breake thorow, is rather gracefull then otherwise. Wherein I finde my Homer-Lucan, as if he gloried to seeme to haue no bounds, albeit hee were confined within his measures, to be in my conceipt most happy. For so thereby they who care not for Verse or Ryme may passe it ouer with taking notice thereof, and please themselues with a well measured Prose. And I must confesse my Aduersary hath wrought this much vpon me, that I thinke a Tragedie would indeede best comporte with a blank Verse and dispence with Ryme, sauing in the Chorus, or where a sentence shall require a couplet. And to auoyde this ouer-glutting the eare with that alwayes certaine and full incounter of Ryme, I haue assaid in some of my Epistles to alter the vsuall place of meeting, and to sette it further off by one Verse, to trie how I could disuse mine owne eare and to ease it of this continuall burthen which indeede seemes to surcharge it a little too much: but as yet I cannot come to please my selfe therein, this alternate or crosse Ryme holding still the best place in my affection.

Besides, to me this change of number in a Poem of one nature fits not so wel as to mixe vncertainly feminine Rymes with masculine, which euer since I was warned of that deformitie by my kinde friend and countri-man Maister Hugh Samford, I haue alwayes so auoyded it, as there are not aboue two couplettes in that kinde in all my Poem of the Ciuill warres: and I would willingly if I coulde haue altered it in all the rest, holding feminine Rymes to be fittest for Ditties, and either to be set for certaine, or els by themselues. But in these things, I say, I dare not take vpon mee to teach that they ought to be so, in respect my selfe holds them to be so, or that I thinke it right: for indeed there is no right in these things that are continually in a wandring motion, carried with the violence of vncertaine likings, being but onely the time that giues them their power. For if this right or truth should be no other thing then that wee make it, we shall shape it into a thousand figures, seeing this excellent painter, Man, can so well lay the colours which himselfe grindes in his owne affections, as that hee will make them serue for any shadow and any counterfeit. But the greatest hinderer to our proceedings and the reformation of our errours is this Selfe-loue, whereunto we Versifiers are euer noted to bee specially subiect; a disease of all other the most dangerous and incurable, being once seated in the spirits, for which there is no cure but onely by a spirituall remedie. *Multos puto ad sapientiam potuisse peruenire, nisi putassent se peruenisse*: and this opinion of our sufficiencie makes so great a cracke in our iudgement, as it wil hardly euer holde any thing of worth. *Caecus amor sui*; and though it would seeme to see all without it, yet certainely it discernes but little within. For there is not the simplest writer that will euer tell himselfe he doth ill, but, as if he were the parasite onely to sooth his owne doings, perswades him that his lines can not but please others which so much delight himselfe: *Suffenus est quisque sibi*

> *—neque idem vnquam*
> *Aeque est beatus, ac poema cum scribit.*
> *Tam gaudet in se tamque se ipse miratur.*

And the more to shew that he is so, we shall see him euermore in all places, and to all persons repeating his owne compositions, and

> *Quem vero arripuit, tenet, occiditque legendo.*

Next to this deformitie stands our affectation, wherein we always bewray our selues to be both vnkinde and vnnaturall to our owne natiue language, in disguising or forging strange or vnusuall wordes, as if it were to make our verse seeme another kind of speach out of the course of our vsuall practise, displacing our wordes, or inuenting new, onely vpon a singularitie, when our owne accustomed phrase, set in the due place, would expresse vs more familiarly and to better delight than all this idle affectation of antiquitie or noueltie can euer doe. And I cannot but wonder at the strange presumption of some men, that dare so audaciously aduenture to introduce any whatsoeuer forraine wordes, be they neuer so strange, and of themselues, as it were, without a Parliament, without any consent or allowance, establish them as Free-denizens in our language. But this is but a Character of that perpetuall reuolution which wee see to be in all things that neuer remaine the same: and we must heerein be content to submit our selues to the law of time, which in few yeeres wil make al that for which we now contend Nothing.

BIBLIOGRAPHY

GENERAL

Allen, J. W. *A History of Political Thought in the Sixteenth Century.* London: Methuen, 1957.

Atchity, Kenneth J., and Rimanelli, Giose, eds. *Italian Literature: Roots and Branches.* New Haven: Yale University Press, 1976.

Atkins, J. H. *English Literary Criticism: The Renascence.* London: Methuen, 1947.

Auerbach, Eric. *Mimesis: The Representation of Reality in Western Literature.* Translated by Willard R. Trask. Princeton: Princeton University Press, 1968.

Bates, B. W. *Literary Portraiture in the Historical Narrative of the French Renaissance.* New York, 1945.

Benesch, Otto. *The Art of the Renaissance in Northern Europe.* Cambridge: Harvard University Press, 1945.

Berger, Harry, Jr. "The Renaissance Imagination: Second World and Green World." *The Centennial Review* 9 (1965): 36–78.

Bindoff, S. T. *Tudor England.* New York: Penguin, 1969.

Bloch, Mark. *Feudal Society.* Translated by L. A. Manyon. Chicago: University of Chicago Press, 1961.

Bloor, R. H. U. *The English Novel from Chaucer to Galsworthy.* London: Nicholson and Watson, 1935.

Bond, R. W. *Early Plays from the Italian.* Oxford: Oxford University Press, 1911.

Bowers, F. T. *Elizabethan Revenge Tragedy 1587–1642.* Princeton: Princeton University Press, 1940.

Brown, G. K. *Italy and the Reformation to 1550.* Oxford: Oxford University Press, 1933.

Buckley, George T. *Atheism in the English Renaissance.* Chicago: University of Chicago Press, 1932.

Buxton, John. *Elizabethan Taste.* New York: Macmillan, 1964.

Cabeen, D. C., ed. *A Critical Bibliography of French Literature.* Syracuse, N.Y.: Syracuse University Press, 1956.

Cameron, Alice. *The Influence of Ariosto's Epic and Lyric Poetry on Ronsard and His Group.* Baltimore: Johns Hopkins University Press, 1930.

Caspari, Fritz. *Humanism and the Social Order in Tudor England.* Chicago: University of Chicago Press, 1954.

Cassirer, Ernst. *The Individual and the Cosmos in Renaissance Philosophy.* Translated by Mario Domandi. Oxford: Blackwell & Mott, 1963.

―――; Kristeller, Paul O.; and Randall, John Herman; eds. *The Renaissance Philosophy of Man.* 12th edition. Chicago: University of Chicago Press, 1971.

Castor, Grahame. *Pléiade Poetics: A Study in Sixteenth-Century Thought and Terminology.* Cambridge: Cambridge University Press, 1964.

Chastel, Andre. *The Age of Humanism.* New York: McGraw-Hill, 1963.

Clemen, Wolfgang. *English Tragedy Before Shakespeare.* Translated by T. S. Dorsch. New York: Barnes and Noble, 1961.

Cody, Richard. *The Landscape of the Mind.* Oxford: Oxford University Press, 1969.

Colie, Rosalie. *Paradox Epidemica: The Renaissance Tradition of Paradox.* Princeton: Princeton University Press, 1966.
Craig, Hardin. *The Enchanted Glass: The Elizabethan Mind in Literature.* Oxford: Blackwell & Mott, 1960.
Crane, R. S., ed. *Critics and Criticism, Ancient and Modern.* Chicago: University of Chicago Press, 1952.
Crane, William G. *Wit and Rhetoric in the Renaissance.* New York: Columbia University Press, 1937.
Davis, Natalie Z. *Society and Culture in Early Modern France.* Stanford: Stanford University Press, 1975.
De Sanctis, Francesco. *History of Italian Literature.* Translated by Joan Redfern. 2 vols. New York: Harcourt Brace, 1931.
Doran, Madeleine. *Endeavors of Art: A Study of Form in Elizabethan Drama.* Madison: University of Wisconsin Press, 1954.
Durling, Robert M. *The Figure of the Poet in Renaissance Epic.* Cambridge: Harvard University Press, 1965.
Eliot, T. S. *Selected Essays.* London: Faber & Faber, 1972.
Fish, Stanley E., ed. *Seventeenth-Century Prose: Modern Essays in Criticism.* New York: Oxford University Press, 1971.
Fowler, Alastair. *Conceitful Thought: Interpretation of English Renaissance Poems.* Edinburgh: University of Edinburgh Press, 1975.
Giamatti, A. Bartlett. *The Earthly Paradise and the Renaissance Epic.* Princeton: Princeton University Press, 1966.
Gilbert, Neal W. *Renaissance Concepts of Method.* New York: Columbia University Press, 1960.
Haggis, D. R., ed. *The French Renaissance and Its Heritage: Essays Presented to Alan M. Boase.* London: Methuen, 1968.
Harbison, E. Harris. *The Christian Scholar in the Age of the Reformation.* New York: Scribner's, 1956.
Hardison, O. B., Jr. *The Enduring Monument: A Study of the Idea of Praise in Renaissance Literary Theory and Practice.* Chapel Hill: University of North Carolina Press, 1962.
Hathaway, Baxter. *The Age of Criticism: The Late Renaissance in Italy.* Ithaca: Cornell University Press, 1962.
Haydn, Hiram. *The Counter-Renaissance.* New York: Grove, 1960.
Hazlitt, William. "Lectures on the Dramatic Literature of the Age of Elizabeth." In *Works,* vol. 6, edited by P. P. Howe. London: Dent, 1931.
Helgerson, Richard. *The Elizabethan Prodigals.* Berkeley: University of California Press, 1976.
Herrick, Marvin T. *Comic Theory in the Sixteenth Century.* Urbana: University of Illinois Press, 1964.
Highet, Gilbert. *The Classical Tradition.* New York: Oxford University Press, 1957.
Ing, Elizabeth. *Elizabethan Lyrics.* London, 1951.
Keating, L. Clark. *Studies on the Literary Salon in France, 1550–1615.* Cambridge: Harvard University Press, 1941.
Kernan, Alvin. *The Cankered Muse.* New Haven: Yale University Press, 1949.
Kristeller, Paul O. *Renaissance Thought: The Classic, Scholastic, and Humanist Strain.* New York: Harper & Row, 1961.

Lee, Judith. "The English Ariosto: The Elizabethan Poet and the Marvelous." *Studies in Philology* 80 (1983): 277–99.
Lewis, C. S. *English Literature in the Sixteenth Century*. Oxford: Clarendon Press, 1954.
Molinaro, J. A., ed. *Italian Criticism and Theatre from Petrarch to Pirandello*. Toronto: University of Toronto Press, 1973.
Montgomery, R. L., Jr. "Allegory and the Incredible Fable. The Italian View from Dante to Tasso." *PMLA* 81 (1966): 45–55.
Preminger, Alex, et al., eds. *Princeton Encyclopedia of Poetry and Poetics*. Princeton: Princeton University Press, 1974.
Quinones, Ricardo J. *The Renaissance Discovery of Time*. Cambridge: Harvard University Press, 1972.
Raysor, Thomas M. *Coleridge's Miscellaneous Criticism*. Cambridge: Harvard University Press, 1936.
Rice, Eugene F., Jr. *The Renaissance Idea of Wisdom*. Cambridge: Harvard University Press, 1958.
―――, ed. *Medieval and Renaissance Studies*. Ithaca: Cornell University Press, 1959.
Scaglione, Aldo. *Nature and Love in the Late Middle Ages*. Berkeley: University of California Press, 1963.
Seigel, Jerrold E. *Rhetoric and Philosophy in Renaissance Humanism*. Princeton: Princeton University Press, 1968.
Simone, Franco. *The French Renaissance: Medieval Tradition and Italian Influence in Shaping the Renaissance in France*. Translated by Gaston Hall. London, 1969.
Smith, Hallett. *Elizabethan Poetry*. Cambridge: Harvard University Press, 1964.
Spingarn, Joel E. *A History of Literary Criticism in the Renaissance*. New York: Columbia University Press, 1899.
Symonds, John A. *The Renaissance in Italy*. New York: Modern Library, 1935.
Thompson, John. *The Founding of English Metre*. New York: Columbia University Press, 1961.
Tilley, Arthur A. *Studies in the French Renaissance*. Cambridge: Cambridge University Press, 1922.
Tillyard, E. M. W. *The English Epic and Its Backgrounds*. London: Chatto & Windus, 1954.
Tuve, Rosemond. *Elizabethan and Metaphysical Imagery*. Chicago: University of Chicago Press, 1968.
Weinberg, Bernard F. *A History of Literary Criticism in the Renaissance*. 2 vols. Chicago: University of Chicago Press, 1961.
Whitfield, J. H. *A Short History of Italian Literature*. London: Cassell, 1962.
Wood, Charles T. *The Age of Chivalry*. New York: Universe Books, 1970.

BOCCACCIO

Barricelli, Jean-Pierre. "Satire of Satires: Boccaccio's *Corbaccio*." *Italian Quarterly* 18 (1975): 95–111.
Bergin, Thomas G. "An Introduction to Boccaccio." In *The Decameron*, edited by Mark Musa and Peter Bondanella. New York: W. W. Norton, 1977.

_____. *Boccaccio*. New York: Viking Press, 1981.
Branca, Vittoro. *Boccaccio: The Man and His Works*. Translated by Richard Mongos. New York: New York University Press, 1976.
Brown, Margery L. "The *Hous of Fame* and the *Corbaccio*." *Modern Language Notes* 22 (1917): 411–15.
Carswell, Catherine. *The Tranquil Heart: Portrait of Giovanni Boccaccio*. New York: Harcourt Brace, 1937.
Chubb, Thomas C. *The Life of Giovanni Boccaccio*. New York: Albert and Charles Boni, 1930.
Clements, Robert J. "Anatomy of the Novella in the *Decameron*." In *The Decameron*, edited by Mark Musa and Peter Bondanella. New York: W. W. Norton, 1977.
Cottino-Jones, Marga. *An Anatomy of Boccaccio's Style*. Naples: Cymba, 1968.
_____. "The *Corbaccio*: Notes for a Mythical Perspective of Moral Alienation." *Forum Italicum* 4 (1970): 490–509.
Dombrowski, Robert S., ed. *Critical Perspectives on the "Decameron."* New York: Barnes and Noble, 1977.
Griffin, Robert. "Boccaccio's *Fiametta*: Pictures at an Exhibition." *Italian Quarterly* 18 (1975): 75–94.
Hollander, Robert. *Boccaccio's Two Venuses*. New York: Columbia University Press, 1977.
Hutton, Edward. *Giovanni Boccaccio: A Biographical Study*. London: J. Lane, 1910.
Kahane, H. and R. "Akritas and Arcita: A Byzantine Source of Boccaccio's *Teseida*." *Speculum* 20 (1945): 415–25.
Kern, Edith G. "The Gardens in the *Decameron*." *PMLA* 66 (1951): 505–23.
Layman, Beverly J. "Eloquence of Pattern in Boccaccio's Tale of the Falcon." *Italica* 46 (1969): 3–16.
MacManus, Francis. *Boccaccio*. New York: Sheed and Ward, 1947.
McWilliam, G. H. "On Translating the *Decameron*." In *Essays in Honor of John Humphreys Whitfield*, edited by H. C. Davis et al. London: St. George's Press, 1975.
Mazzota, Giuseppe. "The *Decameron*: The Literal and the Allegorical." *Italian Quarterly* 18 (1975): 53–73.
Perella, Nicholas J. "The World of Boccaccio's *Filocolo*." *PMLA* 76 (1961): 330–39.
Symonds, John A. *Giovanni Boccaccio as Man and Author*. London: J. C. Nimmo, 1985.
Tournay, Gilbert, ed. *Boccaccio in Europe*. Proceedings of the Boccaccio Conference, Louvain, December 1975. Louvain: Leuven University Press, 1977.
Wright, Herbert G. *Boccaccio in England from Chaucer to Tennyson*. London: Athlone Press, 1957.

PETRARCH

Bergin, Thomas G., ed. *Petrarch: Selected Sonnets, Odes and Letters*. Arlington Heights, Ill.: AHM Publishing, 1966.
_____. *Petrarch*. New York: Twayne Publishers, 1970.
Bernardo, Aldo S. "Petrarch's Attitude Toward Dante." *PMLA* 70 (1955): 488–517.

———. *Petrarch, Scipio and the "Africa."* Baltimore: Johns Hopkins University Press, 1962.

———. *Petrarch, Laura and the "Triumphs."* Albany: State University of New York Press, 1974.

Billanovich, Giuseppe. "Petrarch and the Textual Tradition of Livy." *Journal of the Warburg and Courtauld Institutes* 14 (1951): 137–208.

Bishop, Morris. *Petrarch and His World.* Bloomington: Indiana University Press, 1963.

———, ed. *Letters from Petrarch.* Translated by Morris Bishop. Bloomington: Indiana University Press, 1966.

Durling, Robert M. "The Ascent of Mt. Ventoux and the Crisis of Allegory." *Italian Quarterly* 18 (1974): 7–28.

———. *Petrarch's Lyric Poems.* Cambridge: Harvard University Press, 1976.

Forster, Leonard. *The Icy Fire: Five Studies in European Petrarchism.* Cambridge: Cambridge University Press, 1969.

Foster, Kenelm, O. P. "Beatrice or Medusa: The Penitential in Petrarch's *Canzoniere.*" In *Italian Studies Presented to E. R. Vincent.* Cambridge: Heffer, 1962.

Freccero, John. "The Fig Tree and the Laurel: Petrarch's Poetics." *Diacritics* 5 (1975): 34–40.

Kadish, Emilie. "Petrarch's *Griselda*: An English Translation." *Medievalia* 3 (1977): 1–23.

Minta, Stephen. *Petrarch and Petrarchism: The English and French Traditions.* New York: Harper & Row, 1980.

Phelps, Ruth S. *The Earlier Later Forms of Petrarch's "Canzoniere."* Chicago: University of Chicago Press, 1925.

Roche, Thomas P., Jr. "The Calendrical Structure of Petrarch's *Canzoniere.*" *Studies in Philology* 71 (1974): 151–72.

Scaglione, Aldo, ed. *Francis Petrarch Six Centuries Later: A Symposium.* Chapel Hill: University of North Carolina Press, 1975.

Seigel, Jerrold E. "Eloquence and Silence in Petrarch." *Journal of the History of Ideas* 26 (1965): 147–74.

Shapiro, Marianne. "Petrarch, Lorenzo il Magnifico and the Latin Elegaic Poets." *Romance Notes* 15 (1973): 172–75.

———. *Hieroglyph of Time: The Petrarchan Sestina.* Minneapolis: University of Minnesota Press, 1980.

Tatham, Edward H. R. *Francesco Petrarca, the First Modern Man of Letters, His Life and Correspondence: A Study of the Early Fourteenth Century (1304–1347).* 2 vols. London: Sheldon, 1925–26.

Thompson, David, and Nagel, Alan F., eds. *The Three Crowns of Florence: Humanist Assessments of Dante, Petrarca, and Boccaccio.* New York: Harper & Row, 1972.

Watkins, Renee Neu. "Petrarch and the Black Death: From Fear to Monuments." *Studies in the Renaissance* 19 (1972): 196–223.

Whitfield, J. H. *Petrarch and the Renaissance.* Oxford: Oxford University Press, 1943.

Wilkins, Ernest H. *The Making of the "Canzoniere," and Other Petrarchan Studies.* Rome: Edizioni di Storia e letteratura, 1951.

_____. *Studies in the Life and Works of Petrarch.* Cambridge, Mass.: The Medieval Academy of America, 1955.
_____. *Petrarch's Eight Years in Milan.* Cambridge, Mass.: The Medieval Academy of America, 1958.
_____. *Petrarch's Later Years.* Cambridge, Mass.: The Medieval Academy of America, 1959.
_____. *Life of Petrarch.* Chicago: University of Chicago Press, 1961.

ERASMUS

Aldridge, John W. *The Hermeneutic of Erasmus.* Richmond, Va.: John Knox Press, 1966.
Allen, Percy S. *Erasmus: Lectures and Wayfaring Sketches,* edited by Helen M. Allen. Oxford: Clarendon Press, 1934.
_____. *The Age of Erasmus: Lectures Delivered in the Universities of Oxford and London.* New York: Russell & Russell, 1963.
Bainton, Roland H. *Erasmus of Christendom.* New York: Scribner's, 1969.
Bouyer, Louis. *Erasmus and the Humanist Experiment.* Translated by Francis X. Murphy. London: Geoffrey Chapman, 1959.
Campbell, William E. *Erasmus, Tyndale, and More.* London: Eyre and Spottiswoode, 1949.
Dorey, T. A., ed. *Erasmus.* London: Routledge and Kegan Paul, 1970.
Froude, J. A. *The Life and Letters of Erasmus.* New York: Scribner's, 1925.
Giese, Rachel. "Erasmus' Knowledge and Estimate of the Vernacular Languages." *Romantic Review* 28 (1937): 3–18.
Huizinga, Johann. *Letters of Erasmus.* London: Phaidon Press, 1952.
Kaiser, Walter J. *Praisers of Folly: Erasmus, Rabelais, and Shakespeare.* Cambridge: Harvard University Press, 1963.
May, Harry. *The Tragedy of Erasmus: A Psychohistoric Approach.* St. Charles, Mo.: Piraeus Publishers, 1975.
Murray, Robert H. *Erasmus and Luther: Their Attitude to Toleration.* London: Society for Promoting Christian Knowledge, 1920.
Olin, John C., ed. *Desiderius Erasmus, Christian Humanism and the Reformation: Selected Writings.* New York: Harper Torchbooks, 1965.
Panofsky, Erwin. "Erasmus and the Visual Arts." *Journal of the Warburg and Courtauld Institutes* 32 (1969): 200–27.
Phillips, Margaret M. *Erasmus and the Northern Renaissance.* New York: Macmillan, 1950.
_____. *The Adages of Erasmus: A Study with Translations.* Cambridge: The University Press, 1964.
Rabil, Albert, Jr. *Erasmus and the New Testament: The Mind of a Christian Humanist.* San Antonio: Trinity University Press, 1972.
Sowards, J. Kelley. *Desiderius Erasmus.* New York: Twayne Publishers, 1975.
Thompson, Craig R. "Erasmus and Tudor England." In *Actes du Congrès Erasme, Roterdam 27–29 Octobre 1969.* Amsterdam: North-Holland Publishing Co., 1971.

Woodward, William H. *Desiderius Erasmus Concerning the Aim and Method of Education.* New York: Teachers College Press, 1964.
Zweig, Stefan. *Erasmus of Rotterdam.* Translated by Eden and Cedar Paul. New York: Viking Press, 1934.

GIRALDI CINTHIO

Gilbert, A. H. "Fortune in the Tragedies of Giraldi Cinthio." *Philological Quarterly* 20 (1941): 224–35.
Horne, P. R. *The Tragedies of Giambattista Cinthio Giraldi.* Oxford: Oxford University Press, 1962.

JOACHIM DU BELLAY

Belloc, Hillaire. "Joachim du Bellay." In *April, Being Essays on the Poetry of the French Renaissance.* New York: Dutton, 1904.
Clements, Robert J. "Anti-Petrarchism in the Pleiade." *Modern Philology* 39 (1941): 15–21.
―――. *Critical Theory and Practice of the Pleiade.* Cambridge: Harvard University Press, 1942.
Coleman, Dorothy Gabe. *The Chaste Muse: A Study of Joachim du Bellay's Poetry.* Leiden: E. J. Brill, 1980.
Dickinson, Gladys. *Du Bellay in Rome.* Leiden: E. J. Brill, 1960.
Fucilla, Joseph. "A Sonnet in Du Bellay's *Antiquitez de Rome.*" *Modern Language Notes* 61 (1946): 260–62.
Griffin, Robert. *Coronation of the Poet: Joachim du Bellay's Debt to the Trivium.* Berkeley: University of California Press, 1969.
Keating, L. Clark. *Joachim du Bellay.* New York: Twayne Publishers, 1971.
Lapp, John C. "Mythological Imagery in Du Bellay." *Studies in Philology* 61 (1964): 109–27.
Merrill, Robert V. *The Platonism of Joachim du Bellay.* Chicago: University of Chicago Press, 1925.
―――. "Considerations on *Les Amours* of Joachim du Bellay." *Modern Philology* 33 (1935–36): 129–38.
Pater, Walter. "Du Bellay." In *The Renaissance, Studies in Art and Poetry.* New York: Boni and Liverwright, 1919.
Renwick, W. L. "Mulcaster and Du Bellay." *Modern Language Review* 17 (1922): 282–87.
Silver, Isidore. "Did Du Bellay Know Pindar?" *PMLA* 56 (1941): 1007–19.
―――. "Du Bellay and Hellenic Poetry: A Cursory View." *PMLA* 60 (1945): 66–80, 356, 363, 670–81.

ROGER ASCHAM

Dees, Jerome S. "Recent Studies in Ascham." *English Literary Renaissance* 10 (1980): 300–10.

Greene, Thomas M. "Roger Ascham: The Perfect End of Shooting." *Journal of English Literary History* 36 (1969): 609–25.
Ryan, Lawrence V. "Roger Ascham's *Toxophilus* in Heroic Verse." *Huntington Library Quarterly* 22 (1959): 119–24.
——. *Roger Ascham*. Stanford: Stanford University Press, 1963.
Saintsbury, George, ed. "Roger Ascham (1515–1568)." In *A Letter Book: Selected With an Introduction on the History and Art of Letter-Writing*. New York: Harcourt Brace, 1922.
Salamon, Linda B. "*The Courtier* and *The Scholemaster*." *Comparative Literature* 25 (1973): 17–36.
Smith, John H. "Roger Ascham's Troubled Years." *Journal of English and Germanic Philosophy* 65 (1966): 33–46.
Strozier, Robert M. "Roger Ascham and Cleanth Brooks: Renaissance and Modern Critical Thought." *Essays in Criticism* 22 (1972): 396–407.
Tannenbaum, Samuel A. *Roger Ascham: A Concise Bibliography*. New York: S. A. Tannenbaum, 1946.
Vos, Alvin. "The Formation of Roger Ascham's Prose Style." *Studies in Philology* 71 (1974): 344–70.
——. "Form and Function in Roger Ascham's Prose." *Philological Quarterly* 55 (1976): 305–22.
——. "The Humanism of *Toxophilus*: A New Source." *English Literary Renaissance* 6 (1976): 187–203.
Wilson, K. J. "Ascham's *Toxophilus* and the Rules of Art." *Renaissance Quarterly* 29 (1976): 30–51.

LODOVICO CASTELVETRO

Charlton, H. B. *Life of Castelvetro and a Theory of Poetry*. Victoria University Publications in Comparative Literatures, XV, 1. Manchester, 1913.
Melzi, Robert C. *Castelvetro's Annotations to the Inferno*. The Hague: Mouton, 1966.

GEORGE GASCOIGNE

Adams, Robert P. "Gascoigne's *Master F. J.* as Original Fiction." *PMLA* 73 (1958): 315–26.
Ambrose, Genevieve. *See* Oldfield, Genevieve Ambrose.
Bowers, F. T. "Notes on Gascoigne's *A Hundred Sundrie Flowres* and *The Posies*." *Harvard Studies and Notes in Philology and Literature* 16 (1934).
Bradner, Leicester. "The First English Novel: A Study of George Gascoigne's *Adventures of Master F. J.*" *PMLA* 45 (1930): 16–22.
——. "Point of View in George Gascoigne's Fiction." *Studies in Short Fiction* 3 (1965): 16–22.
Lanham, Richard. "Narrative Structure in Gascoigne's *F. J.*" *Studies in Short Fiction* 4 (1966): 42–50.
Oldfield, Genevieve Ambrose. "George Gascoigne." *Review of English Studies* 2 (1926).

———. "New Light on the Life of George Gascoigne." *Review of English Studies* 13 (1937): 129–38.
Prouty, C. T. "Gascoigne in the Low Countries and the Publication of *A Hundred Sundrie Flowres.*" *Review of English Studies* 12 (1936).
———. "George Gascoigne and Elizabeth Bacon Bretton Boyes Gascoigne." *Review of English Studies* 14 (1938).
———. *George Gascoigne: Elizabethan Courtier, Soldier, and Poet*. New York: Columbia University Press, 1942.
Ward, B. M. "George Gascoigne and His Circle." *Review of English Studies* 2 (1926): 32–41.
———. "The Death of George Gascoigne." *Review of English Studies* 2 (1926).

MONTAIGNE

Boase, Alan M. *The Fortunes of Montaigne: A History of the Essays in France, 1580–1669*. New York: Octagon Books, 1970.
Bowen, Barbara. *The Age of Bluff: Paradox and Ambiguity in Rabelais and Montaigne*. Urbana: University of Illinois Press, 1972.
Bowman, Frank P. *Montaigne: Essays*. London: Arnold, 1965.
Brown, Frieda. *Religious and Political Conservatism in the "Essais" of Montaigne*. Geneva: Droz, 1963.
Burke, Peter. *Montaigne*. New York: Hill and Wang, 1981.
Clark, Carol. *The Web of Metaphor: Studies in the Imagery of Montaigne's "Essais."* Lexington, Ky.: French Forum, 1978.
Frame, Donald M. *Montaigne in France, 1812–1852*. New York: Columbia University Press, 1940.
———. *Montaigne's Discovery of Man: The Humanization of a Humanist*. New York: Columbia University Press, 1955.
———. *Montaigne: A Biography*. New York: Harcourt, Brace & World, 1965.
———. *Montaigne's "Essais:" A Study*. Englewood Cliffs, N.J.: Prentice-Hall, 1969.
Friedrich, Hugo. *Montaigne*. Translated by Robert Rovini. Paris: Gallimard, 1968.
Gray, Floyd. "The Unity of Montaigne in the *Essais*." *Modern Language Quarterly* 22 (1961): 79–86.
Haillie, Philip P. *The Scar of Montaigne*. Middletown: Wesleyan University Press, 1966.
Keller, Abraham C. "Montaigne on the Dignity of Man." *PMLA* 72 (1957): 43–54.
La Charité, Raymond C. *The Concept of Judgement in Montaigne*. The Hague: Nijhoff, 1968.
———. "Montaigne's Early Personal Essays." *Romantic Review* 42 (1971): 5–15.
McGowen, Margaret. *Montaigne's Deceits: The Art of Persuasion in the "Essais."* London: University of London Press, 1974.
Norton, Glyn P. "Image and Introspection in Montaigne's *Essais*." *PMLA* 88 (1973): 281–88.
Regosin, Richard L. *The Matter of My Book: Montaigne's "Essais" as the Book of the Self*. Berkeley: University of California Press, 1972.
Samaras, Zoe. *The Comic Element of Montaigne's Style*. Paris: Nizet, 1970.

Sayce, Richard A. *The Essays of Montaigne: A Critical Exploration.* London: Weidenfeld and Nicolson, 1972.
Tannenbaum, Samuel A. *Michel Eyquem de Montaigne: A Concise Bibliography.* New York: S. A. Tannenbaum, 1942.
Tetel, Marcel. *Montaigne.* New York: Twayne Publishers, 1974.
Winter, Ian J. *Montaigne's Self-Portrait and Its Influence in France, 1580–1630.* Lexington, Ky.: French Forum, 1976.

SIR PHILIP SIDNEY

Amos, Arthur K. *Time, Space, and Value: The Narrative Structure of the "New Arcadia."* Lewisburg, Pa.: Bucknell University Press, 1977.
Barnes, Catherine. "The Hidden Persuader: The Complex Speaking Voice of Sidney's *Defence of Poetry.*" *PMLA* 86 (1971): 422–27.
Buxton, John. *Sir Philip Sidney and the English Renaissance.* New York: St. Martin's Press, 1964.
Connell, Dorothy. *Sir Philip Sidney: The Maker's Mind.* Oxford: Clarendon Press, 1977.
Danby, John F. *Poets on Fortune's Hill: Studies in Sidney, Shakespeare, Beaumont and Fletcher.* London: Faber & Faber, 1952.
Davis, Walter R., and Lanham, Richard A. *Sidney's Arcadia.* New Haven: Yale University Press, 1965.
Denkinger, Emma M. *Philip Sidney.* London: Allen and Unwin, 1932.
Dipple, Elizabeth. "Harmony and Pastoral in the Old Arcadia." *English Literary History* 35 (1968): 309–28.
———. "'Unjust Justice' in the *Old Arcadia.*" *Studies in English Literature* 10 (1970): 83–101.
Donow, Herbert S., ed. *A Concordance to the Poems of Sir Philip Sidney.* Ithaca: Cornell University Press, 1975.
Duhamel, A. "Sidney's *Arcadia* and Elizabethan Rhetoric." *Studies in Philology* 45 (1948): 134–50.
Godshalk, W. L. "Bibliography of Sidney Studies Since 1935." In *Sir Philip Sidney as a Literary Craftsman.* Lincoln, Neb.: University of Nebraska Press, 1965.
———. "Recent Sidney Studies." *English Literary Renaissance* 2 (1972): 148–64.
———. "Recent Studies in Sidney (1970–1977)." *English Literary Renaissance* 8 (1978): 212–33.
Greenfield, Thelma N. *The Eye of Judgement: Reading the "New Arcadia."* Lewisburg, Pa.: Bucknell University Press, 1982.
Hamilton, A. C. *Sir Philip Sidney: A Study of His Life and Works.* Cambridge: Cambridge University Press, 1977.
Kalstone, David. *Sidney's Poetry: Contexts and Interpretations.* Cambridge: Harvard University Press, 1965.
———. "Sir Philip Sidney." In *English Poetry and Prose 1540–1674*, edited by Christopher Ricks. London: Barrie & Jenkins, 1970.
Kimbrough, Robert. *Sir Philip Sidney.* New York: Twayne Publishers, 1971.
Lawry, Jon S. *Sidney's Two "Arcadias:" Pattern and Proceeding.* Ithaca: Cornell University Press, 1972.

Lewis, C. S. "Sidney and Spenser." In *English Literature in the Sixteenth Century.* Oxford: Clarendon Press, 1954.

McCoy, Richard C. *Sir Philip Sidney: Rebellion in Arcadia.* New Brunswick, N.J.: Rutgers University Press, 1979.

Marenco, Franco. "Double Plot in Sidney's Old *Arcadia.*" *Modern Language Review* 64 (1969): 248–63.

Moffet, Thomas. *Nobilis, or A View of the Life and Death of a Sidney.* Translated by Virgil Heltzel and Hoyt Hudson. San Marino, Cal.: Huntington Library, 1940.

Montgomery, Robert L., Jr. *Symmetry and Sense: The Poetry of Sir Philip Sidney.* Austin: University of Texas Press, 1961.

Muir, Kenneth. *Sir Philip Sidney.* London: Longmans, Green, 1960.

Nichols, John Gordon. *The Poetry of Sir Philip Sidney: An Interpretation of His Life and Times.* Liverpool: Liverpool University Press, 1974.

Osborn, James Marshall. *Young Philip Sidney, 1572–1577.* New Haven: Yale University Press, 1972.

Rose, Mark. *Heroic Love: Studies in Sidney and Spenser.* Cambridge: Harvard University Press, 1968.

Rudenstine, Neil L. *Sir Philip Sidney's Poetic Development.* Cambridge: Harvard University Press, 1967.

Stillinger, Jack. "The Biographical Problem of *Astrophel and Stella.*" *Journal of English and Germanic Philology* 59 (1960): 617–39.

Tannenbaum, Samuel A. *Sir Philip Sidney: A Concise Bibliography.* New York: S. A. Tannenbaum, 1941.

Turner, Myron. "The Heroic Ideal in Sidney's Revised *Arcadia.*" *Studies in English Literature* 10 (1970): 63–82.

Washington, Mary A. *Sir Philip Sidney: An Annotated Bibliography, 1941–1970.* Columbia, Mo.: University of Missouri Press, 1972.

Weiner, Andrew D. *Sir Philip Sidney and the Poetics of Protestantism: A Study of Contexts.* Minneapolis, Minn.: University of Minnesota Press, 1978.

Wilson, Mona. *Sir Philip Sidney.* London: R. Hart-Davis, 1950.

Young, Richard B. "English Petrarke: A Study of Sidney's *Astrophel and Stella.*" In *Three Studies in the Renaissance,* Yale Studies in English, 138. New Haven: Yale University Press, 1958.

Zandvoort, R. W. *Sidney's Arcadia: A Comparison Between the Two Versions.* Amsterdam: Swets & Zeitlinger, 1929.

GEORGE PUTTENHAM

Magnas, Laurie, ed. *Documents Illustrating Elizabethan Poetry.* New York: Dutton, 1906.

Puttenham, George. *The Art of English Poetry,* edited with an introduction by Gladys Doidge Willcock and Alice Walker. Folcroft, Pa.: The Folcroft Press, 1969.

NASHE AND HARVEY

Berryman, John. "Thomas Nashe and *The Unfortuante Traveller.*" In *The Freedom of the Poet.* New York: Farrar, Straus & Giroux, 1977.

Crosten, A. K. "The Use of Tragedy in Nashe's *The Unfortunate Traveller*." *Review of English Studies* 24 (1948): 90.

Duhamel, P. Albert. "The Ciceronianism of Gabriel Harvey." *Studies in Philology* 49 (1952): 155–70.

Duncan-Jones, Katherine. "Nashe and Sidney: The Tournament in *The Unfortunate Traveller*." *Modern Language Review* 63 (1968): 37–39.

Harlow, C. G. "Thomas Nashe and William Cotton, M. P." *Notes and Queries* 8 (1961): 424–25.

Hibbard, George R. *Thomas Nashe, A Critical Introduction*. Cambridge: Harvard University Press, 1962.

Johnson, Francis R. "The First Edition of Gabriel Harvey's *Foure Letters*." *The Library*, Fourth Series, XV (1934): 212–23.

_____."Gabriel Harvey's *Three Letters*: A First Issue of his *Foure Letters*." *The Library*, Fifth Series, I (1946): 134–36.

Kane, Robert J. "Anthony Chute, Thomas Nashe, and the First English Work on Tobacco." *Review of English Studies* 7 (1931): 151.

Kocher, Paul H. "Nashe's Authorship of the Prose Scenes in *Faustus*." *Modern Language Quarterly* 3 (1942): 17.

Latham, Agnes M. C. "Satire on Literary Themes and Modes in Nashe's *Unfortunate Traveller*." *Essays and Studies on the English Association* (1948): 85–100.

McGinn, Donald J. "Nashe's Share in the Marprelate Controversy." *PMLA* 49 (1944): 952.

_____. "The Allegory of the 'Beare' and the 'Foxe' in Nashe's *Pierce Penilesse*." *PMLA* 61 (1946): 431–53.

_____. "A Quip for Tom Nashe." In *Studies in the English Renaissance Drama*, edited by Josephine W. Bennett, Oscar Gargill, and Vernon Hall. New York: New York University Press, 1959.

McPherson, David C. "Aretino and the Harvey-Nashe Quarrel." *PMLA* 84 (1969): 1551.

Miller, Edwin H. "The Relationship of Robert Greene and Thomas Nashe (1588–1592)." *Philological Quarterly* 33 (1954): 353–67.

Nicholl, Charles. *A Cup of News: The Life of Thomas Nash*. London: Routledge & Kegan Paul, 1984.

Perkins, David. "Issues and Motivations in the Nashe-Harvey Quarrel." *Philological Quarterly* 39 (1960): 224–33.

Sanders, Chauncey. "Robert Greene and the Harveys." *Indiana University Studies* 18 (1931): 4–58.

Schrickx, W. *Shakespeare's Early Contemporaries: The Background of the Harvey-Nashe Polemic and "Love's Labours Lost."* Antwerp: De Nederlandsche Boekhandel, 1956.

Steane, J. B., ed. *"The Unfortunate Traveller" and Other Works*. Harmondsworth: Penguin, 1972.

Tannenbaum, Samuel A. *Thomas Nashe: A Concise Bibliography*. New York: S. A. Tannenbaum, 1941.

Thomas, Sidney. "New Light on the Nashe-Harvey Quarrel." *Modern Language Notes* 63 (1948): 481–83.

Wilson, Harold S. "The Humanism of Gabriel Harvey." In *Joseph Quincey Adams Memorial Studies*. Washington: Folger Shakespeare Library, 1948.

Young, G. M. "A Word for Gabriel Harvey." In *English Critical Essays, Twentieth Century*, edited by Phyllis M. Jones. New York: Oxford University Press, 1983.

SIR JOHN HARINGTON

Bartley, J. O. "Harington and Saint Basil." *Modern Language Review* 42 (1947): 233–34.

Cauchi, Simon. "The 'Setting Foorth' of Harington's Ariosto." *Studies in Bibliography* 36 (1983): 137–68.

Crais, D. H. *Sir John Harington*. Boston: Twayne Publishers, 1985.

Gilbert, Alan H. "Sir John Harington's Pen Name." *Modern Language Notes* 58 (1943): 616–17.

Grimble, Ian. *The Harington Family*. London: Cape, 1957.

MacKinnon, M. H. M. "Sir John Harington and Bishop Hall." *Philological Quarterly* 37 (1958): 80–86.

Nelson, T. G. A. "Harington and Dante." *Notes and Queries* 16 (1969): 456–57.

———. "Sir John Harington as a Critic of Sir Philip Sidney." *Studies in Philology* 67 (1970): 41–56.

Rich, Townsend. *Harington and Ariosto: A Study in Elizabethan Verse Translation*. New Haven: Yale University Press, 1940.

Sigerist, Henry E. "An Elizabethan Poet's Contribution to Public Health: Sir John Harington and the Water Closet." *Bulletin of the History of Medicine* 13 (1943): 229–43.

Strachey, Lytton. *Portraits in Miniature and Other Essays*. London: Windus, 1931.

TORQUATO TASSO

Boulting, William. *Tasso and His Times*. London, 1907.

Brand, C. P. *Torquato Tasso: A Study of the Poet and of His Contribution to English Literature*. Cambridge: At the University Press, 1965.

Cody, Richard. *The Language of the Mind: Pastoralism and Platonic Theory in Tasso's "Aminta" and Shakespeare's Early Comedies*. Oxford: Clarendon Press, 1969.

Giamatti, A. Bartlett. "Milton and Fairfax's Tasso." *Révue de Litterature Comparée* 40 (1966): 613–15.

Kates, Judith A. *Tasso and Milton: The Problem of Christian Epic*. Lewisburg, Pa.: Bucknell University Press, 1983.

Lord, Carnes. "The Argument of Tasso's *Nifo*." *Italica* 56 (1979): 22–45.

Patterson, Annabel M. "Tasso's Epic Neoplatonism." *Studies in the Renaissance* 18 (1971): 105–33.

Trafton, Dain A. *Tasso's Dialogue on the Court*. English Literary Renaissance Supplements, no. 2. Amherst, Mass.: Dartmouth College and *English Literary Renaissance*, 1973.

GIAMBATTISTA GUARINI

Beall, Chandler. "A Quaint Conceit from Guarini to Dryden." *Modern Language Notes* 64 (1949): 461–68.
Bullough, Geoffrey. "Sir Richard Fanshawe and Guarini." In *Studies in English Language and Literature Presented to Karl Brunner*, edited by S. Korninger. Vienna-Stuttgart, 1957.
Cacossa, Anthony A. "A Bergamask Parody of G. B. Guarini's *Il Pastor Fido*." *Italica* 39 (1962): 182–88.
Hall, H. G. "Guarini in Boileau's Lutrin." *Modern Language Review* 60 (1965): 17–20.
Perella, Nicholas. "Fate, Blindness, and Illusion in the *Pastor Fido*." *The Romantic Review* 69 (1958): 252–68.
———. "Amarilli's Dilemma: The *Pastor Fido* and Some English Authors." *Comparative Literature* 12 (1960): 348–59.
———. *The Critical Fortune of Battista Guarini's "Il Pastor Fido."* Florence: Olschki, 1973.
Whitfield, J. H. "Sir Richard Fanshawe and the Faithful Shepherd." *Italian Studies* 19 (1964).
———, ed. *Battista Guarini: "Il Pastor Fido."* Austin: University of Texas Press, 1976.

GEORGE CHAPMAN

Bartlett, Phyllis B. "The Heroes of Chapman's Homer." *Review of English Studies* 27 (1941): 257–80.
Battenhouse, R. W. "Chapman and the Nature of Man." *English Literary History* 12 (1945): 81–105.
Bottral, Margaret. "Chapman's Defense of Difficulty in Poetry." *Criterion* 16 (1937): 638–54.
Bullen, A. H. "George Chapman." In *Elizabethans*. London: Chapman and Hall, 1924.
Eccles, M. "Chapman's Early Years." *Studies in Philology* 43 (1946): 176–93.
Gilbert, Alan H. "Chapman's Fortune with Winged Hands." *Modern Language Notes* 52 (1937): 190–92.
Goldstein, Leonard. *George Chapman: Aspects of Decadence in Early Seventeenth Century Drama*. Salzburg: Institut fur Englische Sprache und Literatur, 1975.
Lord, George de Forest. *Homeric Renaissance: The Odyssey of George Chapman*. New Haven: Yale University Press, 1956.
Muir, E. "*Royal Man*: Notes on the Tragedies of George Chapman." In *Essays on Literature and Society*. London: Hogarth, 1949.
Perkinson, R. H. "Nature and the Tragic Hero in Chapman's Bussy Plays." *Modern Language Quarterly* 3 (1942): 163–85.
Rees, Ennis. *The Tragedies of George Chapman*. Cambridge: Harvard University Press, 1954.
Schoenbaum, Samuel. "The Widow's Tears and the Other Chapman." *Huntington Library Quarterly* 23 (1960): 321–28.
Smith, James. "George Chapman." *Scrutiny* 3 (1934–35): 339–50.

Spivack, Charlotte. *George Chapman*. New York: Twayne Publishers, 1967.
Swinburne, Algernon. "George Chapman." In *The Complete Works*, volume 12, edited by Sir Edmund Gosse and Thomas Wise. London: William Heineman, 1875.
Tannenbaum, Samuel A. *George Chapman: A Concise Bibliography*. New York: S. A. Tannenbaum, 1938.
Ure, P. "Chapman's Tragedies." In *Jacobean Theatre*, edited by John Russell Brown and Bernard Harris. New York: St. Martin's Press, 1960.
Wieler, John W. *George Chapman: The Effect of Stoicism Upon His Tragedies*. New York: King's Crown Press, 1949.

THOMAS CAMPION

Kastendieck, Miles Merwin. *England's Musical Poet: Thomas Campion*. New York: Russell & Russell, 1963.
MacDonagh, T. *Thomas Campion and the Art of English Poetry*. Dublin, 1913.
Vivian, P. *Campion's Works*. Oxford: Oxford University Press, 1969.
Ward, A. W., and Waller, A. R., eds. "Thomas Campion." In *The Cambridge History of English Literature*. Cambridge: Cambridge University Press, 1909

SAMUEL DANIEL

Blisset, William. "Samuel Daniel's Sense of the Past." *English Studies* 38 (1957): 49–63.
Brady, George K. *Samuel Daniel: A Critical Study*. Urbana: University of Illinois Press, 1926.
Chang, J. "Machiavellianism in Daniel's 'The Civil Wars'." *Tulane Studies in English* 14 (1965): 5–16.
Eccles, M. "Samuel Daniel in France and Italy." *Studies in Philology* 34 (1937): 146–47.
Godshalk, W. L. "Daniel's History." *Journal of English and Germanic Philology* 43 (1964): 45–57.
Gottfried, R. B. "Samuel Daniel's Method of Writing History." *Studies in the Renaissance* 3 (1956): 157–74.
Himelick, Raymond. "*A Fig for Momus* and Daniel's *Musophilus*." *Modern Language Quarterly* 28 (1957): 247–50.
Rees, Joan. "Shakespeare's Use of Daniel." *Modern Language Review* 55 (1960): 79–82.
_____. *Samuel Daniel: A Critical and Biographical Study*. Liverpool: Liverpool University Press, 1964.
Seronsky, Cecil. "Well-Languaged Daniel Reconsidered." *Modern Language Review* 52 (1957): 481–97.
_____. "Daniel and Wordsworth." *Studies in Philology* 56 (1959): 187–213.
_____. *Samuel Daniel*. New York: Twayne Publishers, 1967.
Tannenbaum, Samuel A. *Samuel Daniel: A Concise Bibliography*. New York: S. A. Tannenbaum, 1942.